Storms Brewed in Other Men's Worlds

Storms Brewed

in Other Men's Worlds

The Confrontation of Indians, Spanish, and French in the Southwest, 1540-1795

by ELIZABETH A. H. JOHN

UNIVERSITY OF NEBRASKA PRESS • LINCOLN AND LONDON

First Bison Book printing: 1981
Most recent printing indicated by first digit below:
1   2   3   4   5   6   7   8   9   10

Library of Congress Cataloging in Publication Data

John, Elizabeth Ann Harper, 1928–
   Storms brewed in other men's worlds.

   Originally published: 1st. ed. College Station: Texas A&M University Press,
1975.
   Bibliography: p.
   Includes index.
   1. Indians of North America—Southwest, New—History. 2. Southwest,
New—History—To 1848. 3. Indians of North America—Government
relations—To 1789. I. Title.
[E78.S7J64   1981]   978'.00497   81–3401
ISBN 0–8032–7554–4 (pbk.)   AACR2

The artwork on the title page is reproduced by permission from *Comanche Scout*, a 1940 watercolor by Leonard Riddles (Black Moon), Comanche, in the collection of the Museum of Art, University of Oklahoma.

Published by arrangement with Texas A&M University Press

CONTENTS

ers. Hopi-Spanish impasse. Ute grievances. French pressures on the Apachería. Jicarilla appeals for Spanish protection. Loss of the northern Apachería.

MAPS

PREFACE

The Austin store manager courteously hands me his card, and I mispronounce his unusual surname. He corrects me in the sharp, defensive tone of a man who has heard altogether too many wrong guesses about his name, too many foolish remarks about his ancestry. Suddenly recognizing syllables that I have lately encountered in eighteenth-century documents, I exclaim, "Isn't that Comanche?"

Astonished, but enormously pleased, he demands, "How could you possibly have known that?" My explanation, that I am a historian and that earliest Comanche history is the focus of my current research, pleases him still more. He regrets that he knows little more of Comanche history than the tales his grandmother told him: dim memories of Comanche camps in those last, difficult days before they bowed to reservation life; nothing of what his people were like "in the beginning." He wishes he could teach his children more. Can I recommend a book that will tell him the things he wants to know?

Not really. Although invaluable to scholars, the standard work on his tribe is rough going for the general reader and, like most works on Plains and Southwestern Indians, tells little of the crucial century before the westering American frontier shattered the Comanche universe. Similar difficulty awaits most Indians seeking some whole sense of their own people's experience, especially "in the beginning." Not for the first time I reflect that this may be the ultimate injustice: to know of one's heritage only the last sad defeats, never the vigorous struggles and triumphs.

The encounter sharpens my own growing desire to trace lost Indian worlds and to comprehend them as components in the vast panorama of the national experience. More than the modern Indian quest for identity is involved: millions of non-Indian Americans need, and many desperately want, to incorporate a fair understanding of the Indian experience into their sense of national history. Of course there is temptation, and even considerable pressure, to derive a tidy monograph on the Comanches from hitherto unexploited documents in the Bexar Archives, but what of the many other Indian peoples whose fortunes interlocked with theirs? And how to divorce the Comanches' experience from that of the Spaniards with which they grappled? Isn't it time to attempt a synthesis for the general reader, according Indians the fullest and fairest treatment that our necessarily European sources permit?

My inquiry focuses upon those Indian peoples whose lands and fortunes fell within the spheres of the Spanish provinces of New Mexico and Texas and of the southwesternmost outpost of French Louisiana at Natchitoches. I find it necessary to start from "the beginning," that is, from the earliest documentation of each people, asking how Indian societies coped with that first jolting experience of revolutionary change and seeking some cohesive view of the interplay among diverse Indian peoples and European intruders. This initial account spans two and a half centuries, from earliest contacts in the 1540's to the crumbling of Spanish power in the 1790's.

Indian cultures thus considered range from the advanced societies of settled Pueblos and Caddos to primitive little Coahuiltecan groups whose world collapsed early under the onslaught of mounted Apaches. Their stories illuminate diverse dimensions of Indian experience: Navajos and Comanches forging distinct cultural revolutions from the Spanish encounter; Apaches, Utes, Wichitas, and Tonkawas preserving and perhaps intensifying old patterns, even while assimilating profound changes; Hopis defending old ways through relentless resistance to change; Pueblos conserving basic values through subtle accommodations to imposed change. Uttermost pathos emerges in the story of the Caddos, most cooperative and welcoming of settled Indian peoples, all but destroyed in the maelstrom of change.

The narrative is intended for the general reader seeking historical construction of a key segment of American Indian experience. While it is in no sense an anthropological treatise, the anthropologically oriented reader will note population movements, territoriality, intergroup relationships, factionalism, and various dimensions of culture change. Available population estimates are quoted as given in original sources, even though some clearly must be wide of the mark: for the purposes of this study it is important to understand the numbers assumed by the actors. It is hoped that presentation of such data in its historical context may also prove useful to scholars venturing into the quicksands of early population statistics. Most interesting to the author, and perhaps most relevant to current Indian concerns, is the documentation of political processes in various Indian societies and of the character of Indian statesmanship. The often remarkable initiative and responsibility of Indian leaders two centuries ago merit wider appreciation in this decade of resurgent Indian interest in self-governance.

Inseparable from the Indian experience, and thus a vital thread in this narrative, is the ancestral experience of the Hispanic communities of New Mexico and Texas. Poverty and strife loom large in the annals of those Spanish frontiers. So do fierce pride in the traditional rights of Spaniards, tenacity in their faith, and responsibility to the Indian as a child of the same God, susceptible of civilization in this world and of salvation in the next. Contrary to the Black Legend, and notwithstanding flagrant violations of Indian rights, it is on the Spanish frontier that one finds the earliest commitment to due process for Indians and the only consistent efforts to foster self-governance of Indian communities.

By painful trial and error, Indian and Spanish communities evolved toward peaceful coexistence in eighteenth-century New Mexico and Texas. Santa Fe and San Antonio were seats of lively interaction among Indian allies come to trade and to talk, to nourish the bonds of brotherhood. Unfortunately, most of the hard-won accommodations lapsed at the turn of the century when a decaying Spain could no longer sustain its commitments on that remote northern frontier. A half-century of turbulence followed: revolution on the Hispanic frontier, then the chaotic early years of the Mexican Republic; the slashing decade of the Texas Republic; the westward thrust of the United States—buying Louisiana, annexing Texas, seizing New Mexico; and, always, grievous dislocations of Indian peoples, buffeted against one another by storms brewed in other men's worlds.

It will require another volume to examine the ordeal of Indians caught up in that turbulence and to trace its impact on their worlds. Just as this inquiry has sought Indians coping with European impact, the next should follow these groups to their ultimate confrontation with the United States. The sum of the two efforts should be three centuries' depth of perspective from which to view that grim fourth century which now dominates American perceptions of Indian history. The longer perspective also displays elements of catastrophe, but it gives fairer play to neglected elements of Indian achievement and leadership, of energetic grasping of opportunity, and of constructive, often creative, change. Those should be useful perspectives for this generation, as Indians reach out vigorously to regain control of their own fortunes.

The sources for this study fall into two major categories: documents in the Spanish provincial archives of Texas and New Mexico and microfilm copies from archives in Mexico and Spain; published documents, particularly those massive collections edited by Herbert Eugene Bolton, Charles W. Hackett, George P. Hammond, and Alfred Barnaby Thomas as they blazed the trail of inquiry into Northern Borderlands history. Since the academic purist will surely protest undue reliance upon the latter, I would point out that referring the inquiring undergraduate or general reader to those volumes is very much like giving a hopper of ore to the fellow who needs a dime for a cup of coffee: however richly the gift assays, it falls short of the immediate need. Six decades after Bolton's pioneering *Athanase de Mézières* and four decades after Thomas's *Forgotten Frontiers*, the important contributions of de Mézières, Anza, and the Indian leaders whom they documented have yet to figure in the general understanding of American history. Surely it is neither premature nor pointless to attempt the requisite narrative construction for the general reader.

Although my conclusions may be deemed revisionist, I have derived information and insights from many monographs, principally those produced by historians of the Boltonian school. I am especially indebted to one of their number, Professor Max L. Moorhead of the University of Oklahoma. He directed the master's thesis on the Taovayas that began my ventures in Indian history, suggested as well as directed my subsequent doctoral dissertation on Spanish relationships with northern frontier tribes, and has since been generously helpful.

A researcher's results depend heavily on the nature of his questions. My own perception of the questions to be asked about the Indian experience was influenced by two extraordinarily useful works of anthropologists: Edward H. Spicer's *Cycles of Conquest* and Gene Weltfish's *Lost Universe*. The length and breadth of Spicer's perspective on Southwestern Indian experience and the wholeness of Weltfish's evocation of the Pawnee world seemed to me to point the direction in which the historian should aim.

Further recourse to anthropologists' expertise is represented by the maps, of such vital importance to a study of this scope. They were drawn by ethnobotanist Glendon H. Weir, now a doctoral candidate in the Department of Botany at Texas A&M University, working in association with Professor Vaughn Bryant of the Department of Anthropology.

Over many years in archives and libraries, one accumulates too many debts of gratitude to enumerate. My own searches reached a happy climax at the University of Texas in Austin. There the newly calendared and microfilmed Bexar Archives facilitated my final researches immeasurably, as did the unfailing helpfulness of University Archivist Dr. Chester Kielman and the generous assistance of translator Carmela Leal. I had also the pleasure of working in the Eugene Barker History Center with the hospitable aid and encouragement of Dr. Llerena Friend and invaluable access to the Latin American Collection and the expertise of its director, Dr. Nettie Lee Benson.

There is no remedy for the dearth of primary Indian sources for early tribal histories. However, some twentieth-century Indian painters have purposefully recorded tribal traditions, relying upon personal study and observation and upon the tales of their elders. The sum of their efforts is a growing, permanent treasury of Indian perspective on tribal worlds. The paintings vary widely in style, from relatively primitive, unschooled work characteristic of the earliest years of the Indian art renaissance to very sophisticated work of distinguished professional artists active today; their common denominator is commitment to truthful presentation of the ancestral experience.

On research trips I have enjoyed the assistance and good company of my daughter, Meredith. I am indebted to my husband, Peter, for repeated reading of the manuscript and for indispensable help with the chores of publication. For generally cheerful adaptation to a long project often fraught with domestic chaos, I am grateful to my son, Christopher, as well as to Peter and Meredith.

E.A.H.J.
Austin, Texas
1974

Storms Brewed in Other Men's Worlds

CHAPTER 1

Pueblo World, 1540-1610

Picture now that vast arena stretching westward from the pine-forested great bend of the Red River to the red desert mesas of the Colorado Plateau and southward from the Arkansas River to the Rio Grande. Envision it four centuries ago, homeland of countless small, diverse Indian worlds. Then consider the changes that engulfed those worlds and ponder the power of accident.

Spain made one great purposeful thrust into the Pueblo world in the sixteenth century, to claim those sober, industrious Indians as vassals of Crown and Church. A century later a chastened Spain made a second, half-hearted lunge into the Caddo world, more to balk French expansion than to advance Christendom. Frenchmen came anyway, seeking trade, their packs heavy with implications of revolution for Indian lives.

Thus superimposed on the multiplicity of Indian worlds were the Spanish provinces of New Mexico and Texas and the French province of Louisiana. Measured on the European scale of empire, none of the three ever amounted to much, but they unleashed forces of change that transformed the lives of Indian peoples throughout the arena, most quite remote from the initial, deliberate encounters, outside the ken as well as the intent of the invaders. The complex interplay of Indian and European cultures through two centuries molded the region before Anglo-Americans took it and called it Southwest.

The process began with a prodigious blunder. Spain's intrusion into the Pueblo world was born of a great misunderstanding, only the first of many that claimed a frightful toll of lives and property over the next two centuries. To Spanish frontiers in Mexico came rumors that far to the north lay Indian villages of great wealth, perhaps true in the eyes of people who bruited the reports southward.

Compared with camps of wandering Indians, pueblos were veritable citadels: multi-storied stone or adobe blocks of dwellings, centered upon the plazas where focused the community lives of populations ranging from four hundred to two thousand. The compact village structure lent itself not only to defense but to the cooperative way of life fundamental to Pueblo agriculture. The people of each village shared the labor of the fields and the religious observances they believed essential to their common enterprise. Together the people of the pueblos observed ceaseless rounds of inherited ceremonials to propitiate the ruling spirits of their universe. Properly done, these rituals assured the pleasant, orderly life, the fertility of crops and people, and the protection from violence and sorcery, which was the sum of the villagers' desires.[1]

Those sober, egalitarian societies, built upon principles of harmony among themselves and with the spirits of their universe, vested principal leadership in village headmen, whose duties were primarily religious. So important were their spiritual responsibilities that no quarrels could be brought before them, lest disharmony mar rapport of village with spirit world. To be involved in conflict, even if in the right, tarnished a man's reputation. To seek leadership was considered bad form and could provoke accusations of witchcraft. Such total subordination of individual feelings to group interests cost heavy stress to some individuals, especially those of more ambitious, assertive temperaments. For all their surface harmony, Pueblo communities were gravely vulnerable in their lack of leadership in secular matters and in the absence

---

[1] Discussion of Pueblo culture is based chiefly on the following works: Harold E. Driver, *Indians of North America*; Edward P. Dozier, "Rio Grande Pueblos," in *Perspectives in American Indian Culture Change*, ed. Edward H. Spicer; Elsie Clews Parsons, *Pueblo Indian Religion*; Edward H. Spicer, *Cycles of Conquest*; William Whitman, "San Ildefonso of New Mexico," in *Acculturation in Seven American Indian Tribes*, ed. Ralph Linton.

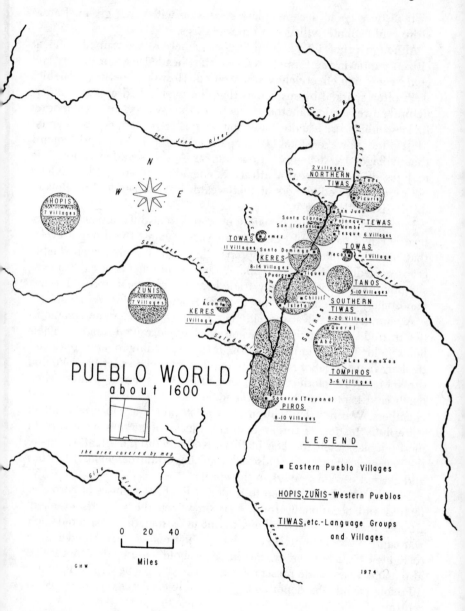

HOPIS
7 Villages

2 Villages
NORTHERN
TIWAS

Taos
Picuris

TEWAS
6 Villages

San Juan
Santa Clara
San Ildefonso
Pojoaque
Nambe
Tesque

TOWAS
11 Villages

Jemez

KERES
8-14 Villages

Santo Domingo

TOWAS
Pecos 1 Village

ZUNIS
7 Villages

Acoma
KERES
1 Village

Puaray
Tiguex

Chilili
Isleta

TANOS
5-10 Villages

SOUTHERN
TIWAS
8-20 Villages

Quarai
Abo
Las Humanas

TOMPIROS
3-6 Villages

PUEBLO WORLD
about 1600

Socorro (Teypana)
PIROS
8-10 Villages

the area covered by map

LEGEND

■ Eastern Pueblo Villages

HOPIS, ZUÑIS – Western Pueblos

TIWAS, etc. – Language Groups
and Villages

0   20   40
Miles

GHW

1974

of realistic ways to accommodate dissension within the group. Latent strife could splinter villages at times of crisis.

Although primarily peaceful Indians, Pueblos maintained efficient citizen militia in the form of war societies headed by war priests and could campaign effectively when aroused. Hostilities between pueblos were often sparked by suspicions that one pueblo had cast evil supernatural power against another. Sometimes they warred upon each other in loose alliances, usually based on linguistic or geographic affinity. Most often, however, Pueblos campaigned in reprisal for raids against their villages by such roving enemies as Apaches and Navajos. The realities of Pueblo wealth attracted nomadic Indian predators long before exaggerated rumors of that wealth lured Spaniards northward in the sixteenth century.

Pueblo wealth consisted mainly of stored foodstuffs, especially corn, hoarded over periods of three or four years against the drought cycles that brought famine to the unprepared. In good years, when Pueblo crops exceeded both storage capacity and requirements of current consumption, the villagers gladly traded for buffalo meat and hides and handsomely dressed deer skins brought from the plains by nomads.

Accumulated textiles were another Pueblo wealth, prime commodities in trade, subject to theft when one people raided another. Their fields yielded scanty crops of cotton, prized according to its scarcity and the long hours of labor required to make it into textiles for basic Pueblo dress. Men wove cloth on their looms in the kivas during winter, when harsh cold kept them below ground in the snug safety of communal chambers. Warmer than cotton, thus most valued as cloak or blanket, were fluffy textiles of turkey feathers. Flocks of turkeys were kept in most pueblos, solely for their feathers. Not only did those feathers make the warmest textiles: they also adorned important ceremonial fetishes and carried certain prayers to the spirits.

Fortunately, nomads liked to trade for Pueblo surpluses of corn and textiles and occasionally for pottery in which the villagers excelled. Besides meat, hides, and tallow, the nomads sometimes bartered their war captives. Many a prosperous Pueblo householder purchased a slave to lighten his labors or expand his household's production. A captive also made a handsome present when a visiting Apache wished to honor a Pueblo friend: the donor could reasonably expect a very nice gift in return.

Thus Pueblos and roving neighbors evolved an interdependence, always wary, sometimes broken by hostilities, but generally permitting each people to specialize in its own best products and to trade for the goods of the other. Some frontier pueblos became trade centers for particular groups of nomads. Winter often found Apaches or Utes camped near the sheltering walls of a pueblo.

Because of the marked similarities of their adaptations to the land, their agricultural practices, their compact multi-storied villages, and their preoccupation with ceremonials, the settled Indians of New Mexico looked deceptively alike. Actually, they were diverse peoples who spoke some four or five mutually unintelligible languages, each with several dialects. Each of the sixty or seventy villages was autonomous. Among them were marked differences of organization and of ceremonial emphasis, although welfare of the community and fertility of its land and people were paramount concerns everywhere. Each little village society had shaped a viable balance with the difficult environment, achieving orderly, purposeful existence well above survival level. No one could have guessed how fragile was the balance or how vulnerable the Pueblo world to a massive intrusion.

Misleading appearances cost the Pueblos heavily. Tales of their similarities to the Indians of Meso-America, in houses, textiles, and crops, led Spaniards to guess that "another Mexico" lay northward. In reality, the Pueblo Indians differed sharply from those of the Valley of Mexico in their egalitarianism, their minimization of war, and the disciplined austerity of their lives. Theirs was not a society or a land that could heap wealth upon conquerors, but misunderstandings persisted even when Spaniards came to stay in New Mexico.

Obvious similarities among Pueblos led Spaniards to miscalculate the complexity and difficulty of Hispanicizing them. Apparent simplicity, even frivolity, of Pueblo rites caused laymen and priests alike to underestimate the power and importance of native beliefs and the dangers of attacking them. Spain's decisions about New Mexico, first to undertake conquest, then to persist despite costly disappointments, derived from false assumptions that Pueblos generated considerable wealth and that they lived in a spiritual vacuum which Christianity could readily fill. Only a century of tragedy would teach Spaniards the true paucity of material resources and the tenacity of traditional beliefs in the Pueblo world.

Nothing in the Spaniards' experience prepared them to understand the Pueblo world they invaded in the sixteenth century, although years of New World experience helped to shape their New Mexican venture. Spaniards were themselves creatures of conflict. Their Hapsburg kings piously resolved to protect New Mexico's natives from such plunder and destruction as had characterized earlier conquests, but that humane royal intent clashed with the conquistadors' expectation that this New Mexico would yield wealth to rival the old. The Crown itself pursued conflicting aims in the New World: its quest for empire, prestige, and wealth required conquest and therefore war, yet its urgent commitment to win the Indians to the Roman Catholic faith could be fulfilled only in peace and conciliation. Thus, policies vacillated, while men and ideas clashed from the court in Madrid to the farthest frontier. Either aim—conquest or conversion—implied disruption of Indian cultures and values: to be caught in their conflict was perhaps cruelest of all Indian dilemmas. Nowhere was the impact greater than in New Mexico, where Spanish expectations were so ill-founded and thus so bitterly disappointed.

New Spain was founded upon the most basic resource of empire—a large, settled native population already profitably exploiting the land. Spaniards seeking slave labor for their Caribbean island mines and plantations had found on the mainland a rich aboriginal empire, seething with internal discontent, as ripe for conquest as it was alluring to fortune hunters. Hernando Cortés commanded only 553 soldiers, but he allied with malcontented nations within the Aztec empire to conquer the Valley of Mexico for Spain. Replacing Aztecs with Spaniards in the ruling class, Cortés built upon established native patterns of administration, tribute, and service. It was eminently successful practice in highly developed areas, applicable throughout Meso-America and Incan regions of South America.

On those aboriginal foundations Iberians built their New Spain, invoking attitudes and institutions of their homeland: legacies of their ancient experience in the Roman Empire and their long struggle to oust Moorish conquerors; customs of the recent feudal past; new practices evolving as Hapsburg monarchs forged from their Spanish inheritance a national state.

Conquest of the Indies raised questions not unlike those Castile had faced while reconquering the Peninsula from the Moors. Rewards to the conquerors for their services to the Crown, defense of conquered lands, protection and management of conquered peoples and their relationship to the Crown—all lent themselves to a familiar solution. The *repartimiento–encomienda,* deeply rooted in Castilian custom, was grafted onto the native structures that Cortés and his peers found so useful. However, the Crown, still struggling to curb feudal powers on the Peninsula in the interest of royal absolutism, modified the *encomien-da* for the New World, lest the Indies also be fragmented among power-ful feudal barons.[2]

The *encomienda* was a grant of the fruits of Indian labor, initially collectable either in personal service or in material tribute. Contrary to Castilian practice, which made peoples in *encomienda* vassals of *en-comendero* as well as king, Indians remained the direct, free vassals of the Crown. They were not attached to the soil, but legally free to move about. They could bring charges against *encomenderos* for abuses of their statutory rights. *Encomenderos* had neither administrative nor judicial authority and were forbidden to live in the Indian towns or to own property within them.

Encomienda had several purposes: to reward the builders of the em-pire and their descendants (usually for one generation); to ensure the permanence of colonization by requiring *encomenderos* to reside in the area of their *encomienda*; and to provide for defense of the area and its inhabitants. Beyond those traditional purposes, the New World *encomienda* entailed obligations not only to protect Indians but also to instruct them in Christianity and the rudiments of Spanish civilization.

Essentially feudal, the *encomienda* had repercussions in the New World beyond Indian rights. It fostered the feudal structure of a fight-ing class, a praying class, and a mass of laborers below to do the work. Spaniards of the New World divided between those who held *en-comiendas*, or hoped to do so, and those who did not. The latter were badly disadvantaged in the scramble for wealth and status, though their problems were trivial compared with those of Indians granted to ruthless *encomenderos*.

In practice, *encomenderos* sorely abused Indians, particularly in early years when *encomenderos* sought to gain perpetual rights of lordship over the Indians, like those enjoyed by feudal barons on the Peninsula during Reconquest. Those abuses, which destroyed countless Indians, sparked a great outcry for reform, led by such clerics as Bartolomé de Las Casas. Emperor Carlos V, who took very seriously his obligation to convert the Indians, heard lurid stories of their de-struction and virtual enslavement by his own people. Debate raged at court for years while the emperor and his councilors tried to evaluate charges and counter-charges, heard the vehement denials of *encomen-deros* and the learned discourses of theologians, and then weighed

---

[2] Robert S. Chamberlain, "Castilian Backgrounds of the Repartimiento-Encomi-enda," *Contributions to American Anthropology and History* 5 (1939): 19–66.

obvious need for reform against practical difficulties of enforcement in the vast distances of the New World.

The principle of reform triumphed in 1542, when Carlos V promulgated the New Laws. Earlier decrees against enslaving Indians were reiterated. Rigid rules were set for new discoveries: no longer were Indians to be brought back as loot; only a governor could levy tribute from newly discovered natives. The most telling reform projected the demise of the *encomienda* with that generation of *encomenderos*. Meanwhile, the law forbade requirement of personal service, so often tantamount to slavery: *encomenderos* thenceforth could legally collect only the fixed tribute in kind specified by their grants.

A storm of protest arose from conquistadors and their successors, defending their privileges against modernizing trends of centralization and reform. Crusading priests had prodded the emperor's conscience to save the Indians, but some religious orders and prelates in the New World now upheld the *encomienda*, arguing that they must retain their own grants of Indian labor to exist. There was danger that the lay *encomenderos*, who had won their privileges by military service and always stood ready to take the field again, would rise up in arms against the reforms. The Crown faced the unhappy prospect of having to conquer the Indies a second time, this time against its own doughty vassals.

Confronted with the limitations of his power, the emperor backed down in 1545 to let the *encomienda* continue and thus negated the heart of the reforms. That reverse was a serious one, both for Indian rights and for the movement to centralize and modernize the Spanish polity. The laws against cruelty to Indians remained on the books, however, and Carlos V reiterated several times the ban on requiring personal service of Indians. Enslavement of Indians remained illegal, though practice on remote frontiers often deviated from the principles of the Crown.

Crimes against Indians continued to plague the conscience of Carlos V and of his son, Felipe II, who succeeded him in 1556. Concern about abuses common in conquest led the Crown to order conquests suspended until some just method of conducting them could be devised. After that pause, 1550 to 1566, viceroys who authorized conquests had to instruct their agents in strict responsibility for the natives' welfare and meticulous enforcement of laws protecting them.

The Hapsburgs' quest for justice in the Indies climaxed with a new ordinance promulgated by Felipe II in 1573. He explicitly banned the term "conquest," preferring instead "pacification." Natives whose lands were singled out for pacification were to be approached with all kindness. Spanish forces were to be led by men of excellent character—more concerned with converting Indians than with material gain—men well qualified to explain to the Indians the obligations which rested upon the Crown of Spain as well as the remarkable advantages bestowed upon Indians who submitted to vassalage. The king took considerable pride in those benefits to the natives: the Christian doctrine and thus the key to eternal salvation; extension of the king's peace to secure his vassals in their civil pursuits; foods, textiles, livestock, tools, arms, and countless other things from Spain; new crafts and trades. Surely Indians who understood those advantages would readily accept Spanish settlements and listen to the Christian gospel. If some should persist in opposition, despite all explanation, then Spaniards might use some force, harming as little as possible. Native vices were to be dealt with very gently, so as not to upset the aborigines and prejudice them against Christianity. Never were captives to be enslaved.[3]

The Law of 1573 thenceforth embodied the governing principle of Spanish conquest, although there were always some Spaniards who thought it permissible to subjugate Indians forcibly because they were infidels. The Crown and the force of Spanish law remained committed to the humane principles hammered out in years of debate: that the Indians discovered in the New World were not beasts or slaves by nature or limited childlike creatures, but men capable of becoming Christians. They should not be enslaved or destroyed, but rather incorporated into Spanish Christian civilization, with every right to enjoy their property, political liberty, and human dignity.

While the king and his councilors and scholars wrestled great questions of principle, the advance of the frontier in the New World brought increasing practical difficulties in dealing with Indians. The conquest of Meso-America had been remarkably swift and easy, grafting upon established native sociopolitical patterns the Castilian feudal *repartimiento–encomienda* and, after 1535, the viceregal administrative structure. Spaniards after Cortés were held more closely accountable to the Crown than the first adventurers, and far more attention was paid to the Crown's responsibility to convert the natives. Missionaries marched alongside, and often ahead of, conquistadors. With astonishing speed Indian villages of Mexico were drawn into Christendom, a

---

[3] Lewis Hanke, *The Spanish Struggle for Justice in the Conquest of America*, pp. 131 ff. This monograph is the main basis of the discussion of principles underlying Spanish policy.

vast New World triumph for Roman Catholicism when forces of Islam and Protestant Reformation threatened its old hegemony in Europe. As vassals of the king of Spain, Mexican Indians adopted his religion and paid him tribute. The tribute was sometimes paid in products, sometimes in labor on Spaniards' mines and ranches, sometimes directly to the king's treasury, sometimes to his Spanish vassals to whom he granted fruits of Indian labor for military services to the Crown. A flow of wealth from the Indies underwrote the Spanish Hapsburgs' defense of their European and African domains, as well as their defense of Roman Catholicism against heretics and infidels who threatened in the Old World from north, east, and south.

The quest for more gold and silver drew Spaniards ever northward from the Valley of Mexico, beyond the twenty-first parallel to the arid expanses of modern northern Mexico. The minerals were there, but the Spaniards found few settled Indians either to exploit or to convert. Instead, less docile Indians, not so firmly tied to the land, fled to the hills and tenaciously defended their freedom. Whereas Meso-American Indians were a human resource on which to base an empire, Indians of the north were a formidable obstacle, exacting a fearful cost for the advance of the frontier. Friars still pressed northward to "reduce" and convert northern Indians, but missions had now to be accompanied, or even preceded, by presidios. Successes were limited and precarious: even converts were frequently subverted or threatened by Indians who remained hostile. On that difficult northern frontier were tested the principles of the Law of 1573.

One great mineral find after another drew Spaniards northward, until the 1570's saw mines, ranches, missions, and presidios in the southern reaches of modern Chihuahua. Around the mines of Santa Barbara clustered tough, ambitious men, some already rich, some determined to be so. They probed ever northward, seeking both new lodes and labor for mines already operating. There was little distinction between parties of mineral prospectors and slave-raiders; enterprising men seized any opportunities they found. The shock of first encounter with those Spaniards spread terror among Indian populations scattered toward the Rockies and the Rio Grande. The humane intentions of Felipe II were a long way from implementation on the remote frontiers of his empire.

Despite rich mineral deposits, Spaniards found the arid north sorely disappointing. Though mines and ranches could operate profitably when Indian hostilities could be held to tolerable levels, there was no accumulated Indian wealth for the taking as in Meso-America. No wonder rumors of another Mexico far to the north sparked such excitement.

These rumors first reached Mexico City in 1536, with Cabeza de Vaca's tattered quartet of shipwreck survivors from the Florida expedition of Pánfilo de Narváez. They had seen no wealth in their trek from the Texas Gulf coast to the Spanish outpost in Nueva Galicia, but they had noted some indications of mineral deposits and Indians had told them of prosperous towns to the north. Their story fitted earlier rumors of Indian trading connections with towns far north. Veteran conquistadors itched to probe northward to investigate those tales, but that was the very thing which Viceroy Antonio de Mendoza had come to prevent.

It was particularly to check the excessive power of the conquistadors and to end their brutal exploitation of natives that the Crown had established the new office of viceroy, assumed by Mendoza in 1535. The New Laws were a few years in the offing, but Carlos V already believed the reformers enough to begin significant efforts to protect the Indians. Mendoza came fully informed of the emperor's views and strictly charged to safeguard Indian rights in New Spain. Any new conquest must be under viceregal control, with due care that it be "apostolic and Christian, and not a butchery." The viceroy thought of probing northward himself, but he could not risk long absences from his duties. Instead, Mendoza appointed a promising young officer who had accompanied him from Spain—Francisco Vázquez de Coronado, already governor of Nueva Galicia, the logical base for an expedition to seek the rumored Indian cities. Mendoza directed Coronado to prepare a major expeditionary force while preliminary reconnaissance was made to ascertain that the undertaking would promote both missionary and economic concerns of the Crown.

To assure peaceful approach to the natives of the new lands, preliminary investigation was entrusted to a Franciscan friar, Marcos de Niza, noted for bravery and selfless zeal. His guide was the vigorous Moor, Estevánico, a former slave who had survived shipwreck to trek back to Mexico with Cabeza de Vaca. They departed from Nueva Galicia in the spring of 1539, with Indian guides who knew the area immediately north, and were well received by Indians along their route. As Estevánico recognized landmarks, he pressed ahead with Indian guides, sending back to Fray Marcos signals of riches far beyond the Spaniards' expectations. Fray Marcos hurried to overtake him, but could never match Estevánico's pace. Suddenly he met members of the advance party, fleeing in panic from the pueblos of Zuñi, presumed to be the legendary Seven Cities of Cíbola. The Zuñis had killed Estevánico and some of his party, for reasons never ascertained. The survivors described a great city of conspicuous wealth. Estevánico's fate ruled out close approach, but Fray Marcos glimpsed from a hill the object of his reconnaissance. Through a haze compounded of distance and his own keen desires, he saw a terraced stone city, larger even than Mexico City. His Indian companions assured him that it was the smallest of the seven cities and also described a populous valley to the east, where townspeople commonly used gold for utilitarian objects. Pausing only to plant crosses symbolizing possession for God and king, Fray Marcos hurried south to report to the viceroy. His tale set Mexico City agog. Cortés embarked for Spain to press his own claim to lead the conquest, but Mendoza promptly authorized Coronado to set out from Nueva Galicia.[4]

The Coronado expedition marked a new style in Spanish conquest, under government control from the beginning and held accountable for the well-being of Indians whose lives it would touch. No Indians could be forced to go on this expedition, but the reports had excited the Indian populace, too, and hundreds volunteered to make the journey. Coronado had to deal with them as freemen and let them turn back anytime they wished. No Indians could be made burden bearers; unlike earlier conquerors, Coronado's Spaniards would have to carry their own gear when they lacked pack animals. Coronado took his responsibilities to his Indian expeditionaries seriously. His prompt, severe punishment of men who abused them created some disaffection among his soldiers.

Mendoza also charged Coronado to protect the rights of Indians whose territory his expedition would cross. Nothing was to be taken by force; any supplies they chose to sell must be purchased at a fair price. This expedition must not live off the land, a principle implying a substantial, unprecedented outlay for its support. The Crown made no such investment, so the venture was privately financed. Mendoza, already wealthy, was its principal backer, but Coronado sank most of his wife's considerable fortune into the venture, and some of his soldiers invested all they had. All expected substantial profits, even under the

---

[4] Discussion of the Coronado expedition is based principally on Herbert Eugene Bolton, *Coronado, Knight of Pueblos and Plains.*

Crown's new rules—not an unreasonable expectation in view of the reports of Fray Marcos.

Recruitment flourished. Spring 1540 found the force wending north through the Sonora Valley toward Fray Marcos' Cíbola. However peaceful the Crown's intentions, the expedition formed a massive intrusion into the Pueblo world. Four friars accompanied the 336 Spanish soldiers, of whom 250 were mounted. A few soldiers brought wives, children, and Negro slaves. With them came hundreds of Indian allies, also armed, serving in many capacities, many traveling with wives and children. More than a thousand horses and mules constituted the pack and remount herds. Indian herdsmen drove vast numbers of cattle and sheep, a great walking commissary. Northward pounded all those hoofs, toward the unfenced fields upon which Pueblo life depended.

Reports of scouts indicated hostility at Cíbola, and Coronado noted worrisome discrepancies between their observations of the region and the previous reports of Fray Marcos. Reluctant to expose the entire expedition to undue risk, Coronado pressed ahead with an advance guard of a hundred Spaniards, many Indians, and friars impatient to reach their new mission field. In July they gazed upon the little stone pueblo of Háwikuh, first of the Zuñi group that Fray Marcos had thought to be the fabled Seven Cities of Cíbola. The poor reality contrasted so shockingly with the friar's reports that soldiers turned upon him in rage. Coronado feared for the Franciscan's safety.

Anger and disappointment notwithstanding, the task of investigation remained. Coronado found the Zuñis ready to resist his call for their peaceful submission to Spanish rule. Men of Háwikuh drew lines of sacred corn meal before their pueblo, forbidding the Spaniards to cross them. A ringing Spanish announcement that Coronado's force had come in peace to protect these Indians as children of their great emperor across the sea did not convince the Zuñis; nor did the pantomime of laying down Spanish weapons and urging the Indians to do the same. The Indians attacked, and a dozen died in the skirmish before the rest retreated to their fortress-like pueblo. The Spaniards stormed the pueblo and took it in short order; Coronado himself was badly wounded in the fray. The Indians signaled their desire to leave and were permitted to depart in peace, though they were assured that they would be unharmed if they would remain. Tired and hungry, the invaders feasted on the pueblo's stores, rested, and hoped for the return of its populace.

Coronado regretted the hostilities, which he deemed a necessary response to an unprovoked attack. Surely the Zuñis saw themselves defending their land against unwarranted aggression; just as surely Coronado saw himself asserting his king's rightful claim to New World dominion (based upon papal donation) and proffering the grace of Christendom to the Indians. He believed that the Indians had been wrong not to render obedience peacefully, but he meant to conciliate rather than punish them.

Forbidding his men to bother the Indians in any way, Coronado sent conciliatory messages to those who had left, made peaceful visits to other Zuñi pueblos, and soon received leaders of all the Zuñi villages. As Coronado interpreted their talks, the Indians rendered formal obedience to the king of Spain and avowed their desire to become Christians. One can only wonder about the Zuñis' understanding of the propositions to which they nodded. Some mentioned an old prophecy that a force like Coronado's would come to conquer their entire country, and they seemed resigned to its fulfillment. Gradually the people of Háwikuh came home. His apparent progress in winning their confidence pleased Coronado.

The economic realities were far from pleasing. Zuñi wealth was fairly represented by their leaders' gifts: a few deer and buffalo skins, a few turquoises, some poor blankets of yucca fiber. Coronado appreciated the spirit of the gifts, which he reciprocated with Spanish manufactures, and he respected the Zuñis' intelligence and industry. Nevertheless, their gifts were poor return for all the pesos and work, the hardship and hopes invested in his venture. He continued conscientiously to investigate the area, but nothing that he saw indicated much of value in that harsh land.

Another seven cities were reported farther north, similar to those of Zuñi, but smaller and built of mud. With volunteer Zuñi guides and interpreters, Captain Pedro de Tovar led a reconnaissance northward to the Hopi villages. They found the Hopis drawn up on their high mesas, ready to resist. Virtual repetition of the Háwikuh episode followed: Spanish call for peaceful obedience to God and king; lines of sacred corn meal drawn by Hopi leaders who demanded that the intruders leave; Spaniards crossing the line to talk with Hopis; a Hopi blow at a Spaniard; Spanish charge; Hopi surrender.

Leaders from all Hopi towns then met with Tovar, bringing presents and formally rendering obedience to the king. The gifts were very like those at Zuñi, plus a bit of cotton cloth. Most useful to the Spaniards was Hopi information about a great river in the west, possibly the avenue to meet the vessels of Hernando de Alarcón, who had sailed from Acapulco with supplies for Coronado's forces. Coronado dispatched twenty-five horsemen with Captain López de Cárdenas to seek the Colorado River and meet Alarcón. Cárdenas rode far enough to discover the Grand Canyon, then turned back from its rim after failing to find a way down to the river. Alarcón was indeed on the lower Colorado River then, but rendezvous was never accomplished. Coronado found himself alarmingly short of supplies as autumn approached.

Meanwhile, friendly delegates from Pecos pueblo visited Coronado at Zuñi. Their leaders, an elder whom the Spaniards called Cacique and a robust, mustachioed young man whom they dubbed Bigotes, offered their friendship in case the Spaniards should wish to visit further east. Their gifts to Coronado were impressive: finely dressed skins, well-made shields and headdresses. When they mentioned vast numbers of woolly cattle east of their pueblos, Coronado remembered the tales of Cabeza de Vaca and ordered a reconnaissance. Captain Hernando de Alvarado led twenty soldiers homeward with Bigotes, allotted eighty days to explore eastward to the great cattle lands and to inform the Indian populations of the benevolent, peaceful purposes of the king of Spain.

Alvarado enjoyed the first truly encouraging experiences of the entire venture. At the formidable sky fortress of Ácoma, the natives let the explorers climb the rock to visit their pueblo and gave them food, cloth, skins, turquoises, and turkeys. A grateful Alvarado reckoned that the Spaniards could have done nothing about it if the Indians had chosen to remain aloof on their high mesa. Three days later the party camped on the Rio Grande, a little north of present Albuquerque. They sent Bigotes north with a cross and peaceful messages for the pueblos upstream, and the next day they enjoyed welcoming visits from men of the twelve pueblos that the Spaniards thereafter called the province of Tiguex. They had in common their Tigua (Tiwa) language and their way of life; Alvarado may not have realized then that each village was an autonomous unit.

Alvarado responded to the peaceful embassies and their gifts with appropriate presents, and he subsequently paid return visits to each friendly pueblo, erecting crosses in each and teaching the natives to venerate them. The visitors found the Indians' response heartwarming though strange: they decorated the crosses with flowers and feathers and offered sacred meal and feathers before them, just as before their native altars.

To Alvarado that September the Rio Grande Valley, shaded with fine cottonwoods, seemed temperate and almost lush in contrast to the Zuñi area. The natives' fields abounded in maize, beans, and squash; their cotton textiles were good. Flocks of turkeys at each pueblo further promised good subsistence. The Zuñis had explained that they kept turkeys only for feathers, never to eat the meat or eggs, but Coronado had simply ignored that, and Alvarado failed equally to comprehend that any people would eschew good fowl.

The Rio Grande pueblos looked to Alvarado very like those of Zuñi, although built more of adobe than of stone. Their people, more numerous and more prosperous than those of Zuñi, also seemed friendlier and more generous. Alvarado dispatched to Coronado his recommendation that the expedition winter in Tiguex.

Continuing with Bigotes as guide and interpreter, the Spaniards rode on to Taos, the northernmost Tiwa pueblo, finding everywhere the same cordial reception. Bigotes also offered to lead them to other pueblos southward on the Rio Grande or westward to Jémez and Zía, but Alvarado inclined eastward toward the woolly cattle. Bigotes obligingly led the Spaniards to his own Pecos, a four-story fortress, then largest of all pueblos. The welcome there was the most enthusiastic yet, with generous gifts of clothing and turquoises to the Spaniards. Like the people of Taos, those of Pecos did not raise cotton or turkeys in the manner of the Rio Grande villagers: their economy was oriented more toward the nearby plains.

Bigotes excused himself from guiding the Spaniards to the plains, but he lent them two slaves as guides. They were Indians from the east, perhaps captured by the Pecos, perhaps traded by Apaches at the pueblo. Ysopete, a young lad, was a native of Quivira; the other, dubbed "Turk" by the Spaniards, hailed from a land farther east called Harahey; both seemed reliable. Four days beyond Pecos, the Spaniards found themselves amid a great herd of buffalo on the Canadian River. Everything about the monstrous "cattle" was awesome: their incredible numbers, their dense woolly coats, their savory meat. Excited to find true at least one tale of Cabeza de Vaca, the Spaniards wondered anew about the other marvels he had reported.

The Turk urged them northeastward, indicating treasures in Quivira. He had picked up a few words from Mexican Indians in the party and could make eloquent signs. Spanish imaginations leaped the language barrier to help him weave a tale of gold, silver, fine textiles, altogether a rich economy in Quivira. As confirming detail, the Turk mentioned a gold bracelet he had brought from Quivira to Pecos only to see it confiscated by Bigotes, who had it still. Gladly would the Turk lead the Spaniards to Quivira to see for themselves. Loath to exceed his instructions, Alvarado declined and turned back to rejoin Coronado. He hoped to get the gold bracelet from Bigotes for solid evidence on which the whole expedition could proceed to Quivira.

Again the Pecos welcomed the Spaniards and gave them fresh provisions. However, Alvarado's inquiries about the bracelet elicited only surprised denials from Bigotes and Cacique. Alvarado decided to take them back to Tiguex to confront Coronado. When they refused, he took them forcibly in chains, along with the Turk and Ysopete. That shocking violation of hospitality brought the Pecos warriors out fighting. Alvarado's force turned them back, but he had sown hostility and distrust where there had been valuable friendship.

Back on the Rio Grande, Alvarado found that Coronado had adopted his recommendation to winter at Tiguex. Captain Cárdenas was already there with a dozen Spanish horsemen, uncounted Indian allies, and Zuñi helpers, preparing a winter camp. The first snow dissolved their intention to camp out: the Indians were asked to vacate one pueblo for the Spaniards' use. They complied, rather grimly. It was but the first of many severe strains on their hospitality. The Cárdenas and Alvarado contingents were soon joined by the rest of Coronado's vanguard from Zuñi, then by the principal force, which had traveled more slowly from Mexico with the main livestock herds.

The Crown had not intended the expedition to live off the natives, but provisions carried by Alarcón's fleet never reached Coronado. New Mexico's winter presented another unanticipated problem. The Spaniards were not outfitted for cold weather; their Mexican Indian allies suffered even more severely in that northern climate. Coronado looked to the twelve pueblos of Tiguex for relief, levying food and clothing from each. The compensation tendered could hardly soothe Indian resentment. That food and clothing were essential to their own welfare; they could not feed their children glass beads or keep them warm with copper bells.

Tension mounted rapidly. The Tiwas must have known of the clashes at the Zuñi and Hopi pueblos and at Pecos and of Bigotes and Cacique, leading men of Pecos, held in chains in the Spanish camp. Indignation deepened when a Tiwa reported his wife raped by a Spanish soldier and the commanders refused to punish the offender because the aggrieved husband could not furnish indisputable identification of the culprit. Each new visit to the pueblos to demand more food and clothing further inflamed the smoldering sense of grievance.

Retaliating Tiwas struck at the horse herd. They killed some in pasture and corralled many more for systematic slaughter, apparently not tempted to seize them for use against the Spaniards. The invaders, whose survival depended upon their horses, resolved to crush the resistance promptly and decisively.

Thus began the Tiguex War. Coronado's force besieged and destroyed the pueblo that had led the resistance, then burned to death survivors of the siege. They brought Bigotes, Cacique, the Turk, and Ysopete in chains to watch the burning, so they could tell their own people the price of defying Spaniards.

The remaining Tiwas fled from their homes. Some took refuge in the mountains despite severe winter weather; others congregated in the large pueblo called Moho, which held out all winter against a Spanish siege. In March 1541 the Spaniards burned Moho and several other Tiwa pueblos. Some captured survivors were distributed among the soldiers as servants, prizes of war.

That proved a costly victory, for Tiguex had been destroyed as a source of supplies. The Spaniards levied some supplies that winter from such Keres pueblos as Zía, and they even had Keres offers of help against the Tiwas, with whom they had an old feud. Nevertheless, it was a winter of hardship and scarcity. In April the Spaniards pulled out of Tiguex altogether, with their herds, their Mexican Indian allies, and their new Tiwa captives. They were off to see Quivira with the Turk. En route, Coronado restored Bigotes to his people at Pecos.

On the plains, the Spaniards met wandering Indians who lived by following the buffalo herds. They called the first group Querechos and noted their habit of wintering at the pueblos where they traded meat and skins. The second group, farther east, were a tattooed people whom the Spaniards called Teyas.[5] Though enemies of each other, both groups cordially welcomed the Spaniards. Coronado's caravan of 1,500 persons and thousands of animals never before seen on those plains must have astonished the nomads.

By the end of May their wanderings had brought them to Palo Duro

---

[5] It has been suggested that the Querechos were almost certainly Apaches and that the Teyas were either Apaches or Jumanos. It seems equally reasonable to speculate that the latter were Wichitan or Caddoan peoples out for the buffalo hunt.

Canyon and to a growing suspicion that the Turk was untrustworthy. The Quiviran lad, Ysopete, had always declared the Turk a liar: now Coronado decided to let Ysopete lead just thirty Spaniards to Quivira. He sent most of the caravan back to Tiguex, there to prepare either for another winter on the Rio Grande or, if events warranted, for a summons to join Coronado in Quivira. By mid-summer the main force was back in the desolated area of Tiguex. At every inhabited pueblo they passed, the Indians were openly hostile; in Tiguex, those Indians who had returned home fled as the Spaniards approached.

Ysopete confidently guided Coronado's party to Quivira, in the great bend of the Arkansas River: in July 1541 he introduced them to the grass-hut villages of Indians eventually called Wichitas. They were cordially received. Coronado reported that the Quivirans pledged allegiance to the king of Spain and accepted his authority. Their own understanding of the event is buried in time, beyond the reach of folk memory.

For twenty-five days Coronado explored the reaches of Quivira, visiting or hearing of twenty-five villages strung along the Arkansas and its tributaries. The valley was beautiful and productive, the Indians of Quivira prosperous with diligent farming and seasonal hunting on the buffalo plains just to the west. But it grew obvious that the Turk had invented his stories of gold and other riches in Quivira, probably to trick the Spaniards into taking him back toward his own homeland. Coronado let his soldiers execute the rogue, not only for that deceit, but also for intriguing with some Quivirans to kill the Spaniards.

In mid-August Coronado turned his party back toward New Mexico with provisions obtained from the Quivirans and six young men of Quivira to guide them to Pecos. Mid-September found Coronado's party back in Tiguex, facing another difficult winter. Supplies had been requisitioned from pueblos in all directions during harvest time, enough to cause suffering in the pueblos, yet inadequate to feed Coronado's large force all winter.

Some talked of riding eastward in the spring to seek possible wealth beyond Quivira, but few expected to salvage anything from the failure of the expedition. Morale crumbled in the Spanish camp. Just after Christmas Coronado fell from his horse and suffered a severe head injury from which he never fully recovered. When most of his men petitioned to return in the spring to Mexico, he gratefully yielded. They set out in April 1542, with the ailing Coronado slung in a litter between two mules.

The friars would not so readily abandon their mission. Fray Marcos had early returned to Mexico, thoroughly discredited, and religious leadership had devolved upon Fray Juan de Padilla, the only ordained priest with the expedition. With him were two lay brothers, Fray Luis de Escalona and Fray Juan de la Cruz, and his two personal aides, Indian lay brothers named Lucas and Sebastián. All five chose to remain when Coronado left. Unable to dissuade them from the risk, the distressed leader left them all possible aid. With them stayed a Portuguese called Andrés do Campo, a mestizo, a free Negro interpreter, and a few other servants. Two Negro slaves, a lad called Cristóbal and a man named Sebastián, with his wife and children, also remained. Fray Juan de Padilla particularly wanted Cristóbal, because he believed that the bright youngster would quickly learn Indian languages and become an invaluable interpreter.

Fray Luis de Escalona went to Pecos with Cristóbal; Fray Juan de la Cruz stayed at Tiguex. Never heard of again, they were presumed martyred. Fray Juan de Padilla returned to Quivira, where he saw an urgently beckoning mission field. With him went the two Indian lay brothers, the Portuguese do Campo, the mestizo, the free Negro interpreter, and a few servants. The six Quiviran braves who had led Coronado back from Quivira to Pecos guided them to Quivira in spring 1542. Warmly welcomed, Fray Juan set up his mission, then ventured further afield to minister also to the Guaes.[6] That decision proved fatal. Strange Indians attacked the party, killing Fray Juan. Lucas, Sebastián, and do Campo escaped and eventually made their way back to the Spanish frontier to relate his martyrdom.

One determined soldier took a Pueblo wife back to Mexico City. As for the rest, Coronado made his men relinquish the Tiguex War captives whom they had held as servants and the consorts whom some had taken among the native women. Given the principles of the Crown and the explicit instructions of Mendoza, it would have been unduly risky to take natives of New Mexico back to New Spain. Thus released in the Rio Grande Valley were many Pueblos who had lived closely with the Spaniards for a year and had even marched with them across the plains to Palo Duro Canyon and back. Some of the Mexican Indian expeditionaries chose to remain at Zuñi, where they were eagerly welcomed into the population.

After a grueling march through Sonora, Coronado disbanded his men at Culiacán and returned to his duties as governor of Nueva Galicia,

[6] A name applied in the eighteenth century to the Skidi Pawnees, or Panismahas.

his health and his fortune forever impaired. He faced several years of litigation; with the New Laws of the Indies now in force, some officials sought to make an example of Coronado's conduct toward the Indians of New Mexico. Coronado himself was ultimately cleared of charges, but some of his subordinates paid heavy penalties for excesses committed in the Tiguex War.

The long investigations of the Coronado expedition registered ample testimony to the forbidding, barren vastness of New Mexico. Men who had seen it agreed that the area would never produce wealth and that no Spanish colony could ever exist there without heavy, continuing subsidy from the Crown. Some missionaries could not forget that many Indian souls awaited conversion in the pueblos and that work begun by three Franciscan martyrs cried for completion. Still, the economic truths revealed by Coronado would help to protect the Pueblo world from Spanish colonization for another generation or two.

Pueblos had much to remember in the interval. The Spaniards could not be trusted; they violated the laws of hospitality; they consumed precious stores like a plague of locusts. They set great store by an emblem of crossed sticks, which they trusted to protect them. Spaniards could be killed and so could their fearsome horses, but the price of resisting them was death and destruction.

At the same time, a similar learning experience had occurred in the region from Florida to the eastern Arkansas Valley. Hernando de Soto had demolished the myth of rich native civilizations. Southeastern Indians had learned an even costlier lesson about the price of Spanish invasion, for de Soto was not inhibited by restraints like those Mendoza laid upon Coronado. Both Coronado and de Soto had piloted Spanish forces to hit-and-run collisions with Indian peoples of the north, with no gain of comprehension between the alien peoples.

While the Crown's investigators documented Coronado's disappointments, new mineral discoveries on the central plateau of Mexico caught Spanish attention. Ironically, the biggest fortune gleaned from the great Zacatecas strike of 1546 fell to Cristóbal de Oñate, the friend of Coronado who had governed Nueva Galicia without compensation for the two years of Coronado's absence. That fortune would finally underwrite the conquest of New Mexico: the Pueblos' reprieve was destined to be brief.

For thirty years the central mining frontier surged northward, carrying its grim complement of illicit slave raiding beyond the fringe of effective Spanish authority. Again, contact with roving Indians yielded reports of settled Indians far to the north. The stories excited missionaries disheartened by the difficulties of reducing nomads to mission life. Laymen who had yet to find their fortunes envisioned another, richer Indian frontier farther on. Coronado's discouraging experiences lay buried in official archives, unknown to adventurers looking north to the Pueblo world from Santa Barbara.

The new investigations of the northern lands began as specified by the Laws of 1573, which emphasized pacification rather than conquest and preferred missionaries with only token military escort as Spain's agents of discovery and conversion. In 1581, Fray Agustín Rodríguez led a trio of friars from Santa Barbara to seek the new mission field, escorted by eight Spaniards under the command of Captain Francisco Sánchez Chamuscado and nineteen Mexican Indian aides.

Even that small party made a conspicuous caravan, moving toward La Junta with ninety horses and six hundred head of livestock. Most Indians fled as they approached, fearing yet another slave raid. However, the Cabris[7] welcomed them on the Conchos River with generous gifts of food. They had heard that the Spaniards would be their friends and would reconcile them with their enemies, who were also at war with the Spaniards. Rodríguez and Chamuscado gave assurance that they had indeed come only to restore friendship between the Cabris and their enemies, help them in their wars, and protect them from their foes. The helpful Cabris had heard of some brave people far to the north who had many houses, lots of corn, beans, and calabashes, and white clothes like the Spaniards'. Anticipating cotton textiles and thus an advanced agriculture, the Spaniards pushed on to La Junta and up the Rio Grande.

Because they sent word ahead that they were coming to restore peace among warring Indians, the Spaniards were generally well received. They lived on foods freely given by the Indians. With them trailed a retinue of three hundred Indians, very much awed by and interested in the horses. They too had heard of well-clothed people living in great houses in the interior but had never actually seen them. The tales had come long ago from the men who hunted the buffalo.

At some boundary visible only to the Cabris, the cordial procession ended. All three hundred turned back, explaining that the people farther upstream spoke another language and were their enemies. Intrusion into their country would make them think the Cabris were coming to fight them.

---

[7] G. P. Hammond suggests that these were Julimes.

Two days upstream the Spaniards encountered the Sumas, a welcoming people who patiently answered their pantomimed inquiries. Their signs indicated a clothed, settled people in large, multi-storied houses seven days upstream, a very brave, warlike, and numerous people who, as members of a different nation, gave the Sumas a great deal of trouble. The Spaniards pressed on to see for themselves.

Fifteen days later they reached the pueblos and initial disappointment: first, a long-abandoned pueblo and then, thirty miles south of present Socorro, a contemporary pueblo whose people had fled. Perhaps they knew of Spanish slave raids in the south; perhaps memories of Coronado's army still stalked the Pueblo world.

Impressed by substantial architecture, good pottery, and well-tended fields, the Spaniards carefully refrained from damages and camped nearby to await an opportunity to make friends. Visitors soon rewarded their patience. A few Indians came to see what they wanted and what manner of men they were. Plying the emissaries with gifts and kind treatment, the Spaniards sent them back with peaceful messages. The pueblo's residents came home, and visitors streamed from other pueblos to see the strangers. Their friendly overtures included gifts: quantities of corn, beans, and calabashes, cotton blankets, and tanned buffalo hides.

Whether Indians or Spaniards first suggested the idea is unclear, but the Spaniards encouraged the Indians to think the intruders children of the sun, which had given them guns for protection. Sometimes they claimed only that the friars were children of the sun, and the soldiers children of the friars. Claim to some godlike status was the same expedient that Alarcón had used to good advantage among Indians of the lower Colorado River forty years earlier. Whether the friars agreed to that pagan invention and how they hoped to reconcile it with the gospel they had come to preach are also unclear.

The Rodríguez-Chamuscado party had entered the Pueblo world at the Piro towns, some twenty in all, which were the southernmost in the Rio Grande Valley. Four days among them gave the Spaniards preliminary acquaintance with patterns of Pueblo life and some information about other pueblos to the north with whom the Piros were at war. The Spaniards proceeded upstream from Piros to Tiwas, gathering information as they went.

It was a hopeful time. The farther they went, the larger the pueblos they found, the better the houses, the more numerous the people. Everywhere the Pueblos greeted the visitors with generous gifts of food. The Spaniards' impressions were overwhelmingly favorable, though their comprehension of Pueblo life was necessarily limited by the language barrier. A literate soldier, Hernando Gallegos, collected some vocabulary in each nation, particularly such key terms as corn and water. Convinced that these friendly, intelligent Indians would readily become Christians if only interpreters were available, he hoped to return to their land himself.[8]

The Chamuscado-Rodríguez party made a far-ranging reconnaissance of more than sixty pueblos, including Ácoma, Zuñi, and the pueblos east of the Manzanos in the saline area. They heard of the Hopi towns, but they did not venture that far. On the Rio Grande they explored as far north as the Keres towns; they also reconnoitered the Galisteo basin and the Jémez area. Ever alert to mining potential, the Spaniards noted in some pueblos interesting rocks acquired from Indians in the buffalo regions and asked to see the source of the specimens. Their hosts refused to guide them for fear of clashing with the plains dwellers. Years of trade had not altered the fundamental enmity of nomads and Pueblos.

The soldiers resolved to visit the plains on their own early in September. Fray Juan de Santa María then decided to return alone to Mexico to report their discoveries, ignoring his companions' vigorous objections. His solitary departure alarmed the Pueblos, who feared that the friar was going to bring more Christians to put them out of their homes. In an exchange limited to sign language, the remaining Spaniards could not adequately reassure the questioning Indians. Only later did they learn that Indians killed Fray Juan a few days after he left the party.

Meanwhile, Chamuscado's group pressed on to the plains without a guide, met Apaches, and overcame their initial hostile suspicions by gunning down forty buffaloes and sharing the meat. Though pressed to join the Apaches for bigger hunts, the Spaniards hurried back to the Rio Grande where they had left the Pueblos in an ominously restive mood.

Their own provisions exhausted by the journey to the plains, the Spaniards made their first request for Indian stores. The Pueblos simply withdrew to their houses. The soldiers quickly conferred. Sensing that any forcible seizure of supplies would precipitate revolt, the

[8] Hernan Gallegos, "Relation of the Chamuscado-Rodríguez Expedition," in George P. Hammond and Agapito Rey, eds., *The Rediscovery of New Mexico, 1580–1594*, p. 83.

eight armed, mounted men nevertheless preferred swift death in battle to a long ordeal of starvation. Displaying a measure holding a half-peck of corn meal, they fired their guns into the air to show that they would have the containers filled, either peacefully or by force. The Indians then brought corn meal from every house in the Pueblo, and the story of their intimidation spread throughout the region. Each pueblo the Spaniards visited after that gave exactly the same amount of corn meal, so that supplies were never again a problem. The Indians also gave so many turkeys that the Spaniards merely thought them little valued by the Pueblos, never guessing their ceremonial import. Gallegos complacently ventured that the Pueblos had now accepted the principle of paying tribute and would willingly do so whenever colonization should occur.[9]

Only when they learned of Fray Juan's death did the Spaniards grow frightened. They had felt secure in the assumption that the Indians believed them immortal children of the sun. Now that the Indians knew a Spaniard could be killed as easily as any other mortal, the soldiers were sure that the natives would conspire to slaughter them, so they resolved to withdraw from the region. The two friars determined to stay, despite the soldiers' protest that missionaries could accomplish nothing without sufficient forces to control the natives.

An armed clash occurred when Indians killed three horses. The Spaniards resolved to prevent further attacks at all costs because they knew as well as the Indians that their lives depended on their horses. On a smaller scale, the circumstance matched that which began the Tiguex War forty years earlier, but Chamuscado tried psychological warfare instead of massive destruction. His soldiers fired guns within several pueblos suspected of complicity in the horse incident, took some captives back to camp, and set up a block on which to behead them before a thousand Indian witnesses. By prior arrangement among the Spaniards, at the crucial moment of the "execution" ceremony the friars rushed in and successfully tussled with the soldiers to effect a triumphant "rescue" of the victims. The Indian crowd carried off friars and prisoners together to protect them from the soldiers. Chamuscado hoped that the charade would create enough gratitude toward the friars to safeguard them after his departure.

Whether or not the stunt improved the friars' standing among the Pueblos, it confirmed the Indians' fear and resentment of the soldiers. They tried to placate them with great quantities of turkeys, alive and

[9] *Ibid.*, pp. 94–95.

dead, as well as Pueblo foodstuffs. Perhaps the Pueblos reckoned that the offerings had the intended effect: for the rest of the soldiers' stay, they took care not to antagonize the natives, lest they endanger the friars who would stay unprotected. On leaving for Mexico in January 1582, Chamuscado charged the natives to look after the friars well, and he promised to return with many more Christians, including women. The Indians professed joy at the news and promised to have the fathers waiting, fat and well, to greet them. All nineteen Mexican Indian aides remained with the missionaries, but no Pueblo Indian would agree to visit New Spain with the soldiers. For the friars' safety, Chamuscado refrained from taking any by force.

The journey home proved onerous. Chamuscado fell gravely ill and died less than a hundred miles short of Santa Barbara. Probably the friars were already dead when the remaining soldiers reached Santa Barbara in April 1582. Word of the martyrdom at Puaray pueblo of Fray Agustín Rodríguez and Fray Francisco López reached Mexico that summer with two Mexican Indian servants who had escaped. So poor were communications, however, that the news did not reach Santa Barbara before a rescue party rode off in November to seek the friars.

Chamuscado's returning men set Santa Barbara ablaze with concern for the friars' safety and lust for the wealth of the north. Inevitably, the reports exceeded the facts. Felipe de Escalante and Hernando Barrado testified that their party had discovered eleven mining areas rich in silver as well as a saline rich in excellent salt. Estimates of populations in the pueblos multiplied as the men looked back on their adventure and multiplied again as the story traveled. The Pueblos' little cotton fields grew vast in retrospect, and the soldiers recalled a gift of 2,000 blankets at one pueblo. They remembered also a veritable ranchers' paradise: abundant woods, pastures, water, and thousands of humpbacked cattle, not very wild or fierce and far tastier than Castilian animals. Escalante and Barrado put enough stock in their own stories to volunteer to settle in New Mexico and help to save the many souls enslaved by the devil in that region. The more ambitious Gallegos hurried to Spain to petition the king to let him conquer New Mexico at his own expense. In Mexico City, Madrid, and Seville, the ponderous machinery of Spanish monarchy slowly began to decide the fate of the Pueblo world.

Frontier people had scant sympathy with the careful processes of government. Fortune hunters schemed to circumvent the laws and claim New Mexico for themselves. Rumors had the friars dead and all pueblos up in arms: the viceroy debated whether to send an official military expedition. The Franciscans, alarmed for their brethren, found the vice-regal deliberation intolerable. They hastily accepted the offer of Antonio de Espejo to head a rescue expedition and sent two friars off to New Mexico with him in November 1582, apparently unaware of their lay benefactor's dubious status.

Espejo, an ambitious Andalusian of some prominence as a cattleman on the northern frontier, was a fugitive from justice, charged with complicity in the murder of two cowhands. He needed a conspicuous good work to redeem his reputation. What better course than to go at his own expense to rescue two missionaries and perhaps establish at the same time his own claim as conqueror of New Mexico? He led the two friars and thirteen assorted laymen off to the Rio Grande with the usual complement of servants, including natives of the Conchos area to serve as interpreters.

The Chamuscado-Rodríguez party had done such a good job of pacification among the Indians of the Conchos Valley and La Junta regions that a year later most of them welcomed Espejo's party peacefully and even enthusiastically. Encouraged by their friendliness and by rumors among them that the friars still lived, the Spaniards hurried upstream, reaching the Piro towns in February 1583.

The Spaniards eagerly observed and inquired, gathering all the information possible through sign language and lines scratched upon the ground to show distances between pueblos and numbers and populations of the pueblos. Piro informants indicated that the Tiwas had killed the two friars, three Mexican Indian boys, and a mestizo at Puaray and were now up in arms. They also recounted Tiwa traditions of Coronado: that they had killed nine of his soldiers and forty horses and that the Spaniards in turn had destroyed all the people in one pueblo. Although Coronado's party had never visited the Piros, tales of his visitation upstream lived vividly among them forty years after the event.

The Piros appeared genuinely hospitable, even eager to be helpful, during the Spaniards' brief sojourn. They plied the visitors with gifts: turkeys, corn, beans, corn meal. Many accompanied the visitors from one pueblo to another, perhaps exercising precautionary surveillance, and for the first time Spaniards encountered problems of theft in the pueblos. The Indians wanted iron so badly that they stole it at any opportunity, a great departure from characteristic Pueblo honesty.

Espejo led his party upstream to the luckless dozen Tiwa pueblos once victims of Coronado, now terrified that these Spaniards had come to avenge the dead friars. They fled to the mountains and rejected all overtures to come back to their pueblos in peace. Nothing in Tiwa experience suggested that any Spaniard could be trusted. Espejo could not even guess their numbers, although his force examined their deserted pueblos and provisioned themselves generously from Tiwa storerooms.

The Keres pueblos just upstream sent emissaries with gifts of turkeys and invited the Spaniards to visit. Moving on north and east, the Spaniards were pleased to find larger, more prosperous pueblos and apparent friendliness. In rapid succession they visited the Keres, eastern Tiwa, Tompiro, and Jémez pueblos. At some they bartered sleigh bells and small iron articles for fine buffalo hides.

Rumors of mines near the Zuñis and Hopis drew Espejo westward via Ácoma, which seemed friendly enough on first contact. Danger from roving Querechos seemed to account for the fortress-like location and the constant vigilance. Though the rugged region around Ácoma looked promising, Espejo did not prospect for minerals, because he understood the mountains to be inhabited by numerous, warlike Querechos, as wild as Chichimecas,[10] who occasionally traded salt, game, and hides at the pueblos.

Communications improved at Zuñi, thanks to Mexican Indians who had come with Coronado forty years ago and still spoke some Spanish. They warned that the Hopis were prepared to fight the Spaniards. Many Zuñis volunteered to accompany Espejo to the pueblos of their traditional enemies, and he accepted eighty warriors. To the considerable surprise and gratification of the invaders and the Zuñis' disappointment, the Hopis decided not to fight. Instead, their elders asked for peace, and the people presented gifts of food to the invaders. When Espejo entered the Hopi towns to take formal possession, he found in the main plaza of each a newly erected cross, decked with feathers and lavishly sprinkled with corn meal. A salvo of harquebuses before the cross celebrated the Spanish triumph while the villagers cowered in their houses.

Hopis gave generously of food, firewood, and their excellent cloth, but they had no silver. Espejo led half his party west to seek the rumored mines, while the other Spaniards returned to Zuñi with the war-

---

[10] Generic term applied by Spaniards to the fierce nomadic peoples of the north Mexican plateau, who remained their standard for Indian "wildness" throughout the conquest.

riors. Mountain people, perhaps Yavapais, fled as the prospectors approached, but soon returned to greet them, singing for peace, with crosses of colored sticks on their heads. With unstinting hospitality, they shared their food and shelter with the Spaniards and showed them mineral deposits. Again, disappointment: there was no silver to be seen, only rather poor copper veins, though Espejo would later report rich silver deposits there.

Once reunited at Zuñi, the Spanish party broke up in dissension. Six, including the friars, turned back to Mexico to report the fate of the martyred missionaries. Espejo, more a creature of ambition than of duty, persuaded nine men to stick with him for one last search for possible mines in the Tiwa area, thence to travel home via the buffalo country.

Hostile Indians harried Espejo's group all the way back to the Rio Grande. Ácomas joined Querechos to oppose the Spaniards as common foe. How the Spaniards had antagonized the Acomas is unclear, but the Querechos' grievance was obvious: the Spaniards held two of their women, one given to a Spaniard by her Hopi captor. Trying to get their women back, the mountain dwellers conducted a running skirmish. The retaliating Spaniards burned a *ranchería* and destroyed a fine cornfield. Some reached the Rio Grande wounded; tempers were running short; missing was the friars' restraining presence. Once more disaster loomed over Tiwas on the Rio Grande.

Again the Tiwas evacuated women and children to the mountains. The few men who stayed to deal with the Spaniards steadfastly rejected Espejo's demand that all the population return to their homes. The invaders found that intolerable impudence. They seized about thirty men at one Tiwa pueblo and executed sixteen, shooting some, garroting others. They burned the rest to death in the course of burning the pueblo. As Diego Pérez de Luxán noted, "This was a remarkable deed for so few people in the midst of so many enemies."

Remarkable indeed! The news spread through the Pueblo world while the Tiwas huddled with their grief and terror in the mountains. Frightened Keresans brought offerings of turkeys to ingratiate themselves with the Spaniards. The invaders rested among the Keres pueblos through June, then moved eastward, noting that the territory looked favorable for mining. They found the Pueblos reluctant to supply food because there had been no rain and the Indians feared they would reap no corn that year. The Spaniards tolerated the refusals until they reached Pecos, then extorted corn by threatening to burn that pueblo to the ground. Once provisioned, they seized two men of Pecos to lead them to the buffalo.

With those captive guides, Espejo's party wandered in the heat all July without seeing a buffalo. They were desperately tired and hungry when they met three Jumano hunters early in August 1583, and gratefully accepted their offer of guidance to the junction of the Rio Grande and Conchos, whence the trip was relatively pleasant. The Jumanos *ranchería* welcomed the visitors joyously with a feast of fish; then the Spaniards progressed from one friendly *ranchería* to another. Only the Tobosos fled in terror. On September 10 Espejo's party reached San Bartolomé, where he began at once to maneuver for the right to return to New Mexico as its official conqueror.

Espejo proved to be an imaginative propagandist, if not a scrupulous reporter. He claimed that he had left the majority of Pueblo leaders in a pleased and grateful mood, eagerly looking forward to his promised return with richer gifts. His official report omitted the clashes, the destruction and intimidation of natives that another member of the party recorded frankly.[11] Espejo described Pueblo life in great detail, praising their cleanliness and order, and reported a political structure very much like those with which Spaniards had dealt successfully in Mexico, hoping thus to suggest ease of conquest. He exaggerated the economic potential of New Mexico beyond all reason, particularly in the matter of minerals. No inkling of the real difficulties could be drawn from his boundless praise of the Pueblos and the natural resources of their homeland.

Who could doubt, on the basis of the Gallegos and Espejo reports, that the Crown's clear interest and duty lay in the colonization of New Mexico? No one dug from archives the testimonies of Coronado's veterans: that New Mexico was a cold, sterile land that would never yield a profit and would cost a fortune to colonize; that its natives were rich only in huge grinding stones with which to break the bones of Spanish soldiers. The question before the Crown was no longer whether Spanish Christendom should embrace the Pueblo world, but how soon and under what leader. In 1583 Felipe II instructed his viceroy in New Spain to appoint a suitable person to reduce the Indians

---

11 Antonio Espejo, "Report of the Expedition . . . to the Provinces and Settle- of New Mexico," in Hammond and Rey, *Rediscovery of New Mexico*, pp. 213 ff.; Diego Pérez de Luxán, "Account of the Antonio de Espejo Expedition into New Mexico, 1582," ibid., pp. 153 ff.

of New Mexico under the principles of the Law of 1573, at no expense to the Crown.

Important considerations of foreign policy nudged the Crown to quick decision concerning New Mexico. That most troublesome English raider, Francis Drake, had made home port in 1580 after circling the globe to escape Spanish vengeance. Rumor was that he had discovered en route the Strait of Anian, the fabled northwest passage. If Spain were to maintain her New World hegemony, she must at once find and control the Strait of Anian. New Mexico seemed the most likely outpost for that venture.

However complex and far-reaching the Crown's motives, any man could see in the recent reports of New Mexico fortunes to be gleaned by settlers with *encomiendas* of industrious Indians and vast mining and agricultural operations. The more ambitious also dreamed of exploring and occupying the country of Quivira and beyond to the Strait of Anian. There was no shortage of contenders for the honor of conquering the new land, even at enormous personal expense. A dozen years of stiff competition for the appointment ensued. In 1595 the contract was awarded to Don Juan de Oñate, heir to a great Zacatecas mining fortune, but vacillations by the Crown delayed Oñate's actual colonization until 1598.

While fifteen years elapsed between the departure of Espejo and the arrival of Oñate, the Crown's delay did not protect the Pueblo world from intrusion all that time. Filibusters from the lawless northern frontier settlements twice sought their fortunes among the Pueblos, only to be pursued and discredited by authorized forces. The incidents broadened Pueblo experience of the Spaniards, but they must also have compounded confusion and apprehension in the Pueblo world.

The first filibustering sprang from the illegal slave traffic on the northern frontier. Despite the Crown's abhorrence of Indian slavery and its repeated bans, traffic in Indian slaves persisted in remote areas. One of the most brutal slaving operations was run by the governor of Nuevo León, Luis de Carvajal de la Cueva, whose henchmen preyed upon unoffending Indians of the lower Rio Grande. When the viceroy had Carvajal arrested to break up the operation, the enterprise continued under his lieutenant-governor, Gaspar Castaño de Sosa, with a gang of sixty soldiers considered by the viceroy "outlaws, criminals, and murderers—who are rebels against God and king."[12]

[12] Viceroy Villamanrique to Don Luis de Velasco, Tezcuco, Feb. 14, 1590, ibid.,

Viceroy Luis de Velasco fell heir to the problem on taking office in 1590 and promptly adopted his predecessor's recommendation for strong measures to break up the gang. He directed Castaño to cease taking and selling Indians as slaves and attached to that order his negative reply to Castaño's petition for permission to go to New Mexico, explicitly forbidding him to leave without authorization.

Seeing his lucrative slave trade and his official position in jeopardy, Castaño defied the viceroy. In July 1590, Castaño headed for New Mexico with a wagon train laden with the trappings of colonization: equipment, supplies, and a full complement of men, women, and children. He had scrounged the capital by promising to repay investors in slaves, to be shipped back as he forged north. Thus, as the caravan wended to a Rio Grande crossing near present Del Rio and on up the Pecos Valley, the Spaniards scoured the countryside, prospecting for minerals and seizing Indians. Although the mineral outlook was disappointing, Castaño reckoned profit in captives, whether kept as servants or sent back as merchandise.

As its haphazard beginning portended, the group was ill-organized and undisciplined. Shortages of provisions and water threatened their survival until Castaño forged ahead to Pecos in December and seized provisions, much as Espejo had done seven years earlier. It was a poor start for ostensibly peaceful colonization, but Castaño left conciliatory messages for the outraged Pecos and rode on to the pueblos of the Rio Grande Valley.

At some pueblos Castaño found a gracious reception, at others distinct hostility. Refraining from provoking battle, he ceremoniously took possession in the king's name at each pueblo that received him. A horde of Indian observers accompanied him from pueblo to pueblo, watching closely as he repeated the ceremony. Castaño pantomimed explanations of his peaceful purpose and the concepts of allegiance to the king and the meaning of the cross: at least, that was his intention. Hearing no dissent or question from the audiences, Castaño assumed them to have understood his proposition and to have pledged themselves vassals of the king, subject to a three-man local government that he appointed in each pueblo. The symbol of their new status was a large cross, raised in the main plaza of each pueblo with sounding trumpets and gunfire. Surely it was an impressive ceremony, but what

---

pp. 296–298. The ensuing discussion of the Castaño, Morlete, and Humaña expeditions relies upon documents in the same collection.

must it have meant to the watching Pueblos beyond the obvious fact that the business satisfied the Spaniards and was to that extent useful?

Castaño established his colony at Santo Domingo pueblo, from which place he continued to explore, prospecting for minerals and taking formal possession of pueblos as he traveled. Though he claimed to have established friendly relations with most of the pueblos he visited, he could not manage his own colony. Dissension ran rife. Castaño blamed his followers' discontent on his virtuous refusal to let them plunder the natives. Some sought and received his permission to return to Mexico, but they dared not attempt the journey for lack of escorts. The troublesome situation was resolved only when Captain Juan Morlete arrived to haul the crew back to Spanish justice.

Viceroy Velasco had been infuriated to learn that Castaño had defied his orders and had penetrated to New Mexico with "all the riffraff left over from the war against the Chichimecas." Not only did their slaving outrage his legal and moral sensibilities; he also feared that their crimes against the natives exposed all the northern provinces to retaliatory wars. Thus, in October 1590, Velasco dispatched Captain Morlete with forty soldiers and a friar to pursue Castaño and to attempt restitution for his crimes. As many as possible of the Indians sold into slavery from Nuevo León were gathered up to accompany Morlete northward. The captain was to accord them every kindness, restore them to their homes, and try, with the friar's help, to convince them of the king's sincere interest in their souls. He was also to arrest men who had received slaves from Castaño, as accessories to his crimes, confiscate their slaves, and ship them to Mexico City for trial.

Captain Morlete pursued his objectives vigorously. Following Castaño's trail northward, he met soldiers and traders returning with Indian captives. In short order, the Spanish offenders were under arrest and the Indians set free. Liberation of those captives reassured other Indians of the area, who received Morlete cordially as he hurried on to the filibusters' camp. At Santo Domingo he found the colonists disillusioned with Castaño's leadership and eager to abandon their misadventure. The Indians of the pueblo were keen to speed their departure, for they had grievances against Castaño and his colonists. Morlete suspected that the Indians would soon have killed the whole sorry company if he had not come to remove them.

Castaño meekly accepted arrest and rode back to Mexico in irons. There, in 1593, he was found guilty of charges including invasion of lands inhabited by peaceable Indians, raising troops, and unlawful entry into New Mexico. His sentence: six years of exile from New Spain, serving the king without salary in the Philippine Islands, under penalty of death for any default. There he died, when Chinese galley slaves revolted on his vessel. Viceroy Velasco was glad to be rid of Castaño, whose presence in New Spain he thought inimical to peaceful, orderly colonization of New Mexico.

What were the Pueblos to make of the Castaño-Morlete episode? It marked the first thrust of viceregal authority into that remote region expressly to protect Indians against abuse by Spaniards. Morlete, struggling to explain his errand with signs, fretted that his lack of interpreters prevented adequate reassurances to his Pueblo hosts. He stayed about forty days, letting his squad rest and prepare for the return journey while he collected evidence against the filibusters. During that time, he talked as extensively as possible with the natives, learning about them as much as he could. Morlete thought the Pueblos quite peaceful and happy on the whole, though he noted some warfare among them. Asking about several deserted pueblos of the Tiwas, he learned that those Indians had fled for fear that Castaño had come to avenge the dead friars.

Pueblos also used the opportunity to observe. Attentive Indian audiences watched Fray Juan Gómez as he celebrated Mass. They found that the Spanish captain listened carefully to their grievances, and they saw him take away the intruders with their leader in irons. His sign language could convey only limited meanings, but his actions bespoke a better Spanish way than Pueblos had seen before.

Two years later Pueblos experienced another casual brush with Spanish filibusters. In 1593, the governor of Nueva Vizcaya sent Captain Francisco Leyva de Bonilla northward with a small force to punish Indians who had been stealing from frontier ranches. Bonilla gratuitously expanded his errand to invade the Pueblo world. Establishing headquarters at San Ildefonso pueblo, he wandered a year among the Pueblos. Disappointed to find no treasure, he led his men over the buffalo plains to the grass villages of Quivira, quarreling en route with Antonio Gutiérrez de Humaña. At Quivira, Humaña murdered Bonilla and took command of the group, only to be destroyed himself by Quivirans. Five Mexican Indians escaped the slaughter to make their way back to the Rio Grande pueblos; one lived a year among Apaches on the way. No special force pursued Bonilla because the official *entrada* to New Mexico seemed imminent. When Oñate set out for New Mexico five years later, he bore orders to arrest the filibusters. The outcome was entirely fortunate for Oñate: the Quivirans had spared him the nuisance of pursuing the criminals, and the few Mexican Indian survivors at San Ildefonso made useful interpreters.

The filibustering episodes dramatized the difficulties of protecting New Mexican natives from the driving greed and ambition of some Spaniards. Pondering the reports of Captain Morlete and Fray Juan Gómez, Viceroy Velasco reconsidered the basic premise of the New Mexican project.

Velasco did not question that pacification of New Mexico looked worthwhile. All indications were that the Pueblos, invariably described as industrious, intelligent, and orderly, merited prompt inclusion in Christendom. Furthermore, strategic considerations now coincided more than ever with religious duty. Concern about the Strait of Anian continued, while a colony of English heretics posed a new threat on the Atlantic coast. They were reported at 37 degrees, the very latitude at which Spaniards reckoned New Mexico. Spanish authorities hoped, once pacification of New Mexico was well underway, to establish a land route to Florida and solidify their line against the English intruders. The distance was thought not very great.

With so much at stake, Velasco hesitated to risk a private contractor in New Mexico. Obviously, no man would undertake that onerous, expensive colonization without assurance of great profit. Just as obviously, the only sure profit in New Mexico lay in *encomiendas* and tribute from the Indians. To let an entrepreneur exact satisfactory profits from the Indians would surely jeopardize the primary objective of conversion and might make it impossible to pacify New Mexico.

Therefore, the viceroy urged that no contract be let. He proposed instead a royal expedition to undertake pacification in the service of both Majesties, commanded by an officer "of high quality, of an age capable of hard work, with a deeply Christian spirit, and a character commanding the respect of his followers." With the Crown already committed to pay the cost of friars and religious instruction, the additional expense would not be great. Velasco prayed the Crown to make that small extra investment to protect the interests of both Majesties, and he postponed award of the New Mexico contract pending a review of policy.

Aging, ailing Felipe II received Velasco's urgent recommendation in 1592. Despite the king's true concern for Indian souls and his crippling passion for detail, New Mexico surely seemed a minor matter among the crises then besetting the Crown. The rebellion in the Low Countries was in its third grueling decade; intervention in religious wars in France bled his purse; the war with England, which had long smoldered undeclared, had erupted only three years before with the disastrous episode of his great Armada. Every peso counted. The king denied the viceroy's plea.

On September 21, 1595, in the closing weeks of his term, Viceroy Velasco awarded the New Mexico contract to Don Juan de Oñate, who pledged one of the great New World mining fortunes to the venture. From the outset, Oñate's ambitions conflicted with the Law of 1573 and with the whole spirit of the reform movement. He wanted power to allot both land and Indians in *encomienda* and to reserve for himself thirty square leagues with their Indian residents. He also demanded the right to levy from the Indians tribute payable in fruits of the land. Viceroy Velasco denied Oñate any powers or privileges exceeding the Law of 1573. Velasco's successor, the Count of Monterrey, stipulated that Oñate could grant *encomiendas* only on a provisional basis; he must account to the viceroy within three years for all grants and obtain approval to make them permanent. Oñate, who hoped to establish a fief independent of the viceroy and accountable only to the king, accepted Monterrey's terms with mental reservations and sent relatives to Spain to plead his case at court.

Oñate began to assemble his expedition in the autumn of 1595, promptly upon winning the contract. Thanks to delays, first of viceroy and then of king, it was summer 1597 before his final authorization reached Mexico, and January 1598 before the final inspector let Oñate march. The delays cost heavily in money and in human hardship. Helplessly, Oñate and other investors in his camp saw their provisions depleted and their colonists' energies and morale sapped. For residents of the staging area, around Santa Barbara, it was like suffering military occupation. Lawless men from Oñate's camp, often penniless, preyed upon the local populace, quite beyond control of the commander or any other authority.

First inspection, in January 1597, credited Oñate with 205 men and more than 4,000 pesos' worth of supplies. A year later, final inspection showed the force dwindled to 129 men.[13] Oñate thus fell short of his contractual commitment by 71 men and considerable quantities of supplies and cattle. The inspector let him make bond for the shortage,

---

[13] The count did not include the numerous servants and the women and children whom some men took with them. The entire party numbered more than five hundred.

which he pledged to make up by subsequent recruitment, rather than delay his departure any longer. The inspector guessed that there were in the area more men who would join the march but who dared not report for inspection because of legal charges against them. It was just such persons who made it unthinkable to detain the caravan there to assemble more: local residents could not reasonably endure their presence any longer.[14]

So Oñate headed north with a rabble too unruly to be tolerated any longer in New Spain, short of supplies, and doomed by untimely departure to reach New Mexico too late to plant crops that year. The strict inspection procedures that had consumed crucial weeks had two objectives: to ensure that the colony carry enough provisions to last until it could produce food in the new land, thus avoiding any necessity to levy supplies from the natives; and to keep careful track of persons who advanced under the Spanish flag. Official delays had undermined the first, but the official muster roll attested to the diversity of the migrants.

The call to muster stipulated, under penalty of death, that no Indian, mulatto, or mestizo present himself without stating clearly his identity. One rich colonist declared in his household three female Negro slaves, one mulatto slave, and other mulatto servants, male and female. Many Indians and mestizos came in diverse roles. The 129 enumerated colonists were themselves a motley crowd: a few men of substantial wealth and social standing, several more of moderate means and aspirations, and many footloose adventurers who brought to the enterprise little more than their own horses and armaments. Some men lacked even those, but attached themselves to the service of Oñate or some other ranking member who would outfit them. Their diverse geographic origins reflected the recent lowering of barriers to non-Castilians in the Indies—a generous sampling hailed from other realms of the Spanish Crown. A striking number were, like Oñate himself, Spaniards born in the New World. Some Peninsular critics of the venture would later scoff that it had been doomed from the outset because it included an inordinate number of Creoles,[15] deemed a particularly dubious risk with a Creole commander. From the very beginning,

---

[14] Count of Monterrey to the King, Mexico, May 4, 1598, in George P. Hammond and Agapito Rey, eds., *Don Juan de Oñate, Colonizer of New Mexico, 1595–1628*, I, 390–392. The discussion of the Oñate period relies upon the documents and analysis in this two-volume work of Hammond and Rey.

[15] I.e., persons of pure Spanish or French blood born in the New World.

Spanish colonists carried a complex heritage of caste and prejudice to New Mexico.

The caravan also carried the tensions between Church and State that ran deep in the Spanish world. Official raison d'être of the New Mexican venture lay in a small missionary contingent—seven Franciscan friars and two lay brothers, led by Father Commissary Alonso Martínez, supported by royal benefaction, and quite independent of Governor Oñate's authority. The Franciscans feared that Oñate's settlers would undermine the conversion by abusing Indians, but the viceroy assured them that Oñate was forbidden to allot any Indians for work and that any levy of tribute would be as light as possible.

If some conflict was anticipated, there was also a moderating interdependence. The friars relied upon Oñate's force for protection and were properly concerned with the emigrants' souls. The colonists looked to the friars for their spiritual necessities, and some were piously interested in the missionary purpose. Oñate and Fray Alonso accorded each other the respectful courtesy due the ranking representatives of the king and the pope on the newest frontier of New Spain.

By April 30, 1598, Oñate had led the whole extraordinary aggregation across the Rio Grande—no mean feat with heavily laden wagons and great herds of livestock. They paused to celebrate the crossing and took formal possession of New Mexico in the name of Felipe II. Then, just as surely as the king's delays had betrayed Oñate's interests, Oñate betrayed the king's instructions. Because the supplies intended to sustain the colony until its first harvest had already dwindled alarmingly, Oñate approached the pueblos in search of food.

Lest he alarm the Indians by advancing with his whole colony unannounced, Oñate moved ahead with a few soldiers and two friars. Of course, Oñate never reported his illegal requisition, but veterans of the march later testified that Oñate loaded eighty pack animals with maize at the southernmost pueblos, to the Indians' manifest sorrow. Oñate only recorded that he renamed Teypana pueblo "Socorro" because it furnished much maize.

Oñate's advance party found succeeding pueblos upstream deserted, but camped in them, presumably commandeering part of their stores, and received Indian visitors from many places. The Spaniards suspected that they came to spy, but the encounters were civil.

A useful breakthrough in communications came with the discovery of two Mexican Indians, Tomás and Cristóbal, who had lived among the Pueblos since the time of Bonilla. They became Oñate's interpreters.

Perhaps their command of Pueblo tongues was no better than their
limited Spanish, but they translated Pueblo speeches into Mexican
Indian languages that more fluent Indians of Oñate's party then translated into Spanish.

That small breach in the language barrier helped the Spanish and
Pueblo leadership grope toward some means of dealing with each
other. Oñate, obligated to deal with the Indians peacefully and not to
harm or annoy them, needed to find authorities with whom to treat.
Probably the leading men of the Pueblos held council in those early
summer weeks to decide their course of action toward the intruders
and to designate spokesmen to meet with them. Somehow, on July 7,
1598, Pueblo leaders met Oñate in a council in the great kiva of Santo
Domingo pueblo.

Oñate had proceeded up the Rio Grande with his new interpreters,
taking formal possession of each pueblo as he went, dedicating each
to a patron saint. He had encountered no overt resistance, but he could
hardly pretend any real conquest. True Spanish dominion, at least in
the eyes of Oñate's company, would begin with this meeting of the
Pueblo leaders, whom he would ask to render obedience and vassalage
to the king of Spain. With scrupulous attention to procedure, interpreters were sworn to faithful performance of their duties. Juan del
Caso Barahona translated Oñate's Castilian into a Mexican Indian
language, which Don Tomás and Don Cristóbal then translated into
local languages.

Oñate announced that he was sent by the most powerful king and
ruler in the world, Felipe II, to save the Indians' souls and embrace
them as his subjects, to protect and bring justice to them. Observing
the Law of 1573, Oñate explained the great advantages to be enjoyed
if the Pueblos should voluntarily submit to the king and become his
subjects and vassals. They would live in peace, justice, and orderliness,
protected from their enemies and enriched in arts and trades, crops
and cattle.

How fared the feudal concepts of vassalage, the complex structure of
mutual obligations, of protection and tribute, in translation from
Castilian to a Mexican Indian language and then to Pueblo tongues?
Whatever they heard, the Pueblo leaders courteously agreed, through
the interpreters, to become vassals of the Most Christian King. Oñate
carefully explained the obligations of vassals: that they would be subject to the wills, orders, and laws of the king; that, if they did not obey,
they would be severely punished as transgressors of the commands of

their king and master. It was a commitment to be made only with the most careful thought. Again, the process of double translation; again, favorable response: the Pueblo spokesmen did indeed wish to submit to His Majesty and become his vassals.

Next serving the other Majesty, Oñate explained that the Spaniards' principal purpose was to save Indian souls. If the Pueblos should become Christians, they would go to heaven to enjoy eternal life of great bliss in the presence of God; if not, they would go to hell to suffer cruel and everlasting torment. All this, he promised, would be further explained by the friars, who represented the pope.

Surely the concepts of Christianity, of heaven and hell and pope, taxed the interpretive skills of Don Tomás and Don Cristóbal, but no one demurred. Indicating that they understood and were ready to become vassals, all the Pueblo leaders knelt to kiss the hand of the father commissary in the name of God and the hand of Oñate in the name of the king. Eminently satisfied with his council, Oñate recorded the Indians' free decision for the peace and satisfaction of the royal conscience.

With what authorities did Oñate actually deal at Santo Domingo? He could not be sure, nor can we in retrospect. There was Pamo, said to be captain of the Keres and of seven pueblos, including Santo Domingo, Cochití, Santa Ana, Zía, San Felipe, and San Marcos. Poquis was said to be captain of the Tiwas and of five pueblos of the west, the names of which do not obviously correlate with modern pueblos. Pestaca was said to be captain of the Jémez, representing eight pueblos of the Jémez and one of Zía. Atequita was identified as captain of the Zía and of two pueblos whose names also do not obviously correlate with any extant. Pacquia was understood to be captain of pueblos called Tziati and Pequen, Cali the captain of a pueblo of Cachichi, and Poloco the captain of five pueblos whose names convey little now. Perhaps they were war captains, perhaps representatives designated for this particular meeting by the councils of elders, perhaps only leaders of certain village factions that favored coexistence with the Spaniards. There did not exist in the pueblos any institution of chieftainship in the sense understood by Oñate. He had in fact achieved at Santo Domingo utter futility: a contract binding nonexistent authorities to obey totally uncomprehended authority.

Oñate had next to find a home for his colony. The wagon train with the main body of the expedition, moving slowly with the livestock, had at last wended up the Rio Grande Valley into the Pueblo world. Rather than build a new Spanish village, Oñate occupied an existing pueblo at the confluence of the Chama and Rio Grande rivers. At his request, the natives vacated Ohke, which the Spaniards dubbed San Juan de los Caballeros. Later, when San Juan proved too small, the Spaniards moved across the stream to occupy the four hundred houses of Yunque pueblo, which they named San Gabriel. Again the natives acquiesced. San Gabriel would remain the capital of New Mexico for a dozen years, until the founding of Santa Fe; San Juan would survive the ordeal of dispossession to endure to the present.

The main party of colonists arrived in mid-August. The sixty-one wagon loads of Spanish goods and domestic gear, the great herds, the families (both Spanish and Mexican Indian) obviously come to stay with their women and children must have astonished the Indians who saw them. Had the Pueblo representatives at the great kiva of Santo Domingo really anticipated intrusion on that scale? If the Indians began to have misgivings about welcoming the Spaniards, they concealed them, filling requests for food and clothing without complaint and making seasonal repairs on the adobe dwellings of San Juan as in all pueblos.

Oñate's earliest troubles were with his own people: most were sorely disappointed by the absence of wealth in the land; some adventurers resented Oñate's firm prohibition against looting or other abuse of Indians. Two days after the wagon train arrived, Oñate discovered a conspiracy of some soldiers to rebel and harshly quashed it. Discontents still simmered within the colony, latent threats to the authority of Oñate and the peace of the land, but surface calm was restored.

To make the borrowed pueblo a proper home, the colonists built an adobe church at San Juan. For its dedication on September 8, 1598, they staged an elaborate fiesta, shared by many Indian visitors. One traditional entertainment, a sham battle between "Moors" on horseback with lances and shields and "Christians" on foot with harquebuses, gave Oñate his first excuse to show the submissive Pueblos Spanish fighting techniques and weapons in action. Perhaps the show reaffirmed lessons taught by Coronado and Espejo before him.

The next day, in the main kiva at San Juan, Oñate convened a second major council of Pueblo leaders. Again, there were present leaders whom the Spaniards understood to be chiefs of the pueblo "provinces" of Tiwas, Puaray, Tsias, Tewas, Pecos, Picurís, and Taos, along with some of their people. Some of the terms indicate language groups; some name specific pueblos. Again, it is impossible to know exactly who was represented and with what measure of authority.

As at Santo Domingo two months earlier, Oñate explained the Spanish Christian view of the world, with its division of authority between the spiritual realm of the pope and the temporal realm of the king, identifying the father commissary as the pope's representative and himself as the king's. He urged the Indians to become vassals of the king so that he might protect them from their enemies and foster their prosperity in many ways, but he warned that vassalage meant subjection to the king's laws and punishment for any infractions. All the delegates affirmed their understanding and willingness.

Oñate suggested that the Indians take missionaries home so that the friars could learn their languages and thus expedite the Indians' religious instruction. They agreed, promising to take good care of them and obey them. In that mission field which had already claimed six Franciscan martyrs, eight volunteered, each to live alone in a pueblo and be responsible for several neighboring pueblos. Some also accepted responsibility for "wild" Indians beyond: Fray Zamora, assigned to Picurís, was also responsible for Taos and all Apaches in the mountains north and east; Fray Alonso de Lugo, stationed at Jémez, was charged with the souls of Apaches and "Cocoyes" of neighboring mountains.

Some Indians were understood to request baptism for their children as they embraced their assigned friars, indeed a heartwarming beginning. That day Don Juan wrote the kind of report that the pious Felipe II liked best to hear of his native children in the Indies, but time had run out for the king.

Whatever the Pueblos understood of the relationship of vassals and king, within a few days the monarchy to which they had sworn allegiance suffered a critical change. On September 13, 1598, Felipe II died, and with him died whatever was left of vigor and ability in the Hapsburg kings of Spain. The succeeding century was a nightmare of decay throughout the realm, with little to protect a remote fringe like New Mexico from the worst corruptions of a bankrupt empire. The closing events of 1598, in Madrid as on the upper Rio Grande, presaged a century of disaster for Pueblos and Spaniards alike.

Oñate's immediate duty was to implement the instructions that Viceroy Velasco had issued three years before; his problem, to reconcile his sworn support of the Crown's benevolent intentions with the imperatives of his own ambitions and those of his men.

Your main purpose shall be the service of God our Lord, the spreading of His holy Catholic faith, and the reduction and pacification of the natives of the said provinces. You shall bend all your energies to this object, without any other human interest interfering with this aim. . . .

Since greater success and better results on the expedition depend on taking the people, provisions, and livestock in good order, . . . you must be extremely careful that the soldiers and settlers go well disciplined, informed, and prepared. Under all circumstances they must treat the Indians well; they must humor and regale them . . . not harm or annoy them nor set them a bad example. . . . You must arrange it so that the provisions and livestock are not lacking when they are needed . . . figuring out first the remoteness of the land and the time that the supplies are desired to last.[16]

But the king and his viceroy and his inspector had forced Oñate to default that obligation. The long delay in camp had left his people in a frame of mind far from "well disciplined, informed, and prepared," and the dwindling of his supplies in that time had forced him from the beginning to demand food from the Pueblos. Fortunately the colony had arrived in summer in a relatively good crop year, so its demands had not yet imposed intolerable burdens on the Pueblos.

The natives must not be compelled to serve against their will, as they resent very much the imposition of personal service. From the very beginning you must endeavor, by all means that seem most suitable to you, to induce the Indians to live in the homes of the Spaniards in order that they may learn trades and help in the necessary labors, both on the farms and in other occupations of the Spaniards. In this manner the Indians will be benefited and will be able to use this knowledge for themselves in farming and building construction, as the Indians in New Spain have learned to do and by which they support themselves and their homes.

Since forcing the Indians to work in the mines results in their running away and abandoning their homes, which is the opposite of what we are trying to do, you must not permit such labor, unless they themselves should want to engage in this work. You shall always keep in mind how important it is to predispose and incline the Indians to live among the Spaniards and help them with their work, and thus avoid the need of employing negro slaves, who mistreat the Indians, and whom they fear for the harm they cause them.

A little progress had been made toward those goals. Indians working

---

[16] Viceroy Luis de Velasco, Instructions to Don Juan de Oñate, Mexico, October 21, 1595, in Hammond and Rey, *Don Juan de Oñate*, I, 65–68. Quoted by permission of the University of New Mexico Press (copyright 1953).

with Spaniards at San Juan on the irrigation ditch and church building had begun to learn something of Spanish engineering techniques and the manufacture and use of adobe bricks. But, instead of building a proper settlement, the Spaniards had dispossessed a whole pueblo. How easy would it be now to attract Indians to stay with Spaniards, except for a pitiful few of San Juan who chose to carry wood and water for the intruders as the price of staying in their own homes? As for the farm work contemplated in the instructions, Oñate's settlers had come too late to plant crops. Moreover, the governor would now focus all energies on exploration for exploitable resources. The question of free Indian labor or Negro slaves in the mines was moot unless mines could be found.

Thus, the colony relied upon the natives for food, perhaps misled by the Pueblos' generous hospitality to visitors at harvest time. At first the Indians were paid for food taken from them, but sales came increasingly under duress as Indians grew reluctant to trade vital foodstuffs for Spanish trinkets. As the bitter cold of a New Mexican winter set in, the colony also requisitioned blankets and skins from the Indians, probably without comprehending at first the scarcity of those items or the hardships created by the demands. Firewood became another source of tension. Spaniards and Mexican Indians, suffering acutely from unaccustomed cold, could not understand how Pueblos warmed their homes and kivas with such tiny fires; for themselves, they required great quantities of firewood. The Pueblos, scrupulously frugal with the resources of their sparse environment, were offended and alarmed by the colonists' careless consumption of wood. Spring planting brought yet another strain: the Spaniards' livestock trampled and browsed through the Pueblos' unfenced fields.

Oñate was absent from San Juan when approaching winter and the settlers' growing demands began to erode Pueblo tolerance. The governor spent the autumn exploring, drawing more pueblos into sworn vassalage while desperately seeking some wealth to justify his enterprise. Five times Oñate repeated the ceremonial acceptance of Pueblo vassals: twice for clusters of pueblos east of the Manzanos, presumably the Tompiro and Jumano peoples; then, proceeding to the three principal groups in the west, at Ácoma, the Zuñi pueblos, and the Hopi pueblos. He searched in vain for the route to the South Sea, but he prospected with some success for minerals in present northeastern Arizona.

Meanwhile, the governor's nephew and principal lieutenant, Vicente de Zaldívar, reconnoitered the buffalo plains, whence he returned no richer but considerably wiser about the prospects of wrangling buffaloes. His brother Juan then rode off with reinforcements for Oñate. As had his uncle, Juan de Zaldívar procured supplies from pueblos on his route. To avert possible bullying or robbing of the natives, he ordered his thirty soldiers to pay for everything they took from the natives and issued sundries to barter for provisions.

Zaldívar followed the governor's trail, probably oblivious to the strain suffered by pueblos required for a second time that season to supply food and firewood for thirty soldiers and corn for their horses. Though reluctance to sell was apparent in pueblos east of the Manzanos, not until the troop reached Ácoma early in December did any Indians actually try to refuse. With his men and horses hungry and feeling keenly the biting cold in their barren campsite, Zaldívar insisted until the Ácoma leaders sadly agreed to provide food, water, and firewood. The principal purchase was to be a quantity of corn meal, which the women had yet to grind. Zaldívar agreed to return the next day for the meal.

On the morning of December 4, 1598, Zaldívar left a dozen soldiers in camp to guard the horses and led eighteen up to Ácoma to purchase the promised supplies. Aware that the natives were loath to sell, Zaldívar carried plenty of attractive trade articles, such as hatchets, and carefully kept his men together, lest some isolated incident mar the transaction. Unfortunately, purchasing meal from women who really did not want to sell proved slow business. To accumulate the needed amount before twilight, Zaldívar finally divided his party to bargain separately in several sectors of the pueblo.

Suddenly, in a sector visited by one squad, a great outcry arose. Violence flared throughout the pueblo. Juan de Zaldívar and most of his men died in the melee. A few hurtled off the great rock, to be picked up from the sand below by the guard left in camp. The Ácomas drew up their long ladders to barricade themselves in their great sky fortress. The surviving men of Juan de Zaldívar's force reported back to his brother, Vicente, then in charge at San Juan. Oñate, who had given up waiting at Zuñi for his reinforcements and started homeward, heard the news from messengers on the trail. He hastened to San Juan to share the grief and terror, the horrible state of shock, that pervaded the colony's first New Mexican Christmas.

Certain that the massacre at Ácoma had been calculated treachery by the natives, the Spaniards resolved to punish them accordingly.

Vengeance and grief demanded it, especially in the heart of Vicente de Zaldívar. So did self-preservation: would not failure to punish Ácoma encourage other natives to slaughter the entire colony?

Oñate argued that the Ácomas were no longer simple savages. They had sworn obedience and vassalage to the king and were subject to his laws. The father commissary and three friars present at San Juan agreed that a punitive campaign would satisfy the four criteria of a just cause: protection of the innocent, restoration of goods seized unjustly, punishment of transgressors of the law, and attainment and preservation of the peace, "which is the main purpose of war."

Vicente de Zaldívar demanded the right to lead the punitive force, and Oñate had not the heart to refuse his nephew's request. Critics would later point out that the grief-stricken brother was a poor choice to administer objective justice. Zaldívar led seventy soldiers to Ácoma in mid-January and demanded surrender. Drawn up for battle on their towering rock, the Ácomas shouted their defiance. In two days' fighting, Zaldívar systematically captured the pueblo, sacked and burned it, destroying most of the population. A few escaped. Some prisoners were hauled to Santo Domingo pueblo for trial: seventy or eighty men, five hundred women and children.

Oñate promptly set the legal machinery in motion, appointing a Spanish attorney for the defendants. Captain Alonso Gómez Montesinos swore to defend them to the best of his knowledge and intelligence, which were among the finest in the colony, and pledged his person and property as performance bond. With Don Tomás sworn in as interpreter, the Indian witnesses stood in turn to tell of the attack on Juan de Zaldívar's party.

Their versions conflicted. Some of the Indians said the Spaniards had been killed because they asked for corn, flour, and blankets. One had heard that the Spaniards set off the melee by killing an Indian; another said the Spaniards started it by wounding an Ácoma Indian. One had heard that it happened because a soldier either asked for or took a turkey. The testimonies suggested general confusion among the Indians about the outbreak more convincingly than they supported the Spaniards' charge of premeditated treachery.

The soldiers testified to Zaldívar's strict care to prevent his men from abusing Indians throughout their journey and to his particular effort to keep them together at Ácoma so none could bother the Indians. Alonso González testified that he had seen a soldier named Martín de Biberos holding a turkey and an Indian woman vociferously complaining. He did not know whether Biberos had paid for the turkey or why the woman objected, but it occurred at the time and place of the war cry that sparked the fray. No one noted how the González testimony dovetailed with that of the Indian Excasi, who had heard in the pueblo that they had killed the Spaniards because a soldier demanded a turkey. González went on to say that the Indians had attacked without provocation and so must have committed premeditated treason.[17]

In the trial records published four centuries later, the affair of the turkey stands out as grave provocation, climaxing a classic tragedy of the failure of one people to comprehend and respect the necessities of another too unlike themselves. Ever since Coronado refused to believe that Zuñis kept turkeys only for feathers, never to eat them, successive Spaniards had considered turkeys merely plentiful foodstuff of New Mexico. No Spaniard had ever grasped the significance of the gifts of turkeys, dead and alive, which frightened Pueblos laid before invaders again and again; from their very quantity they had thought them little valued by the Indians. On the day of reckoning at Ácoma, half a century after Coronado, Zaldívar's hungry soldier surely saw that Indian woman's turkey as a succulent roast. He could not know, and probably would not have cared, that she needed the turkey for even more than the warm cloak its feathers could yield. At Ácoma, life itself turned upon prayers borne by turkey feathers, and certain prayer sticks and ceremonial headdresses could not be made without them. Thirteen Spaniards died the day she howled her outraged protest, and countless Ácomas afterwards paid with their lives or freedom.

Within the next two years, Spaniards would learn the value of turkeys in the Pueblo world. The best of them would suffer in conscience as they saw Indians flee from their pueblos at the approach of Spaniards, abandoning everything except the precious turkeys tucked under their arms as they fled. Some settlers would even understand the provocation suffered by the Ácomas and list the unjust, harsh reprisal among crimes charged against Governor Oñate. But in February 1599, the outcome of the four-day trial was never much in doubt. Although Captain Montesinos surely did his best for his clients, to the Spanish soldiers who sat as judge and jury it was obvious that the Indians of Ácoma were guilty of treason by an unprovoked, premeditated attack. The sentences fitted the crime as they saw it. All male captives over

[17] Testimony of Alonso Gonzales, ibid., pp. 447–449; Statement of Indian Excasi, ibid., p. 467.

twenty-five were condemned to have one foot cut off and to render twenty years' personal service. Boys between twelve and twenty-five and women over twelve were sentenced to twenty years' personal service. Children under twelve were placed under Spanish supervision, the girls charged to the care of Fray Alonso Martínez and the boys to Vicente de Zaldívar.

To deter further rebellions, the Spaniards widely publicized the outcome. They chopped off the feet of men of Ácoma in public ceremonies at several pueblos on successive days. Two luckless Hopis who had chanced to be visiting Ácoma when it fell were sent home with their right hands severed, just to warn those remote pueblos. The women, children, and youths were herded off to San Juan to begin their twenty years of servitude.

Perhaps the public mutilations looked as shockingly barbaric to watching Pueblos as to twentieth-century eyes, though death or servitude was not an uncommon result of clashes between Indian peoples. Mutilation and servitude were not extraordinary penalties in sixteenth-century Spain, particularly for crimes as serious as those of which the Ácomas were found guilty. Although he intended punishment severe enough to discourage any further attack on his colony, Oñate exercised relative lenience when he eschewed the capital punishment that would have befallen a Spaniard judged guilty of the same crime. Whatever his reasoning, Oñate's deterrent apparently worked: the Pueblos would suffer more than eighty years before they again rose up in violence.

A month after the trial, the father commissary departed with the Ácoma children, whom he would deliver to the viceroy to be reared as Christian wards of the king. With him rode three officers, the governor's messengers to the viceroy, and his recruiting agents. Oñate reported lavish resources in New Mexico, just waiting for Spaniards to exploit them, and asked permission to recruit new settlers and more missionaries. The viceroy granted his request.

With its minimum of truth about New Mexico, Oñate's report carried maximum effect as recruiting propaganda. Enlistments went well: at the end of summer 1600, seventy-three new Spanish colonists set out for New Mexico, most with wives, children, and many servants. With them traveled seven more Franciscans. Thanks to Oñate's well-publicized report and his agents' propaganda, all were enormously hopeful of success in the new land.

Like the original colony, the reinforcements were closely inspected at Santa Barbara. Great quantities of goods procured by Oñate's kinsmen were loaded into the wagons; like the new colonists, they helped make up the contract shortages for which the governor had made bond in 1598. Many of the colonists brought substantial personal wealth. Their livestock, plus Oñate's increment, made a huge herd. Inspectors invited local residents to satisfy themselves that none of their own stock was being rustled off to New Mexico.

As in 1598, racial identities were carefully checked. Many Mexican Indians went, most as servants; a few went independently. A mulatto, branded on the face, was challenged to produce his reason for going and certified that his owner had given him permission to serve on the expedition with *caudillo* Juan Bautista Ruano. An unmarried mulatto woman named Isabel, traveling alone, anticipated annoyance and asked the inspectors for an affidavit of her free status as the legitimate daughter of a free Negro father and an Indian mother, producing three sworn witnesses who had known her parents. Affidavit won, she journeyed to New Mexico legally armed against abuse on racial grounds.

A tall mulatto youth showed his affidavit of freedom from his owner, Mateo Montero of Los Angeles, who gave his slave both his own name and his freedom, on condition that he join this expedition to New Mexico. Mateo, purchased in childhood, would remain a slave if he stayed in Mexico, so at twenty he headed northward with the slave's brand on his face negated by the certificate of freedom in his hand.[18]

While the caravan rolled toward the Pueblo world, Oñate's colony prepared to welcome the sorely needed increment. Deeming San Juan too small to accommodate the newcomers, the settlers moved across the river to the larger pueblo of San Gabriel. The newly dispossessed Indians of San Gabriel were told to join those of San Juan, who now could reclaim their own homes; most did, though some stayed in their own pueblo as servants of the Spaniards.

The new colonists arrived on Christmas Eve 1600 for a brief season of joyous celebration, the new arrivals thankful to end their arduous journey safely, the first settlers heartened by reinforcements and sup-

---

[18] A New Mexican scholar advances an elaborate hypothesis that Mateo's progeny included the prime instigator of the Rebellion of 1680 and figured prominently in other disorders. The present writer doubts that available evidence supports that hypothesis, but the article provides an interesting analysis of interracial complexities and tensions in colonial New Mexico. See Fray Angelico Chávez, "Pohé-Yemo's Representative and the Pueblo Revolt of 1680," *New Mexico Historical Review* 42 (1967): 85–126.

plies. But the newcomers soon discovered shocking discrepancies between the recruiters' stories and actual conditions. The rich resources reported by Oñate were nowhere to be seen; the colony had achieved almost no agricultural development. Worst of all was the pitiful condition of the Indians, who nevertheless remained so docile that it had been unnecessary to build any kind of fortification at San Gabriel. Oñate had not granted any *encomiendas*, much to the settlers' dismay, but he had required a great deal of labor from the Indians and had exacted so much tribute that the native economy was ruined.

The friars had urged the governor to establish extensive common fields to feed the colony, and the Indians had been willing to do the work in order to protect their own supplies, but Oñate had not come to New Mexico to farm. Instead, he instituted monthly requisitions, sending squads of soldiers to take from the pueblos enough corn to feed his colony of more than five hundred men, women, and children. Oñate also levied an annual tribute of blankets and hides, much of which he distributed to the colonists according to needs. That left the Indians in dire poverty, not only short of food but also stripped of protection against the cold. The effect of the corn levies grew even worse in 1601, a drought year, for the colony's demands had consumed the stores of corn customarily hoarded against drought. Squads of soldiers even ferreted out the Pueblos' sacred seed corn. Indians followed piteously behind to pick up kernels falling from sacks as the soldiers rode away. Often the Indians fled as the soldiers approached a pueblo, leaving behind everything but the turkeys they could carry in their arms, hiding in the highlands until the visitors left with their loot.

The colonists realized that their own hardships were as nothing compared with those of the Pueblos, and some worried intensely. Not only did the abuse of the Indians weigh heavily upon their consciences; they feared that the Indians must surely rise up one day to end their suffering by killing all the Spaniards.

The Indians' suffering also appalled the friars, who felt little hope of converting people who fared so badly at the hands of Christians. Even with Indians who responded somewhat to their ministry, the friars proceeded very cautiously about baptism. Doubting the colony's permanence, they hesitated to baptize souls that might later be left without the sacraments and the means of fulfilling their Christian duties —better leave them unbaptized innocents than expose their souls to the worse risk of apostasy. By March 1601, only one hundred Indians were baptized, mostly San Gabriel residents closely associated with the Spaniards.

The colonists lived sharply divided among themselves that spring. Many young, single men, restive in their disappointment, wanted to abandon the province. More stable members, mostly married men burdened with family responsibilities, were willing, or at least resigned, to settle down to work for the modest living that the land would yield, and they wanted to build a proper Spanish town. For them, the best prospect that life now afforded was to make the most of the New Mexican venture on which they had gambled all they owned. A few, richer and with fewer responsibilities, wanted to concentrate on exploration, still dreaming that if only they could search far enough some great wealth would be discovered.

Oñate led seventy of the most optimistic and adventurous to Quivira in June 1601, unaware that in Mexico City the viceroy was interrogating messengers from New Mexico and beginning to doubt the colony's viability. Like Coronado before him, Oñate reached the grass villages of Wichitan bands on the Arkansas River, where the only "gold" to be seen lay in their fields of pumpkins and corn, and turned back disillusioned.

Meanwhile, drought shriveled that summer's crops at the pueblos and brought to a climax the human ordeal in the upper Rio Grande Valley. Harsh levies stripped the pueblos of food, yet did not yield enough to feed the colonists. Their corn and blankets gone, the Pueblos had nothing to trade to Apaches for meat, and in their starving condition they lacked the strength to go hunting. Emboldened by desperation, the Pueblos began killing livestock. The Spaniards guessed that they themselves would be slaughtered if they did not first starve to death.

In September the colonists convened to examine their plight. Many feared for their souls as well as their lives. Friars cited scriptures proving that mortal wrongs had been done the Indians; the settlers protested that they had been forced to do those things lest their own women and children perish and sadly admitted that they would repeat the sins if they stayed. Abandonment seemed the only remedy. A majority agreed to return at once to Mexico, lay their case before the viceroy, and trust his mercy against the possible charge of criminal desertion. They left early in October, ahead of the winter's cold and Oñate's certain wrath.

Not until he reached San Gabriel on November 24, 1601, did Oñate learn the heavy cost of his Quiviran quest. Of the colony on which he had gambled his fortune and reputation, only twenty-five Spaniards awaited him. He dispatched a hard-riding force to arrest the defectors, but they beat their pursuers to Santa Barbara and the viceroy's protection.

The defectors' testimony utterly damned Oñate. Although the viceroy's investigators allowed for the witnesses' personal grievances against their governor and their obvious stake in justifying their unauthorized departure, their stories fitted all too well with other reports from New Mexico in the past two years. His doubts about Oñate and about New Mexico's economic potential confirmed, the viceroy ordered a study of the desirability of abandoning the conquest.

Once more the ponderous, creaking machinery of the Spanish Empire began to grind toward a decision on New Mexico; once more the rotation of viceroys, which had so ruinously delayed the first caravan, impeded the process. The Crown waited to receive the unprejudiced recommendations of a new viceroy, the Marqués de Montesclaros, who succeeded the Count of Monterrey in 1603. He took two years to study the complex, unfamiliar problem. Evaluation of his recommendations by the king and his council took yet another. Montesclaros judged the New Mexican venture a costly fiasco and advised disengagement, but the king's Christian obligations forbade total abandonment. As long as there existed in New Mexico a single baptized Indian, there remained the duty of protection. While Spanish officialdom wrestled with that dilemma, assuming the conditions reported in 1601, circumstances changed on the Rio Grande.

The departure of most of the Spanish population reduced the pressure on Pueblo food supplies, to the advantage of both peoples. The drought cycle ended. The dwindling of the livestock further diminished the Spaniards' ability to feed themselves, but it also minimized damages to Pueblo fields. Somehow the two peoples coexisted for eight more years, while the Spaniards wondered whether they would receive permission to leave or reinforcements to enable them to stay. Meanwhile, the pressure of Apache raiders against the Pueblos worsened until some feared that the Spaniards' departure would be an even greater calamity than their presence.

Apache raids were an old problem to Pueblos, long antedating Spanish occupation. Indeed, the Spaniards had understood that their relatively easy initial acceptance by the Pueblos stemmed partly from the Pueblos' desire for allies against the Apaches. Particularly at harvest time, Apaches had often preyed upon pueblos while leaving their women and children safely hidden in the mountains.

Perhaps Spanish presence did serve for the first few years to deter raids on the Rio Grande pueblos, for the Spaniards then knew Apaches mostly as traders who sometimes camped near the pueblos to barter meat and hides for Pueblo produce. However, within three years of Oñate's invasion, Pueblos suffered more than ever from Apache raids. Spanish requisitions of corn and blankets had spoiled the Pueblos' stock for the Apache trade and thus wrecked established trade patterns. Pueblos weakened by starvation were hard-pressed to fend off raiders, and the faltering Spanish colony afforded little support to the king's newest vassals.

Just when the Spaniards' exactions weakened the Pueblos, the goods they brought attracted raiders. Metal implements lent themselves to Apache uses, as domestic tools, as ornaments, and as weapons. Some were to be found in the pueblos, where Spaniards had once bartered them for food. The livestock also tempted Apaches, and they began to take a toll, first killing horses, cattle, and sheep indiscriminately for food, then making off with the horses and sometimes their trappings. In the Apache world, revolution began, based on horses and metal.

For Pueblos it was a new testing time: what of those protections promised them as recompense for the burdens borne as vassals of the Spanish king? Oñate, who had so zealously exacted tribute, fell woefully short on the reciprocal obligation of defense. He created a few belated *encomenderos*[19] to spearhead campaigns against marauders, but he could not even secure San Gabriel against Apache raiders. In 1607 Oñate submitted his resignation, warning that his fifty colonists could not remain past June 1608 without help. Fray Lázaro Ximénez carried the governor's resignation to Mexico and explained to Viceroy Velasco, who had just returned for a second term, that the Spaniards' inability to defend the Pueblos as promised had earned the natives' contempt for all things Spanish, even the gospel. Appalled by the breakdown of responsibility to the Crown's Pueblo vassals, Velasco ordered the governor to defend New Mexico and sent eight soldiers to shore up his forces.[20]

[19] France V. Scholes, "Juan Martínez de Montoya, Settler and Conquistador of New Mexico," *New Mexico Historical Review* 19 (1944): 337–342.

[20] Don Luis de Velasco, Instructions to Don Pedro de Peralta, Who Has Been Appointed Governor and Captain General of the Provinces of New Mexico in Place of Don Juan de Oñate Who Has Resigned the Said Office, Mexico, March 30,

Perhaps that gesture toward improved protection bolstered confidence in the Spanish alliance. Perhaps terror of other Indians drove the Rio Grande Pueblos to strengthen their Spanish connection. Picurís, Taos, and Pecos Pueblos leagued with Apaches to extirpate those Pueblos who had accepted Spanish dominion and who would not heed the call to throw off the invaders' yoke.[21] The Rio Grande Pueblos responded in 1608 with a sudden surge toward Christianity. Where the friars had counted only four hundred Indians baptized in 1607, they counted seven thousand in 1608, with more clamoring for baptism when Fray Lázaro Ximénez left New Mexico to report the new situation to Viceroy Velasco.

At that point the government had nearly decided to abandon New Mexico and escort the four hundred Christian Indians to Mexico for protected, subsidized resettlement, but that would hardly be practicable for seven thousand or more. Reluctantly, the viceroy decided to maintain the worrisome province at government expense, expressly to defend the baptized Indians and provide them ministry.

While obligations to Christian Pueblos ruled out abandonment of New Mexico, the known limitations of the province forbade continuation under Oñate or any other entrepreneur. Thus, in 1609, the compromise decision: maintain New Mexico as a royal colony with fifty married soldiers, but eschew further explorations. Twelve friars would be sent to continue teaching and ministering to the Indians; if they wished, they could peacefully and discreetly seek converts in outlying regions. A new governor, seasoned, reliable, sympathetic to friars and colonists alike, would be appointed. No Oñate would ever again be permitted any connection with New Mexico.

Don Pedro de Peralta arrived in 1609 to take charge of the colony, which had been practically leaderless and adrift since Oñate's resignation in 1607. Oñate and his lieutenants returned to Mexico in 1610, stood trial, and sustained heavy penalties for their misdeeds in New Mexico, among which the excessive punishment of the Ácomas counted heavily. Courts did not levy the grimmest penalty that Oñate paid for his New Mexican venture: in a skirmish on the way back to Mexico, *indios bárbaros* killed his only son. Oñate lived another twenty years in Mexico, bereft of realm and heir.

1609, in Hammond and Rey, *Don Juan de Oñate*, p. 1089; Viceroy Don Luis de Velasco, Order Requiring the Governor of New Mexico to Send a Squad of Men to Defend the Spaniards from the Apaches, Mexico, March 6, 1608, ibid., p. 1059.

[21] Fray Francisco de Velasco, April 9, 1609, ibid., p. 1094.

Could the Crown repair the havoc Oñate had wrought in its name? Not unless it could send New Mexico a succession of extraordinarily able and just royal governors, with missionaries as compassionate and forbearing as zealous in the faith. And given such miraculous personnel to mend the torn fabric of the Pueblo world, could the Crown quell or conciliate the Apaches whose threat to the Christian Pueblos had denied it the choice of prudent disengagement? Presuming the usual success of handfuls of Spaniards against countless Indians, the king and the viceroy expected Governor Peralta to eliminate the Apache threat with his allotted fifty men-at-arms.

Spaniards had only a hazy notion of the Apache frontier and comprehended their own national dilemma even less. The able Velasco could not know that the tide had turned against Spain, that rottenness and incompetence in government at every level would dissipate power and wealth, that rivalry between secular and religious forces and conflicts among classes would rend the society from top to bottom. Nor could anyone have anticipated how remarkably the tiny, remote Spanish colony in New Mexico would mirror and even magnify the parent society's weaknesses. Its confrontation with Apaches was singularly ill-timed for Spain.

Apaches, on the other hand, were catching a rising tide—revolutionizing their lives with horses and metal, expanding their ranges and prowess, scoring against old enemies and new rivals on every side. Perhaps the seventeenth century was as exhilarating for Apaches as the sixteenth had been for Spaniards, though Apaches too would feel the abrupt shock of ebb tide in the next century.

CHAPTER 2

New Mexico, 1600-1680

Apaches and Spaniards were strangers when their destinies interlocked. Unknowing Apache warriors determined that Spain must persevere in New Mexico at the same time that unknowing Spaniards' horses and metal stuff sparked a revolution in Apache worlds.

"Apache" perhaps derived from the Zuñi word for enemy. Spaniards applied the term to those uncounted Athapaskan-speaking Indians who roved the peripheries of the Pueblo world, sometime raiders, sometime traders. Thus, "Apache" denoted peoples of diverse life styles, not any single polity or society.

North and west of the Rio Grande pueblos were corn-planting mountain dwellers whom Spaniards learned to distinguish as "Apaches of Navajo" and finally as Navajos. On the plains east of the pueblos, and then northward, roved the buffalo hunters whom Spaniards first dubbed Vaqueros for their dependence on the woolly cattle. Less visible were the mixed life styles characteristic of most Apaches: a summer agricultural cycle spent in sheltered valley camps, farming crops of corn, beans, and squash and gathering wild fruits; summer and fall buffalo hunts on the plains. The rigors of winter brought some to camp outside the sheltering walls of frontier pueblos, trading hides or captives for Pueblo foodstuffs.

How often quarrels precipitated fights between Apaches and Pueblos, or how often accumulated stores at pueblos tempted raiders in precolonial times, is uncertain, but Apaches were usually cautious fighters and pueblos were formidably defended bastions. As long as their capacity to attack and to escape depended solely on their own swift moccasins and as long as the amount of loot could not exceed that which a man could carry on foot, the scale of Apache depredations against Pueblos was necessarily limited. The scale of trade was limited, too, as long as hunting ranges had to be traveled on foot, the take of meat and hides dragged by dog-drawn travois, and captives from enemy camps led in on their own unwilling feet.

Acquisition of the horse meant expanded capacities for hunting and fighting and for raiding and trading. To some Indian peoples it would mean revolution. Among Athapaskans, it was the Navajos who would build a new pastoral life style, adopting sheep as well as horses and becoming more settled and agricultural than before. For most Apaches, the horse meant triumphant intensification of old patterns: capacity to move farther and more often, to dominate long-contested hunting grounds, to terrorize old foes and to attack new ones at greater distances, to carry off more loot and captives, and to accumulate more wealth. Still, old patterns of social organization remained remarkably unchanged, and old values held fast. The horse was readily assimilated into Apache lifeways and even into their myths. They soon treasured it as the precious gift of their own gods rather than the accidental largess of Spaniards.

So very small was the scale of Apache social organization, so extreme the independence of each unit, that it baffled the Spaniards and, subsequently, Anglo-Americans who were absorbed in their own concepts of national entities and well-defined political authority. In three centuries the more massively organized societies would crush the smaller, but at first considerable advantage lay with the Apaches. Spaniards found pursuing the myriad Apache raiders little more rewarding than chasing the gossamer lint of the cottonwood trees in the valleys.

The basic unit of Apache life was the extended family: parents, their unmarried sons, their daughters, and their daughters' husbands and children. They camped together under the leadership of the head of the family, essentially a self-sufficient economic unit. Several family groups usually remained together within a limited territory, cooperating in hunting and warfare and in other activities requiring larger numbers. Leadership of the local group fell by common consent upon the man who had proven himself wisest and bravest over the years, but he was a respected advisor rather than a commanding authority. Several local groups ranging within a feasible distance usually made up a band, the highest level of Apache organization. They convened for important social and ceremonial functions and sometimes cooperated in war. The most notable local group leader emerged as band chief, but the other local headmen served with him as a council, and no one exercised binding powers.

Apache organization was extraordinarily fluid. The dissatisfied could easily shift to another local group or even another band. Nomenclature was fluid, too. Local groups and bands were often known by the name of a noted leader or some feature of their territory. As leadership changed or people moved, old names often fell into disuse and new names emerged. Most persistent were names derived from cultural traits, such as Mescalero or Jicarilla, but the actual composition of those groups must also have shifted considerably during the turbulent seventeenth and eighteenth centuries.

Apache life centered in family camps, humming with the unceasing round of work and ritual that spelled their survival. Men devoted their lives to hunting, raiding, and warfare, ever alert against surprise attack upon the camp or intrusions into their range. To women fell the manifold chores: farming tiny plots of corn, beans, and squash; gathering seeds and fruits; processing the varied foodstuffs and caching surpluses against less abundant times. Women also carried wood and water, cured and tanned animal hides, and manufactured clothing and utensils. Seeing them work so hard, some observers thought Apache women little valued, and never comprehended how much the men's more impressive tasks revolved around feeding, clothing, and protecting the women and children. A highlight of Apache ceremonial life was the girl's puberty ceremony, celebrating each new hope of the people's continuity, and it was through the female line that Apaches counted family descent.

The horse increased the responsibilities and widened the horizons of Apaches. Men had to make horse trappings as well as weapons and bore intensive pressures to raid for horses and metal. Unless they could delegate the chore to children or captives, Apache women had to care for the horses their men brought home. They had to move more often because horses exhausted pasture around a camp even faster than humans consumed local game and wild fruits. However, with horses to carry the people and drag the travois, Apaches could move camp farther and faster, and a group's seasonal rounds could encompass wider territory. They encountered more people and had more stuff to barter. Larger groups could meet more readily for buffalo hunts or such important seasonal events as gathering mescal. The horse not only made it easier to hunt food, but it also became food. Especially when Apache groups were driven from the buffalo plains in the next century, horseflesh became the preferred meat of many.

Horses became a prime medium of exchange, particularly necessary to pay for ceremonials or the bride price for a good marriage. Among both Apaches and Navajos, ownership of horses became the principal measure of wealth and prestige: a man's reputation as a warrior depended directly upon the horses he acquired. If a man or his relatives had to go without horses, it was presumed that he was too cowardly to raid for them. Raids for horses became the endurance test by which men were judged, and lads were accepted as men only after they performed creditably on a raid or war party. Horse racing became their principal sport. Even in death, they believed, a man needed a good horse: his favorite was slain at his grave so he could ride it in the next world.

Highly formalized customs and taboos grew up around the quest for horses. Like raids of earlier times, those for horses grew directly out of the peoples' economic necessities. Navajos and Apaches alike deemed them sacred missions to bring home "the things by which men lived."[1] Solitary raiding was not permissible, for the rituals required to protect raiders from harm and their people from revenge could be celebrated only by several men working together. The magic and rituals used on horse raids were much like those which had always been used in hunting, for in essence they were trying to capture the animals of the enemy, in either case pursuing sacred quarry.

As the horse pervaded the daily lives of Apaches and Navajos, it fixed in their mythologies. It puzzled them at first that Spaniards had been given the horse when they had not, for they knew their own gods had given them the "things by which men live." Myth soon resolved doubt, explaining that the deities had possessed the horse first,

---

[1] LaVerne Harrell Clark, *They Sang for Horses: The Impact of the Horse on Navajo and Apache Folklore.* Other sources for this discussion of the Apaches are Grenville Goodwin, *Social Organization of the Western Apache,* and Harold E. Driver, *Indians of North America.*

before allowing any men to have them, and the gun as well. The Athapaskan culture heroes had chosen wrongly in the beginning, failing to
accept the horse and preferring the bow to the gun. Eventually the
deities gave horses to their Indian children, too, but the Spaniards,
having received them first, had great numbers. The Indians, lacking
enough for their barest needs, began stealing horses and thus waxed
prosperous and happy. They deemed raids no ordinary theft, but a
grand ritual sanctioned by the spirits. Marvelous steeds abounded in
Navajo and Apache myths. Some Apaches relied upon a guardian
horse spirit, mastered the "power of the horse," and used that on raids.
Pueblos, aware that Apaches and Navajos used magical powers in
raiding for horses, tried to invoke countervailing magic against them.

Both Navajos and Apaches formed small, highly organized raiding
parties from the local group. Navajo raiding parties usually numbered
three or four, never more than ten. An Apache raiding party might
have as many as forty men, but usually no more than ten. Although
Spaniards, or perhaps even Pueblos, did not appreciate the distinction,
raiding expeditions were quite separate in purpose from war parties.
Raiders tried to avoid direct encounters; their sole purpose was to seize
enemy possessions. However, the episodes inevitably turned into fights
if victims overtook raiders fleeing with plunder.

Most war parties were formed solely to avenge the death of a kinsman killed by an enemy people, although chances to pick up booty
were rarely ignored if they did not interfere with the central purpose.
A Navajo war party had from thirty to two hundred men; an Apache
war party might involve the warriors of a whole band if many dead
or a very important chief had to be avenged.

Every death at the hands of an enemy required the victim's kin to
kill at least one of the same enemy people. Others might join the kinsmen in the venture, perhaps to fight a hated enemy, to win personal
glory, or to pick up whatever loot might be taken from the enemy. Only
an established leader could head a war party. Preparation involved
whole camps in two nights of war dancing and an intervening day
spent in feasting, sweat bathing for ritual purification, speech making,
and planning.

However distinct the purposes of the war party and the raiding
party, raids were fraught with potential war because a man killed in
the course of a raid or subsequent pursuit had to be avenged. Irate
Spanish and Pueblo pursuers were quite likely to fall upon a group un-
connected with the raid, and those Apache casualties would also re-

quire vengeance. Countless occasions for vengeance also arose from forays of Spanish slavers into Athapaskan ranges. Every encounter that flared into hostility almost inevitably occasioned subsequent war parties.

The tempo of the raids accelerated in proportion to the pressures upon every man to go after horses. From the widely scattered local groups, countless little parties headed toward the Rio Grande to grab the horses, sheep, and metal goods beckoning from pueblos and every *rancho*. No wonder Spaniards and Pueblos felt themselves besieged.

Probably most Apache and Navajo "attacks" upon Pueblos and Spaniards were raids, specifically to seize the prized horses and metal goods. Spaniards condemned all raiders as predators, even while some Spaniards preyed upon Athapaskan camps to seize women and children. In each case, the raiders threatened the well-being and even the survival of the victims, and the victims reacted accordingly.

Reports of governors and missionaries and testimonies of settlers all vividly document the impact of Apache and Navajo incursions in New Mexico throughout the seventeenth century. Less documented, but surely no less important, was the effect of the Spanish slave trade upon Athapaskans and other Indians beyond the province. The illegal character of the trade ruled out formal record keeping, but there were countless references to "Apache" slaves owned by governors and settlers and to even more "Apaches" shipped south to be sold in the mining provinces. It is impossible to know how many of the "Apache" slaves of the documents were actually Apaches or Navajos, and how many were instead captives taken by the Apaches from other "wild" tribes whom they raided, sometimes expressly to garner merchandise for the slave trade.

Most captives were women and children. What must have been the impact of those losses upon the small Apache family camps whose future they embodied? How many simply ceased to exist, their remnants assimilated into some other camp, after an overwhelming loss? How many Apache families had to seize and adopt women and children of other peoples to replace their own lost women and children? What was the effect upon the Caddoan village peoples at the eastern edge of the plains and upon other peoples, still without the horse, whose women and children were seized by Apaches? How many women and children of Pueblos and Spaniards of New Mexico, stolen by raiders, were assimilated by Apaches struggling to survive? Of the "Apaches" sold south, how many lived to be assimilated into the populations of the mining provinces? What happened to those whom viceroys ordered freed down south, stranded far from home among alien peoples? The questions stand unanswerable, but they suggest tremendous ferment among all peoples affected and a much wider circle of involvement than was immediately obvious. Undoubtedly those were tragic times for peoples with so strong and sure a sense of their own group identities as Apaches and Navajos. That they survived and for a time even prospered under such conditions suggests that the extraordinary decentralization and fluidity of their societies, so often scored as weakness, were curiously advantageous in that early testing time.

The teeming, disjointed activities of the Athapaskan raiders and warriors, so unlike warfare practiced by Europeans, baffled the Spaniards. At any given time, there could be any number of small raiding parties out looking for horses or metal, some distinctly separate war parties out to avenge dead kinsmen, and still peaceful bartering at some pueblos with Apache trading parties coming to do business as of old. Probably there was never a total breakdown of communication among Athapaskans and Pueblos and even Spaniards, although tensions were rife and contacts were always fraught with possible hostilities. Apaches and Navajos, sometimes as visitors at the pueblos, sometimes as hosts to Pueblo fugitives from Spanish dominion, had ample opportunities to observe both the losses and gains of Pueblos embraced, willy-nilly, by Spanish Christendom.

The Crown's reform program for New Mexico soon improved the lot of the Pueblos, who had been so badly affected by the turmoil, the uncertainties, and the scarcities in the Spanish colony. At least the Spaniards no longer dispossessed Indians to house themselves, and they established fields and gardens to produce their own food. As instructed, Governor Peralta promptly founded a proper villa, marking for the colonists the restoration of their right to elect their local government and live under Spanish law. Santa Fe, established in 1610, embodied the colonists' hope for stable, dignified lives at last, after a dozen years of uncertainty and hardship in expropriated pueblos.

Governor Peralta bore prime responsibility for protecting the Indians' legal rights; of all Spaniards, only he and his lieutenant had any jurisdiction over them. He could allot Indians in *encomienda* to settlers as compensation for services, but he had to account to the king for the *encomenderos'* services and qualifications. Distressed by reports of excessive tributes brutally collected from New Mexican Indians, Felipe III desired Peralta to moderate both the manner of collection and the sum of tribute from Indians in *encomienda*, as well as to protect them from hostile Indians. The two matters were closely related. *Encomenderos* would be the principal means of defending the Pueblos.

The viceroy also expected Peralta to encourage consolidation of pueblos too small to defend themselves adequately or too exposed on the Apache frontier, choosing new sites both defensible and promising for agriculture. To facilitate Indian affairs, Velasco wished the natives to be taught Spanish or, failing that, the one language most widely spoken in the land.

In the matter of teaching Indians, as indeed in most responsibilities related to Pueblos, Peralta's instructions impinged upon the privileges and duties of the missionaries, who were quite independent of gubernatorial authority. Triumphantly aware that the secular colony now existed only to support their work and alert against any infringement either of their own prerogative or of the rights and welfare of Indians under their tutelage, the Franciscans were quick to challenge Peralta and his successors. Authorities of Church and State in New Mexico soon developed a rivalry so contentious and embittering as to bar wholesome development of the province. Every resident suffered in consequence, but the costs in body and in spirit were particularly grave for Pueblos caught between the contending forces. Intended beneficiaries of the Spanish missionary enterprise, they fell victims to its defects.

Both Franciscans and the Crown could take just pride in much of the missionary program. Assuming full costs, the Crown poured a million pesos into the program from 1609 to 1680. Supply caravans came at roughly three-year intervals, bringing new friars to the field and returning others to Mexico. They brought, too, the supplies agreed upon for the friars' maintenance and such religious necessities as wine, tapers, oil, and church ornaments. Each friar going for the first time to New Mexico was issued a full complement of vestments and altar accouterments and a kit to build his church: axes, nails, hinges, latches, and carpenter's tools. He also received the basic equipment of a rural Spanish household: kitchen utensils; needles, awls, scissors, yarns; hoes, coarse axes, and a dozen horseshoes. He carried basic surgical instruments and medical supplies for a simple infirmary. He would build or maintain a church as necessary; would indoctrinate his flock; and would teach domestic and agricultural skills to support his mission and enrich the lives of his congregation.

The friars emphasized material benefits, both to lure neophytes and to found the orderly Spanish way of life they deemed inseparable from the faith that they lived and preached. Disciplined service to God began with construction of mission buildings, and friars taught their charges new building skills as they worked. Adobe bricks in the pueblos date from that time. While directing the planting of gardens and orchards, the friars introduced new crops and agricultural techniques. They established herds of cattle and sheep to feed converts as well as priests, and with that improved diet Pueblos also acquired herdsmen's skills. Wool from the flocks lent itself to the weaving techniques Pueblos had long applied to their scant cotton crops and wild plant fibers, so that the quality and quantity of textile production improved immeasurably. Some missions ran workshops for weaving and for such newly introduced crafts as leatherwork, metalwork, and carpentry. In mission kitchens Indian women added European culinary skills to those of their Pueblo tradition.

The mission enterprise flourished for a decade or two. In 1620 the sixteen Franciscan friars claimed 17,000 converts in the pueblos; by 1626, their books showed 20,181. At least twenty-seven churches and seventeen convents stood in the pueblos, all built and decorated by Indians working under the friars' directions. Serious resistance flared at Taos and Zuñi, where the Indians actually destroyed churches and killed two priests, but 1,200 Zuñis asked to have priests again, and even at Taos some 600 souls were counted won. Undaunted at seeing two of their brothers join New Mexico's list of Franciscan martyrs, the friars asked their Order for forty more.[2]

For a while there seemed almost no limit to the accomplishments of those zealous missionaries, who instructed the Indians in doctrine and led them in a full round of daily religious observances. Determined to enhance their worship with all the arts, the friars trained instrumentalists and choristers among the Pueblos. Thirteen churches boasted organs; several had a good array of other instruments. The friars supervised decoration of the churches by Indian artists and when possible embellished their missions with paintings and statuary in the European

[2] Fray Gerónimo de Zárate Salmeron, Report, in France V. Scholes, "Documents for the History of the New Mexican Missions in the Seventeenth Century," *New Mexico Historical Review* 4 (1929): 46–51. The principal source for this period is the work of Scholes, set forth in a series of articles in the journal cited: "Church and State in New Mexico, 1610–1650," 11 (1936): 9–58, 145–179, 283–294, 297–349; 12 (1937): 78–106. See also "The Supply Service of the New Mexican Missions in the Seventeenth Century," 5 (1930): 93–115, 186–210, 386–404.

tradition. As their enterprises flourished, the friars shipped products south for sale, enriching their missions beyond the austere basic level of the Crown benefaction. The busy round of work and worship in which priest and congregation served together and the obvious material enrichment of Pueblo life seemed tangible justification of their missionary program. The friars were little inclined to brook interference from governor, colonists, or recalcitrant Indians. Nor did they comprehend that the mission program, for all its benefits, cost the Pueblos dearly.

Demands of work and worship in the mission routine grew burdensome. Pueblo days had been well filled with work and necessary ritual in precolonial times. Added now were requirements of labor and tribute to support the Spanish secular colony as well as the friars' disciplines. The friars contested secular demands upon the Indians, but they never considered that mission neophytes would need also to observe their ancient pagan duties. Again there was misunderstanding: Pueblos were willing to add Christian beliefs and practices, as they understood them, to their own religious traditions; Franciscans were determined to supplant pagan ways with their one true faith, oblivious to any shade of compromise.

Even the economic benefits of the mission program had uncalculated side effects. The Pueblos' improved skills and expanded productivity made them all the more vulnerable to exploitation by Spanish laymen and Indian predators. The mission herds, intended by the Franciscans to stabilize and enrich their congregations' subsistence, were magnets to *bárbaros* raiders, who waxed more dangerous to Pueblos with every horse they stole.

While the Crown benefaction and Franciscan energies got the missionary enterprise off to a flourishing start, the secular colony settled down to a stagnant existence terribly frustrating to ambitious men. Chief among them were about thirty-five *encomenderos*, soldier-settlers who constituted the principal defense of the province and were granted Indian services as pay. They had to report at the governor's call, mounted and armed at their own expense, without limit to the days of service required, distances traveled, or expenses incurred. They levied tribute from the fields and stock of the Indians in their *encomiendas*; some required "their" Indians to work as household servants, herdsmen, or farm laborers on their own lands, often illegally. Although small, *encomienda* proceeds were a distinct advantage in the limited provincial economy, and the *encomenderos* became a kind of local aristocracy, dominant in the government of the villa of Santa Fe and held in some awe by less fortunate Spaniards.

Neither *encomenderos* nor missionaries could legally interfere with the Pueblos' right to live under local governments elected by themselves, just as other vassals of the king. The Crown forbade any Spanish presence in pueblos on the January 1 election day, lest outside pressures diminish the Indians' freedom of choice. Spaniards had admired the Pueblos' remarkable civil order since their earliest contacts, but the invaders had never discerned the natives' leadership structure because key Pueblo officials held aloof from outsiders. The Spaniards therefore decreed a new structure of local government on the Spanish model: a governor, an *alcalde*, and other officers elected by majority vote in each pueblo, then formally installed by the royal governor of the province. In practice, the traditional Pueblo religious leaders chose the slate of "Spanish" officers, which evolved as a convenient set of "outside" officers to tend the pueblo's temporal, external affairs while the old theocracy carried on the vital functions of leadership in their ancient tradition. The Pueblos managed the business so discreetly that the Spaniards never realized the subordinate role of the governments they installed in the pueblos, and thus never worried about it. The pattern served Pueblos well through successive occupations, right into the twentieth century.

Beside the Pueblos' discreet reconciliation of religious and secular offices, the Spaniards of New Mexico afforded spectacular, often painful, contrast. A stormy petrel, Father Commissary Ordóñez, set the tone early, hotly challenging Governor Peralta's collection of tribute from the Pueblos. In his zeal, he nailed a notice of Peralta's excommunication to the church door in Santa Fe and hurled the governor's chair into the street; later he arrested Governor Peralta and displayed him in irons at Sandía, Santo Domingo, and Zía, deliberately maximizing his humiliation before Pueblos. Father Ordóñez was even quicker to quarrel with Peralta's successor, Governor Bernardino de Ceballos, whom he excommunicated in 1617.

Carried away with power and self-righteousness, the father commissary also arrogated jurisdiction in the pueblos. When Jémez Indians killed a Cochití man, Ordóñez hanged one Jémez and ordered several more hanged, thus bringing the Jémez to the brink of revolt. Some friars, appalled by his excesses, tried to leave the province. Ordóñez arrested them, too.

The climax came in 1618 with a new governor, Don Juan de Eulate, as belligerent as the father commissary. The pair quickly brought the unseemly wrangle between Church and State to such a disgusting pitch that the Crown intervened to rebuke both and set new guidelines to protect Pueblos from such jurisdictional tussles.[3]

Deploring the Franciscans' scandalous actions against the governors of New Mexico, the Crown reminded them that their jurisdiction was solely ecclesiastical and that they had no right to interfere with the collection of agreed tributes from the Pueblos. The Crown desired the Franciscans to reform their own treatment of the Pueblos: to limit their demands on Indian time and labor; to moderate necessities of church and convent; to stop sending the Indians off to the mountains to harvest cash crops of piñon nuts; to cease over-zealous discipline; and particularly not to wound Indian sensibilities by cutting off their hair as punishment. The Crown required good treatment and consideration for the Indians and was sorely displeased that the Franciscans had fallen short of that standard.

Equally displeased with gubernatorial lapses, the Crown admonished the governor not to interfere in religious matters but to enforce all laws protecting the Indians against their Spanish neighbors. Excessive demands for Indian labor, failure to pay fair wages, exploitation of Indian women—all must be stamped out. There should be scrupulous care to prevent livestock damages to Pueblo property, and prompt, fair restitution for any damages wrought. Again the Crown certified its humane intent toward the Indians and its appreciation of their difficulties with Spaniards sent to teach and protect them.

Unfortunately, neither governors nor friars heeded the royal admonition to work together for the good of the Indians. The Franciscans gained a potent new weapon in 1626 when the Inquisition designated the head of the New Mexican missions also commissary for the Holy Office of the Inquisition in that province. Thus armed, missionaries would defy civil authorities and terrify many colonists. Pueblos were mercifully exempt from the Inquisition.

At the same time that an unhealthy concentration of power vested in the missionary establishment, the quality of the governors reflected the deterioration of administration throughout the empire. Three- or

---

[3] King Philip, Cedula to Father Fray Esteban de Perea, signed by the Viceroy at Mexico, January 9, 1621, in Lansing B. Bloom, "The Royal Order of 1620 to Custodian Fray Esteban de Perea," *New Mexico Historical Review* 5 (1930): 288–298; Marqués de Gualcazar, Viceroy, to Don Juan de Eulate, Governor of New Mexico, Mexico, March 10, 1620, in Lansing B. Bloom, "A Glimpse of New Mexico in 1620," *New Mexico Historical Review* 3 (1928): 357–380.

four-year gubernatorial terms derived from the Hapsburg practice of short terms and regular rotation of officials, a practice calculated to minimize corruption and abuses of authority. Not very successful in that respect, the practice did assure that such a unique province as New Mexico would usually be governed by men, often of low competence and integrity, unfamiliar with its people and problems. Roughly every third or fourth year yet another governor arrived, determined to profit enough during his short term to compensate for the rigors of the journey and the ordeal of service in a hardship post. Often he needed also to recoup a sum paid to procure the appointment and to set aside enough to bribe his successor not to expose his crimes in office. Successive governors vigorously exploited New Mexico's economic possibilities, which were essentially limited to the primitive products the land would yield to native labor and to the actual persons of the natives. Pueblos bore most of the human costs, but colonists were exploited, too, and Apaches came in early for a share of both the agony and the profit.

An ambitious governor with active cohorts and small conscience could amass a surprising variety and quantity of goods to ship south to the markets of Parral. Most involved Pueblo labor, often exploiting the new skills and products introduced through mission enterprises. Santa Fe hummed with the governors' workshops: Indian carpenters building carts and wagons to carry goods south; and Pueblo artisans weaving woolen and cotton textiles, knitting stockings, and manufacturing leather goods. Pueblo workers collected salt from salines east of the Manzanos and piñon nuts from the sierras. Though law forbade governors any agricultural enterprise, Pueblos tended livestock and crops of governors as well as *encomenderos*. Some of the best herdsmen drove cattle and sheep south to market with the caravan, often to remain stranded for want of provision for their homeward journey.

The carts also hauled buffalo hides and antelope skins to market. Most came from roving Indians of plains and mountains, some acquired through traditional channels of Pueblo trade, but ever-increasing quantities procured by Spanish traders and raiders. Apaches quickly learned about the Spanish market. Even more in demand than meat and hides were Apaches and their captives. Even New Mexico's primitive economy could employ astounding numbers of hands, but the truly insatiable market for labor lay southward in the mining provinces. Missionaries vigorously protested enslavement of Indians and could largely protect their Pueblo charges from that illegal fate, but no power on the northern frontier could prevent enslavement of "wild" Indians when governors connived to evade the law. Slave traffic figured quietly but importantly in New Mexico's internal and external commerce and that too involved Pueblo fortunes.

The Spaniards' demand for slaves intensified patterns of warfare and enslavement of captives long antedating the Spanish occupation. Taking captives, either to hold in one's own group or to trade to another, was a common feature of Indian warfare and had figured in intermittent Pueblo-Apache hostilities. Apaches had also marketed their captives, as well as meat and hides, at the pueblos. Spaniards were soon involved through their commitment to defend the Pueblos. Spanish squads sallied forth to punish raiders, usually with warriors from the injured pueblos, and successful retaliation often involved captures. Spaniards enslaved their own captives and often purchased those taken by Pueblos.

Excuses to campaign against Apaches were seldom wanting after 1601, thanks to the Spaniards' disruption of established Pueblo-Apache trade and the new lure of metal goods and livestock in the pueblos, but Spaniards sometimes went slave hunting on the plains without Apache provocation. Pueblos often served on those expeditions, sometimes to render required service to an *encomendero*, sometimes just to strike a blow at an old foe. Apache vengeance usually fell upon pueblos, which were handier targets than Santa Fe. There evolved an endless round of Apache attacks on pueblos and any unguarded livestock, followed by Spanish-Pueblo campaigns against Apaches, which sparked yet more Apache raids.

With Apaches they captured and captives they purchased from Apaches, some Spanish entrepreneurs turned a nice profit in slave marts down south. Over the years, their success cost New Mexico's population, both Pueblo and Spanish, a heavy price in Apache vengeance. Apache raids particularly impaired the quality of Pueblo life. The frequent need to defend the pueblos from attack and to pursue raiders bore heavily upon Indians already oppressed by the demands of the missionary program, duties of tribute and service to their *encomenderos*, and the governors' often grueling exactions.

In their suffering, most Pueblos turned increasingly to the consolations of their native religion, trusting ancient rituals to restore the shattered harmonies of their world. Outraged, uncomprehending friars blamed the governors for their neophytes' disaffection and battled them for control of Pueblo time and energies; at the same time, they invoked

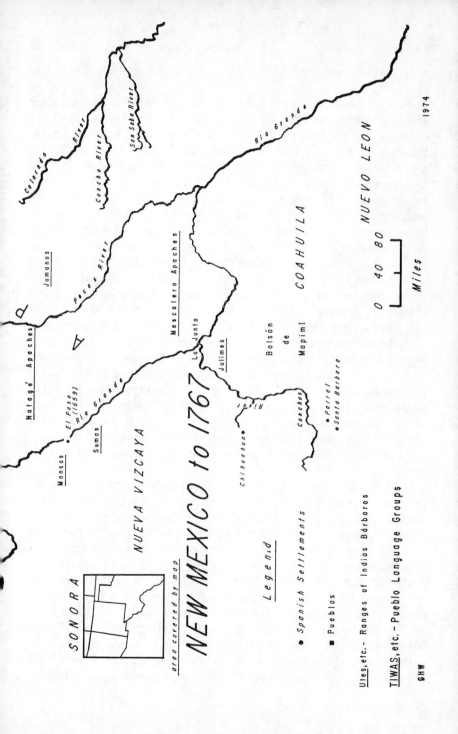

NEW MEXICO to 1767

area covered by map

SONORA

NUEVA VIZCAYA

Mansos

Sumas

●El Paso
(1659)

Rio Grande

Natagé Apaches

Jumanos

Pecos River

Mescalero Apaches

La Junta

Julimes

Chihuahua●

Conchos River

●Parral
●Santa Barbara

Bolsón
de
Mapimí

COAHUILA

Colorado River

Concho River

San Saba River

Rio Grande

Rio Grande

NUEVO LEON

0   40   80

Miles

1974

Legend

● Spanish Settlements

■ Pueblos

Utes, etc. - Ranges of Indios Bárbaros

TIWAS, etc. - Pueblo Language Groups

GHW

ever harsher methods to beat the devil in the struggle for Indian
souls.

Both the fanaticism of the friars' assault on native customs and their
scandalous quarrels with the governors outraged Pueblo ideals of
harmony and moderation. By those standards, the Christian religion
thrust upon them by the Spaniards seemed sadly deficient. Taking
sanctuary underground in their kivas, most of the disillusioned Pueblos
hardened their loyalties to the old ways. Some fled to the sierras to take
refuge among old Athapaskan enemies, preferring those uncertain
mercies to the ordeal of coercion in the pueblos. As disaffected Pueblos
bore their tale of exploitation and abuse to Apache and Navajo camps,
they also brought knowledge of new goods and skills, especially livestock management, thus diffusing change even as they fled it.

In the first two decades of the royal colony, many Athapaskans saw
the Spanish regime at closer quarters. Despite intensified raiding, old
visiting and trading relationships still flourished at the frontier pueblos,
and Apaches experienced missionary contacts. Pecos, long a principal
trade center for Apaches from the plains, was by 1617 the regular gateway of Spanish entrepreneurs seeking plains Apache trade. Taos and
Picurís were traditional markets for more northerly Apaches, probably
Jicarilla forebears. The Franciscans, who had always understood their
responsibility to include conversion of "wild" Indians as well as Pueblos,
welcomed Apache visitors and encouraged them to watch and ask
about the interesting, often impressively colorful, rituals and paraphernalia of the mission chapels and to enjoy the hospitality of mission
kitchens.

In 1626 a new leader, Fray Alonso de Benavides, brought fresh im-
petus to missionary interest in the Apaches. Even more strongly than
most Franciscans, Benavides considered it his mission to wrestle the
devil for possession of the souls of all the unfortunate natives who had
been in Satan's power ever since God created them. Confident that
miraculous aid would be forthcoming and that success must attend a
missionary enterprise founded upon the blood of ten Franciscan martyrs, Benavides saw New Mexico as a base from which to convert all
natives of North America. Assuming the Rio Grande's source to be at
the North Pole and Virginia nearby, he feared that English and Dutch
heretics then settling on the Atlantic coast would not only corrupt the
seaboard natives but would also reach out to contaminate those of New
Mexico unless the Roman Catholic faith were speedily and firmly es-

tablished there. He therefore launched a vigorous expansion of the
missionary program in New Mexico.

A forceful penman, Benavides let his dreams for the future override
current realities in his reports.[4] He wrote of 500,000 converts in New
Mexico, firmer in the faith than Europeans who had been Catholics
for generations; he also described remarkable wealth in New Mexico,
especially rich mines. Published promptly, his reports not only excited
the Spanish court but also aroused such interest that French, Dutch,
Latin, and German editions quickly followed. In his enthusiasm, Benavides made New Mexico attractive to the very elements, Catholic
and heretic, most inimical to his own pious purpose.

If Benavides' dreams were outsized, his capacity for work was real.
Not content just to supervise the twenty-seven missions and numerous
visitas already serving Pueblos, Benavides advanced the mission frontiers. He sent priests back to Jémez and Picurís, where hostility had
earlier disrupted the mission program, and then began his own work
in the Piro pueblos downstream from the established missions of the
Rio Grande Valley. There he met Apaches not previously in contact
with missionaries.

Gila Apaches had long frequented Piro pueblos, for their territories
on the headwaters of the Gila River lay not far west of Senecú. A
sociable Gila leader, Sanaba, regularly visited Senecú to gamble.
Hearing Benavides preach there, Sanaba grew receptive to missionaries
for his own people. In 1628 Benavides dispatched Fray Martín del
Espíritu Santo to Sanaba's territory for an extended visit. Though he
did not achieve the desired mass conversion, the Gilas entertained him
cordially, and he helped them plant some crops.

His Piro work also brought Benavides into contact with southeasterly
Apaches called Apaches del Perrillo after the spring by which they
camped. Their relations with the Piros had been strained, but a visitor
from the group heard Benavides preach at Senecú and was so impressed that he brought a hundred of his people to the pueblo for
instruction at the same time that Sanaba's people came to hear the
missionaries.

No wonder Benavides envisioned vast conversions in New Mexico,
given his successes among the Piros and the encouraging receptivity
of the Gilas and Apaches del Perrillo. More encouragement came from

[4] Alonso de Benavides, *Fray Alonso de Benavides' Revised Memorial of 1634*,
ed. Frederick Webb Hodge, George P. Hammond, and Agapito Rey.

the north, when Captain Quinia visited Benavides to request baptism. Head of an Apache *ranchería* less than thirty miles beyond Taos, he had maintained friendly, interested communication with Fray Pedro de Ortega at the Taos mission since 1621. His growing interest in Christianity had divided his camp so badly that one of his own people shot Quinia in the heat of argument. The missionaries at Taos, one of whom was skilled in surgery, heard of the incident and visited Quinia's camp to treat his wound. Both the friars and Quinia believed that divine intervention healed the chief, and Quinia resolved to become a Christian; hence his appeal to Benavides in 1627 and Benavides' subsequent visit to his camp. In 1628 Quinia went to Santa Fe to escort Fray Bartolomé Romero to his homeland to found a mission. In Santa Fe he proved his seriousness of purpose by arranging two baptisms, that of his own son and that of a valorous Indian war captive, Quinia's most cherished possession, christened Bernardino.

Governor Phelipe Sotelo Ossorio readily grasped the importance of a new mission north of Taos. Briefly forgetting the crippling rivalries of Church and State, he led fifty Spanish soldiers to escort Fray Bartolomé to Quinia's camp. All one day governor and missionary worked with soldiers and Indians, hewing and carrying logs, erecting a church, and plastering its outer walls. Then, aglow with good will and great accomplishment, they parted, governor and soldiers riding back to Santa Fe, and Fray Bartolomé remaining alone in his new mission to convert the Apaches.

The new mission seemed successful enough at first and attracted another Apache leader called Manases. The Apaches soon soured on the experiment, however, and even Quinia threatened to kill the priest. Aided and protected solely by the faithful Bernardino, Fray Bartolomé stuck to his post until the Apaches quit the site to be rid of him. Thus deserted, he reluctantly left his mission, but he tried again the next spring with Fray Francisco Muñoz. A new governor, Captain Francisco Manuel de Silva Nieto, escorted them with twenty soldiers. They visited the camps of both Quinia and Manases, enjoyed friendly receptions, and reported some requests for baptism, but they won no permanent successes among those Apaches. Perhaps their brief experience of a mission in their territory had convinced them that Catholic discipline was incompatible with Apache life. Their Pueblo acquaintances would hardly have encouraged them to persist in a mission experiment, for those Apaches dealt principally with Taos and Picurís, pueblos seething with antagonism toward Spaniards and all their works. Nor could they draw encouragement from the Vaquero Apaches' fleeting experiment with Christianity.

Missionaries assiduously cultivated the Vaquero Apaches who regularly traded at eastern frontier pueblos. Intrigued by tales of an elaborately adorned, much revered representation of the death of the Virgin that Benavides had placed in the church at Santa Fe, Vaquero headmen went to see it. The friars arranged that the Apache leaders first viewed the image at night, the chapel ablaze with candlelight and resounding with music. Deeply impressed, the chiefs joined in veneration of the image and subsequently talked with Benavides about learning to be Christians. The friar urged them to settle down to permanent village life to facilitate first their instruction and then their observance of Catholic obligations. The Vaqueros dutifully chose a site and began the work of establishing a large settlement.

Benavides concluded that the devil himself inspired Indian enemies to attack the new settlement, kill the principal leader and many inhabitants, and then carry the rest off to be peddled as slaves. His first report of the calamity charged the governor with instigating the attack and claimed that only a public outcry against the crime prevented the governor from selling the captives for his own profit, but Benavides later dropped that accusation. Perhaps on mature reflection the friar realized that he lacked evidence. Whatever the truth, the treacherous attack naturally provoked attacks upon Spaniards and Pueblos by Apaches bound to avenge their dead kinsmen. Peaceful relations were restored about 1629, presumably after requirements of tribal vengeance were satisfied. Benavides noted some renewed interest in Christianity among Vaqueros, but there was never again any report of substantial progress toward their conversion.

Fray Alonso succeeded better on the northwestern frontier of New Mexico. In 1626 he reestablished the Jémez mission, although Jémez had been up in arms against both Spaniards and Christian Tewas for three years. He assigned Fray Martín de Arvide to Jémez and required him also to visit and preach to nearby Navajos. Fray Martín reported substantial interest in baptism among them. More productive contact with Navajos followed when Benavides determined to solve peacefully the problem of Navajo attacks upon converted Tewas. Civil authorities had sought to check the war by stealthy campaigns into Navajo country and destructive surprise attacks on their homes. The Navajos proved difficult to surprise and usually mustered formidable resistance, so the "search and destroy" approach did little but spark more attacks.

Benavides believed that the Navajos had been provoked by Tewa intruders and would respond to sincere peace overtures. He moved to the mission at Santa Clara, a Tewa pueblo often struck by Navajos, and persuaded those villagers to send a dozen delegates to the Navajos with arrows symbolizing peace. The embassy found the Navajos preparing a war party, but they were well received. Navajo leaders came to Santa Clara to talk and, after airing deep grievances against the Christian Tewas, agreed to end hostilities. The armistice apparently endured several years. A missionary worked among those Navajos in 1629, though without appreciable results.

There were other hopeful signs for the missionary program in 1629. Priests were accepted, albeit uneasily, at the Zuñi and Hopi pueblos, and even Ácoma was gathered into the missionary fold. Atop the high rock now dwelt 2,000 Indians: some remnants of the Keres who had peopled Ácoma before the calamity of 1599, some fugitives from other pueblos who had found Spanish rule intolerable. Fray Juan Ramírez had now to teach the people of Ácoma about the loving God of the Spaniards and bring them willingly to His service, an extraordinarily challenging assignment in light of their earlier experience of Christian charity.

Benavides gave high priority to missions for the Tompiro pueblos east of the Manzano Mountains, which he first assigned to Fray Juan de Salas of Isleta mission. Again, expansion into frontier pueblos gave opportunity also to reach "wild" Indians who traded there. Jumano Indians from the southern plains had long traded at the Tompiro pueblos.[5] They apparently liked what they heard of the missionaries there. In 1629 fifty Jumanos went to Isleta to invite Franciscans to visit their people.

With escorting soldiers, Fray Juan de Salas and Fray Diego López traveled more than 250 miles across Vaquero Apache ranges to reach the Jumanos' camp somewhere on the southern plains of Texas. It was an exhilarating experience for the friars, who attributed the Jumanos' invitation to the good works of a noted Spanish nun said to have flown miraculously to the New World to minister to the natives. Though they accomplished no wide conversion, they enjoyed a cordial, extended visit with the Jumanos and learned of other interested nations to the south and east. Quiviras and Aixaos were also said to have received the

---

[5] Of all the thorny problems of Indian nomenclature, "Jumano" is one of the most complex. The most complete recent analysis is that of W. W. Newcomb, Jr., *The Indians of Texas*, pp. 225–236, supported by a thorough bibliography.

remarkable nun, and their very existence in settled villages seemed to invite missionaries.

In 1632, with another friar and a military escort, Fray Juan again braved the plains to visit the Jumanos, then living on the Colorado River of present Texas. So cordial was the reception that one priest stayed six months, in which time he considerably broadened the Spaniards' awareness of the diverse Indian populations of the area. The Jumanos, industrious traders, ranged from the Gulf coast to La Junta as well as to the Tompiros. Within limitations imposed by language barriers, they could teach a visitor much about Indians from the Gulf of Mexico to the Rocky Mountains. That was more fuel for missionary ambitions.

Even on the established route to New Mexico from the south, new mission fields beckoned the Franciscans. Benavides noted early that Mansos and Sumas around El Paso del Norte looked ripe for conversion. The Order's contract with the Crown committed them first to complete conversion of the Pueblos, but Franciscans resolved not to neglect too long the numerous, apparently docile souls to the south. They believed that conversion of the Mansos and Sumas at El Paso would be the key to conversion of savage peoples scattered from the Rio Grande to the sea.

Few of those great dreams of conversion would be realized in the Spanish centuries, but it is important to remember that in the beginning the missionaries found the *indios bárbaros* approachable. Centuries of "Apache wars" have obscured the fact that once, about 1630, Franciscans in New Mexico had very real hope of converting Apaches and Navajos. There seems to be no reason to doubt the *bárbaros'* sincere willingness to listen to missionaries. It was obvious to them, as indeed to Pueblos, that the Spaniards must have very powerful gods who had given them many wonderful things. The mission churches, as richly adorned as the friars could manage, candlelit and filled with music, the solemn rituals, and the priests' earnest harangues all attested a power that merited close inquiry, and the New Mexican colony included several hundred Mexican Indians witnessing that it was not a power for Spaniards alone.

Swept by the momentum of their own compelling faith, the friars too readily assumed that their gospel, once heard, must surely be accepted. Nothing in their very differently structured universe prepared them to comprehend such enormous cultural barriers as those between Apache ways and the disciplines of Christian life that the friars expounded. Thus, Benavides could write of 500,000 converts in New Mexico because he saw in each encounter with the *bárbaros* a promise of converting all their people, whose numbers he could only guess. He tempered his claim with the admission that only 86,000 Indians were actually baptized, and, despite his optimism, he recognized that certain conditions in New Mexico impeded conversions. As soon as his tour of duty in the province ended, he hurried to Spain to advocate reforms required for the Christianization of all peoples in New Mexico.[6]

Benavides presented the court a blunt analysis of New Mexican problems. The most direct, persistent affront to *bárbaros* was enslavement of war captives, not only those taken in "just" war, but also many seized in deliberate slave raids. Benavides proposed instead to place all captives in convents or in exemplary Christian Spanish or Indian households, to be converted by kind example. Of course, escapes would occur, but he hoped escapees would report their good treatment to their people, perhaps paving the way for future conversions. The thrust of Benavides' argument was that disposition of captives should not be an economic matter but rather a charitable act for purposes of conversion, a wise, compassionate proposal, quite unenforceable on that remote frontier of poverty.

Benavides also denounced virtual enslavement of Pueblo children. Orphans were often taken forcibly from pueblos to serve in Spanish households, on pretext of charitable care. Benavides contended that no Pueblo child was truly orphaned, because extended-family households included grandparents and aunts who reared a child as their own in the event of parental deaths. That Spaniards preyed upon Pueblo children was a keen grievance among Pueblos and well known to their Apache visitors. With neither people did it advance the cause of Christianity.

Exactions of tribute and service from Christian Pueblos also discouraged new conversions among outlying pueblos and *bárbaros*. Households in converted pueblos paid annual tributes of one blanket or skin and two-and-a-half bushels of corn. Other Indians were naturally loath to assume such burdens. Converted pueblos were deteriorating as families consolidated in larger households to minimize tributes and let empty houses crumble. To counter that evasion, some *encomenderos*

---

[6] Benavides' petitions regarding tribute and personal service by the Indians appear in translation in Appendix 16, pp. 168–177, *Benavides' Revised Memorial of 1634*, ed. Hodge, Hammond, and Rey.

levied tributes on individuals instead of households, thus increasing tributes to levels never contemplated by the Crown.

Again, Benavides proposed reforms of substantial merit if only Crown authority could be enforced in New Mexico. Tributes should be deferred for at least five years after an entire pueblo had been baptized. Pueblos should have total freedom to move as they pleased, and only after a year's residence in a pueblo should they pay taxes to that pueblo's *encomendero*. Benavides hoped thus to spark a competition of kindness and justice among *encomenderos* vying for residents in their *encomiendas*. In no case should *encomenderos* collect tribute from individuals: they would have to accept fluctuating numbers of households in a pueblo as part of the natural order.

Benavides reminded the Crown of abuses of Indian property rights, especially encroachment on their lands and damages to their fields by livestock. But he pointed out that *encomenderos* often suffered abuses, too. Spanish law entitled settlers who served five years at their own expense in New Mexico to the dignity of *hijodalgo* and to the compensation of an *encomienda* in the pueblos. But newly arrived governors often expropriated *encomiendas* earned by bona fide settlers and conferred the income upon members of their personal retinues, who would contribute little to the province and would depart with the governor. Benavides wanted no one granted an *encomienda* before serving five years in New Mexico, and preference given native sons and daughters of the province in order to encourage more families to settle there permanently at their own expense. Clearly, Benavides meant to foster a stable Spanish population in New Mexico, with incentives for kind, responsible treatment of Indians.

Benavides spent several years in Spain and in Rome as an eloquent propagandist for development of New Mexico. He persuaded the Crown to approve in 1635 some important reforms: exemption of all New Mexican Indians from tribute and personal service for ten years after baptism; permanent exemptions for principal Indian leaders; and exemption during term of service from both tribute and service for Pueblo aides of both civil and church administrations.

Had New Mexico been destined to progress as Benavides envisioned, or indeed as he sometimes implied had already happened, his further suggestion of a bishopric there would have followed logically. Although abortive, his proposal led the Crown to enlightening examination of its New Mexican problem.

The Crown liked the idea that New Mexico could now support a bishopric: the mission program was costly and the province yielded no revenue to the Crown. Felipe IV was perenially short of money, and drains upon the Crown's resources constantly multiplied. The Moslem threat continued in Africa and eastern Europe, Dutch rebels took a heavy toll of Spanish shipping, and Spain was continually embroiled in Italy and the Low Countries, both theaters of the Thirty Years' War. When Benavides attended upon the Court, Cardinal Richelieu was just bringing France into the war against Spain, thus beginning a quarter-century of open war between the two powers. On the Iberian Peninsula both Catalans and Portuguese threatened to rebel against the revenue demands of Felipe IV. Perhaps the problems of New Mexico looked very small and remote by comparison, but Benavides' proposal implied that a province that could support a bishopric could sustain its own missionary activities. Indeed, if his reports of its wealth and population were accurate, New Mexico should even produce revenues for the Crown. The proposition merited investigation.

The inquiry revealed astonishing unanimity among Franciscan veterans of New Mexico and its most recent ex-governor.[7] Grueling poverty gripped Pueblos and Spaniards alike in New Mexico, and there was no prospect of improvement. No one denied Benavides' reports of fertile lands and probable mineral veins, but what were New Mexico's few beleaguered inhabitants to make of them? Perhaps there had been 60,000 baptisms among Pueblos over the years, but by 1638 disease, famine, and war had reduced inhabitants of the pueblos to some 40,000. The Spanish colony amounted to fifty households at Santa Fe and another dozen on farms downstream on the Rio Grande. They could muster perhaps two hundred men-at-arms to defend the Pueblos against Apaches. All raised grain and cattle for their livelihood; *encomenderos* had also the bleak little annual tribute of a blanket and corn from each Pueblo household. All New Mexicans, Pueblo and Spanish alike, lived forever on the defensive against Apaches. It was difficult to imagine that they would ever have the energies, the time, or the heart to develop any wealth. Even Pueblo conversions were precarious, easily reversible if new demands should be imposed or other conditions worsen. Those who knew the province agreed that, if the

---

[7] Petition of Father Juan de Prada, Convent of San Francisco, Mexico, September 26, 1638, in Charles Wilson Hackett, ed. *Historical Documents Relating to New Mexico, Nueva Vizcaya, and Approaches Thereto, to 1773*, III, 106–115; Petition of Francisco Martínez de Baeza, Mexico, February 12, 1639, ibid., pp. 118–120.

Crown contemplated any changes of policy toward New Mexico, it had better increase its aid, not its demands.

The investigation seemed to make nonsense of all Benavides had said. Resigned to a continuing financial drain in New Mexico, the Crown turned its attention back to more pressing problems of empire. Unfortunately, the new information on New Mexico came in confidential documents and never circulated abroad to counter the effect of the Benavides *Memorials*. Thus, unseemly and largely unwarranted interest in New Mexico persisted at some foreign courts.

Perhaps the most interested observers of events in New Mexico were the Apaches and Navajos of whose impending conversion Benavides had felt so sure. Even Fray Alonso's optimism would have been sorely tried had he served in New Mexico another decade, for the 1630's saw disaster piled upon disaster. Watching Apaches and Navajos could see little evidence that adherence to the new religion had brought the Pueblos any benefits.

Indians expected definite results from proper ceremonial obeisance to specific gods, but everything seemed to go wrong in the pueblos. The rains failed year after year, and the drought cycle brought famine. Many people died. Weakened by starvation, they suffered from repeated epidemics of smallpox and of the fever that Mexicans called *cocolitzli*. When troubled Pueblos tried to perform their old ceremonials to make things right in their world again, the friars objected, and there were dreadful times when friars broke up Pueblo meetings and destroyed sacred masks and fetishes. Some Pueblos fled to Apache and Navajo camps; some who stayed in their homes took strong measures to end their troubles. In 1632 Zuñis rid themselves of missionaries by murdering two. Toward the end of the decade, Taos and Jémez revolted, killing their priests and destroying much of the mission properties. All pueblos seethed with tension and fear. The friars did their best to feed the hungry during famines, but on the whole there was little to envy in the lives of "converted" Pueblos.

Anyone could see that the Spaniards had brought the Pueblos some important things they had never had before and that the friars had tried to give much to the Indians. But even those material benefits were doubtful gains when other Spaniards took so much away from the Pueblos. The Apaches could hardly fail to know of the blankets and corn that *encomenderos* collected annually, because Pueblos had so much less to trade to Apaches; but they also saw *encomenderos* turn out with their horses and guns to lead Pueblos against their enemies. The worst problem was damage inflicted by governors of the province, often upon Spanish settlers as well as Pueblos, and there was no visible compensation for that. Observing the lot of vassals of the Spanish king in New Mexico, whether Pueblos or settlers, Apaches and Navajos must have learned to prize their place outside the new system.

Particularly shocking by Indian standards was the disastrous quality of Spanish leadership in New Mexico. Apache custom vested leadership in their bravest or wisest men and readily replaced those who failed to lead effectively. In contrast, the royal governorship of New Mexico, one of the least desirable jobs in a decaying imperial structure, often fell to the sorriest products of the infinitely larger and more complex Spanish civilization. The people of the province lay at the mercy of those governors until routine rotation of terms relieved the situation. Not available to Spanish settlers was the easy Apache option of moving away from an unrespected leader, nor could they so easily depose a leader who displeased the community. Only the missionaries could safely challenge the arbitrary exercise of gubernatorial power, and the running conflict of church and state officials generally deepened the miseries of settlers caught in the cross fire. That some governors were later tried and punished by Crown or Inquisition could not alleviate their appalling impact on lives and fortunes in New Mexico and beyond.

Governors in the 1630's varied only in degree and style of rapacity. Francisco de la Mora y Ceballos (1632–1635) systematically plundered the province, expropriating possessions of settlers as well as Indians. He shipped to Santa Barbara's markets nine wagon loads of loot and much of the livestock of the province, and three years later he left impoverished, demoralized New Mexicans to cope with a devastating cycle of famine and disease. His less rapacious successor, Francisco Martínez de Baeza (1635–1637), was largely content to peddle textiles produced in his Santa Fe workshops by Pueblo and captive Indian labor.

Finding little of value in the stricken province, Governor Luis de Rosas (1637–1641) exploited the natives much more intensively to make his fortune. He set several whole pueblos to weaving for him, while employing captives in his Santa Fe weaving shops. Flaunting the law against agricultural enterprise by governors, he used Indian labor for extensive plantings. For maximum exploitation of the Apache trade, Rosas deposited stocks of metal goods with agents at such frontier pueblos as Pecos, where he hoped to garner every possible hide for the southern market. His greed soon led him to subvert his own enterprise: seizing captives for his workshops and the slave marts down south, he provoked Apaches in all directions. On an expedition toward Quivira, Rosas attacked friendly plains Apaches, killing some and capturing others. Escorting friars southwest of Zuñi, where they hoped to find new converts, he gratuitously sacked some Gila *rancherías*, wrecking the missionary venture and bringing the friars back to Santa Fe heartbroken and furious with the governor. Rosas also made an unprovoked foray north of New Mexico against Utes who had harmed neither Spaniards nor Pueblos, killing several and capturing eighty, some to be sold and some to be placed in his Santa Fe workshops. All those crimes sparked retaliation, particularly against frontier pueblos, but Rosas never bothered to protect the victims.

Rosas' abuses soon precipitated a break with the friars; then *encomenderos* defied the governor and supported the clergy. Indians witnessed one outrageous spectacle after another, beginning when the governor rose in church in Santa Fe to shout "Liar!" at a critical priest, then stalked out as the priest cursed him in the names of God and Saint Peter and Saint Paul. By 1640 the split was so deep that the leading Franciscans and many *encomenderos* gathered at Santo Domingo to establish a separate, dissident government. When they sent two friars to Santa Fe to talk with Rosas, he threatened to kill the pair and packed them off with a severe beating. Again, public scandal reverberated throughout the province.

Fearing the governor's wrath, some friars abandoned their missions to seek refuge at Santo Domingo, a shattering experience for Pueblo converts suddenly deprived of the sacraments they had been taught requisite to their salvation. San Ildefonso, Santa Clara, and Nambé, for example, had no friars for a year, and they suffered economic as well as religious crises. As missionaries abandoned pueblos, Rosas confiscated mission herds. When *encomenderos* defected to the friars, Rosas declared their *encomiendas* forfeit and seized the tributes. To enforce the new order, he established a garrison at San Ildefonso and set about wringing maximum yield from the expropriated *encomiendas*.

Bewildered, helpless pawns in the conflict, Pueblos heard Rosas rail against the friars, denouncing all they taught and urging the Indians to ignore them. Some watched him desecrate mission altars at Sandía, Cuarac, and Socorro. The imbroglio outraged every value held by Pueblos, whether aboriginal ideals of harmony or new Christian tenets. Some became restive: Indians of Taos and Jémez killed their friars. Moving at leisure, Governor Rosas finally led a squad to Taos, ostensibly to punish the insurgents, and looted the pueblo. Many Taoseños, surfeited with the lot of vassals of the king of Spain, fled northeast on the plains to establish a new pueblo among Apaches.

Meanwhile, no force barred the vengeance of Apaches and Utes whom Rosas had provoked. The governor was indifferent to the fate of the populace; most *encomenderos* had abandoned their charges in their civil conflict. Raiders swept New Mexico in 1640, burning an estimated 50,000 bushels of corn, essentially wiping out the provincial stores. That same year a new epidemic killed 3,000 Indians, an estimated 10 percent of the Pueblo population.

By 1641 authorities in Mexico realized the scandalous situation in New Mexico. Both the Franciscan Order and the viceroy sent new leaders to mend the difficulties. A viceregal decree fixed the number of *encomenderos* at thirty-five, and within that limit the confiscated *encomiendas* were restored. *Encomenderos* rallied to campaign against Indian marauders; Franciscans furnished them mounts from mission herds because raiders had nearly wiped out the horse herds in private and government ownership. Both friars and *encomenderos* cooperated with the royal governor to secure the province.

Only when the raids were substantially checked did Governor Alonso Pacheco de Heredia (1642–1644) assess the recent rebellion. To the Franciscans' great dismay, he ruled that the *encomenderos* had usurped Rosas' authority for their own purposes, on pretext of protecting the friars. He had eight soldiers beheaded and displayed one head on a gibbet to discourage future rebellions, then pardoned everyone else involved in the insurrection. Pueblo leaders were reported impressed and even pleased by the dramatic execution of justice. Perhaps they welcomed any sign of restored order in the Spanish community, for Pueblos had suffered grievous repercussions from the tumult. The episode proved that harsh sentences were meted out to Spaniards as well as to Indians and that Spaniards too could be held accountable for crimes against the laws of their faraway king.

If the Pueblos were much encouraged by Governor Pacheco's early measures, he soon disillusioned them, mercilessly extorting higher tributes and quarreling with the missionaries as vociferously as any predecessor. In August 1643, Governor Pacheco sent soldiers to Santo Domingo to read to the Indians his proclamation forbidding them to obey the friars, thus flinging down the gauntlet to the Franciscans whose headquarters were at that pueblo. Dazed and terrified, many

Santo Domingans hid in their fields and nearby heights. A week later, calmed by a Franciscan emissary, Governor Pacheco himself rode to Santo Domingo, summoned the Indians, and publicly rescinded the order, explaining that he had only issued it because he was angry and had wanted to test their obedience.[8]

The whole sorry episode could only deepen the fear and distrust in Santo Domingo and every other pueblo to which the story traveled. The tale found its way to the *bárbaros*, too, as more and more Pueblos fled to old enemies to escape the increased tributes and dangerous whims of Pacheco. By the end of his term there were only 43 pueblos left in New Mexico, a steep decline from the estimated 110 to 150 at the beginning of the Spanish occupation. Some pueblos had been consolidated at the instance of missionaries or *encomenderos*, to facilitate indoctrination or defense, but the main factor was population decline, born of war, disease, famine, and desperate flight.

Even worse was Pacheco's successor, Governor Fernando de Argüello (1644–1647), who had paid 9,000 pesos for the office and meant to squeeze enough from New Mexico's Spanish and Indian populace to realize a profit. He did. So did Governor Luis de Guzmán (1647–1649), who next purchased the office in 1647. Both systematically raided Apaches and Navajos for slaves, thus provoking retaliation against the Pueblos. Apache warriors killed forty and captured eight in a single attack on a pueblo, a devastating loss for a small community.

Four decades later Pueblos would recall Argüello as the governor whose intolerable abuses ignited the fires of rebellion that smoldered in the pueblos until 1680. When some Jémez killed a Spaniard, Argüello proclaimed them guilty of treasonable conspiracy with Navajos, publicly hanged twenty-nine men of Jémez, and lashed many more. The event long symbolized in Pueblo minds Spanish injustice and perfidy.

By mid-century old enmities among Pueblos and Athapaskans paled beside their common grievances against the Spaniards. Some conspired in 1650 for the general uprising always dreaded by Spaniards. Knowing how the religious obligations of Holy Week preoccupied Spaniards, some Pueblos arranged to turn the horse herds of their districts over to Apache and Navajo confederates on Holy Thursday evening, when all colonists attended church services, thus setting the stage for general attack on the assembled Spaniards. The Tiwas of Sandía and Alameda actually disposed of the horses of their districts

[8] Quoted in Scholes, "Church and State in New Mexico, 1610–1650," *New Mexico Historical Review* 12 (1937): 94.

before an alert colonist spotted unusual activity around a herd of mares and discovered the plot. Isleta, San Felipe, Cochití, and Jémez were also found involved. Nine leaders from those pueblos were hanged for the plot; many were sentenced to ten years' personal servitude.

Perhaps the swift, severe penalties made Pueblos more cautious, but they did not end conspiracies. Governor Hernando de Ugarte y la Concho (1649–1653) found Christian Pueblos and Navajos apparently plotting together when he campaigned in Navajo territory early in the 1650's.[9] In the same decade, Taoseños circulated two deer skins painted with a call to revolt, but Hopi rejection damped that effort. The spirit of revolt smoldered on in the pueblos, awaiting some extraordinary leader to unite the suffering Indians for freedom, and the obvious storm signals inspired no reforms in New Mexico.

Despite the Pueblos' hardened resolve to be rid of the Spaniards, they worked harder than ever before for governors and friars in the third quarter of the seventeenth century. They also suffered more damage from *bárbaros*, despite tentative efforts to collaborate with them against the Spaniards.

By mid-century there was seldom a time when some Apache or Navajo group did not have cause to send a war party against the Spaniards or Pueblos. Furthermore, there always prevailed the incentives to raid that sent little groups of men out to fetch "the things by which men live." Since the Spaniards made no distinction, it is impossible to know how many of the countless "attacks" they reported were actually raids for horses, but by the mid-1650's the Spaniards, with the help of Pueblo warriors, were openly attacking both eastern Apaches and Navajos, and Athapaskans were striking hard and often at persons as well as property.

In response to a Navajo attack that cost Jémez 19 dead and 35 captured, Governor Juan de Samaniego y Xaca (1653–1656) surprised a Navajo ceremonial and, whether or not they were the same Navajos who attacked Jémez, killed several and captured 211. Governor Bernardo López de Mendizábal (1659–1661) targeted Navajo cornfields for destruction from the outset of his term. Jémez relations with the Navajos worsened considerably when Mendizábal had Navajo warriors admitted to Jémez in peace only to slaughter them, then sent soldiers to seize the women and children those Navajos had left behind for safety.

9 Jack D. Forbes, *Apache, Navajo, and Spaniard*, p. 145.

Mendizábal was also charged with gross violation of the terms under which certain Apaches had come to live at Taos and Jémez, perhaps to escape famine in the Apachería. When he learned of their presence in the pueblos, the governor ordered the men killed and enslaved their women and children. Apache kinsmen and Pueblo witnesses long remembered treachery of that magnitude.

One of the most ambitious of the gubernatorial entrepreneurs, Mendizábal launched extensive Apache trade operations, using Pueblo agents on the trail as well as in the pueblos. His most notable employee was Don Esteban Clemente, a distinguished Tompiro who exercised some leadership in the Tiwa and Tompiro villages of the Salinas district and frequently visited Apaches in the Siete Ríos area. Mendizábal supplied stocks of goods for Don Esteban to trade when he visited his Apache friends and also helped him to organize trading parties to the plains, to their mutual profit.

Despite his great interest in the Apache trade, Mendizábal soon launched a major aggression against them, again involving many Pueblos. In September 1659, with eight hundred Christian Indians and only forty Spaniards, the governor scoured Apache territory for captives to ship south to market. The folly of that September expedition was immeasurable, for it was harvest time, when Pueblo men were needed at home to work in their cornfields and to guard their pueblos during the seasonal visits of countless Apache groups.[10] The 1659 corn harvest was particularly critical because drought had ruined the preceding year's crops. The drought had also affected the *bárbaros'* subsistence so badly that some had brought in all their captives from other nations to sell, and some had even offered their own children to the convents for a little meat or flour. The missionaries had nearly bankrupted themselves making those purchases, in order to save the children's lives and rear them as Christians. Mendizábal was infuriated when the friars refused to let him ship the little Indians to the Parral market, and perhaps his pique sparked his sudden, ill-timed invasion of the Apachería.

The friars charged that Mendizábal shipped seventy Apaches south in that autumn's caravan. The next year Mendizábal sold 12,000 pesos' worth of Apaches in Sonora, at a time when a strong youngster ten or twelve years old fetched thirty or forty pesos. The Audiencia of Guadalajara spotted that 1660 transaction and forced refunds to the purchasers and liberation of the slaves. Given that financial setback and

[10] Declaration of Captain Andrés Hurtado, Santa Fe, September 1659, in Hackett, *Historical Documents*, III, 186–187.

a very specific, strongly worded ban on the sale of Apache captives, Mendizábal abruptly suspended all military action against *bárbaros*. Consequently, neither Pueblos nor settlers received even the slightest protection from the governor against the Apache and Navajo attacks he had provoked.

Mendizábal's successor, Diego Dionisio de Peñalosa Briceño y Berdugo (1661–1664), claimed that he obeyed the *audiencia's* order to free the Indians sold and enslaved by his two immediate predecessors, but it was a dubious freedom. He "gave the Indians as free men to other persons to be indoctrinated, informing them that the Indians were free and not subject to servitude."[11] Governor Peñalosa himself seized forty Apaches who had belonged to Mendizábal and shipped several to Mexico City with other New Mexican products as gifts for personal friends and influential persons whom he wished to cultivate. Peñalosa kept numerous slaves. The count of enslaved Indians swelled steadily as plains Apaches marketed increasing numbers of Quivirans at Pecos; the price for an Apache woman in New Mexico dropped to twenty-six pesos.

Peñalosa undertook little aggression against the *bárbaros*, but Apaches and Navajos had so many scores to settle against Spaniards and Pueblos that no area was safe from attack. Any Apache or Navajo presence grew so ominous that Governor Peñalosa finally decreed that no *bárbaros*, even those at peace, should be allowed to enter the pueblos.[12] With tensions running so high in New Mexico's populated areas, people dared not gamble on telling at a glance a friendly Athapaskan visitor from a hostile one. On the other hand, to cut off trade entirely was only to disrupt the economy of those *bárbaros* who had long depended on Pueblo trade and to remove every incentive to peaceful commerce as the alternative to raiding. Peñalosa's cure boded worse than the disease.

The 1660's also brought hardships to Pueblos who had fled their troubled homeland. The last of the Taos Indians who had fled northeast to the Cuartelejo Apache territory gave up their attempt at independent existence and declared their desire to be brought home. They had built a pueblo on the plains, had established some trade with the Quivirans,

---

[11] Reply of Diego de Peñalosa, Mexico, October 22, 1665, ibid., 262.

[12] Order of Diego de Peñalosa, January 1664, in Ralph Emerson Twitchell, comp., *The Spanish Archives of New Mexico*, II, 2, cited by Frank D. Reeve in "Seventeenth Century Navaho-Spanish Relations," *New Mexico Historical Review* 32 (1957): 48.

and through them had acquired some metal goods, presumably the fringe effect of French trade then thrusting down from Canada into the Mississippi Valley. But theirs was an uncomfortable position amid the traditional enmities of Quivirans and Apaches, and the Taoseños found themselves too much at the Apaches' mercy. Don Juan de Archuleta led twenty New Mexican soldiers with a force of Pueblo auxiliaries to escort the thirty-three survivors home to Taos. They razed the fugitives' pueblo at El Cuartelejo and, while they were about it, destroyed Apache property, too.

The Taos fugitives returned to conditions nearly as unhealthy as the civil war they had fled a quarter-century before. The Franciscans, freshly outraged by gubernatorial abuses, had learned how to use the Inquisition to dispose of offenders, and in the process they terrorized settlers as well as governors. The rapacious Mendizábal had been hauled off in chains in 1662 to face trial by the Inquisition in Mexico, where he died in jail two years later as his trial dragged on. The next year Governor Peñalosa and Father Commissary Alonso Posada quarreled so bitterly over *encomiendas* that the governor rode to Pecos to arrest the father commissary and jailed him at the Governor's Palace. In protest, the clergy of Santa Fe and some missions closed down churches, consumed the Host, and thus deprived their congregations, Spanish and Indian, of the sacraments. When Peñalosa returned to Mexico in 1664, the Inquisition tried him, found him guilty of blasphemy and heresy, stripped him of all possessions, and exiled him forever from New Spain and the West Indies. Already a fugitive from justice in his native Peru, Peñalosa sailed for England and then France to peddle treasonable schemes for invading New Spain.

Peñalosa's successor, Juan de Miranda, could not govern the turbulent colony. Within a year the Santa Fe *cabildo* deposed him and held him prisoner at Picurís pueblo. What a pitiful spectacle Spanish authority had become! In the space of three years, the Pueblos had seen one governor leave the province in chains, raving like a lunatic, and had seen the head missionary imprisoned by the next governor; now, at Picurís, they saw another governor jailed by the settlers.

Never was vigorous remedy more urgent, but the ailing Spanish Empire lacked that capacity. The new climax of civil strife in New Mexico coincided with the accession of the infant Carlos II, a congenital invalid doomed to incompetence either to rule or to sire an heir. His reign dragged on from 1665 to 1700, the deathwatch of the Hapsburg dynasty in Spain. It was not a likely time for strong initiatives or administrative reforms. The chief outside contribution to calm New Mexico's strife was a decision to do nothing. By 1665 the leadership of the Inquisition in New Spain suspected that their representatives in New Mexico had been guilty of excesses. Thenceforth, the Inquisition pointedly refrained from interfering in New Mexico, and missionaries tempered their actions accordingly.

The friars' zeal found a new outlet southward, healthily remote from gubernatorial friction, in a field which had beckoned since the time of Benavides. In the 1650's they founded at El Paso del Norte the long-desired mission for the Mansos.[13] Fray García de San Francisco brought ten families of Christian Indians from Senecú pueblo to help found the mission and later, in 1664, obtained six Manso boys and girls who had been servants in a Spanish household in New Mexico. Reared as Christians, familiar with Spanish language and customs, they too could teach their compatriots. More than four hundred Indians attended the festive dedication of the church building at Mission Nuestra Señora de Guadalupe in January 1668. Some of the crowd were Mansos already deemed converts; some were neighboring peoples being wooed by the missionaries. Thirty miles downstream a mission for the Sumas was already underway.

Meanwhile, the populace of the New Mexican heartland suffered yet another ordeal, a drought cycle that lasted from 1666 to 1671. Starvation increased unrest among both Pueblos and Athapaskans, and infectious stories of revolt spread from the south. In 1666 a major Indian uprising swept Nueva Vizcaya; the next year brought a flurry of rebellion among the Mansos at the El Paso mission. The El Paso insurrection was quickly and harshly quelled, but unconverted Mansos and their Apache friends roved about the area in a turbulent mood, jeopardizing New Mexico's communications with the provinces to the south.

Soon the normally docile Piros, southernmost of the Rio Grande Pueblos, rebelled in concert with Apache allies. The *alcalde mayor* and four other Spaniards died in an ambush for which the Piros paid dearly. Spanish forces quickly quashed the disorder: six leaders hanged for the crime in the plaza of Senecú. Others burned at the stake, condemned as sorcerers as well as traitors. Some lived only to be sold into slavery.

[13] Annie E. Hughes, "The Beginnings of Spanish Settlement in the El Paso District," *University of California Publications in History* 1 (1914): 308–309; Scholes, "Documents for the History of the New Mexican Missions in the Seventeenth Century," *New Mexico Historical Review* 4 (1929): 195–201.

If the Spaniards thought to inflict penalties so terrible as to make rebellion unthinkable, their strategy failed. Across the Manzanos, in the Salinas district of the Tompiros, an established leader tried to revive the plot that failed in 1650: to drive to the sierras on Holy Thursday all the horse herds and then to slaughter the Spaniards. His conspiracy discovered, Don Esteban Clemente hanged for it.[14]

The Piro and Tompiro pueblos did not long survive those abortive efforts at liberation. With their leadership destroyed and their numbers decimated, they could not withstand the famine and epidemics and the devastating surge of Apache hostility that beset them from 1668 to 1671. *Encomenderos* did what they could, repeatedly taking the field with Pueblo warriors to punish the enemies, but even that remedy posed hazards. Piro and Tompiro men were then so few that departure of any useful number left their people and property exposed to raids by watchful Siete Ríos Apaches. Gila Apaches also preyed upon the Piros, and the Gilas and Siete Ríos seemed to conspire in harrassing the wagon route from El Paso to Senecú. Life grew so intolerable that Piros and Tompiros drifted away from their homes, some to other pueblos, some to the distant sanctuary of the El Paso missions. By the end of the 1670's, the Pueblo world was nearly dead east of the Manzanos and its southern reaches on the Rio Grande were shrinking.

While devastation was worst on the southern and eastern frontiers of the province, no quarter escaped the onslaught of the *bárbaros* in that decade. The pueblos bore the brunt of the attacks, but not even Santa Fe was immune. Response to their acute common dangers finally restored some unity among the New Mexicans. Old quarrels between church and state officials and rivalries of friars and laity receded as they confronted the crisis together. Governors as well as *encomenderos* spent much of their time on campaign with the Christian Indians against the *bárbaros*. Missionaries, helpless to check the destruction of their congregations, their mission buildings, and even some of their own Order, appreciated and supported those efforts. Laymen ceased to oppose the missionaries' farming and ranching now that mission stores preserved colonists as well as Pueblos from starvation.

The epidemic of 1671 killed livestock as well as people, and the next year Apache and Navajo raiders focused particularly upon livestock. By the end of 1672, the province was virtually stripped of livestock.

[14] Declaration of Diego López Sambrano, December 22, 1681, in Charles Wilson Hackett, ed., *Revolt of the Pueblo Indians of New Mexico and Otermín's Attempted Reconquest, 1680–1682*, II, 299–300.

In their extremity, both Pueblos and Spaniards ate hides, even consuming the leather suspension straps of their carts. Soaked and washed, then toasted with corn or boiled with herbs and roots, that pitiful diet saved half the people from starvation.

Among the Pueblos, the ordeal of death and destruction evoked a resurgence of their old religion stronger than any before. The principal leaders were Tewa shamans, but the movement affected every pueblo. Spaniards, friars and settlers alike, were frightened and dismayed by the apparent surge of witchcraft. Half a dozen priests and several settlers died mysteriously, presumed victims of witchcraft; it was whispered that the priest at San Ildefonso was bewitched. Throughout the Tewa pueblos and at the outlying pueblos of Zuñi, Ácoma, and Taos, friars found "idolatry" so prevalent that they could no longer perform their ministry.[15]

Against a foe identified as witchcraft, surely the appropriate remedy should have been exorcism, but of such response no record remains. The friars approved of the forceful reaction of Governor Juan Francisco Treviño (1675–1677), who dispatched soldiers to seize the leaders, confiscate their religious paraphernalia, and burn their kivas. They hanged three shamans of Nambé, San Felipe, and Jémez. Another despairing soul hanged himself. Forty-three more leaders of the movement were publicly whipped, then jailed at Santa Fe, and sentenced to be sold into slavery for the crime of idolatry.

To the Spaniards' amazement, the Pueblos rallied to save their shamans. A horde of warriors appeared at Santa Fe, and seventy entered the Governor's Palace, weapons in hand, to demand release of the imprisoned leaders. Quiet, courteous, but in deadly earnest, they prevailed. Governor Treviño released to them the prisoners and all went home to their pueblos, but nothing was ever the same after that. Scars on flogged backs healed, but wounds in pride and spirit did not. The strongest leaders plotted more earnestly than ever before. Many Pueblos would continue to avoid strife at nearly any price, but now they could all remember a time when they had stood together to defend the Pueblo way and had made the Spaniards bow to their will.

Spaniards would later recall that quiet, compelling confrontation in the Governor's Palace in 1675 and know that it foreshadowed the holocaust.[16] But at that moment the overriding threat was imminent

---

[15] Forbes, *Apache, Navajo, and Spaniard*, p. 171.

[16] The recollections appeared in the *autos* taken in December 1681 when Otermín interrogated the veterans in his force about their understanding of the

destruction of the province by *bárbaros*, and Treviño needed every able-bodied man in New Mexico to defend the frontiers. He dared not risk battle with Pueblos.

By autumn 1676, the leadership of the province united in a desperate appeal for help. When Custodian and Procurator General Fray Francisco de Ayeta journeyed to Mexico for the triennial mission supply caravan, he carried the warning of the governor and *cabildo* that, barring major Spanish reinforcements, the Apaches would soon destroy New Mexico. Ayeta quickly won the point: the Crown would supply men, arms, and horses. As rapidly as possible, Ayeta assembled the authorized reinforcements, also organizing meanwhile the triennial supply caravan that was his regular responsibility. He left the capital in February 1677 and reached Santa Fe nine months later. Although the viceroy had responded with extraordinary speed and Ayeta had followed through with exceptional ability and dedication, more than a year had passed since he had carried that urgent plea to Mexico City.[17]

Ayeta purchased and transported north a thousand horses, a hundred guns, a hundred hilts for swords and daggers, and fifty saddles with bridles and spurs. The viceroy had authorized him to recruit fifty soldiers, plus a commander and a sergeant, but New Mexico's problems were so notorious that only three raw recruits volunteered for the dangerous, unrewarding job. For the rest, Ayeta scoured the jails for convicts sentenced to armed service on the northern frontier. Seven escaped along the way; the other forty-nine reached Santa Fe in carts, ignominiously fettered. Only the two officers and the three volunteers arrived mounted and armed. Nevertheless, Governor Antonio de Otermín (1677–1683) promptly mustered in all the reinforcements and deployed them to frontier trouble spots.

The increment helped temporarily. Pueblo families reoccupied the abandoned pueblos of Las Salinas, Senecú, Cuarac, and Chililí, under protection of Spanish soldiers stationed at those spots. For a few months, hostilities subsided, but by autumn 1678 Apaches were again hitting hard. When Ayeta went back to Mexico for the next supply caravan, he carried another appeal for help.

There had been just one hopeful development. Utes, who had injured the northern pueblos from time to time, made peace at Taos in 1678,

---

causes of the rebellion and the attitudes of the rebels. See Hackett, *Revolt of the Pueblo Indians*, II, 255 ff.

[17] Petition of Father Francisco de Ayeta, 1678, and Reply of Fiscal, Mexico, September 11, 1678, in Hackett, *Historical Documents*, III, 287.

and they kept the pact so faithfully that Governor Otermín hopefully anticipated their conversion. However, the primary problem of Apache and Navajo attacks seemed only to worsen with time, despite repeated Spanish-Pueblo campaigns. The toll of Pueblos killed or captured by Athapaskans and the Spaniards' patent inability to protect the Pueblos cast increasing doubt upon the value of vassalage to the Spanish king.

Fray Ayeta sought permanent remedy, encouraged by reports that the Crown had approved the viceroy's earlier assistance and had asked to be kept informed of the New Mexican situation. Ayeta requested fifty more men to defend the frontier at once and perhaps someday to reduce the *bárbaros* to peace. If necessary, he would cart another fifty convicts north to shore up defenses, but he realized now that New Mexico's survival required more than sporadic, piecemeal reinforcements and haphazard reliance upon *encomenderos* and other settlers. Ayeta therefore urged establishment of a presidio at Santa Fe for ten years, with a fifty-man garrison, as had been done to check Indian wars in Sinaloa.

Succinctly, Ayeta defined the stakes in New Mexico: its territory, 450 miles north from El Paso to Taos, 400 miles west from Las Salinas to the Hopi pueblos; its population, forty-six pueblos of Christian Indians and twenty-five convents of missionaries, altogether some 16,000 Christian Indians, male and female, of whom only 6,000 could use the bow and arrow. The Spaniards and others of various castes, even including the last relief contingent, could muster only 170 men who could use arms; of those the governor could summon only 20 on short notice because most were stationed on the frontier or lived on scattered farms.

Authorities in Mexico City balked, not because Ayeta failed to convince them of New Mexico's need, but because they would not establish a presidio without specific authorization from Madrid. In vain did Ayeta point out the wide discretionary latitude in New Mexican affairs that early seventeenth-century decrees had vested in the viceroy. Timidity prevailed in Mexico City, and the question of a presidio was forwarded to Spain. Pending an answer from the Crown, New Mexico would receive no further reinforcements. Heartsick, Ayeta marshaled his mission supply caravan and departed from Mexico City in September 1679.

With luck, a caravan could reach Santa Fe in six months, but big supply trains were vulnerable to many delays, and this proved a difficult year. The next August found the caravan marking time at El Paso, held up by unseasonal high waters in the Rio Grande. With it waited twenty-seven New Mexican soldiers under Pedro de Leiva, sent by Governor Otermín to escort the caravan up the dangerous road to Santa Fe. At eight o'clock on the morning of August 25, 1680, stunning news reached Leiva and Ayeta: general Pueblo revolt in New Mexico.

Details were sparse. The dispatches came from the southern district. The fate of Otermín and the colonists and friars in the north was unknown. The southern survivors were evacuating the province and would rely upon Ayeta for succor. He promptly pledged his mission supplies to unstinting relief for the refugees, while Leiva and his men prepared to ride north. They would deliver emergency supplies to the refugees, then continue north to Santa Fe, either to rescue or to find the bodies of their families and the governor. Meanwhile, Ayeta prepared to receive the refugees at El Paso, using Mission Guadalupe as his base of operations. By early October all the refugees, including many survivors led south from Santa Fe by Governor Otermín, were encamped at El Paso, there to assess the nightmarish events of the past eight weeks and to consider the urgent matter of reconquest.

Indios bárbaros loomed large in the discussions. What, if any, role had they played in the rebellion? Would Apache and Navajo warriors rush to obliterate their Pueblo foes now that the Spaniards and their guns were gone? Or would they rally to help the Pueblos fend off reconquest? With the buffer province of New Mexico destroyed, how soon would the *bárbaros* sweep southward to plunder Sonora and Nueva Vizcaya?

Apaches and Navajos could indeed rejoice in the Pueblos' success. Expulsion of the Spaniards rid them of the slavers who had preyed upon their women and children. It also eliminated Spanish leadership of punitive campaigns against Apache and Navajo raiders. While there remained in the Pueblo world the livestock and metal goods that had been the *bárbaros'* great gain from the Spanish occupation, there was no longer the Spanish presence to distort the patterns of trading and raiding by which the *bárbaros* lived. The Pueblos, weakened from years of stress and notoriously factious, posed little threat to their neighbors: their property and their women and children lay pitifully vulnerable to raiders. It was a time of relative freedom for Athapaskans to consolidate their gains and to exploit the new ways of life founded upon the Spanish imports.

CHAPTER 3

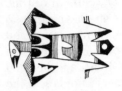

New Mexico, 1680-1704

Looking back from El Paso that autumn, Governor Oter-
mín was still amazed at the revolt. No one denied that the Pueblos had
had grievances in the past, but New Mexico had lately enjoyed greater
tranquillity. Otermín had carefully protected the Pueblos from excessive
demands, requiring them only "to assist in the cultivation of the soil
in order to obtain the necessary subsistence."[1] Spaniards had enjoyed
cordially cooperative relationships with many Pueblos. Some groups
had preferred their *encomenderos* to live in or near their pueblos for
maximum security against *bárbaros*. Even the Apaches and Navajos
had been less troublesome than usual that year, and the Utes had kept
their peace pact of 1678 so faithfully that Otermín had thought their
conversion imminent.

Utterly incomprehensible to Otermín was the depth of rancor rooted
in old grievances, although he came to Santa Fe only two years after
the crucial episode of 1675. Among the shamans rescued from Governor

[1] Governor Antonio de Otermín to the Viceroy, Paso del Río del Norte, October
20, 1680, in Charles Wilson Hackett, ed., *Revolt of the Pueblo Indians of New
Mexico and Otermín's Attempted Reconquest, 1680–1682,* I, 206.

Treviño by the Tewa warriors had been Popé, who carried home to San Juan pueblo a grim determination to destroy the Spaniards. His persistent invocation of traditional spirits and his burning hostility to Spaniards made him suspect in San Juan, so Popé moved north to Taos. There he secluded himself in a kiva, communing with spirit messengers of the old war gods, who made Popé their envoy to all Pueblos. In the summer of 1680 he proclaimed their message throughout the Pueblo world: rise up together to destroy the Spaniards or drive them out forever, then forget all they taught you and discard all they brought. Go back to ancient ways.

Popé had negotiated many months with like-minded Pueblo leaders and perhaps with *bárbaros*, too. He brooked no resistance. When he suspected that his son-in-law, the governor of San Juan, would report him to Spanish authorities, he killed the man in his own house. When at last Popé issued the call to revolt, he threatened to have Apaches destroy any pueblo that failed to join in the rebellion.

Runners carried the message to all pueblos, as far south as Isleta. A knotted thong told the days that must pass before they would rise together on August 11, first destroying all Spaniards in their own vicinity, then converging on Santa Fe to finish off the colony.

The response was far from unanimous. Although many shared Popé's longing for liberation from the Spanish regime, there were compelling arguments against his scheme. Many Pueblos preferred peace above all else, and they dreaded a return to the old days of internecine strife. Although few practiced the exclusive devotion the Franciscans expected, some valued Christianity as they understood it and were loath to lose the sacraments or harm the friars. Some Pueblos had ties of blood or friendship in the Spanish community. The indigenous and colonial populations had mingled for eight decades; many Pueblos and Spaniards cordially acknowledged kinsmen of the other race. While Pueblo labor had often been abused, some pleasant and even close relationships had grown between employers and workers. Some *encomenderos* had won the gratitude of the Indians they protected during the years that Pueblos and Spaniards fought side by side against the *bárbaros*. Most Pueblos had become involved in the more complex economy introduced by the Spaniards: many would find it difficult to revert to the limited old economy.

Even Pueblos without personal ties to any Spaniard raised questions. Perhaps the Apaches and Navajos would indeed help them to get rid of the Spaniards, but what if they should afterward attack the

Pueblos when the soldiers and their guns were gone? And what of Popé himself? Such a self-assertive, overweening man was the very antithesis of the Pueblo ideal, perhaps a dangerous sorcerer. Would they be better off at his mercy than under Spanish rule? Many doubted it, some so vehemently that they warned the Spaniards.

Leaders of five nearby pueblos[2] rode to Santa Fe to warn Governor Otermín on August 9, the same day that he received warning messages from the two priests and the *alcalde mayor* at Taos. Meanwhile, at Pecos, Governor Don Felipe tried in vain to convince the priests and soldiers stationed there of the impending revolt. The story did confound Spanish minds: no Pueblo group totally uninvolved in the plot, Apache allies poised on the rim of the province to support the rebels. But Popé's two runners, intercepted by Spaniards, confirmed the plot.

Their arrest precipitated the rebellion a little prematurely. The Indians of Tesuque murdered their missionary, rounded up the cattle and horses, and fled to the mountains. Every pueblo north of Isleta erupted. Once the die was cast, many who had opposed the plot saw no choice but to join in the fray. Some dispersed settlers were warned in time to escape, but many Spanish families suffered devastating losses. About a thousand survivors in the northern district took refuge in the Governor's Palace at Santa Fe; those in the southern district flocked to loyal Isleta pueblo, certain that no one could have survived the bloodbath in the north.

Ácoma, Zuñi, and Hopi warriors did not trek to Santa Fe to join the siege, but no Spaniards survived at those remote pueblos or at Picurís. Even at Taos, where the plot had been discovered, only two soldiers managed to fight their way out after their families were killed. They reported at Santa Fe that the Apaches del Acho[3] had joined the forces of Picurís and Taos.

On August 13, a sizeable body of Tano warriors formed across the river, just south of Santa Fe's main plaza. Their leader, a Spanish-speaking Tano resident of Santa Fe called Juan, parleyed with Governor Otermín in the plaza. The governor appealed to the rebels' Christian consciences, promising pardon if they would abandon the insurrection, but to no avail. Juan boasted of reinforcements coming from the other pueblos and from the Apaches, all sworn to destroy the villa, and demanded that Otermín choose between a red cross, signifying war, and a white cross, signifying abandonment of the province. The gover-

---

[2] Galisteo, San Cristóbal, San Lázaro, San Marcos, and La Ciénega.
[3] A people who lived just north of Taos, probably Jicarilla forebears.

nor chose to fight that day, before those reinforcements could arrive. Battle swirled through the Barrio Analco,[4] around the church of San Miguel. Otermín claimed victory over the Tanos, but as they fled their allies arrived: Tewas, Taoseños, and Picurís.

More followed. By August 16, 2,500 Indians surrounded Santa Fe. For nine days they besieged the Spanish community, barricaded with their livestock in the Governor's Palace. No Spanish soldiers died, but many were wounded. The Indians had seized the guns and ammunition of Spaniards slain throughout the province and they used them to good effect. The soldiers' leather armor repelled arrows but not shot. Himself wounded in a desperate, futile charge from the Palace on August 20, Otermín took stock of his situation.

Of more than a thousand persons in the Palace, less than one hundred were men who could fight. The sole hope for the lives of all those women and children was to walk to Isleta to join the other survivors. On August 21, they evacuated the Palace and marched toward Isleta. The Indians gleefully swarmed to sack the Palace, apparently content for the moment despite their heavy casualties. More vindictive rebels would have pursued Otermín's rabble of refugees to wipe them out, but those Pueblos were satisfied just to see them go: "We are at quits with the Spaniards and the persons whom we have killed; those of us whom they have killed do not matter, for they are going, and now we shall live as we like and settle in this villa and wherever we see fit."[5]

The fleeing colonists progressed mournfully downstream from one deserted pueblo to another, past haciendas gruesome with corpses of families known to all the marchers. Mounted Indians watched from the heights, carefully herding numerous horses and cattle, more eager now to keep livestock than to kill Spaniards.

To the governor's chagrin, Isleta also lay deserted. Runners were sent ahead to order the retreating southern survivors to wait, and the group trudged on. Grimly aware now that they trod Apache country, Otermín pressed to consolidate the two groups at the earliest possible moment, but it was September 13 before he reached the southern refugees' camp at Fray Cristóbal, forty miles below Socorro.

Otermín had hoped there to muster enough soldiers to turn back and quell the rebellion, but none had any stomach for the venture. At most, 155 men could bear arms; they had only 471 horses and mules,

---

[4] Traditional quarter of the Mexican Indian population of the colony.
[5] Declaration of an Indian rebel, Place of the Árroyo de San Marcos, August 23, 1680, in Hackett, *Revolt of the Pueblo Indians*, I, 19.

most in bad shape. Of the estimated 2,500 persons in camp, most were women and children, suffering agonies of hunger and fatigue. With winter imminent, they had to be escorted safely to El Paso. Bowing to those arguments, Otermín led his wretched band on to El Paso.

The fugitives were a heterogeneous lot. A few Spaniards were householders of substance; most were desperately poor; many were servants attached to some household. Much of the non-Spanish population had chosen to stay on in New Mexico. Only six convicts made the trek south: few had had time to finish their sentences since Ayeta delivered them to Santa Fe less than three years before, so the sentence to New Mexico must have proved a death sentence to most of the forty-nine.

With the retreating colonists trudged 317 Christian Indians of all ages and sexes from the pueblos of Isleta, Sevilleta, Alamillo, Socorro, and Senecú, plus one Tewa couple with their six children. Since the Isletas had not honored the call to revolt and since the Piros had not even been invited, they had every reason to fear the Pueblos upstream. Enmity between northern Pueblos and Piros long antedated the Spanish presence: apparently the old distrusts endured.

Of the 380 Spaniards killed in the uprising, 73 were men of military age, a telling blow to a colony that had rarely boasted more than two hundred men-at-arms. The Franciscans had grave shortages to repair if they were to restore their ministry, for twenty-one priests had died at the pueblos.

Many of the fleeing settlers would gladly have escaped deeper into New Spain to forget New Mexico forever. Anticipating that, and determined that these colonists would spearhead prompt reconquest, Fray Ayeta had taken steps to hold them. Although they crossed the Rio Grande into Nueva Vizcaya to establish their camp, Ayeta had arranged for Otermín's jurisdiction to cover the refugees south of the Rio Grande, too. Any deserters fleeing deeper into Nueva Vizcaya would be rounded up and returned to El Paso. No matter how sick they were of New Mexico, or how grievous their losses, or how little they had to go back for, they must camp on the Rio Grande to await reconquest. Fray Ayeta promised to support them with every resource at his command until the Crown could assume the responsibility.

No one doubted that a hard year lay ahead, but it was unthinkable that the reconquest be delayed more than a year. The Franciscans agonized over six thousand baptized Indian souls hovering on the brink of apostasy, and the Crown shared their concern. Strategic considerations also dictated prompt reconquest. Elimination of New

Mexico as a buffer province exposed Sonora and Nueva Vizcaya to a southward sweep of *bárbaros*, which probably would stimulate uprisings among Indians now settled in missions. Equally alarming was the thought of French and English frontiersmen relentlessly probing southward and westward from their original settlements toward the silver mines of New Spain.

Reconquest would be regrettably expensive, but the Crown had eighty years of investment at stake in New Mexico. Immediate reconquest could be organized around the nucleus of men familiar with the land and people of New Mexico, able to communicate with them and to anticipate their stratagems. So reasoned the viceroy when he authorized a fifty-man presidio at El Paso. He meant to transfer the post to Santa Fe after reconquest, but for the moment it was needed to protect the sprawling refugee camps and missions at El Paso from raiders and to prevent incursions by the *bárbaros* into Sonora and Nueva Vizcaya. The Crown endorsed the viceroy's decision. Never again would New Mexico's defense depend solely upon *encomenderos* and a citizen militia. Spain had paid dearly to learn the worth of Ayeta's proposal of 1679.

By the end of the summer of 1681, authorization for the presidio and some resources were in Governor Otermín's hands. In September he enlisted men for the new presidio and also recruited a force to reconquer New Mexico. He paid the latter in goods worth 250 pesos, plus a ploughshare, an axe, and four hoes apiece. After victory, it would be their duty to establish homes once more.

Many former residents ignored the summons to enlist for the return. Most colonists had known little but hardship and heartbreak in New Mexico. They realized that invaders would confront Pueblos who were not such easy game as those conquered a century earlier. Pueblos now had horses and guns and knew how to use them. No longer would the sight of mounted soldiers or the crack of gunfire terrify them. Many spoke Spanish, a lingua franca bridging the old language barriers that had earlier made it hard for them to unite against invaders. Many common grievances would unite Pueblos and perhaps Apaches against the Spaniards. If the Spaniards should prevail, the Indians would surely run away forever. Of what use would the land be without people to make it produce? How would it profit any Spaniard to own a piece of the wreckage of New Mexico?

What of personal ties between the Spanish and Pueblo communities? What of their fellow communicants in the faith? Everyone could echo the stunned report of a priest who had survived the bloodbath: "The Indians who have done the greatest harm are those who have been most favored by the religious and who are most intelligent."[6] Few could cherish any illusion of comity after the bloody lesson of August 1680.

Otermín was infuriated that his New Mexican veterans were so reluctant to enlist. He marched, nevertheless, early in November 1681, with too few men and too little equipment, believing it better to fail than to make no attempt at all. Sixteen of his 146 soldiers were raw recruits; ages ranged from fifteen to ninety-six. They took more than nine hundred horses and mules and the usual herd of cattle.

Like most "Spanish" expeditions, Otermín's force had important Indian components, each with its own leader: twenty Mansos, fifty-four Piros, thirty Tiwas, eight Jémez. Many Piros had come to El Paso with the fugitives in 1680; probably the Tiwas were of the Isleta group who had come at that time. Surprising is the Jémez contingent led by Governor Francisco, who apparently had led an exodus of a few who would not countenance the uprising.

Fray Ayeta himself led a small group of friars. More hopeful than Otermín of the outcome, he expected that the Pueblos had come to their senses over the year and would welcome the chance to repent their awful sins and receive the sacraments. He also thought it likely that the Pueblos had by now suffered so much at the hands of *bárbaros* that they would be humbly grateful to live again under Spanish protection.

Though less sanguine than the friars about the redeeming force of the faith among Pueblos, Otermín too hoped that the Pueblos would welcome the Spaniards back to fight the *bárbaros*. So much of Spanish energy and treasure had been expended over the years against the *bárbaros*, so sorely had Pueblos needed protection from raiders, that it was difficult to imagine that the old hostilities vanished when the Spaniards left.

True, Popé had threatened to turn Apaches on pueblos that failed to revolt, but perhaps he had bluffed. A survivor from Taos had reported Utes as well as Apaches del Acho involved in the conspiracy, but Otermín had seen no sign of Apache participation in the siege at Santa Fe. The Tano leader, Juan, had demanded all Indians in the besieged villa, Mexicans as well as Pueblo servants, and particularly Apache servants, warning that Apaches in his force would raze Santa

---

[6] Fray Antonio de Sierra to Father Francisco de Ayeta, Fray Cristóbal, September 4, 1680, ibid., 59.

Fe if their kinsmen were not restored. Otermín had thought Juan lied; he saw no Apaches in the crowd. If there had indeed been support from *bárbaros*, it had not been conspicuous, and his own experience in New Mexico led the governor to doubt that any alliance of Apaches and Pueblos could have endured many months. He also guessed that the unbridled tyranny of leaders like Popé would have grown so onerous that many Pueblos would prefer Spanish rule restored.

Nursing their separate hopes, Governor Otermín and Fray Ayeta led their expedition northward to look for miserable penitents in the pueblos. Ahead lay great shock and disappointment.

Leaders of the rebellion had worked hard all year to consolidate their gains. Popé and his lieutenants had promptly sought to erase every trace of the Spanish regime and restore the old ways in absolute purity. At his direction, people waded into streams to scrub themselves with yucca root, so as to purge themselves of Christian baptism. Churches were destroyed, sacred images defaced, religious accouterments put to homely uses. Building new kivas and bringing ritual paraphernalia out of hiding or fashioning it anew, the people celebrated an intensive round of rituals to restore the old, essential harmonies among Pueblos and the spirits of their universe.

When Popé urged Pueblos to repudiate marriages based on the Christian sacrament and choose any mates they wished for however long they wished, some gladly returned to the older, more flexible Pueblo style of marriage. But Popé's fanaticism carried him too far when he told them to relinquish everything the Spaniards had brought. Many of the innovations had enriched the Pueblos' material lives, and they had gladly expropriated the colonists' possessions. Cattle, sheep, oxen, and especially horses and mules were carefully husbanded. No one wished to quit using carts and teams, or to eschew plows and hoes in favor of pointed sticks, or to abandon the friars' better irrigation methods. Worst of all was Popé's demand that the Pueblos destroy the seeds of crops the Spaniards had introduced. Who would willingly renounce the wheat, the melons, the tomatoes, and the chiles[7] which the Spaniards had brought to New Mexico? Who would destroy the orchards of apple and peach and apricot and pear trees, sacrificing not only their luscious fruits but their pleasant green shade about the pueblos?

[7] Tomatoes and chiles were indigenous to the New World but not previously known to the Pueblos.

Nor would people discard their new skills. Traditions of fine crafts-manship were old in the Pueblo world, but they had gained much from the Spaniards. Now Pueblo weavers turned out fine woolen tex-tiles; some were skilled carpenters and metalworkers. Pueblo black-smiths were competent to run the Spanish smithies and to repair and manufacture weapons and tools as long as the metal supply should last.

Nor would Pueblos go back to old ways of fighting. They had care-fully salvaged the arms of slain Spaniards: swords, lances, daggers, and armor, as well as guns. Some would meet Spaniards on equal terms in any future encounter, armed like Europeans and mounted on horses that they could handle well. With that complement, those Pueblos who, by choice or necessity, battled on foot with their bows and arrows would stand all the firmer. Even if the Spaniards should never return, what rational people would cling to old-style warfare now that Apaches, Navajos, and Utes rode horses and fought with metal weapons?

Popé had been a useful leader against the Spaniards, but he was dangerous to anyone who opposed his ideas, and he was in some ways conspicuously unwise. He soon became such a nuisance that his own people killed him. Even in the early stages, while Popé stirred men's minds like a whirlwind with his nativist crusade, more practical leaders labored to assure the Pueblos' safety.

The *bárbaros* held the key to peace and security. Their minimal response to the revolt had been disappointing. Would they now be friends and allies of the Pueblos and help them to prevent the Span-iards' return, or would they seize the chance to even old scores against Pueblos? Would their raiders now grab all the wealth Pueblos had won from the Spaniards? Apache and Navajo leaders parleyed many times with Pueblo leaders in the year after the revolt, but they made no commitment either to forgo raids or to fight alongside Pueblos against Spaniards. Thoughtful Pueblos dreaded the outcome.

Uncertainty about the *bárbaros* was not the Pueblos' only difficulty in their first year of liberation. Despite all their dancing, the rains did not come. A scant corn harvest cast doubt on the validity of Popé's spiritual leadership. The specter of famine loomed over people plagued with doubts about their standing with the ruling spirits and about the intentions of both *bárbaros* and Spaniards. Many fled the dilemma, seeking refuge principally among Navajos.

In the autumn of 1681, Pueblo leaders schemed to stave off famine and at the same time conciliate the Apaches. They would conquer

Isleta by trickery, sack its granaries, kill its men, and present the Isleta
women and children to Apaches in compensation for Apache women
and children lost to Spaniards and Pueblos over the years. Isleta would
be destroyed for its failure to join in the rebellion, and the handsome
gift might win the Apaches' friendship and alliance. The plot involved
twenty-six pueblos: Tanos, Tewas, Keres, and those of Ácoma and
Jémez.

Into that volatile situation rode Governor Otermín and Fray Ayeta,
much encouraged by their initial observations. They found the Piro
pueblos totally deserted, rife with Apache signs. Assuming that the
residents had abandoned them for fear of the Apaches, the Spaniards
burned the four pueblos. On the trail were signs of Apaches driving
herds of livestock, which suggested that interior pueblos also had
suffered losses.

Isleta was the first pueblo they found occupied. The Isletans put up
little show of force before complying with Otermín's call for surrender
and later explained that they had first thought Apaches were attacking.
The Spaniards were outraged to see the church a charred ruin and
sacred articles put to profane uses, but the Isletans explained that, too.
It was the work of leaders of the rebellion, the Tewas and the people
of Taos and Picurís, who had swept the land, burning every vestige of
Christianity and bidding the people live as in the old days. Though
Pueblos no longer had to obey priests or governors or Spaniards, they
did have to obey the leaders of the rebellion.

The Isletans seemed truly penitent. Fray Ayeta hastened to absolve
five hundred souls in the pueblo, baptized infants born since the rebellion, and urged loyalty to Christian marriages. He had big crosses
erected in the plazas and little crosses hung about the people's necks; all
paraphernalia of idolatry was burned. There seemed hope, after all,
that the last year's awful damage to souls could be undone.

Otermín sent runners upstream to the other Tiwa pueblos, Alameda,
Puaray, and Sandía, where rebellion had been so long plotted and so
violently consummated, with his command: *wait in your pueblos for the
Spaniards and surrender to them peacefully*. Those Pueblos fled. There
would be no more easy conquests like that at Isleta.

While Otermín established headquarters near Isleta, Juan Domínguez de Mendoza led half the army upstream, only to find Alameda,
Puaray, Sandía, San Felipe, Santo Domingo, and Cochití deserted. A
rumor that the Spaniards had slaughtered the Isletans had spread
through the pueblos and did not seem inconsistent with the history of

Spanish reprisals against Pueblo insurgents. All chose to take their chances in the sierras, even when winter storms came and sharp sleet drove the cold into their shivering bodies. Fleeing with their livestock as the Spaniards approached, the Pueblos left most of their food in their storerooms. Gnawing hunger worsened their ordeal, but no one surrendered to the invaders.

Mendoza achieved no meaningful contact with the rebels until he camped at Cochití, where on nearby heights congregated a thousand Indians. Their principal leader was Alonso Catití, a Santo Domingo mestizo influential among Keres, who had helped to promote the rebellion. Many of his crowd hooted down to the Spaniards, gesticulating their desire to fight, but Catití calmed them and took a few leaders down to parley with Mendoza's party.

Catití's task was to stall for time until his people could dispose of the Spaniards by trickery or muster an overwhelming force against them. Given enough days, Governor Luis Tupatú of Picurís could organize an assault force and Popé could throw his powers into the struggle. Meanwhile, Catití gulled Mendoza by promising to call off the rebellion and to lead his people back to their pueblos within two days.

Captain Mendoza promised the rebels the king's pardon; Fray Guerra urged them to confess and receive absolution. Catití acknowledged his great sins and professed concern for the awful jeopardy to his soul, but he questioned the worth of Spanish promises. Did not all Pueblos remember the slaughter at Jémez of Apaches whom Spaniards had promised peace? Catití's delegation voiced the causes of their rebellion, stressing particularly the harsh repressions of their native religion that climaxed under Governor Treviño.

Mendoza had served thirty-eight years in New Mexico and had seen fourteen governors at work. He acknowledged the truth of the Pueblos' grievances and trusted in the sincerity of their repentance. Although Otermín had ordered him to disarm all rebels, he let them keep their weapons because they pleaded fear of Apaches in the mountains. Not for several days did he realize that Catití had feigned a peace agreement with him. Again, sharply divided loyalties among Pueblos betrayed their cause. Several Pueblos alerted Spanish friends to their danger. Mendoza retreated downstream to Otermín's camp.

The governor had not been idle. Within sight of his camp lay the smoking ruins of Alameda, Puaray, and Sandía. Mendoza's moderation infuriated Otermín. The old New Mexico veteran had not even burned kivas, much less pueblos; he had taken supplies for his men from the deserted pueblos, but he had not sacked them. Otermín deliberately destroyed all food he could not carry away, lest fugitives in the sierras sneak down for provisions. While Mendoza had sought reconciliation, Otermín had attempted reconquest.

Most soldiers were ready to give up any idea of reconquest. All information from friendly visitors and interrogated prisoners documented Pueblo determination to exterminate the invaders. Pueblos had debated for more than a year the policy to be followed in the event of the Spaniards' return. Some had advocated a cautious, conciliatory reception, but the strongest leaders had prevailed with their determination to destroy the enemy. Dread of the struggle had caused many peace-loving Pueblos to flee to the Navajos. Now the Spaniards, disabused of the notion that repentant sinners waited to welcome them with open arms, also bowed to that fierce determination and left the Pueblo world.

Profound sadness filled the heart of Fray Ayeta, whose five cherished assumptions lay shattered. No pueblo had been destroyed by Apaches; indeed, the *bárbaros* had done relatively little damage, though the long-time foes had made no actual alliance. The Pueblos were not anxious to be rid of their own leaders. No pangs of conscience beset them. On the contrary, they had shown total commitment to their old paganism. Every act underscored their determination: their desperate flights from homes and property; their stubborn two-week sojourn in the mountains, starving and shivering, with only a few poor hides to shelter them from falling snow. The good treatment accorded Isleta had not reassured other Pueblos. Ayeta gloomily conceded that, after more than eighty years of life with the Spaniards, Pueblos whom he had thought Christian preferred death to restoration of the Spanish regime. Men like Catití would speak of repentance and absolution, but they only manipulated words they knew the Spaniards wanted to hear. In truth, they gloried in their apostasy.

That realization shook Ayeta to the very depths of his being. Though he deplored the soldiers' lack of zeal and offered to give all he possessed to any who would persist in the reduction of the apostates, he had to admit that he saw no real hope. Otermín could do nothing about the apostates except burn their empty pueblos.

While the Spaniards argued their next move, the rebels looked to Isleta. On the night of December 23, fifty mounted Pueblos, led by Don Luis Tupatú himself, circled about Isleta, urging its people to join the rebels and promising to destroy all who refused. For a week the terrified Isletans sent messenger after messenger to Otermín to beg protection, but they saw no sign of response. Many Isletans renounced their recent absolution and fled to the apostates. Only 385 remained by the time the Spaniards decided to take them to El Paso to save their lives and preserve them from apostasy.

Otermín persuaded the Isletans to join his force with whatever they could carry for the journey, then burned their pueblo to keep it from the hands of the rebels. More than 2,500 bushels of corn and countless beans went up in smoke as the people started toward El Paso and safety on January 2, 1682.

The triumphant Pueblos remained in undisputed possession of their snow-covered world. Eight pueblos lay in charred ruins and three more had been stripped of foodstuffs, but the people still had their liberty. They had now to establish enough order and security to make life good again. Questions of relations among pueblos remained unresolved. *Bárbaros* loomed on all their frontiers. No one knew whether or when Spaniards would come again. But the combined Pueblo forces had won some time in which to work out their own destinies.

The population at El Paso also confronted new realities. Otermín had shown how fatuous was the dream of immediate reconquest by a few ill-equipped men. Still, no one in power, either in Church or State, thought of writing off New Mexico as a permanent loss, though the plethora of demands upon the Crown's resources would long delay the necessary support. Those who had not escaped the dreary refugee camps had to be settled into villages and organized into some semblance of economic sufficiency. Otermín doubted that it could be done. The Spanish New Mexicans had long been nearly ungovernable, and they preferred to live on scattered homesteads, the better to pasture their animals and avoid the constraints of town life. Unfortunately for those thorny individualists, their El Paso refuge quickly became a major focus of Apache raiders.

Horses had become the prime desiderata of Apache life, and their prime source was the Spanish frontier. When the Spanish frontier fell back three hundred miles in New Mexico, Apaches readily adapted. As usual, raids escalated into war. Governor Jirónza Petriz de Cruzate, who succeeded Otermín in 1683, found it necessary to campaign against Apaches. He killed many, captured twenty-two, and congratulated himself that he had terrified the rest. He had in fact laid the foundation for war, because all those Apache losses had to be avenged.

The southward sweep of Apache raiders bore heavily upon both

Indian and Spanish populations of the region, none of which were in any condition to withstand continual harassment. The Spanish refugees had fled southward in a state of shock bordering upon hysteria. Even before they reached El Paso they heard rumors of Mansos plotting with Pueblos to finish the colony's destruction. The Mansos had revolted before, and some Spaniards descried danger in the friendly visiting between Christian Mansos and those still pagan.

Pueblos at El Paso were another source of anxiety. Many pueblos were represented in the established population at Mission Guadalupe; now hundreds of Piros and Tiwas had joined the Spanish population in the retreats of 1680 and 1682. How loyal were they? Some visited the rebel area to see about their compatriots, and they reported that the Indians who had won their freedom now lived much better lives than before. Otermín's failure to punish the rebels in 1681 made a great impression. Some of El Paso's Indian population muttered of imitating the insurgents. Some cooperated with Apache raiders and plotted with them for a total sweep of Spanish lives and property.

As usual, the issue of rebellion against the Spaniards divided the Indians. The principal conspirators were Mansos, who gave the intruding Piros and Tiwas two choices: to join the revolt and then have the privilege of returning to their original homes upstream or to hold aloof from the conspiracy and die with the Spaniards. The plot came to a head in the spring of 1684 and, like the Pueblo conspiracy of 1680, was betrayed by Indians. Tiwa and Piro leaders whom the Manso conspirators had approached, as well as some Manso converts, informed Governor Cruzate that the Manso leaders planned to revolt with the help of Apaches, Tiwas, Piros, Janos, and Sumas.

Speedy arrests and death sentences for eight principal conspirators momentarily checked the plot at El Paso, but the Sumas and Janos nearby revolted, and turbulence soon flared from Casas Grandes on the west to La Junta on the east. Many Christian Mansos fled from their El Paso settlement to join their heathen compatriots. A confused state of war prevailed through 1684, though few actual encounters occurred. Apaches with old scores to settle against Governor Cruzate joined enthusiastically. Several times hostile groups from as many as ten tribes were reported ready to sweep down upon El Paso and destroy it, possibly with help from the Pueblo rebels of New Mexico. Violence never materialized on any significant scale, but the very idea panicked many survivors of the bloody catastrophe upstream.

Actually, friction plagued the rebels. The Christian Mansos had trouble with their pagan compatriots, and their women especially wanted to return to the settled life they had enjoyed at El Paso. Mansos and Sumas quarreled, blaming each other for their difficulties.

Cruzate and his officers campaigned several times with Indian allies, principally Tiwas and Piros of El Paso, seizing every chance to send single captives back to their people with invitations to peace and alliance with the Spaniards. Gradually those efforts bore fruit. By the spring of 1685, most Sumas and Conchos made peace because they were hungry and tired of hiding. Peace with the Mansos was on-again-off-again through 1686.

The two years of war levied devastating penalties upon the Spanish community at El Paso. The hostilities of 1684 sharply curtailed the harvest; food stores ran out within six months. The next year drought made the harvest even slimmer. By April, 1685, they had no breeding stock left: rebel Indians had grabbed more than 2,000 horses and mules and another 2,000 cattle and sheep. The Crown finally granted 2,500 pesos for the relief of El Paso's citizenry late in 1685, but those who could fled, defying official and priestly opposition. They found the richer areas farther south sustaining even larger losses: an estimated 6,000 horses were taken from Parral, and no mission or hacienda herd escaped the raiders. The result was a great increase in the number of horses in Indian hands, many of which were traded to far distant points, clear across to the Mississippi.

The costs of remaining on that hostile northern frontier far exceeded any expected return on the investment, but fear of French intrusion made its abandonment unthinkable for the Crown. Besides the new presidio at El Paso, five more marked the line across Sonora and Nueva Vizcaya where Spain relied upon force to control the indigenous population and to ward off the *bárbaros*.[8] Each had its horse herd, virtual lodestars for raiders.

Unseemly French interest in the northern frontier of New Spain also spurred the Spanish government to spend considerable sums trying to reconquer New Mexico after 1685. Former New Mexican governor Peñalosa, whom the Inquisition had exiled, penniless, from New Spain in 1668, was in France peddling schemes for invasion and conquest of the northern provinces of New Spain. The exact intentions of the French Crown were unknown, but somehow the schemes of Peñalosa seemed entangled with the colonizing ambitions of Robert Cavelier, Sieur de La Salle, discoverer of the mouth of the Mississippi River.

[8] Jack D. Forbes, *Apache, Navajo and Spaniard*, pp. 200–211.

Suddenly the vacuum in New Mexico looked intolerably dangerous to Spain's interests. Again Spanish forces probed the Pueblo world.

In 1688 and 1689 Governors Reneros de Posada and Jirónza de Cruzate led forces northward and laid waste the pueblos of Santa Ana and Zía. The fighting was bloody, particularly at Zía: hundreds of Indians died; four captured leaders were shot to death in the plaza; many Pueblos were carried off as captives. Thus encouraged, the Crown decided upon permanent reconquest. For that purpose, it entrusted the governorship of New Mexico in the fall of 1690 to Diego de Vargas, the ambitious scion of a distinguished Spanish family.

Vargas took charge at El Paso on February 22, 1691, pledged to reconquer the province immediately at his own expense, but he found his colony in no condition for his enterprise.[9] The poverty-stricken settlers, living on the edge of starvation and ever menaced by Indian raiders, were hardly up to grand adventure. Even the soldiers of the presidio had neither the arms nor the horses to do their jobs. Furthermore, Vargas soon had to assist in campaigns in Sonora and Sinaloa, where Indian uprisings persisted, and in his own district he had to sally forth against Apaches as well as suppress restive Mansos.

Nevertheless, Vargas persevered in his preparations for a venture ominously similar to that of Oñate a century before. Vargas too dreamed of carving in New Mexico a fief to enhance the wealth and fame of his family. He too would expend his very considerable ambition, ability, and money in that formidable land, only to find grief the principal prize. And, once again, the Pueblo world lay divided, ill-prepared to repel purposeful invasion.

After a decade of freedom, the pueblos downstream lay deserted, largely in ruins. Upstream, Santa Fe remained the rebels' stronghold, occupied principally by Tanos from Galisteo, but still a rallying point for the Tewas and Tanos who were at war with most other Pueblos. The Keres, who had borne at Santa Ana and Zía the brunt of Spanish incursions in 1688 and 1689, now feared the Tewas and Tanos at least as much as they feared the Spaniards. They had virtually abandoned their pueblos, taking refuge in heights nearby. The Keres had some support from the Jémez, who were also sorely dislocated, and from some old Navajo associates. Some Keres, with a mixture of other Pueblo fugitives, lived aloof on the formidable rock of Ácoma, counting as friends only some nearby Navajos. On the eastern rim of the Pueblo

[9] J. Manuel Espinosa, ed., *The First Expedition of Vargas into New Mexico, 1692.*

world, Pecos and Taos were also at war with the Tewas and Tanos. Pecos counted the Faraon Apaches as allies. Of the strong leaders who had engineered the triumphs of 1680 and 1681, only Don Luis Tupatú of Picurís still lived, and, although he could influence, he could not command.

The Pueblos' tragedy was that the trials of freedom had nearly outweighed the joys. Support for the revolt had never been unanimous. As troubles occurred, recriminations arose inexorably. Crops still failed, enemies still raided, and critics of the rebellion recalled that friars and soldiers had been useful in such crises. Since Pueblo society had never developed any practicable way of handling dissent within a village, major issues inevitably spawned bitter factions. The quarrels within and among pueblos, the stresses of enemy raids and warfare, the realities of hunger, and the shadowy apprehensions of Spanish vengeance led many to flee, either to the remote Hopi territory or to the Navajos.

Ironically, the principal beneficiaries of the revolt were the Apaches and Navajos who had not rallied to support it. For the far-riding Apaches, it was a time to claim vast new hunting grounds, scouring away weaker peoples, driving them to seek nearly any refuge from oblivion. Some of their victims sought alliance with other Indians; some looked southward to the Spanish frontier for protection. There the livestock herds of missions and presidios beckoned to Apache raiders, who exploited the opportunity to the hilt. Some retaliatory campaigns from Sonora and El Paso struck *rancherías* of the Gila and Siete Ríos Apaches, but, for the most part, Apache raiders enjoyed in the late seventeenth century a wide choice of targets and relative safety from retaliation.

Far to the north, safely remote from Spanish forces for two valuable decades, Navajos shrewdly assimilated people and goods, ideas and skills, with which they evolved their own unique, enduring way of life.[10] The most recent Athapaskan migrants to the region, not many centuries earlier than the Spaniards, Navajos had found the Pueblo example powerful. Their folk memory has it that they acquired corn from the Pueblos; many of the myths and rituals by which Navajos live reflect Pueblo influence. However, Navajos never wavered from their

[10] The discussion of Navajo culture and geography relies principally on the following sources: Evon Z. Vogt, "Navajo" in *Perspectives in American Indian Culture Change*, ed. Edward H. Spicer; Laura Gilpin, *The Enduring Navaho*; Frank D. Reeve, "Early Navaho Geography," *New Mexico Historical Review* 31 (1956): 290–310.

strong sense of identity as a people. Always they were selective adapters, not slavish imitators of the more advanced culture. Their work of selective adaptation continued when Spaniards intruded so many novelties upon the Pueblo world. While Pueblos suffered the traumas of imposed change, Navajos freely made important choices that transformed their own lives.

The Navajo homeland lay just northwest of the Pueblo heartland. Its well-guarded mesatop dwellings and canyon farms offered a natural refuge to Pueblos fleeing the periodic turmoils after the Spanish occupation. The flow of Pueblo refugees climaxed with the many who abandoned their homes forever during the final agonizing sequence of revolt, chaotic independence, and eventual reconquest. By virtue of their numbers, the refugees partly compensated for Navajos lost over the years to Spanish raiders. Even more significant, however, were the skills the Pueblos brought to Navajos when the Navajos were reorienting their lives around the livestock introduced by Spaniards in New Mexico.

Pueblos had learned from Spaniards how to use the fleece of the tough, wiry little sheep, and they brought that complex of skills to the Navajos: the shearing, the washing with yucca root, and the carding and spinning, which precede the weaving or knitting of finished textiles. Weaving was an old skill among Pueblo men, who had readily adapted to use of woolen yarns on the stationary looms with which they had long made cotton textiles. Woolen textile weaving rapidly became important among Navajos, too, but in their world the weavers were women, and they did not adopt either the stationary loom of the Pueblos or the treadle loom of the Spaniards. They preferred the distinctive portable loom, which they perhaps knew when they came to the Southwest. With that loom and the wool of their ever-increasing flocks, Navajo women became peerless weavers. The women owned the sheep and, with their children's help, herded, sheared, and butchered.

While ownership and management of sheep brought new focus to the lives of Navajo women, horses transformed the men's lives. They owned and herded the horses, and they used them for the hunting, raiding, and warfare that remained prime duties of men. Men also had primary responsibility for farming, although women and children helped to tend crops when their shepherd duties permitted.

Navajos proved good husbandmen: their herds grew with natural increase as well as raiding. The need for pasture, especially for the voracious sheep, dictated new patterns of Navajo life, ranging over wider expanses of grassland, yet revolving about the little farms and orchards that grew ever more important to Navajo life. New crops introduced by Spaniards and adopted by Pueblos had come also to Navajos. Some innovations, especially peach orchards, grew nearly as vital as the sacred crops of corn, beans, squash, and tobacco.

The Navajos' new riches required their geographic expansion just when the horse widened their practicable range of operations. Thus, Navajos expanded westward, establishing farmsteads in sheltered, watered canyons, settling their matrilocal extended families in little clusters of hogans from which family members ranged in accord with seasonal requirements of their livestock. The lands into which they moved had been home centuries earlier to Pueblo forebears. Navajos lived in respectful proximity to the ruined homes of the Ancient Ones, reverently grinding ancient potsherds to temper new Navajo pots made with techniques learned from contemporary Pueblo guests.

New Navajo clans descended from Pueblos who came to stay and married with Navajos.[11] Perhaps some aspects of the matrilineal clan system developed then among Navajos influenced by the Pueblo increment. Certainly the newcomers shared more than techniques of farming, animal husbandry, and pottery and textile production, for Pueblos were rich in ceremonial concepts and practices. Many Pueblo ideas permanently fused into Navajo understanding of the origins of life and of the proper ways of doing things.

Thus, it was a richer Navajo people who expanded over the vast, varied lands bounded by four sacred mountains: Sisnaajiní (Mount Blanca) on the east; Tzoodzil (Mount Taylor) on the south; Doko'-ooslíid (San Francisco Peaks) on the west; Dibéntsaa (Mount Hesperus) on the north. In its vastness they sought security for their families and for the farms and flocks that rendered them fearfully vulnerable to enemy depredations.

From that base they sallied forth to raid and to fight. Honor and necessity would always require men to go forth for horses and sometimes for women. Strict rules of clan exogamy so limited a young man's choice of mates in his own locality that it was sometimes necessary to steal a wife from another people. Utes, Hopis, indeed most Pueblo groups, would occasionally lose women to the Navajos; no horse or sheep in the herds of any neighboring people would ever be quite safe from the exigencies of Navajo life.

---

[11] E.g., the Jémez clan, the Zía clan, and the Black Sheep People who traced their ancestry to San Felipe pueblo.

For the land, too, a new era began. Navajos lived in careful harmony with nature as they understood it, but they could not foresee the destructive impact of their expanding flocks upon the land they claimed. The shattering accidents of change attacked another fragile balance, this time with thousands of sharp hoofs and voracious mouths.

Beyond the Navajos, just across the San Juan River, Southern Utes also caught the tide of change that surged from Spain's intrusion. The catalyst of change in Ute life was the horse. Neither the agricultural example of Pueblos and Navajos nor the pastoral life style the Spaniards introduced with cattle and sheep ever prompted the Utes to imitate. The horse transformed the scale of their economy, their social organization, and their relations with peoples on every side of their homeland.[12]

Southern Utes lived thinly scattered in little family camps in sheltered mountain valleys, dispersed so that each family could gather enough food to survive in that sparse environment. Massive mountain barriers separated Southern Utes from Northern Utes, and it was largely geography that delimited their three bands. West of the Continental Divide, below the Gunnison River and down toward Navajo country, lived the Wemintucs, isolated by the formidable Divide. They camped mainly in the San Miguel and La Plata ranges or on the western slope of the San Juans. East of the Divide lived the Kapotas, around the San Juans and the Sangre de Cristos. Farther east lived the Mowatsis, who occupied the territory between the Sangre de Cristo and Culebra ranges and ranged as far west as a line that now would stretch from Denver south to Raton. Mowatsi and Kapota warriors sometimes cooperated to defend their territories against enemy Indians from the plains, and occasional intermarriages helped to perpetuate among the three Southern Ute bands some sense of oneness as a people. Even a single band convened only once a year, for the bear dance in spring; meetings had to be brief, so quickly did a band gathering deplete food in an area. Since it was impracticable to camp or move as a band, responsibility for defense was a local matter.

Though a Ute's highest allegiance was to his band, he recognized that other Utes spoke the same language and shared his fundamental views of life. No common authority linked the bands, but they respected each other's bounds. Friendships and marriages across band lines kept open cordial lines of communication.

The real roots of Ute life lay in the camp of the extended family,

[12] The principal source on Ute culture change is Morris Opler, "Southern Ute," in *Acculturation in Seven American Indian Tribes*, ed. Ralph Linton.

where the elders were the leaders. No higher authority existed. Directed by its elders, the family moved as the seasons required, camping within the territory recognized as its own for hunting and gathering. Life revolved around three paramount concerns: food, health, and rapport with the supernatural forces of their universe. So few were the Utes, so difficult their environment, and so dangerous their enemies that each year's survival was a fresh triumph.

In spring, families moved to the mountain ranges, camping beside the springs and rivers of sheltered valleys. Through summer those well-hidden camps were the safest retreat from Indian invaders from the plains. When snows began, the Utes moved southward to the level plateaus, following the antelope herds that were their winter meat. All winter Ute families roved, foraging for food. Sometimes they ventured south to trade for corn and beans at northern pueblos, particularly Taos, Picurís, and San Juan. Their trade with Pueblos tended to lag because Utes lacked a dependable surplus; often their hunters could not procure enough meat and hides for their families' own use. Yet, despite their very real needs, Utes rarely raided pueblos in the old days. Nor did they depend very much on buffalo meat from the nearby plains. A hunting trip to the plains on foot was unduly hazardous and strenuous for the men of the small family group, and the difficulties of making the kill and transporting the meat and hides back home dwarfed possible gains from the venture.

Horses changed all that. Introduction began peacefully, for early Spanish colonization did not intrude upon the southernmost limits of the Utes' winter range and thus spared the Utes any territorial affront. Spanish enterprise in the Pueblo world gave the Utes new opportunities for trade. By the 1630's both Spanish and Pueblo traders were leading pack trains north to Ute camps, purchasing as many pelts as Ute hunters could glean in their home territory. Utes began to learn the valuable uses of the horse.

Initially desirable as a key to improved subsistence for the Utes, the horse became necessary for survival as soon as Apache and Navajo warriors adopted its use. The insatiable market for captives at Santa Fe portended extinction of any Indian group that could not hold its own against Athapaskan warriors or against Spanish and Pueblo slaving parties.

Governor Rosas broke the even tenor of Ute relations with New Mexico with his gratuitous attack in 1639. The Utes sought appropriate vengeance, but Ute hostilities never reached the sustained pitch of the

Apache wars. During the mid-century Utes played the prevailing game of raiding–trading–war in New Mexico and thus acquired enough horses to survive and even to flourish.

Once the Utes had horses, they could go to the plains for buffalo. They could also escape when enemy Indians from the plains invaded Ute territory. Suddenly it became possible, and even necessary, for bands to live together in the large camps not previously feasible. Men formed large hunting parties to bring meat and hides from the plains for the whole band. The greatest war leaders headed the band camps, exercising authority hitherto nonexistent among Utes. Suddenly the scale of Ute life had exploded: their subsistence, warfare, and social organization. But everything hinged upon plenty of horses.

The beginning was very hard. The price in meat and hides that Spaniards charged for horses was nearly prohibitive to Utes still hunting on foot in the mountains. Short of meat and hides to trade, some Utes bartered their children for horses. Spaniards wanted Ute youngsters to herd their livestock, and two factors disposed some Ute parents to sell: Ute society had precedents for giving away children; in the changing circumstances parents could not protect their children without horses on which to escape with the band when invaders struck their camp. Thus, young Ute herdsmen shared the rough lives of Spanish frontier settlers, and by the standards of that frontier, or indeed of Ute camps, they did not fare badly. The willing presence of Utes in Spanish households perhaps furthered the communication and understanding that grew between those two very unlike peoples.

The pace and scale of Ute life changed remarkably. The band's social life, once a fleeting excitement at the spring bear dance, became a year-round condition. Formerly isolated family camps now sprawled together for as much as half a mile along a stream. From that base, groups of women scoured the countryside for plant foods while large parties of men frequently went out to hunt buffalo or to raid. The concentrated population consumed much meat, and horses had to be obtained to facilitate the hunting, raiding, and war on which their lives turned. War focused more on loot than prestige, but leaders won their reputations by outstanding service in war and by generosity in distributing their loot at camp. A leader's authority lasted only so long as his camp believed he served wisely and well, so that political pressures demanded a high level of activity in band camps. To maintain his popularity, a leader needed to initiate many hunts and war parties. Circumstances easily turned many hunting parties on the plains into raiding or war parties, so that the men sometimes brought back horses and other loot as well as meat and hides. Scouts rode ahead to notify the camp of a successful party's return, and the people turned out to praise the warriors and claim a share of the loot. As long as anyone in camp was in need, a prosperous man could honorably keep only the scalps he had taken. The more horses he gave away, the better the chance that someday his band would call him chief.

The Utes did not actually expand their ranges much with their new mobility, but they made much better use of plains resources. Their seasonal cycle changed accordingly. In fall the band hastened to complete its antelope drives in the foothills, cached as much meat as possible, then forged on to the plains to hunt buffalo. While the men were gone, scouts guarded the band camp, where women, children, and old people were much safer than they had ever been in the small family camps with warriors away. When their men were off to raid in enemy country, women packed up camp and stood poised to flee in case of a retaliatory raid. Whenever possible, Utes avoided a standing fight in their own territory, but, when one occurred, the older women donned headdresses, picked up weapons to join the fray, and afterward scalped and stripped fallen enemies. Loot was distributed throughout the camp; a scalp was sewn upon the shirt of the man credited with the kill.

Some Southern Utes concluded that a peaceful trading relationship with the Spaniards, even if erratic, was preferable to war. Perhaps they were helped to that decision by their stringent contest with Navajo and Apache raiders for horses and captives. In 1678 Utes rode to Taos to negotiate a peace with Governor Otermín; at the time of the revolt in 1680 they were deemed to have kept their agreement faithfully. Rumors that they were involved in Popé's conspiracy were never substantiated. On the contrary, the record suggests that the Utes, unlike other *bárbaros*, were sorely inconvenienced by the Spaniards' expulsion. The chaotic years of the rebellion found the Utes at war with Pueblos as well as with Navajos and Jicarilla Apaches.

During their brief independence, some Pueblos hunted buffalo in territory claimed by Utes. Mounted Pueblos posed as Spaniards, wearing the leather jackets and hats, carrying the firearms, and even blowing the bugles that were their booty from the 1680 rebellion. Utes always attacked the intruders; the transparent ruse of the Spanish garb only intensified their annoyance with the Pueblos. Utes raided pueblos freely in those years. By the 1690's they regarded the Tewas, Tanos, Picurís, Jémez, and Keres as their enemies from time immemorial.[13]

By the turn of the century, the once poor Utes had plenty of hides and meat to market. They even had enough horses to trade the animals to their distant Comanche kinsmen in more northerly ranges of the Rocky Mountains. Thus, the forces of change surged farther northward, fomenting yet another revolution by accident. The yeasty ferment of new possessions, new values, new relationships among compatriots, and new tensions among enemies, all derived from the Spanish intrusion a century before, lay quite beyond the ken of the Spaniards who now reasserted dominion in New Mexico. Vargas marched northward in autumn 1692, pledged to impose upon the Pueblo world forever the changes that a dozen years ago had somehow gone awry.

Vargas prudently broke his project into two parts, beginning with a military expedition to reconnoiter, to pacify where possible, and to conquer where necessary. Afterward would come the colonizers: settlers with their families and possessions, missionaries, and soldiers to safeguard the province.[14]

Vargas could recruit few Spaniards on that turbulent, poverty-ridden frontier, but he found at El Paso a hundred Pueblo warriors glad to march north with him.[15] Most were Tiwas and Piros, refugees from Isleta, Senecú, and Socorro, who would trek with him through their abandoned, desolated homeland into the territory of Keres and Tewas, ancient enemies whose leadership they had spurned in the rebellion a dozen years before. A few were Keres, whose reports of Pueblo strife and Apache depredations spurred Vargas to forge ahead with his fraction of an army, gambling that the Pueblos would either welcome peace or be too divided to offer effective resistance.

Eerie emptiness awaited them in the Pueblo world. Smokes rose from the heights to remind them that Apaches watched, but no attack came. Vargas could only glimpse fleeing Pueblos. A hasty chat with a San Felipe fugitive revealed that the Keres would welcome the Spaniards' peaceful return, in the hope that Spaniards would help the Keres to kill the Tewas and Tanos. Vargas assured him of his peaceful intent

[13] J. Manuel Espinosa, "Journal of the Vargas Expedition into Colorado, 1694," *The Colorado Magazine* 16 (1939): 81–90.

[14] Principal sources on the reconquest are Espinosa, *The First Expedition of Vargas*, and idem, *Crusaders of the Rio Grande*.

[15] Oakah L. Jones, Jr., *Pueblo Warriors and Spanish Conquest*, pp. 38–40.

and rode on to Santa Fe, where he sang out praise for the Blessed Sacrament and called upon the rebels to surrender to both Majesties.

Tanos swarmed to Santa Fe's walls and rooftops to shout their scorn of Vargas' promises of pardon. They remembered too much of Spanish rule: Apaches hunted down and killed after Spaniards promised them peace; the work of building houses and churches for the Spaniards, all of which they would have to do again if the Spaniards should return; the floggings when they did not obey the Spaniards; the injustices of certain officials. Vargas answered patiently, but the long dialogue appeared only to gain time for the rebels. More Indians appeared from the north, bearing long metal-tipped lances. Vargas issued an ultimatum for surrender of the villa within two hours, then parleyed with the new arrivals.

Governor Domingo of Tesuque led the delegates from his own pueblo, Santa Clara, and San Lázaro. Vargas assured them that he had come to pardon, not to punish, and would not remove present officials of the pueblos. They were glad to make peace on those terms. Domingo carried the message into Santa Fe, but he returned to say that the occupants of the villa would not make peace, despite his warning that their stubbornness might cost them their lives. More Indians arrived to make peace. One last exhortation from Vargas brought some people out of Santa Fe to join in the embraces and handshakes that marked the beginning of reconciliation between Spaniards and rebels. The next day Vargas entered Santa Fe to pardon the Indians, to receive their new pledge of vassalage to the king, and to possess the villa again in the name of Carlos II. Fray Francisco Corvera led the Spaniards and Indians in devotions, blessed the Indians, and absolved them of apostasy.

The bloodless reconquest gained momentum. By noon that day, Domingo informed Vargas that all the Tewa and Tano pueblos pledged their loyalty to Spain. Their acknowledged leader, Don Luis Tupatú, was on his way to meet the governor. That most powerful Pueblo had reason to fear punishment for his outstanding role in the rebellion, but Vargas promised to receive him as an honored guest.

Don Luis arrived the next day with three hundred Pueblo warriors. Ceremoniously and cordially, the two leaders conferred, drinking chocolate together and exchanging valuable gifts. Vargas promised Don Luis that he would not interfere with his leadership of the Indians so long as he tried to bring the people back into true allegiance to both Majesties. Don Luis accepted those terms and returned the next day with the leaders of all pueblos that recognized his authority. All knelt to receive absolution. Then the Spanish and Indian leaders planned together for the future.

Pueblo factions were indeed at war in the upper Rio Grande region. Don Luis had moved from his native Picurís to San Juan, the better to direct his alliance of Tewas, Tanos, and Picurís. Among his enemies to the east he counted Taos, Pecos, and their Faraon Apache allies; to the west, the Jémez and the Keres of San Felipe, Santo Domingo, and Cochití. He would have liked a simple alliance to conquer his foes, but Vargas meant to make peace with and among all Pueblos.

Vargas proposed to visit all the pueblos to give the king's pardon and reaffirm Spanish possession, taking priests along to absolve apostates and baptize children born since the revolt. Don Luis therefore asked him to enjoin the Pecos and Taos people to be the friends of his people. If they should refuse, he would send warriors to help the Spaniards reconquer them. Vargas agreed to intercede with Pecos and Taos on behalf of Don Luis' people and also offered to mediate for them with the Jémez and Keres. Apparently satisfied, Don Luis and the other leaders set off for their respective homes.

At every pueblo northward from Santa Fe to San Juan, the people quickly responded to Don Luis' summons to come down from the mesas and reoccupy their homes. Vargas seemed well on the way to restoring "normality" in New Mexico by Spanish standards. Part of that process was religious. The many children born in the pueblos since 1680 needed to be baptized as soon as possible. On the morning of September 17, the priests baptized 122 souls at Santa Fe. Vargas himself stood godfather for the three daughters of Santa Fe's Governor José and for six other infants whose mothers thrust them into his arms. Soldiers served as godfathers for the rest, and a spirit of genuine harmony seemed to prevail.

Meanwhile, the young people fled from Pecos, rejecting their elders' arguments in favor of peace and threatening to kill any who should welcome the Spaniards. The elders stood their ground until they learned how many men marched with Vargas from Santa Fe: his original fifty Spanish soldiers and fifty Pueblo allies; three hundred armed warriors led by Don Luis and his brother, Don Lorenzo of Picurís; fifty fresh Spanish soldiers just arrived from Parral to reinforce Vargas' army. Panic-stricken, most of the remaining Pecoseños fled, leaving only a few too feeble to travel. Vargas tried for five days to coax the fugitives home, but the young Pecos majority held firm against peace.

Vargas then withdrew his forces, leaving in the pueblo all the Indians' property, scrupulously respected, a few residents who had been very kindly treated, and a standing offer to make peace whenever the Pecos people were ready, with assurances that the Tewas and Tanos wished peace, too.

A Keres messenger carried to the mountain hideout of the people of Santa Ana and Zía Vargas' proposal of peace and his invitation to an early peace meeting at Santo Domingo. Meanwhile, Vargas turned northward to affirm possession of the Tewa and Tano pueblos for Carlos II and to assist in the reclamation of souls. At each pueblo in turn, the friars absolved the apostates, and then Vargas stood godfather for the leaders' children while other Spaniards sponsored the rest, until 728 were baptized. When the governor admonished the people to say the four prayers morning and evening, to wear crosses, and to honor their Christian marriage vows, they seemed to concur solemnly. The faith appeared restored on the upper Rio Grande.

At San Juan delegates from all the Tewas, Tanos, and Picurís begged Vargas to conquer and burn Taos. They had suffered much robbery and murder at the hands of the Taoseños and feared to leave their homes lest their wives and children be clubbed to death in their absence. Vargas promised either to win the friendship of the Taos or to vanquish them, but he devoutly preferred the former.

The Taoseños fled to their mountain hideout east of the pueblo as the Spaniards approached with their Pueblo enemies. Vargas rode to the mouth of the canyon, laid his arms on the ground, and parleyed with Josephillo, a Spanish-speaking Taoseño who carried the governor's rosary and his promises of pardon back to the people several times. Gradually they responded and came back to the pueblo with their governor, Don Francisco Pacheco. Vargas presided over a ceremony of reconciliation in the plaza, where the Taos leaders and Don Luis, Don Lorenzo, and other Tewa and Tano leaders all embraced and shook hands.

Since Taos and Pecos were friends, Vargas arranged for two Taos messengers to convey his peaceful intentions to Pecos. Taos warriors promised to accompany his forces the next week to Pecos for another effort at pacification.

Vargas rode back to Santa Fe, whence he dispatched to Mexico news of his successes thus far and his recommendations for recruitment of colonists to hold the region. He designated Don Luis governor of the thirteen pueblos already conquered, ceremoniously presenting the staff of office to him in the presence of leaders from all those pueblos. Don Luis vowed to uphold both Majesties.

Miserable weather conditions forced Vargas to modify his plans. Snows had begun in the first week of October, and men and horses felt the strain of traveling over slippery terrain in piercing cold. Vargas sent most of his men and equipment to a new base camp at Santo Domingo before he learned that the promised Taos, Tewa, and Tano warriors would not accompany him to Pecos after all. He rode on to Pecos with very few men, and his risk paid off in a heartwarming reception.

The whole populace turned out to greet him and asked him to install officers for the pueblo as in earlier Spanish practice. He asked them to elect officers, then installed the governor and seven other functionaries whom they chose. The restoration of order, on terms respecting their right to choose their own leaders, seemed to please the people of Pecos very much. If the pueblo still harbored young dissidents, Vargas did not see them.

When the snowfall slackened, Vargas hurried on to Santo Domingo to deal with the Keres. Some Keres leaders visited him there; others invited him to their camps in the mountains, where he was cordially welcomed. All gladly agreed to reoccupy their proper pueblos if the Spaniards would guarantee them protection from the Tewas, Tanos, and Picurís whose raids had driven them from their homes. The priests' ceremonies of absolution and baptism were readily accepted. Some of the refugees danced to celebrate the restoration of order that Vargas seemed to promise.

The Jémez people, ensconced atop a mesa in a new pueblo, greeted Vargas' troop in a rowdy, truculent fashion, with warriors painted and armed, women and children hidden. Vargas doggedly delivered, through interpreters, his usual harangue about peace and pardon. To his great relief, the Jémez responded favorably. At their leaders' signal, the men put down their weapons and the women and children came to the plazas. None held aloof from absolution or baptism of the children. A large number of "Apaches"[16] discovered hiding in the pueblo also tendered their obedience. Vargas promised them he would be back in a year and warned that he would not want their friendship if they would not become Christians.

Relieved to have escaped hostilities at Jémez, Vargas rejoined his

[16] Probably these were Navajos, the Athapaskans nearest Jémez and frequently associated with them.

main force on the Rio Grande. He had yet to account for the remote western pueblos, but most of his forces were in no condition to journey so far. Vargas sent most of them back to El Paso with seventy-four persons, mostly Spaniards taken in the revolt, whom he had rescued from captivity. Retaining only eighty-nine Spaniards and thirty Indians, he headed for the Zuñi and Hopi pueblos.

Bárbaros shadowed his fortunes as he struck westward from Isleta. Apache and Manso messengers warned the Ácomas that Vargas would feign peace only to hang or behead them. Only with great difficulty could the governor finally persuade them to let him ascend their rock with a few friars and officers for the ceremonies of repossession, absolution, and baptism. They proved cordial, generous hosts and bade the Spaniards friendly goodbyes, warning them to beware of Apaches who were waiting to destroy Vargas' force. The Ácomas themselves now counted some nearby Navajos their only real friends.

Faraon Apaches did filch a few cows from Vargas' herd as he continued to Zuñi, where he enjoyed an exuberant welcome. Apache raids had lately been so severe that the Zuñis had abandoned five pueblos to consolidate in one, and the Apaches continued to take a heavy toll of Zuñi food and horses. The Zuñis rejoiced in the prospect of Spanish protection against the *bárbaros*.

Meanwhile, Navajos warned the Hopis not to make peace, charging that the Spaniards would only feign friendship in order to kill all the men and capture the women and children. The Hopis drove their livestock to the mountains for safety and decided to resist the Spaniards. Vargas heard that news at Zuñi and sent messages assuring the Hopis of peace and pardon, then headed northward with only the sixty-three soldiers now fit to travel.

Rowdy throngs of armed warriors awaited him at each Hopi pueblo; at Walpi the crowd included Utes and Havasupais. Vargas managed to enact the forms of repossession and the friars performed absolutions and baptisms at each, but the Hopis' reduction was obviously precarious. Governor Miguel of Aguatovi, who welcomed Vargas courteously and did his best to protect him, predicted privately that his people would kill him as soon as Vargas left for having been friendly to the Spaniards. He warned of a plot to kill the entire force, but Vargas insisted nevertheless on visiting the rest of the pueblos, stopping short of Oraibi only when his horses were exhausted by severe weather and rough terrain. Discretion forbade Vargas to press his luck among the

Hopis much farther, so he rode back to Zuñi for the soldiers and horses whom he had left to recuperate.

Apaches had constantly watched the Spaniards' camp at Zuñi, and they had driven off horses the force could ill afford to lose. Zuñis warned that a great Apache war council had met to plot destruction of the Spaniards. It had broken up in dissension, but a Salinero Apache chief who had visited Vargas to talk of peace was fomenting trouble. Vargas decided to return to El Paso at once. He had achieved at least the semblance of reduction of all pueblos. Nothing could be gained by exposing his men to a winter of attrition by Apaches and storms.

Vargas hired a Zuñi guide to take him southeast to old Senecú on the Rio Grande, where he could pick up the familiar trail to El Paso. Apaches harried them all the way; one snowy night they stole fourteen horses. The Zuñi guide and his three companions decided to go back to Zuñi via Ácoma rather than cross that Apache territory again. Vargas' party clashed with Apaches before they reached El Paso on December 20. There two Apache raids had cost the community twenty horses during the governor's four-month absence.

Still, Apache harassment amounted to little more than inconvenience by comparison with Vargas' triumph among the Pueblos. He had reclaimed twenty-three pueblos for both Majesties, had rescued seventy-four captives, and had overseen baptism of 2,214 Indians, mostly children. Eager now to affirm the reconquest by permanent occupation, Vargas lost no time in laying the foundation for his new colony. He had no idea that upstream his splendid achievements crumbled.

Pueblos gathered at San Juan that winter to listen to the mestizo Tapia, who had accompanied Vargas as an interpreter. Tapia convinced them that upon the Spaniards' return they would slaughter all Pueblo leaders to avenge the deaths of 1680. The story was as tragically plausible as it was false, consistent with Spanish actions Pueblos had seen before and with their own ideas of vengeance. The rumor spread swiftly, and most Pueblos spent the next summer making arrows and darts for a massive resistance. The Tewas, Tanos, Picurís, Taos, and Jémez prepared for war; the Ácomas and Hopis were hostile, too. Santa Ana, San Felipe, and Zía decided to honor their peace commitment to Vargas, but the issue rent the other Keres pueblos. Governor Juan de Ye of Pecos prevailed over a substantial anti-Spanish faction to keep his pueblo loyal to the Spaniards. Some Apaches and Navajos plotted with the hostile Pueblos against the Spaniards. Others hastened to prey on Pueblos pathetically vulnerable in their dissension and dislocation.

Though ignorant of the turmoils upstream, Vargas had now seen enough of New Mexico to realize that he could not finance the colonization in the style of Oñate. A small-scale occupation could only invite repetition of the disaster of 1680. He would require enough settlers and settlements to make the Pueblos feel both secure against the Apaches and afraid to revolt again: at least five hundred families and a hundred presidials. Vargas proposed substantial buffer settlements at key points of Apache and Navajo ingress: one hundred families at Taos, fifty at Pecos, fifty in the vicinity of Santa Ana, one hundred at Jémez, and one hundred more on the river road near deserted Sandía and Puaray. He hoped to anchor the southern frontier by restoring El Paso's refugee Tiwas and Piros to their old pueblos of Isleta and Socorro. He would write off as lost old Senecú, so exposed to Apache attack, and thought distant Zuñi and Ácoma best left alone. Unless quicksilver mines should be discovered in the Hopi district to warrant settlement, those Indians could be brought back into the fold only if moved to abandoned pueblos on the Rio Grande. Missionaries could expect tolerable safety only in districts that could be well populated and were within reasonable range of the presidial force.

Both the viceroy and the Crown readily endorsed Vargas' recommendations, not only because they were logical and well presented, but also because his widely publicized triumphs in New Mexico had made him a considerable hero, both in New Spain and in the homeland. The viceroy authorized him to recruit in the northern provinces both his presidial garrison and the necessary colonists, and he promised all financial support required to consolidate the reconquest.

Vargas hoped to recruit his colonists from those who had fled in 1680, in order to avoid dredging the jails. By January 1, 1693, he had visited every household at El Paso and revised his cost estimates upward. Pitifully destitute, most were willing to settle in New Mexico if definitely assured government assistance. The government would have to supply every necessity: transportation, provisions, seeds and breeding stock, allowances for clothing and other basic equipment. Again, the viceroy promised full support.

Through the spring and summer of 1693 Vargas scoured the northern provinces, seeking out former New Mexican residents, enlisting soldiers, and inviting settlers. Public proclamations promised royal aid and favors to those who joined the colony: those formerly of New Mexico who would return were guaranteed restoration of their lands and the distinction of conquerors for their families forevermore. Buying up livestock and other supplies, paying soldiers' salaries and settlers' subsidies, Vargas spent 40,000 pesos by mid-summer and was dismayed to find that the treasuries would honor no more drafts for want of sufficient funds, viceroy's promise notwithstanding. He turned back to El Paso with his hundred soldiers and fifty settlers, many with families, and paused only three weeks before setting out for Santa Fe on October 4.

Even better than Oñate before him, Vargas realized that his colonists were too few and their provisions too scant for the task ahead, but hesitation could only compound his risks. The longer he delayed return, the less could he rely on last year's peace with the Pueblos. El Paso's marginal economy could not long support the would-be settlers; Apache raids there would only worsen if the livestock destined for Santa Fe were pastured at El Paso. Banking heavily upon the viceroy's promise to send more colonists from Mexico City, Vargas headed north.

Like the Oñate colony a century before, Vargas' seventy families were a microcosm of the complex society of New Spain. A few were former settlers of New Mexico: after years of near paupery in El Paso, and in some cases for generations before that in New Mexico, they could anticipate high status and relative wealth if the reconquest were successful. At the other end of the economic and social scale were twenty-seven families of Negroes and mestizos whom Vargas had signed on very cheaply. A fresh start on a new frontier offered their only hope of better lives for themselves and their children, and for that they would gamble their lives. Some Indian allies accompanied the group; most were Pueblos who wanted to return home. Eighteen friars came to rebuild the shattered mission program.

Vargas managed to raise only half the sum he deemed necessary for provisions. Most went for the herd: over two thousand horses, one thousand mules, nine hundred head of cattle, sheep, and goats, at once indispensable to the colony's success and a terrible danger to it. They were, in effect, four thousand invitations to raiders.

Like Oñate before him, Vargas had meant to carry provisions enough to support the colony until crops could be planted the next spring, but his food supplies were dangerously low by the time he reached the deserted southern pueblos. He sent a Zía messenger northward from Socorro to inform the Keres of the Spaniards' arrival and to ask them to sell food. Meanwhile, when Indians visited the caravan, the hungry settlers traded their arms, jewelry, horses, anything the Indians would accept for grain and vegetables. Vargas required payment of a just price for all goods purchased from the Indians. He would permit no forced sales or confiscations to mar his relations with the Pueblos.

Just below Isleta, on November 10, his Zía courier brought him news of the hostility upstream. Only Santa Ana, San Felipe, and Zía adhered to last year's peace; they lived under constant fear of attack by the Jémez, Tewas, and Tanos. Vargas dispatched his thanks to the loyal Keres and asked them to be ready to sell him corn and meal at a just price. Then he sent letters of greeting and rosaries to the Tano and Tewa leaders, to be answered in six days.

Governor Vargas rode on with fifty soldiers to San Felipe, where he was welcomed generously. Recognizing visiting Keres from Cochití, he dispatched them with invitations for their leaders to visit him. Meanwhile, Pecos Governor Juan de Ye brought a few delegates to greet Vargas, and he explained the cause and extent of the Pueblos' hostility.

Appalled by the mischief Tapia had wrought, Vargas decided to consolidate his people at Santo Domingo and from that base seek accommodation with the hostile groups. He was confident that he could convince the leaders that Tapia had lied if only he could talk with them. Juan de Ye volunteered to remain with Vargas to render any possible help; other Pecos warriors joined him at Santo Domingo.

Indian messengers reported a mounted, heavily armed force of Tewas, Tanos, Taos, Picurís, Navajos, and Río Colorado Apaches[17] in the area, trying to incite the still uncommitted Keres to join them in attacking the Spaniards. Some reported division among the Tewas who had taken refuge atop Black Mesa, a hopeful sign for the Spaniards. Vargas prepared to repel attack, but none came. Instead, a Tewa rider announced the approaching governors of San Juan, Picurís, San Lázaro, and Tesuque. Although they had been on cordial terms with Vargas a year before, they rode into his camp heavily armed, led by Don Luis Tupatú. It was a cautious, correct courtesy call, but no rapport developed. Vargas remained alert for attack and took comfort in the knowledge that Pueblos found effective, sustained cooperation very difficult.

Governor Vargas rode west to the mesatop camps of Keres and Jémez, all of whom received him cordially and let him purchase badly needed food to pack back to the colonists. Most would promise to re-

---

[17] Apparently a reference to the Apaches del Acho (Jicarilla forebears) from the small stream above Taos called Colorado.

occupy their old pueblos if Vargas could guarantee them protection against the raids of Tewas, Tanos, and all sorts of Apaches.

Many friendly Indians warned Vargas of a great convocation of Indians plotting to destroy the Spaniards en route to Santa Fe. Pecos, Jémez, and many Keres would not cooperate, so the militants formulated an alternative plan to dig in at Santa Fe and eventually destroy the Spaniards' military capacity by stampeding their horses away in the night.

A glum Luis Tupatú rode again to Santo Domingo to see Vargas, in his capacity as supreme governor of all Tewas and Tanos, and explained how angry all his people were about Tapia's tale. Vargas vehemently denied the story and boasted that the Virgin whose banner he carried would protect him against any number of angry Tanos and Tewas. More conferences with the troubled Pueblo leaders followed there in the forsaken pueblo of Santo Domingo, as Vargas tried desperately to scotch Tapia's lie. Meanwhile, he sent pack trains off to Pecos and Santa Fe to try to buy supplies and assess the people's attitudes.

The Indians at Santa Fe were divided toward the Spaniards: some wanted them back so they could hunt deer and plant crops without fear of the Navajos, who had murdered a boy and stolen some horses there only a week before. They sold the visitors twenty-three sacks of corn.

Vargas decided to take his entire colony on to Santa Fe to confront the Tano-Tewa problem, for he dared not divide his forces to protect the women and children in some valley camp. Supplies furnished by Jémez and Keres friends sustained them as they slogged through heavy snow to Santa Fe. There, at midday on December 16, 1693, they found a quiet, ceremonious welcome but no obvious enthusiasm. Rather than risk any friction between soldiers and Indians, Vargas refrained from occupying the villa at that time. Instead, he ordered his people to pitch camp a little way north at the foot of the mountains.

Morale sagged in the Spanish camp. Juan de Ye reported conspiracies of Tewas and Tanos with Apaches to destroy the Spanish camp and volunteered to bring reinforcements from Pecos; obvious sullenness in Santa Fe seemed to confirm his warning. Meanwhile, camping out in winter with inadequate food and shelter, the women and children suffered dreadfully. The *cabildo* demanded the right to reoccupy the government buildings in Santa Fe and house the families whom they had brought to repopulate the town. They found intolerable the governor's hesitation and his consideration of the Indians' feelings before the welfare of Spanish families. Still, Vargas played for time. Don Luis Tupatú and several other important northern Pueblo leaders came to render obedience. All the pueblos now sold meal and corn to the Spaniards, but all that they could spare was not enough to feed the Spanish camp.

Infants and children died; frantic parents knew they would lose the rest without swift remedy. With twenty-two buried under the snow, they made Vargas call a general council and forced the issue, demanding that the Tanos return to their old pueblo of Galisteo and vacate Santa Fe for Spanish occupants.

Tanos watched from the walls of the villa, well aware of the meeting's purpose, then posted sentinels and convened their own meeting in the kiva. Men of Taos and Picurís rode into Santa Fe, heard the leaders calling for destruction of the invaders, and boldly declared their own loyalty to the Spaniards, but to little effect. Some Tanos advocated retreat to the mountains instead of battle in the villa, lest their children be injured, but their leaders scorned that argument. They would destroy or be destroyed, but they would not suffer the Spaniards to take their homes and food. Suddenly the warriors rushed, howling, to the walls of Santa Fe, hurling missiles and insults toward any Spaniards who appeared.

Vargas rode to the wall with the *cabildo* and most of the soldiers, loudly singing praise to the Blessed Sacrament, only to provoke rude answers. He ordered the Tanos to quit the villa. They shouted their vow to fight, alongside all other Indians of New Mexico, until they killed or enslaved every Spaniard. Meanwhile, Juan de Ye arrived from Pecos with 140 warriors who proved invaluable that day. On the morning of December 29, 1693, the battle of Santa Fe began.

The defenders of Santa Fe were not as lucky with reinforcements. The Spaniards had won about half the villa by late afternoon, when a large Indian force arrived to help the Tanos. In two brief, fierce encounters, the Spaniards fought them back, killing four; the rest fled without further ado. After a tense night, with each force in control of one square, the Spaniards renewed the attack before dawn. By morning Santa Fe was theirs. Governor José hanged himself; Antonio Bolsas led most of the women and children out. A house-to-house search ferreted out the rest of the populace and revealed plenty of corn and beans in the storerooms. The colonists were assigned quarters in the villa, and the food was taken to a central warehouse in a big kiva, whence the *cabildo* distributed rations.

The Tanos paid dearly for their resistance. Vargas ordered seventy executions: Antonio Bolsas and the sixty-nine dragged out of hiding. The 400 who had surrendered voluntarily were distributed among the Spaniards for ten years of servitude, under terms protecting them from chattel slavery. Unfortunately, the executions seemed to many Pueblos to vindicate Tapia's story. Two Tanos escaped to spread the story that all Pueblos would be treated so. Vargas never ceased to defend his act as a necessity of war; eventually the highest authorities upheld him. But throughout New Mexico, Pueblos who earlier had become conciliatory and even helpful toward Vargas now retreated into sullen, uncompromising hostility. Only the Pecos and the Keres of Santa Ana, Zía, and San Felipe remained loyal to their commitment to Vargas, and even at Pecos the opposing faction waxed alarmingly strong.

Again people left their pueblos to fortify themselves atop the mesas. Most of the hostile Keres rallied to Captain Malacate on the mesa of Cochití, where they were reported plotting with the Jémez and Navajos to stampede the Spaniards' horses and then attack the colony.

Even more threatening was a large concentration of Tewas and Tanos on the Black Mesa of San Ildefonso. Vargas visited the site twice, trying to persuade them to return peacefully to their pueblos, but they were convinced they would be slaughtered like the seventy Tanos at Santa Fe. No words of Vargas could offset the enormity of his recent act.

Raiders crept down from the mesa to Santa Fe by night, taking food for their people and steadily eroding the horse herds upon which Spanish soldiers depended. One night they seized 70 horses and 144 mules. By late February the thefts were so intolerable that Vargas resolved to bring the rebels down by force. He tried to storm the mesa, failed, then besieged it till mid-March, and finally gave up.

Everyone suffered as the hostilities continued into spring planting time. Neither Indians nor colonists dared work in the fields. A long starving time loomed ahead. Vargas systematically searched abandoned pueblos for corn to pack back to Santa Fe. There soon remained little to be found by either Indian or Spaniard in pueblos north of Santa Fe.

Bárbaros made capital of the turmoil. Although the rebels always threatened the Spaniards with attack by Apaches, they had little reliable cooperation from their alleged allies. Apaches from the northeast pitched five tents on the Rio Chama, their base for raids on the Santa Fe herd. Neither they nor other raiders saw much reason to distinguish between Spanish and Pueblo property when they found opportunity to take a horse. Ute raiders also came south and drove some Tano fugitives from the Truchas River to join the rebel camp on Black Mesa.

Bárbaros also preyed on western Pueblos. The Zuñis fortified themselves upon the mesa of Kiakima and thus survived both war with the Apaches del Mechón and a concerted attack by Hopis, Utes, and Havasupais. In the spring, when they needed to come down from the mesa to plant and till their fields, they appealed to Vargas for protection from their enemies. Unable to spare forces for duty two hundred miles from Santa Fe, Vargas could only suggest that the Zuñis move to the vacant pueblos on the Rio Grande below Isleta, where he could more reasonably hope to protect them.

Plains Apaches welcomed the Spaniards' return as an economic boon. In March and in May, Apache parties waited at Pecos while Governor Juan de Ye escorted their chiefs to Santa Fe to call upon Governor Vargas. They presented him with handsomely dressed pelts and camp tents to celebrate renewal of their relationships; despite the crucial shortage of mounts, he reciprocated with gifts of horses. Apaches, Pecos, and Spaniards eagerly anticipated harvest time and resumption of the old trade fair at Pecos.

The plains Apaches' enthusiasm for the Spanish trade boded ill for Indians whose ranges bordered theirs. An Apache leader who lived fourteen days from Santa Fe told Vargas of the Tejas territory only seven days beyond his camp; he knew that Spaniards had been there briefly. More important to him was Quivira, where his people often went to fight and to capture youths whom they could barter for horses. Once Apaches were assured of renewed Spanish demand in New Mexico, there would be little security in Indian villages on the eastern margins of the plains.

Vargas could spare little thought to the far-reaching repercussions of Spanish presence in New Mexico. By June 1694, his eleven hundred colonists exhausted their livestock supply; their horse herd had dwindled to five hundred. They existed on meager rations of corn from captured enemy stores. The friendly Keres were about to abandon Santa Ana, Zía, and San Felipe under threat of attack by hostile Keres, Jémez, Tewas, and Apaches. To protect them, Vargas campaigned against the hostile Keres on Cochití mesa, routing them and razing their pueblo. He captured 342 and executed 13 leaders. These executions only reinforced the determination of Tewa leaders never to fall into Spanish hands.

Even after that victory, friendly Pueblos and settlers could plant their fields only when Vargas stationed mounted, armed guards to protect them. The Jémez harassed the friendly Keres so relentlessly that Vargas seconded ten mounted soldiers, whom he could ill spare, to protect workers in the fields of those three pueblos.

Late in June, Santa Fe's population received a badly needed boost: sixty-six and a half[18] families sent by the viceroy from Mexico City. However welcome the increment, feeding 220 more mouths posed an immediate problem. Vargas ventured to Picurís and Taos in search of food, hoping to purchase it, willing to seize it if necessary.

Juan de Ye's army of Pecos warriors accompanied Vargas' hundred Spaniards. Finding Picurís abandoned, they continued to Taos, while the Taoseños took refuge in their mountain canyon. Vargas hoped to conciliate Governor Pacheco, who was reported coerced into unwilling alliance with the Tewa rebels. As he rode to the mouth of the canyon to contact Pacheco, plains Apaches greeted the Spaniards with friendly handshakes. They had been trading at Taos when news of Vargas' approach reached the pueblo and had accompanied the fleeing Taoseños toward the canyon. They seemed quite neutral.

Juan de Ye, interpreting for Vargas, shouted to Pacheco to come down to negotiate. A sullen Pacheco emerged with many warriors and would talk only to Juan de Ye, whom he invited into the canyon to parley. Vargas objected to the risk, but Don Juan insisted and went into the canyon unarmed, never to be seen again. When Don Juan did not return the next day and Pacheco would not parley again, Vargas issued an ultimatum: the Taoseños must come out by noon or have their pueblo sacked. When no response came, the Spaniards and their Pecos allies made good the threat.

The stores of Taos were rich. Vargas' men worked all night, hulling corn and loading it on pack mules. They now had food for the colony, if only they could get it to Santa Fe. The heavily laden pack animals were so vulnerable to attack and the land between Taos and Santa Fe so rife with hostile Indians that the New Mexican veterans recommended a roundabout route northward through Ute territory. Vargas agreed. Although much longer, the safer route would also afford opportunities to contact the once-friendly Utes and to take some buffalo meat.

Taos warriors harried them northward as far as Colorado Creek.

---

[18] That peculiar "half-family" unit consisted of three Frenchmen, survivors of La Salle's abortive Texas coast colony, who had been taken prisoner by the Spaniards and would serve life sentences on this bleak northern frontier.

Even across the Colorado, the Spaniards made all possible speed through that land of the Apaches del Acho, dreading their cordial welcome more than hostile reception. Given the bitter enmity between Utes and Apaches del Acho, the Spaniards dared not risk a friendly encounter that might suggest to Ute spies some alliance of Spaniards and Apaches. Not until they reached the San Luis Valley of present southern Colorado did they dare to relax and camp beside the San Antonio River. For two days they rested their tired pack animals and hunted buffalo and deer, meanwhile sending up smokes to attract Utes.

Just before dawn on the third day, as the men broke camp, three hundred Ute men and women assailed them with bows and arrows and war clubs. Six Spaniards were wounded and eight Utes killed before the attackers fled across the river and waved a buck skin for truce, calling out in Ute, "My friend and brother!"

When the Spaniards signaled a friendly response, the Utes recrossed the stream and courteously explained their mistake: they had assumed Vargas' men were just another bunch of Pueblo hunters poaching on Ute land in Spanish garb. The Utes always attacked such Pueblo intruders, and they had not realized until in the midst of the skirmish that these hunters were bona fide Spaniards.

Vargas gave appropriate presents to the territorial hosts: corn, dried meat, some European trinkets, and the indispensable horse. They exchanged pledges of friendship, and the Utes seemed especially pleased by his invitation to come to Santa Fe to trade, as they had done before 1680. All seemed cordial, the eight Ute deaths forgiven as the product of their own error.[19]

Four days later the party delivered eight hundred bushels of corn to the *cabildo*'s warehouse in Santa Fe. The Spanish colony was assured subsistence for weeks to come; the rebels' resources were correspondingly weakened. Vargas looked again to the two menacing mesatop aggregations of rebels.

He first targeted the Jémez–Santo Domingo stronghold on the mesa of Jémez, even though Cochitís and Navajos attacked Santa Ana as he formulated his strategy against the hostile Keres. Friendly Keres warriors joined Vargas to assault that mesa on the evening of July 23, 1694, and swiftly won. Only seventy-two rebels escaped, some wounded; some fled to Taos or to Cochití, a few to the Navajos. Three captive warriors died before the firing squad: a Jémez, an Apache,

[19] Espinosa, "Journal of the Vargas Expedition into Colorado," 81–90.

and a Santo Domingan. The remaining 346 captives, women and children, were shipped off to Santa Fe with six hundred bushels of corn from Jémez stores. The Keres allies received a similar quantity of corn, more than welcome in their three beleaguered pueblos. They ransacked the vanquished pueblo, burned, and razed it.

Within three weeks of their debacle, the Jémez submitted. Their wounded governor sent two emissaries to Santa Fe to sue for peace. Vargas promised full pardon and restoration of their women and children if they would rebuild their church, reoccupy their old pueblo, renew their vassalage to both Majesties, and prove their loyalty by joining his campaign against the rebels on Black Mesa. They agreed.

Now Vargas was ready to vanquish the last rebel stronghold. He delayed briefly because plains Apaches came to Pecos for the traditional August trade fair, and neither his Pecos allies nor enterprising Spaniards wanted to miss that opportunity. Vargas stipulated that no Spaniard could trade horses; they were too scarce in the colony to be spared.

Half the Jémez warriors served in his campaign while the rest stayed home to protect their pueblo. When Vargas rode north to Black Mesa on September 4, 1694, his force included 150 warriors from Jémez, Pecos, and the friendly Keres pueblos. Hostile shouts greeted his approach, so he attacked at once.

The battle wore on indecisively for two days. However, the rebels had planted their crops down in the valley. Their anguish and rage knew no bounds when they were cut off from their fields and from above saw Vargas' men and their horses consume the ripening corn. The rebels launched another fruitless attack and suffered grievous losses. They sued for peace the next morning, September 8, and Vargas set surrender terms.

The leaders were obviously scared, but, when Vargas approached unarmed and hailed them in friendly fashion, they responded with the appropriate "Glory be to the Blessed Sacrament!" Seeing the Spaniards' pleased reaction, the rebels then came down unarmed, and the erstwhile enemies gratefully embraced one another. The Pueblos again pledged themselves to become good Christians and faithful vassals of the Spanish king. Governor Vargas stipulated that they must reoccupy their proper pueblos within eight days; subject to that condition, he granted all of them full pardon.

More impressive than his words were Vargas' actions in the week after the battle. Promptly honoring his promise to Jémez, whose warriors had faithfully served in the campaign, Vargas restored their women and children, held in servitude since the capture on July 23. The Jémez spoke eloquently of their gratitude and loyalty, and their good news spread through the Pueblo world. Within a few days, prominent Tano and Tewa leaders presented to Vargas some mules they had obtained from Cochití Keres, who had captured them from Apaches, who in turn had taken them from a Spanish supply train. To that conciliatory gesture, Vargas responded with gifts of hats, ribbons, and other ornaments suitable for chiefs. When they reported their people busy rebuilding their pueblos, Vargas presented the rods of office in formal recognition of their positions as governors and war captains of their pueblos and administered the oaths of office. They returned the next day to attend Mass with him. At last, internal peace seemed a reality in the New Mexican heartland.

Vargas visited each reoccupied pueblo to install its elected officials. At the instance of their friar, he petitioned the viceroy for special privileges for the extraordinarily loyal pueblo of Pecos. The last rebels of the Rio Grande Valley, Keres of Cochití and Santo Domingo, voluntarily rendered obedience and joined in the general reconstruction. Vargas gradually released all captive Pueblo women and children from servitude, to the considerable annoyance of some colonists who resented the loss. Santa Fe had a steady stream of Pueblo visitors, mingling amiably and trading with the settlers. The Tewa and Tano governors were Vargas' guests for the Christmas 1694 holidays.

Yet, trouble was already brewing in the pueblos. All available friars had been assigned early in the autumn to the missions that the Pueblos were dutifully rebuilding and had launched vigorous programs of instruction and worship. Morning and evening, mission bells called the Pueblos to church for prayers and indoctrination, usually in Spanish because few friars knew the Pueblo tongues. No absences were tolerated. Those who stayed away without good reason suffered public penance; some were lashed by the *fiscal* at the friar's order. In some pueblos, the children gathered regularly at noon to pray. The Franciscans saw some results: a few baptisms and marriages performed; some non-Christian marriages sundered.

The Indians supported their missionaries with gifts of tortillas and game, much as they had long supported their native shamans; they tilled the mission fields and tended the mission herds as well as their own. Most attended faithfully their duties in both kiva and church and found no serious conflict.

Not content with that patient cooperation, the missionaries strove to root out all pagan practice and belief. They tried to make the church rather than the kiva the community meeting place, and they objected to native religious observances that they saw, principally offerings of feathers and sacred meal at the stone altars found in every pueblo. The friars' admonitions drew the retort that these were ancient, necessary practices, and the pointed reminder that efforts to abolish them had contributed to the catastrophe of 1680. Since the friars could regard the Pueblos' beliefs and their marital practices only as idolatry and concubinage, no real sympathy was possible. Resentments festered in both church and kiva.

Still, the Franciscans' year-end reports indicated satisfactory progress.[20] Unaware of the danger signals, Vargas anticipated 1695 cheerfully. Santa Fe had its presidio of a hundred soldiers, many with families, and 130 families of settlers. As soon as the caravan should bring more settlers and the necessary farm implements, the governor would deploy Spanish settlement more widely. He had already assigned some ranches to be occupied in the coming summer and was surveying more grants. He had established *alcaldes mayores* over most pueblos to stabilize administration. Unfortunately, Vargas grew so preoccupied with advantageous distribution of his colonists that he decided to relocate two pueblos and thus sparked the anger and distrust of all the rest.

The matter seemed trivial to Vargas because the Indians of San Lázaro and San Cristóbal had not long occupied the sites from which he ordered them. Most were Tanos who had lived southwest of Santa Fe before 1680. They had lived a few years at San Juan to be nearer their Tewa allies, then had joined some Tiwas and Piros to build new pueblos on the foundations of former Spanish haciendas shortly before the reconquest. Vargas, committed to restore all former Spanish possessions, ordered the Tanos out in March. The people of San Lázaro were to reoccupy their communal dwelling at San Juan, with permission to plant fields at Yunque;[21] those of San Cristóbal were to move to Chi-

[20] The missionaries counted the natives served as follows: San Ildefonso, 188, and the *visita* of Jacona, 40; Santa Clara, 249; Zía, 279; Santa Ana, 168; San Felipe, 240; at Santo Domingo, about 20 persons coming to Mass and most still living on the mesa of San Juan de Jémez; Tesuque, 183, with many still living elsewhere; Cochití, 500; San Juan de los Cabelleros, 172; Pecos, 736. There were still too few friars to provide missionaries for Taos, Picurís, and Jémez (Espinosa, *Crusaders of the Rio Grande*, p. 216).

[21] The pueblo across the river from San Juan that had housed San Gabriel, first capital of New Mexico.

mayó. The latter petitioned to remain for that crop season because they had already dug their irrigation ditches. Vargas let them stay through the harvest season, provided they would move immediately afterward, then subsequently directed them to move to Galisteo instead of Chimayó. Outraged, the people of San Lázaro and San Cristóbal ran away to the mountains to protest their loss. Though they let themselves be persuaded to come back and receive pardon, their grievances rankled widely.

In April, Vargas deployed sixty-six families who had arrived from Mexico City the preceding summer, founding a new town on the site just vacated by the Tanos of San Lázaro: Villa Nueva de Santa Cruz de Españoles Mexicanos del Rey Nuestro Señor Carlos Segundo, usually called Santa Cruz or La Cañada. The colonists brought seed to plant and requisite farm implements, but theirs was very much a frontier outpost. They had a military government and a resident squad of soldiers; their *alcalde mayor* had charge of a town armory of firearms, gunpowder, and lead.

In May, forty-four families of new settlers from Nueva Vizcaya reported to the governor. Disregarding official instructions to keep his settlements compact for better defense, Vargas established Bernalillo downstream on the Rio Grande and a mining camp at Los Cerrillos. He also granted lands to many individuals who wished to live on haciendas as in the old days.

His optimism ill suited the actual condition of the colony. Crops failed in 1695, due to insects and drought. The livestock herds had never been properly rebuilt after the war in 1694. Thus, the winter of 1695–1696 was another grim starving time for New Mexico. Epidemics worsened the ordeal. Settlers bartered their possessions and even their labor to the Indians for food and piteously appealed to the viceroy for succor. His response, slow and minimal, included a curt notice that New Mexico would receive no further aid.

It was a trying winter for Pueblos, too. They could see how starvation and disease weakened the colony and how ill-equipped the soldiers and militia were to defend it. Some leaders talked again of revolt and found no shortage of grievances on which to play. The dispossession of the Tanos of San Lázaro and San Cristóbal suggested that no pueblo was really secure on its lands if the Spaniards should desire them.

Even more telling was the religious issue; friction between missionary zeal and native values grew with each passing day. An awful incident worsened matters. Devoted Fray Diego Zeinos of Pecos Mission accidentally shot and killed an Indian there. Although another missionary hastily replaced him, the affair heightened animosities toward the friars. Alarmed, Vargas ordered strict enforcement of the law against selling arms to Indians.

In that climate, hysterical rumor had a field day, especially that old story of a Spanish plot to kill all Pueblo men and enslave their women and children. All winter the issue of rebellion agitated the Pueblos with deeply divisive effect, both within pueblos and among neighboring groups.

Many Indians objected, some from fidelity to their vows to the two Majesties, but probably more from their grim understanding of the suffering and hardship that revolt entailed. Even among those most eager to revolt, deeply rooted enmities prevented effective cooperation to set off a rebellion or to see it through.

The friars were first to apprehend the revolutionary ferment. Some Indians grew extraordinarily truculent, even blasphemous, and openly threatened that events of 1680 would soon repeat themselves. Sympathetic Indians quietly warned their priests of plots on their lives. Tesuque's Governor Domingo, in an open meeting in the church, spoke frankly of revolutionary councils in the hills to the north. A plot to kill the priests on Christmas Eve and sack the missions in the western Rio Grande pueblos narrowly failed. Thereafter the situation deteriorated rapidly. In March, the Franciscan custodian of New Mexico notified Governor Vargas that revolt was imminent and that the friars must have military guards or be slaughtered.

Vargas was woefully short of men when the Franciscans demanded protection, but he promised to do his best for them and asked the custodian to determine the absolute need of each. The missionaries' requests totaled sixty men, but the governor had at his disposition just six not assigned to other duties. Of his hundred presidials, two squads of thirty each were required to guard the garrison and the horse herd and another ten to man the towers and gate of the villa of Santa Fe. Of the remaining thirty, Vargas had currently dispatched two dozen south to El Paso to escort urgently needed caravans of supplies and livestock. To ward off Ute raids on the northernmost pueblos, he had lately found it necessary to establish thirty armed militiamen at Taos. Somehow he juggled his manpower so as to station four-man squads at each of the six frontier pueblos the friars deemed most restive. Unfortunately, the men he sent were so poorly armed and so obviously half-starved that they only dramatized in the pueblos the weakness of the Spanish colony.

The native shamans scored an important victory, at least temporarily. Convinced that bloody rebellion would occur momentarily, the friars left their missions to take refuge in the three Spanish settlements and vowed not to resume their stations without proper protection. Conceding that Vargas truly had not the means to protect their missions, the Franciscans asked him instead to send soldiers to remove sacred objects from the missions and evacuate the livestock and other valuable property.

Vargas rejected such a move as a provocative gesture of distrust and a flagrant confession of weakness. On the same grounds, he deplored the friars' abandonment of their posts, suggesting that they had panicked unnecessarily over unsubstantiated rumors. His only concession to their fears was to move all livestock from the northernmost missions to the settlement of Santa Cruz, explaining it to the Pueblos as a precaution against Ute raids. Some friars quietly returned to their missions, resentful of the governor's skepticism but prepared to die defending the sacred articles and serving their few faithful communicants. They found conditions even scarier than before: when the custodian read their reports, he gloomily warned his superiors in Mexico that the missions again stood on the brink of destruction.

Most ominous of all was disaffection among the Pecos, who had been such staunch allies throughout the war of reconquest. Fray Domingo de Jesús, their new priest, suffered ridicule and bullying, but he stuck to his post until a sympathetic Indian warned him of a plot to behead him. If the Pecos should revolt, would not their Faraon Apache friends join them? When the priest fled, one *ranchería* of the Faraones were actually in the pueblo and more were camped nearby on the banks of the Pecos River.

Rebellion erupted on Monday, June 4, 1696, with the murder of priests at five missions: Taos, San Cristóbal, Nambé, San Ildefonso, and San Diego de Jémez. Twenty-one settlers and soldiers died, too. Most Pueblos fled to the mountains. Even those who had opposed the plot were now terrified by the prospect of Spanish retaliation and by the rebels' ugly threats of reprisals against those who failed to join them. Although the leaders of Taos and Picurís had opposed the plot, they led their people to mountain hideouts. The people of Santo Domingo, who had been loath to rebel, yielded now to grim pressures from Cochití and fled to the heights. Only five pueblos stood fast against the rebels' pressures: Santa Ana, Zía, San Felipe, Tesuque, and Pecos.

At the time of the outbreak, three rebel leaders from Jémez and Nambé were recruiting at Pecos. They harangued a general meeting in the kiva and won the hostile faction led by Cacique Don Diego and several war captains, but loyal Governor Felipe managed to retain control of the pueblo. Don Felipe had already warned Vargas of the considerable rebel faction at Pecos, and he had asked and received permission to hang the ringleaders. Now he hanged Don Diego and hauled the visiting agitators off to the Santa Fe jail; by summer's end, he hanged four more leaders of Pecos' rebel faction and beheaded a fifth. When Vargas appealed on the day of the outbreak for a hundred Pecos warriors, Governor Felipe responded within twenty-four hours. For the rest of 1696 there were rarely less than eighty men of Pecos on campaign with Vargas' forces.

At Tesuque, Governor Domingo stood firm against the rebels. A prime leader of the opposition in 1693, he had served since the peace as governor general of all Tanos and Tewas. He enjoyed a good working relationship with Vargas and believed that another rebellion could only bring his people death and destruction. In mid-June, Domingo asked for protection. He had been warned that warriors from Santa Clara and San Ildefonso would kill him for his loyalty to the Spaniards and to the faith and then force the Indians of Tesuque to join the rebels. Vargas responded, and with his Indian allies he chased the rebel warriors off as they approached Tesuque. Thenceforth, Tesuque furnished Vargas all the warriors who could be spared from defense of the pueblo, and Domingo himself proved a shrewd strategist when he led his men on campaign.

Vargas concentrated the Spanish population as best he could at Santa Cruz and Santa Fe, and he also ordered the downriver settlers to the capital. The people of Bernalillo refused because they would not abandon their livestock, and they could not convey animals across the Rio Grande, then running high and fast. Vargas offered to escort the friendly Keres to Santa Fe for better security, but they too elected to remain in their homes, and their missionaries stayed with them at Santa Ana, Zía, and San Felipe. The other missionaries stayed with the settlers, supported by the voluntary generosity of Vargas and of loyal Indians who brought them food and firewood as often as possible. The friars' gratitude allayed some of their recent suspicions and resentments.

All that summer and fall the colony was an armed camp, most of its men in the saddle, the rest on guard at the settlements. Under such prolonged stress, the settlers grew so embittered that Vargas found them nearly as obstreperous as the rebels. Over his strenuous objections, the people of Santa Cruz petitioned the viceroy for permission to leave the province. Actually, the colonists were relatively secure in the compact towns as long as Vargas could scrounge enough corn from the fugitives' caches.

One by one, Vargas campaigned against the principal enemy strongholds. By summer's end he had won significant victories. Equally important were his successes in ferreting out the rebels' food caches. Each load of corn that his mules packed back to Santa Fe was of life or death importance to the settlers because the previous year's crop failures had left their granaries empty. The fresh hostilities prevented proper cultivation of the new season's crops, and another drought was fast ruining the small plantings that they had achieved.

Up in the mountains, the Indians needed that lost corn just as badly, for the summer war cost them the year's crops, too. Already many fugitives were going hungry. The prospect of a winter in the mountains without food was terrifying. Many fled to the Navajos; others moved to Zuñi or to the Hopi mesas; some took their chances with Apaches. The governor of San Juan journeyed to the Navajos to buy corn for his people, but his purchase fell woefully short of their need.

Dangerous tensions remained between the Jémez-Keres coalition on the west and the Tewa-Tano group on the north, and the fugitive populations moved uneasily about the mountains. No one knew what to expect of the *bárbaros*. Navajos and Apaches actively peddled the story of a Spanish plot to slaughter the Pueblo men and enslave the rest. Navajos were reported enthusiastic about general war, urging all other peoples to join in it. Apaches had attended planning sessions, but those of the northeast had gone off to attend a dance in their own territory. The Tewa and Tano rebels could only wait and hope that those Apaches would return to help destroy the Spaniards. There were said to be promises of help from Ácoma, Zuñi, the Hopis, their Apache neighbors, and Utes, too, but only after the green corn harvest. The only plan for any concerted action against the Spaniards revolved about the old scheme for an Apache sweep of the horse herds, to be followed by an overwhelming general assault on Santa Fe.

There was also doubt about the attitude of the westernmost pueblos. Reports from Zuñi conflicted, but it appeared that the principal leaders wanted only to be left alone to farm in reasonable security and that the few warriors who went off to join the Jémez forces defied their leaders' wishes. Hopi warriors and some from Ácoma also joined the people at Jémez in time to be badly beaten by Vargas' forces. The Hopis fled home terrified and opted out of the rebellion. The Ácomas suffered eleven deaths in the battle and went home so angry that their great rock once again became a prime resort for dissidents. Apaches were said to go there to plot against the Spaniards and the friendly Keres. Vargas besieged the rock in vain for three days, then laid waste the Ácomas' fields and rode back to Zía.

By summer's end the rebellion seemed doomed to failure: dissension ran rife in the insurgents' ranks; the leadership was collapsing. Some rebel leaders had been captured or killed; a few had voluntarily surrendered. Ahead of the weary fugitives loomed a winter in the mountains without food or shelter. Gradually, fearfully, some stole back to their pueblos.

That fall Vargas campaigned against the last rebel concentrations at Taos and Picurís. Although their leaders had originally opposed rebellion, they had consistently spurned Vargas' offers of peace and pardon, fearing a Spanish plot to kill their men and enslave their women and children. Vargas invaded the Taos hideout in the canyon above the pueblo, burned their log huts, and devastated their fields. As snow began to fall, some Taoseños crept back to their pueblo, defying adamantly hostile leaders. Soon Governor Pacheco came down to surrender, rather than see his people die of cold and hunger in the mountains. Vargas received them kindly, spent two days reassuring them of his genuine pardon and good will, then left them in peaceful occupation of their pueblo.

Many Picurís also came down from the mountains in a conciliatory mood and reoccupied their pueblo. However, they soon fled to the plains for fear they would be blamed and punished for a horse theft committed by Apaches who visited Santa Cruz with some Picurís. Some Tewas and Tanos fled with the Picurís, all in company with plains Apaches. Vargas pursued the fugitives, overtook them, killed some, and captured more. Others surrendered the next day. Picurís Governor Lorenzo and some others escaped eastward to Apache territory, where they fell into the unhappy predicament of slavery to the Cuartelejo Apaches.[22]

Toward the end of 1696, the pueblos were gradually reoccupied and their surviving leaders pardoned. No longer did fugitives roam the

[22] They requested rescue in 1706, and the Spaniards obliged. (See below, p. 228.)

mountains, but many never returned to the Rio Grande pueblos from their new homes with Navajos, Apaches, or far western Pueblos. Early in 1697 the Tanos remnants from San Cristóbal and San Lázaro obeyed Vargas' directive to resettle at Galisteo, there to remain until the late eighteenth century, when *bárbaros* raiders would drive the few survivors to move to Santo Domingo. Isleta, reoccupied during the reconquest, stood as the sole surviving southern Tiwa pueblo.[23]

The schism at Pecos did not readily heal. Relatives and friends of the dissidents executed by Governor Felipe plotted vengeance. In 1700 they were carted off to the Santa Fe jail, whence they escaped to flee to the mountain camps of Jicarilla Apaches. Pecos stayed split into hostile factions. Only with difficulty did Governor Felipe prevent bloody clashes. Some irreconcilables petitioned for permission to move to Pojoaque. Nevertheless, Pecos endured until 1838, when ravages of the *bárbaros* drove the surviving remnant to Jémez.

The westernmost pueblos remained aloof and antagonistic longer, but their remoteness permitted the Spaniards to wait for reconciliation. In 1698 the Keres fugitives from La Cieneguilla, Santo Domingo, and Cochití descended from their bastion at Ácoma to found nearby the new pueblo of Laguna. In July of that year, Zuñis, Ácomas, and Lagunas all made peace with the Spaniards, tendering submission to both Majesties. By 1700 missionaries were stationed at each. With eleven soldiers stationed at Zuñi to protect the mission from the very active Apaches, the Zuñis felt secure enough to leave their mesatop fortress and reoccupy their old pueblo of Alona.

The Hopis felt their isolation keenly. Theirs were the only pueblos not entitled to the protection of Spanish vassals and not included in the trading economy of the Spanish province. In May 1700, Hopi war captains visited Santa Fe to sue for peace, protesting their attachment to Christianity and asking for missionaries. The governor granted peace and pardon and promised them missionaries. Meanwhile, the cacique of Oraibi invited Fray Juan de Garaicoechea of Zuñi mission to visit the Hopis and reinstate them in the faith.

Fray Garaicoechea rode with Fray Antonio Miranda to Aguatovi, the Hopi community nearest Zuñi, where they were warmly welcomed. They baptized many and were encouraged to found a new mission there. All seemed to go well until the foremost Hopi leader, Cacique Espeleta, heard rumors that all his emissaries had been slain in Santa

23 That remained true until 1741, when refugee Tiwas returned from the Hopis to occupy Sandía.

Fe. Abruptly he bade the priests begone, pending definite news of the fate of the Hopi war captains. By the time the Hopi envoys arrived home, quite well and safe, another faction had prevailed. They too wished peace and commerce with the Spaniards but were determined to avoid involvement with Christianity.

So much of the Hopi way hinged on their independence. Theirs was a sparsely populated, tightly self-contained little universe atop three mesas. Each Hopi village was an independent unit within which the people tended to marry, thus reinforcing their sense of separateness and uniqueness. They had accepted Tewas and other Pueblo fugitives from the rebellion and had let them establish the village of Hano, but Hopi identity never blurred. No political structure bound their villages together, but they shared a commitment to the Hopi way of life, embodied in their myths and traditions and sustained by an elaborate system of training and initiations. Life centered around the rituals required for the proper relationship with the god of life and death, Masau'u, whom they understood to be the giver of lands and crops. Survival from year to year depended upon the proper rain ceremonies. For fifty years before the revolt, Hopis had tolerated friars in their villages, but they could not reconcile mission life and the exclusive disciplines of the Catholic faith with the spiritual necessities of their own tradition. In 1700 the Hopi leadership wavered briefly in the face of economic and military pressures, then firmly resolved to brook no more Christian intrusion into the Hopi world.

In September, Cacique Espeleta himself led twenty Hopi delegates to Santa Fe to seek peace without missionaries. When he understood that the Spaniards considered submission to Christianity indispensable to peace and pardon and would entertain no compromise, the Hopis departed, never to resume negotiations.

Espeleta's grim resolve spelled tragedy for the people of Aguatovi, who had welcomed the friars. He led a hundred warriors to destroy their village, slaughtered the men, and enslaved the women and children.

In the summer of 1701 New Mexico's Governor Pedro Rodríguez Cubero led a punitive campaign against the Hopis. Briefly he held three hundred captives hostage, but the Hopis convinced him that they would not compromise their independence. Cubero gave up and led his forces home to Santa Fe. Sporadic efforts to reduce them later in the century fared no better. The remoteness that enabled the Hopis to hold aloof from the Spanish system also made them vulnerable to increasing pressures from mounted Navajos, Utes, Apaches, and even hostile Pueblos, but they chose to risk oblivion at the hands of Indian enemies rather than jeopardize the integrity of the Hopi way.

Revival of the Zuñi mission was short-lived, because of the overbearing, abusive behavior of soldiers stationed there and of three settlers exiled to service on that dangerous frontier. Fray Garaicoechea warned Santa Fe that trouble was brewing and urged withdrawal of the offending Spaniards, arguing that he would be safer alone than guarded by ruffians who injured his congregation. Navajos informed Governor Cubero in 1702 that Zuñis planned to kill the trouble-makers, but he shrugged their tale off as a false alarm.[24] By March 1703, the Zuñis could brook no more. They killed the three settlers at Mass on Sunday; the soldiers escaped because they were away at the time. The Zuñis carefully spared the priest. Anticipating reprisal, most of the community fled to the mesa of Kiakima. The ringleaders of the plot fled with the mission sheep to Hopi country and settled near Walpi.

Fray Garaicoechea insisted that the Zuñis were loyal and protective toward him and had acted only under intolerable provocation, but Governor Cubero sent forty soldiers to escort him back to Santa Fe. For all practical purposes, the Spaniards abandoned Zuñi. Henceforth, its people could be nearly as aloof and independent as the Hopis.

In the Pueblo heartland, the diminished population settled into a pattern of existence that would serve them well as long as Spaniards ruled New Mexico and for a century beyond. They clung as tenaciously as ever to old Pueblo values, but they kept their activities discreetly underground in the kivas and dutifully observed Catholic forms. Friars baptized, married, and buried them; they went to Mass as well as kiva. Native religious leaders headed the villages as of old, and in effect they selected the officers whom the Spaniards installed annually to carry on the secular and external affairs of the pueblos. The new position of governor filled an important need in Pueblo life, managing the everyday affairs that could not properly be brought before the cacique and constituting an authority with whom outsiders could deal. Major policy decisions still rested with the traditional council of leading men. Meanwhile, prime leadership remained with the cacique, whose devotions established proper harmonies with the spirit world and maintained the orderly universe of the Pueblo ideal. Down in the kivas, the young men

[24] Frank D. Reeve, "Navaho-Spanish Wars, 1680–1720," *New Mexico Historical Review* 33 (1958): 213–214.

learned the old principles: never quarrel; always give visitors enough to eat, even when there is hardly anything to eat yourself.

Secured on their lands by decrees of the Spanish Crown, surviving Pueblos were richer farmers than before. Those innovations that appealed to their sense of economy and did not offend their sense of fitness became so well assimilated that their alien origins faded from memory. New crops came to be accepted as "Indian food," eaten in the kivas and named in rituals and prayers. The flocks of goats and sheep, the cattle herds, and the chickens were important new riches; the horses and mules and the two-wheeled carts revolutionized transportation and travel in the Pueblo world.

New tools and new skills enriched the village economies, stimulating trade within and among the pueblos and bringing people together in such Spanish trade centers as Santa Fe. Thus, Pueblo horizons were far wider than before. They had in the Spanish language a lingua franca, and in the turbulent years of the rebellions the diverse Pueblos had grown to know each other better than before. People of many pueblos campaigned with the Spaniards against the *bárbaros* and grew to feel some of the unity of common cause.

Pueblos faithfully met their military obligations as vassals of the Spanish Crown, and they in turn relied upon Spanish authorities to keep peace among the pueblos and defend them against the *bárbaros*. Rarely did either Spanish or Pueblo forces take the field without the support of the other; neither had sufficient numbers to campaign against their elusive enemies and still protect their homes. As the *bárbaros'* raids increased their mutual dependence, overt antagonisms dwindled.

Out of the bloodshed and anguish of revolt, the Pueblos had won one overwhelmingly important victory. Never again after 1680 were they subject to *encomienda*. Even the one *encomienda* granted for the services of Vargas was never put into operation. It ceased to exist even on paper when the Vargas heirs had that grant converted to a pension. Thus vanished the greatest economic grievance of the Pueblos and the worst source of friction between Spanish and Pueblo populations.

Religious frictions eased, too, partly because Pueblos had learned valuable lessons of discretion and partly because friars were less powerful and aggressive than before. Even more than the uprising of 1680, the revolt of 1696 had taught the friars the limitations of force against deeply held convictions. When, after a century's instruction in the faith, the intelligent, industrious Pueblos still adhered to their ancient beliefs despite dire warnings of hellfire and damnation, the Franciscans had reluctantly to abide that subtle coexistence of old and new traditions which the Pueblos had themselves evolved.

The Franciscans' new moderation stemmed from changes in the Spanish world as well as recognition of the stubborn realities of Pueblo thought. Powerful new secularizing trends diminished the power of the Church. Investigators of the revolt had blamed much of the Pueblos' disaffection upon vexations inflicted by friars as well as governors. In the new climate of thought, missionaries could expect from the government more criticism than support for attacks upon Indian rituals.

If the Pueblos and the Franciscans had learned much from their experience, the settlers had not. Reconquest was hardly complete before the colony lapsed into the sordid wrangling that had always crippled its progress and discredited it in Indian eyes. Demoralized by the hardships and disappointments of recent years, angered by their continuing poverty, the colonists turned on Governor Vargas. Some resented his distribution of the limited relief supplies that arrived in April 1697: only the poorest two-thirds received livestock, clothing, and blankets, though all 1,500 needed help. The more prosperous, particularly the New Mexican veterans, chafed at his enforcement of prohibitions against use of Indian labor. They especially resented Vargas' insistence upon releasing Pueblos captured in the recent turmoils instead of holding them in prolonged servitude. In June 1697, when a new governor, Don Pedro Rodríguez Cubero, arrived, the *cabildo* and many settlers lodged extreme charges by which they hoped to ruin Vargas in his *residencia*.

Delighted to cooperate, Cubero placed Vargas under house arrest, confiscated his goods, and levied a heavy fine against him. The conqueror's plight was unknown in Mexico until the end of 1698, when the retiring Franciscan custodian informed the viceroy and petitioned for Vargas' release. At court in Madrid, where Vargas was much praised and honored for his accomplishments in New Mexico, his imprisonment was unknown until 1701, a year after he was released at the viceroy's order. Vargas, who had lived three years a prisoner, jailed in irons for the last four months, rode to Mexico City to win vindication in the courts.

Meanwhile, Spanish authority in New Mexico again presented a sorry spectacle. Not content with having jailed his predecessor, by 1699 Cubero was also at odds with the Franciscans, whom he accused of incompetence and meddling. Civil affairs received little of Cubero's attention. Settlers and soldiers were soon widely dispersed, with no provision for emergency defense.

Had there been much spirit of revolt left in the Pueblos, surely the disrupted Spanish community invited disaster. But leaders of western pueblos visited the capital to deal peacefully with Cubero, missionary activity expanded, and the colony gradually rebuilt its shattered economy in cooperation with the Pueblos. The overriding need of Pueblos and Spaniards alike was cessation of strife: they learned now to live together, despite new follies, because they had no other choice.

Internal problems soon paled by comparison with the external menace. Before Cubero's term expired, *bárbaros* raids again posed a serious problem on every side. Even those who had welcomed the returning Spaniards so cordially, the Utes and the northern and eastern Apaches, found the incentives for raiding irresistible. Just as surely as the young men of the *bárbaros* had to raid the livestock, especially horses, so the Spaniards had to protect that property, whether it belonged to Crown or to settlers, to missions or to Pueblos. Raids did not necessarily begin in a spirit of hostility, but out of them wars were born. New Mexico would experience little peace from that time forward.

During Cubero's administration, Navajo and Faraon Apache raids grew troublesome enough to warrant punitive action, but Cubero dropped a projected campaign against the Navajos when one of their war captains sued for peace at Taos. He never got around to acting against the Faraones who systematically preyed upon livestock in the Bernalillo area. Cubero also failed to protect the northern frontier, where Ute and Apache raids became so damaging that the strategically important settlement of Santa Cruz was virtually abandoned.

Late in 1703, after two years of litigation in Mexico City, Vargas returned to Santa Fe to resume the governorship for another five-year term, fully vindicated by the courts and wearing the new dignity of Marqués de La Nava Bracinas. Cubero fled the province as his successor approached, and the *cabildo* hastily repudiated its charges against Vargas.

Vargas at once confronted the complex problem of relations with the Apaches, in which there was rarely a clear-cut pattern of war or peace. Settlers from Santa Fe had resumed trade with the Jicarillas, whose lands they visited to sell horses and buy captives.[25] Any commerce was

[25] Antonio de Aguiloa et al., Petition to the Cabildo, Santa Fe, November 26, 1703, Spanish Archives of New Mexico (hereafter cited as SANM), no. 91.

important to New Mexico's primitive economy, but how, if at all, did that trade relate to the Apache raids that menaced every head of livestock in the province? How could one identify marauders so as to punish them without risking alienation of friendly Apaches?

Vargas saw one unquestionable target: Faraon Apaches, camped in the Sandía Mountains to raid in the Bernalillo area. In the spring of 1704, he campaigned against them with fifty Spanish soldiers and a sizeable troop of Tewa, Pecos, and Keres warriors. Faraon lookouts spotted their approach. In a week's hard pursuit, Vargas' forces found only the fresh trails of their fleeing quarry. The campaign ended abruptly when Vargas sickened and died on April 8, 1704.

The death of Vargas was a singularly ill-timed blow to the fortunes of New Mexico. Momentous changes were afoot in the Spanish Empire; the capable Vargas, favorably known at both viceregal and imperial courts, might have made the most of them for New Mexico. The Hapsburg Crown had first sent him to New Mexico to reclaim the province in the style of the grand conquistadors, and he had served them well. He had returned for a second term to govern for the Bourbons. His record suggests that he would have performed fairly and well, bridging for his province the transition between old and new orders. Even the reinvigorated Bourbon administration would not afford New Mexico a governor of comparable ability for at least three generations. New Mexico, in its first century the creature of the best intentions and the worst performance of the declining Hapsburg dynasty, had now to mark time until the improved Bourbon administration could reach the fringes of the empire.

The Bourbon era in Spain began in the fall of 1700, when the pitiful Carlos II died at last, leaving his throne to the grandson of Louis XIV of France. Felipe V vigorously set about renewing royal leadership in his decaying empire, bringing to the task skilled administrators from France. Under the Bourbons, both the economy and the government of the Spanish Empire would be revitalized and reformed, but all that would take time, and Felipe had first to fight a war to validate his claim to the Spanish throne. Austria, Great Britain, and Holland joined forces to oppose the dynastic triumph engineered by Louis XIV, and the War of the Spanish Succession ensued. Spain and France fared poorly in the war. In 1714 Felipe V had to cede Spain's possessions in Flanders, Luxembourg, and on the Italian Peninsula. He substantiated his claim to the Spanish throne, however, and his losses were in some respects salutary for Spain and her American empire. Too long Spain and the

Indies had been drained and neglected while the Hapsburgs fought their European wars: there was advantage for the people of Spain in a narrower focus of their monarch's interests and resources. Felipe V, with his Italian wife, unfortunately dissipated too much money and energy trying to regain control of the Italian Peninsula, but he was rid of the Lowlands problem, and the able sons who succeeded him were more content to focus their interests on Spain and the Indies and to avoid unnecessary European wars.

As speedily as the exigencies of war allowed, the Bourbon regime in Spain attacked its inherited problems of political corruption and economic decay and, in the large time scale of the European political arena, progressed with all reasonable speed. Urgent problems on the Iberian Peninsula demanded first priority; difficulties of distance and slow communications further delayed reforms in the New World. Problems had to be defined and studied before solutions could be devised. Although the Bourbons early sent some good professional administrators to the colonies, it was half a century before a thorough study of New World problems began and another quarter-century before significant structural reforms were effected.

Measured in lives on the northern frontier, an eternity passed before the Bourbons really mattered. Meanwhile, Indian cultures knew revolution in a generation, and for some groups a season or two spelled oblivion. Some small, vulnerable groups were swiftly wiped out by European frontiersmen ranging beyond the control of their own national states; others were destroyed by rival Indians who acquired the new technologies first. Attrition by war, starvation, or disease drove dwindling groups to merge for survival. Cherished identities blurred and vanished, traditional territories were lost, but out of the turbulence some Indian peoples emerged with unprecedented power. As compared to ponderous shifts of power in Europe, the volatile balances of Indian power changed in the twinkling of an eye.

Time also ran swiftly for the Spanish frontiersman, whose own safety and prosperity were entwined with the volatile Indian world. The years and miles away from the sources of his own culture changed him, too. The unrelenting struggle to survive on a hostile, neglected frontier shaped a tough, rustic population, little amenable even to improved management by a distant Crown.

Time was not the sole dilemma of scale that plagued New Mexicans. Their capacity for defense, the quality of their government, and the health of their economy depended heavily upon decisions ground out by the massive political machinery of the Spanish Empire, and shifting factors far from the frontier weighed heavily in the result. The state of relations with rival powers, the success of the harvest in other parts of the empire, the turbulence or calm of Indians in other provinces, the momentary progress of the vast administrative restructuring, the condition of the imperial treasury, all helped determine whether the Crown would answer New Mexican pleas for help.

Beyond the provincial frontiers, the *bárbaros* lived on a very different scale. Individuals decided at the instant to raid or attack, depending upon their own need for horses or prestige or vengeance. They had only to persuade a few others to join their enterprise, perhaps spend a day or two on the rituals of preparation, then sally forth against the goods and persons of Spaniards and Pueblos. Countless little parties swarmed over the province with devastating effect, and before them the forces of empire were nearly helpless. Spaniards could find among the *bárbaros* neither authorities with which to negotiate peace nor armies against which to campaign.

Just as Faraon Apaches eluded pursuit in the Sandías on Vargas' last campaign, most *bárbaros* raiders escaped the punitive forays of his successors. Spain never found a military solution to the problems of the northern frontier, but eventual accommodation grew out of the dynamics of the Indian world. Even in the early eighteenth century, when New Mexico seemed doomed to destruction by the raids of Apaches, Navajos, and Utes, countervailing forces developed. Comanches ventured southward to New Mexico for horses, while French traders carried the ferment of revolution to countless Indian villages along the banks of the Mississippi River system. The disparate forces of change moved toward collision in the arena of the plains, where no human entity would be large enough to control the outcome or small enough to escape the impact.

CHAPTER 4

Caddo World, 1673-1700

The specter of French invasion brooded over the Spanish colony in New Mexico for nearly two centuries. Somewhere—perhaps from the wilds of New France, perhaps from the coast of the Gulf of Mexico, at some incalculable distance—an indeterminable number of Frenchmen were periodically thought to threaten the silver mines of New Spain. Imperial strategists at Madrid and Mexico City saw New Mexico as their line of defense against that aggression. The responsibility loomed appalling at Santa Fe, for France was a very great military power and Frenchmen were reputed diabolically clever at manipulating Indians. Beset with internal problems, woefully conscious of their weakness and isolation, New Mexicans started at the very shadow of intruders on the vague periphery of their province.

The reconquest was hardly complete when the alarms began again. Apaches trading at Picurís in September 1695 mentioned white men far to the east. *Alcalde mayor* Matías Lujan hurried to Santa Fe to tell Governor Vargas that Apaches had reported many Frenchmen advancing across the plains and a general Apache retreat toward New

Mexico to escape the frequent attacks upon them by the Frenchmen.[1]

Vargas' subsequent inquiry revealed a story quite unlike Lujan's excited first report. The Apaches were not falling back before a French onslaught. They had only heard of the white men from enemy nations whose people the Apaches frequently enslaved, those of Quivira and perhaps others. Seven nations, far beyond Apache territory, told of certain white men who came to the bank of the water and made war on the people of Quivira and other parts. Again and again they had come to make war, but they had always gone away afterward. Presumably those white men were very far off, since the far-ranging Apaches had never seen them. Nevertheless, Vargas reported the possibility of French invasion and requested two pieces of artillery to defend New Mexico. Shortly afterward there blazed the last Pueblo revolt, real trouble to divert the governor's attention from anticipated ones. The requested artillery pieces never came from the viceroy, but neither did the French invasion.

Perhaps the New Mexicans were spooked by their own shadows; the visitors' tale could have described the Quiviran experience of Spaniards. Beginning with Coronado, then Humaña, then Oñate, and others at later intervals, Spaniards had reached the villages of Quivira on the banks of the Arkansas; clashes had occurred; the Spaniards had gone away. Surely those periodic visitations of armed white strangers were recounted in the grass huts of Quivira on winter nights over the century. The captives' version carried to Picurís by the Apaches would have been filtered through barriers of language and years until only faint outlines remained.

If it was a false alarm that the Apaches' tale excited in 1695, French presence in the Mississippi Valley was real enough. That very spring, reinforcements for the New Mexican colony had included three Frenchmen, survivors of La Salle's abortive Gulf coast colony, sentenced to serve out their lives on New Spain's northern frontier. Thus, Santa Fe had for the next quarter-century its resident experts to consult about rumors of French intruders and to use as interpreters should the expected confrontation ever come.

As it turned out, New Mexico's century and a half of anxious vigilance against French invasions were nearly wasted: only two small exploring parties and a few straggling traders ever reached Santa Fe. The actual confrontation of Spain and France occurred far to the southeast, in the

[1] Frederick Webb Hodge, ed., "French Intrusion toward New Mexico in 1695," *New Mexico Historical Review* 4 (1929): 72–76.

pine-forested world of the Caddo peoples, where Spain founded another buffer province, Texas, to counter French advances. New Mexico's fortunes, and those of neighboring Indian populations, were sooner affected by the impact of French fur traders surging into the Mississippi Valley from New France in the last quarter of the seventeenth century.

French commerce bore revolutionary consequences for Indians far beyond the range or even the ken of the traders. Southward and westward swept currents of change loosed by the fur trade, meeting tides of change surging northward and eastward with the horses from the Spanish frontier. It was a turbulent time for Indian peoples caught in the convergence of change, but some caught the tide and for a while rode it to greatness.

The forces of change converged in the Mississippi Valley, a world of small, relatively stable Indian villages, where people had farmed with wooden hoes for perhaps a thousand years. Each village was largely a self-sufficient economic unit, but there was trade in luxury and specialty articles and in captives bartered as slaves from one tribe to another. The streams of the Mississippi system formed great natural highways along which goods moved great distances, sometimes through many neighboring hands, sometimes in the packs of Indian traders who ventured far from home. When Europeans introduced novelties that suited Indian needs or desires, those items also moved along old channels of trade. Horses and metal goods began to move from the northern frontiers of New Spain toward the Indian villages of the Mississippi Valley by the seventeenth century; soon afterward goods introduced by French traders began to move southward and westward from Quebec. Some of the goods and much of the jolting impact of change reached Indians in the interior long before they saw either Frenchman or Spaniard.

Frenchmen were relatively easy to welcome because they came first as traders rather than conquerors. They offered very real advantages, both goods and help against enemies, without the painful imposition of cultural change suffered by Indians on the Spanish frontiers. Although Jesuit missionaries figured importantly in French explorations and Indian relations after 1632, France had no great national commitment to convert the Indians, either to the Roman Catholic faith or to the French way of life. Frenchmen came primarily to garner the valuable products of the land for the European market, which in the northern reaches of the continent meant principally furs. They found Indians indispensable, both as collectors of furs and as allies in the struggles to control territories. Guns and ammunition figured importantly in the trade, not only because Indians wanted them badly enough to pay many pelts for them, but also because firearms enhanced their prowess as hunters and as warriors. France needed Indians in both those roles.

From 1608 onward, Indians flocked each summer to Quebec to trade their winter's catch of furs for French merchandise. There seemed no limit to the traders' tempting array: iron knives, axes, and hoes; needles and brass kettles; colorful blankets and textile yardage to replace hide robes and enhance the wearer's prestige; glass beads to replace porcupine quills in Indian embroideries; copper bangles and bells and vermilion to gratify personal vanities. None was necessary to Indian life in the beginning, but the sum of it was convenience and prestige. All that, and guns and brandy, too.

Indians in the Quebec region soon became middlemen, bartering French merchandise for the furs of more distant Indian hunters at considerable profits. Thus, incentives for intensive hunting spread far beyond the Quebec traders' actual range, and Indians of the interior competed ever more keenly for hunting grounds. Conflicts blazed, and war captives also could be traded to other Indians or sometimes to Frenchmen for desired goods. Indians who obtained guns terrorized those who did not yet have them. Just as mounted Apaches grabbed captives to barter for horses and metal in New Mexico, Indians to the northeast sought captives to trade for goods from Quebec.

From the early posts in the St. Lawrence Valley, the second and third generations of traders thrust westward into the Great Lakes region, then beyond, lured by fabulous quantities of fine pelts to be gleaned from relatively untouched hunting grounds. By-passing the ever more sophisticated Indian middlemen of the St. Lawrence Valley, they reached new Indian customers prepared to pay exorbitant prices for French goods.

Above all, there was the westward push of Indian wars and, by mid-century, the race against the British for an empire in the heartland. French traders were involved in Indian wars from the beginning, for they arrived to find the Algonquians and their allies contesting with the Iroquois for control of the St. Lawrence Valley. The new commerce intensified the old wars, as control of hunting grounds became more important than ever and access to French trade became another point of rivalry among enemy nations. Frenchmen sided with Algonquians against Iroquois from the outset and tipped the balance for a quarter-century, until the 1640's, when Dutch traders and then Britons in New York brought guns, and therefore new advantage, to the Iroquois.

Aggressive Iroquois warriors drove many Indians westward from the Ohio Valley to the lands of the Sioux in the upper Mississippi Valley, a process only temporarily slowed when Frenchmen mediated a truce in 1653. Displaced Indians who had earlier enjoyed trade goods from Quebec wanted to resume trade, so they invited French traders to their new homelands. In 1656 French traders reached the Wisconsin area, where they heard tales of Indian populations along the Mississippi River system. At the same time, other traders thrust northwestward to discover rich prospects in the Hudson's Bay region: splendid furs and Indians primitive enough to trade a stack of pelts for a single metal knife.

The fur potential seemed unlimited, matching traders' ambitions and Indians' desires, but mismanagement in Paris stunted development of the trade. New France had never amounted to more than a commercial concession. Court favorites who owned the fur-trade monopoly were unwisely restrictive and unfairly exploitive toward the men who actually did the work and ran the risks of the business. Some of the best traders quit in disgust in the 1660's, and two dissidents promptly turned up on Hudson's Bay with British backing. Their first winter's trapping yielded such enormous profits that Great Britain chartered the Hudson's Bay Company forthwith. From 1670 on, the fur trade and thus the Indian populations of the northern wilderness loomed large in the Franco-British contest for empire.

Louis XIV, who took charge of the French government in 1661, realized the importance of trade and colonies in the great power rivalries, though his own interests focused on European wars and dynastic politics. He made New France a royal province in 1663 and turned it over to an extraordinarily able intendant. Jean Talon, who arrived in 1665, revitalized the fur trade and encouraged colonial development of the St. Lawrence Valley. He had first to check a new Iroquois war. His smashing victory over the Iroquois in 1666 established Talon's own prestige among Indians and strengthened Indian confidence in French prowess and the worth of French alliance.

As he revitalized the fur trade, Talon found it necessary to regulate traders' activities in order to control Indian affairs and to collect the expected revenues. He devised a system of licensed traders that prevailed in New France for the next century, when and where the law could be enforced. Always there were some men who found legal restrictions irksome and chose to take their chances operating in the wilderness beyond the law. They ranged from particularly able, strong-willed individuals to shiftless, even criminal, dregs of frontier society; their impact upon the Indians where they roved was correspondingly uneven and unpredictable. In effect, Talon's regulations formalized the risk he sought to avoid: in those *coureurs de bois* operating outside the system, France loosed in the wilderness a force beyond control.

Economically calculated for maximum use of a limited number of men, the system kept to an absolute minimum the Crown's expenditures in the colony from which it expected large returns.[2] The prime link between trade headquarters at Quebec, and later at Montreal, and the wilderness post was the licensed *voyageur*, who transported the entrepreneurs' trade goods to the wilderness and brought back furs. His license specified the number of canoes he could take, the route he could cover, the number of employees he could take, and the duties of each, as well as the compensation he would collect in pelts. Besides the trade cargo, he had to carry in each canoe a specified quantity of goods for the Crown, destined to supply the commander of a fort, a missionary, or perhaps an interpreter, in effect the price he paid the government for his license.

With the *voyageur* traveled the *mangeur de lard*, often a raw recruit, who signed on to work for five years as a common laborer at a minimal wage. Most could not live on their pay and thus fell into a trap: they could not leave as long as they were in debt, and they had little chance of working their way out of debt. Some resigned themselves forever to marginal existence in the wilderness at the mercy of an exploitive company, but others escaped into back country to live by their wits among the Indians.

Voyageurs delivered their principal cargos to trading posts on the larger streams in the wilderness, each managed by a *bourgeois* who had absolute authority over the territory of his jurisdiction. Local relations with Indians were his responsibility; it was he who dispatched messengers or agents to various Indian groups. Thus, the quality of the Indians' experience of French contact depended very much on the quality of the *bourgeois* in their area and of the men in his employ.

[2] John Anthony Caruso, *The Mississippi Valley Frontier: The Age of French Exploration and Settlement*, discusses the French trade system on pp. 371 ff. A perceptive analysis of the impact of trade appears in Preston Holder, "The Fur Trade as Seen from the Indian Point of View," in *The Frontier Re-examined*, ed. John Francis McDermott.

Some furs were trapped by Frenchmen whom the *bourgeois* dispatched in teams to work designated streams. Most were purchased from Indian hunters and middlemen. Entrepreneurs found it most profitable to carry the trade to the Indians; Indian time and energy were better spent hunting and preparing pelts than in long treks to market. Collection in the wilderness usually yielded pelts in better condition and at cheaper prices. On-the-spot collection also helped foil competition, whether from English traders or from bootleg French traders who opted out of the royal government's restrictive system. It sometimes paid, therefore, to serve distant Indians with a subordinate post in the interior, usually run by a *commis*, or clerk, working his way up to *bourgeois*. Under the direction of the *commis* worked the *hivernants*, old hands in the trade who roved among the Indians during the winter trapping season, swapping goods for pelts.

It was often safest and most economical to base wilderness trading operations in established Indian villages, where the *commis* lived as a guest, usually in the lodge of an Indian leader, with his stock of trade goods. The *hivernants*, too, lived mostly with Indians. Their success, or even survival, depended upon mastery of Indian languages and extraordinary adaptability to the customs and conditions of Indian life. Many traders and trappers became very like Indians themselves in dress, travel, and work; some took Indian wives and sired Indian children. Many came to prefer wilderness life and spent minimum time in touch with the wider world when they journeyed downstream to exchange accumulated pelts for a new stock of trade goods.

No one ever knew exactly how many Indian villages had French residents, what distances the traders ranged, or what streams they explored, for the intensely competitive fur business fostered secrecy. Individual fortunes lay in exclusive knowledge of prime sources of pelts and in personal contacts in Indian villages. Even those men who operated within the system did not necessarily share much of their knowledge with company bosses or government officials. After 1696, many operated as virtually independent agents. During the succeeding century, those *coureurs de bois* were an imponderable force in the burgeoning of change in the interior.

Talon sent his first group of twenty-five licensed traders into the Great Lakes country by 1670. In Wisconsin, he claimed the interior in the name of the king and negotiated trade alliances with the Indians of the region, who already knew and wanted French trade goods. Those Wisconsin alliances marked only the beginning of the French thrust into the Mississippi Valley. When Indians spoke of the great river to the west, some French listeners surmised a possible northwest passage or at least a highway to the fabled Indian kingdoms of Quivira and Gran Teguayo and to the rich mines of New Mexico, so widely known from the reports of Fray Alonso de Benavides. In 1673 Father Jacques Marquette and Louis Joliet set out to explore the stream, hoping to reach Spanish settlements and the Pacific Ocean. With five men, they portaged from the Fox River to the Wisconsin, then paddled their birch canoes down the Wisconsin and onto the Mississippi River. Most Indians along the way received them kindly enough, though each group tried to dissuade them from going further.

The explorers pressed on to the mouth of the Arkansas, where Indians[3] gave them information that convinced them that the Mississippi must empty into the Gulf of Mexico, not the Pacific. Rather than push on to the Gulf and needlessly risk capture there by Spaniards, they turned back to report their news to Quebec. Father Marquette noted the obvious importance of the Missouri River, and he picked up enough information about the Platte and Colorado rivers to surmise that the route to the Pacific must lie along those streams. He resolved to pursue the matter in the future and returned with Joliet via the Illinois and Lake Michigan, reaching Quebec early in 1674.

Father Marquette did not live to pursue his quest for a route to the Pacific, but his exploit with Joliet had far-reaching results. At Quebec, the new provincial governor, Louis, Comte de Frontenac, and a successful trader, Robert Cavelier, Sieur de La Salle, saw in the report of the Mississippi River the key to French possession of the heartland of the continent and to their own fortunes in fur. They proposed a system of posts across the Lake country and down the Mississippi, each commanded by a trader who would collect furs from the Indians of his region. Large vessels would sail each year on the Great Lakes and the Mississippi to collect the year's catch for export, either from Quebec or from a settlement to be made at the mouth of the Mississippi. The Crown readily approved the scheme and granted the pair a five-year monopoly.

From 1675 onward, La Salle worked to build his trade empire. Although he suffered grave setbacks with renewed Iroquois wars, an insurrection at one of his own posts, and the loss of his first fur-laden

---

[3] Perhaps Quapaws (called Arkansas in the eighteenth century), who were driven from their earlier homeland east of the Mississippi by the wars of the period and found a new territory at the Arkansas-Mississippi junction.

vessel, in the spring of 1682 he journeyed downstream to the mouth of the Mississippi. After claiming all its drainage basin for France, he returned upstream to found a fort on the Illinois River, where Indians flocked, eager for trade. There remained for La Salle the crucial task of colonizing the mouth of the Mississippi, to secure French control of the stream and to provide a year-round port for his trading enterprise.

It was more practicable to launch that large undertaking from the mother country, so La Salle assembled his colonists and equipment in France, whence they sailed, four hundred strong in four vessels, early in 1684. Stormy weather and dissension in the group plagued the colony clear across the ocean. Their crowning misfortune was a mistaken landing, not at the mouth of the Mississippi River, but at Matagorda Bay. Apparently the ships departed before the error was discovered, but it was suspected in some quarters that the "accident" was deliberately contrived to establish a base for invasion of New Spain. Spanish authorities reacted vehemently to reports of the French settlement.

In reality, La Salle's colony was hardly a base for any grand invasion.[4] The people worked hard to establish a proper settlement, but they had landed in a hard environment, appallingly remote from any civilized contact. In 1685 La Salle sought the way to the Mississippi and his Illinois post. He managed to buy a few horses at Caddo villages, but, before he could fulfill his purpose, some of his own men murdered him. An epidemic killed half his colonists; Indians of the coastal region massacred most of the remainder. A few survivors straggled back to the Illinois to tell the story; a few others, in no position to face French authorities, found refuge in Caddo villages. Spaniards picked up some of the latter in 1689.

Indians sacked and razed the settlement. When Spaniards finally found the place in 1689, there remained only a few mutilated corpses and some torn remnants of finely bound books. A patch of asparagus and some excellent endive grew there still, pathetic testimony to a little fragment of French civilization once transplanted to that bleak coast.

After La Salle's fiasco, French interests largely ignored the lower Mississippi Valley and poured their energies into the fierce competition against the British for control of the trade and the Indians in three more critical areas: Hudson's Bay, the Great Lakes, and the Ohio Valley. Under Frontenac's leadership, the traders of New France seemed to be winning their contests, but in 1696 the Crown repaid their efforts with

[4] The Texas Memorial Museum excavated the site on the west bank of Garcitas Creek in eastern Victoria County, Texas, in fall 1950.

an order canceling all western trade operations, its short-sighted response to a slump in the European fur market.

The lower Mississippi Valley became a major arena after 1697, when the Treaty of Ryswick[5] left the American issues between France and Britain dangling so conspicuously that another war to resolve them seemed inevitable. Louis XIV rescinded his foolish order of 1696 and reopened the interior to the legitimate French fur trade; by 1700 *voyageurs* were swarming back into the Great Lakes region. Missionaries, traders, and even French farmers developed the settlements of Kaskaskia and Cahokia, which made the Illinois country the principal focus of French and Indian contacts on the upper Mississippi system.

British traders pushed westward from the Carolinas. By 1698 they were on the middle reaches of the Mississippi, trading with the Chickasaws and smaller nations around the mouth of the Arkansas.

The crucial prize was the mouth of the Mississippi, which the three great colonial powers raced to win. Pierre Le Moyne, Sieur d'Iberville, who had already distinguished himself in New France, won the contest for Louis XIV in the spring of 1699, when he built the first of his quick series of three posts to control the outlet of the great stream on the Gulf of Mexico. Thus began French Louisiana.

Thenceforth the forces of change encompassed the Indians of the Mississippi Valley: N, NE, New France; NE, E, the English seaboard colonies; SE, the tenuous Spanish settlements in Florida; S, the new French colony of Louisiana; SW, W, the frontiers of New Spain. Even on the northwest quadrant, not yet penetrated by Europeans, horses from New Mexico set in motion toward the plains potentially powerful Indian groups, while toward them from the northern wilderness moved the guns of the fur traders and the Indian populations pushed westward by colonial wars. The episodes of change were countless, as varied as the modes and purposes of the European intruders and the life styles of the Indian peoples involved, and as intricate as the European power politics that hammered the shifting framework of distant confrontations.

Within the great circle of converging change, there occurred no greater drama than that played in the southwest quadrant, where rival thrusts of Spanish and French frontiers transformed lives in Indian villages and camps from the Red River to the Rocky Mountains and

5 The Treaty of Ryswick ended the War of the Palatinate, called in the English colonies King William's War, which broke out in 1689, the first of four great wars in which France and Britain battled for empire on the North American continent.

from the Arkansas River to the Rio Grande. The agents of France and Spain first confronted one another in the Caddo world late in the seventeenth century, but intimations of change had preceded them by at least half a century.

It was the Caddo world that had long glimmered among Spanish frontier myths as the "great kingdom of the Tejas." The reality was a settled, agricultural population of perhaps eight thousand Indians, extending northeastward in the woodlands beyond the Trinity River and around the big bend of the Red River. They had in common the Caddo language, with dialectal variations, and an impressively developed culture descended from more splendid ancestral attainments of several centuries past.[6]

There was no all-embracing Caddo polity. Of some twenty-five identifiable groups, most were loosely leagued in one of three "confederacies." Westernmost was the largest confederacy, the Hasinai, who occupied the upper reaches of the Neches and Angelina rivers. They were the first Caddo peoples encountered by Spaniards, and it was they whom the Spaniards called *Tejas* through the first century of contact. At the end of the seventeenth century this confederacy had some eight component groups: Hainai, Neches, Nacogdoches, Nacono, Namidish, Nasoni, Anadarko, and Nabedache.

Northeastward, the Kadohadacho confederacy dominated the big bend region of the Red River. They had only four component groups: Kadohadacho, Nanatsako, another Nasoni group, and the upper Natchitoches. Although a smaller confederacy, the Kadohadachos enjoyed greatest prestige, for they were deemed the ancestral group, the "true Caddos."

The third and smallest confederacy was the Natchitoches, downstream from the Kadohadachos on the Red River. When floods dispersed them early in the eighteenth century, the upper group joined the Kadohadachos and the lower group went down to the Mississippi to seek French help. Under French aegis, the lower Natchitoches maintained their separate identity, returned to their original homeland, and in time gave sanctuary to a Yatasi segment dispossessed by Chickasaw raiders. Other Yatasi refugees joined the Kadohadachos, as had the upper Natchitoches before them. There were at least two other in-

---

[6] John R. Swanton, ed., *Source Material on the History and Ethnology of the Caddo Indians*, is the principal source of information on the Caddos, complemented by the most recent modern summary of Caddo culture and history in W. W. Newcomb, Jr., *The Indians of Texas*, pp. 279–313.

dependent Caddo groups, somewhat less advanced culturally: the Adaes, a little north of the Natchitoches in the Red River Valley, and the Eyeish (or Hais, or Ais) in the area of present San Augustine, Texas.

Conflicts among Caddo groups were not unknown, but they employed well-defined legal and diplomatic procedures to keep frictions to a tolerable level. Sometimes they banded together to fight the enemy nations who nearly surrounded them. Perhaps their oldest enemies were the Choctaws. Caddo tradition held that Choctaw warriors had prevented them from living nearer the sea in earlier times, and Choctaw incursions always continued to be a matter of dread. In the late seventeenth century, Chickasaw raiders plagued northeastern Caddo groups, while Osage raiders from the north imperiled the Kadohadachos' very existence. On the west and northwest were historic enmities with the Wichitan groups and the Kichais, despite their linguistic kinship with the Caddos. On the west, the Caddos were traditionally on hostile terms with roving Tonkawan peoples, and by the mid-seventeenth century Apaches posed new dangers for the Caddos. Only to the southwest could the Caddos look to friendly neighbors, Atakapan peoples who held the more advanced Caddos in some awe. They could sometimes be called upon for assistance in war or for the services of their noted medicine men.

Caddo warriors were formidable, as De Soto's men learned painfully in the mid-sixteenth century. Men who had won distinction in war composed an honored caste, titled *amayxoya*, who wore on their leather shirts the carefully tanned scalps of enemies they had slain. The drive for personal glory and the duty to avenge slain kinsmen impelled Caddo men to war. War parties were volunteers, bound to obey the group's elected leader only for the duration of their common purpose. Preparation for war was serious and demanding: the party lived for a week in a special house, fasting, praying, dancing, planning, recruiting; at their departure, the house was burned. Once on the road to the enemy, they moved carefully, using scouts intensively and communicating by smoke signals. Surprise was a key element in their wars, the hit-and-run raid their favorite tactic. They killed most captives, often with extreme tortures, and the people ate some in rituals designed to enhance the power of their own people and diminish that of the enemy.

Yet, for all the ferocity of their warfare and the high honor accorded warriors, the Caddos were not an aggressive people, and their culture never centered upon war as did many others. Much of their warfare was defensive or retaliatory, and the lives and land they defended were largely devoted to peaceful farming and hunting. In the late seventeenth century, Spaniards and Frenchmen were cordially welcomed to the Caddo world, and, despite severe strains on their hospitality, Caddos were rarely goaded into hostilities against the Europeans.

European visitors found much to admire in the Caddos' well-ordered, productive society. Although the "kingdom" of Fray Benavides' report did not exist, the Caddo polities were rudimentary theocracies with clearly defined structures of authority. At the head of each major grouping was a *Grand Xinesi*, the high priest whose duties were primarily religious. He tended the eternal fire in the temple and served as an intermediary between the people and the gods. As the interpreter of divine will, he exercised a virtually unassailable power. The office was hereditary in the male line and cast an aura of greatness upon all the family to which it belonged.

The actual conduct of temporal affairs fell to a *caddi*, a principal chief heading each component group. That office, too, was hereditary in the male line. In groups large enough to need more officials, the *caddices* were assisted by one or more subchiefs called *canahas*, and they, in turn, had assistants called *chayas*. Each group had its law-enforcement officers, called *tammas*.

That well-defined hierarchy with orderly hereditary succession was relatively easy for Europeans to comprehend and to respect. So too was their religion: the Caddos believed in an omnipotent deity, the creator, who punished evil and rewarded good behavior. The similarity to Christian belief suggested to European minds a superior intelligence and encouraged missionaries to believe that Caddos would convert easily to Christianity. Since other, lesser spirits, both good and bad, figured in Caddo belief, they were neither surprised nor offended to hear Europeans talk of still more gods. Tensions arose only when Christian missionaries insisted that theirs was the one true God and that belief in all others must be discarded.

The productive Caddo economy also commanded respect. Their agriculture was a communal enterprise, producing two varieties of corn, half a dozen kinds of beans, squash, sunflower seeds, and tobacco. Only the *Grand Xinesi* was exempt from labor. The people planted his fields first, brought him their first fruits, and supplied all his material needs. All other men and women, regardless of rank, joined in preparing and planting the fields. Moving from the fields of the *Grand Xinesi* to those of their respective *caddices* and *canahas* and so on down in order of descending importance, everyone labored methodically until the fields of even the lowest-ranking members of the group were planted. After that, women assumed responsibility for tending the fields, while men pursued their duties as hunters and warriors. Black bears (hunted mainly for their fat), deer, countless small animals, and fish were all important foodstuffs. Buffalo became more important as the Caddos acquired horses, but the westernmost Caddo groups in particular had always hunted buffalo to some extent. The wilderness also yielded important crops of nuts, berries, and fruits, which the women gathered and processed for storage. In a good year, the Caddos' well-filled storage bins and the lavish feasts they spread for visitors conveyed an impression of great wealth and industry. In poor years, the discipline and cohesiveness of their society were manifest in the unstinting generosity with which they shared all that they had and in their diligent protection of the precious seed corn for another year.

The Caddos were a well-housed, elaborately dressed people. Always heavily tattooed, they also painted themselves for special occasions. Their deer-skin clothing was handsomely tanned to a dark luster, and their costumes for special occasions were lavishly ornamented. Their homes, skillfully constructed for individual owners by community enterprise, were large dome-shaped frameworks of wood, thatched with grass. The interior furnishings were simple but functional and often beautiful: high bed platforms, wooden stools, well-organized storage facilities, and an abundance of fine pots, baskets, and reed matting. The homes of leaders and such special public buildings as temples and council houses were larger models of the same construction. They sometimes gave temples commanding height by building them upon the great earth mounds that survived from ancestral mound-building cultures.

Only when serious problems of defense forced consolidation did Caddos dwell in compact villages. Because they liked their fields on rich, arable bottom lands and required ample running water for domestic use, their settlements were usually strung out along streams, little clusters of houses interspersed among fields. The clusters probably comprised extended family groups; clan affiliation sometimes figured in settlement patterns. Visitors to the Caddo world glimpsed those clusters of handsome houses among carefully tended fields, often in settings of great natural beauty, and heard of countless more farther on. No wonder many visitors, Indian and European, carried away from the Caddo world impressions of great power, beauty, and wealth.

Although the Caddo peoples were less numerous than most outsiders guessed, their world was remarkably self-sufficient and well ordered. Together they produced all they needed for an abundant existence, and they shared responsibility for the welfare of all. The sick received solicitous care by family, by neighbors, and by village. Well-established civil routines governed such communal enterprises as farming, gathering, hunting, and building. Shirking, a rarity, was promptly punished by the *tammas*. More serious crimes, such as theft, were severely punished within the tribe. Offenses by a member of one group against a member of another were handled by the leaders through formal procedures of complaint and restitution, so Caddo groups did not suffer such constant internecine wars as those which decimated more primitive peoples, such as Coahuiltecans.

Caddos' external affairs primarily involved matters of trade and war. Some of their resources, especially salt and the wood of the bois d'arc,[7] were widely in demand; so were products of Caddo craftsmen, especially bows and pottery. They welcomed traders from other tribes, particularly at the harvest celebrations, but only on the periphery of their lands. The internal peace and security of the Caddo world were scrupulously guarded against intrusion.

Yet, by the late seventeenth century, Caddos were prepared to welcome Europeans into their lands and even to let them live there. The attractive goods that the Europeans proffered, as presents and in trade, surely helped to break down Caddo reserve, but far more important were growing external pressures upon the Caddos. With horses revolutionizing Indian life and warfare to the south and west of them, and guns upsetting balances of power among Indians to the north and east of them, the Caddos needed powerful new friends. In that critical time the well-armed strangers came, inviting the Caddos to pledge themselves vassals to great kings across the sea and to receive in return presents and protection from their enemies.

Except for their unpleasant brush with De Soto's force in the 1540's, the Caddos suffered no European intrusions before the time of La Salle. However, during the seventeenth century, the roving Jumanos of the southern plains became brokers of change between the Spanish and

---

[7] Now commonly known as Osage orange, a tree whose wood was preferred for bows.

Caddo frontiers. Jumano traders had long bartered Pueblo textiles and turquoises to Caddos, and Caddo bows in turn to Pueblos, as well as their own take of buffalo meat and hides to both village peoples. With the horse, Jumanos gained effectiveness as hunters and long-distance traders, and horses and metal goods from the Spanish frontier in New Mexico enhanced their stock for the Caddo trade.

On their western borders, Caddos held great summer trade fairs, which attracted Jumanos and many other groups annually. Because Caddo policy forbade aliens to penetrate beyond the border villages, Jumanos gleaned only limited knowledge of life in the Caddo world. Nevertheless, they saw and heard enough at the fairs to form an impression of a great, wealthy population of many villages and many warriors, ruled by an all-powerful chief whose lieutenants were themselves great chiefs.

Like other peddlers, Jumanos carried news as well as goods, and they were typically ready to embellish stories when inspired by listener interest or their own purposes. Thus, it was a lavishly gilded picture of the Caddo "kingdom" that they painted for Spaniards whom they met through their trade contacts at the Tompiro pueblos east of the Manzanos. The Spanish presence in the Pueblo world was equally newsworthy. Though the Jumanos' direct contacts with Spaniards were also very limited, their view of developments in seventeenth-century New Mexico must have generated memorable tales at the Caddo trade fairs.

The Jumanos' own early experience of Spaniards was relatively favorable. Their invitations in 1629 and 1632 had led to cordial visits by Franciscans from New Mexico. Given the Jumanos' expressed desire for conversion and the possibility that their conversion might pave the way to conversion of the important settled Tejas populations of which they spoke, some friars wanted to expand their mission to the Jumanos. Although the New Mexican friars were never granted support or even permission to attempt it, their evident good will and enthusiasm for the Jumano project pleased the Jumanos. As long as Jumanos frequented the pueblos, missionaries hospitably treated them as prospective converts. So sturdy were the friendly relations between Jumanos and Spaniards that they even survived two military probes from New Mexico in 1650 and 1654.

Some resources in Jumano ranges warranted secular interest: freshwater pearls in the western tributaries of the Colorado River and countless buffalo. Even more interesting was the possibility that the Jumano country could be a base for trade with and perhaps conquest of the land of the Tejas. Like the missionaries, Spanish officialdom at mid-century lacked resources to pursue the opportunities in the Jumano country, but during the next quarter-century small Spanish trading parties went annually from New Mexico to trade with the Jumanos.

For perhaps half a century after 1630, the Jumanos prospered as never before. They were near enough to the Spanish frontier to gain horses and metal goods rather easily yet distant enough to avoid abrasive contacts with the Spanish population, thus ideally placed to expand their traditional role as middlemen between the Pueblos of the Rio Grande and the Caddos beyond the Trinity. But the halcyon days of the Jumanos ended abruptly. Their commerce with New Mexico collapsed with the destruction of their traditional market, the Tompiro pueblos, and the subsequent expulsion of the Spaniards. Even had they sought new trade connections with other pueblos, southward-moving Apaches barred the Jumano routes to New Mexico. Worse, Apaches invaded their customary hunting grounds on the southern plains, raided their camps, and stole their horses and people.

While the Jumanos were sorely tried by Apache aggressions, many weaker Indian groups were threatened with imminent extinction. Most vulnerable of all were the hundreds of small Coahuiltecan groups who had for centuries eked out a marginal subsistence by intensive hunting and gathering in the arid country rolling southward from the Balcones Escarpment and the San Antonio River.[8] It was they who first cried out to the Spaniards for help.

Coahuiltecans camped in small family groups, constantly moving in quest of food. Only rarely did some seasonal abundance permit an entire band to convene briefly for a communal hunt or harvest enterprise. Each band claimed a territory as its own range and guarded it jealously against all trespassers.

Internecine war was rife among Coahuiltecans, rooted in fierce competition for too-sparse territorial resources. To destroy enemy people and assure the survival of one's own were their overriding concerns. Cannibalism figured importantly in the struggle, as a matter of magic effect rather than foodstuff. Infant daughters were often discarded at birth as worse than useless to the family group. Incest taboos would prohibit their marriage within the group, and self-interest forbade the

---

[8] See Newcomb, *Indians of Texas*, pp. 29–57, for a discussion of Coahuiltecan culture and a brief summary of their history.

risk of letting them grow up to become mothers of warriors in some rival group.

Although wars among Coahuiltecans exacted a cruel toll, they were waged under well-understood customs, and the combatants met on fairly equal terms. Far more devastating were the raids of mounted Apaches, who swooped down without warning or provocation and all too easily wiped out the people of a family camp or even a band. The Apache onslaught created an insoluble dilemma for the Coahuiltecans whose homelands they penetrated in the late seventeenth century. They could not build effective fortifications because they had to move camp so frequently in quest of food; nor could their relentless round of hunting and gathering be sustained by men and women forced to guard constantly against attacks on their camps. They could huddle together for protection and starve, or they could disperse to gather food and risk slaughter.

Nowhere could a threatened group flee: territories south and east of the ever-widening Apache thrust were claimed by other groups who would fight off trespassers. Hope for survival seemed to lie only in Spanish missions, which proffered sanctuary and sustenance as well as salvation. In the 1670's many Coahuiltecan emissaries visited the Spanish frontier to plead for missions for their people. Some went beyond Saltillo to Guadalajara and even to Mexico City in search of a sympathetic hearing.

Coahuiltecan groups had experienced Spanish contacts off and on for a century, often unhappily. They had been preyed upon by Nuevo León slavers back in the freebooting days of Carvajal and Castaño de Sosa and probably by others since. More recently, some Coahuiltecans had raided Spanish frontier establishments in Nuevo León and Nueva Vizcaya; in the 1650's they had provoked at least two punitive military expeditions north of the Rio Grande. Some Coahuiltecan groups had members who had visited or lived in Spanish settlements. Perhaps some had escaped from slavery; perhaps some had been freed in the periodic viceregal campaigns against illegal Indian slavery. Some had been baptized; more had at least a minimal acquaintance with the Spanish frontier and some knowledge of the mission program. They had carried smallpox, as well as information, back to their homeland: the disease early took its recurring toll in Coahuiltecan camps beyond the Rio Grande.

When they came to plead for missions, considerations of both piety and strategy demanded serious attention to their request. Coahuiltecans had never been considered promising mission prospects. Since the time of Cabeza de Vaca, Spaniards had thought them hopelessly scattered, primitive peoples, addicted to war and superstition. However, their need for protection was now urgent, and their avowed desire for Christianity had to be presumed sincere. To reduce and convert them would help to calm a troublesome sector of the northern frontier, and of course there was the lure of the more promising Tejas "kingdom" said to lie just beyond Coahuiltecan territories. Coahuiltecans who traded goods from the Spanish frontier to the Tejas villages were willing, if not accurate, informants about that tantalizing land. Missions for the Coahuiltecans would probably save few souls in proportion to their cost, but, if they should become stepping stones to conversion of the Tejas, both Majesties could reap good returns on the investment. Tentative response to the Coahuiltecan plea began in 1670.

Fray Juan Larios ministered alone to Indians on the Coahuila frontier for three years before two more friars and some soldiers from Saltillo came in 1674 to help him found two mission settlements. The province of Coahuila was established to support their venture, with settlers, livestock, implements, provisions, and a coterie of Hispanicized Coahuiltecans, all drawn from Saltillo.

All winter and spring, 1674–1675, the friars labored to reduce the Indians to settlements. Many band chiefs came to make formal submission to Spanish vassalage and to receive pardon for past misdeeds and promises of future aid and protection. But profound enmities among Coahuiltecan groups made it impossible for the settlements to thrive, and the situation seemed likely to worsen. The leaders spoke of many more Indians beyond the Rio Grande who wished to settle at mission to Spanish vassalage and to receive pardon for past misdeeds groups. Both lay and religious leaders of Coahuila decided to investigate for themselves before getting further enmeshed in the tangled web of Coahuiltecan wars.

Thus, in the summer of 1675, Fernando del Bosque and Fray Larios led about ten Spaniards and a dozen times as many Indians across the Rio Grande to take formal possession for God and King and to collect all possible information about the population. Indians flocked to meet them as they traveled, pleading their desire for Christianity, listening patiently to religious instruction, and proffering their children for baptism. They explained that enemy Indians made it impossible for them to travel to the Spanish frontier for religious instruction, and they also explained the impossibility of settling with, or even near, enemy Indians. Bosque began to comprehend how virulent their enmities were and what explosive situations could be created by unwise combinations of Coahuiltecans in settlements. At the same time, he knew that available resources would not stretch to support missions for each little band, so he proposed a compromise to reconcile Coahuiltecan antipathies with sound mission economy. His report became the basis of a more systematic, albeit still insufficient, approach to the Coahuiltecan problem.[9]

Bosque identified three principal sectors of Coahuiltecan population; other observers differentiated a fourth that he had not discerned. Each sector comprised many small units, but in at least two a prestigious chief exerted region-wide influence that created some cohesiveness within his sphere. The considerable numbers within each sector, the deep hostilities between sectors, and the complexity of their linguistic differences led Bosque to urge a separate mission settlement for each of his three major categories, with four missionaries at each and a presidio with seventy soldiers to oversee the lot. The Bishop of Guadalajara endorsed the proposal enthusiastically, largely because he thought it an avenue to convert the Tejas. As a result, the 1670's saw four missions established on the Coahuila frontier, each meant to serve an identified sector of Coahuiltecan population running north-south across the Rio Grande.

By 1683, Jumanos also sought Spanish help against the Apaches. The New Mexican Spaniards with whom they had dealt in years past were now refugees at El Paso, and the El Paso mission community had long included a few Jumanos. Thus, it was not entirely as strangers that two Jumano delegations visited the interim capital of New Mexico. They asked Governor Otermín for help against the Apaches, and they also asked for resumption of Spanish trading expeditions to Jumano country.

New Mexicans could fully empathize with victims of Apache raiders, but the El Paso community was then no likely source of help to anyone. Still reeling from the emotional and economic shock of the revolt, stunned by the total failure of the previous year's attempt to reconquer the Pueblos, the New Mexicans could hardly keep order in El Paso and defend it from Apache raiders. Nor, in their extreme poverty, could they gather much to trade with anyone. However, Otermín politely referred the petitioners to his successor, expected soon.

In mid-October a new delegation rode to El Paso to present to Gover-

[9] Diary of Fernando del Bosque, 1675, in Herbert Eugene Bolton, ed., *Spanish Exploration in the Southwest, 1542–1706.*

nor Cruzate a far more elaborate proposal. The seven delegates included other Indians from La Junta besides Jumanos. Its Jumano leader, Juan Sabeata, claimed to speak not only for the Jumanos at La Junta and on the buffalo plains, but also for some thirty nations farther east, including the "great kingdom of the Tejas." In the name of all those people, he requested missionaries, as well as help against the Apaches who now had a *ranchería* near La Junta. It was precisely the kind of appeal that Spaniards could not deny, and Juan Sabeata knew that very well.[10]

Perhaps Juan Sabeata should be remembered as the prototype of the Texan wheeler-dealer. For a whole crucial decade he maneuvered back and forth across the broad expanse from El Paso to the Neches River, trying every conceivable tactic to retrieve the Jumanos' declining fortunes and make capital of the Spanish and French newcomers. He possessed extraordinary powers of leadership and a discomfiting sophistication in manipulating Spaniards.

Sabeata had sometime been at Parral, where he had been baptized. In 1683, he lived at La Junta with a Jumano group settled there with the Julimes, but he was in close touch with those Jumanos who lived on the plains six days beyond La Junta. He had visited El Paso with the first delegation, and apparently he had used the intervening time to consolidate a position of leadership among the Jumanos and others beyond the Rio Grande. The late summer trade fair at the western rim of the Caddo country would have given him an opportunity to expound his knowledge of the Spaniards and to propose to all tribes menaced by Apache incursions his scheme to win Spanish help.

Whatever the state of Sabeata's faith in 1683, he knew that soldiers usually accompanied missionaries, and he knew how to bait missionaries. He embellished his appeal with a wondrous tale of the appearance to the Indians in battle of a great cross in the sky, which secured for them a bloodless victory. How could missionaries not minister to a people so divinely favored? It was rather sad the next year when Sabeata had to admit that he had concocted the story to inveigle a Spanish escort for his people on the hazardous buffalo plains.

Sabeata also knew how to hook Spanish officials. To Governor Cru-

[10] Governor Cruzate's account of Juan Sabeata's declaration, as interpreted by Captain Hernando Martín Serrano, appears in Charles Wilson Hackett, ed., *Pichardo's Treatise on the Limits of Louisiana and Texas*, I, 137–139; J. Charles Kelley, "Juan Sabeata and Diffusion in Aboriginal Tribes," *American Anthropologist* 57 (1955): 981–995, analyzes the career of Sabeata in terms of cultural diffusion.

zate he emphasized the importance of the invitation to the kingdom of the Tejas, some fifteen or twenty days' journey beyond La Junta, where a powerful king ruled and where the people raised so much grain that they even fed it to horses. Better still, he said the Tejas were close neighbors of Gran Quivira, where they visited back and forth almost daily.[11] That was irresistible: the old myth of fabulous wealth in Quivira had never died, despite several discouraging experiences to the contrary. Furthermore, Sabeata quoted Tejas reports of "Spaniards" sailing to the coast in wooden houses and bartering with the Tejas. It was obvious to Cruzate that he spoke of French vessels.

The governor dispatched to the viceroy news of the glorious opportunity to win two great kingdoms for the Spanish Crown and sent an expedition to Jumano country without awaiting further instructions. Captain Juan Domínguez de Mendoza, who suddenly remembered some remarkable exploits as a member of the New Mexican expedition to the Jumanos in 1654, led the party. He was charged to foster its missionary purpose, reconnoiter the country, and make the most of any commercial possibilities.

While Mendoza assembled his force of twenty Spaniards and uncounted Indian allies, missionaries hurried downstream to La Junta to answer the Jumanos' appeal. Franciscans had long known of the La Junta populace, with whom they had made some tentative, unproductive efforts in the 1670's. Now Fray Nicolás López, custodian of the El Paso missions, and his two confreres found nine Indian groups clustered there, two with churches already built and altars made to measurements they had taken in El Paso. Each group demanded its own mission. In short order, the friars founded seven, using grass huts of Indian style for churches and priests' dwellings. The missions marked a potential sanctuary at the confluence of the Conchos and Rio Grande for Indians whose roving life styles had ceased to be viable, as well as another focus for far-riding Apache raiders.

When Mendoza followed in mid-December, he encountered many *rancherías* of Sumas en route, all pleading for help against the Apaches. Many professed an inclination to become Christians; some were already beginning to build pueblos on the Rio Grande because Apaches now barred them from their accustomed ranges north of the river.

At La Junta, Fray López and Fray Juan de Sabaleta of the Holy Office joined Mendoza for the trek to the plains, leaving Fray Antonio

[11] Actually, the Caddo and Wichitan groups lived at considerable distances from each other and were often on hostile terms.

de Acevedo behind to serve the new mission district. With Jumanos and other Indians acting as guides, escorts, and hunters, Mendoza's force left La Junta on January 1, 1684.

Juan Sabeata awaited them with other Indian leaders at a Jediondo[12] *ranchería* on the Pecos River, where he meant to negotiate a pact with the Spaniards against the Apaches. The Jediondos helped him to give the Spaniards a rousing welcome when they arrived on January 17, and they urged Mendoza to stay with them for protection against an expected Apache raid on their horse herd.

Juan Sabeata's larger purpose emerged two days later, when he led a delegation of all the chiefs to Mendoza's camp and formally asked permission to speak with the captain on their behalf. Mendoza summoned his officers and soldiers to witness, then heard the chiefs petition him, "for the love of God . . . make war on the hostile Apaches . . . enemies of theirs and of the Spaniards."[13] They were not just asking him to fight their battles for them; they wished to campaign with him. Finding their argument convincing, Mendoza agreed to make war on the Apaches, to the enormous pleasure of the chiefs. Juan Sabeata came back to the camp the next day to give the ill-equipped Spaniards seventeen deer skins to fashion into armor, and he promised more as soon as they could be cured.

Apaches did raid the horse herd of the Jediondos within a few days and scored a considerable success, despite the vigilance of the forewarned Indians and their Spanish friends. On January 24, the motley allies pursued: Mendoza, the two friars, and their ragged troop from El Paso; Juan Sabeata and assorted Indians, including perhaps all the Jediondos. Indians called Arcos Tuertos[14] soon joined them; by mid-March sixteen Indian groups were represented in Mendoza's camp, not counting the Indian allies from El Paso. They were on the move most of the time, enjoying good buffalo hunting and a nicely varied diet of small game, pecans, and fruit. The priests toiled faithfully among the Indians and sang Mass in camp at least daily. Those Indians who were already Christians dutifully assisted; the rest seemed genuinely responsive.

Though a pleasant hunting trip, it was not a plausible war cam-

[12] Apparently a band of the Jumanos.

[13] Itinerary of Juan Domínguez de Mendoza, 1684, in Bolton, *Spanish Exploration in the Southwest*, p. 331. Other documents concerning the expedition, including accounts by Fray López, appear in Hackett, *Pichardo's Treatise*, II, 328–366.

[14] Twisted Bows.

paign. In a month Mendoza guessed that Sabeata had lied about making war on the Apaches so as to lead the Spaniards on for his own purposes. Sabeata always had scouts out looking for Apaches, but they reported Apache signs just often enough to keep the Spaniards from giving up the campaign, and the alarms always proved false. When, on February 19, yet another scout announced at a choice hunting spot that the party should stop because Apaches were near, Mendoza bluntly accused Sabeata of faking and set two Piro Indians from El Paso to watch him.

After that episode, there was much more intensive buffalo hunting by both Spaniards and Indians and much less expectation of serious action against the Apaches. Perhaps that had been the main purpose of Sabeata and his friends anyway: to have a Spanish escort for safer hunting on the grounds from which Apaches sought to drive them, meanwhile making their way toward the Caddo fair. If so, the stratagem had worked nicely.

On March 16, the entire company halted for six weeks of intensive hunting, while they awaited the arrival of more than forty-eight Indian "nations," which, through their own ambassadors or others, had asked to parley with Mendoza. The men from El Paso and the sixteen Indian groups camped with them brought into the camp a total of 4,030 large buffalo and never bothered to tally calves taken. They also left countless carcasses to rot on the plains, collecting only their hides.

The camp centered about a two-room structure that Mendoza had built on a high hill, its lower room a chapel dedicated to San Clemente, its upper room a fortified lookout to safeguard all the camp and the horses.[15] The two missionaries set a strenuous pace of religious services and instruction, drawing heavily upon the assistance of Christian Indians whom they discovered among the visitors. They sang all the services of Holy Week with gratifying effect: all the Indians in the camp asked to become Christians.

The camp soon became a target of Apache raiders from the north and others from the west, those known in Nueva Vizcaya as Salineros. Mendoza consulted his officers and the friars, and they agreed to turn

[15] Bolton, in *Spanish Exploration in the Southwest*, p. 338, suggests that the campsite must have been near present Ballinger, Texas. More recently, Seymour V. Connor, in "The Mendoza-López Expedition and the Location of San Clemente," pp. 25–29, argues that they must have camped on the San Saba River, and suggests that a curious rock ruin on the river west of Menard, about six miles from Fort McKavett, is the remnant of their chapel-lookout.

back to El Paso. With so few soldiers and little ammunition, they had no chance of decisive action against the marauders. There was little to be gained by staying on to suffer attrition of their men and their prestige among the Indians.

Fortunately, messengers were on hand from most of the nations whose coming Mendoza had awaited for six weeks.[16] He sent them home with his promise that he would return to meet them the next year. The great encampment broke up, largely in friendly spirit. Most of the Indians dispersed toward their homelands. A few Indian families traveled with the Spaniards, hunting back toward the Rio Grande until vegetation and buffalo dwindled.

Fray Sabaleta rejoined Fray Acevedo at the La Junta mission cluster. Mendoza presented rods of authority to four Indian governors there, implying extension of New Mexico's civil jurisdiction as well as the authority of the Church. He and Fray López then hurried on to El Paso to report to Governor Cruzate, skirting their former route because the Sumas were up in arms.

Fray López wanted to return to the plains to found missions among the Jumanos and beyond in the Tejas "kingdom"; Mendoza wanted to establish a colony. Given the apparent eagerness of the many Indian groups for Christianity and the rich economic potential of the river valleys and the buffalo plains, such a colony seemed to both men more promising than reconquest of New Mexico. They had promised in all sincerity to return in a year; both the custodian and the captain hoped to take enough people and resources to remain there permanently.

They found Governor Cruzate and the people of El Paso totally occupied with combating the spreading Indian revolt. There were neither people nor resources to spare for any new enterprise, no matter how promising. Fray López and Captain Mendoza persisted; they

---

[16] Mendoza recorded the names of the Indian nations as follows: "First, the Jumana nation; the Ororosos, the Beitonijures, the Achubales, the Cujalos, the Toremes, the Gediondos, the Siacuchas, the Suajos, the Isuchos, the Cujacos, the Caulas, the Hinehis, the Ylames, the Cunquebacos, the Quitacas, the Quicuchabes, Los que asen Arcos, the Hansines. These nations are those who are accompanying us. Those for whom we are waiting are the following: People of the Rio de los Tejas, who had sent me a message that they would come, the Huicasique, the Aielis, the Aguidas, the Flechas Chiquitas, the Echancotes, the Anchimos, the Bobidas, the Injames, the Dijus, the Colabrotes, the Unojitas, the Juanas, the Yoyehis, the Acanis, the Humez, the Bibis, the Conchumuchas, the Teandas, the Hinsas, the Pojues, the Quisabas, the Paiabunas, the Papanes, the Puchas, the Puguahianes, the Isconis, the Tojumas, the Pagaiames, the Deto-Abas, the Bajuneros, the Nobraches, the Pylchas, the Detobitas, the Puchames, the Abau, the Oranchos" (*Mendoza Itinerary*, pp. 339–340, in Bolton, *Spanish Exploration in the Southwest*).

spent much of 1685 and 1686 in Mexico City petitioning higher authorities,[17] each strongly supporting the other as best candidate for governor or head missionary. Here, they urged, was a unique opportunity to form a great barrier against the Apache onslaught: seventy-five friendly Indian nations would help them to secure the region with only two hundred Spaniards. Without prompt Spanish action, the Apaches would surely sweep those friendly nations off the buffalo plains, then hurl their full strength against the Spanish frontier. Surviving Indians east of the Apache range would surely fall under the influence of French traders already intruding among the Tejas. The captain and the custodian argued that all New Spain lay at stake.

Their proposal was carefully heard at the capital. It might have won approval in a less crisis-ridden time, but not in 1686. With revolt raging across the northern frontier, from Sonora to Coahuila, it was impossible to find a base for expansion, much less spare men and money to support it. Even worse, the French menace suddenly loomed larger than ever before in New Spain, with the news in 1685 of La Salle's colony on Matagorda Bay. Intensive searches began in 1686; in the next four years four expeditions by sea and five by land sought the French colony. Coahuila was the base for those land operations and thus for Spain's penetration of the "kingdom of the Tejas." The possible relevance of the Jumano project to the French problem faded from official view. López and Mendoza returned to El Paso completely disappointed.

The spring of 1685 must also have disappointed the Indian peoples to whom the captain and the custodian had promised permanent help. Not only did their expected allies fail to return, but the revolt raging along the Spanish frontier meant they could find no haven southward throughout 1685 and 1686. La Junta fell into turmoil, with most of its populace involved in revolt. The few Christian Indians of those missions stood loyal to both Majesties and escorted their two priests and their sacred articles to safety in Parral just in time to forestall their destruction. The missionaries resumed work at La Junta at the first lull in the insurrection, but communications with the beleaguered Indians of the southern plains were disrupted for two crucial years.

[17] Memorial of Juan Domínguez de Mendoza, Mexico, November 18, 1685, in Charles Wilson Hackett, ed., *Historical Documents Relating to New Mexico, Nueva Vizcaya, and Approaches Thereto, to 1773*, II, 354; Fray Nicolás López to the Señor Secretario Don Antonio Ortiz de Otalua, Mexico, April 24, 1686, ibid., pp. 359–360; April 25, 1686, ibid., pp. 363–364.

Meanwhile, Juan Sabeata continued to organize resistance to the Apaches and to carry on the traditional Jumano trading enterprises as best he could. He chanced to be with a Jumano delegation among the Caddos in the late spring of 1686 when La Salle visited the Hainai village with a party of ten men. The Frenchmen, seeking a way from their misplaced colony on Matagorda Bay to their proper destination on the Mississippi, were delighted to find that they could buy horses from the Caddos. They were also intensely interested to find the Caddos well informed about the Spaniards, although not in direct contact with their settlements, and to learn that they reckoned the Spanish frontier only six days distant. In addition to considerable numbers of horses, many with Spanish brands, the Caddos had divers Spanish articles: money, silver spoons, all kinds of laces and clothing, even a bull from Rome exempting Spaniards of New Spain from fasting during the summer.[18]

La Salle's party understood from the Caddos that their contact with the Spaniards was through their Jumano allies, who were always at war with New Spain and who had sometimes been joined by Caddo warriors in their wars on New Mexico. While not consistent with the history of Jumano relations with the Spaniards, the story perhaps reflected their bitter disappointment after the Mendoza-López visit. The Jumano delegation visited the French guests of the Hainais, displayed impressive knowledge of Roman Catholic customs, then invited the Frenchmen to join them in war against the Spaniards or at least to give the Jumanos some guns for that purpose. Whether Juan Sabeata seriously intended war against the Spaniards is doubtful. Perhaps he meant only to use the Frenchmen as he had used Mendoza two years before, as his escort for safe travel and hunting across the Apache-ridden southern plains.

Whatever Sabeata's purpose, La Salle declined. He needed to reach his own compatriots on the Mississippi, not to stir up gratuitous trouble with Spaniards. La Salle led his men farther eastward into the Caddo country on the unsuccessful errand from which they returned, downhearted, to their colony in the fall. Juan Sabeata and his Jumanos resumed their regular business, insofar as Apache raiders and insurrection on the Spanish frontier permitted. Sometime the next winter they turned up at the revived missions of La Junta. In the spring of 1687

---

[18] The account of Fray Anastasius Douay, a member of La Salle's party, appears in Swanton, *Source Material on the History and Ethnology of the Caddo Indians*, pp. 38–40.

they asked Fray Agustín de Colina for a letter to take to the foreigners whom they expected to see on their annual visit to the Tejas trade fair. The missionary warily put them off, suggesting instead that they bring him a letter from the strangers, which he would gladly answer. The Jumanos agreed and set off on their annual travels.

Fray Colina heard no more until September 1688, when Cíbolos visiting La Junta mentioned strangers who traded axes to the Tejas for horses and slept in wooden houses on the water. They told of one foreigner who had deserted the rest to live with a nation near the Tejas. His hosts found him an asset in war with his armor and his harquebus. He had helped them to destroy half of a nation called Michi.

Fray Colina had too many urgent problems at La Junta to worry unduly about strangers in the distance. The Indians of his area were under such constant pressure to defect from the missions and join the rebellious Indians that conversion was gravely impeded. That fall the Sumas grew so turbulent that the Franciscan superior at El Paso ordered the missionaries to withdraw from La Junta for safety. With a company of loyal Indians and his assistant, Fray Colina regretfully moved down to Mission San Pedro de Conchos in Nueva Vizcaya, making no secret of his conviction that the fault lay more with Spaniards than with Indians. He had seen too many Indians taken from La Junta to work in the mines of Parral and the haciendas, under conditions forbidden by the Crown, and had known too many kept waiting interminably for their just pay. Those abuses seemed to him greater impediments to conversion than any passing rebellion. He petitioned for their correction.

Nueva Vizcayan officials ignored those concerns of Fray Colina, but they sprang into action when the two priests and the Indians from La Junta mentioned the rumors of strangers and interrogated them under oath. The energetic new governor, Juan Isidro de Pardiñas, ordered the presidial commander at San Francisco de Conchos, General Juan de Retana, to hurry to La Junta with a very large force and asked the missionaries to return with them. He ordered Retana to consolidate Indian loyalties to Spain throughout that area and to find and arrest the intruders.

Julimes Governor Don Nicolás rode to the Conchos presidio to inform Retana that Cíbolos were reported en route to La Junta with letters from the foreigners and with one of the strangers who had fled the rest. The strangers were said to have visited the Tejas again, trading axes and clothing for horses, and to have gone away again.

Retana sent Indian runners to La Junta with his promises to those people: he would bring back their priests; then, with his big army he would campaign throughout the region to punish the enemies who were killing and robbing them. Henceforth, they would enjoy the protections due vassals of the king of Spain.

Retana did not proceed directly to La Junta after all. His scouts spotted a camp of three rebel bands up in the hills, and Retana decided that he must attack because they had been wreaking havoc in Nueva Vizcaya. He was successful, killing many and routing the rest, recovering many horses whose brands would make it possible to return them to their owners. Unfortunately, the delay cost him the opportunity to talk with the principal leader of the Jumanos and Cíbolos.

Juan Sabeata was pleased to receive Retana's message when he turned up at La Junta late in the fall, an invitation to wait for Retana and then, with many bowmen, help the general seek the foreigners who had come to deceive the Indians. However, after many days' wait, he heard that Retana had gone to fight the rebel Tobosos. Juan Sabeata then decided to go downstream to check on rumors of foreigners who had brought gifts to several Indian camps, asked many questions, and disparaged the Spaniards. Traveling down the Rio Grande, he collected reports of several visits by strangers in canoes, acquired a few traveling companions who had experienced those visits, and then journeyed on to the Caddo trade fairs. There he learned that coastal Indians had destroyed the French settlement and that they intended to repeat the deed for all who should come in wooden houses on the water thenceforth. There survived only a few Frenchmen who had been trading at the Tejas villages at the time of the massacre.

Since the friar at La Junta had told him that the foreigners were bad men coming to deceive the Indians, Sabeata assiduously collected every possible scrap of information, visiting many *rancherías* for the purpose. At the Tejas villages he talked with four or five Frenchmen who asked permission to go with him when they learned that Sabeata lived among Christian Spaniards. They traveled with his party three days, then turned back in fear of hostile Indians along the way, asking Sabeata to report them to the Spaniards so that a rescue party might come for them. Sabeata agreed and set off for La Junta with his evidence: two sheets torn from French books and a painting of a frigate upon a parchment, all carefully wrapped in a wide lace neck-cloth.

Meanwhile, General Retana reached La Junta in mid-winter to find an alarming story current among the Indians: Frenchmen had prom-ised the *rancherías* downstream that they would soon return with wagons, which they would drive clear to Parral. Determined to head off any such incursion, he sent Indian scouts from La Junta to recon-noiter a route to the French camp. They returned sooner than he had expected to report that Juan Sabeata was already en route to La Junta from the Tejas with letters and a full report of the strangers. Unable to contain his impatience, Retana rode from La Junta to meet him, quite prepared to continue to the coast if the news should warrant the journey. Four days later, early in March 1689, General Retana met Chief Juan Sabeata on the Pecos River.

Delighted to see so many Spaniards in his country, Sabeata hospitably inquired about Retana's purpose. He reported the French colony destroyed and said he would carry the papers and the lace to Governor Pardiñas. It was his opportunity to meet the Spanish governor, of whom he had favorable reports, and he would not spoil it by surrender-ing his evidence to a subordinate officer. Retana sent runners to Par-diñas for further instructions. Pardiñas ordered Retana to expedite with every courtesy Juan Sabeata's journey to Parral with his leading asso-ciates, furnishing them provisions and horses at government expense. Since Parral had no interpreter competent in the Jumanos' tongue, Pardiñas also requested that Julimes Governor Don Nicolás accom-pany them, with one other person competent to interpret for them.

Toward dusk on April 10, 1689, Don Juan Sabeata, governor of the Cíbolo and Jumano nations, rode into Parral as an honored guest of the governor of Nueva Vizcaya.[19] With him rode Miguel, said to be chief of those Jumanos and Cíbolos who lived on the Rio Grande, and other leaders from unidentified *rancherías* farther downstream. The visitors paid their compliments to Governor Pardiñas, briefly reported the de-struction of the Frenchmen, and handed over the papers and lace that Juan Sabeata had so carefully preserved as evidence. Governor Par-diñas embraced and thanked them, then gave instructions for their lodgings and refreshments, and asked them to return for formal in-quiries the next day. That conversation and subsequent formal pro-ceedings were marked by good will and by a wide margin for misun-

[19] The *autos* covering the Jumano reports at La Junta and Parral, 1688–1692, appear in Hackett, *Historical Documents*, II, 233–289.

derstanding. Julimes Governor Don Nicolás, who spoke little or no Spanish, interpreted the Jumanos' speech into a Mexican Indian language that an official Spanish interpreter translated into Castilian.

Despite those difficulties, Juan Sabeata's testimony convinced Governor Pardiñas of more than the destruction of the French colony by the Indians. The zeal with which Sabeata had collected information for the Spaniards and his eagerness to cooperate with them left no doubt that the chief was a valuable ally whose good will should be cultivated. His companions' testimony gave a sobering glimpse of the ease with which intruders could penetrate remote *rancherías*. They were astonished to hear that their visitors had been bad men, coming only to deceive them and to turn them against their Spanish friends. After all, the strangers had been the same color as Spaniards, they had carried rosaries, and they had spoken of God, just as did the mission fathers. The only notable oddity had been their steel doublets. They had been delightful guests, had run and danced with the Indians, had brought them nice presents, and, most unusual of all, had taken nothing away from their Indian hosts.

Pardiñas resolved to spare no effort to consolidate the loyalties of the Indians north of the Rio Grande and to encourage them to report promptly to La Junta or Parral any news from their region. There seemed little urgency concerning the five French survivors in the Tejas village. Sabeata's associates advised against setting out for the Tejas country before early summer because spring floods on the major streams made the coastal plain a vast, impassable swamp. On April 12, the grateful Governor Pardiñas presented gifts to Juan Sabeata and his company, providing supplies for their journey and handsome new uniforms for each chief from the provincial budget for war and peace. He asked Sabeata to convey new orders to Retana at his camp on the Pecos, recalling the general to home base, and then to continue his praiseworthy service to their mutual sovereign. Sabeata gladly agreed. He enjoyed the important role of roving envoy on the plains, and he had his own uses for Spanish forces.

Just ten days after Juan Sabeata left Parral, Spaniards finally discovered the ruined French fort on Matagorda Bay. Alonso de León, leading his fourth expedition from Coahuila for that purpose, reached the macabre scene on April 22, 1689. In his company traveled Fray Damian Massanet, attracted to the region by Benavides' report of the miraculous work of Mother María de Jesús de Agreda among the Tejas. As the priest and the officer investigated the region, they picked up a few survivors of the French colony and met a Tejas chief and eight of his compatriots.[20] The chief's dignity and intelligence impressed Massanet, as did all reports of the Tejas country. He urged the chief to receive priests to instruct his people in Christianity. The chief indicated that he would gladly welcome Massanet in his land. The missionary promised to return with more priests in the planting season next year.

Back home by mid-summer, both Massanet and de León filed glowing recommendations of the Tejas project. The viceroy, still mindful of the French shadow, personally pledged utmost support for the venture. With the concurrence of the Junta, the viceroy ordered de León to proceed to the Tejas with 110 soldiers, 150 loads of flour, 200 cows, 400 horses, 50 long firelocks, and a generous supply of powder and shot. His duty would be to escort Fray Massanet and three priests of his choice, to penetrate the Tejas country cautiously, and to leave the priests there only if the Tejas ruler should freely consent. Fray Massanet asked only for some wine, wafer boxes, and wax, but, when it was time to assemble the expedition after Christmas, the viceroy sent him twenty mules laden with wine, wax, and clothing and tobacco to give to the Indians.

That spring, while Spaniards prepared to expand their mission frontier to the Tejas, the Caddo world received a new French visitor, far more impressive than La Salle's luckless colonists. Henry de Tonti, commander of the French establishments in the Illinois country, sought survivors of La Salle's debacle. For that he came too late, but he rendered important services to the eastern Caddos and promised more.

Arkansas Indians at the mouth of the Arkansas gave Tonti two Kadohadacho women, apparently captives rescued from the Osages, to escort back to their homeland. That fortunate commission guaranteed him a grateful welcome. More luck awaited him at the Taensa village, where the leaders begged him to arbitrate their quarrel with the Natchitoches over some valuable salt deposits. He took thirty Taensa delegates to the Natchitoches villages, where he mediated a peaceful settlement much appreciated by both peoples. Tonti also mediated an end to a war between the Yatasís and the Kadohadachos, to the joy of all concerned.

The Kadohadachos, still mourning heavy losses suffered in a recent Osage raid upon their settlements, clamored for Tonti's help to avenge their slain kinsmen. To calm them, he agreed in principle, although

[20] Accounts by Fray Massanet and Captain de León appear in Bolton, *Spanish Exploration in the Southwest*, pp. 347–423.

he had with him neither men nor equipment to campaign at that time. Leaving the Kadohadachos assured of his good intentions, he pressed on to the Hasinai, or Tejas, country to seek seven Frenchmen reported living with the Nabedaches.

That visit proved unfortunate. No Frenchmen were visible among the Nabedaches. When Tonti asked about them, the women began to wail, while the chief gave a jumbled account of some slain by hostile Indians and others gone with a hunting party. Perhaps the lack of competent interpreters and the limitations of sign language created confusion. Tonti concluded that the Nabedaches had actually killed the Frenchmen. He bluntly accused his hosts, and their women wailed all the louder. To emphasize his displeasure, Tonti refused to smoke the calumet with them. When he demanded that they furnish him horses and guides to take him to the site of La Salle's fort, they supplied four horses readily enough but balked at giving him guides. Since his party was not strong enough to force the issue, Tonti turned back to the Kadohadacho settlements. After a week's rest, he started homeward to the Illinois on May 17, 1690, promising the Kadohadachos he would return.

Perhaps Tonti left hope among the Kadohadachos; surely he left dread among the Tejas, for refusal to smoke the calumet was a very ominous gesture. The alarm and dismay that Tonti stirred in the Nabedaches' village probably ensured the phenomenally cordial reception of the Spaniards who arrived later that month to found missions for the Tejas.

De León and Massanet left Monclova in March 1690 for an uneventful journey over the previous year's route. They burned the remains of La Salle's fort, then sought the Tejas, whose lands they had never seen. They soon chanced upon the hunting camp of a Tejas family, who notified the Tejas leaders of their approach. The chief of the Nabedaches and fourteen leading men greeted them on the Trinity River in mid-May 1690. After a cordial parley, the Spaniards outfitted the chief with a suit of Spanish clothing so that he would wear that mark of their esteem as they entered his village the next day.

The formal entry to the Nabedache village seemed a happy occasion, despite some unfortunate breaches of hospitality by the soldiery. The priests led all the Spaniards in solemn procession to the chief's house, displaying cross and banner and singing a litany. The chief invited them to live as guests in his imposing lodge, but he took no offense when the priests explained that they must build a church and dwell beside it. He gave them free choice of building sites. When the friars selected a beautiful wooded spot beside a brook in the midst of the settlement, the Indians diligently set to work on the church and the priests' dwelling. Only a week after their arrival, the priests dedicated the finished church of San Francisco de los Tejas before a great crowd of Indians.

Meanwhile, de León attended his secular offices, raising the Spanish flag in the settlement, accepting the assembled residents' pledge of obedience to the king, and promising them in turn the king's aid and friendship. Thenceforth the Tejas bore the name of vassals of the king of Spain. Only time could tell what it would mean to them.

It seemed at first an ideal mission field, because the Tejas were amiable and conspicuously intelligent. Since they lived in a well-ordered society and acknowledged a supreme, if not a sole, deity, the priests were confident that they would grasp the principles of Christianity as soon as the language barrier could be surmounted. Furthermore, their active trade brought many other Indians from a vast area to their villages, making the Tejas missions bases for conversion of untold numbers of far-flung nations. Again, language seemed the only barrier. The priests strove to master the Caddo language as rapidly as possible.

To Fray Massanet's dismay, de León proposed to leave fifty soldiers behind to guard the new mission. The Tejas had been so friendly that the priests felt no need of protection, and some of the soldiers' offenses against the Indians outraged the priests. Fray Massanet balked. The Nabedache chief backed him, indicating that he did not wish to entertain so many men for so long in his village. De León reluctantly agreed to leave just three soldiers to guard the mission, with nine horses and some guns and ammunition.

Early in June, Fray Massanet headed back to Monclova with de León, leaving behind three priests and a lay brother. He meant to return the next spring with reinforcements to found missions throughout the Caddo village world. Meanwhile, the missionaries were to develop a mission program and a livelihood. They had for capital twenty cows, two yokes of oxen, ploughs, axes, and spades, and such miscellaneous necessities as chocolate and sugar. Their duty was to fit into the agricultural life of the village and, where feasible, to foster improvements. Above all, they must learn to speak Caddo.

Zealous Fray Francisco Casañas de Jesús María quickly expanded their task, founding a new mission five miles away on the Neches River: Santísimo Nombre de María, intended to serve the Hainai settlement. His vigorous, often aggressive, approach to the delicate task of conversion soon strained the Indians' hospitality. His direct challenges to established religious leaders and medicine men earned powerful enemies.

That was the very blunder that the Nabedaches and Fray Massanet had deliberately avoided. When the first mission was founded, the chief took particular care to send people to pay ritual tribute to the *Grand Xinesi,* lest the attentions to the missionaries offend him. The chief's emissaries brought the *Grand Xinesi* to the mission as an honored visitor. With the chief's pleased permission, Massanet sat beside the *Grand Xinesi* at the dedication feast and gave him the finest possible presents of clothing for himself and his wife. Both the Nabedache chief and Fray Massanet realized that the mission could not flourish if the *Grand Xinesi* should resent it.

Fray Casañas, neither perceptive nor discreet, soon outraged custom. He barged into the *Grand Xinesi's* temple improperly dressed, ridiculed his most sacred fetish, and threatened to toss it into the sacred fire. He also challenged the medicine men, hurled exorcisms to counter their curing magic, and found himself credited with the death when one target of his exorcisms died within a day. Fray Casañas was complacently amused that the medicine men feared him after that and gave him a wide berth, but the episode hardly endeared him to the Tejas.

That proved an unfortunate time to challenge Caddo medical beliefs. The first smallpox epidemic swept the settlements in the winter of 1690–1691, leaving the Indians terrified and bewildered. More than three hundred persons died in the mission area, including Fray Fontcuberta and a soldier; deaths in the entire Caddo world numbered perhaps three thousand.

Native religious leaders and medicine men suggested that the priests caused the sickness, perhaps with the holy water of baptism, perhaps through the outrageous behavior of Fray Casañas. When a delegation of leading men confronted him with the charge, Casañas chuckled at their notion that illness was the work of evil spirits; he serenely explained that the smallpox epidemic and other such phenomena were actually pestilences willed by God. Their great astonishment amused him more, but, when they asked him to clarify his meaning, he patiently repeated, as carefully and as simply as he could, that God's will caused the epidemic. The leaders rushed off to tell everybody in all the villages. Attitudes toward Fray Casañas, which had been cooling for months, became very icy indeed, and the reaction also affected his unlucky colleagues.[21]

Cultural tensions and smallpox were not the missionaries' only worries in that lonely first year. In the summer of 1690 they heard of a French establishment somewhere north of the Kadohadachos, whose personnel would visit the mission before February. What if they meant to avenge La Salle's colony? Three soldiers could hardly fend off an attack, and there was no time to fetch help from Coahuila. Thus, it seemed to Fray Fontcuberta truly a blessing when, at summer's end, Juan Sabeata turned up at Mission San Francisco de los Tejas.

Sabeata had heard of the friars when he came to the summer trade fairs, and, true to his charge from Governor Pardiñas, came to investigate a possible new intrusion. Communication was difficult. The priests had scant knowledge of Caddo, and Sabeata had little or none; signs were the principal bridge between his Jumano and their Castilian speech.

The Jumano chief conveyed that he was a Christian, had lived with Spaniards, and would return to a place where Spanish priests lived. Unaware of La Junta mission, the priests assumed that he came from El Paso and were immeasurably relieved when they understood him to say that he lived only five days away from their mission. Help seemed very near after all. When Sabeata offered to carry a letter to the missionaries at his home, Fray Fontcuberta gratefully addressed a letter to the custodian of New Mexico at El Paso, requesting troops to defend the mission against possible French attack.[22]

Perhaps Fray Fontcuberta still expected troops from El Paso when he died the next February, but his letter never reached El Paso. Indeed, it was only by chance that Juan Sabeata delivered it nearly two years later at Parral. He had no idea of its urgent content, and he was satisfied that these were bona fide Spanish missionaries. Thus, he felt no need to hurry back to Governor Pardiñas with the report and spent the next ten months pursuing his own affairs among various nations. Apparently he had occasion that spring to call at the mission again. In the summer of 1691 he was carrying two more letters from the missionaries, detailing troubles at San Francisco de los Tejas and reporting

---

[21] Letter and report of Fray Francisco Casañas de Jesús María to the Viceroy of Mexico, Santísimo Nombre de María, August 15, 1691, in Swanton, *Source Material on the History and Ethnology of the Caddo Indians*, pp. 241–263.

[22] Fray Miguel Fontcuberta to the Custodian, San Francisco de los Techas, September 4, 1690, in Hackett, *Historical Documents*, II, 284.

the death of Fray Fontcuberta. He turned those two letters over to Governor Domingo Terán, who happened in mid-June upon the Guadalupe River camp where Juan Sabeata had gathered about him some two thousand Jumanos and allies.

Governor Terán, of Coahuila, was escorting Fray Massanet back to the Tejas country to establish seven more missions with twenty-one more missionaries. Upon reading Sabeata's letters, the missionaries rushed ahead to help their colleagues, while Terán followed more slowly with the main force and the livestock herds. The new priests apparently adapted satisfactorily to Caddo customs, for a Tejas *caddi* welcomed Terán quite cordially when he arrived on August 4. The governor repeated the ceremony of the king's formal possession, then distributed presents lavishly among the new vassals of the Crown.

In the three weeks that Terán's force camped among the Tejas, the Indians grew openly resentful of the Spaniards. The most worrisome manifestations were increasing attacks upon cattle and horses. The Spaniards apparently made no effort to pen their livestock or to herd them at a reasonable distance from the Indian settlements. Probably the numerous horses and cows, trampling and grazing across ripening crops, annoyed the Indians even more than the various abuses by the soldiers or the indiscretions of over-zealous friars.

Late in August, Terán led most of his men down to Matagorda Bay to pick up supplies shipped from Veracruz. In addition to supplies for the missions, Terán received new orders requiring him to explore the rest of the Caddo country before returning to Coahuila.

Back at the Tejas settlements, Terán found tensions worsening. Attacks upon the livestock were greater than ever. The once cordial *caddi*, absent with a war party, had bluntly warned the missionaries to leave his country before his return. Some of the friars were discouraged enough to give up, but Terán's new instructions ruled out immediate departure for Coahuila.

The governor surveyed the surrounding country as quickly as possible, then pushed on to Kadohadacho territory with thirty men, including Fray Massanet and other missionaries. They reached the Kadohadacho towns at the end of November in sleet and snow and were kindly welcomed. The original plan had been to establish four missions among the Kadohadachos, but simply shortages made that impossible. The missionaries could only cultivate friendly relations with the Indians, whose character and attitude they liked, and promise to return later to give them missions. Terán explored the countryside for a week and took soundings of Red River. The return trip to the Tejas missions consumed three hard weeks, during which storms cost the party nearly all their horses.

Early in January, Terán started homeward, taking for his party's subsistence much of the livestock and other provisions earmarked for the new missions. Most of the missionaries went, too. Only Fray Massanet and two other friars remained, with nine soldiers.

Ahead of them lay a grim two-year ordeal. Floods ruined their crops; an epidemic killed most of their cattle and some of the Indians. The winter of 1692–1693 found the missionaries and their soldier escorts without provisions, amid increasingly restive Indians. Floods that spring destroyed Mission Santísimo Nombre de María. The three priests and the soldiers huddled at San Francisco de los Tejas, meaning to leave as soon as the streams should subside enough to make travel possible.

A supply train arrived from Monclova on June 8, 1693, just in time to forestall their departure. The ninety-seven pack loads of provisions and gifts for the Indians would make it possible to hang on a little longer, but Fray Massanet had concluded that the Tejas were not really ready for conversion because they stubbornly clung to belief in their own supreme deity. That they were willing to concede the existence of another great God who had given the Spaniards many fine things in no way appeased him. Their unshakable loyalty to old Caddo beliefs, combined with their repeated threats to kill all the Spaniards, led the head missionary to recommend abandonment of the field, unless the viceroy would establish there a large garrison of soldiers.

Before permission to quit could arrive from Mexico City, with an armed escort to take the missionaries to safety, the Tejas took matters into their own hands. In October 1693, the *caddi* warned the Spaniards to get out immediately unless they wished to die and convinced them that he meant it. They buried the sacred objects, packed up their meager gear, set fire to the mission, and left on October 25.

A menacing horde of Indians shadowed their retreat for several days but never attacked. Four soldiers deserted the group to stay with the Indians. Joseph de Urrutia spent seven swashbuckling years leading sundry Indian warriors against the Apaches before he returned to the Spanish frontier to make a career as an expert on Indian affairs.

The rest of the fugitives wandered for four months, lost much of the time, nearly starving; they reached Monclova on February 17, 1694. One survivor, Fray Francisco Hidalgo, had opposed the departure. From the moment he reached the Spanish frontier, he was determined to return to the Tejas. Fray Hidalgo's resolution would prevail in time, but for the next dozen years the Caddos were rid of the Spanish presence.

More than distance separated Caddo country from the Spanish frontier in that time. Those were climactic years in the Indian struggles for control of the lands from the Rio Grande to the Brazos. Apache aggressions from north and west threatened to close the southern buffalo plains to all the nations that had hunted there from time immemorial, and to some extent they rallied together to combat the common foe. It was that resistance which Juan Sabeata worked so hard to organize from his bases at La Junta and on the upper Colorado and which Joseph de Urrutia helped to lead during his sojourn among Tonkawas and Xaranames in the 1690's.

Caddos and Spaniards were peripherally involved in those struggles. Caddo warriors took a limited part in the wars to control the buffalo hunting grounds, for they were less dependent upon the buffalo than the rest and thus had less immediately at stake. Spaniards felt the repercussions when fugitives from the struggle fell back upon the Spanish frontier, sometimes to seek sanctuary at the missions, sometimes to raid or to fight for new living space. Especially the Spaniards felt the tragedy of the Coahuiltecans: growing Apache pressures on their territories intensified their complex internecine wars, and the question of their relations with the Spaniards became another bloodily divisive issue. As fugitives and as marauders, Coahuiltecans shaped the history of the Coahuila mission frontier in the last decade of the seventeenth century and the first decade of the eighteenth. The friars could only guess at the complexities of the struggles beyond the Rio Grande and grasp occasional rumors of the Tejas that floated across the vast battle arena.

Increasing turmoils so beset the Jumanos and Cíbolos that in midsummer 1692 Juan Sabeata rode to the Julime pueblo on the Conchos to seek help. Warriors of several nations, principally Satapayogliglas and Sisimbles, had killed some of Sabeata's people because they refused to join in a war against the Spaniards. Juan Sabeata had been called home from his travels among the eastern nations to lead a vengeance campaign, and the war was still in progress. He hoped to persuade the governor of the Julimes to bring four or five hundred warriors from his own pueblo and La Junta to help the Jumanos.

Since his business brought him to the vicinity of Parral, Sabeata took the occasion to deliver to Governor Pardiñas the letter that Fray Fontcuberta had entrusted to him nearly two years before. He patiently weathered a long formal interrogation about events in the interior, then accepted gifts of clothing and other articles with the governor's formal praise and thanks. Though distressed that the friars' urgent appeal had been delayed for two years, Governor Pardiñas found it neither fair nor expedient to blame Juan Sabeata. He only asked the chief to continue to act with his usual zeal and care and to bring quickly any news that he should hear in future.[23] The two leaders parted cordially.

Perhaps that was the last year of Juan Sabeata's remarkable career; certainly it was his last official visit to the Spanish frontier. Whether the hazards of war or epidemic or simply of age finally overtook him is unknown. When General Retana went to La Junta the next year to lead campaigns against the hostile Indians, it was Chief Nicolás of the Julimes who led the Cíbolos of La Junta.

On the battlegrounds of the southern buffalo plains, Jumano warriors joined others who fought the Apaches under the leadership of Joseph de Urrutia. That Spanish deserter probably appeared at just the right time to replace Sabeata as the coalition's war leader.

That was the Jumanos' last stand against the agressors from the north. Sometime between 1700 and 1718 the Jumanos of the plains gave up the struggle against the Apaches and threw in their lot with their former enemies so completely that they came to be known in some quarters as Jumano Apaches. Men like Urrutia, who had known the depth of Jumano hatred for the Apaches, were astounded to learn of their rapprochement.

Fray Hidalgo never ceased to work toward restoration of the Tejas missions, but there was no practicable hope of another Spanish thrust across that dangerous arena of Indian wars. Meanwhile, the Franciscans rallied to succor the beleaguered Coahuiltecans with new mission settlements. Fray Antonio Margil de Jesús took the lead, sending Fray Hidalgo north to begin the new work in 1698. Insurrections, flights of neophytes, and chronic thefts of livestock disrupted their first efforts. The friars blamed the influence of Indians in the turbulent interior and boldly moved, unauthorized, north to the Rio Grande in 1700. Captain Diego Ramón, a veteran officer on that frontier, escorted them. The missionaries found that they could not remain on that advanced frontier without permanent protection. By 1703, a presidio, San Juan

23 *Auto* of Pardiñas Interrogation of Juan Xaviata, Parral, July 7, 1692, ibid., pp. 285–289.

Bautista, evolved from the flying company established to protect the Rio Grande missions; Captain Ramón became commander of the presidio.[24]

Quite outside any intentions of the government, a cluster grew at a strategic point on the Rio Grande: Presidio San Juan Bautista, its small supporting settlement, two missions, and Indian settlements at each mission. It proved such a useful listening post that the viceroy accepted the *faits accomplis*. Father Hidalgo and his confreres took care to supply the viceroy with rumors of French activities in the Tejas country and for another decade prayed and planned to return to their forsaken mission.

[24] The founding of San Juan Bautista and its supporting role in the founding of Spanish Texas are detailed in Robert S. Weddle, *San Juan Bautista.*

CHAPTER 5

Louisiana and Texas, 1700-1721

After a hiatus of more than a decade, a curious convergence of Spanish evangelism and French mercantilism revived the momentum of change in the Caddo world. French explorers visited Caddo villages within a year after founding the colony of Louisiana in 1699, but it took a nudge from Fray Hidalgo to prompt a permanent French establishment a dozen years later.

Louisiana's founder, Pierre Le Moyne d'Iberville, planned from the beginning to make the Indian trade in skins a major facet of Louisiana's economy. He meant to traffic in buffalo hides as well as beaver pelts, and for that purpose built special flatboats to float the heavy bales of hides down the Mississippi for transshipment to France. From its very first year, 1699, Biloxi had a good trade in hides from the upper Mississippi.[1]

---

[1] The standard work on Louisiana's development is N. M. Miller Surrey, *The Commerce of Louisiana during the French Régime, 1699–1763*. The complex missionary matter is treated in Jean Delanglez, *The French Jesuits in Lower Louisiana (1700–1763)*. A useful summary and analysis of Louisiana development appear in John W. Caughey, *Bernardo de Gálvez in Louisiana, 1776–1783*.

Iberville hoped eventually to establish trade with the mining areas of northern New Spain, but his most urgent priority lay far upstream. He needed to establish traders among the Sioux tribes at once, both to forestall British competitors moving south from Hudson's Bay and to preempt the mineral resources known to exist on the northern reaches of the Mississippi system. In the fall of 1700, one party of his men built a fort on the Blue Earth River, where they wintered, hunting, trading, and prospecting for minerals.

Iberville expected to gather scattered Indian nations at strategic points, both to bar British expansion and to develop trade. His Canadian experience had taught him the importance of dealing with the Indians in their own languages. Since Jesuits had proved extraordinarily proficient in Indian languages and diplomacy, Iberville asked that Jesuit missionaries be assigned to his colony. Unfortunately, a jurisdictional wrangle broke out between the Jesuits and the Priests of the Foreign Missions early in the 1700's, so bitter as to stunt religious development of the colony. The Jesuits would found missions only if granted exclusive jurisdiction in a separate district. Since they failed to win that point, only a few transient Jesuits passed through lower Louisiana in its crucial early years, and no effective substitute ever materialized. Neither the Crown nor the successive concessionaires to whom it granted the colony ever made any significant provision for support of missionaries. Thus, the experience of Louisiana Indians was almost solely with laymen of France and of New France. There could have been no greater contrast to the powerful missionary component of neighboring Spanish frontiers.

Nor had Louisiana any substantial counterpart of the Spanish presidial system. Iberville had projected a chain of forts, adequately garrisoned, to stabilize his clusters of Indian population and hold the line against British expansion. However, the colony was hardly founded before France plunged into the long War of the Spanish Succession. Given that serious drain on its manpower and materials, the French government allowed Iberville few forts and troops for Louisiana and gave him in lieu some pious generalities about preferring missionaries to control Indians. Since the government never financed a viable missionary program either, Louisiana's early development devolved upon a motley assembly of soldiers, experienced traders, and adventurous novices, who never numbered much more than two hundred.

Iberville, and after him his brother, Jean Baptiste Le Moyne de Bienville, made the most of those few men, deploying them widely to learn with all possible speed the nature of the country and the people. Because youngsters most readily learned new languages and because Indians were particularly kind and protective toward children, Iberville used the half-dozen young cabin boys who had sailed on his vessels from France, placing each in a key Indian village to live in the home of a leading man and learn the language and customs of the people. Some were apt enough to master one language quickly, then be moved to another village, then another. Meanwhile, men of the colony improved their own competence with Indians. Autumn after autumn, when the colony faced a winter of deprivation because expected supplies failed to arrive from France, as many as fifty men dispersed into the wilderness for the winter. They fended for themselves, hunting and living in the homes of friendly Indians. In spring they returned to base with their winter's haul of pelts, welcome supplies of meat for the colonists, and valuable new knowledge of Indian lives and languages. Many established friendships among the Indians, while the Indians learned much about French frontiersmen.[2]

Caddos first saw the Louisiana company in 1700, when Bienville led a reconnaissance group up the Red River as far as the Natchitoches settlements. His party included the exceptionally able young officer, Louis Juchereau de St. Denis, whose destiny was to be closely linked with the Caddos for more than forty years. The Natchitoches mentioned Spaniards among the Kadohadachos, so St. Denis soon returned with twenty-five men, assigned to observe any Spanish activities and, if possible, to learn the route to the mines of Mexico. He persuaded a Natchitoches leader to guide him to the Kadohadachos, only to learn that no Spaniard had been seen in that area for more than two years.

St. Denis returned downstream to take command of Fort Mississippi, a base from which he broadened his acquaintance and his trade among the tribes. His trade relationship with the Natchitoches was continuous from 1701, and he won their complete confidence. When, in 1702, floods destroyed their crops and they abandoned their traditional locality, the lower Natchitoches went downstream to Fort Mississippi to ask St. Denis to let them live nearby. He helped them to settle on the north shore of Lake Pontchartrain near another refugee group, Acolapissas, whom Chickasaw raiders had recently driven from their home on the Pearl River.

Shortly afterward, Governor Bienville ordered St. Denis to abandon

---

[2] A valuable first-hand account of such an experience appears in André Pénigault, *Fleur de Lys and Calumet*, ed. Richebourg Gaillard McWilliams.

Fort Mississippi and move his men and supplies to Mobile, but his relations with tribes in the area remained strong. Natchitoches and Acolapissas warriors helped St. Denis campaign against the Chitimachas. Both groups cordially lodged Frenchmen who wintered with them in succeeding years.

Iberville and Bienville made a great point of coming in peace to the Indians and of fostering peace among tribes. Their Canadian experience had shown that trade could flourish only in a peaceful climate: tribesmen could not devote themselves to hunting in times of war, nor could French traders move among them safely.

Nevertheless, important wars did break out, principally with the Chitimachas and the Alibamons, each sparked by a small party of Indians murdering a small party of Frenchmen. Bienville reacted vehemently, calling upon all friendly nations to go to war against the offending tribes and offering ten crowns for each enemy scalp or live captive brought to the French leaders. Great horrors ensued: one coarse black scalp lock looked much like another, and some grew upon the heads of Frenchmen, particularly some of the *métis* from Canada.

Activities of the British in the Carolinas and the Spanish in Florida had already dislocated tribes, exacerbating old enmities among the various nations. The added complication of French wars against the Alibamons and Chitimachas, with bounties for scalps, helped to make the first decade of the eighteenth century very turbulent indeed in the eastern reaches of the lower Mississippi Valley. Worst of all for long-range French interests, Choctaws tricked the French into apparent responsibility for the deaths of thirty-five Chickasaw leaders, thus throwing the Chickasaws permanently into the British camp in the developing power struggle.

Caddo groups, other than the Natchitoches on Lake Pontchartrain, usually ignored those tangled conflicts, although Chickasaw raiders occasionally scored on the northeastern margins of the Caddo world. The Kadohadachos remained so isolated from the French traders in Louisiana that as late as 1711 they obtained French merchandise principally by bartering horses to the Illinois Indians.

The problem was one of default. As in New France in the previous century, the Crown expected large returns on little or no investment. Despite its superb economic potential, the Louisiana colony stagnated for want of men and goods. In the autumn of 1712, the Crown granted Antoine Crozat a fifteen-year monopoly on the Louisiana trade, with

TEXAS to 1774

LEGEND

● Spanish Establishments
☩ Spanish Missions
⊕ Spanish Presidios
⌂ French Towns and Posts
▲ Indian Settlements

TONKAWAS, etc.—Ranges of Roving Indian Groups

area covered by map

the expectation that he would develop the economy. He did bring supplies and a few settlers, but unduly restrictive management and ill-considered greed for immediate returns ruined his enterprise within five years. Nevertheless, it was the Crozat regime which launched French trade in the Caddo world.

Crozat sent Louisiana an able governor, Antoine de Lamothe Cadillac, another veteran of service in New France. One of his principal charges was to sound out possibilities for trade with the Spanish colonies, either through the port of Veracruz or overland to the mining provinces. Cadillac's agents were rebuffed at Veracruz, but at that juncture a curious letter from Fray Hidalgo reached Mobile. The former missionary to the Tejas had so completely despaired of support from his own government that in 1711 he addressed to the governor of Louisiana an inquiry about the welfare of the Tejas and asked him to support a mission for them. Hidalgo's letter reached Mobile in 1713, perfectly timed for Cadillac's purposes. He wanted to expand trade among Indians as well as Spaniards, and he thought missions desirable to foster trade relations. Why not find the enterprising Fray Hidalgo and, if possible, collaborate with him?

Cadillac summoned St. Denis, now a private trader at Biloxi but always ready to serve the colony, and made an attractive proposition. He wished St. Denis to revisit the Caddo territories, using his old contacts among the Natchitoches and Kadohadachos to make his way to Fray Hidalgo's "Tejas," then continue to Mexico. The governor would underwrite the venture with ten thousand livres' worth of merchandise and twenty-two men. St. Denis gladly agreed. While he returned to Biloxi to make his own preparations, he sent André Penigault to Lake Pontchartrain to ask the Natchitoches to accompany him back to their old homeland.

The Natchitoches readily agreed, but the Acolapissas burst into a jealous rage when they heard the news. They massacred seventeen Natchitoches and seized more than fifty women and girls, while the rest fled in terror. Penigault saved the life of the Natchitoches chief by shielding him with his own body and afterward managed to gather some of the survivors, including thirty warriors, whom he took to St. Denis. Outraged, St. Denis vowed someday to avenge the crime. For the present, he had to hurry to the Tejas country to find the mysterious Fray Hidalgo.

St. Denis bought food from the Tonicas and hired their chief, with fifteen of his best hunters, to accompany his party up the Red River.

More Natchitoches who had escaped the Acolapissas' attack joined them as they neared the old village site. With them came about two hundred men of the Soustionies, another Caddo group that had once lived in association with the Natchitoches but had refused to join their trek downstream in 1702. They had wandered ever since, hunting and gathering, and welcomed a chance to settle down anew.

When the people celebrated their homecoming at the old village site, St. Denis promised that Frenchmen would always live with them from that time onward. As long as they should stand closely united, they would have nothing to fear from other Indians. St. Denis would distribute grain to the Indians so that they could sow their fields again; the Indians, in turn, would be responsible for feeding the Frenchmen. He distributed hatchets and picks for construction of the new settlement. With logs cut by the Indians, the Frenchmen built a warehouse for their merchandise and a larger building for their quarters. Ten stayed to guard the merchandise when St. Denis forged on to the Tejas.

St. Denis' party of a dozen Frenchmen, fifteen Tonicas, and fifteen Natchitoches came as a considerable surprise to the Tejas, but they graciously welcomed them with a three-day calumet ceremony. They had plenty of cattle and horses. St. Denis traded profitably with them in both livestock and hides and reckoned that discovery of this new market made his trip worthwhile even if he should never see a Spaniard.

The Tejas had seen no Spaniards for more than five years, but four of them agreed to guide St. Denis to the nearest Spanish outpost. Unfortunately, the Tejas did not have surplus food to sell that spring, and the party had to spend so much time and energy living off the land that the journey took six weeks.[3]

On July 19, 1714, St. Denis politely handed his passport[4] to the as-

---

[3] Ibid., pp. 144–152. Pénigault was a member of the St. Denis party. His account of the encounter with the Tejas differs considerably from those preserved in Spanish records of the official interrogations of St. Denis.

[4] The original French document was translated into Spanish in Mexico City in June, 1715; that translation was transcribed by Pichardo, and thus rendered in English by Charles Wilson Hackett, ed., *Pichardo's Treatise on the Limits of Louisiana and Texas*, IV, 310: "We permit the lord of St. Denis and the twenty-four Canadians who are with him to take at their choice the number of Indian savages which he considers necessary to go to the Red River and wherever he thinks best, to search for the mission of Fray Francisco Hidalgo, Recollect religious, according to his letter written to us on the 16th day of January, 1711, in order to buy oxen, horses, and other cattle for the colony of the province of Louisiana. We pray all those that, in doing this, it may be to our purpose to permit the said

tonished commandant at Presidio San Juan Bautista, announcing that the governor of Louisiana had sent him to open trade with the Spaniards. He asked where he might find Fray Hidalgo. The visit flouted the standing order against foreign intrusion, but Captain Diego Ramón could not be certain of his ground. A grandson of the king of France now sat upon the throne in Spain, and the two powers had been allies during the War of the Spanish Succession. What if there were new accords affecting commerce in the Americas, not yet published in the northern provinces? Captain Ramón sought advice from the governor of Coahuila. Pending the result, St. Denis lived comfortably with the commandant's household, cultivating the friendship of the influential Ramón family and courting the seventeen-year-old granddaughter, Manuela.

After consulting the governor of Nueva Vizcaya, the governor of Coahuila brought St. Denis to Monclova for interrogation, then shipped the puzzling intruder under heavy guard to Mexico City in the spring of 1715. St. Denis sent back to Penigault at San Juan Bautista an order to lead the party back to the Natchitoches without him. Regretfully, they left the comfortable hospitality of the presidio and spent the next two months living off the land, working their way back to Tejas country.

Few men greeted them at the Hasinai settlement; one hundred and fifty had ridden off to war against the Kichais. Penigault's party stayed a few days to rest and buy provisions and saw the war party return with two Kichai prisoners. Four others were said to have been eaten on the way back. Shocked and sickened, the Frenchmen witnessed the elaborate ritual tortures and finally the cannibalism in which all the villagers took part. They also learned a bit about the Indians' mounted warfare, so different from war practices of Indians in woodlands farther east. The mounted warriors of the Tejas counted among their enemies others who fought on horseback, not only the Kichais, but also the Tawakonis[5] and the Kadohadachos, all their linguistic relatives and culturally similar. The Frenchmen were glad to hurry away from that war arena toward the Natchitoches.[6]

En route they found a Yatasí group reduced from twenty-five hun-

---

lord of St. Denis and the other members of his party to pass, without offering them any obstacle."

[5] A Wichitan band, probably then residing on the lower reaches of the Canadian River.

[6] Pénigault, *Fleur de Lys and Calumet*, pp. 153–157.

dred to five hundred by Chickasaws and epidemics. Penigault invited them to come to live with the Frenchmen at the Natchitoches villages and escorted those who wished to come with their women and children, their livestock, stores of grain, and personal possessions. Some chose instead to go to the Kadohadachos. The Natchitoches welcomed the refugees graciously and they lived congenially, side by side, from that time onward.

Penigault's party settled in with the Frenchmen who had stayed at Natchitoches and there awaited St. Denis. The fifteen Tonicas returned to their homes downstream after two years' absence.

Meanwhile, St. Denis laid his case before the viceroy, vowing his ignorance of any legal barriers to trade between the French and Spanish colonies. He reported that the Tejas had begged to have their missions restored and had pleaded especially for the return of Fray Hidalgo and Captain Urrutia. The Spanish authorities envisioned many practicing Catholics among the Tejas, languishing for pastoral care.[7]

That was precisely what Fray Hidalgo and some of his confreres had contended for years, so the Franciscans found pleasing vindication in the Frenchman's testimony. Secular officials fumed at the outrageous manner in which Fray Hidalgo had defied the national interest by inviting French attention to the Tejas, but they could not punish him. Now that the French had penetrated the Tejas settlements on friendly terms and opened trade, the Spaniards had to counter with missions and presidios enough to fill the dangerous vacuum. If the Tejas specified their preference for Fray Hidalgo, the government dared not jeopardize the venture by shipping the bold priest off to some punitive assignment elsewhere.

Late in the summer of 1715 the highest councils in Mexico City authorized a substantial effort: four missions to be established among the Tejas, under Fray Hidalgo's leadership; a supporting garrison of twenty-five soldiers, commanded by Alférez Domingo Ramón, a son of the commandant of San Juan Bautista, soon to be St. Denis' uncle by marriage. St. Denis himself was hired as commissary officer of the expedition, at a salary equal to that of the commander. He had declared his intention to settle on the Spanish frontier and go into business there; he would soon marry Manuela Ramón. The viceroy had every reason to think he had gained a valuable member for the service of New Spain.

[7] The declaration of St. Denis, as drawn up by Licenciado Don Gerardo Mora, in Hackett, *Pichardo's Treatise*, IV, 305–309.

In the fall and winter of 1715 San Juan Bautista became the staging post for the return to the Tejas. It would continue to be the principal base of supply and communication. That was a splendid reward for the dedicated labors of Fray Hidalgo, who had helped to develop the northern Coahuila missions during the years he had waited to resume his Tejas mission. It also afforded a notable opportunity to realize the dreams of Fray Antonio de San Buenaventura y Olivares, who had grown obsessed with the importance of establishing missions beyond the Rio Grande for the northernmost Coahuiltecans.

Since 1707, Fray Olivares had often crossed the Rio Grande to recruit Indians for mission communities decimated by epidemics and wars. Many Indians had pleaded for Christianity and promised to settle down in missions if only they could have them in their home territories. In 1709 Fray Olivares had discovered an ideal spot for the venture: San Pedro Springs, at the head of the San Antonio River, earlier admired by Terán for its extraordinary beauty and promise. Nearby lay a large *ranchería* of perhaps five hundred Indians: Sipuans, Chaulaames, and Sijames. Olivares had no doubt that the locale could support many more Indians and, indeed, could become the site of a great city. He had traveled clear to the court in Spain to plead for new missions beyond the Rio Grande, only to find indifference in high places. He had returned to the mission province, discouraged, about the time that a despairing Fray Hidalgo launched into the wilderness three copies of his appeal to the French governor of Louisiana.

Now, in 1716, Fray Olivares capitalized on the new importance of the Tejas missions to establish as a vital way station his own long-cherished project at the head of the San Antonio River. The fiasco of the 1690's had proved the importance of adequate communications and supply links for distant outposts. Fray Olivares thus found a sympathetic hearing when he declined the opportunity to go to the Tejas missions and asked instead for permission to move flagging Mission San Francisco Solano north from the Rio Grande to the San Antonio River. He expected to concentrate three thousand Indians in a pueblo there, mostly Coahuiltecans whom he considered very promising mission material.

Since Apaches now controlled territories not far north and west of that site, Fray Olivares requested a squad of ten soldiers for protection. He also desired some settlers, both for numerical strength and for their example of Spanish agricultural life style. The viceroy and the junta agreed.

What a curious venture they launched late in April 1716: Spanish reoccupation of the Tejas country to bar French expansion, under the aegis of an agent of French Louisiana. St. Denis had exaggerated surviving Catholic sentiment among the Tejas to promote restoration of the missions. Now he would conduct the expedition from the Rio Grande to the Neches, where he would serve as intermediary to assure a Tejas welcome to new Spanish establishments on a scale far exceeding those of 1690.[8]

About seventy-five people made the trek: nine missionaries, twenty-five soldiers, and assorted settlers, drovers, and muleteers. Eight married women went along, but Manuela Ramón y St. Denis remained at her grandfather's house in San Juan Bautista to bear her first child. With her remarkable bridegroom rode her uncle, Alférez Domingo Ramón, commanding the military force, and her father, the younger Diego Ramón. Whatever the outcome, the Ramón family fortunes were deeply involved in this strange meeting of Spanish and French frontiers in the Caddo world.

The sizeable herds—sixty-four oxen, four thousand horses and mules, and one thousand sheep and goats—slowed their progress. They paused for three days in June near the Brazos River to visit the Ranchería Grande, an extraordinary offshoot of the great struggles for control of the southern buffalo ranges.[9] More than two thousand Indians of widely assorted groups, some mere fragments of once viable bands, clustered together for survival. Some had been active in the wars on the Spanish frontier, but all now shared the overriding bond of enmity with the Apaches, and they welcomed the Spaniards as a counter to Apache power.

As the caravan neared Tejas territory late in June, St. Denis rode ahead to assemble the Tejas leaders. He returned a few days later with five *caddices* and twenty-nine leading men prepared to smoke the calumet in formal welcome. St. Denis, interpreting for the Indians and advising the Spaniards, was in an excellent position to set a pleasant tone for the affair and to avoid possible areas of friction.

Nearly a hundred more Indians joined the second day's festivities, bearing gifts of food: corn, tamales, watermelons, and pots of cooked vegetables. In return, the Spaniards distributed blankets, sombreros,

---

[8] Gabriel Tous, trans., "Ramón's Expedition: Espinosa's Diary of 1716," *Mid-America* 12 (1929): 339–361.

[9] The Ranchería Grande is discussed in Herbert Eugene Bolton, *Texas in the Middle Eighteenth Century*, pp. 144–145.

tobacco, and flannel. The missionaries meant underwear made of that flannel to be an early step toward Hispanicizing the Tejas. As news of the pleasant celebration spread, more and more Indians came to dance and to exchange their gifts of Indian foodstuffs for Spanish clothing.

The cheerful spirit prevailed even when the serious business of settling the Spaniards began. The *caddices* allowed them free choice of building sites. When Alférez Ramón selected his presidio site just east of the Neches River, the Indians generously built a grass house for him. Allocation of the four missions among the several settlements was left up to the Indians, whose decisions St. Denis interpreted to the Spaniards. They declared that they could not assemble at the missions before their harvests were completed, but they willingly built the rude structures of grass and logs in which the missions would begin. The efficiency of their well-directed cooperative enterprise made a great impression on the Spaniards.

Within a month, four missions stood in the settlements designated by the Tejas leaders. First was the new San Francisco de los Neches (or de los Tejas), under Fray Hidalgo's charge, for the Neches and Nabedaches; the presidio of Nuestra Señora de los Dolores de los Tejas stood nearby. A little less than thirty miles northeast lay the mission for the Hainais, Nuestra Señora de la Purísima Concepción. Nuestra Señora de Guadalupe, founded in the Nacogdoches village, would serve the Naconos, too. San José de los Nazones in the Nasoni settlement was intended also for the Nadacos.[10] Within the year Fray Antonio Margil de Jesús founded two more: one among the Adaes and one among the Ais. The diligent Tejas built small wooden churches and very adequate dwellings for the priests at each mission. The forms of Spanish civil government were established in each of the prospective mission communities. Each group elected its captain general, to whom Alférez Ramón presented the cane of office. Indeed, they had by summer's end all that missions needed except neophytes, and those they were never to have.

The Indians promised to settle at the missions if St. Denis would come to live among them, and he promised to bring his wife and make his permanent home there. There is every reason to think that St. Denis meant to keep his word. He built a great wilderness career by

[10] Anadarkos.

dealing honestly and fairly with Indians. He could see a unique trade opportunity on that colonial Franco-Spanish frontier, given influential in-laws commanding the nearest Spanish establishments and his own extraordinary rapport with the settled, productive Indians athwart the frontier. He dreamed of a wilderness seigneury far surpassing that which his father had carved in Canada.

As soon as he had overseen the Spanish-Tejas negotiations and had helped initiate construction of the missions and presidio, St. Denis hurried on to Mobile. He reported his success to the governor there in August 1716, then liquidated his assets at Biloxi to invest his all in the new venture, and organized a trading company to pursue his advantage. By autumn he was on his way back up the Red River to Natchitoches with a big cargo of merchandise, much of it intended for Spanish markets.

St. Denis rested briefly at Natchitoches in November, then went on to the Tejas settlements for the winter. In spring he took much of his merchandise on to San Juan Bautista, transporting the contraband on the Spanish Crown's own mules. Those animals had packed provisions for the founding expedition; neither the commanding Ramón nor St. Denis was so thriftless as to send them back without a pay load. With St. Denis traveled his father-in-law, the younger Diego Ramón.

Rumors of Ramón family complicity in contraband trade ran rife on the frontier and, unluckily, down to Mexico City. When St. Denis reached San Juan Bautista in April 1717, some of his goods were seized as contraband; in no other way could old Captain Ramón have hoped to salvage his own reputation and those of his sons. St. Denis hurried south to protest to the viceroy, only to find himself detained, part of the time in prison, while the case was deliberated. Extensive investigations tended to confirm St. Denis' contention that he honestly intended to settle down as a merchant on the Spanish frontier. Nevertheless, the viceroy decided to eliminate any chance of conspiracy for contraband trade by removing the Ramóns from their frontier command posts and banishing St. Denis and his Manuela to Guatemala.

Fortunately, St. Denis escaped from Mexico City in the autumn of 1718. By the time the decision was announced, he was back in Louisiana. It was thenceforth out of the question for him to live in Spanish territory, but he reestablished himself in the Louisiana service. In 1721 Manuela joined him at Natchitoches, where they lived out their lives.

The loss of St. Denis undermined the Spaniards' Tejas mission effort. In the spring of 1718 Fray Hidalgo appealed to the viceroy and to his own ecclesiastical superior to send St. Denis back to the area in any office that could be devised.[11] He saw no hope whatever that the missions could succeed without the Frenchman's persuasive influence among the Indians. He judged St. Denis a man of excellent character, and he knew that the Indians bore him extraordinary affection. When the viceroy ignored Fray Hidalgo's plea to retain St. Denis' unusual talents for the Spanish service, he virtually assured that he would be employed in the service of France.

Although the fortunes of French Louisiana fluctuated sharply in succeeding years, St. Denis created in the next quarter-century an extraordinarily successful sphere of influence in a wide region centering upon Natchitoches. Furthermore, he and Manuela produced a little wilderness dynasty that perpetuated his remarkable influence among the Indians long past his death and even past the demise of the French Empire in America.

During St. Denis' second sojourn in New Spain, important changes had occurred in Louisiana. In 1717 Antoine Crozat relinquished the proprietorship of the stagnating colony. The Crown conferred a similar monopoly on a newly formed "Company of the West," with rights to Illinois as well as Louisiana. Reorganized the next year as the Company of the Indies, it became the developmental arm of John Law's Mississippi scheme.

That Scottish financier convinced the regent, the Duke of Orleans, that development of the Mississippi Valley could restore the financial health of France. He formed a great corporation for colonial trade, in which he sold shares, with the idea that the proceeds could be used to liquidate the national debt. His bank issued paper money based on assumed values in the Mississippi Valley. A two-year surge of speculative fever drove the price of the company stocks to absurd heights before confidence in the scheme broke down and Law's financial bubble burst.

Meanwhile, however, the Company of the Indies made substantial efforts toward genuine development of Louisiana. The able, experienced Bienville, appointed governor in 1718, moved the capital from Mobile to the better located new settlement of New Orleans on the Mississippi. Extensive land grants, called concessions, were allocated to concessionaires, whose responsibility it was to bring out settlers and provide

---

[11] Fray Francisco Hidalgo to the Viceroy, San Francisco de los Tejas, April, 1718; and Fray Francisco Hidalgo to Fray José Diez, San Francisco de los Tejas, March 11, 1718, in Hackett, *Pichardo's Treatise*, IV, 316-317.

means of production and development on their concessions. Some concessionaires made considerable investments to import workers and equipment. The Company of the Indies sent many ship loads of settlers and merchandise; on the return voyage, the vessels carried cargos of pelts, lumber, and tar, and in later years rice and tobacco, too.

Because few Frenchmen would voluntarily leave home to pioneer in the wilderness, some concessionaires filled their quotas of settlers from prisons and sundry correctional institutions. Some, like Law himself, imported Swiss and German workers, often highly skilled. Upstream in the Illinois country, the company imported miners and equipment. Many Negro slaves were imported, largely from the West Indies, to form the principal labor force on the projected plantations. In a short time Louisiana's colonial population jumped from only seven hundred to more than five thousand.

Since the concessions usually lay near Indian settlements, tensions arose in localities where French developments impinged too closely upon Indian interests. No such friction troubled the Caddo world: its relative remoteness shielded it from the more ambitious development projects in the brief era of the concessions. The brothers Brossart, merchants from Lyon, were granted a concession at the Natchitoches and came to develop it themselves with only ten persons. Bénard de La Harpe, of St. Malo, brought twenty-five persons to develop his concession in the Kadohadacho region in the spring of 1719.[12]

The few newcomers posed no great shock to the Caddo societies. As St. Denis had promised in 1713, there had been a continuous, though small, French presence in the Natchitoches village. Bienville stationed a squad of half a dozen soldiers and a sergeant to protect French interests there in January 1717, only a month after St. Denis left on his second journey to the Tejas and San Juan Bautista. One of St. Denis' associates, Claude du Tisne, remained in charge of the Natchitoches Post until 1718, when Bienville sent Philippe Blondel to take command at Natchitoches in order to transfer du Tisne to the Illinois. There du Tisne joined Pierre Dugué de Boisbriant in the company's effort to develop the Illinois trade with the western Indians and perhaps with Santa Fe. Thus, Blondel was in charge at Natchitoches when in the spring of 1719 came the news that Spain and France were at war.

Spain's new Bourbon king, Felipe V, had stirred up a hornet's nest through unwise indulgence of his Parmese wife's appetite for Italian

---

[12] Pénigault's *Fleur de Lys and Calumet* is a usefully detailed source on the brief era of the concessions.

territories and his own clandestine efforts to supplant young Louis XV as successor to their grandfather's throne in France. In August 1718, the Quadruple Alliance of England, France, Holland, and Austria moved to check Felipe's ambitions. In little more than a year they beat him soundly. By the Treaty of the Hague, 1720, he renounced his Italian claims, probably to the long-range benefit of his Spanish subjects, and he ceased to maneuver for the French throne.

When news of the war reached Natchitoches in June 1719, Lieutenant Blondel decided upon precautionary seizure of the Spanish establishments among the Tejas. He had the advantage of surprise, since Spaniards on that frontier had yet to hear of the war. With his seven-man squad, he easily overpowered the two men on duty at the Adaes mission and made it his, but one escaped to alert the other five missions and the presidio.

The Spaniards, laymen and religious alike, felt hopelessly vulnerable. They had been hampered all along by failure of supplies due them from Mexico, and they had been unable to establish rapport with the Tejas. Ready access to the French traders at Natchitoches put guns in the hands of many Indians. If general conflict between Spain and France should blaze along that frontier, there was little reason to expect Indians to side with Spain. Uncertain and fearful, the Spaniards withdrew from the Tejas country. They paused on the Trinity River, hoping that supporting forces would arrive to escort them back to the missions, then retreated in despair to the new Spanish establishments at the head of the San Antonio River. The refugees reached Mission San Antonio de Valero and its supporting Presidio de San Antonio de Béxar in the autumn of 1719, there to mark time for more than a year.

For the French garrison at Natchitoches, the war was practically over. The Tejas assured the Frenchmen of their neutrality; Blondel's attack upon guests in their country had not offended them. So slight had been the role of the missions among the Tejas that their abandonment probably made little difference to either the Indians or their French neighbors. The French agents felt free to pursue the principal aims of the Company of the Indies, which in the Caddo area meant further expansion of trade.

St. Denis did not participate in the first phase of the new development. He had returned from Mexico to find his old associates gone from Natchitoches, and his own relations with his kinsman, Governor Bienville, somewhat strained. He settled at Biloxi to rebuild the fortune he had lost in his venture into the Spanish trade. During the war he led Indian allies from the Biloxi region in the French campaign against Pensacola and so distinguished himself that reports of his unusual merit reached the Crown. The next year, 1720, ships from France brought St. Denis well-earned rewards: the Cross of St. Louis and an appointment to command the Natchitoches Post.

Meantime, Bénard de La Harpe widened the sphere of French operations from their base in the Caddo world. He functioned in two capacities. As an agent of the Company of the Indies, he was expected to establish a post among the Kadohadachos and from that base to explore possibilities for trade alliances with the unknown tribes north and west. As a concessionaire at the Kadohadachos, he would reap private profits from any economic development he might foster in the area.

The Kadohadacho bands gathered at the Nasoni village in April 1719 to welcome La Harpe with a feast of smoked fish. They gladly let him select a site for his post, and he chose a spot near the home of the Nasoni chief, on the south bank of the Red River. The chief sold La Harpe either the land or the right to its use. Perhaps the French and the Indian understanding of the transaction did not exactly coincide, but the Kadohadachos prized the post so much that no friction over its status ever occurred.

With the Indians' help, La Harpe built a stockaded post. He was uncertain whether enemies of the Kadohadachos might attack and even more uncertain whether the Spaniards would contest his presence there. Once Blondel had routed the Spaniards from the Tejas country and ascertained the friendly attitude of neighboring Caddo groups, La Harpe felt free to explore north and west.

The first reconnaissance up the Red River proved encouraging. Du Rivage led the small exploring party, which reported back to the post in July 1719. They had encountered several wandering bands, including the principal Tonkawan groups, who lived mainly by hunting buffalo. All the Indians had welcomed the Frenchmen very cordially. Two Kichais accompanied Du Rivage back to the post to visit La Harpe.

The Kadohadachos had already mentioned to La Harpe the peace they had recently made with the wandering nations, including an errant westerly Caddo group called Naouydiches. If that peace should prove stable and the French could maintain the cordial tone of their first encounter with the wandering bands, the prospect for development of a major trade center at La Harpe's new post would indeed be bright. The obvious next step was to contact the nations to the north-

west, so La Harpe readily accepted the services volunteered by two
visitors from the Kichais and the Naouydiches. They would guide him
to the villages of the Touacaras, despite the danger of Apaches prowling the regions beyond the Kadohadachos.

La Harpe set out on August 11, 1719, his small party a virtual
microcosm of the emerging colonial society of Louisiana. From his
own Nassonite Post came two officers and three soldiers, one of whom
was competent in some Indian languages, two common laborers, and
two Negroes, the property either of La Harpe or the company. They
had three Indian companions: a Nasoni and the Kichai and Naouydiche
braves who came to guide them. They took a dozen horses laden with
provisions and merchandise. Though a Naouydiche scout warned them
of sixty Apache raiders in the area, they traveled more than two weeks
without incident.

The principal chief of the Naouydiches, en route to the Touacaras
with forty warriors, had camped on the Boggy River to dry some
meat. La Harpe's party joined forces with them. Thus, it was a considerable group that reached the Touacaras' village on the lower South
Canadian River on September 3, 1719.

La Harpe could hardly have realized that he had reached the southeastern margin of fabled Quivira, nor could he know that in the same
month du Tisne was penetrating Quivira's northern reaches with a
party from Illinois. The actual grass-hut villages of Wichitan bands
along the Arkansas River and its tributaries accorded as oddly with
the rich myth of Grand Quivira as did the Caddo settlements with
the legendary Great Kingdom of the Tejas.

The Wichitas spoke a Caddoan language and had many cultural
similarities to the Caddos, but on the whole theirs was a ruder culture.
They had no equivalent of the Caddo "confederacies" and recognized
no authority higher than the band. Nor did they possess a stable
leadership structure comparable to the Caddos' hereditary priests and
chiefs. Wichitan band structure was probably more fluid than that of
the Caddos, and the economic and military pressures of the eighteenth
century sharply diminished the number of bands, with many changes
in nomenclature.[13]

No people had been more sharply penalized by the convergence of

[13] For a discussion of Wichitan culture, see W. W. Newcomb, Jr., *The Indians
of Texas*, pp. 247–277. The history of the Taovayas and Wichita bands is detailed
in a series of three articles by Elizabeth Ann Harper. The location of sites is
discussed in Robert E. Bell, Edward B. Jelks, and W. W. Newcomb, Jr., *A Pilot
Study of Wichita Indian Archaeology and Ethnohistory*.

changes flowing from the Spanish frontier in New Mexico and the French frontier on the Great Lakes. The Wichitas were more than ready to enjoy at first hand some of the advantages of change. They had figured in earlier French plans for development of Louisiana. Iberville had learned of the Wichitan peoples of the Arkansas Valley in his earliest investigations of Louisiana's trade potential and had included them in his grand design for structuring trade with the Indians and with New Mexico. He had calculated that five hundred livres' worth of hardware would induce the Wichitas[14] to congregate at the villages of the Mentos, 250 miles up the Arkansas River, at a site that could always be reached by water. He believed that, once settled, they could be persuaded to stop warring against New Mexico and would form an important base for extension of French trading operations to Santa Fe.[15]

Iberville did not identify the source of his information about the Wichitas, but there must have been some reported French contact with them on which to base his assumptions. Perhaps the Wichitas had already glimpsed about 1701 a tantalizing prospect of French trade establishments in their own territory, only to be disappointed when Louisiana's development flagged for nearly two decades. Meanwhile, many guns from the French and British traders had reached their enemies on the north and east, and equestrian Comanches had emerged as powerful new enemies to the west, northwest of Wichitan territories. The visits of La Harpe and du Tisne in 1719 were indeed timely.

La Harpe found himself negotiating with chiefs of nine Wichitan bands gathered at the village: Touacaras, Toayas, Caumuches, Aderos, Ousitas, Ascanis, Qustaquois, Quicaquiris, and Honenchas.[16] The Toayas appeared most numerous and their elderly chief the most respected leader. La Harpe estimated the population at more than six thousand, but it is unlikely that so many people lived there permanently. Perhaps they had come together for a harvest festival or

[14] He called them Panis, as did most Frenchmen until the latter eighteenth century.

[15] Pierre Le Moyne d'Iberville, *Memoire*, in Pierre Margry, ed., *Découvertes et Établissemenets des Français dans l'Ouest et dans le Sud de l'Amerique Septentrionale, 1614–1754*, IV, 599.

[16] It is probably reasonable to equate four of these band names with those which survived late in the eighteenth century: i.e., Toayas = Taovayas; Touacaras = Tawakonis; Ousitas = Wichitas; Ascanis = Iscanis. The rest of the names lapsed during the period of reorganization and consolidation in the first half of the eighteenth century.

perhaps to celebrate their recent great victory over the Apaches in the Red River Valley.

The chiefs welcomed La Harpe's party with gracious ceremony, and the people danced the calumet for him the next day. The old Toayas chief spoke in favor of the alliance with the French that La Harpe proposed. He reasoned that only a very powerful nation could have dared to send such a small party so far without fear of enemies along the way. Everyone concurred. The assembled Wichitan bands made that day an alliance with the Frenchmen, which endured to their mutual advantage as long as France possessed Louisiana.

Only when he asked about continuing to New Mexico did La Harpe meet disappointment. The chiefs admitted that the Arkansas was navigable in winter as far as Spanish territory, but they would not make the journey because Comanches now frequented the Arkansas and Canadian headwaters. Spaniards were said to visit the same area for gold, furs, and slaves, but it had been many years since Wichitan peoples had seen any Spaniards.

La Harpe stayed ten days among the Wichitan bands, learning much about their way of life. From March until October they lived in their villages to tend their crops, and they were very successful farmers, who annually dried and braided great quantities of tobacco. Once crops were harvested and stored in the fall, they became roving hunters, following the buffalo. They owned many horses, some quite beautiful, and used saddles and bridles. The horses carried them to war as well as to the hunt. They pursued a particularly hot vendetta against the Apaches who lived west of them. When the chiefs presented gifts to the departing visitors, the old Toayas chief gave the French commander a little Apache slave about eight years old. He apologized for the smallness of his gift and assured La Harpe he would have received many more if only he had come a month sooner. The Wichitas had eaten seventeen Apache captives at a great public feast.[17]

La Harpe left the French flag flying over the Tawakoni village when he started back to the Kadohadachos on September 13, 1719. Thenceforth the Tawakonis cherished that flag and the alliance that it symbolized. When time and weather wore the banner thin, they called upon the Frenchmen for replacements, many times over the decades. During some of that time Frenchmen lived in their village, to trade and, when possible, to protect Tawakoni lives and property. When enemy

[17] Bénard de La Harpe, *Relation du Voyage*, December 12, 1719 in Margry, *Découvertes*, VI, 289 ff.

Indians made life intolerable in the pleasant Canadian Valley, the Tawakonis moved southward to live in the protective sphere of Natchitoches.[18]

Other Wichitan bands lived northward and westward, nearer the plains. La Harpe heard of two villages, one of the Wichitas proper and one of the Iscanis, some 150 miles north, northwest from the Tawakonis. Perhaps those were the two that du Tisne reached from Illinois just as La Harpe started back to the Kadohadachos.

Those people told du Tisne of more villages west and northwest of their own, but he lacked the time to visit them and did not estimate their strength. The villages he saw were perhaps three miles apart, on the same side of a small tributary stream west of the Arkansas. The first village had 130 houses and perhaps two hundred warriors; the second appeared somewhat stronger. Altogether they had about three hundred horses, which they prized so highly that they were loath to sell any. They had yet to acquire enough horses to mount every warrior, a dangerous dilemma for peoples vulnerable to Comanche raiders on the one side and Osages on the other. However, they had only six guns, and they desperately wanted more. Du Tisne bartered three guns, powder, and some picks and knives for two horses and a mule with a Spanish brand. He also bought an old silver cup, perhaps a relic of long-ago Wichita visits to New Mexico. They no longer ventured so far west because Comanches barred the way.

Du Tisne's trip to the Wichitas on the Arkansas was far more difficult than La Harpe's cordial progress with Kichai and Caddo escorts to the welcoming Tawakoni village. Du Tisne first crossed the territory of Osages, who welcomed him in their own midst but strenuously opposed his visit to the Wichita villages 130 miles beyond their own. They wanted to deny their neighbors access to French guns. When du Tisne would not be dissuaded, the Osages tried trickery: they warned the Wichitas that the Frenchmen were coming to catch them for slaves. Du Tisne thus found the Wichitas sullenly suspicious until he persuaded them of his peaceful intent. Then they gladly contracted an alliance with the Frenchmen and let du Tisne raise the French flag over their villages.

The Wichitas were dismayed to learn that du Tisne also wanted to

[18] El Cavallero Macarty to Martos y Navarrete, Natchitos, September 10, 1763, copy in Bexar Archives, University of Texas (subsequently cited as BA). Internal evidence suggests that the Spanish copyist erred in reading the signature and that the author of the letter was probably Athanase de Mézières, in charge at Natchitoches after the death of Césaire de Blanc.

visit Comanches. They had a very live war with the Comanches and did not want French guns to reach their enemies. Du Tisne heard the Wichitas mention a big Comanche camp just five days west, and in six days he found it for himself. The Comanches welcomed him graciously. He planted a flag of truce in the Comanche camp on September 27, 1719, and came away convinced that the way to New Mexico would be clear if peace were effected between Wichitas and Comanches.[19] The key to alliance with the Comanches would be plenty of presents and, most important of all, restoration of all the Comanches who had been captured and enslaved by village tribes to the east.

Although the French trade sphere included the Wichitan bands from 1719 onward, no records survive to answer the many questions about that important time of change. What was the volume of trade? Who were the traders, and from which posts did they come? When and how did the bands consolidate, and how many village moves were made to accommodate the Wichitan economy to the new conditions? How soon did French guns tip the balance in the war of Wichitas against Apaches or of Osages against Wichitas? If the Wichitan villages had indeed become key outposts in a Louisiana trade with New Mexico as Iberville had once dreamed and as du Tisne and La Harpe proposed to the Company of the Indies, they would surely have figured in many important reports. Instead, the ambitious scheme to develop an Arkansas River route to New Mexico collapsed along with most of Louisiana's economy in the 1720's, and the Wichitas thenceforth ranked low in the priorities of French officialdom.

John Law's Mississippi bubble burst in 1720. The Company of the Indies, under new management, continued for another decade to run the colony, but Law's debacle had so thoroughly discredited the colonial enterprise that investment capital virtually ceased to flow. With the agricultural and mineral development of the colony nearly at a standstill, the Indian trade and the uncertain hope of commerce with the Spanish provinces were almost the only assets left to the Company of the Indies. Officers of the company necessarily focused their limited resources on the trade areas of greatest strategic importance, especially among the Sioux. In 1722, Frenchmen were trading with only five of the twenty-five–odd Sioux groups; British traders from Hudson's Bay

---

[19] *Voyage Fait par M. Du Tisne en 1719, chez les Missouris pour aller aux Paniassas, Extrait de la Relation de Bénard de la Harpe*, in Margry, *Découvertes*, VI, 311–312.

had most of the rest. In 1724, the company established a new post, Takamamiowen, in the Sioux country in order to improve their stance on that frontier.

The Indians on the lower Missouri River grew so disgusted with inadequate French trade efforts by 1723 that they took the warpath and plundered French traders in their region. Obviously, that situation had to be corrected, but no officer of the company felt equal to the job. They called back from pleasant retirement in Paris Étienne Veniard de Bourgmont, formerly a ranking official in the Canadian-based trade, who had lived for several years among the tribes of the Missouri. He had left many friends among them and a family as well; no man stood a better chance of restoring French ascendancy among those Indians. Furthermore, Bourgmont had been among the first Frenchmen to report Comanches ranging from New Mexico to the Black Hills. He had heard of them in 1714 when he traveled among the Osages, Kansas, Pawnees, and Otoes and far up the Missouri to the Arikaras. If anyone could negotiate the general peace with the Comanches that du Tisne and La Harpe had deemed prerequisite to trade with New Mexico, Bourgmont probably was the man.

By the end of 1723 Bourgmont established Fort Orleans on the Missouri River in present Carroll County, Missouri. The Osages gladly welcomed him, for they had a big accumulation of pelts to trade. So many new guns in Osage hands boded ill for the tranquillity of tribes within their striking range.

In spring 1724, Bourgmont sallied forth to establish peace with the Comanches, escorted by eight Frenchmen, sixty-four Osages, and a hundred Missouris. They went first to the Kansas village, where Bourgmont presided over a great ceremonial to establish friendship among the Kansas and Missouris and Osages. Many Indians accompanied Bourgmont when he left the Kansas village to seek the Comanches, but he fell so ill that he had to return by canoe to Fort Orleans. One of his subordinates, M. Gaillard, went on to the Comanchería with fifty Kansas warriors to return two Comanche captives, a young woman and a boy, whom the Kansas had been holding in slavery. That good-will gesture enabled Gaillard to preside over a great peace ceremony between the Comanches and the Kansas and to leave with a grateful Comanche assembly Bourgmont's proposal for a general alliance embracing the Comanches, the French, and all the tribes at peace with France. The Comanches wanted very badly to fire the guns that Gaillard and the Kansas carried, but they did not know how.

Gaillard won many friends among the Comanches by giving them lessons in musketry and helped inaugurate a new era in plains warfare.

By autumn, Bourgmont recovered enough to travel to a Kansas village for a big peace meeting of Otoes, Osages, Iowas, Panismahas, Missouris, Illinois, and Kansas. Then, with delegates from all those allied nations, he rode on to the Comanche camp to embrace them in the peace and general alliance. It was a landmark achievement. Bourgmont did well to have the *Te Deum* chanted in gratitude for the Comanche peace when he returned to Fort Orleans on November 4, 1724.

Those Comanches agreed to live at peace with all those allies of France and to share with them the benefits of trade. They also conceded Frenchmen free passage through Comanche territory to trade with the Spaniards of New Mexico. Bourgmont had hoped to continue to New Mexico from the Comanche camp, but his illness and difficulties in finding the Comanches had delayed his accord with them until too late in the season to permit the trip to Santa Fe. Bourgmont returned to Fort Orleans a bit disappointed, but confident that he had opened the way for trade with New Mexico. He went home to Paris that winter, taking his Indian daughter and one chief each from the Otoes, Osages, Missouris, Illinois, and Michigameas. The chiefs came home in good time with wondrous tales for their people, but Bourgmont never returned to the New World.[20]

Many other able men left the company's service in the 1720's. La Harpe, who had returned to the Arkansas River in 1722, urged development of a post for the Tawakonis and other enterprises downstream in the vicinity of Tonti's decaying Arkansas Post. He left, unsuccessful and discouraged. The Indians of the Arkansas Valley, never troublesome to the French, fared poorly in the company's allocation of its limited resources when posts and goods were so urgently required to keep order among tribes of the Missouri and northward. When Bourgmont seemed to have breached the Comanche barrier to New Mexico by mediating peace among tribes north of the Arkansas, he erased the company's incentive to mediate peace and alliance between the Comanches and Wichitas. Southwestern Louisiana became a commercial backwater.[21]

---

[20] Étienne Veniard de Bourgmont, *Relation du Voyage de la Rivière Missouri, sur le Haut de Celle des Arkansas et du Missouri aux Padoucas*, June 25, 1724– November 1, 1724, ibid., VI, 312 ff.

[21] In 1725, when the Louisiana fur trade (excluding pelts from the Sioux,

Trade in upper Louisiana was widely disrupted in 1727, when the Fox sparked an insurrection against the French. Shortly afterward, the trade in lower Louisiana was badly affected when the Natchez rose in anger against the French settlers of their area, and war blazed over much of the lower Mississippi Valley. In 1731, the company acknowledged its failure and turned the declining colony back to the Crown. Louisiana became a royal colony, with about 800,000 livres' annual subsidy. Much of that money went to purchase peace with the Indians, through annual presents paid as a kind of tribute in exchange for the privilege of doing business in their territories.

The Natchitoches Post and the Caddo world formed an island of comparative stability in those turbulent years of the Louisiana colony. St. Denis, who took command at Natchitoches in 1720, remained in charge until he died in 1744. The Caddo peoples' extraordinary affection and trust toward him only grew with time.

St. Denis was conveniently able to consolidate friendly trade with the Tejas during the Spaniards' absence. When La Harpe's concession among the Kadohadachos lapsed, the Nassonite Post fell to St. Denis' jurisdiction; so too did the substations established at the Yatasí and Petit Caddo settlements. He carefully inculcated the principle that Indians who were at peace with or allied with the Frenchmen must live at peace with other Indian friends of France. The result was an end to wars among the Caddo groups and wide extension of peaceful relations among the Caddos and such former enemies as the Kichais and the Wichitan bands.

St. Denis distributed at Natchitoches the annual presents to the Indians of his jurisdiction. Thanks to the importance of his area as a barrier to Spanish expansion, he was able to maintain a reasonable flow of trade goods. Neither the company nor the Crown dared risk antagonizing the Indians of that important frontier by wrecking the trade on which they had come to depend.

The Spaniards suspected that St. Denis took advantage of their expulsion from the frontier to cultivate the friendship of Indians south and west of the Caddos in lands claimed by Spain. That made reoccupation of the Tejas country all the more urgent, and the task was assigned the Marqués de Aguayo, newly appointed governor of Coahuila and Texas. Truce between France and Spain in 1720 meant that

---

Missouri, and Illinois Indians) amounted to 50,000 skins, only one thousand each were derived from the Indians on the Red River, those on the Arkansas, and the Tonicas.

no actual hostilities should occur, but Spanish officialdom reckoned they would need a stronger Spanish presence than ever to contain the expansive St. Denis. In the spring of 1721, Aguayo led a large force toward the Tejas settlements, uneasily aware that somewhere on the Brazos River St. Denis was holding council with many Indian groups.

No untoward incident marred the journey from San Antonio to the Tejas. The Indians at the old mission sites received the Spaniards graciously, but some leaders voiced in their welcoming addresses their apprehension that the Spaniards' stay would again be only temporary. The Indians brought their customary gifts of food and in return had the most lavish array of presents ever distributed among them by Spaniards. The *caddices* received complete new suits of Spanish clothes and the silver-mounted canes symbolic of governorship. The forms of Spanish civil government were thus reestablished in the Tejas settlements. The Indians promised once more to form large, compact pueblos at the missions after harvest, and they cheerfully rebuilt the mission structures.

St. Denis came to visit Governor Aguayo and declared his willingness to observe the truce if Aguayo would do so. The Spanish governor agreed, on the condition that St. Denis pull his frontier back from Los Adaes to Natchitoches. The Frenchman reluctantly complied.

Aguayo not only restored the six missions among the Tejas and rebuilt the presidio of Dolores, but he also founded, over St. Denis' protest, the new presidio of Los Adaes,[22] much nearer Natchitoches. So that the governor could deal directly with any emergency on the frontier, Los Adaes became the capital of Texas and remained the capital as long as the province lay on an international boundary.

To forestall further French activities on the coast, Aguayo established another new presidio on Matagorda Bay, at the site of La Salle's ill-starred fort. Near the coastal presidio, La Bahía del Espíritu Santo, he established a mission for the roving Karankawas who made the coast so perilous for all intruders.

Perhaps the Spanish presidios could be counted successful, inasmuch as the French frontier encroached no nearer New Spain, but the missions were almost total failures. Some Tejas adopted the custom of requesting baptism for the dying, but they rarely came to the missions as healthy neophytes. Strongly committed to their native religion, all the Caddo groups rejected the missionaries' demand for exclusive

---

[22] Near present Robeline, Louisiana.

devotion to Christianity. The missions could not tempt the Caddos with the measure of material and civil security that sometimes lured less civilized Indians. Caddos had long enjoyed material sufficiency and a high degree of civil order, with a tradition of mutual assistance among themselves in times of sickness or want. As to protection from their enemies and access to European goods, the French traders from Natchitoches served their needs far better than the Spaniards, and the French did not impose unwelcome cultural change.

While Spaniards on the eastern frontier endured their dreary little exercise in failure, San Antonio became the principal focus of action in Texas. The missions for the Coahuiltecans and the protecting presidio were hardly founded before their herds became the target of Apache raids. There ensued a lively war with the eastern Apaches, its intensity mounting as Comanches and Wichitas and others encroached upon the Apachería from the north. Those invaders were not seen for another generation at San Antonio, but they embodied still more sweeping forces of change.

Mission San Antonio de Valero had its formal beginning on May 1, 1718. Fray Olivares and three more missionaries from the College of Querétaro,[23] assisted by a few Jarame Indian converts from San Francisco de Solano on the Rio Grande, built huts for a temporary chapel and dwellings near San Pedro Springs. Just four days later, Governor Alarcón founded the Presidio and Villa of San Antonio de Béxar nearby. Only six of the ten soldiers brought families, but there were ten families of civilians, and twenty more joined them later. As Fray Olivares had suggested, free land and water rights were offered near the mission to encourage permanent settlers.[24]

The enterprise began with a typically acrimonious running quarrel between its civil and religious leadership. Fray Olivares grew angry with Governor Alarcón months before they actually went to San Antonio, so, when the Indians were slow to gather at the mission in its first summer, he assumed that the governor's brutality to an Indian was solely to blame.

The first auspicious development occurred at the end of August, when Fray Espinosa and Alférez Ramón came from East Texas to greet

[23] The Franciscan apostolic colleges were specialized missionary units that took much of the responsibility for converting and civilizing the Indians on the frontiers from the late seventeenth century onward. The Texas missions were the work of the colleges of Querétaro and Zacatecas.

[24] Marion A. Habig, *The Alamo Chain of Missions*, pp. 38 ff.

the governor. They brought the leaders of twenty-three Indian groups, many formerly hostile to the Spaniards, to welcome the governor and offer allegiance to the Spanish Crown. By the end of the year, there were enough Payayas and Pamayas at the mission to form a viable settlement. San Antonio took on an air of permanence as the people dug irrigation ditches for the mission and presidial communities. In January 1719, Governor Alarcón called all the neophytes together to distribute gifts and installed the Indian officers of the mission pueblo. Thenceforth the Indians would live under the forms of Spanish civil government as well as the pastoral care of the missionaries.

In the autumn of 1719, refugees from the East Texas missions swelled the San Antonio community. The missionaries built temporary huts at Mission San Antonio in which to mark time until the governor could bring soldiers to escort them back to their stations.

Fray Antonio Margil de Jesús, president of the three Zacatecan missions in East Texas, soon encountered three groups in the vicinity who desired mission life but who would not enter Mission San Antonio because they disliked the Indians already settled there. To accommodate them, Fray Margil established another mission more than seven miles downstream from Mission San Antonio, far enough to avoid friction between either the unfriendly Indians or the rival missionary colleges.

His Mission San José began on February 23, 1720. The civil offices of the mission pueblo were carefully divided among the leaders of the interested nations: Chief Juan of the Pampopas as governor; Chief Nicolás of the Suliajames as judge; Chief Alonso of the Pastías as sheriff; two others as councilmen. More than two hundred Indians settled at the mission, began their irrigation ditches, and planted corn that spring; within two years they were marketing surpluses. When the Zacatecan friars returned to East Texas with Aguayo, they could count Mission San José an important new link in their chain of mission enterprises.[25]

When Governor Aguayo traveled to Texas in 1721 to reoccupy the eastern frontier, he bore other, rather surprising instructions: to seek not only peace but also alliance with the Apaches. Spanish knowledge of Texas thus far suggested that the new province was more likely to be another front in the wars with the Apaches than an avenue to peace. After all, the Apaches were long-standing enemies of the king's Tejas vassals, and Spanish soldiers had helped Tejas warriors campaign

[25] Ibid., pp. 83 ff.

against Apaches in 1692.[26] The Coahuiltecans, for whom the San Antonio missions were founded, had sought that sanctuary because Apaches infested their accustomed ranges; they, too, were now entitled to the protection of the king's arms. The Presidio of San Antonio de Béxar had been established chiefly to protect the mission communities from possible Apache harassment.

The twenty-three Indian groups who had pledged their loyalty to Governor Alarcón in 1718 were enemies of the Apaches, too. It was mainly because they deemed Spanish forces a counter to Apache power that they were prepared to welcome their intrusion. Furthermore, San Antonio's livestock herds would be magnets to Apache raiders.

There had always been some who envisioned the San Antonio River mission project as a possible avenue to solution of the Apache problem. Friars had argued for the foundation as a base for conversion of the Apaches. Now, developments in New Mexico had persuaded the viceroy that the Apaches could be made the friends of the Spaniards and might indeed form the barrier needed to seal New Spain's frontier against French intruders and their Indian allies. Although Apache raids remained a serious problem in New Mexico, there now loomed on the northern and eastern perimeters of the Apachería enemies dangerous to both Spanish and Apache interests. Some Apaches had appealed for help. Given careful encouragement, perhaps they would eventually bring all their compatriots into peaceful alliance with Spain.

[26] William Edward Dunn, "Apache Relations in Texas, 1718–1750," *Texas State Historical Association Quarterly* 14 (1911): 204.

CHAPTER 6

New Mexico, 1705-1733

An Apache alliance would have seemed a peculiar nostrum indeed to New Mexicans at the turn of the eighteenth century. Although trade with the Apaches flourished again once the reconquest was complete, raids also burgeoned. By spring 1705, a year after Governor Vargas died in his abortive pursuit of Faraon raiders, the Pueblos were virtually besieged by *bárbaros*, especially in such exposed locations as Zuñi, Ácoma, Laguna, Jémez, Pecos, Picurís, Taos, Santa Clara, and La Alameda.[1] Apaches were deemed the principal culprits, though Navajo and Ute raiders were also taking many horses. New Mexico's scanty resources were so speedily depleted that a general defensive war was unthinkable. The presidials lacked both arms and horses, and so did the settlers who had to supply much of the manpower for any expedition. Governor ad interim Francisco Cuervo y Valdés, the *cabildo*, missionaries, and settlers appealed jointly to Mexico City for help.

[1] Rael de Aguilar, Certification, Santa Fe, January 10, 1706, in Charles Wilson Hackett, ed., *Historical Documents Relating to New Mexico, Nueva Vizcaya, and Approaches Thereto, to 1773*, III, 367.

The viceroy and his council wearily noted that New Mexico now cost the Crown 77,500 pesos annually, in addition to any funds the religious could draw into the province, and that neither any profit nor any end to the drain was in sight.[2] Nevertheless, they agreed to ship powder and balls to the beleaguered province and to transfer thirty additional soldiers to the Santa Fe garrison. However onerous the responsibility, the Crown would extend all feasible protection to its New Mexican vassals.

Meanwhile, Governor Cuervo pursued raiders as promptly and as vigorously as the provincial resources allowed, with encouraging success. In the spring of 1705 he mustered the settlers to punish Apache horse thieves.[3] Cuervo also sent a company of soldiers after two large Navajo parties that had been stealing horses from San Ildefonso, Santa Clara, and San Juan. Subsequently he established the practice of sending just a token Spanish contingent with Pueblo forces to punish Navajos for raids against the Pueblos.[4] Squads of soldiers, deployed to frontier pueblos, helped the Pueblos pursue raiders with all possible speed and effectiveness in the districts most afflicted.

That program pleased the Pueblos tremendously. They exacted proper vengeance and reparations through spoils they took on the governor's campaigns, and by the end of the year they felt themselves virtually free of Apache and Navajo raids. Furthermore, the governor treated Pueblo officials with unfailing courtesy and generosity and forbade all Spaniards to bother the Indians in any way. On King's Day 1706, when the elected Pueblo officials reported to Santa Fe for formal installation in office, they presented the *cabildo* with a petition that they wished forwarded to Mexico City. Finding themselves defended, happy, and secure, the Pueblos unanimously petitioned for Governor Cuervo's continuation in office.[5]

By the summer of 1706 Governor Cuervo claimed that his campaigns had indeed achieved a general peace among the Navajos and Apaches.[6] He recalled to Santa Fe most of the soldiers he had deployed to the frontier pueblos and was even so sanguine as to push the frontiers of settlement a little farther southward, founding the new settlement of Albuquerque. He took the precaution of posting ten soldiers there

⸺ Duke of Alburquerque, Junta, Mexico, February 28, 1706, SANM, no. 122.

[3] Francisco Cuervo y Valdés, Bando, Santa Fe, March 10, 1705, SANM, no. 110.

[4] Aguilar, Certification, Santa Fe, January 10, 1706, in Hackett, *Historical Documents*, III, 367.

[5] Ibid.

[6] Duke of Alburquerque, Mexico, July 30, 1706, SANM, no. 24.

because Albuquerque lay near the frontiers of three Apache groups: Chilmos, Faraones, and Gilas.[7]

Much less encouraging was the outlook on the northern periphery of New Mexico. Ominous new pressures in that area came to light in the summer of 1706, when Governor Cuervo sent General Juan de Ulibarri northeastward with forty Spaniards and a hundred Pueblo warriors on an errand of mercy. En route, they found the Taoseños braced for a joint attack upon their pueblo by Utes and Comanches. Ulibarri notified the governor of the danger and continued his mission with grave misgivings about taking so many men away from the province.

Their destination was El Cuartelejo, and their purpose was to rescue the Picurís who had fled there in panic during the revolt of 1696. After a decade of unhappy servitude to their Cuartelejo Apache hosts, they had appealed to Governor Cuervo to fetch them home. The pious governor was financing the expedition from his own purse; the few remaining residents of Picurís had supplied all the blankets and horses they could gather to facilitate the homeward journey of their suffering kinsmen.[8]

Ulibarri found the Apachería humming with activity in late July, the people tending their crops and harvesting wild fruits that flourished along the streams where they lived. They welcomed the Spaniards cheerfully, grateful that they entered their lands without doing them any harm. First encountered were people who frequented Taos: Conexeros, Achos, and Río Colorados, probably all Jicarilla bands. They warned him against hostile Apaches farther on, especially those called Penxayes, Flechas de Palos, Lemitas, and Nemantinas, who had always been very bad thieves and sometimes injured the Jicarillas. Ulibarri explained that he could trust his God to preserve his people from harm and rode on, leaving suitable presents and his courteous thanks for their advice.

More Apaches came down from the mountains: Jicarillas, Flechas de Palos, and Carlanas, with chiefs of varying ranks. They promised to have ready for him on his return many raisins, an item they supplied to all Indians of the region. Ulibarri gave them tobacco, knives, and

---

[7] Frank D. Reeve, "Navaho-Spanish Wars, 1680–1720," *New Mexico Historical Review* 33 (1958): 224.

[8] Diary of Juan de Ulibarri to El Cuartelejo, 1706, in Alfred Barnaby Thomas, ed., *After Coronado: Spanish Exploration Northeast of New Mexico, 1696–1727*, pp. 59–77.

biscuits and entrusted to their care some horses too exhausted to continue the journey.

As Ulibarri journeyed on into present eastern Colorado, the Penxayes, against whom the Jicarillas had warned them, approached somewhat fearfully. When they saw his manifest good will, however, and noted that he permitted no injury to their fields, they welcomed him cordially. Two days and fifty miles farther into their territory, Ulibarri saw for the first time signs of difficulty with enemies beyond the Apachería. A Penxaye Apache man, with two women and three little boys, scurried by, rushing to join the rest of their band for defense against Utes and Comanches said to be coming to attack. Ulibarri heard that same story of expected Ute-Comanche incursions the next day from a woman and a little girl of the Penxayes, out gathering cherries along a creek.

The Spaniards pushed on across the Arkansas River, and within three days they found themselves among the *rancherías* of the Cuartelejo Apaches. Everywhere the people greeted the visitors with gifts of bison meat and roasting ears, true feasts for men many days on the trail.

Deep within El Cuartelejo, at a large *ranchería* marked with a tall cross, Ulibarri found and embraced Don Lorenzo and his people, who wept for joy when they understood the general's errand. The Apaches readily agreed to hand over the Picurís, although they needed time to round up all those scattered about in other *rancherías* and away with hunting parties. They asked Ulibarri to go with them meanwhile to fight Pawnees, seven days distant.

Loath to exceed his instructions so radically, Ulibarri protested that he must deliver the Picurís home before the snows came and before his horses were exhausted. He promised to come back another time, in spring, to aid them against their enemies. The Cuartelejos accepted that excuse and asked him instead to leave them a gun because the French were now giving guns to their enemies. Ulibarri swapped one of his guns for a big French gun that Apaches had taken that summer from a white man they had scalped when he and his woman lagged behind a Pawnee party. The Cuartelejos had a few other firearms, including three carbines seized from Pawnees.

Ulibarri talked at great length with the Cuartelejos about the advantages of peace and alliance with the king of Spain, meanwhile learning all that he could of their affairs. They seemed to him more truly inclined toward the Catholic faith than the Pueblos. Many wore crosses, medals, and rosaries, old but very carefully preserved, and

believed them possessed of magical powers to protect them in battle.
They said they had acquired them many years before, when they had
traded with the Spaniards. Many knelt an hour and a half with the
Spaniards and Pueblos for nightly prayers and kissed the chaplain's
sleeve as they departed, just as they saw the Christians do.

The docility and good will of the people, the excellent streams and
the fertile land, the abundance of game, all suggested to Ulibarri a
useful, appropriate expansion of the province of New Mexico. If
Frenchmen were indeed living and trading among their enemies, the
matter was urgent.

The Cuartelejos spoke of many tribes dwelling on streams beyond
them, all enemies of each other, but all trading with white men farther
east who sold them many metal goods. The Cuartelejos could not say
whether the traders were British or French, but the guns they had
were of French manufacture. Pawnees and Jumanos[9] were their principal enemies. Pawnees customarily captured women and children
from the Apaches to sell them to white men in the east, just as Apaches
sold Pawnee captives to Spaniards in New Mexico.

Ulibarri asked about the distance from El Cuartelejo to the seas of
the north and east, but Cuartelejos knew of seas only by hearsay. They
thought a sea lay three long days' journey beyond a people called
Pelones, by a grassless route across dunes of very fine sand.

Ulibarri left the Cuartelejos formally pledged to obey the king of
Spain and claimed their lands pacified for his domain. He bestowed the
staff of command as Captain-Mayor of all Apachería upon a promising
young man of distinguished family. They promised to venerate the
cross he had erected.

In mid-August Ulibarri started back to Santa Fe with sixty-two Picurís headed by Don Lorenzo. In two weeks they reached the Jicarilla
ranchería where they had left their worn-out horses. Chief Coxo and
his associates turned the animals over in good condition and generously
entertained the visitors. From them Ulibarri learned that Utes and
Comanches had indeed attacked the Apachería: one *ranchería* of the
Carlanas and Sierra Blancas, another of the Penxayes.

The New Mexicans hurried homeward. On August 31, 1706, Ulibarri
delivered the displaced Picurís to the pueblo they had fled a decade
before. Everyone rejoiced in the reunion of the long-suffering Picurís:
the priest came from Taos to absolve the apostates, and the *alcalde*

---

[9] In this, as in most subsequent New Mexican contexts, Jumano refers to the
Wichitan peoples.

mayor officially received them for the Spanish Crown. Picurís was on its way back from the brink of oblivion.

What of Ulibarri's promise to return to El Cuartelejo? Its worth depended upon decisions remote from New Mexico. His proposal to extend the faith and the king's government to El Cuartelejo was approved in Mexico City, subject to the king's consent. Pending a verdict from Madrid, the viceroy enjoined the New Mexicans to cultivate the friendship of those promising Apaches. But before the matter reached the Crown's attention, Comanche and Ute invaders swept the northernmost Apaches from their pleasant valley homes and pounded at the northern frontiers of New Mexico.

Utes had occasionally raided for horses in northern New Mexico since the mid-seventeenth century, just as Spaniards had sometimes preyed upon Ute camps for slaves. Utes had generally preferred friendly trade to hostilities, however, and they had cheerfully welcomed the Spaniards' return in 1693. By that time Utes had reorganized their lives around horses and were purveying the animals to other Indians farther north.

Most receptive to the equestrian life were the Comanches, aggressive, rustic, linguistic kinsmen of the Utes, who lived in the Rocky Mountain ranges of present northern Colorado and southern Wyoming. They soon appeared in New Mexico with Utes, both raiding and trading. Spaniards first learned of the Comanches when some turned up at the Taos trade fair with Ute companions early in the eighteenth century.

The turn of the century marked an epoch of change in the Southern Ute world. Northward expansion of Spanish settlements, as at Santa Cruz, spelled the first Spanish encroachment upon the winter ranges of the Utes. At the same time, Utes, mounted and operating in large bands, were able to use their range more effectively than ever before, and they could more than hold their own against the mounted Navajos and Apaches who had long preyed upon their camps. When Comanches came in increasing numbers to join forces with them, the Utes commanded an unprecedented potential for raiding and for war.

With countless old scores to settle against Athapaskans and Pueblos and with horses inviting raiders to every corral and pasture in New Mexico, the temptations to act were overwhelming. Thus, by 1706, the people of Taos lived in dread of Ute attack, and there was no security for any Apache *ranchería* within striking range of the Utes and their Comanche allies. Navajos also felt the impact of the new Ute power and regretfully came to know their Comanche allies. Spanish interests suffered last and least from the Ute-Comanche incursions. Although they lost occasional horses to the raiders, the Spaniards' involvement derived chiefly from their obligation to defend Pueblos against their Indian enemies and from the new issue of defending the Apaches of La Jicarilla and El Cuartelejo.

Even with their exciting new prowess, the Utes still preferred at least the semblance of peace with the Spaniards. During the gubernatorial term of the Marqués de la Peñuela,[10] Utes and Comanches solicited formal peace with the Spaniards and were, of course, granted it.[11] Utes and Comanches continued to steal horses throughout those years of "peace," but the losses remained at a level the Spaniards had learned to tolerate as the price of coexistence with *bárbaros*. Chronic friction between Utes and Pueblos climaxed in a grave incident at Taos pueblo in 1714, beginning with horse theft and ending in bloodshed. Governor Flores Mogollón[12] intervened to avert a general war, arranging restitution for damages and calming both Utes and Taoseños.[13] Though Utes and Comanches did not cease their horse thefts in New Mexico after Flores Mogollón pacified them in 1714, they focused their actual warfare against their enemies among the *bárbaros*, especially the Navajos and the Apaches of La Jicarilla and El Cuartelejo. Those beleaguered peoples soon looked to Spanish protection from the fierce Ute-Comanche pressures.

The Navajos' changing life style with their flourishing horse herds and flocks of sheep, their rising agricultural productivity, and their accumulated textiles of cotton and wool made them increasingly vulnerable to raiders.[14] Navajos built their homes away from their fields, atop adjacent mesas, so they could defend their persons relatively well against attack. But they suffered untold anguish when Spaniards or enemy Indians came to lay waste their fields and to destroy all the food and livestock they could not carry away. The more their lives revolved around their flocks of sheep and their horse herds, the more

[10] Admiral Joseph Chacón Medina Salazar y Villaseñor, Marqués de la Peñuela, 1707–1712.

[11] Christóbal de la Serna, Opinion in Council of War, Santa Fe, August 19, 1719, in Thomas, *After Coronado*, p. 105.

[12] Don Juan Ignacio Flores Mogollón, 1712–1715.

[13] "Relaciones de Nuevo Mexico, Año de 1707. Gobierno del Marqués de la Peñuela y Almirante," in *Documentos para la historia de Méjico*, ser. 3, I, 201.

[14] Willard W. Hill, "Some Navaho Culture Changes during Two Centuries (with a translation of the early eighteenth century Rabal Manuscript)," in *Essays in Historical Anthropology of North America*, p. 397.

they needed within their homeland the peace that would guarantee Navajo women and children safety to tend their flocks in far-flung pastures. Governor Cuervo's repeated punitive thrusts into their territory in 1705 and 1706 grew insupportable. By 1706, many Navajo leaders sued for peace, avowing the willingness of their people to accept baptism and reduction to formal settlements. Cuervo agreed gladly and let them ransom their captive women and children. Thenceforth, Navajos came to trade peacefully with the Spaniards and Pueblos.[15]

What Navajo leaders sought peace with Governor Cuervo? For what Navajo groups did they speak? Cuervo assumed one "principal captain" of the Navajos, but no such office existed. Cuervo's successors soon learned that no authority could commit all Navajos to a long-term peace.

When New Mexico received a new governor in the autumn of 1707, Navajos took the initiative to continue the peace with the new leader. In the spring of 1708 four Navajo delegates presented themselves as ambassadors "of all the captains of the *rancherías* and mountains of Navajo," come to renew their peace arrangements with the Spaniards. Delighted, the Marqués de la Peñuela presented to their principal spokesman the cane of office symbolizing gubernatorial authority over all Navajos.[16] Perhaps the governor assumed that the man had greater authority than actually existed in Navajo society; perhaps he simply wished to encourage the development of such authority.

That peace did not last the year. Whether it fell victim to the strong compulsions upon young Navajo men to raid for horses and captives or whether some Spaniards or Pueblos gave provocation is unknown, but by the end of 1708 Navajos were robbing, killing, and capturing, both at frontier settlements and at pueblos.[17] Spanish authorities felt betrayed: the viceroy demanded greater caution in the future in admitting either Navajo or Hopi groups to peace, lest they feign peace only to gain access to the settlements and pueblos.[18]

San Ildefonso, San Juan, and Santa Clara pueblos first bore the brunt of Navajo raids, and prompt pursuit of the thieves gained them

---

[15] Cuervo, Santa Fe, August 16, 1706, in Hackett, *Historical Documents*, III, 382.

[16] Reeve, "Navaho-Spanish Wars, 1680–1720," p. 224.

[17] "Relaciones de Nuevo Mexico, Año de 1707," in *Documentos para la historia de Méjico*, ser. 3, I, 197.

[18] Duke of Alburquerque to the Marqués de la Peñuela, Mexico, December 4, 1708, SANM, no. 152.

little relief.[19] Even worse, in June Navajos attacked their erstwhile friends at Jémez, sacked their houses, destroyed the church, and desecrated the sacramental vessels.[20]

That was the intolerable affront. The Marqués de la Peñuela gathered all the forces of the province, Pueblo and Spanish, to carry the offensive into Navajo territory.[21] Half a dozen campaigns ensued before the Navajos finally sought a new truce with the Spaniards in 1710.[22]

That truce endured through Peñuela's term, but, within the year after Flores Mogollón succeeded him in autumn 1712, Navajos began stealing stock and capturing Pueblos. Governor Flores Mogollón sent Captain Cristóbal de la Serna into Navajo country with 50 presidials, 20 militiamen, and 150 Pueblo warriors, charged to pursue the raiders as far as necessary, but to be ready to talk peace if the Navajos would release their Pueblo captives. The force mustered at Jémez and pursued the escaping Navajos nearly forty miles. They laid waste cornfields and took about thirty captives, but they could not persuade the Navajos to talk peace.[23]

Navajos struck Jémez again the following March and killed one of its leaders. To retaliate, Governor Flores Mogollón dispatched fifty soldiers, a few militiamen, and 212 Pueblos. Captain Roque de Madrid led the force up the Chama Valley, then swept back down through the Navajo country to Jémez. At every opportunity, he attacked Navajos: thirty-odd died; seven were captured. The invaders carried off five hundred bushels of corn, some other foodstuffs, and 110 sheep. The exchange began to cost the Navajos dearly, but they raided and endured the punitive campaigns through 1716. After that, the Ute and Comanche pressures against them grew so severe that the Navajos came to prefer the peace and protection the Spaniards proffered their Indian friends. By 1720, Navajos were no longer reckoned among the enemies of New Mexico.[24]

[19] Marqués de la Peñuela to Sargento Mayor Juan de Ulibarri, Alcalde Mayor de Santa Cruz, Santa Fe, February 21, 1709, SANM, no. 154.

[20] "Relaciones de Nuevo Mexico, Año de 1707," in *Documentos para la historia de Méjico*, ser. 3, I, 197.

[21] Marqués de la Peñuela, Santa Fe, December 8, 1709, SANM, no. 154.

[22] "Relaciones de Nuevo Mexico, Año de 1707," in *Documentos para la historia de Méjico*, ser. 3, I, 197.

[23] Juan Ygnacio Flores Mogollón, Santa Fe, May 13, 1713, SANM, no. 193; Autos and Junta de Guerra on thefts committed by the Navajo Apaches, Santa Fe, October 18–23, 1713, SANM, no. 199; Reeve, "Navaho-Spanish Wars, 1680–1720," pp. 226–228.

[24] Reeve, "Navaho-Spanish Wars, 1680–1720," pp. 229–231; Donald E. Wor-

Although they would never accept missionaries, the Navajos remained until the late eighteenth century the most consistently friendly of the nations surrounding New Mexico. Their trade in textiles, skins, baskets, and war captives grew to major importance in the commerce of the province.[25] The Spaniards, at least the missionaries, never ceased to hope, and indeed to expect, that a people so rational and industrious would surely be converted to the faith sometime soon.

In contrast, Faraon Apache raiders rampaged unchecked throughout the second decade of the eighteenth century. Spaniards and Pueblos along the eastern frontier of New Mexico suffered heavy losses, but the Faraones wreaked their worst havoc upon their northern neighbors, the Jicarillas, who were gravely weakened by the Ute-Comanche onslaught and thus vulnerable to any foe. By 1714, New Mexicans began to consider including Jicarilla warriors among the friendly Indians who campaigned with the Spaniards against the Faraones.[26]

In the summer of 1714 Faraones perched in the Sandía Mountains, whence they preyed so heavily upon the livestock, especially around Bernalillo and Alameda, that by August neither Spaniards nor Pueblos dared postpone retaliation until after harvest as they had hoped. Settlers from Albuquerque and La Cañada and Taos, Pecos, and Keres Indians joined thirty-six presidials from Santa Fe for a punitive campaign, with some success.[27] The Faraones sued for peace at both Pecos and Isleta.

The New Mexicans had won only a fleeting respite. Within months, Faraones were taking advantage of the peace granted them at Isleta to enter the settled area, where they committed more robberies and kidnapped a Spanish child. Governor Flores Mogollón summoned the leading citizens to council on the Faraon problem, and they debated through the summer of 1715.[28] Everyone agreed that the outrages demanded punishment, but how could they identify the actual offenders? How could they find their mountain hideouts? Governor

cester, "The Navaho during the Spanish Régime in New Mexico," *New Mexico Historical Review* 26 (1951): 112.

[25] "Apuntamientos," in *Documentos para la historia de Méjico*, ser. 3, I, 108.

[26] Auto and Junta de Guerra on the matter of war with the Apaches Faraones, Santa Fe, June 30–July 6, 1714, SANM, no. 206.

[27] Ibid.; Junta de Guerra on campaign against the Apaches Faraones in the Sandia Mountains, Santa Fe, August 9–14, 1714, SANM, no. 209.

[28] Junta de Guerra against the Apaches, Albuquerque and Santa Fe, June 16–September 14, 1715, SANM, no. 224.

Flores Mogollón invited Don Gerónimo Ylo, lieutenant-governor of Taos, and Don Lorenzo and his lieutenant-governor of Picurís to identify the attacking band and to suggest a plan of action.

Don Gerónimo explained that the raiders were Chipaynes or Lemitas, called Sejines by the Taos, but identical with the people whom the Spaniards dubbed Faraones and the very same ones who had fled Pecos at the time of the conquest. Don Lorenzo called them Lemitas or Trementinas. They generally visited Pecos at the time of ransoming,[29] mingled unobtrusively among other, truly peaceful Indians from the plains, and then took advantage of their access to the province to rob and kill. They also preyed upon the Jicarillas, who were therefore willing to furnish both scouts and warriors for a campaign against them.

The Taoseños had long wanted to pursue and punish the offenders, but they lacked sufficient arms. Don Gerónimo was eager now to guide the Spaniards and warriors from the Tewa, Taos, and Picurís pueblos,[30] with Jicarilla allies, to attack the Faraon *rancherías* on the plains. Don Lorenzo declared that the first *ranchería*, some thirty wooden houses plastered with mud, lay on the Canadian River only ten days from Picurís. Time was of the essence: the New Mexicans should strike in mid-August, just as the moon waxed full. The Faraones would be busy then, shaking the grain from their ears of corn. As soon as they could cache their shelled corn, they would depart for the buffalo hunt, not to return until planting time at the beginning of May. In the interval they would live wherever hunting was good. During those months New Mexicans would see Faraones only when a need for corn should impel them to raid.

Even as the council debated, the New Mexican situation deteriorated further. Worsening Apache raids on the western frontier required the governor to deploy twenty-five soldiers to defend the Zuñi area.[31] Then Apaches made off with the horse herd of Picurís, with the young men of the pueblo in hot pursuit. Flores Mogollón tried to send help as soon as he heard of it, but the presidial herd was grazing far north on the Chama River. Before the soldiers could round up mounts to join the

---

[29] The "ransoming" was the periodic gathering of the *bárbaros* at the frontier pueblos to market their captives.

[30] Don Gerónimo advised against taking Pecos warriors on the grounds that they were kin to, and therefore sympathetic with, the Faraones. He also considered the Keres likely to warn the enemy. Perhaps his warning reflected traditional Pueblo enmities more than current realities, for Pecos warriors acquitted themselves well in this and subsequent campaigns.

[31] Flores Mogollón, Decree, Santa Fe, September 27, 1715, SANM, no. 231b.

chase, another messenger brought word that the men of Picurís had recovered their herd and that the enemy had fled to the plains.

Regardless of their garrison's inauspicious showing in the latest crisis, the council agreed that something must be done to check the depredations of the Faraones. Unfortunately, they scheduled the attack for mid-September, a month later than Don Gerónimo advised. Their own harvest would not be finished before that, and they doubted the Taoseño's report that corn planted as late as May could be harvested and stored by mid-August.

The force mustered on the plaza of Picurís, early on the morning of August 30, 1715, under command of Don Juan Páez Hurtado: 37 soldiers, 18 settlers, 146 Pueblos.[32] Thirty men of Pecos came, despite Don Gerónimo's doubts that they could be trusted against the Faraones; Taos, Picurís, Nambé, Tesuque, San Juan, Santa Clara, and San Ildefonso furnished the rest. Thirty Jicarilla warriors and one Cuartelejo joined the party as it rode through the Mora Valley toward the plains, where they would follow the Canadian River.

Ten days passed before they saw any Apache signs at all, and they never spotted a *ranchería*. They found only old tracks of many people and large herds. Several times their Indian guide was obviously lost and confused. By the fifteenth day, Páez Hurtado was so exasperated that he gave the man fifty lashes and turned the force back toward Santa Fe. He assumed that the Faraones had heard of the expedition at Pecos and had therefore fled from the Canadian. No one recalled Don Gerónimo's warning that the Faraones would have finished their harvests and departed a month earlier. The month-long exercise in futility was significant only because it marked the friendly northeastern Apaches' first participation in a Spanish campaign. Failing contact with the enemy, the Jicarillas and Cuartelejos had no chance to show their mettle and ample reason to grow disgusted with Spanish management of the effort.

The Spaniards had little time to brood over their failure. That fall smoldering difficulties between Governor Flores Mogollón and the Santa Fe garrison blazed to a climax. In November, the governor surrendered his post to Captain Félix Martínez, who served ad interim until the viceroy sent his replacement more than a year later. Martínez desperately needed some outstanding achievement to vindicate his role in ousting the lawful governor, and Indian affairs appeared the

[32] Council of War and Diary of the Campaign of Don Juan Páez Hurtado against the Faraon Apaches, 1715, in Thomas, *After Coronado,* pp. 80–98.

main chance. He campaigned against the Faraones with a little success, and against the Gilas with none, but events in the distant Hopi country soon shaped a better target for his ambitions.

Since the Hopis had staved off reconquest, their independence had entailed certain penalties. As vulnerable as any Pueblos to the growing effectiveness of mounted Ute, Navajo, and Apache raiders, Hopis lacked the recourse to Spanish arms that the reduced Pueblos enjoyed. Nor had they access to the burgeoning New Mexican trade so useful to Christian Pueblos. At first they mitigated their isolation through trade fairs with northern Pimas, whose towns lay only three days distant, but about 1715 some incident sparked a great fight between Pimas and Hopis at the Sobaipuris fair. Many Hopis died in the fray; trade and communication with Pimas ceased. The Pimas regretted the breach and wished to restore peace and trade, but Gila Apaches, enemies of both nations, occupied a key pass on the trail and cut off their access.[33]

Greater misfortune followed. A fourth year of drought made Hopi food supplies critically short in the winter of 1715–1716. Already there were too many stresses on the population: the terrors of *bárbaros* raids; the uncertainty whether or when the Spaniards would again try reconquest; the internal divisions among Hopis about the best response to the Spaniards and their God; the tensions inherent in the presence of refugee Pueblo groups not always on good terms with each other and unaccustomed to the powerful Hopi leadership; and, always, the rigors of wresting a livelihood from the stark Hopi land. By the spring of 1716, some refugees were disheartened and homesick enough to brave the return to their native pueblos. Sixteen Jémez families at Walpi sent three men to Jémez to request escort home. Thirty Zuñi refugees and two Hopis trekked to Zuñi to stay. Ten went home to Laguna, five to Isleta. All departed with the permission of Oraibi's new young cacique, whose aged father had willed him the office with a mandate to make peace with the Spaniards. Everyone in the Hopi country was sick of war.

Governor Martínez first learned of the new developments late in April 1716, when two men from Jémez brought to the Governor's Palace the three emissaries of the refugees and asked permission to take twenty men from Jémez to fetch the sixteen families home from Walpi.[34] Martínez not only granted permission, he also ordered the

[33] Rufus Kay Wyllys, ed., "Padre Luis Velarde's *Relación* of Pimería Alta, 1716," *New Mexico Historical Review* 6 (1931): 139.

[34] Lansing B. Bloom, ed., "A Campaign against the Moqui Pueblos under the

people of Zuñi, Ácoma, Laguna, and Zía to accord the refugees every assistance, and he sought further information from Fray Francisco Yrazábal of Zuñi mission. Reduction of the apostate Hopis had been for twenty years a prime desire of both Church and Crown. One New Mexican governor after another had failed in the attempt. If Martínez could now solve the Hopi problem, his own position would be unassailable.

The missionary's response was most encouraging. On the basis of talks with the returning Zuñi refugees, he believed that famine had rendered the Hopis vulnerable to reconquest at last. They were still terribly afraid of Spaniards, but Fray Francisco was sure that in time the Hopis would see that Catholics had "good hearts" toward their fellows, and he had no qualms about seeing them starved into submission.

Don Juan Nicolás, governor of Zuñi, rode to the Hopi towns as New Mexico's envoy to the Hopis and the Tano, Tewa, and Tiwa refugees, carrying a cross to signal desire for peace and a generous array of gifts. Hopi and refugee leaders convened at Oraibi to welcome him, earnestly expressing their own desires for peace and assuring him that the refugees were free to leave. His report further encouraged Governor Martínez to seize the opportunity to reestablish both Majesties' authority among the Hopis. Cristóbal, leader of the 113 Jémez refugees who arrived home in June, declared that the other refugees would have come home too if only they had enough horses to bring out their women and children.

Accordingly, at the beginning of August, Governor Martínez summoned all the forces he dared spare from the province: 70 soldiers from the presidio; 41 militiamen from the three villas, including all the Santa Fe *cabildo*; 282 Indians from twenty pueblos. Provisioning such a big force was no trivial problem, and Martínez expected to bring out many refugees, all of whom would need food. He sent eleven soldiers ahead with a hundred cattle, and he arranged through Fray Francisco Yrazábal to purchase 250 bushels of corn at Zuñi, half ground and half kernels.

Most of the force mustered at Albuquerque's plaza on August 20, 1716. The Indians from Laguna, Ácoma, and Zuñi joined the force as it reached their home localities. Tension arose when the governor of

Picurís spotted in the possession of a Jémez man a horse that Utes had stolen from him a year before, and demanded that Governor Martínez order it returned. Questioned, the Jémez said he had acquired the animal in a horse trade with a Ute. It was his lawful property, which he had no idea of relinquishing. To avoid friction among his Indian allies, Governor Martínez gave one of his own horses to the governor of Picurís. That incident was but the first of many severe strains upon the limited patience of Martínez.

At Zuñi, on August 29, Governor Martínez held council with the leaders of each pueblo represented in the force. He asked them to select the sixteen most capable Indians to carry the cross and his offer of peace and pardon to the Hopis and to invite the refugees to return under his protection to their original pueblos. Having anticipated his request, the leaders readily agreed upon appropriate emissaries. Governor Martínez gave the envoys careful instructions, a cross painted on paper, and appropriate quantities of tobacco to be given to the Hopi leaders in his name. Don Cristóbal Caiquiro of Zía led the delegation off to the Hopi mesas.

To minimize strain upon the scant water and pasture of the Hopi country, the rest of the force followed in three separate divisions. They rendezvoused at the ruined Hopi pueblo of Aguatovi, destroyed in 1700 by conservative Hopis. A dozen Hopis and Tiwas, including two war captains, greeted the vanguard there and offered peace and friendship. They promised that people would come from all the pueblos next day to greet the governor. The sixteen Pueblo envoys sent word that they were happily received on the mesas and that perfect peace would be achieved.

On September 3, leaders from Oraibi, Mosonavi, and Walpi came to express their desires for peace to Governor Martínez. He assured them of his protection and friendship. Fray Antonio Camargo harangued them about the benefits of eternal salvation. To avoid offense to the Indians, Martínez proclaimed harsh penalties for any member of his force who should harm any of the Indians' fields or other property: two years' banishment to the Zuñi frontier for any Spaniard, soldier or civilian, who offended; one hundred lashes and a humiliating ride through the camp on a burro for any Indian offender. Then he waited to receive the penitent refugees.

The Tano refugees at Walpi had remained stubbornly silent when the Pueblo emissaries presented the peaceful proposals of Martínez. Within two days their doubts began to infect others. Martínez heard that the people of Walpi were withdrawing to their rock, suspicious that war would soon be waged against them. He sent a Tano from his force to talk with his fellow Tanoans, but to no avail. Although leaders of every other group in the Hopi area came to talk with Martínez, the Tanos held aloof.

Other problems arose. About to reap a good harvest after four years of crop failures, the refugees were loath to return home at once with the governor's force. His insistence that they abandon their crops and the long harangues of both Martínez and Fray Camargo about the damnation into which the devil had tricked them served to remind everyone of the disadvantages of dealing with Spaniards.

A week's dickering exhausted the governor's patience and the Indians' confidence. On September 8, the governor called a council of war and won its unanimous approval to declare war on the Hopis. He did not try to storm their mesas, but for ten days he systematically devastated fields, confiscated herds, and seized captives. Some Hopis and others died in the attempt to protect their property; most watched in anguish from the mesatops as their first harvest in five years fell victim to vengeful self-righteousness. Fray Yrazábal had been wrong: it was not, after all, the year to convince the Hopis that Catholics had good hearts.

Governor Martínez returned home to Santa Fe in mid-October with a costly, humiliating failure on his record at best; at worst, he could be called to account for indefensible, illegal assault upon Indians who had in no way attacked his province. More than ever, he needed a conspicuous triumph to vindicate his governorship. Within a week, he grasped at another chance to win distinction, this time at Ute expense.

Martínez had ridden off on his Hopi campaign aware that Ute and Comanche raiders were enjoying an active summer. Early in July ten Ute visitors stole four horses at Jémez. For the rest of the summer, Utes and Comanches wandered into villages and pueblos, committed petty thefts, and seemed to spy on the settled area. Absorbed in his preparations for the Hopi venture, Martínez ignored all reports and made no effort to correct the difficulty, much to the dismay of the afflicted Pueblos and settlers.

Less than a week after his return from the Hopi country, on October 14, Governor Martínez announced that the Ute and Comanche culprits were camped by San Antonio Mountain, less than a hundred miles north of Santa Fe. His hastily summoned council endorsed war against the Utes and Comanches because they had been stealing livestock from settlers and friendly Indians. One factor in their decision for war was their expectation of help from friendly Jicarilla and Sierra Blanca Apaches, sworn enemies of the Utes and Comanches.

The force assembled at Taos: fifty soldiers, a dozen settlers, and fifty Tewas, led by Captain Cristóbal de la Serna.[35] They surprised the camp at the foot of San Antonio Mountain and wrought havoc, killing some, capturing many, and putting the rest to flight. Governor Martínez speedily dispatched his brother south with the captives, to be peddled in Nueva Vizcaya.

The story of that campaign sparked a great public outcry against Martínez and became the basis of a move to oust him.[36] Those Utes had camped to await an answer to a peace overture they had sent to Santa Fe. Whether Martínez already knew of the peace proposal and how specifically he had directed Serna's attack was never ascertained. By the time the matter was investigated during the *residencia* of Martínez, key witness Serna was dead, and other testimonies conflicted. There seemed no doubt that Serna fell upon a peaceful Ute camp without giving them any warning or opportunity to come to peaceful terms, nor was there any doubt that Martínez hastened to turn a profit by selling the captives. He was found guilty of inhuman conduct and required to repurchase and return the captives to New Mexico at his own expense.

Unfortunately, restitution proved impossible. Most of the captives had died of smallpox; the few survivors were already baptized and thus could not be shipped back to the pagan life. The aggrieved Utes, who came to make peace with acting Governor Juan Páez Hurtado in January 1717, counted upon recovering their lost kin.[37] Perhaps the later trend to more serious hostilities reflected their grim disappointment in 1717. The fact that the *residencia* rendered a strong judgment against Martínez in 1723 availed little to either his Ute or his Hopi victims of 1716.

The Utes observed the new peace reasonably well for a year and a half. Visiting Utes and Comanches committed occasional thefts, but that cost was negligible in comparison with the serious losses of life and

[35] Council of War Concerning an Expedition against the Utes and Comanches, Santa Fe, July 2–October 15, 1717, SANM, no. 279.

[36] Isidro Armijo, ed., "Information Communicated by Juan Candelaria, Resident of This Villa de San Francisco Xavier de Alburquerque, Born 1692—Age 84," *New Mexico Historical Review* 4 (1929): 290.

[37] "Gobierno de D. Félix Martínez," *Documentos para la historia de Méjico,* ser. 3, I, 106–107.

property inflicted by Faraon and Gila Apaches on the eastern and southern frontiers of the province. The war parties and big raiding parties of Utes and Comanches rode against Navajos and the Apaches of La Jicarilla and El Cuartelejo until they drove them in desperation to seek the protection of the Spaniards. Not until mid-summer 1719 did the Ute and Comanche activities in New Mexico take a truly menacing turn.

Suddenly, Utes and Comanches penetrated much more deeply into the province than ever before, in much larger numbers, stole more property, and, most unusual of all, murdered. They left a Taoseño in Arroyo Hondo bristling with arrows and seized four horses and a little boy from El Embudo. Terror swept the Taos Valley.

Some twenty Utes killed a Cochití man in a canyon near his pueblo. When the *alcalde mayor* led forty Indians after the criminals, they found the trail of a hundred men, six women, and some dogs. The surge of worrisome reports from many quarters puzzled Governor Antonio Valverde y Cosío. Promiscuous killing had never been a Ute practice, and he knew of no reason for the sudden change. He sent a squad to protect Taos and summoned twenty-eight provincial leaders to council at Santa Fe on August 19.[38]

All but three councilors recommended immediate war upon the Utes. Most agreed that the Comanches were probably just as much involved and just as deserving of punishment, if only they could be found. One settler from Pojoaque, Juan de Mittas, objected that the Utes had always kept the peace with New Mexico and did so even now: they were killing only to avenge kinsmen killed by Pueblos, a permissible act. Mittas also suspected that the Ute and Comanche intruders were in collusion with the Apaches or the slaves of the Pueblos, and that the latter might set off a revolt in the heart of the province if they should see the troops march off for a long campaign.

Captain Sebastián Martín, a Rio Arriba settler with thirty-four years' service in New Mexico, cautioned that the Utes were probably being wrongly blamed for crimes committed by Comanches. He advised the governor to station armed squads of Spaniards and Pueblos at spots where the *bárbaros* entered the settlements in order to ascertain whether the culprits were Utes or Comanches. Martín feared that rash

---

[38] Testimonios which were made in the matter of the campaign against the Utes for their murders and thefts in New Mexico, called by Governor Valverde y Cosío, Santa Fe, August 11, 1719, SANM, no. 301; Council of War, Santa Fe, August 19, 1719, in Thomas, *After Coronado*, pp. 100–110.

punishment of innocent Utes would bring down a bloody, altogether unnecessary war upon New Mexico.

Alférez Ygnacio de Ruybal, a veteran of twenty-six years at the presidio, agreed with the majority that a force must march against the Utes and Comanches, but he argued that they should only deliver a peaceful reprimand upon overtaking the enemy. Only if the enemy should take up arms against them would the force be justified in making war upon them.

The other twenty-five stood firm for war. None mentioned the grave wrongs inflicted upon Utes less than two years before, nor did any acknowledge Mittas' point that perhaps the Utes were acting now within a permissible framework of vengeance in tribal warfare. Even those from areas where no murders had occurred were heartily sick of losing livestock to Utes and Comanches. Many insisted that the thefts and killings would only increase until those two nations were punished. Some recounted their long toleration of thefts to maintain peace with the Utes. Now, they reasoned, by acts of murder the Utes had deliberately declared war. Surely the incursions of large parties so far from home could only signal active intent to pursue hostilities.

Valverde concurred with the majority. Convinced that it would be dangerous to tolerate the depredations any longer, he announced a campaign to drive the enemy back to their own lands and thus to liberate New Mexico from their terror. The governor himself would lead the force.

Governor Valverde mustered his men at Taos pueblo on August 19, 1719.[39] Forty-five ragged, ill-equipped settlers volunteered to ride with the sixty presidial soldiers from Santa Fe; 465 Pueblo warriors answered the call. As they marched northward, 165 Apache warriors joined the great war party, delighted to hope for vengeance on the Utes and Comanches. Their combined horse herds totaled more than a thousand; the provisions included a drove of sheep. They progressed slowly and conspicuously.

The motley crowd of men and beasts traveled two months and a thousand miles and never saw a Ute or a Comanche. On the Arkansas River, between present Pueblo and La Junta, they found traces of two big Comanche camps, one with more than sixty fires and another with more than a hundred. Valverde's scouts guessed that a thousand Indians had camped there. Thence the trail pointed northeastward,

[39] Antonio de Valverde y Cosío, Diary, September 15–October 22, 1719, in Thomas, *After Coronado*, pp. 110–133.

across the arid plains. Both Apache and Pueblo scouts warned that the enormous horse herd would not find enough water to survive. The soldiers and settlers worried that the winter snows would soon close the mountain routes back to New Mexico. Valverde turned his men back toward home, leaving the Utes and Comanches unscathed.

Even so, the expedition proved important. Valverde brought home to Santa Fe the first appreciation of the newly critical state of affairs in the northern reaches of the Apachería, and he left behind promises, more reassuring than realistic, of protection for the Apaches. He also gleaned alarming tales of new French activities among the Apaches' Indian enemies to the north and east.

Ute and Comanche warriors had reduced life to a misery of fear and want in the once pleasant *rancherías* of La Jicarilla, the Sierra Blanca, and El Cuartelejo. The Apaches' semi-sedentary agricultural way of life made them terribly vulnerable to raiders. Perhaps the Pueblo example, particularly during the sojourns of the fugitives, had influenced those Apaches toward a more settled, agricultural life style, though Apaches had done some farming as long as men could remember. Beginning with the first of the Jicarilla *rancherías*, near present Cimarron, Valverde found some Apaches living in adobe homes, sometimes clustered, sometimes even terraced, and he saw irrigation ditches in some of their fields. Many Apaches venerated Christian religious articles. Such Apaches appeared genuinely ready to be baptized and to occupy permanent settlements under the protection of Cross and Crown.

Some Jicarillas had proposed as much to the missionary at Taos early that year. Convinced of their sincerity, he persuaded Governor Valverde to endorse the request and forward it to the viceroy for decision. The viceroy's affirmative reaction had not yet reached Santa Fe, but Governor Valverde talked with the Jicarillas about the importance of settling down to the Christian life, and they readily promised to do so. Events of recent years had saddened and discouraged the Jicarillas overwhelmingly. Utes and Comanches had killed so many of their men and captured so many of their women and children that all bands were gravely weakened, and they no longer knew anywhere that they could go to live in safety.

One of the saddest places was the *ranchería* of Chief Coxo. Just a year earlier, Utes and Comanches had attacked there, killed sixty, captured sixty-four women and children, and destroyed everything. Now Chief Coxo had ridden to the Navajo country, perhaps to negotiate for help or refuge, while his people dreaded the enemy's return any day to finish the bloody ravages begun the year before.

While Valverde was among the Jicarillas, Chief Carlana came from the Sierra Blanca with three other leaders of his band. They were leading half the Sierra Blanca Apaches to seek the Jicarillas' help against the Utes and Comanches. The other half of their people had already given up the struggle to hold their territories and had fled farther into the interior to take refuge among Apaches led by Chief Flaco. Delighted to learn of Valverde's campaign against the Comanches and Utes, Carlana offered the services of his people to aid the Spaniards in penetrating the enemies' haunts.

True to his word, Chief Carlana brought sixty-nine painted warriors to join Valverde on the Purgatoire River late in September. They danced most of their first night in camp, then settled down to the serious business of scouting for enemy signs. They were on familiar ground, for this had once been their best source of pelts. Now their hunters dared not venture into the area, lest they fall victim to Utes or Comanches. Their failure to find the enemy for Valverde to trounce was a crushing disappointment for Carlana and his men, but they had no stomach for a hopeless campaign on the plains.

The Spaniards had already pointed homeward when ten Apache messengers from El Cuartelejo overtook them. Their chiefs had been on the Arkansas River with all their people, more than two hundred tents, when they learned of Valverde's campaign from Cuartelejos who had been trading at Taos in September when the governor's force mustered there. The Cuartelejos had spread the word to other Apaches farther east. Now they all wanted to come and join in his effort. The Cuartelejos were on their way en masse, with untold numbers of Calchufines Apaches.

It was unthinkable to hurry home without seeing them. Governor Valverde sent men to Taos to fetch more provisions and promised to await the Cuartelejos on the Arkansas River, just downstream from present Las Animas.

The Apaches arrived within the week and pitched camp across the stream from Valverde's own. They had more than two hundred tents and three hundred armed men, with a total population of perhaps a thousand. Although they had horses for hunting and war, dogs still hauled their household goods and tents in the old way. They told of still more Apache tribes on the way to see the governor, and he promised to wait as long as he could.

The Apaches had hardly arrived before someone notified the governor that a Paloma Apache chief in the camp had a gunshot wound. Investigation revealed an alarming story: the wounded man had been planting corn with his people in their homeland beyond El Cuartelejo, on the farther borders of the Apachería, when they had suffered a surprise attack by Frenchmen, Pawnees, and Jumanos. The Palomas had managed to escape with their lives, but their enemies had held their lands ever since. The Palomas had come to the upper Arkansas to take refuge with their kinsmen.

Their information about the French was fragmentary and largely second-hand: two new pueblos, each as large as Taos, in which Frenchmen lived with the Pawnees and Jumanos; long guns given to those Indians, with lessons in musketry; three more French settlements across the Mississippi, from which they brought guns and other goods to the new ones recently built; French alliances with Kansas, Tejas, and Pawnees; a first French settlement among the Kadohadachos; two other settlements up the large river on the north bank. Reports of the farther French posts derived from Apache women, sometime captives sold to Frenchmen, who had escaped to return to their own people. The accounts of more recent developments apparently reflected the September visits of La Harpe and du Tisne, and the new trading activities spurred by the Company of the Indies.

With such news for the viceroy, Governor Valverde dared wait no longer for other Apaches. He left important promises: the Spaniards would expel the French from all of these lands, which rightfully belonged only to the king of Spain and his vassals and the Apaches. The king would protect the Apaches' right to live securely on their own lands. The Apaches appeared consoled and pleased, although sadly disappointed that Valverde could not wait to see the other bands.

Valverde hurried back to Santa Fe to send to the viceroy his own appeal for help: trained officers and artillerymen, munitions, and usable artillery, all lacking in New Mexico. Its rustic soldiers, settlers, and Pueblos could manage well enough in Indian warfare, but they would need training and equipment if they were to meet a French army on the plains.[40]

Viceroy Valero could hardly discount the French threat to New Mexico. Only that summer Lieutenant Blondel's little squad had routed Spaniards from Tejas country; French activities were now suspected

[40] Antonio de Valverde y Cosío to Valero, Santa Fe, November 30, 1719, ibid., pp. 141–145.

among most tribes north and east of San Antonio. The viceroy had already dispatched in August orders to the missionary at Taos and to Governor Valverde to do anything necessary to cultivate the Jicarillas' friendship and thus to lay the groundwork for alliance with them against the French.[41] Now, in January 1720, after evaluating the autumn reports of Governor Valverde, the viceroy and his council proposed a far more dramatic thrust into the Apacheria to forestall French incursions.

Off to New Mexico went the new order: establish a presidio and a mission at El Cuartelejo. Man it with twenty-five of Santa Fe's best soldiers, all married, and send their families for permanent settlement there. Send several missionaries to convert the Apaches. Form a perpetual alliance with the Apaches to protect the frontier. "In view of the fact that these Indians are so widely dispersed that they extend as far as the Texas and the Mississippi River, we can make use of their assistance in those parts for defense and for impeding the ingress of the French."[42] The governor of Texas would be instructed to make similar alliances with the Apaches on that frontier. Thus, a great Apache barrier would bar the French from New Spain.

Valverde found the order thoroughly irresponsible; so did his council of New Mexican veterans. Most had seen El Cuartelejo with Ulibarri when he rescued the Picuris in 1706, and they minced no words. El Cuartelejo was 330 miles northeast of Santa Fe, much too far to supply satisfactorily from the capital; its natural resources were inadequate to support a community of any size; its climate was too harsh for year-round occupation. Twenty-five soldiers with their families and a few priests would be helpless there if the Indians should ever league against them, for Apaches alone could rally two or three thousand warriors. To assign Spaniards to such a post would be tantamount to human sacrifice.

Valverde and the council unanimously protested the order and urged instead that the presidio be established at La Jicarilla, less than a hundred miles northeast of Santa Fe and conveniently near Taos. The Jicarillas had long inclined toward Christianity; their land was well watered and wooded and its soil productive. Even there a garrison of fifty men would be needed if the Jicarillas were to be adequately protected against Utes and Comanches on the one hand and Faraones

[41] Marqués de Valero, Order, Mexico, August 1, 1719, ibid., pp. 138–139.
[42] Junta de Guerra, Mexico, January 2, 1720, in Charles Wilson Hackett, ed., *Pichardo's Treatise on the Limits of Louisiana and Texas*, III, 204–205.

on the other and if the Spaniards were to be safeguarded against a possible surge of antagonism among the Jicarillas.[43]

The New Mexicans won their point. The viceroy ordered Valverde to establish the presidio at La Jicarilla to facilitate the conversion of the Jicarillas and the establishment of a "perpetual alliance" with the Apaches.[44]

That decision, which the Jicarillas had awaited nearly two years, should have spelled sanctuary for the beleaguered northeastern Apaches. However, events on the northern frontier again outran New Spain's processes of official decision. In January 1720 the viceroy ordered the presidio at El Cuartelejo; in June the council at Santa Fe filed its protest; in September the viceroy assented to the Jicarilla location. But by mid-August, New Mexico had suffered a crushing military blow that virtually ruled out any new venture.

Lieutenant-governor Pedro de Villasur led a large reconnaissance force northeast from Santa Fe in June 1720 to spy out French forces on the farther rim of the Apachería. In August, attacking Indians[45] nearly wiped out the force near present North Platte, Nebraska, with the reported assistance of Frenchmen. Only a dozen Spanish survivors, badly wounded, stumbled back to El Cuartelejo to be succored by the Apaches, who grieved with them and promised to help them avenge their dead.[46]

There was little chance that the Cuartelejos would see a great Spanish war party avenge Villasur's men as they expected. The fiasco had cost New Mexico thirty-two of its best presidial veterans, nearly a third of its garrison. The province lay an easier mark than ever for Utes, Comanches, and Faraones. Unable to protect their own frontiers, the New Mexicans could hardly check enemy raids against the Apaches of the northeast.

Mexico City read further-reaching implications into Villasur's calamity. The Treaty of the Hague had ended the war with France in February 1720. The reported attack by Frenchmen on Villasur's force

[43] Valverde to Valero, Santa Fe, May 27, 1720, in Thomas, *After Coronado*, pp. 154–156; Council of War, Santa Fe, June 2, 1720, ibid., pp. 156–160; Valverde to Valero, Santa Fe, June 15, 1720, ibid., pp. 160–162.

[44] Valero, Order, Mexico, September 26, 1720, ibid., pp. 234–239.

[45] The Spaniards assumed they were Pawnees. However, a French deserter from the Illinois country testified in Santa Fe in 1750 that it had been Kansas Indians, notably proficient with firearms, who had routed the Spaniards in 1720 (Hackett, *Picardo's Treatise*, III, 315).

[46] Valverde to Valero, Santa Fe, October 8, 1720, in Thomas, *After Coronado*, pp. 162-167.

thus appeared an outright violation of the truce, which could portend general renewal of hostilities between the two powers. Anticipating the worst, the viceroy planned immediate reinforcements for New Mexico and ordered prompt establishment of the presidio at La Jicarilla.[47]

Valverde balked. After losing thirty-two soldiers to the Pawnees, he could hardly spare another twenty-five for the Jicarilla project, and he considered it suicidal to station less than fifty men at an isolated outpost in the Apachería.[48] His arguments moved the council in Mexico City to authorize fifty men for La Jicarilla's garrison, to be recruited wherever Valverde could find them. A further concession to Valverde was the order to supply the soldiers with provisions in advance of the severe winter season.[49]

It was a hollow victory for the governor. New Mexico had neither the potential recruits nor the supplies necessary to implement the council's order. Valverde instead mustered the forces of the province against the Faraones, in the hope that a vigorous campaign might make them regret and even limit their "continuous insults and robberies on the frontiers and population of the province."[50] He summoned all settlers, as good vassals of the king, to present themselves with their arms and horses to carry out the campaign.

Officials in Mexico City ceased to pursue the matter of the Jicarilla presidio after the summer of 1721, when Spain made an alliance with France. An Apache barrier no longer seemed urgent. New Mexico's leadership was paralyzed by public clamor for a scapegoat for the Villasur fiasco, calling into play all the ugly animosities that had rent the Spanish community for years. It led first to Valverde's dismissal from the governorship, then to investigation by Visitador General Pedro de Rivera. The affair ultimately cost Valverde fines of 200 pesos, although he was never found guilty, as charged, of dereliction of duty.[51]

The Apaches of the north could not so easily forget the sweeping promises of Spanish protection. Their enemies marauded unchecked, and every year their territories dwindled and their survival grew more doubtful. The summer of 1723 brought the worst Comanche on-

---

[47] Master Sainz to Valero, Mexico, November 4, 1720, ibid., pp. 167–169.

[48] Valverde to the Viceroy, Santa Fe, February 3, 1721, in Hackett, *Pichardo's Treatise*, III, 215.

[49] Junta de Guerra, Mexico, July 14, 1721, ibid., pp. 218–219.

[50] Valverde, Bando, Santa Fe, August 9, 1721, SANM, no. 313.

[51] Revolledo to Casa Fuerte, Mexico, May 29, 1727, in Thomas, *After Coronado*, pp. 241–244.

slaught yet. Weakened Apache *rancherías* lay nearly defenseless while the enemy slew their men and carried off their women and children to captivity. When his Sierra Blanca group could no longer hope to hold their mountain ranges, Chief Carlana threw in his lot with the Jicarillas and that autumn rallied the surviving leaders and their people to devise some plan of survival. Once they reached agreement, Carlana and two other chiefs rode to Santa Fe to lay before the new governor, Don Juan Domingo de Bustamente, a nearly irresistible proposition.

They admitted frankly that they had come because they could no longer survive alone in their accustomed territories and they could find no sanctuary. Thus, they wished to place themselves under the protection of the king of Spain and his God, just as the Pueblos had done and as they themselves had often been urged to do. They wished to settle in pueblos in the Valley of La Jicarilla, to grow crops as the Pueblos did, and to have an *alcalde mayor* for their district and missionaries to instruct and baptize them. Years of close contact with Pueblos had taught them the obligations incurred by the king's vassals in return for his aid and protection, and these Apaches were now prepared to pay that price in order to survive against their Indian enemies. They wanted Bustamente to come at once to designate sites for their pueblos, so that they could plant their fields in the coming spring.[52]

Bustamente was preparing for a campaign against the Faraones, whose raiders had taken their usual autumn toll along the eastern frontier of the province. However, he quickly called a council to consider whether he should abandon the Faraon campaign in order to respond to the Jicarilla appeal. Carlana and his associates waited for the verdict, which was quick and favorable. The council agreed with Bustamente that this was an incomparable chance for distinguished service to both Majesties. Perhaps the Jicarilla example would inspire other Apaches also to become settled Christian vassals of the king, and the resulting Apache settlements would form valuable buffers against French intrusion.

The council agreed that Governor Bustamente should ride to La Jicarilla with Fray Antonio Camargo and fifty soldiers to survey the situation. If all the Apaches of the area truly supported the proposals of Carlana's delegation and if their lands seemed suitable, the governor would be justified in designating pueblo sites and promising them

---

[52] Governor Juan Domingo de Bustamente, Decree, Santa Fe, November 8, 1723, ibid., pp. 193–195.

protection. No one doubted that Mexico City would approve such a pious and strategic move.[53]

Governor Gerónimo Ylo of Taos, the Jicarillas' sympathetic intermediary and interpreter, explained the decision to the waiting chiefs, then asked them to go home and summon their people to council with Governor Bustamente. Chief Carlana had a welcoming party ready when Governor Bustamente reached La Jicarilla two weeks later. Bearing a cross, half a dozen chiefs and fifty young warriors rode out to greet the Spaniards. Three days of negotiations followed. Some young men of the welcoming party dispersed to the scattered *rancherías* to discuss with their people the prospect of living like Pueblos under Spanish protection, while Chief Carlana escorted Governor Bustamente and Fray Camargo to the *rancherías* of the most influential chiefs.

Some uncertainties were not easily resolved. Many Apaches were so scattered that they could not be expected to come to La Jicarilla until the following spring. Bustamente had to content himself with the assurances of others that the absent tribesmen would accept the new life style. The complexities of absolution had to be explained to Chief Coxo and his people, who were actually not new converts, but apostates. They cheerfully acquiesced.

Many obviously did not share either the clear understanding of the life of a Christian vassal or the driving determination of Chief Carlana, but somehow they all reached amicable consensus. Bustamente's ensign waved the royal banner over the land to signify its possession by the king, and the troop fired a three-gun salute to affirm the act. Then the governor received into the royal protection all Apaches present and even those members of their bands who were absent. Jicarillas had much to think about when Governor Bustamente led his troop back to Santa Fe: their new status as vassals of the Most Christian King; the promise that priests and an *alcalde mayor* would come in the spring; the promise of tools and seed for the spring planting; and, above all, the promise that the Spaniards would protect them from their enemies.

The worth of those promises depended upon the viceroy's reaction to the governor's recommendations: a presidio with fifty soldiers to protect the Jicarillas from the Comanches and, incidentally, to keep them safely obedient to the missionaries; tools, seeds, and a year's subsistence to keep them settled until their own production could support them; and full support and equipment for the missionaries whom the

[53] Council of War, Santa Fe, November 9, 1723, ibid., pp. 195–197.

Apaches had so urgently invited to instruct them. But it was January 1724 when Bustamente sent his dispatch to Mexico City, April when the *fiscal* ruled favorably on it, and July when the *auditor* endorsed the proposal and recommended that fifty experienced soldiers be transferred from Santa Fe to garrison La Jicarilla.

Unfortunately, neither Comanche nor Apache calendars allowed time for the methodical processes of decision in Mexico City. Bustamente's recommendations hardly had time to reach the viceroy before Utes and Comanches returned to the attack in La Jicarilla. On February 1, the Jicarillas reported the raids to Bustamente and called upon him to honor his promise to protect them.

Bustamente was again preparing to campaign against the Faraones, whose punishment he had forgone in November in order to visit La Jicarilla. Although Faraon raiders were harrying the Albuquerque district unmercifully, the governor again called a council to weigh the Jicarillas' appeal against the Faraon problem. Again the council found defense of the Jicarillas a greater opportunity for service to both Majesties. Indeed, Bustamente's commitments of November clearly obliged them to defend the Jicarillas as the sworn vassals of the king.[54]

Again deferring punishment of the Faraones, Bustamente led the New Mexican forces northward in pursuit of the Comanche and Ute raiders. He somehow recovered sixty-four captured Jicarilla women and children and restored them to their grateful kinsmen. Still, terror stalked the *rancherías*. As the planting season passed without any sign of the promised presidio, the Jicarillas threatened to move to the Navajo country for safety. Bustamente urged them to give him time to make good his promises and warned the viceroy that if the Jicarillas should disperse into the Navajo region it would become virtually impossible ever to settle and convert them.[55]

It was the last day of May 1724 when Bustamente warned the viceroy of the new Jicarilla crisis and appealed for immediate instructions. Late in October the *fiscal* noted that he had not enough information on the matter to make any firm policy recommendation. He surmised that it would be worthwhile to reduce the Jicarillas before they escaped to the Navajo country and that perhaps they should be given lands near the Pueblos and subsistence for the first two years.[56]

---

[54] Junta de Guerra, Santa Fe, February 1–February 11, 1724, SANM, no. 324.
[55] Bustamente to Casa Fuerte, Santa Fe, May 30, 1724, in Thomas, *After Coronado*, pp. 208–209.
[56] Fiscal to Casa Fuerte, Mexico, October 20, 1724, ibid., p. 209.

Astonishingly, the viceroy only referred the question to Brigadier Don Pedro de Rivera, then slated for a general inspection of the northern frontier, and postponed decision until Rivera should supply more information.[57]

It was June 1726 when Rivera finally reached Santa Fe, and September 1727 when he reported to the viceroy.[58] By then it hardly mattered that his recommendation concerning the proposed presidio at La Jicarilla was negative: the Comanches were completing their triumphant ouster of the Apaches from their northeastern ranges. Rivera scoffed at the notion of using Spanish arms to protect the Jicarillas or Cuartelejos or any other victims of the Comanches. He considered the Comanches formidable and the Apaches both cowardly and insincere in their quest for baptism. The hazards of Comanche occupation of the New Mexican frontier apparently did not figure in his calculations.

Remnants of the Jicarillas settled in the vicinities of Taos and Pecos, with a subsidy of tools and subsistence; most northeastern Apaches dispersed to unknown locations. Comanches took over the region of La Jicarilla, and for the next half-century the New Mexicans found them very dangerous neighbors indeed.

Fragments of news recorded on the frontiers of Louisiana, Texas, and New Mexico trace the rapid expulsion of eastern Apaches from their vast ranges north of the Red River; Apaches left no records to attest the terror of the ordeal in their scattered *rancherías*. Certainly the fatal pincers of change were at work by 1706, when mounted Utes and Comanches struck *rancherías* of the Carlana–Sierra Blanca and Penxajes on the northwestern sector of the Apachería while Pawnee and Wichita enemies appeared with French rifles on the borders of the Cuartelejo territories on the northeast. Ulibarri's promises to protect El Cuartelejo against the Indian allies of the French were less practicable than well meant. What hopes did he arouse in El Cuartelejo? What adventures did his rash promise inspire?

The fragmentary nature of Apache organization and active enmities among some Apache groups lessened their capacity to defend the Apachería against hostile incursions. Best documented is the damage Faraon raiders inflicted on the Jicarillas; not easily assessed is the toll of lives and property taken by internecine wars among other Apache groups on the remote plains. Páez Hurtado's dismal failure to

[57] Casa Fuerte, Order, Mexico, October 21, 1724, ibid.
[58] Pedro de Rivera to Casa Fuerte, Presidio del Paso del Norte, September 26, 1727, ibid., pp. 209–217.

overtake and punish the Faraones sorely disappointed the Jicarillas and Cuartelejos; possibly their participation in his effort cost them more raids of revenge.

The critical turning point on the north came in 1719. As the year began, Jicarillas sought the sanctuary of a Spanish mission and presidio for themselves. By summer, the Sierra Blancas were driven from their territory, one segment seeking refuge with the Jicarillas, the other fleeing much farther south on the plains to escape the Comanche hordes. The Palomas, easternmost of Apache bands, retreated to the upper Arkansas to seek refuge with the Cuartelejos, abandoning their homes to Pawnee and Wichita aggressors armed with French guns. The tide of disaster for Apaches was not confined to their northernmost regions, however, for the Tawakonis and their eight associated bands in the lower Canadian River Valley celebrated a great victory over their Apache enemies in the summer of 1719.

The situation on both eastern and western margins of the Apachería deteriorated still further in the autumn of 1719. Valverde's campaign from Taos against Ute and Comanche marauders dramatized the Spaniards' helplessness before those equestrian raiders. The new burst of activity by Frenchmen from Law's Company of the Indies brought new trade alliances to Wichitan and Pawnee groups, assured them of more arms, and gave them new incentives to hunt and raid on the plains. Du Tisne even reached a Comanche camp with his guns and shooting lessons and initiated a long French effort to woo Comanche allegiance. On the southeastern sector after 1719, French guns and help would flow from Natchitoches to the Caddos, Kichais, and other enemies of the Apaches in the Red River Valley. Apaches fleeing the terrors of the Arkansas Valley would find scant comfort with kinsmen on the upper Red River.

Among the northernmost Apaches, one disappointment followed swiftly upon another. In 1720, Cuartelejos saw Villasur's Spanish-Pueblo force cut to pieces by Indians with French guns, then waited in vain for another force to avenge the honor of Spain and its vassals. From 1721 onward, Jicarillas pinned their hopes of survival to a settled life under the protection of a presidio often promised but never realized. The Carlanas and Jicarillas pledged themselves vassals of the king of Spain in 1723 and did once in 1724 know the satisfaction of having a Spanish force recover their captured women and children from the Comanche and Ute invaders. But when 1724 passed without any practical steps toward protection of their *rancherías*, hope died in

La Jicarilla. Perhaps also they heard of Bourgmont's triumph on the eastern plains, his big peace meeting at the Kansas village, when Comanches came to terms with France and its Indian friends and agreed to share the advantage of the trade that would bring them guns and powder and balls.

By 1726 the Jicarilla remnants gave up the old ways to settle under Spanish protection in the neighborhoods of Pecos and Taos. In 1733, the Franciscans at last won permission to found a mission for them on the Rio Trampas, a dozen miles north of Taos. Fray Juan Mirabal argued that the Jicarillas could thus be mustered for war against the Comanches and Utes, since the Jicarillas, as Christians, would have a sound moral right to make war on non-Christian Indians.[59]

Governor Gervasio Cruzat y Góngora endorsed the project at its inception, but he dealt the new mission community a death blow when he proclaimed sweeping restrictions upon trade with all the *bárbaros*. Although his principal target was the Comanche and Ute trade, his policy soon ruined the trade in hides that was the livelihood of the Jicarilla neophytes. Thoroughly disheartened, they scattered, seeking safety from the Utes and Comanches wherever they could find it. They had little reason any longer to expect Spanish support in their struggle to survive.[60]

Apaches who stayed on the plains knew defeat even sooner. The Comanches carried their triumphant sweep of the northern plains to the upper reaches of the Red River system early in the 1720's. The climactic struggle lived afterward in Apache tradition as a nine-day battle, at the end of which the Apaches fled the region.[61] They fell back to the area between the western reaches of the Brazos and Colorado

[59] Ralph Emerson Twitchell, comp., *The Spanish Archives of New Mexico*, I, 19–20.

[60] Fray Juan Agustín de Morfi, "Geographical Description of New Mexico," in Alfred Barnaby Thomas, ed., *Forgotten Frontiers: A Study of the Spanish Indian Policy of Don Juan Bautista de Anza, Governor of New Mexico, 1777–1787*, p. 97.

[61] Domingo Cabello, Ynforme, San Antonio de Béxar, September 30, 1784, Archivo General y Pública de la Nación, Mexico City (cited hereafter as AGN), Provincias Internas, vol. 64. Cabello, an assiduous student of Indian history and culture during his term as governor of Texas, perhaps drew this information from earlier records then available to him in the archives at San Antonio, or perhaps he obtained the story in the course of his many long conversations with Apache leaders. In either case, the ultimate source would appear to be Apache tradition, and the exact locale of the battle is doubtful. Cabello says that the battle occurred in the foothills of the "Gran Cierra de el fierro," which gives rise to the river of that name. The Rio del Fierro in the usage of later years is usually equated with the Pease or the Wichita.

rivers, a pleasantly fertile region in which they established themselves without an ordeal of serious contest with previous occupants. Even there, however, they could not feel that they would long be safe from the advancing Comanche hordes. Thus, they determined to explore southward in the hope that they could move even farther beyond the Comanches' thrust. Their explorations soon carried them to the new Spanish establishments at San Antonio, where a new chapter in Apache relations with Spaniards began.

CHAPTER 7

Texas, 1718-1759

The first encounter between the fleeing Apaches and the Spaniards of Texas was as accidental as it was fateful. About 1720 a few Apache explorers ventured through Elotes Pass, northwest of San Antonio, and stumbled upon two settlers from the presidio, out looking for missing horses. The settlers, thinking them friendly local Indians, approached them, only to be attacked. Thanks to his fleet horse, one escaped to shout the alarm at Béxar presidio. Captain Nicolás Flores y Valdes promptly sent fifteen soldiers in pursuit, but they found only the mutilated corpse of the other settler. The assailants had vanished with his horse, all his clothing and equipment, and his scalp.

The stunned San Antonians could not know the identity of the attackers, but they vaguely assumed them to be Apaches, and they read too much into the incident. Supposing that the atrocity signaled a deliberate hostile invasion, they braced for a bloody war like those reported with Apaches on other provincial frontiers.

Vagueness and miscalculation figured among the Apaches, too. On the basis of first reports, they favored that area around San Antonio as a possible future home. Since their scouts had taken so easily a scalp from people whom they did not know, and the rest of whom they had not seen, and had also acquired a badly needed horse, the Apaches decided to keep probing in that direction. The next year they slipped through the same pass, stole several horses, and killed a Spaniard only a couple of miles from the settlement. After that encouraging success, they raided more boldly and more often.[1]

The cheap successes did not long continue. Pursuing the thieves whenever possible, the Spaniards occasionally brought back horses, and, once, the heads of four Apache raiders. Not until August 1723, however, did the Spaniards mount a punitive campaign into the Apache territory. In the dead of night, Apache raiders broke into the presidio's locked corral, despite ten guards, and grabbed eighty horses. Immediate pursuit of the raiders failed, but Captain Flores could not let such a flagrant offense go unpunished. Two days after the raid, he left Béxar with thirty soldiers and thirty mission Indians, determined to track the raiders to their *rancherías*.

Five weeks and 330 miles later, he found a camp of some two hundred Apaches, probably in the vicinity of modern Brownwood. They came out to meet him. Whether the Apaches intended to greet the visitors peacefully was never known; the angry captain and his men had come to fight. They joined battle at once, and in six hours the Spaniards won. The chief and thirty-four warriors of the Apache camp lay dead; twenty of their women and children were captives. The plunder included 120 horses and mules, thought to be stock stolen from San Antonio, and a quantity of saddles, bridles, knives, spears, and other articles, many also stolen from Spanish sources. The San Antonians, who sustained only four light wounds, rode triumphantly back into Presidio Béxar in mid-October.[2]

The nature of the triumph was soon questioned. Flores was accused of surprise attack upon innocent Apaches. Fray Joseph González of Mission San Antonio de Valero insisted that he had sent the mission Indians to pursue the Apaches on the understanding that the campaign

[1] Cabello, Ynforme, San Antonio de Béxar, September 30, 1784, AGN, Provincias Internas, vol. 64. This account, which must reflect the Apaches' own understanding of the beginning of hostilities, is interestingly at variance with the interpretation drawn from Spanish documents by William Edward Dunn in his pioneering study, "Apache Relations in Texas, 1718–1750," *Texas State Historical Association Quarterly* 14 (1911): 198–274. A more recent summary of Apache relations with San Antonio occurs in Curtis D. Tunnell and W. W. Newcomb, Jr., *A Lipan Apache Mission: San Lorenzo de la Santa Cruz, 1762–1771*, pp. 154 ff.

[2] Dunn, "Apache Relations," pp. 207–208.

objective was to establish communication with the Apaches and pave the way for their peaceful conversion. The captain's betrayal of his just and pious intent so outraged Fray González that he carried his grievance clear to the viceroy. That cost Flores his command for a year.[3]

Although the slaughter made a dubious beginning for a peace overture, Captain Flores did try afterward to establish communication with Apaches, perhaps yielding to the angry insistence of Fray González. The captives taken in that battle afforded the first opportunity to probe the reasons for the Apache raids at San Antonio. Thus the Spaniards inquired as thoroughly as their scant interpretive resources allowed.

Their best informant was a woman about forty years old. Asked why the Apaches were hostile to the Spaniards of San Antonio and kept coming to steal their horses, she was understood to say that it was because of the Apaches' trade with "other Spaniards" to the north, to whom they sold horses and slaves. Although she must have referred to the market for captives and horses on the New Mexican frontier, the San Antonians leaped to the conclusion that she meant the long-dreaded trade with the French. The specter of French activity among Apaches prodded the Texas Spaniards to seek accommodation with them.

The woman assured Captain Flores that the Apache leaders would like to be friends with the Spaniards. He therefore decided to send her home as his emissary, bearing his promise to release the other captives if the chiefs would come to make peace. Glad to undertake the mission, she promised to ride to the head chief and return within twenty days. She left on October 7, 1723, riding a horse given her by Captain Flores and carrying his propitiatory gifts to the chiefs.

When the woman arrived home with news of the Spaniards' friendly intent and their desire to live at peace with the Apaches, her chief called four other chiefs into council. They decided that one chief should go to see if the woman spoke the truth; another gave him a gold-tipped cane to carry to the Spaniards. If he should return with a favorable report, then all five chiefs would ride to San Antonio to make peace.

True to her promise, the woman returned to San Antonio just twenty-two days later, with the designated Apache chief, his wife, and three

3 Robert S. Weddle, *San Juan Bautista*, p. 169.

other Apache men. When Flores rode out from the presidio to greet the party, the chief handed him the gold-tipped cane, exclaiming, "Dios! Dios!"

The Apaches received presents and three days of the best hospitality the settlement afforded, but want of interpreters limited the usefulness of the talks. The six Apaches left on November 1, promising that all five chiefs would surely come to make the peace, but nearly two months passed before Flores heard from the Apaches again. Meanwhile, San Antonio teemed with rumors that the Apaches only feigned peaceful intentions in order to regain their captives and would attack as soon as they had their women and children back.

Late in December Fray González welcomed thirty Apache visitors to Mission San Antonio de Valero. The missionary wanted to turn the captive women and children over to them, but Captain Flores insisted upon keeping them hostage until all five chiefs should agree to peace. The priest and the soldier shouted their argument to a furious climax before the Apaches, so alarming the guests that they rode away, leaving a twelve-year-old girl as an additional hostage. They were understood to say that four of the chiefs would come to make peace as soon as the cold weather should end, but that the fifth did not wish to be the Spaniards' friend.

Perhaps the fifth chief won the others to his point of view. No one arrived to make peace that spring. Scattered depredations in March and April were attributed to Apaches. Convinced that the un-Christian conduct of Captain Flores had provoked the Apaches, frays González and Hidalgo pleaded for permission to go into the Apachería to work toward converting them. Meanwhile, the mission Indians and their herds at San Antonio began to suffer from marauding Apaches. Much harsher raids befell the Coahuiltecan peoples still surviving on the upper Nueces and Medina rivers. Many were soon driven to seek refuge either in the missions or at the Ranchería Grande.

With the Jicarillas and associated bands beseeching alliance and protection in New Mexico, the viceroy would not believe that it could be very difficult to conciliate the Apache bands in Texas. He continued to urge Texas' Governor Fernando Pérez de Almazán to secure an alliance with the Apaches by gentle means. In 1725 the viceroy denied the Texans permission to campaign against Apaches. His judgment seemed vindicated when Apache raids subsided substantially in the San Antonio area from 1726 to 1731.

During that lull, in 1727, Brigadier General Rivera made his tour of inspection in Texas.[4] The year before, in New Mexico, he had found the Jicarillas and their associates unworthy of protection; now he shrugged off any possible dangers from the few Apaches in the hill country northwest of San Antonio. At worst, they seemed likely to steal a few horses, but only if soldiers were unduly careless. Rivera recommended that Béxar's garrison be reduced by ten, down to forty-three soldiers. To the missionaries' chagrin, the visitador general also recommended that soldiers no longer be assigned to protect the missions or help the friars to control their neophytes and retrieve runaways. He did suggest that twenty-five families of settlers be imported to increase the numerical strength of San Antonio.

Rivera most disapproved of the dismally unsuccessful Spanish establishments in East Texas. At his recommendation, Presidio Dolores was abolished and the three Querétaran missions it had guarded were removed to the San Antonio area, where Indians seemed more receptive to the faith and works of the friars. The presidio of Los Adaes remained, with a reduced garrison, to remind the ambitious Frenchmen at Natchitoches of Spain's prior claim in that area. With it persisted the three Zacatecan missions, though virtually without neophytes.

On the basis of Rivera's recommendations, Viceroy Casafuerte reduced the garrisons of the frontier presidios and issued a general statement of policy that bound frontier officials for the next forty years. The Regulation of 1729 forbade any attack on Indians, whether friendly, hostile, or neutral, until every possible means to persuade them to peace had failed. Spanish forces could side with one non-Christian tribe against another only when one of the two specifically requested help. Soldiers must neither foment unrest in Indian villages nor exploit Indians for economic gain, nor should they ever separate families captured in war. Whenever Indians sued for peace, the Spanish commanders were required to honor the request, under a signed, written agreement obtained from the Indians.

In short, after its first major review of the northern frontier, the new Bourbon regime reiterated the principles of conciliation and forbearance toward Indians to which the Hapsburg kings had subscribed

---

[4] Pedro de Rivera, "Informe y Proyecto," in *Diario y Derrotero de lo Caminado*, ed. Vito Alessio Robles, pp. 168 ff.; see also Lawrence C. Wroth, "The Frontier Presidios of New Spain: Books, Maps, and a Selection of Manuscripts Relating to the Rivera Expedition of 1724–1729," *The Papers of the Bibliographical Society of America* 43 (1951): 191–218.

since the time of Las Casas. Unfortunately, the difficulties of reconciling principles with practice among the diverse peoples of the northern frontier proved no less difficult for Bourbons in the eighteenth century than for Hapsburgs in the sixteenth and seventeenth. Apaches soon put their peaceful assumptions to the test in Texas.

Apache raids resumed early in January 1731 with parties of fifty to eighty, the largest ever seen in Texas. One woman was killed, one boy was captured, and a couple of soldiers were wounded during that season, but the principal focus of the raids was horses. Most were stolen from parties traveling between San Antonio and the Rio Grande presidio, but one bold group broke into Mission San Antonio de Valero to carry off fifty burros, and another invaded Mission San José to scatter the congregation and steal the entire horse herd. The terrified San Antonio community braced against the specter of a full-scale war, but the raids ceased in mid-April, as abruptly as they had begun. It was planting time at the *rancherías* deep within the Apachería, and the men would not sally forth again until mid-September, when their harvest lay safely cached beneath the ground.

In the spring of 1731, at the height of the Apache raiding season, San Antonio experienced a growth spurt. In March the Querétaran friars arrived from East Texas to reestablish their missions on the San Antonio River under the aegis of Presidio San Antonio de Béxar. Within a few days, there also arrived fifty-six persons from the Canary Islands, recruited after Rivera recommended more civil settlers for San Antonio.

The friars brought their ecclesiastical furnishings and their herds of cattle, horses, mules, and burros from the Neches and Angelina rivers. Upon arriving at San Antonio, they purchased 250 more cattle and 1,280 bushels of corn from Mission San Juan Bautista on the Rio Grande. With generous land grants in the San Antonio Valley for their missions, they were ready to begin work as soon as they could round up neophytes. Two extended recruiting trips among scattered Coahuiltecan camps netted nearly a thousand Indians willing to try mission life. By May they were hard at work, building temporary thatched shelters, digging irrigation ditches, plowing new fields, and sowing corn. Purísima Concepción, San Juan Capistrano, and San Francisco de la Espada (formerly San Francisco de los Neches) were going concerns with perhaps three hundred Indians each.[5]

[5] Marion A. Habig, *The Alamo Chain of Missions*, pp. 124–125, 162, 202–204.

The sixteen Canary Islands families fared less happily, although they too were granted land. Rejecting the designated townsite west of the presidio as too exposed to Indian attack, they laid out a plaza between the presidio and the river, where they founded the Villa of San Fernando de Béxar, the first civil jurisdiction in Texas. They were chagrined to find that the five mission grants had preempted much of the choice land along the river, that the missions competed with them for the produce market at the garrison, and that the friars rigorously opposed economic exploitation of the Indians by settlers. The Islanders, as first settlers, received the title of *hidalgos*, but the missions' competition for land, labor, and market suggested that few would ever make a fortune to match the dignity of their rank.

The Islanders vented their discontent in strident quarrels on all sides: with the missionaries, whose removal from the area they repeatedly demanded; with the presidial captain, whose general competence and specific decisions they often challenged; and with the earlier settlers of the presidial community, whom they offended by their pretensions to distinction. For many years, acrimonious squabbling absorbed energies that might better have fostered development of that promising region. The mission Indians and the *bárbaros* who later frequented the settlement knew in San Antonio a community notably contentious, even by Spanish frontier standards.

Growth made San Antonio at once more attractive and more vulnerable to Apache raiders. The herds of the Canary Islanders, pastured north and west of the presidio, and those of the new missions downstream freshly tempted raiders. The mission congregations, chiefly composed of Coahuiltecan groups long plagued by Apaches, drew to the San Antonio Valley the pursuit of old vendettas. The outlying missions of San Juan and Espada suffered particularly, but the presidial garrison was ill-equipped to expand its protective services after its 20 percent cut by Rivera.

After the raids ceased in April 1731, the San Antonians endured a summer of apprehension. Dread worsened after early August, when a captured Apache declared that many of his people were gathering to mount an attack upon the settlement.[6] His boast and the Spaniards' fears seemed confirmed at noon on September 18, when Apache raiders snatched sixty horses from the presidial herd. The twenty-five Spaniards who gave chase engaged about forty Apaches, only to see

6 Dunn, "Apache Relations," pp. 225 ff.

another five hundred arrive, all mounted and well armed. Two hours' fighting cost the Spaniards two deaths and thirteen serious wounds. They feared none would survive, but the Apaches suddenly abandoned the fight, apparently convinced that their own cost in casualties would outweigh any likely gain.

Presidial Captain Juan Antonio Pérez was astonished that the Apaches did not finish off his little band of soldiers, then sack the missions and presidio. With fourteen soldiers absent on assignment in Coahuila, the whole settlement had lain open to extermination. To identify the puzzling enemy, he collected arrows from the battlefield and showed them to the Apache held captive at the presidio since August.

The prisoner readily identified the arrows of Apaches, Pelones, and Jumanes, and he assured his captors that all three nations were very numerous and very warlike. Old Joseph de Urrutia, now stationed at Béxar, was amazed to hear of those groups allied: in the 1690's he had known the Jumanes and Pelones to be among the fervid enemies of the Apaches. That they should now combine forces against the Spaniards was indeed alarming. Some soldiers at the presidio began to talk of moving their families to safer places.

In an effort to discourage further incursions, central authorities granted the Texans permission to campaign against the Apaches. They also gave tacit permission to enslave captives, thus giving settlers incentive to help but hardly furthering reconciliation of the warring peoples. Squabbles over the right to lead the campaign and the size of the force needed delayed the campaign for a year. It was late October 1732 when a new governor, Juan Antonio de Bustillo y Zevallos, led an army from San Antonio, resolved to find the Apaches if he had to ride clear to New Mexico.

Bustillo's was the vaguest of undertakings: to search unknown territories for enemies whose identities and motives he could only conjecture. Spaniards along the frontier clear to Sonora shared his dilemma, for the nature of Apache warfare had changed and intensified everywhere. Many blamed the difficulty on Rivera's pennywise reduction of presidial strength, but the crux of the matter lay deep within the Apachería.

The Utes and Comanches, the Pawnees and Wichitas, and the guns of French traders not only ousted the Apaches from their former ranges north of the Red River; they also left them sadly impoverished. Enemy raiders relentlessly diminished Apache horse herds. They also seized metal goods when they attacked the *rancherías*. The worst damage was inflicted by Comanches, who could easily strike Apache *rancherías* during the spring and summer agricultural cycle. Apaches found it much harder to retaliate against the completely nomadic Comanches. Comanche supremacy on the buffalo ranges curtailed Apache hunting. At the same time, weakened Apache forces could no longer take the quantities of captives that they had previously traded in Spanish and Pueblo markets. Thus, they had neither the quantities of hides and meat nor of slaves that had previously been their chief stock in trade with Spaniards and Pueblos. To compound their woes, Utes and Comanches spoiled their access to Taos, Picurís, and Pecos, traditional marketplaces of plains dwellers. Apaches grew more and more desperate for guns, which Spaniards were forbidden to sell even to Indians who could manage the price and access to the marketplaces. The less they could depend on trade, the more Apaches stole the articles they needed.

The result was nearly continuous raiding, which soon evolved into an almost constant state of war between Spaniards and Apaches on every front. The hazards, as well as the pace, of the conflict mounted. In the beginning, raiders had usually concentrated on running off horses, without much close contact or loss of life on either side. While raids for horses remained necessary to recoup losses to enemy Indians, new demands reshaped the old raiding patterns. It was necessary to come into close contact, often killing the victim, in order to seize from his person or his dwelling the guns, ammunition, and metal goods that the Apaches needed. The results were much larger raiding parties and much greater loss of life, particularly for Spaniards.[7]

New Mexico suffered the impact first. The Faraones, who had raided the province since the beginning of the century, had more than once escaped punishment because Spanish forces digressed northward to protect Jicarillas and other Apaches from Utes and Comanches. But, by 1724, the increasingly grave character of their crimes around Albuquerque made it impossible to tolerate the Faraones any longer. At the very climax of the Jicarilla crisis, Governor Bustamente found it necessary to send fifty of his soldiers into the Sandías with 150 Pueblos to punish the Faraones.[8] That, and perhaps subsequent action, moved the

[7] Frank Raymond Secoy, *Changing Military Patterns on the Great Plains (Seventeenth Century through Early Nineteenth Century).*

[8] Juan Domingo de Bustamente to Captain Antonio Tafoya, Santa Fe, June 20, 1724, SANM, no. 329.

Faraones to make formal peace with the province, but the cloak of friendship only made it easier for them to enter the settled areas, and the losses of life and property worsened. By mid-summer 1731, the problem was so grave that the governor convened a council in Santa Fe to determine a course of action.[9] Without much hope of success, they sent a token expedition to the Sandías to find and punish the offending camps.

Those forays into the mountains after Apache raiders were grueling and nearly hopeless for Spanish forces. Unaccustomed to move on foot as the terrain often required and handicapped by the very short range of their guns, they were woefully ineffective in combat in the rare event that they found Apaches. Yet, the Faraones did find it necessary to fall back from the Sandías. By 1744, when their raids again took such a grievous toll that the New Mexican governor could not ignore citizens' complaints, it was the Ladrones and Magdalenas ranges to the south that the punitive force scoured in search of the Faraones.[10] The southward thrust of the Comanches was as inexorable as the little Spanish armies were impotent.

As they retreated southward, the eastern Apaches regrouped. Many old identities lapsed into meaninglessness: traditional localities were lost to enemies; outstanding chiefs lay dead, victims of the enemy, of disease, or of grief and years. Fragments no longer able to sustain independent existence, the displaced and the dispossessed, merged with each other or with more fortunate bands. Some forsook old enmities to band together against common foes. It must have been a bewildering time of crisis within the Apachería. Certainly the situation challenged the comprehension of San Antonians seeking to identify and punish their attackers and to find some authority with which to negotiate peace.

Governor Bustillo of Texas had remarkably little information upon which to proceed in the autumn of 1732. The negotiations of 1723 had indicated five bands present. Béxar's recent Apache captive had bragged of an alliance of Pelones and Jumanes with Apaches, and the raiding parties in 1731 had been much bigger than any seen before in Texas. Not knowing what huge concentration of enemies he might find, Bustillo took 157 Spaniards and 60 mission Indians, vainly hoping that Tejas warriors would join his force. Uncertain what time and

---

[9] Junta de Guerra, Santa Fe, July 15–July 18, 1731, SANM, no. 362.
[10] Joachín Codallos y Rabál, Santa Fe, December 2, 1744, SANM, no. 495.

distance the search would involve, Bustillo took 140 pack animals laden with supplies and 900 horses and mules.

Six weeks out of San Antonio, on December 8, the mission Indian scout Asencio spied a big concentration of Apaches on the San Saba River. Bustillo led a hundred men on a night march, then attacked early the next morning. The surprised Apaches rallied bravely and stood their ground for five hours, but they could not overcome the advantage of the Spaniards' guns. Most women and children fled as the battle began, so Bustillo captured only thirty. He guessed that two hundred Apache warriors died in the battle, but he had no accurate count because friends threw their bodies into the river as fast as they fell. The battle turned with the fall of a conspicuous leader, whose death demoralized the Apaches at once. The fallen chief bore a silver-headed cane: had he or a predecessor once been recognized as chief of the Indian vassals of the king?

Along nearly two miles of the stream spread four separate *rancherías*, with about four hundred tents and perhaps seven hundred warriors. Their losses were grievous: perhaps two hundred dead, thirty women and children captured, unknown numbers wounded. The San Antonians took about seven hundred horses and a hundred mule loads of hides and other property. Even so, the Apaches were not routed. Bustillo feared an attack from their remaining five hundred warriors. As soon as he could reassemble his own forces, he hurried back toward San Antonio, harried all the way by Apaches. Though the rough terrain ruled out any major attack, the Apaches stole horses at every opportunity.[11]

When he reached San Antonio at the end of December, Governor Bustillo learned that Apache raiders had often preyed upon the settlement's livestock. Terrified that worse crimes would follow, the settlers petitioned the governor not to distribute the Apache captives as he had planned, but to keep them as hostages and to send one or two of the women back to their kinsmen with a peace proposal. If peace by negotiation should fail, then the citizens wished the governor to campaign again with three hundred men. The Apaches must somehow be brought to terms if life in San Antonio were to endure.

Fray Gabriel de Vergara, mission president, vigorously supported the settlers' demand for peace overtures. Though hostile Apaches jeopardized the very existence of the missions and settlement, the priest in-

---

[11] Dunn, "Apache Relations," pp. 230 ff.

sisted that Apaches, once conciliated, could become valuable vassals of both Majesties. Bustillo's prisoners reinforced Fray Vergara's impression that the Apaches were a truthful, good-natured people. He began to advocate establishment of missions for them.

Governor Bustillo yielded to the pressures of the citizenry and missionaries. Early in January 1733, two female prisoners rode out of the presidio to carry Bustillo's letters to their chiefs. The governor gave them horses and provisions for the journey. Twenty soldiers and a priest escorted them across the Guadalupe River, then watched them vanish into the rugged hills. The Spaniards could only await the result of their gamble.

So much hinged upon the luck, the courage, and the good faith of those two Apache women: whether they would find their kinsmen before some chance encounter with enemy Indians spelled death or capture; whether they would indeed convey to their leaders the peaceful intentions of the Spaniards or would instead urge some awful vengeance. For that matter, what good could they do if they wished? Who were their leaders? For which of the raiding Apaches could they speak? Even if they wished it, had they the authority to make peace? Was the enemy toward which the San Antonians now groped actually one people or some vast coalition of hostile *bárbaros*?

In 1723, Captain Flores' Apache captives had spoken of five separate groups, each with its own chief, all subject to a common "great chief" farther north. The five chiefs cooperated for raids. Each group furnished about a dozen men, who divided the booty among themselves, but their expeditions hinged upon permission of the "great chief." A decade later, Governor Bustillo had found four distinct groups camped side by side along the San Saba and had learned their names: Apaches, Ypandis,[12] Ysandis, and Chentis. The latter two were said to be newcomers, who had only recently joined the longer established bands in the region. The two messengers belonged to the older groups: one called herself Apache; the other said that she was of the Ypandis, also called Pelones. Yet old Captain Urrutia insisted that the Pelones, like the Jumanes, had been enemies of the Apaches only a quarter-century ago.[13] How bewildering it all was!

---

[12] Usually equated with the later usage, Lipan.

[13] Note above, p. 230, that the Cuartelejos in 1706 described to Ulibarri the Pelones as a people who lived three long days' journey from the sea, across a land of grassless dunes. In 1743, Fray Santa Ana spoke of the Pelones as an Apache group who had lived on the Red River until ousted by Comanches (Dunn, "Apache Relations," p. 256).

Late in January, the Apache woman returned with three warriors. As she had promised, they signaled their approach with smokes two days from San Antonio. The leader of the party, apparently a man of some distinction, declared that his chief, the head of the Apaches, had sent him to see whether the two women had spoken truly about the Spaniards' desire for their friendship. Meanwhile, the great chief was calling together all his people so that they could concur in a peace agreement. If the emissaries should report favorably, four chiefs would soon bring many people to San Antonio to celebrate the peace. Such a peace would be no trivial achievement: the spokesman claimed there were thirty-seven groups along the road to New Mexico who bore the name Apache.

Their cordial reception seemed to satisfy the Apache delegates completely. They wanted to return at once to inform their great chief that the prospect of peace looked genuine, but Bustillo insisted upon entertaining them for three days. While he lavished San Antonio's best hospitality upon them, he tried to know them better and to impress upon them more firmly the sincerity of the Spaniards' peaceful intentions. They left on February 5, 1733, promising to return within two moons.

For a few weeks peace seemed at hand. Little parties of Apaches freely visited the settlement to trade; once they had transacted their business, a small squad of presidials escorted them out of the settlement. On March 27, three warriors and a woman came to trade. As they rode away from the presidio with three escorts, buffalo appeared in the distance; one soldier turned back to alert hunters at the settlement. Confident of the Apaches' peaceful intent, the remaining pair of soldiers escorted the four visitors another five miles and took no precautions when they saw two dozen more Indians riding toward them. Swiftly, the newcomers surrounded and felled the soldiers, stripped the flesh from their bodies, and vanished. Raids on the livestock resumed at once. No one could safely venture beyond the walls of the presidio or the missions.

The horror of the incident, with its implication that Apache peace talk meant nothing, demoralized the entire San Antonio community. The mission Indians wanted to flee for their lives; those whom the friars persuaded to remain would no longer venture out of the mission compounds to tend livestock. The soldiers of Béxar petitioned for permission to remove their families south of the Rio Grande for safety, though they vowed their own willingness to stay and to die if necessary. Both the *cabildo* of Villa San Fernando and Fray Vergara, as head of the missions, petitioned the viceroy for reinforcements to stave off impending doom. With twenty-eight Apache captives still held at the presidio, no one doubted that their kinsmen would soon strike to liberate them, and no one believed that the settlement could survive a determined assault.

The viceroy would allot Texas no more soldiers, but he did second to Béxar fifteen men each from the presidios of La Bahía and Los Adaes for the duration of the Apache threat. He appointed Don Joseph Urrutia captain of Béxar and charged the old soldier to muster his Indian friends for a decisive campaign against the Apaches.

Urrutia led no great campaign, nor did he rally his old friends of the 1690's to the Spanish standard. Probably few had survived that crucial quarter-century; probably he and they knew all too well the chances of success on such a campaign and the costs of Apache revenge for any success they might gain. The San Antonio community lived in dire uncertainty for many years. Sometimes little groups of Apaches came to the settlement to trade their meat and hides in peaceful fashion. Nevertheless, livestock disappeared regularly in and around the settlement, and unwary Spaniards and mission Indians who ventured out alone or in too small groups often paid for their carelessness with their lives.

Security regulations forbade any citizen to discharge a gun unless he saw Indians entering the place, so that a gunshot could be presumed to signal Indian attack. A man who needed to fire his gun to clean it had to procure special license from the captain of the guard. Anyone moving about the streets after curfew was presumed to be an Apache, up to no good.

San Antonians were not the sole sufferers, for all the herds of their community could not match the lust for horses in the Apache world. Horses became more than the key to success and survival of warriors and hunters and the measure of wealth and manliness. As Apaches lost the good buffalo ranges to Comanches, they turned increasingly to horse meat as a substitute; for many it became the preferred diet. Whether lost to enemy raiders or consumed by Apaches, Apache herds had constantly to be replenished.

After decimating herds in New Mexico and Texas, Apache raiders looked southward to the better developed provinces with more settlements, more presidios, more missions, producing mines, and vast ranches. Each had herds of livestock, and horses were as vital to their functioning as to Apache life style. By mid-century, Apaches and Spaniards joined battle along a new front south of New Mexico and Texas, competing for horses and thus for survival. New Spain confronted the appalling possibility that Apaches would destroy its northern mining provinces.

Some Apache bands concentrated their raids southward on the Coahuila frontier. Seven chiefs were said to have established their *rancherías* on the Rio Grande for that purpose. Severely harassed by Apaches, frightened citizens at the Rio Grande presidio began to think of moving away, as had those of San Antonio. By 1735, even as far south as Monclova and Saltillo, no horse herd was secure against the bold, fast-moving Apache raiders.

Meanwhile, western Apaches had brought Sonora to the brink of destruction. Their raids dated from the turn of the century, when the Spaniards had quelled the Pima Revolt and the concomitant general uprising of 1695–1697, only to find themselves caught up in a long series of Seri wars beginning in 1699. At best, Spanish forces could spare only peripheral attention to the new Apache problem. By 1724, Apaches had grown so bold and their raids so frequent that all Sonora anticipated ruin if defenses were not improved, but the Crown temporized through another crucial decade.

By the 1730's, many mines in Sonora were abandoned in the face of relentless Apache raids. Prospectors no longer explored the hills for metals, lest they be ambushed; even traffic on the roads dropped to a very low volume. The quality of mission life suffered because the converts had to keep arms ready to defend themselves against Apache and Seri attacks.[14] Abandonment of the northern missions and ranches seemed imminent, because they had lost most of their livestock to the raiders; if that should occur, there would remain no impediment to Apache passage to the remote interior. Spanish control rested on the lone presidio of Corodeguachi, whose fifty soldiers had to patrol some seven hundred miles of hostile frontier as well as to police and protect the Seris and Pimas Altas.[15]

Persuaded that they could not hold Sonora without more soldiers and presidios, the government founded two new presidios in 1741: Pitic, or San Pedro de la Conquista,[16] to check the Yaquis, Seris, Pimas,

---

[14] Ignaz Pfefferkorn, *Sonora: A Description of the Province*, ed. Theodore E. Trautlein, p. 207.

[15] Don Agustín de Vildosola, Statement, Real Nuestra Señora de Aranzazu, July 26, 1735, in Donald Rowland, "The Sonora Frontier of New Spain, 1735–1745," in *New Spain and the Anglo-American West*, I, 156.

[16] On the site of modern Hermosillo.

and Tepocas; and Terrenate, or San Bernardo Gracia Real, to protect the missions of Pimería Alta from Apache raids.[17] Like all other presidios founded to hold the line against Apaches, they furnished new targets for the raiders. The garrisons were soon occupied chiefly with guarding their own horse herds from raiders and convoying supplies through the hazards of Apache ambush.

As Apache depredations worsened in Coahuila on the east and Sonora on the west, they also spread into Nueva Vizcaya. Since 1707, El Paso had borne the principal brunt of the Apaches' southward surge in the central sector, but by the 1740's the raiders thrust beyond that buffer, and Nueva Vizcayans faced the dilemma with which New Mexicans had lived for the last quarter-century. The danger to the province exceeded any immediate damages that the raiders might inflict, for the disturbances posed a grave danger of uprising by Indians native to the area. Most were nominally reduced to mission life, but under the stress of war they could explode at any moment to destroy the interior provinces.[18] By 1748, signs of marked decline appeared in Nueva Vizcaya: serious loss of population and a dangerous slump in the morale of the remaining residents. Many ranches lost so much of their livestock, particularly mules, that they virtually ceased to function.[19]

Texas and New Mexico found themselves more isolated than ever as Apache marauders drew new battle lines to the south of them. Their importance as barriers to French expansion and as executors of the Crown's obligations to the Christian Indian populations did not diminish, but more Christian Indians were at stake in the newly threatened provinces, and the immediate threat to the valuable mines and ranches down south was more pressing than any latent French menace. From the 1730's onward, the two northernmost provinces lay, for all practicable purposes, beyond the prime line of defense. Each of them wrestled with its unique Indian problems with little help and much restriction from the ruling powers in Mexico City and Madrid.

Apache marauders kept the San Antonio community in stagnation and misery for nearly two decades. Effective pursuit of the raiders was rarely practicable; to dispatch an adequate force to chase one party

---

[17] Hubert Howe Bancroft, *History of Texas and the North Mexican States*, I, 528.

[18] *Autos* compiled for the Marqués de la Peñuela, Santa Fe, October, 1707, SANM, no. 135.

[19] Hugo de O'Conor, *Informe de Hugo de O'Conor sobre el estado de las Provincias Internas del Norte, 1771–1776*, ed. Francisco R. Almada, pp. 20–22.

exposed the settlement and the missions to the depredations of countless others. The identity of raiders was seldom ascertained, but scattered bits of information convinced Captain Urrutia that Cabellos Colorados was a principal leader in the relentless depredations. Rumor had it that Cabellos Colorados had made a pact with the "great captain" of the Apache tribes to steal all the horses from the presidios of Béxar, Rio Grande, Coahuila, and Sacramento and then to slaughter the inhabitants of those regions.[20]

Late in 1737, Captain Urrutia managed to capture a party of sixteen Apaches, half of them women, led by Cabellos Colorados. At the chief's request, Captain Urrutia let one of the captured women carry the news of his arrest to his band, with the idea of having the stolen horses returned in exchange for the prisoners. The resulting negotiations dragged on for months. Apaches occasionally came to check on the prisoners' condition, declared they would have the horses soon, and vainly coaxed Urrutia to let them have the prisoners back on their word to return the horses later. In mid-winter, scouts reported a thousand armed Apaches in the vicinity, prepared to pounce if the Spaniards should send soldiers out to fetch horses that Apache messengers claimed to have nearby.

Meanwhile, for ten months after the capture of Cabellos Colorados, San Antonio suffered no Apache depredations. That seemed to confirm his guilt as a prime mover in the raids. When raids resumed in October 1738, Cabellos Colorados and his fellow prisoners, including his two-year-old daughter, were shipped off to Mexico City, not to be heard of again.

The Cabellos Colorados affair clinched Captain Urrutia's allegations of Apache guilt and incorrigible bad faith. He won permission to make a major campaign against the Apaches and to sell any captives to meet the expenses of the venture. To encourage volunteers, he declared he would share the booty with all. Urrutia campaigned clear to the San Saba River in the winter of 1738, and captives were his only result. Indeed, Fray Benito Francisco Fernández de Santa Ana charged that it amounted to nothing more than a slaving expedition and that it only provoked the Apaches to new crimes of vengeance.

Apaches continued to plague San Antonio after Captain Toribio de Urrutia succeeded his father in the presidial command. By 1742 he was pressing for permission to make a new series of campaigns against

[20] Dunn, "Apache Relations," pp. 244 ff.

them. Officials with Texas experience joined missionaries in opposing his plan: all of San Antonio's experience with the Apaches suggested the folly of giving them fresh grievances. As the argument wore on, the missionaries reported in 1744 that the depredations were slackening significantly. Many Apaches were coming to request missions for themselves; some had let the priests baptize their children. Fray Santa Ana, who spent a great deal of time with Apache visitors at Mission Concepción and with captives held in the settlement, learned of an incident early in the 1740's indicating that Apaches were growing desperate under increasing Comanche pressures. It helped to account for their growing interest in missions.

A Comanche war party had ventured into the Apachería only to meet an overwhelmingly superior Apache party. Instead of fleeing hopeless odds, they stood their ground until all but one Comanche died in the battle. The Comanches' brave stand impressed the Apaches more than ever with the dangers of the war raging between the two peoples. They spared the last man and sent him home to tell his people of his comrades' fate, gambling that the Comanches would find the episode a warning to stop their aggressions against Apaches. Fray Santa Ana guessed that their already vast territorial losses to Comanches and the dread of more to come would make the Apaches flock to a presidio and mission in their own country. He anticipated quick relief from the pressures on San Antonio and, in the foreseeable future, the long-desired conversion and reduction of the Apaches.

Fray Santa Ana also concluded that the Apaches were less numerous than was generally thought. In 1743 he understood that the three divisions in the region—Apaches, Ypandis, and Pelones—could muster altogether no more than 1,300 warriors. By 1745, he revised his estimate sharply downward: the Ypandis claimed only 166 warriors and the Natagés (i.e., Apaches proper) only 100. The dimensions of San Antonio's Apache problem began to look more manageable.

Nevertheless, Captain Toribio de Urrutia campaigned northwest from San Antonio in the spring of 1745 and fell upon a Lipan *ranchería* beyond the Colorado River. He took enough captives to make his venture a financial success, but he outraged both missionaries and Apaches. Four Apache women carried their leaders' message to San Antonio: the Spaniards had proved they had no wish to be friends, and the Apaches would observe no peace.

The entire community paid dearly in succeeding weeks, in lives lost and property stolen. Only Mission Concepción, whose Fray Santa Ana had been especially kind to Apaches, escaped their vengeance. At the end of June 1745, 250 Lipans and Natagés launched a determined, systematic attack on the presidio. A rescue party of a hundred Indians from Mission San Antonio de Valero routed them in time to save the presidio, but the subsequent pursuit failed. The direct attack upon the presidio, such a great rarity in Indian warfare, suggested the depth of the grievance those Apaches meant to avenge. Fortunately, healing influences developed.

In the confusion of the attack, an Apache captive slipped away from Mission San Antonio to rejoin his people. He assured the worried Lipan chief, whose seven-year-old daughter was among Urrutia's captives, that the prisoners received every kindness and that the Spaniards truly wished to become friends of the Apaches. At that news, the Lipan chief called off the hostilities, over the vehement objections of the Natagé chief. The Lipan chief prevailed, and for the next two months no marauders bothered San Antonio.

At summer's end, when the dread war might logically have resumed, an Apache woman, bearing a cross, came to San Antonio with one boy. She brought presents to Captain Urrutia and the welcome assurance that her people wished to keep the peace. That truce endured for several years. Livestock disappeared occasionally, but lives were reasonably safe in the San Antonio area.

Fray Santa Ana tried, through the little captive daughter, to persuade the Lipan chief to enter a mission, and the approach seemed likely to bear fruit. By October 1745, the Lipan chief made his third request for a mission in his own territory, either with or without a presidio. Late the next January, an Apache chief's wife came with two boys to present to Fray Santa Ana a request for missions. Only three days later, another messenger arrived: an Indian girl from the Ranchería Grande, whom Apaches had captured, was sent to announce that two chiefs were on the way to San Antonio to make a permanent peace. The girl reported that the Lipans wished a mission and a presidio but that the Natagés objected.

Whatever the course of the debate among the Apaches about the wisdom of seeking missions, Fray Santa Ana had small luck with his advocacy of an Apache mission project. Indeed, a startling turn of events involved the Spaniards in new missions for assorted enemies of the Apaches, right on a principal route to the Apachería.

For more than a decade, Fray Mariano Francisco de los Dolores y Viana, of Mission San Antonio de Valero, had maintained friendly contacts with little-known Indian groups to the north-northeast, where he traveled to recruit neophytes. He had often made overtures to the Deadoses, Yojuanes, Mayeyes, and the aggregation of Hierbipiames and others called the Ranchería Grande and had tried to visit them at least annually. His patient efforts bore fruit in June 1745 when four chiefs and thirteen others from those groups visited Mission San Antonio to ask that a mission be founded for them in their own country. Delighted by this response to his prayers and work of many years, Fray Mariano proposed to found two or three missions to accommodate the diversity of languages and customs among Indians of the region. He also requested a presidio with a thirty-man garrison to protect the missionaries from the Indians and the prospective neophytes from Apaches.[21]

Captain Urrutia questioned the visitors closely. Once convinced of their sincere interest in Christianity, he urged them to settle in a separate, new mission that he would provide for them at San Antonio. They refused steadfastly even to consider going so far from their friends and relatives, their lands, and their trade with the Tejas upon whom they relied for guns and other merchandise. That was a telling argument, for all the delegates were armed with French guns. Urrutia relented and promised, in the name of the king, to protect them from their foes. Fray Mariano promised to start a mission in their country as soon as possible.

The delegates left contented, promising Fray Mariano to bring their people to meet him at a designated spot in their country at the beginning of winter. They would expect him then to choose a site and instruct them in preparations for their mission. The mission Indians who escorted the visitors home reported back to San Antonio before the end of July: the four groups had been delighted with the news brought back by their chiefs and had begun at once to look for a mission site. A second delegation visited San Antonio later that year to report that a place had been selected and that many other nations had agreed to join the promised missions.

Fray Mariano and Captain Urrutia had made rash commitments, for there was no guarantee that they could persuade the Crown to support such a venture. After all, Fray Santa Ana and his predecessors had long pleaded in vain for a mission and presidio for the Apaches.

A timely combination of circumstances pushed Fray Mariano's proposal ahead. It was in the very month of the first petition that

[21] Herbert Eugene Bolton, *Texas in the Middle Eighteenth Century*, pp. 149 ff., traces the history of the San Gabriel missions in great detail.

Indians of Mission San Antonio de Valero rescued the presidio and villa from the Apache assault. That episode dramatized the dangers and difficulties of dealing with Apaches and the critical importance of friendly Christian Indians. Furthermore, the petition coincided with the official visitation of San Antonio's missions by Fray Francisco Xavier Ortiz. That important official witnessed Captain Urrutia's formal interrogation of the petitioners. When he reported back to head-quarters, his informed advocacy of the project weighed heavily with the deciding powers, both religious and secular. The College of Querétaro had resources available just then for a new mission because they had lately turned over to secular clergy an older mission down south. If the viceroy would commit reasonable military support, the Querétaran friars stood ready to carry the faith into the Texas interior.

The number and diversity of Indians in the new region posed important challenges and opportunities for both Majesties. By 1745, the four groups requesting the new missions numbered no more than 1,228 souls: epidemics of measles and smallpox and the tribal wars of the last half-century had sadly decimated their ranks. However, they claimed that many other nations would come to join them, and on those claims, plus other fragments of information gathered over the years, the friars based their expectation that the new missions would reach some 6,000 Indians in the interior.[22] Most were yet unknown to the Spaniards, but all were enemies of the Apaches and were either directly or indirectly involved in the French trade network based at Natchitoches. Many of those Indians depended upon the Tejas as their middlemen in the French trade. The friars ventured that, once converted, they would in turn convert their stubborn Tejas friends, who had rejected the faith for half a century. What more glorious service to God than to convert those thousands to the faith? What better service to the king than to divert them from the pernicious French influence and make them a stable counterweight to the Apaches on the Texas frontier?

The list of prospects for the new missions were a veritable catalogue of the woes converging upon eastern Apaches. There were the Wichitan groups (Tawakonis and Taovayas, and others) moving into the

---

22 Fray Ortiz forwarded to King a list of twenty-two groups: Vicais, Caocos, Lacopseles, Anchoses, Tups, Atais, Apapax, Acopseles, Cancepnes, Tancagues, Hiscas, Naudis, Casos, Tanico, Quisis, Anathague, Atasacneus, Pastates, Geotes, Atiasnogues, Taguacanas, and Taguayas. He alluded to unnamed "others who subsequently asked for baptism" (Bolton, *Texas in the Middle Eighteenth Century*, p. 154).

valleys of the Trinity, the Brazos, and the Red rivers; the Kichais, who had been in the area longer; the Tonkawas, prepared to cooperate with their Mayeye and Yojuane kinsmen; the Bidais of the lower middle Trinity, ready to join their Deadose kinsmen in a mission; Cocos and Tups from the assorted Karankawas of the lower Colorado and the Gulf coast; others whose identities time has blurred to meaninglessness. Many had once been enemies of each other and of the Tejas, but, thanks partly to their common enmity to the Apaches and partly to the French trade, they were now friends and trading partners of the Tejas and had from them the guns forbidden to Indians on the Spanish frontier.

If Fray Mariano and Captain Urrutia were permitted to keep their promises, all those Indians would soon enjoy the right to Spain's protection against their enemies, and their warriors would take to the field as vassals of the king of Spain. All of this loomed northeastward, while northwestward Comanches already swept down the plains once dominated by Apaches.

The value of the promises made at San Antonio hinged upon deliberations in Mexico City, which dragged on for more than two years. Although the proposal won a generally sympathetic reception, New Spain had committed all resources immediately available to a more important advance on the northern frontier. In the autumn of 1746, José de Escandón explored the coastal region from Tampico northward to Matagorda Bay, preparatory to establishing the new province of Nuevo León. Because there was reason to fear French occupation if Spain should leave a vacuum on that strategic coast, the Escandón project had irreducible priority.

The reasons for the delay were valid and, in the time scale of Spanish administration, a two-year period was trivial. Unfortunately, two years could be tantamount to eternity in the volatile world of the Indians of the northern frontier. Afraid that the Indians' enthusiasm could not survive a long waiting period, Fray Mariano started a primitive, de facto mission without authorization and thus without adequate support.

There were serious difficulties from the beginning. The Indians had picked a spot on the Brazos in the Cross Timbers region, but for a while that winter floods made the site inaccessible from San Antonio. When a survey party of Spaniards and mission Indians finally managed to reach the Brazos area chosen by the Indians, they found it hopelessly deficient in irrigation potential. Arguing that a mission could never sustain its population if it could neither irrigate fields nor depend upon regular access for pack trains from San Antonio, the Spaniards recommended irrigable sites on the San Gabriel River.[23] That brought the project conveniently nearer San Antonio but also much nearer the Apaches. The San Gabriel lay just below a pass by which Apaches regularly descended from the hill country to the prairies to hunt buffalo.

Surprisingly, the Indians consented to the move. Either they did not realize that Apaches now frequented that area, or they had complete confidence in the protection promised by the Spaniards. In January 1746, they gathered on the San Gabriel, near its confluence with Brushy Creek. Fray Mariano met them there, with a squad from Béxar presidio to guard them and some mission Indians from San Antonio de Valero to help them prepare the site. To his great delight, the Cocos had come, in addition to the four initiating groups, and they too promised to enter the projected missions. The first mission began, in effect, that spring, with the preparation and planting of fields. Fray Mariano supervised their work and instructed them in the faith as long as he dared neglect his primary duties at Mission San Antonio de Valero. When he returned to his station, he left well-trained mission Indians on the San Gabriel to tend the crops, which would be needed to support the prospective neophytes.

As the summer wore on, the would-be converts repeatedly sent spokesmen to San Antonio to ask when they would receive the friars and the supplies promised them. Embarrassed that he could give no satisfactory answer, Fray Mariano feared they would give up in disgust, but, with the help of the San Antonio mission Indians, they stuck to their purpose. That summer they began to construct their mission buildings. Fray Mariano diverted as much as he dared from the resources of Mission San Antonio de Valero: forty cargos of supplies, yokes of oxen, Indian workmen and guards, equipment of all sorts. He spent $5,083.50 that year on the unauthorized project and seconded friars there from Mission San Antonio whenever he could spare them.

The San Gabriel mission project survived its first serious mishap. After the Cocos talked with Fray Mariano in the spring of 1746, some started homeward to the lower Colorado River to fetch their families. Unluckily, their path crossed that of a force led by Captain Joaquín

---

[23] In the eighteenth century the San Gabriel River of today was called the San Xavier; thus, documents of the period refer to the San Xavier missions. The contemporary usage is preferred here as less confusing for the modern reader.

Orobio Bazterra of Presidio La Bahía, who had been out searching for French traders reported on the lower Trinity River. Orobio, apparently both uninformed and trigger-happy, attacked the Cocos, killed two, and captured others.

As soon as the news reached San Antonio, the missionaries protested to Captain Urrutia and asked him to order the captives released. Captain Urrutia not only made Orobio give up the prisoners at once, but he also organized a delegation of mission Indians to convey his apologies and explanations to the Cocos and their friends gathered on the San Gabriel. Apparently his amends sufficed: some Cocos did later enter the San Gabriel missions.

The Indians necessarily dispersed in the winter of 1746 to live off the land, but in the spring of 1747 a creditable number of Deadoses, Cocos, and Yojuanes turned up at the site on the San Gabriel. A Spanish citizen, Eusebio Pruneda, came from San Antonio with Indians from missions Valero and Concepción to help them plant crops. The work progressed smoothly until the workers needed meat early in May.

Twenty-two Coco hunters rode out for buffalo and met Apache hunters. A clash ensued. The Cocos held their own and killed one Apache, but they brought back alarming news of many Apache camps along nearby Brushy Creek. For the next three days, the congregation on the San Gabriel braced against the Apache attack that they thought must surely follow. None occurred, but dread overwhelmed them: all the neophytes fled. They notified Fray Mariano that they would not return until he could send the promised missionaries and other Spaniards to the San Gabriel but that they would then bring back with them several more tribes from the interior.

That same week, a courier reached San Antonio with the viceroy's order of February 14, 1747, approving temporary assignment of soldiers to protect the San Gabriel enterprise: ten to be detached from Los Adaes, twelve from Béxar. The courier had been delayed two months at the Rio Grande by the hostilities of Apaches and other *bárbaros* who had plagued the Coahuila and Nueva Vizcaya frontiers for a year.

San Antonio was also grappling with a resurgent Apache problem. In April, Apache raiders had driven the horse herds off from three of the missions. Urrutia knew that many Apaches were camped near the San Gabriel. He had the *cabildo*'s appeal to Mexico City for reinforcements, dated April 29, ready for the mail courier. Meanwhile, citizens had petitioned him to summon fifteen or twenty men from Los Adaes to reinforce the settlement against an expected Apache assault. Captain

Urrutia dared not honor the viceroy's order to second a dozen soldiers to the San Gabriel to guard neophytes who had already fled.

Like the attack anticipated at the San Gabriel mission site, the dreaded assault on San Antonio did not occur. Perhaps the May planting time diverted Apache energies; perhaps they stayed in the hills to mull over the congregation of their enemies on the San Gabriel together with Spaniards and mission Indians. At any rate, San Antonio experienced no catastrophe that year. Meanwhile, over the vigorous objections of the governor of Texas, the viceroy sanctioned the San Gabriel mission project. On December 23, 1747, he ordered three missions founded on the San Gabriel within the next eight months and authorized a thirty-man garrison to protect the enterprise until a permanent fifty-man presidio could be established.

Fray Mariano lost no time reassembling his neophytes. On February 7, 1748, he formally founded Mission San Francisco Xavier on the San Gabriel River, near present Rockdale. In March, twenty-eight of the promised soldiers arrived, under command of Lieutenant Juan Galbán of Béxar; soon thereafter, the families of the married soldiers joined them, as the viceroy ordered and the friars preferred.

Controversy swelled about the project. The Zacatecan friars objected that the Mayeye country where it was founded was not well suited to agriculture and that the Querétarans had let the Yadoxas sell them false information about the nations of the north. Zacatecan information was that the Tawakonis, Kichais, Tonkawas, and Yojuanes lived entirely too far north to be affected by a mission on the San Gabriel. If they really wanted anything more than Spanish help against the Apaches, those nations and the Bidais, too, could be better served by the existing missions of Nacogdoches and Los Ais in the Tejas country. Governor Pedro del Barrio y Espriella, who disapproved of the San Gabriel project, refused to protect or assist the friars and their charges in any way and actively strove to undermine the venture.

Worst of all was the Apaches' vigorous displeasure. On May 2, 1748, more than sixty Apaches struck the mission, ransacked the houses, and tried to stampede the horses. The soldiers and more than two hundred of the Indians rallied to corral the horses as the Apaches rode off shouting threats. A Yojuane who had once been a captive of Apaches interpreted: they would be back with more warriors to destroy the place. The departing raiders met two mission Indians returning from the hunt with buffalo meat and killed the pair. At the mission, the Indians talked of fleeing to the woods for safety.

Just three days later, the Apaches did return in larger numbers, and that time they ran off the entire horse herd. Two more raids followed that year: each cost the enterprise horses; four neophytes died at the hands of the raiders. When Governor Barrio callously ignored Fray Mariano's appeals for help, the missionaries recruited fifteen or twenty mission Indians from San Antonio to bolster defenses.

Supplies and missionaries en route from Mexico for the new missions were long delayed by bad weather and by Apache hostilities on the Rio Grande. It was late December 1748 before they finally reached the San Gabriel. The Indians had to scatter again that winter to live off the country.

In spite of all the terror and deprivation, they came back in the spring of 1749. Because Fray Mariano was ill, Fray Santa Ana supervised the founding of two more missions: Mission San Ildefonso, about three miles downstream from Mission San Xavier, and Mission Nuestra Señora de la Candelaria, about three miles upstream.

True to missionary custom, Fray Santa Ana tried to apportion the Indians among the missions according to linguistic and cultural similarities. At Mission San Francisco Xavier, he left the Mayeyes, Hierbipiames, and Yojuanes, whom he classified as kinsmen and allies of the Tonkawas. Since the Bidais, Deadoses, and Akokisas camped together, conversed with no apparent difficulty, and seemed much intermarried, he congregated them at Mission San Ildefonso. Mission Candelaria was allocated to the Cocos and such kindred peoples as they should attract. While Mission Candelaria was under construction, the Cocos fled to their old home between the Brazos and the Colorado, angered by some soldiers' abuses. Fray Santa Ana coaxed back those who survived bouts with measles and smallpox at their old home, but the incident foreshadowed chronic offenses by the garrison and desertions by the neophytes.

Fortunately, the Apaches did not compound the serious internal problems of the new missions that year. They had their own troubles: the Spaniards answered their raids of 1748 with punitive campaigns into the heart of their own territory. Late in the summer of 1748, Coahuila's Governor Pedro de Rábago y Terán led a campaign against the Apaches. He came from Monclova by way of San Antonio to recruit soldiers and settlers for his force, then led them into the Apachería, clear to the San Saba River. Apaches easily spotted the large force and fled to safety, so few captives were taken, and Rábago had an embarrassing failure charged to his record.

Captain Urrutia opposed Rábago's project. He had come to agree with Fray Santa Ana's argument that harsh campaigns only provoked the Apaches to worse retaliations.[24] He therefore ordered that in all subsequent campaigns no Indians should be killed except in self-defense and that all captives taken must receive the most humane treatment. Early in February 1749, apparently with Fray Santa Ana's approval, Urrutia led from San Antonio a force of two hundred men, mostly mission Indians, to test the new approach in Apache country.

The campaign began mildly enough. Not far from San Antonio, the force found a small camp that put up very little fight and brought back three old women and five children as prisoners. Meanwhile, Apache raiders struck Mission Concepción and made off with many cattle. Urrutia decided to pursue them, and he headed north with three hundred men. On the Guadalupe River they found the hunting camp of some four hundred Apaches. Most were off hunting, so Urrutia's force easily captured all who remained in camp: thirty men, ninety women, and forty-seven children.

Urrutia and Santa Ana could have asked no better opportunity to test the new policy of mildness. Back in San Antonio, the captain jailed the Apache men and distributed the women and children among the settlers' homes and the missions, stipulating that they must be treated kindly but not allowed to escape. Then the captain and the missionary picked two women and a man as envoys to carry a peace proposal to the Apaches. If the chiefs would promise to live henceforth in peace and friendship with the Spaniards, the Spaniards would release all the prisoners they had taken on the Guadalupe that March and all those taken earlier. The captives reacted very favorably to the idea.

The three messengers rode off to the Apachería in mid-April, promising to return within three moons and predicting that all their people would come with them to make peace. Early in August the three returned with a man of apparent distinction. They represented a large party now camped on the Guadalupe: two Lipan chiefs and two Apache chiefs, with a hundred people of each tribe. They wished to make peace and to receive their captive kinsmen as soon as Captain Urrutia would designate a time.[25]

Captain Urrutia assured the messengers that their chiefs would be

[24] Dunn, "Apache Relations," pp. 259 ff.
[25] Cabello, Ynforme.

welcome whenever they chose to come. He only wished them to send smoke signals first, so he could arrange a suitable reception. Obviously very pleased, the envoys carried the message back to camp. A week later smoke signaled the approach of the entire delegation.

San Antonio spared no effort to entertain the Apache visitors. On the outskirts of the settlement, the authorities constructed a big hall. For this occasion, it would house the chiefs' retinue and serve as a conference place; thenceforth, it would stand ready to accommodate Apache visitors whenever they wished to come. Lavish quantities of beef, corn, squash, and fruit stocked the reception hall for the ceremonial feasting required to celebrate brotherhood. At no time would the Apaches find San Antonio's hospitality stinting.

On the morning of August 16, 1749, Captain Urrutia and Fray Santa Ana led a welcoming party northward to greet the Apaches. Most of the troops from the presidio, the officials of Villa San Fernando and most citizens of the settlement, the five missionaries, and many mission Indians rode out to honor the visitors and to attest their desire for peace and brotherhood with the Apaches. They met joyously, five miles north of the settlement. The visiting chiefs embraced Captain Urrutia and the friars, all the leaders voiced cordial sentiments, then everyone rode into San Antonio together. Shown to the quarters especially built for them, the warriors feasted on several freshly slaughtered beeves and seasonal fruits from San Antonio's fields and gardens. Only the chiefs entered the presidio, where two of them lodged at Captain Urrutia's home. The other two continued with Fray Santa Ana across the river to Mission San Antonio de Valero to enjoy the friars' hospitality. The gracious arrangements for the entire delegation and the special honors paid the chiefs pleased the guests; these Spaniards were showing a grasp of the niceties, very like that expected of Apache chiefs.

The second day began with Mass in the parish church of Villa San Fernando, with Fray Santa Ana officiating and the four chiefs attending, along with the soldiers and all the settlers. Afterward the four chiefs and the Spanish leaders opened their formal negotiations. The discussions went so smoothly that the next day the most recent prisoners were handed over as a first step in the restitution of prisoners. One day later formal ceremonies sealed the peace.

That August 19 was a momentous day for Apaches and Spaniards alike. Upon their ability to make good their peace agreements might hinge the survival, tranquillity, and even prosperity of their communities. All had suffered too much over the last quarter-century; all had a tremendous stake in the success of the peace. They buried the war in a ceremony to match the import of their pact.

Early that morning people flocked to the presidial plaza. On one side gathered the Spaniards: missionaries, soldiers, settlers. On the other side assembled the Apaches: chiefs, warriors, newly released captives. While the assembly watched, workers dug a great hole in the middle of the plaza. In it were placed the instruments of war: a live horse, a hatchet, a lance, half a dozen arrows. The four chiefs joined hands with Captain Urrutia and circled three times around the hole, solemnly looking down into it; twice the chiefs repeated the act, first with the missionaries, then with a settler. Each returned to his place. Then, at a signal, everyone rushed to the pile of earth beside the hole to hurl clods upon the luckless horse and the weapons. When they were buried, and the war thus symbolically buried, the Indians gave a great whoop. The Spaniards shouted back, "Viva el Rey! Viva el Rey! Viva el Rey!"

No incident marred the harmony of the occasion. The Apaches started homeward the next day, eager to restore the captive women and children to their kinsmen. They were escorted out as ceremoniously as they had been escorted in, with many demonstrations of friendship and with the assurance that they would be welcome to visit this and other settlements of their Spanish brothers whenever they wished.

From that time forward, the Spaniards and Apaches in Texas were, for better or for worse, at least nominal "friends and brothers." Apaches often visited the presidio on the terms defined that August. Within a year some of them moved nearer San Antonio to be safer from their enemies. In May 1750 some Apaches established camp on the Medina River, twenty miles southwest of San Antonio, making their rearguard barrier the large hills running northwest to the Guadalupe River. Such close proximity disquieted Captain Urrutia and the citizens of San Antonio, but the Apaches promised to cause the Spaniards no difficulty. As they explained, they were so grateful to escape the Comanches who had plagued them since the Great Battle of the 1720's that they would do nothing to jeopardize their peaceful sanctuary at the Spanish settlements.

Just a few days after they moved to the Medina, the Apache leaders asked Captain Urrutia and Fray Santa Ana for letters of recommendation to the captain of Presidio La Bahía del Espíritu Santo and to the missionary there, so they could visit there to make peace. As soon as they received the letters, the Lipans and Natagés each sent one chief and a hundred followers to establish relations at La Bahía. They were welcomed encouragingly at both the presidio and the mission. During that visit they also celebrated peace with the Akokisas, Mayeyes, Cocos, and Bidais who frequented that presidio. Happy and satisfied, they returned to the Medina.

Certainly the Apaches needed all the friends they could find. At the time of the peace, they had very few horses. Those who visited San Antonio neither had guns nor knew how to use them. They claimed they had never seen firearms before they began to fight with the San Antonians, but they wanted desperately to acquire them. Though they tipped their lances with sharp iron points, they still depended primarily upon the bows and arrows that they used expertly. They had shields for themselves and armor for their horses, made of buffalo skins; the devices would turn arrows, but bullets easily penetrated them. Now French guns were reaching the Comanches, against whom the Apaches had never been able to hold their own. To compound their troubles, the prairies north of San Antonio now swarmed with Indians, all well supplied with French guns, all enemies of Apaches since time immemorial.

Even as Apaches moved to the Medina and looked to the shelter of Spanish presidios, their enemies gathered on the prairies. In mid-June 1750, four Tejas brought to the San Gabriel missions the rumor that the interior nations were assembling to campaign against the Apaches. On August 2, a large party arrived on the San Gabriel: Ais, Hasinais, Kadohadachos, Nabedaches, and Yojuanes. They reported the great chief Sánchez Teja in the area, rallying Tawakonis, Yatasís, Kichais, Nasonis, Tonkawas, and many others. The visitors conferred day and night with the mission Indians, especially at San Ildefonso. Little by little, the neophytes left with groups of the visitors, until the priest found himself alone. Guns, vermilion, and other trade goods helped lure them away. Fray Ganzábal thought he spotted a French trader among the Indians from East Texas. The neophytes promised to return in two months, but a year and two months elapsed before any kept that promise.

The great campaign did not occur. Perhaps the Apaches' new rapprochement with the Spaniards gave their enemies pause. Still, the Apaches could not feel entirely safe, even on the Medina. In April 1751 some of them moved southward to the territory between the Nueces and the Rio Grande, in the jurisdiction of Coahuila rather than Texas.

The Lipans and the Natagés quarreled among themselves after their move beyond the Nueces and parted company, after many years of living side by side. The Lipans stayed on the Nueces; the Natagés, of whom there were perhaps twice as many, moved on southward to the Rio Grande and beyond. In 1755, the Natagés negotiated a peace with the Coahuila settlements and formed an alliance with the Julimeños located at Mission del Dulze Nombre de Jesús de Vizarron. The Lipans, who remained in communication with the Natagés after their separation, learned of the new peace and alliance and sent delegates southward to subscribe to the terms. The separation continued, however, and the Lipans continued to deal principally with the Texas Spaniards while the Natagés dealt principally with those of Coahuila.

Those Apaches most favorably disposed toward mission life continued to cluster in the San Antonio area, camping on the Medina, San Antonio, San Marcos, and Guadalupe rivers. Some pleaded for a mission at San Antonio, but the missionaries worried that a concentration of Apaches there would jeopardize the successful existing missions. Fear and hatred of Apaches were so general among nations served by those missions that the converts were likely to flee and prospective neophytes to reject residence there if San Antonio should become a mission center for Apaches. The friars redoubled their efforts to win permission for a major effort to convert the Apaches with a new mission and presidio well within their own territory. The Apaches' excellent record in keeping the peace of 1749 bolstered the friars' arguments.

Most of the San Antonio missionaries thought the Pedernales River the likeliest place for an Apache mission, so the government sent two expeditions to evaluate that area. First, in the summer of 1753, Lieutenant Juan Galbán and Fray Miguel de Aranda of Mission Concepción probed the Apachería with a small party from Béxar. They found the Pedernales deficient in water and in agricultural potential; so was the Llano River. Not until they reached the San Saba River did they find (near present Menard) a defensible area with enough agricultural potential to support missions. Many Apaches welcomed them there and assured the Spaniards that they would indeed flock to any missions established there. Lieutenant Galbán reported favorably on the San Saba location, recommending that the Béxar garrison be transferred there.[26]

The missionaries endorsed Galbán's recommendations, but some

[26] Robert S. Weddle, *The San Sabá Mission*, pp. 25–27.

officials questioned his assumption that San Antonio would need no military protection once a mission and presidio were established in Apache country. Others opposed the whole Apache project on principle. The viceroy required yet another assessment from Don Pedro de Rábago y Terán, a former governor of Coahuila lately assigned to command the presidio at the turbulent San Gabriel mission project.

Rábago inspected the area late in December 1754 with a friar and twenty-five men from San Antonio. Like Galbán and his associates, they found the Pedernales and Llano unsuitable and pressed on to the San Saba, where they camped near a cross erected by Galbán in summer of the previous year. They concurred with his judgment: this San Saba locality could support a substantial presidio and missions to serve the several thousand Apaches who clamored for them. On the way back to San Antonio, they encountered two bands of Apaches, who cheerfully promised to enter the proposed mission.

Captain Rábago wrote a sweeping recommendation of the San Saba project. Conversion of Apaches was not the sole benefit he envisioned. Nearby ranged Comanches, who might also be converted from that base. Direct communication and commerce between the isolated provinces of Texas and New Mexico could be fostered, to the financial and military advantage of all concerned. French traders, currently worrying New Mexico, could be kept out. Since there appeared to be great mineral resources in the San Saba area, a presidio there could spark development of mines.

The Apache mission project won considerable support from San Antonio settlers and from Captain Urrutia, who estimated four thousand potential converts. News that both Galbán and Rábago had noted probable mineral deposits, especially silver, quickened their interest. The prospect of silver mines also helped the viceroy sympathize with Apache needs. In short, the project enjoyed a rare spread of support among Apaches and settlers, soldiers and priests, and high authorities. Even so, discussion and preparation dragged on another two years before the San Sabá mission and presidio were accomplished.

Those were confusing, difficult years for Apaches. Missionaries at San Antonio had long urged them to come to missions. Spanish actions since the peace of 1749 had at least implied promises of missions for the Apaches: the careful quizzing of countless Apaches to test the sincerity of their desire for missions; the exploring parties sent to check potential mission sites within the Apachería; and the efforts of friars at San Antonio to encourage the Apaches' enthusiasm for missions during the inevitable time of waiting for authority to minister to them. Apaches had good reason to camp around Spanish establishments, pinning their hopes for the future on the fulfillment of the implied promises.

Some Apaches carried their quest for assistance and reassurance to the missions on the San Gabriel. Fray Francisco Aparicio, stationed at Mission Candelaria from 1752 to 1755, unexpectedly found himself presiding over an arena of potentially explosive contact between Apaches and at least ten nations deeply hostile to them.[27]

Fray Aparicio was perhaps the first Spaniard to know at first hand the long-reported Nations of the North. Seeking new converts and trying to recover runaways, he traveled extensively in the homelands of Indians served by the San Gabriel missions. During his several journeys, he met some Tawakonis, Kichais, and Comanches, learned to recognize them by sight, and apparently established cordial relations with them.

A party of Kichais, Tawakonis, and Comanches stopped at Mission Candelaria to visit Fray Aparicio and mentioned that they were looking for Apaches, whom they intended to massacre. It was an awkward situation, for at that very time Mission San Xavier had a considerable number of Apache visitors. Fray Aparicio harangued his guests about the evil of killing people and about the awful wrath of God toward those who broke His holy law. Whether momentarily convinced or merely polite to their host, the Tawakonis, Kichais, and Comanches promised Fray Aparicio that they would not, after all, kill the Apaches. Although those people were their natural enemies, they would refrain out of their high esteem for the fathers and the Spaniards. Seizing the opportunity to mediate peace, Fray Aparicio then brought all the visitors together for a ceremony; they all sang together and touched weapons to attest their new friendship.

The amenities observed by the several visitors could hardly offset the deep-seated hatreds and the necessities of tribal revenge on either side. Soon after Fray Aparicio left the San Gabriel, Indians told him that the war raged on. Worse still, the Yojuanes, Tonkawas, Kichais, and Comanches had begun to hate the Spaniards as well because of their friendship with and kindnesses to the Apaches. Rumor had it that those

---

[27] Statement by Fray Francisco Aparicio to Colonel Parrilla, San Luis de las Amarillas, April 5, 1758, in Paul D. Nathan, trans., and Lesley Byrd Simpson, ed., *The San Sabá Papers*, p. 129.

nations had leagued to exterminate the Apaches; if the Spaniards should defend the Apaches, they would fight the Spaniards, too.

Certainly the Apaches' enemies had reason to grow embittered toward the Spaniards during the 1750's. While Apaches flocked to San Antonio to trade and to enjoy the hospitality of the missions and took shelter from their enemies in the shadow of Spanish presidios, the Indians at the missions on the San Gabriel saw their hopes for security shattered by one misfortune after another. At the humiliating climax of their ordeal, the resources once pledged to their missions were diverted to a mission for Apaches: the presidio, with all the soldiers; the missionaries, the sacred objects that had furnished their chapels, and the bells.

Few neophytes were left on the San Gabriel when the end came, but hundreds who had come and gone over the decade had a sorry experience to remember and to recount in Indian camps and villages of the interior. There was never enough food at the San Gabriel missions: crops were consumed as they ripened; supply shipments never arrived in good time or in adequate quantity. More often than not, neophytes had to disperse in order to live by gathering, much as they had always done. Smallpox and measles epidemics struck the missions several times; from 1753 onward polluted water supplies spawned typhoid epidemics each summer.

The men of the temporary garrison were an undisciplined rabble. Early in their tour of duty, the governor ordered their families back to their home presidios, ostensibly for safety from Apaches. As the outraged missionaries predicted, the soldiers then virtually moved in with the neophytes, took Indian mistresses, and by undisciplined example undermined the teaching of the friars. Matters worsened after establishment of the regular presidio in 1751, for its commanding officer, Captain Felipe de Rábago y Terán, indulged in gross personal misconduct, abused the Indians, flaunted the rights of the soldiers, and quarreled violently with the priests. The spring of 1752 was a sordid time on the banks of the San Gabriel: Captain Rábago's flagrant adulterous affair; murder, apparently with the captain's collusion, of the cuckolded soldier and of the priest who had objected; excommunication of the soldiers. All but one missionary fled after that, and most of the remaining neophytes fled, too.

The missions endured for three more miserable years, but they never recovered any usefulness. The missionaries soon returned to their stations and tried to retrieve the scattered neophytes, but they could never again congregate many. Some Indians returned briefly: some came just long enough to steal guns and horses; some attacked and wounded a soldier. Even patient Fray Mariano abandoned all hope of success on the San Gabriel and talked of moving the missions to a more healthful site at the San Marcos Springs or at the Comal Springs. He was quite prepared to move the few remaining neophytes by force if necessary. When Captain Pedro Rábago y Terán came in August 1754 to take command of the presidio wrecked by his infamous kinsman, he supported the friars' petition to leave that location.

Captain Pedro Rábago could cite many reasons to abandon the San Gabriel venture. He found the presidio a mockery: its men housed in thatched huts, short of supplies, short of horses, under-equipped in every respect. The missions were in even worse shape. Only San Francisco Xavier had any neophytes left, a mere seventy. That fall, Captain Rábago recommended removal of the neophytes to the San Antonio missions, which could easily accommodate more Indians. That would free all the resources of the San Gabriel enterprise, religious and military, to support the long-discussed Apache mission project on the San Saba.

The soldiers of the San Gabriel garrison did not wait for the viceroy's decision. When the plague struck again for the fourth summer, worse than ever before, they demanded that the captain move them to save their lives. The missionaries concurred, and Captain Rábago yielded. By the end of August 1755, he had moved the soldiers, priests, and a few neophytes to the San Marcos River. Most of the neophytes chose instead to return to the camps of their kinsmen.

The new place was simply not tenable for the erstwhile neophytes of the San Gabriel. A thousand Apaches met the missionaries on the San Marcos, hungry and clamoring to have the presidio brought to their own country on the San Saba.

Fray Mariano sent many emissaries to coax the neophytes back and managed for a while to collect at Mission San Antonio de Valero some families formerly of Mission San Francisco Xavier and Mission Candelaria. The Cocos of the latter seemed content to settle at Valero, but those of San Francisco Xavier were another matter. Their kinsmen did not come to join them as the friars had hoped, and three-fourths of those recovered soon left again. Once Fray Mariano realized that the Mayeyes would never settle down at Mission Valero, many of whose Indians were their traditional enemies, he established a new mission for them on the Guadalupe River, at present New Braunfels, Texas. The Akokisas and other tribes formerly at San Ildefonso were not a worry: they would be commended to the care of the new mission, Nuestra Señora de la Luz, just established in the Akokisas' homeland on the lower Trinity.

Fray Mariano arranged to have the salaries of six soldiers appropriated to protect his new mission, but he used the money to subsidize colonization there by exemplary Spanish families who would instruct as well as protect the Indians. The few Mayeyes still at San Antonio de Valero readily agreed to settle there permanently and promised to bring their friends. Four Spanish families moved with them to the Guadalupe in 1756, with two priests and some mission Indians to help with the work. Since the resources once allocated to the San Gabriel project were diverted to the Apache mission on the San Saba, the mission of Nuestra Señora de Guadalupe never amounted to more than an underfinanced appurtenance of the San Antonio missions. It did not survive the fresh turmoils set in motion by the new Apache mission enterprise.

It was May 1756 by the time the viceroy authorized the Apache mission project, and yet another year passed before the priests and soldiers came to build the mission and presidio. By then, time was running out for Apaches in the San Saba region, too.

Captain Pedro Rábago did not survive the lengthy wait. After he died, command of the presidio passed to Colonel Diego Ortiz Parrilla. Although a stranger to the eastern Apaches and, indeed, to the entire Texas situation, he did not lack relevant experience. Parrilla had known troubles with western Apaches as governor of Sinaloa and Sonora and had suffered the disastrous shock of the Pima uprising of 1751.[28] He had tended then to sympathize with the native rebel leader, Luis, against the Jesuits, and, through his acceptance of the Indian point of view, he had negotiated a settlement. The Jesuits had vigorously protested his attitudes and actions, and the resulting wrangle had dragged on through five years of official investigations. The episode marred the record of the ambitious officer. Though entrusted meanwhile with founding the new presidios of Tubac (1752) and Altar (1753) in the Pima country and promoted to the rank of colonel, Parrilla yearned for success in an important new assignment. The San Saba project seemed to offer that chance. From his experience in

---

[28] Russell Charles Ewing, "The Pima Uprising of 1751: A Study of Spanish-Indian Relations on the Frontier of New Spain," in *Greater America: Essays in Honor of Herbert Eugene Bolton*, pp. 265 ff.

Sonora, the colonel brought a capacity for sympathetic understanding of Indian viewpoints, a consciousness that even the friendliest of Indians could turn upon the Spaniards without warning, and the determination not to become embroiled in controversy with the Franciscans of Texas as he had with the Jesuits of Sonora.

The religious head of the project was Fray Alonso Giraldo de Terreros, no stranger either to Texas or to the Lipan Apaches. He had been named to head the San Antonio and San Gabriel missions in 1752, when his Order hoped that his notable wisdom and prudence might heal the appalling breach between the soldiery and the missionaries on the San Gabriel. That situation reached its explosive climax before he could assume his duties, and he was permitted to return to his post as president of the Rio Grande missions. Perhaps he carried back from San Antonio a strong conviction that the Apaches should have missions without further delay; perhaps he reached that conclusion as he studied Apaches surging southward upon the Coahuila frontier in the early 1750's. At any rate, he founded a mission for Lipans in Coahuila in December 1754, just as Captain Rábago set out to inspect potential mission sites in the Apachería. Mission San Lorenzo, near the presidio of San Fernando de Austria, seemed successful at first, but, when other duties called Fray Terreros away, the Lipan neophytes lost their enthusiasm for the experiment. In October 1755 they burned the mission and fled.

Those who had always doubted the possibility of converting Apaches saw their doubts vindicated by the episode. Proponents of the mission to the Apaches blamed the difficulty on the location, too far from the Apaches' homelands, and argued all the harder for missions within the Apachería.

Fray Terreros' own confidence in the Apaches held firm, and he enlisted the support of his cousin, Don Pedro Romero de Terreros, one of the richest men in New Spain and a notable philanthropist. Don Pedro volunteered a generous subsidy for missions within the Apachería: he would underwrite all expenses incurred in founding three missions and support them for three years, on condition that Fray Terreros be in charge.

The Crown, responsible only for the presidial expenses for the first three years, generously allocated a hundred soldiers: fifty from the defunct San Gabriel garrison, twenty-two to be detached from Béxar, and twenty-seven to be enlisted by the commander on his way north to Texas. By January 1758, Parrilla had his force assembled at San Antonio and preparations for the trek to the San Saba well underway. Fray Terreros joined him there with four more priests and nine Tlaxcaltecan families, brought from Saltillo to instruct the neophytes at San Sabá.

The party marked time for three months at San Antonio, completing their preparations and waiting for cold weather to end. Apaches flocked there to visit them, in groups as large as two or three hundred. The friars gave them corn, tobacco, and loaves of brown sugar, all dedicated to the eventual harvest of their souls, and yearned to begin their work in the Apache country.

Observing those Apaches for the first time, Colonel Parrilla grew to doubt the feasibility of settling them in missions. Some San Antonio missionaries encouraged his doubts. Fray Terreros fretted that they would reach the San Saba too late to plant crops for harvest that year; he suspected that Colonel Parrilla deliberately delayed the journey in order to undermine the project. Both Fray Terreros and Colonel Parrilla were too sophisticated to indulge in the open wrangling that had marred so many important ventures on the Spanish frontier, but they took care to put their doubts on record with superior authorities. Relations between them were as strained as they were polite by the time they rode off to San Sabá in April 1757.

Colonel Parrilla's doubts multiplied when they found no Apaches at all on the San Saba River. He wanted to abandon the project and return to San Antonio, but the missionaries would not hear of it. The colonel resigned himself to making the best of an unpromising situation. They started building the first mission and the presidio, three miles apart, on opposite sides of the stream. Anxious to avoid the corrupting influences of soldiers among their neophytes, the friars dismissed Colonel Parrilla's worry about defending a mission so far from the presidio.

Early in May the frontier grapevine explained the dearth of Apaches: Tejas warriors had struck the Apaches on the Colorado River and forced them to flee the region. Encouraged to feel that the Apaches' absence did not imply indifference, the friars briefly thought their persistence rewarded in mid-June, when three thousand Lipans and Natagés camped nearby. They accepted presents when the priests went out to welcome them, but they would not enter the mission. They were going to hunt buffalo and then campaign against the Norteños.

The Apaches were neither unanimous nor altogether negative in their response to the friars' overtures. One Lipan chief, El Chico, expressed his own willingness to enter the mission, but another chief, Casablanca, insisted upon tribal vengeance against the Comanches and Tejas who had killed his brother during the recent battle on the Colorado. They compromised: the band would complete their hunt, strike the necessary blow against their enemies, and then return to enter the mission. They left with the priests several sick Apaches, one of whom they let the priests baptize.

The hunt was a great success. The Apaches soon returned laden with meat, but they stayed only a few days, obviously edgy, then hurried southward. They had little to say to the priests, but it appeared that they had struck their enemies and feared pursuit.

The friars grew to share Parrilla's doubt that missions could succeed at that place. Three priests gave up the effort and returned to Mexico, a luxury not permitted the soldiers. The rest of the company awaited a decision from the viceroy and Don Pedro Terreros; even Fray Terreros was prepared to concede failure. However, Don Pedro remained willing to risk his considerable funds. The viceroy ruled that the two able, experienced leaders should carry on the San Sabá project. The Apaches would be given every possible chance to respond to their patience and kindness.

That autumn many small Apache groups paused to visit the mission, but they hurried on southward, and their promises to return no longer encouraged the friars. They all seemed so fearful. Soon the Spaniards on the San Saba heard that the northern nations were gathering to destroy the Apaches. The incredible detail was that the Norteños expected to find them on the San Saba. Since Apaches had never lived at the mission, the Spaniards wasted little worry on that rumor.

The leaders spent the winter months well, displaying responsibility all too rare in Church-State relations on the Spanish frontier. Fray Terreros and Colonel Parrilla jointly sought permission to travel to Mexico City to discuss their problems with the viceroy. Fray Terreros also worked toward eliminating the resentments of the San Antonio missionaries toward his project, and he welcomed their advice on the best methods of congregating Apaches. Out of their cooperative efforts and their limited experience of the Apaches grew some hope of success if only the project were revised to fit the realities of time and place. Fray Terreros credited Colonel Parrilla's personal management of Indian relations with winning the Apaches' friendliness and their tentative interest in mission life. He did not as readily understand the very real difficulties that hindered Apaches inclined to a mission experiment.[29]

Reconciling the fluid Apache society to the demands of settled community life posed no trivial problem, nor did the internal dissensions precipitated by questions of revolutionary change. The illnesses that Fray Terreros suspected were pretexts for delay were serious deterrents: a grave epidemic ravaged Apache camps during October, November, and December of 1757. Colonel Parrilla ceased to expect that they could keep their promise to return before the favorable hunting time of May and June,[30] but even he failed to realize how well founded were their fears of enemy attack.

Colonel Parrilla and Fray Terreros never had a chance to test their new ideas about converting Apaches: their enemies swarmed into the region late in February 1758. The Norteños first snatched fifty-nine horses from the presidial herd on February 25; a few days later, twenty-six warriors attacked a supply train from San Antonio as it approached the San Saba. Lieutenant Juan Galbán recognized the raiders as Tonkawas, Yojuanes, and Bidais, peoples he had known during his years at the San Gabriel station.

Daily, more smoke signals wafted from the hills to the north and east. Colonel Parrilla urged the missionaries to move to the presidio, but they refused, even when the commander personally came to persuade them on March 15. He could only leave them a guard of eight soldiers, all he could spare from other pressing duties, and worry. Parrilla had 237 women and children to protect in his presidial community of 300-odd persons, and livestock that must be guarded if his people were not all to perish.

At dawn on March 16, two thousand warriors surrounded the mission. Half carried French guns, which they fired in the air as they circled the stockade. However, they spoke pleasantly to the guards, assuring them that they intended the Spaniards no harm: they only sought the Apaches who had killed some of their people. Some of the Indians spoke Castilian, and some soldiers and priests who had served in East Texas conversed in the language of the Tejas. The Spaniards

[29] Fray Alonso Giraldo de Terreros, President of the Mission of San Sabá, to the Marqués de las Amarillas, Viceroy of New Spain, San Sabá, February 13, 1758, in Nathan and Simpson, *San Sabá Papers*, p. 3.

[30] Colonel Parrilla to the Marqués de las Amarillas, San Luis de las Amarillas, April 8, 1758, ibid., p. 132.

recognized Tejas, Bidais, Tonkawas, and others from the interior; some whom they could not recognize were identified by other warriors as Comanches.

Disregarding the visitors' scary war dress and obviously excited mood, the priests took them at their word and let them enter the gate. From that moment, the thirty-five Spaniards and Indians of the San Sabá mission lay at the mercy of the intruders. Fray Terreros, Fray Santiesteban, and half a dozen more died before the warriors turned their full attention to sacking and burning the mission. The survivors, several of whom were seriously wounded, escaped to the presidio in the darkness of night.

With only fifty-nine soldiers available in the presidio, Colonel Parrilla had no chance to rescue mission personnel from two thousand well-armed Indians. He gathered his people within the presidio to await the Norteños' next move and dispatched appeals for reinforcements. None ever came. Fortunately, the Norteños did not mount another massive assault. Some came to taunt the Spaniards at the presidio, but the soldiers carefully stayed inside the stockade. After two days, the Indians abandoned the sport. Within a few days they turned homeward to celebrate their victory and to mourn their seventeen dead, then pondered the consequences of their deed.

The victorious Indians hardly had time to worry before waves of terror swept the northern provinces. The destruction of one more mission paled to insignificance beside the extraordinary aspects of the episode: the amazing numbers and diversity of Indians united in the attack; the quantities of firearms that they possessed and the skill with which they used them; the unprecedented Comanche attack on the Texas frontier.

Throughout Spain's New World experience, tens of Spaniards, relying upon their firearms and their leather armor, had confidently confronted hundreds of Indians armed with bows and arrows and had generally prevailed, or at least survived. None relished the new odds, figuring thousands of hostile Indians, well supplied with guns and ammunition and skilled in their use.

Of the Comanche hordes they had scant information, all alarming. They had terrorized Spanish and Indian populations on the northern frontier of New Mexico for several decades and had relentlessly dispossessed Apaches from their homelands. If Comanches now leagued with Indians of the Texas frontier and shared their access to the guns of Natchitoches, what Spanish force could resist their onslaught? What role would France play in such a war?

From the time of the attack, when he first notified San Antonio, Parrilla assumed that foreign agents had incited it. Although false, his assumption fitted logically with the Francophobia that had pervaded New Spain for a century and had welled afresh over the last decade.

Captain Urrutia accepted Parrilla's fears at face value and relayed them to Coahuila with appeals for help. With only five soldiers to guard Béxar presidio and three more at each mission, San Antonio's forces could not go to rescue those at San Sabá. Captain Urrutia could only escort the mission community from the Guadalupe to San Antonio, sharpen vigilance at Béxar, and brace his command against the possibility of a concerted Indian attack.[31]

Some mission Indians fled from San Antonio, terrified by rumors that the enemy intended to destroy the mission on the Guadalupe and then invade those of San Antonio and that the numerous Apaches camped on the Medina were plotting to kill the Spanish soldiers if they should scatter to defend the various outposts. The friars at San Antonio heard that there had been turmoil among the Indians at La Bahía, that its missionaries had taken refuge in the presidio, and that a general Indian uprising was in the wind. They feared loss of all the mission Indians.[32]

The reaction in Coahuila was neither sympathetic nor helpful nor even logical. Apache groups were crowding upon that frontier, suing for peace, which Crown policy obliged the presidial commanders to grant, despite their profound distrust of all Apaches. Afraid that those Apaches would ravage the province if they should see troops leave Coahuila to reinforce San Sabá and San Antonio, the commanding officers spurned the appeals of Parrilla and Urrutia and even ignored viceregal orders. Coahuila's officials oddly construed the San Sabá disaster as fresh proof of Apache perfidy. Just a week after the attack, contorted, conflicting notions flowed from the councils of Coahuila: that the attackers at San Sabá had actually been Apaches; that Apaches had known of the impending attack well in advance and with deliberate malice had refrained from warning the Spaniards in order to see them destroyed; that the Apaches' failure to resist the Comanche in-

[31] Don Toribio de Urrutia to Señor Don Ángel Martos y Navarette, San Antonio de Béjar, March 20, 1758, ibid., pp. 8–9.
[32] Fray Mariano Francisco de los Dolores to Colonel Don Diego Ortiz Parrilla, San Antonio Mission, March 30, 1758, ibid., pp. 123–126.

vasion belied their claim of enmity between those nations; and that the northern frontier could be secured only when a vigorous Spanish offensive should either destroy or subdue the Apaches.[33]

No bloodbath ensued, either in Coahuila or in Texas, nor was there any marked deterioration of relations between Apaches and Spaniards in Texas. Two Apaches had survived the horrors of March 16 at Mission San Sabá, carefully concealed and protected by Spaniards who might have bought safety for themselves by giving them up to their enemies. The Spaniards' professions of brotherhood with the Apaches had passed a stringent test.

On the other hand, in the week after the attack, when no Spaniards dared go from San Antonio to San Sabá, Apaches from the camps on the Medina promised Fray Mariano that they would go to Parrilla's relief if the friars would take care of their families. That party of nine Apaches reached the presidio on March 27 with the first response from San Antonio since the disaster. They informed Colonel Parrilla that Fray Mariano had sent them to check on conditions at his presidio and to scout the area for enemy presence. Parrilla hesitated to trust them: he still had no news of his messengers' fate, and he was not sure that these Apaches could have learned of his plight at the San Antonio missions. Fray Mariano also had doubts about the Apaches' sincerity, but he tested them repeatedly during the crisis, sending them out to scout the San Antonio region, and they served him well. Many Apaches rallied to San Antonio to help defend the missions against possible enemy attack.[34]

Neither priests nor soldiers who knew the situation at first hand took the occasion to write off the hope of converting Apaches, although everyone agreed that missions could not succeed on the San Saba. No one could any longer think the Apaches' dread of their enemies frivolous, and no one believed that Spain could maintain enough forces to protect them in that exposed region. Fray Aparicio, who went from San Antonio in April to take charge of mission responsibilities on the San Saba, agreed with Colonel Parrilla. There had never been a more favorable time to convert the Apaches. The opportunity would be irretrievably lost, however, if they were not promptly given the chance to settle

---

[33] See letters and formal statements from the governor and presidial commanders of Coahuila, March 23, 24, and 25, 1758, ibid., pp. 13–27.

[34] Statement of Colonel Parrilla, San Luis de las Amarillas, March 27, 1758, ibid., p. 99; Fray Mariano Francisco de los Dolores to Colonel Don Diego Ortiz Parrilla, San Antonio Mission, March 30, 1758, ibid., p. 124.

in an area less exposed to their enemies, closer to protective concentrations of Spanish population, and in a milder winter climate.[35]

However the viceroy might dispose of the Apache mission project, Colonel Parrilla believed that Spain's hold upon Texas depended upon successful military response to the Norteños' attack. He volunteered to lead the campaign himself, arguing that his four years' service in North Africa prepared him to deal with the extraordinary new Indian enemies. Parrilla thought the Norteños very like the Moors: skilled horsemen and marksmen, innumerable, rich, sophisticated in their knowledge of Frenchmen and Spaniards, and in all ways superior to other Indians of New Spain.[36]

That summer, the viceroy and his council decreed that Spanish honor forbade abandonment of the San Sabá presidio, which they deemed vital to the security of Coahuila and Nuevo Santander. Since Don Pedro Terreros would still foot the bill, more missionaries would be assigned to the Apache project on the San Saba, but for safety they would live at the presidio rather than build a new mission.

Only one of Colonel Parrilla's recommendations prevailed. The viceroy authorized him to lead a punitive campaign against the Norteños and required the governors of Coahuila and Texas to go to San Antonio to plan the campaign with Parrilla and other leading officers. They convened in January 1759 and planned an expedition to begin in June, so as to assure plentiful grazing for the horses. It was August 1759 before the force actually set out.

Meanwhile, the garrison at San Sabá lived in constant fear of another attack, and the establishment was useless to Apaches. Small parties of Apache raiders or hunters often stopped at the presidio, but they soon scurried away, lest their enemies discover them there. In summer 1758 a large war party of Norteños struck an Apache band near the presidio and killed more than fifty. In December, Norteños of eleven nations slaughtered more than half a party of thirty-four Apaches who ventured into the presidio's vicinity.

All that winter and spring the province seethed with rumors of new conspiracies among the Norteños. A dozen nations were said to have vowed to destroy the presidio in the spring. Missionaries and French traders picked up the story at Indian villages in East Texas and warned

[35] Fray Aparicio, Statement to Colonel Parrilla, San Luis de las Amarillas, April 5, 1758, ibid., p. 129; Colonel Parrilla to the Marqués de las Amarillas, San Luis de las Amarillas, April 8, 1758, ibid., pp. 131, 140, 144–147, 148–151.
[36] Ibid., pp. 137–138.

authorities; friendly Indians carried similar tales to San Antonio and San Sabá. Parrilla braced his garrison as best he could to resist another attack like that which had destroyed the mission the year before.

The actual event involved no attack on the presidio at all, but a massive raid on its horse herd, pastured far downstream. On March 30, 1759, a big party of Norteños slaughtered the guards and seized seven hundred animals. Several warriors fell to the guards. With only twenty-seven horses left, Parrilla dared not pursue so many Indians. He waited until June for reinforcements. They never came, but neither did the dreaded attack to finish off the presidio. The Norteños had achieved their purpose, at least temporarily. In June, Colonel Parrilla rode to San Antonio to organize his expedition against the Norteños.

Nothing could have suited Apache purposes better. Tribal vengeance required them to campaign against their enemies, and by autumn 1758 they were devoting themselves singlemindedly to that end. They refrained from establishing fixed *rancherías* in order to evade enemy attacks, but one chief assured Parrilla that they would be ready to congregate in missions as soon as they could complete their campaign. They failed to achieve a grand-scale revenge to match the scores of deaths they had suffered, so 134 Apache warriors insisted upon joining Parrilla's campaign the following summer. Their families withdrew southward to safer campsites while the men rode off to satisfy tribal honor.

Parrilla and other leaders had qualms about using Apache warriors. Besides old doubts about Apache reliability, they had disquieting warnings from missionaries in East Texas. Such priests as Fray José de Calahorra y Sáenz of the Nacogdoches mission knew and respected many Norteños, understood how much damage Apaches had dealt them over the years, and knew the innumerable provocations Norteños had suffered since the Apaches found shelter in their peace with the Spaniards in 1749. To identify Spain with Apache interests seemed to those missionaries the ultimate folly: it could only antagonize the Norteños, whom the missionaries considered superior Indians and much more likely converts than the Apaches. They urged the government not to plunge into a dangerous war against a dozen nations who had gone to war only to avenge their own legitimate grievances.

That warning was not inconsistent with Parrilla's information from East Texas veterans in his San Sabá garrison and from such missionaries as Fray Aparicio that the formidable Norteños had turned upon the Spaniards solely because they saw them aiding and protecting

Apaches. Nevertheless, the colonel believed that Spain's honor required punishment of the Norteños, and he had no practicable way to keep the Apaches out of it. To deny them the right to participate in the campaign would infuriate them. He dared not risk some rearguard action by outraged Apache warriors as he marched off to the north.

It was an impressive force to which the 134 Apaches attached themselves at San Antonio in August 1759. They were all that Texas and Coahuila could muster for an offensive: 139 presidial soldiers and officers, 241 militiamen, 30 Tlaxcaltecan Indians, and 90 mission Indians, with 2 priests. Their horses, mules, and cattle numbered more than 1,600. Slowly, conspicuously, they moved northward, while Norteños braced for the confrontation.

CHAPTER 8

Comanches in New Mexico to 1767

Parrilla's campaign of 1759 marked a new epoch in the convergence of change. Now Spain's Texan frontier impinged upon the world of the Wichitan bands and thus upon the southeasterly reaches of the Comanchería. Through an accident of Apache wars, Spaniards and Wichitas met as adversaries, a mutual misfortune for peoples who could so ill afford war on a new front. For Comanches, at first, the Texan imbroglio was trifling compared to their more urgent necessities of extirpating Apaches and juggling trade and war in New Mexico.

The people of the Wichitan villages had enough challenge in the mid-eighteenth century just grappling with the changes set in motion by the French trade: on the one hand, intensifying their hunting in order to reap the wealth and power wrapped in the traders' packs; on the other, battling for survival against old enemies, especially Osages, who had more firearms because they lived nearer trade centers. The necessities of defense and of big hunts brought the people together in larger villages, carefully located for maximum advantage in hunting, trade, and defense. Du Tisne and La Harpe saw or heard of more than a dozen Wichitan villages in the Arkansas Valley in 1719; by 1750 there remained only two or three villages on the Arkansas, located at the head of navigation for the convenience of French traders and on the margin of the buffalo plains for the convenience of hunters. The Wichitan groups of the lower Arkansas had coalesced under Tawakoni leadership, then retreated to the Red River to escape enemy pressures.

From the time of La Harpe and du Tisne in 1719, Frenchmen counted the Wichitan groups among their loyal allies and trading partners. The villagers found themselves penalized by the periodic scarcities of goods and spasmodic disorders that plagued Louisiana after Law's fiasco. Although the Wichitas soon acquired guns in useful numbers and grew to depend upon them, they could never count upon powder and balls or prompt replacements for broken guns. That was a dangerous dilemma for people beset by enemies on every side.

Northward lay several village tribes of the Missouri River system. Particularly aggressive were the Osages, enemies of long standing, who enjoyed two advantages: easier access to French trading posts and, by mid-century, the useful alternative of British traders pressing in from the Atlantic seaboard colonies and from Hudson's Bay. The eastern margins of the Wichita world were subject to incursions by Chickasaws, well armed by their British friends and frequently at war with the French and all their Indian allies. On the south and west roved Apache enemies, ever a danger to Wichitas despite their retreat before the Comanche onslaught. That Comanches now occupied the northerly reaches of the former Apachería afforded Wichitas scant comfort, for Comanches were fiercer enemies than Apaches.

By the late 1730's, the Tawakonis bowed to overwhelming pressures on the northern and eastern reaches of the Wichita world and moved south to the Red River. They established a village upstream from the Kadohadachos, expecting to enjoy better access to trade and the protective French presence in the Natchitoches sphere. But within a decade their enemies from the north made the Red River location untenable, too. In the late 1740's the Tawakonis established a new village farther south, on the Sabine River. There they asked Commandant Césaire de Blanc of Natchitoches to assign a squad of soldiers to their village, a usual French service to Indian allies in that area. Such men not only protected but also served as resident traders and provided liaison between Natchitoches and its allies. It was a mutually advantageous system, and de Blanc readily granted the Tawakonis' request to join it.[1] Neither de Blanc nor the Tawakonis worried that the Tawakonis had planted themselves in Spanish territory. Several years passed before the Spaniards of Texas realized that an Indian village in their province lived under the protection of the French flag.

While the Tawakonis sought safety in the sphere of Natchitoches and its Caddo allies, the Taovayas, Iscanis, and Wichitas entrenched their settlements upstream toward the big bend of the Arkansas River. There they hunted on a large scale, welcomed burgeoning French trade at their villages, and found new security in rapprochement with Comanches.

Since the time of La Harpe and du Tisne, Louisiana authorities had realized that safe development of commerce with New Mexico hinged upon establishing peace between Comanches and Wichitas or some more northerly village Indians on the perimeter of the Comanchería. Bourgmont's peace of 1724 between Comanches and several village tribes of the Missouri River system did not long survive his departure for France, but Louisiana authorities did not again pursue the matter seriously until the late 1730's. Then, primarily to strengthen the colony against British pressures, the Crown made new efforts to develop Louisiana's economy. Again colonial officials eyed the Spanish frontier as their prime commercial prospect. Given the first Family Compact, which made Spain and France allies after 1733, Louisianans assumed that New Spain's barriers to French trade would fall. Both private and official enterprise probed toward Santa Fe, across the Comanchería, reaching out from their trade base in the Wichitan villages on the Arkansas.

Those pioneering Frenchmen gambled their lives and fortunes upon the Comanches' tolerance of intrusion and their courtesy in guiding visitors across the plains to the New Mexican frontier. The risks were awesome. Perhaps they would never have been undertaken had the difficulties been fully understood.

The Comanches were a people as diffuse as their territories were

---

[1] The story of the Tawakoni migration derives chiefly from the letter of de Mézières which appears as El Cavallero Macarty to Martos y Navarette, Natchitos, September 10, 1763, in a copy in the Bexar Archives. The date of the first move from the Canadian River to the Kadohadachos area derives from a report of 1741 in *Extrait des Lettres du Fabry de la Bruyère à l'Occasion du Voyage Projeté à Santa-Fé*, in Pierre Margry, ed., *Découvertes et Établissements des Français dans l'Ouest et dans le Sud de l'Amérique Septentrionale, 1614–1754*, VI, 474. The Sabine River location is identified in Leroy Johnson, Jr., and Edwin B. Jelks, "The Tawakoni-Yscani Village, 1760: A Study of Archaeological Site Identification," *The Texas Journal of Science* 10 (1958): 405–422.

vast. Almost as little was known of the people as of the land, but the ferocity of their warriors was already legend in New Mexico and in Texas. Spaniards knew the Comanches as triumphant aggressors, but Frenchmen in Louisiana knew more of their difficulties than of their formidable character, knew how long and often Comanche families had lost women and children to raiders from the eastern villages armed with guns and how badly they needed firearms to defend themselves and wreak vengeance on their enemies. They would appeal to the Comanches' self-interest, but with whom were they to come to terms, and how?

Comanches counted themselves as numerous as the stars. Perhaps their very numbers ruled out cohesive organization. In essence, they were a vast set of proud individuals, each man entitled to rise to leadership on the basis of his demonstrated capacities in war, and none bound to accept any authority higher than himself except by his own choice. As the small Shoshonean hunting and gathering groups had come down from the mountains to the plains to build a successful pastoral society around the newly acquired horse, they had tended to come together in larger bands. Nevertheless, their society continued to function with a minimal political structure, bound together largely by speech and customs, deeply conscious of their likeness and like-mindedness as Comanches and of their supremacy within the bounds, more felt than defined, of the Comanchería.[2]

The Comanche bands fell into vast major divisions, of which there were three in the latter half of the eighteenth century: the Yupes and Yamparicas, who ranged northward from the Arkansas River, and the Cuchanecs, who ranged southward from the Arkansas as they drove the Apaches back, first beyond the Red River, then beyond the Brazos, then beyond the Colorado. It was the division called Ietan, either equivalent to or a major part of the Cuchanecs, who came to terms with the Wichitas and their French allies. They thus bridged the gap between frontiers of New Mexico and Louisiana, but no one could be sure of the stability or the extent of the arrangement.

The great divisions had a flexible structure, nicely geared to conditions of nomadic life on the plains, lending itself well to varying adjustments required by movements of the buffalo and changing

[2] The principal secondary source for the discussion of Comanche society is Ernest Wallace and E. Adamson Hoebel, *The Comanches: Lords of the South Plains*; see also W. W. Newcomb, Jr., *The Indians of Texas*, pp. 155–191. Contemporary Spanish sources on Comanche culture are cited subsequently.

necessities of protection and warfare. The amorphous, composite bands changed in size and leadership as situations changed. Successful leaders attracted large numbers to their camps; groups afflicted with deficient leadership tended to fade away.

The basic unit of Comanche life was the family encampment, each with its own peace chief or headman, who advised rather than commanded. One family headman was head peace chief of the band; all of them together served as the advisory council for the whole band. In effect, the head peace chief functioned as chairman of the council.

A Comanche peace chief emerged gradually as a leader on the basis of his demonstrated excellence in the required qualities. When others emerged to surpass him, his leadership faded away. The office was not openly sought, for aggressiveness was not a desirable quality for a peace chief. On the contrary, he must epitomize tranquillity and order for his group. His people must know him to be generous, kind, eventempered, knowledgeable about his territory, wise in council, and a persuasive spokesman. Recognition of those qualities in a man led his people to seek his advice, and, when he became the one whose advice was sought most, he became peace chief for his group.

It helped, of course, to have a fine physique and a record of daring and firmness in battle as well as leadership in camp. The reputation of a peace chief often began with an earlier record as a war leader, though the qualities of a peace chief were strikingly at variance with the Comanche warrior ideal.

The peace chief's power was limited to internal and civil matters. He had no power over the life of any member of the nation. His only definite power was to decide the time and destination of a camp move. In theory, the peace chief was superior to the war chiefs, but he could not prevent a war party from taking the trail. In the camp of an aging, decrepit peace chief, a vigorous and popular war chief was likely to have more real influence.

Any headman could call a council meeting of his own band. A joint council of two or more bands could be convened if the separate headmen of each band called a meeting. There existed neither a regular tribal council nor a principal chief with whom another people could negotiate binding, all-embracing commitments for alliance or trade with all Comanches.

Important affairs of a band were considered in its council of peace chiefs, which included all the old men who had stood out as warriors or leaders. In theory, the council was supreme, but in practice it often handed down indefinite decisions. Unanimous agreement was the ideal, for generally a majority was loath to try to impose its will on a minority. Council members took careful soundings of public sentiment, and their decisions usually expressed a consensus. The old men were slow to take any radical action, and they coerced no one. A man who disliked the way things were being run in his own group could freely withdraw to live independently or join another group more to his liking.

The council dealt with civil matters: decisions to move camp, the time and place of the summer hunt, community religious observances, allocation of supplies to widows and needy persons, and regulation of trade with outsiders. They also considered questions of tribal war and peace and of alliance with other peoples to wage war against a common enemy. The council disposed of spoils derived from band warfare, but never of the spoils acquired by a raiding party.

Warriors generally tended to obey decisions of the council, not because they had any awe of authority, but because they were reluctant to arouse the anger of the chiefs and the supernatural powers. However, the nomadic life made it impossible for chiefs always to keep in touch with their warriors or even to know whether their commitments were honored. Usually, offenders were merely rebuked or admonished.

Not only was Comanche civil leadership diffuse and limited. One of the basic principles of Comanche life was separation of civil and military leadership. War chiefs were men with established war records, who had displayed outstanding personal courage and skill. Each band tended to recognize its leading war chief, selected by the warriors' consensus and sanctioned by the council of elders, but there were many lesser war chiefs. Still, the prosecution of war was a matter of individual discretion. In theory, at least, any Comanche could lead a war party, and no power could restrain him.

A warrior who wished to lead a war party simply announced his intention. If he had a good military reputation, if he was known to have powerful "medicine," or to be liberal in dividing spoils, he had little difficulty in recruiting an adequate number. Inexperienced warriors had to serve under others until they acquired enough skill and reputation to attract followers, so they had every incentive to respond to invitations.

On a raid or war party, the leader had supreme authority over all activities, but even then coercion was absent. Warriors followed only leaders in whom they had confidence; they were free to withdraw if they lost confidence. The leader set the objectives of the expedition and designated scouts, a cook, and water carriers. The party camped where he chose and rested at his order. The leader planned tactics and divided booty. At his discretion, he could order the expedition to turn back and could make truce with the enemy, though he could bind no one except his own party.

The supernatural was important in Comanche warfare. It was not required that a leader's venture be sanctioned by a vision, but often that was the inspiration. Certainly a leader needed strong medicine and confidence that his medicine was working for success. A man who contemplated leading a war or raiding party usually made medicine to determine the time and place of the raid. Then he called in his friends and the older men to discuss the matter and, unless dissuaded, then issued the general invitation. Such decisions were usually made very quickly, with departure that same night. A war dance or vengeance dance drummed up support for the venture. From a big camp, several parties might go out the same night under different leaders, each quite independent of the others. The war dance and departure never occurred by day, for that was deemed very bad medicine. If an entire band undertook a campaign against a distant enemy, the warriors took along a few women and some small tipis to set up a temporary base for a series of attacks.

Comanches conducted war parties and raiding parties in much the same fashion, distinguished only by the stated purpose. A raiding party that met an enemy would fight, and it was a rare war party that eschewed the chance to grab horses or other booty. Only the vengeance party moved with terrible singleness of purpose.

Vengeance was a tribal imperative. A Comanche parent who lost a son to the enemy could never rest content without an enemy scalp to even the score. A bereaved father or brother of fighting age could lead a vengeance party or seek a scalp alone. An older father or widowed mother with no son left could ask some war leader to avenge the lost son, and no honorable man could deny such a request. When the revenge party took one scalp, the leader turned his warriors back, ignoring any further opportunities: their objective was the single scalp required for the scalp dance. The death of a distinguished chief or some grave affront to the honor of the band could spark an extended, bitter vendetta, which required many scalps and horses to satisfy Comanche honor.

Every consideration impelled the young Comanche male to war, for that was the route to power and glory. The plunder he took could make him rich; the generosity with which he shared it could help to establish him as a leader. The record of valor and of generosity he compiled could make him an honored warrior, then a war chief, perhaps ultimately a peace chief. He could avenge the grievances of his family or his nation, help his people to control the rich buffalo plains, and scourge their enemies from the earth. He preferred glorious death in battle at the height of his powers to the miseries of old age, and he knew that death was not the end. He expected to enjoy an afterlife replete with all the pleasures of this world and none of its problems and in good time to be born again to the splendid life of a Comanche warrior. Only those things that jeopardized his immortality could intimidate him: to lose his scalp after death, to strangle, to die in the dark, to drown, or to suffer mutilation.

Thus his possible gains on the warpath far outweighed the risks, and most of those gains depended upon the horses he stole. He had to have good horses to ride for war and hunting and many more to move his camp. He had to be able to pay a bride price in horses: the more desirable the girl, the more horses required. His principal wealth would be his horses, which were a general medium of exchange. With them he could meet all his necessities. He could buy bows and arrows and sometimes guns, could pay for the services of medicine men and even buy medicine powers for himself. If he committed a civil offense within his tribe, he could pay restitution in horses to the aggrieved party. He would need horses for giveaways marking special personal and family occasions or for his share of the tribe's ceremonial gift to another people at the making of peace. All his life, his prestige would be measured in terms of his horses and the valor with which he had acquired them, and, when he died, the best of them would be slain over his grave to mourn him and to carry his spirit into the next world.

The life of the Comanche male thus centered first around warfare and raiding, and second around hunting. The ideal adult male was a vigorous, aggressive, self-reliant warrior, and every youngster coming of age strove toward that image. In the contest for prestige, any willingness to arbitrate differences or to overlook offenses was scorned as a sign of weakness. The Comanche warrior was touchy and belligerent, vying for personal honors against all comers.

Ideally, in middle age he grew above the struggle for prestige and strove to counsel his people toward peace and tranquillity. His new role was to work for the welfare of the nation by giving sage advice, smoothing over quarrels, and trying to prevent his people from making new enemies. Then he must be wise and gentle, willing to overlook slights and even to tolerate abuse if need be. It was a terribly difficult transition, and some old men who could not make it waxed malevolent in their failure. Those who succeeded were often men of impressive quality by any standard.

French colonial strategists could not have known the complexities involved in seeking stable peace and alliance with the Comanche nation. All Comanche peace chiefs must be persuaded to agree on behalf of their separate groups; in turn, they must persuade every man in the nation that maintenance of the peace served his own best interests and those of his people. Each individual must be so convinced that he would make the personal sacrifice of forswearing raids and war parties against French traders and tribes allied with them, no matter how tempting the goods they carried or the horses they rode or how deeply ingrained the old tribal enmities. To foster peaceful commerce, the French design even postulated an end to marauding on the New Mexican frontier, a condition hardly conceivable to ambitious young men in the Comanche world.

Comanches had raided and traded in New Mexico ever since their Ute relatives had introduced them to the northern frontier settlements early in the eighteenth century. By 1730, when the Comanches and Utes had swept the Apaches from their old northern ranges, they enjoyed virtually unimpeded access to the province. They brought hides, meat, and captives to market at eastern frontier pueblos, as Apaches had done for centuries before them, with similar effect. The exchanges generated friction: Spaniards and Pueblos tended to exploit their less sophisticated customers; Comanche visitors often abused hospitality by stealing horses and other goods in the province. Extortionate prices for goods, fees for the privilege of trading at a pueblo, restrictions upon sale of such items as guns and horses, discourtesies to visitors, all invited violent responses. Raiding episodes and subsequent pursuits were also fraught with possibilities of violent encounter. Once a death or injury invoked Comanche tribal vengeance, all New Mexicans were subject to grave penalties in lives and property.

New Mexico needed commerce so desperately that officials and settlers encouraged the Comanche trade, despite the dangers. The Taos fair became the hub of commerce from the plains. Some governors tried to minimize friction by supervising trade, partly in response to missionaries' criticisms. In 1725, Governor Bustamente ordered *alcaldes mayores* to supervise trade closely in order to prevent disturbances to the peace, but he also cautioned them to respect the settlers' right to trade freely with the Indians.[3] Seven Spaniards were prosecuted for causing trouble with *bárbaros* who came to market captives and skins at Pecos in the summer of 1726, but the problems continued.[4] The government tried more elaborate regulations to curb unethical competition, even specifying hours at which settlers could trade with Indians and banning shady competitive practices among rival traders.[5] Those too proved inadequate. New laws in the mid-1730's forbade anyone to trade with *indios bárbaros* without a royal license, whether Pueblo, Spaniard, or mestizo, under penalty of stiff fines.[6]

The new restrictions, especially designed to prevent unauthorized visits to the camps of the *bárbaros*, tended to undermine their own pacific intent. Most Indians valued visits as manifestations of friendship, so the sharp curtailment of visits dislocated relationships with Utes and friendly Apaches as well as with Comanches.

Sometime before 1735, a breach occurred between the Comanches and their erstwhile allies, the Utes.[7] For the next half-century, the vendetta of Utes and Comanches worsened the turbulence of New Mexico's northwestern frontier. Utes tended thenceforth to compose their old differences with Pueblos and Jicarillas and to present with the Spaniards and their Indian allies a united front against the Comanche menace.

Every clash between Comanches and Indians of New Mexico was fraught with dangerous consequences for the Spaniards. Their obligations to the Pueblo and Jicarilla vassals of the king affronted the Comanches, who resented the Spaniards' protective services to their enemies. By the 1740's, the manifold stresses sparked a wave of Comanche hostilities upon the eastern frontier of New Mexico, so unsparing that it gradually depopulated that area. Unbearable pressures against their ranches and villages led many settlers to move to

[3] Bustamente, Bando, Santa Fe, September 17, 1725, SANM, no. 340.

[4] Proceedings against seven Spaniards, Santa Fe, August 3–September 7, 1726, SANM, no. 340a.

[5] Criminal proceedings against Diego Torres, Teniente de Alcalde Mayor of the Chama jurisdiction, on charges of violating trade regulations, Santa Fe, April 13–May 7, 1735, SANM, no. 402.

[6] Governor Henrique de Olvide y Michelena, Bando, Santa Fe, January 7, 1737, SANM, no. 414.

[7] Proceedings against Diego de Torres, Santa Fe, April 13–May 7, 1735, SANM, no. 402.

Santa Fe. The population of the capital climbed from 120 families in 1744 to 274 in 1779.[8]

In response to the depredations, the Spaniards mounted some punitive campaigns against the Comanches in the 1740's. The hatreds aroused by the raiders led some Spaniards to such violent excesses when they found any *bárbaros* that the governor acted to curb them. An order of 1741, applicable to settlers as well as soldiers, banned any maltreatment of women, children, and infirm in defenseless enemy camps, on the ground that such acts were inconsistent with Catholic principles.[9] A new governor reiterated the ban three years later, reminding the New Mexicans that the chief objective of Spanish policy wherever possible was to attract the infidels to the faith. All violators were subject to heavy fines; even heavier penalties applied to soldiers. A soldier guilty of a second offense was subject to beating and expulsion from the presidio.[10]

Some incident early in the 1740's sparked a fierce Comanche vendetta against the pueblos of Pecos and Galisteo, even while they continued to trade at Taos. During the five-year term of Governor Joachín Codallos y Rabál, Comanche warriors killed 150 Pecos Indians. Having found that neither regulation of trade nor restraint in retaliation would stem the tide of Comanche depredations, Governor Codallos tried the desperate expedient of prohibiting the Comanche trade to all New Mexicans in 1746.[11] Santa Fe authorities suspected that Comanches trading at Taos pueblo were informed of Spanish troop movements by Taoseños who liked to encourage depredations against Spaniards. Thus, a new decree forbade Taos Indians to go more than three miles beyond their pueblo, on pain of death. Either the trade ban outlived its usefulness or the governor found the policy unworkable: by 1748 he had readmitted Comanches to the privilege of trade at Taos.[12]

Restoration of trade relations did not mark an end to depredations. One of the worst incidents occurred late in 1749, on the very day that

[8] Fray Juan Agustín de Morfi, "Geographical Description of New Mexico," in Alfred Barnaby Thomas, ed., *Forgotten Frontiers*, pp. 91–92.

[9] Governor Gaspar de Mendoza, Bando, Santa Fe, March 21, 1741, SANM, no. 438.

[10] Governor Joachín Codallos y Rabál, Bando, Santa Fe, May 30, 1744, SANM, no. 455.

[11] Governor Joachín Codallos y Rabál, Santa Fe, February 14, 1746, SANM, no. 495.

[12] Ralph Emerson Twitchell, comp., *The Spanish Archives of New Mexico*, II, 227. (The document, no. 497 in the Twitchell catalog, is now missing from the archives in Santa Fe.)

ten parties of Comanches left Taos after a peaceful trading session. Comanches made a major raid on Galisteo, and many other lesser damages occurred in the area. Spanish authorities wavered, uncertain which Comanches to punish for the offenses and afraid that a move against any Comanches would provoke a general assault upon the province by all of them. They reluctantly conceded that it was impracticable to punish Comanche raiders at that time.[13]

Governor Tomás Vélez Cachupín, who inherited the problem in 1749, found it necessary to make Pecos and Galisteo veritable fortresses, surrounding them with entrenchments, erecting towers at the gates, and posting thirty presidials there as consistently as his limited manpower permitted.

Meanwhile, when Comanches visited Taos to trade, Vélez Cachupín seized the opportunity to reproach them for the depredations and to hear their side of the story. Invariably, they disclaimed all knowledge of the crimes and blamed warlike chiefs who persisted in injuring the New Mexicans regardless of the objections of many peacefully inclined Comanches.[14]

Armed with that clue to the problem, Governor Vélez Cachupín systematically interrogated captives whom Comanches marketed at Taos and learned the names of chiefs whose bands preyed upon Pecos and Galisteo and upon the frontier in general. He left those names with the *alcalde mayor* of Taos, with orders to arrest them if they should come to trade and to put them to the sword if they should resist, hoping that the example would make the rest keep the peace.

Unfortunately for the governor's purposes, the Comanches had already found another trade connection, which diminished their dependence upon Taos. Just as Comanche hostilities in New Mexico mounted to new intensity, French traders launched new efforts in that direction. In 1739, a Frenchman who had once lived among Comanches persuaded some traders in the Illinois country that it would be practicable and profitable to cross the Comanchería to Santa Fe. The Mallet brothers, Pierre and Paul, led nine Frenchmen across from the Platte to the upper Arkansas, and from there to northeastern New Mexico. Although the man who had lived among the Comanches remembered

[13] Lieutenant Carlos Fernández to Governor Don Tomás Vélez Cachupín, Taos, December 31, 1749, SANM, no. 509.

[14] Vélez Cachupín to the Viceroy, Don Juan Francisco de Güemes y Horcasitas, Santa Fe, March 8, 1750, in Charles Wilson Hackett, ed., *Pichardo's Treatise on the Limits of Louisiana and Texas*, III, 328.

fifty or sixty Comanche camps scattered on the plains, the Mallet party met no Indians at all until the fortieth day of their journey, when they encountered Ietan Comanches on the plains northeast of Picurís.

Nine months in New Mexico convinced the French visitors that the populace would welcome commerce from Louisiana and that the Comanches, then very dependent upon the New Mexican trade, could easily be won over with French merchandise. Two of the party married that winter and chose to remain in New Mexico, but the Mallets led the other five to Louisiana, via the Canadian River, in 1740 to inform Governor Bienville at New Orleans.[15] Within the decade, officials of New Spain regretted that they had let the Mallets return home. Their news of commercial opportunities in New Mexico and of relatively easy transit sparked official efforts to develop the trade and lured to Santa Fe some drifters who found it necessary or desirable to leave Louisiana.

Given the Franco-Spanish alliance under the first Family Compact and the tolerant reception of the Mallet party at Santa Fe, Governor Bienville concluded that trade could flourish between Louisiana and New Mexico if the Indians along the route could be pacified.[16] To lay the foundations, he dispatched André Fabry de la Bruyère in 1741 to explore the Arkansas River route, which seemed most promising for year-round travel, and to persuade the Osage, Wichita, and Comanche bands to stop warring with each other and attacking New Mexico. His sixteen companions included the Mallet brothers, sufficiently convinced of their own story to carry a good quantity of merchandise. Because of adverse travel conditions, and perhaps mismanagement by Bruyère, the expedition disintegrated far short of the Comanchería.[17] They only discussed Governor Bienville's purpose with an Osage war party on the Canadian River and with Tawakonis and Kichais on the Red River above the Kadohadachos. Another decade passed before a new Louisiana governor, the Marquis de Vaudreuil, sent Pierre Mallet back to Santa Fe with new commercial overtures. In the interval, important changes occurred within the Comanche and Wichita worlds.

Around 1746, when the Comanches found the New Mexican trade

---

[15] *Voyages des Frères Mallet, avec Six Autres Français, depuis la Rivière des Panismahas dans le Missouri jusqu'a Santa Fé (1739–1740), Extrait du Journal,* in Margry, *Découvertes,* VI, 455–462; see also the Pierre Mallet testimony of June 26, 1751, in Hackett, *Pichardo's Treatise,* III, 346–352.

[16] Jean Baptiste Le Moyne Bienville et Salmon, Lettre, New Orleans, April 30, 1741, in Margry, *Découvertes,* VI, 468.

[17] Fabry de la Bruyère, *Extrait,* ibid., pp. 472–492.

entirely closed to them, they reached an accord with the Wichitan bands and thereby gained reliable access to French trade. The new alliance fulfilled French desires of thirty years' standing: both Louisiana officialdom and private traders encouraged and capitalized on the arrangement.

The Wichitan villages on the Arkansas soon became centers of Comanche trade.[18] They were veritable fortresses, their grass houses clustered closely, stockaded with stakes and earth, with loopholes for gunfire, built to withstand raids of Indian enemies. They made splendid trade depots. Up the river from Tonti's old Arkansas Post, the traders paddled canoes laden with the stuff of economic revolution. They returned downstream with hides, tallow, and lard of buffalo, bear, and deer. Some Frenchmen ventured out to Comanche *rancherías* with Wichita guides, and some lived briefly in Comanche camps, but most trade occurred in those fixed, fortified Wichitan villages, with their comfortable lodges and ample stores of food. Comanches rode there to sell hides, meat, horses, and captives, sometimes to French traders, sometimes to Wichitas.

Since the Wichitas themselves were excellent hunters and well placed for access to buffalo, they were most interested in purchasing horses and captives from Comanches. The Wichitas bartered their farm surpluses to French traders and to Comanches, who especially liked the conveniently portable mats of dried pumpkin strips that Wichita women wove. Wichita women's work multiplied: accelerated hunting meant countless hours spent preparing hides; new markets for their crops encouraged them to plant more and thus to spend more time processing produce. The traders brought them plenty of incentives to work. Every household welcomed hoes, kettles, knives, needles, awls, cloth, beads, mirrors, paint, and all the other conveniences and ornaments from French factories. The Comanches peddled solutions to their labor problems, for the far-ranging Comanche warriors seized more captives than were needed for the work of nomads' camps, and they had never adopted the Wichitas' custom of eating captives. Slaves, usually purchased from Comanches, played useful roles in busy Wichita villages.

Horses, stolen from New Mexico and from enemy Indians, and guns from Louisiana combined with the Comanche alliance to strengthen Wichitan war potential. They soon organized important initiatives

[18] Two Wichitan villages, with some five hundred warriors, were reported in 1749; French visitors mentioned three in 1751.

against their principal enemies. About 1750, the Wichitas resolved their differences with the Pawnees, then mediated peace between the Pawnees and Comanches.[19] Early in 1751, warriors of the three nations surprised a Grand Osage village when some of its people were away on a buffalo hunt and killed many Osages, including twenty-two leading men. The attackers lost only twenty-seven.[20]

The Comanches' participation shook the Osages, for they dreaded them more than any other nation. They promptly sought help. The French commandant at Fort Chartres heard out the mournful indignation of an Osage delegation and gave a small present to cheer them up, but he intervened firmly when the Osages tried to persuade the Illinois to help them avenge their people. Pointing out that the Pawnees, Wichitas, and Comanches were all allies of the French and could hardly be blamed for avenging themselves for years of Osage aggressions, he suggested that, if the Illinois really wished to make war, they should fight Chickasaws to avenge all the Illinois and French blood those Indians had spilled.

Fort Chartres' commandant did more to moderate the Indian wars that disturbed the plains. In the autumn of 1750 he negotiated an alliance with the Panismahas of the Missouri River,[21] a people at war with the Comanches in 1749.[22] Within two years, the Pawnees, Wichitas, and Comanches extended their accord to the Panismahas.[23] Happily relieved of pressures from the Pawnees and Panismahas, the Comanches and Wichitas waged vigorous joint campaigns against the Osages and Kansas and pursued their common vendetta against the eastern Apaches. The Comanches also sustained their private wars against the Utes and Pecos and Galisteo. Probably their frequent raids in New Mexico did not amount to war by their own standards, but the distinction was unduly subtle for New Mexicans who suffered losses.

Continuing turbulence in the Comanchería boded ill for the proposed trade between Louisiana and New Mexico. The French accord

---

[19] Declaration of Luis Feusi, Santa Fe, August 9, 1752, in Hackett, *Pichardo's Treatise*, III, 369. Details of the Comanche-Wichita rapprochement appear in the interrogations of French and Spanish travelers who reached New Mexico from Louisiana, 1749–1752, and related correspondence (ibid., pp. 299–370).

[20] Le Jonquière to the French Minister, Quebec, September 25, 1751, in *Wisconson State Historical Collections* 18, pp. 85–88.

[21] Ibid.

[22] Declaration of Luis del Fierro, Santa Fe, April 13, 1749, in Hackett, *Pichardo's Treatise*, III, 304.

[23] Vélez Cachupín to Revilla Gigedo, Santa Fe, September 18, 1752, in Alfred Barnaby Thomas, ed., *The Plains Indians and New Mexico, 1751–1778: A Collec-*

with the Comanches was not reliably established in all quarters, and safe conduct through the Comanchería often depended upon introduction and recommendation by the Wichitas. Several French hunters who ventured independently, and probably illegally, from the Arkansas Post by way of the Wichita villages reached Santa Fe safely in 1749 and 1750, but the first official envoys from Louisiana came to grief at the hands of Comanches.

Pierre Mallet set out from Natchitoches in late summer of 1750 with three fellow traders, bearing Governor Vaudreuil's official proposal for trade between the two provinces and letters from New Orleans merchants to prospective correspondents in New Mexico. Since Mallet had returned from Santa Fe in 1740 via the Canadian River and had liked that route, he purchased horses in the Kadohadacho area, rode to the Canadian, and followed it toward Pecos. His decision to forgo the Wichita help available on the Arkansas route proved unwise. On the western plains, Mallet's group met more than a hundred Comanche warriors, out spying on a group of Pecos hunters. The Comanches greeted the Frenchmen amiably enough, but they turned ugly when they learned the purpose of the journey. They denounced the Spaniards, vowed they would not permit the trade, and advised the Frenchmen that it would be safer just to trade with Comanches. The four Frenchmen were helpless against the hundred: the Comanches seized most of their goods and ripped up their papers. Grateful to escape with their lives, Mallet's quartet continued with a fraction of their wares and fragments of their papers. Friendly Jicarilla hunters guided them to Pecos in February 1751. Taken at once to the governor in Santa Fe, Mallet explained their misfortune, then outlined the proposals that the angry Comanches had destroyed.

Governor Vélez Cachupín was appalled. News of the Comanches' gun trade with the Wichitas had been distressing enough. Vélez Cachupín had worried for the last two years about ten deserters from Louisiana who had come with Comanche escorts from the Wichitan villages to Taos, and he had deplored Governor Mendoza's error in letting the Mallets carry reports of New Mexico back to Louisiana in 1740. Though the governor feared that more Frenchmen would surely follow if tales of easy access to Santa Fe spread among the *coureurs de bois*, he had let the first ten deserters settle in the province. New Mexico

---

tion of *Documents Illustrative of the History of the Eastern Frontier of New Mexico,* pp. 108–110.

needed people badly, and the interlopers brought such scarce, valuable skills as carpentry, tailoring, and barbering.

Mallet's proposition exceeded the governor's worst fears. If the New Mexican government would permit trade, the Louisianans were prepared to ship merchandise worth 100,000 pesos, with an intelligent merchant to draw up contracts with New Mexican entrepreneurs. They assumed that it would be necessary for the two provincial governments to provide safe conduct for the goods through the Comanchería and were prepared to negotiate a division of responsibilities on the route. Upon receiving satisfactory agreements, the French proposed to build warehouses on the Arkansas River above the Wichitan villages and to transport goods that far by canoe. Governor Vaudreuil pledged 2,500 armed men to safeguard the trade. He would even place them at the disposal of the governor of New Mexico if that should be necessary to control the Comanches.

Although skeptical that Louisiana's governor actually commanded so many men, Governor Vélez Cachupín resolved to let Mallet carry no more encouragement back to New Orleans. He confiscated the party's remaining goods and shipped the four to Mexico City to be interrogated and disposed of by the viceroy.

The next year ten French traders tried to open trade between Illinois and New Mexico, across the Pawnee country to the Comanchería and on to Pecos. Only two of that group, Jean Chapuis and Luis Foissy, persevered past the Pawnee villages. They fared a little better than Mallet had with the Comanches, but even worse with the Spaniards. A lavish bribe smoothed the way when Comanches threatened to bar their passage to New Mexico, but at Santa Fe the unlucky pair found their goods confiscated and the proceeds used to send them to Mexico City. The viceroy shipped them to Spain under guard. Their offense warranted the death penalty under Spanish law, but the Council of the Indies decided in 1753 just to imprison Chapuis and Foissy, to lodge a strong protest with the French Crown, and to demand severe punishment of the Fort Chartres commandant who had licensed them to explore toward New Mexico.[24]

His interrogation of Chapuis and Foissy gave Governor Vélez Cachupín further ground for worry. They had spent a leisurely ten months en route from Illinois, visiting and trading in Osage, Missouri, Kansas, and Pawnee villages. The Osages, Missouris, and Kansas had

---

[24] Council of the Indies to his Majesty, Madrid, November 27, 1754, ibid., pp. 82–89.

had French residents in their villages for eight years. Although the French claimed no control of the Pawnees, they had enjoyed some trade with them for ten years, and their relations were friendly. The two travelers had perfect confidence in the friendship of all those nations. They doubted that the Comanches would ever be perfectly reliable, but they thought trade feasible, given convoys of fifty or sixty men to see goods through the Comanchería. They confirmed earlier Comanche tales of a new accord among Pawnees, Wichitas, and Comanches. All that amity among Frenchmen and Indians on the plains seemed to Governor Vélez Cachupín to threaten the very existence of New Mexico.

Encouraged by authorities in Mexico City, Vélez Cachupín resolved to head off that threat by winning the friendship of the Comanches. His first opportunity to conciliate them had occurred in the summer of 1751. As he was inspecting Taos pueblo, Comanches arrived to barter hides and captives. Governor Vélez Cachupín let them trade, but he warned that he would make war on them if they should steal horses or attack Pecos. They promised so convincingly and behaved so contritely that the governor lavished presents and praise upon them. Their chief seemed so pleased by the good reception and so determined to persuade all his people to keep the peace that Vélez Cachupín thought the truce might really endure. They did keep their promises all that summer, while Vélez Cachupín kept Indian scouts on precautionary patrol at all customary entry points. In mid-autumn, when vigilance slackened, more than three hundred Comanches surprised Pecos at dawn, trying to enter and sack the pueblo. Ten Spanish soldiers stationed there helped the Pecos warriors repulse that attack and another soon afterward. The Comanches killed only a dozen cows pastured outside the pueblo and suffered six deaths and several wounds.

Determined to make good his promise to answer any attack on Pecos with war, Vélez Cachupín sallied forth two days later, on November 5, 1751, from Santa Fe with fifty-four soldiers, thirty militiamen, and eight Pueblos. His Indian scout picked up the trail at Galisteo, whence it led in a southerly direction to the plains, then forked northeast and southwest. Vélez Cachupín turned southwest, overtook some 145 fleeing Comanches, and scored an extraordinary victory. He trapped them in a box canyon and drove them back toward a deep pond at the head of the canyon, until they had no choice but to drown, hurl themselves back toward the Spaniards' guns, or surrender. Most died in the pond. Forty men, six women, and three children gave themselves up, all weeping with terror and many wounded.

The Spaniards built fires and wrapped the shivering prisoners in blankets, doing their best to assure them that they would not be slaughtered. To see fierce Comanche warriors quivering in abject terror amazed and touched the witnesses. They could not know the peculiar horror with which Comanches regarded death by drowning, which they believed to trap the spirit within the corpse and thus destroy its immortality. Vélez Cachupín could have gunned down ten times as many warriors without inflicting a comparable blow on the nation's morale.

Although he did not realize the full effect of the episode, the governor was encouraged once his captives were dry and calm enough to talk. The chief who had urged the attack had died in the battle; the survivors seemed more inclined to repudiate than to avenge him. They confirmed Vélez Cachupín's earlier understanding that each chief acted upon his own inclination and that some were so peacefully disposed that they restrained their followers from even the slightest offenses.[25] He had indeed been right to pursue and identify the attackers instead of declaring war on all Comanches.

Now the governor needed to pursue the other party northeastward, but the three hundred–mile chase had left his horses exhausted, and his eight wounded men needed to be taken home. Vélez Cachupín therefore gambled on contacting the more amicably disposed Comanche leaders to see whether they could now persuade all their nation to peace. Keeping only four hostages, he released the rest of the captives to carry their story back to the Comanchería. With them he sent a gift of tobacco for their chiefs and his demand that they keep the peace and return the Spaniards whom they had captured at Abiquiú in 1747.

When the Comanche survivors reached home, their tale of the awful havoc in the pond sent waves of shock and terror through the nation. Now thoroughly scared of the "boy captain," as they called the youthful Vélez Cachupín, the Comanches paid his message serious attention. El Nimiricante Luis, who had been one of the most belligerent chiefs, took the lead that December among several Comanche chiefs who sent messengers in all directions to call their nation together. When

[25] Report of Vélez Cachupín to Conde de Revilla Gigedo, Santa Fe, November 21, 1751, ibid., p. 74.

the principal leaders gathered and smoked the tobacco sent them by the governor, those who had convened the council explained his demands. Their discussions took a long time, because they remembered many years of hostilities with New Mexicans and harbored many very real grievances against them. Some losses still cried for vengeance. Nevertheless, those who had been most belligerent were among the first to advocate perpetual peace with the Spaniards, arguing that it would be better to stop the wars and make the most of the profitable trade fairs. The council of chiefs sent the message to all *rancherías*: be friends of the Spaniards; do them no injury by stealing horses or committing other hostilities; those who have captured Spanish women should turn them over to be restored to their people.[26]

El Oso, foremost of the chiefs, planned to take all his *rancherías* to Taos to formalize the peace with Governor Vélez Cachupín in autumn, at the regular time for ransoming captives. Meanwhile, he tried to collect the three women and two little boys from Abiquiú whose restoration the governor had demanded. Chief Nimiricante helped round up the captives. One of those women now belonged to his own brother, who rejected Nimiricante's offer to compensate him with an Apache woman in lieu. They quarreled sharply. Nimiricante told his brother to get out of his *ranchería* or be punished; he did not wish his people to suffer another defeat like the one they now mourned, because it made them faint-hearted. Nimiricante promised El Oso that he would come to Taos just as soon as he could persuade his brother to relinquish the woman.

Just as Nimiricante could not compel his brother to give up his property for the good of the nation, the other chiefs could not guarantee the behavior of their people and could not even hope to know of all their actions. Some were so lawless that they even stole horses from their own people and sold them at other *rancherías*. There was little likelihood that all the young men would forswear poaching upon the tempting horse herds in New Mexico. Despite the difficulties, the Comanches wished to try for peace. They had in Governor Vélez Cachupín an unusually understanding and responsive authority with whom to deal.

---

[26] This report of Comanche reactions came from a Kiowa woman, then a captive among them, whom the Utes captured from the Comanches a few months later and sold in August to a resident of San Juan pueblo. Her response to interrogation gave Governor Vélez Cachupín an independent check on Comanche reports of their peace councils, as well as interesting insights into the internal problems of the

All winter Governor Vélez Cachupín awaited some result from his November overture, meanwhile taking steps to secure the province in case the Comanches and their Wichita allies should concert an offensive against the New Mexican frontier. The first sign of response came on April 6, 1752, when a small Comanche *ranchería* arrived at Taos. Vélez Cachupín talked with the chiefs and found their tone so encouraging that he decided to send his four hostages home that very month, without awaiting the return of the captive Spaniards. One of the four refused to go back to his people; he preferred to remain with Vélez Cachupín, in whose home he was very happy. Two of the three who did go home, Antonio and Cristóbal, assiduously spread word of their excellent treatment in the governor's home. They assured the Comanches that the fourth man's decision to remain in Santa Fe was indeed his own, a testimony to the generous hospitality that they had enjoyed. Antonio particularly focused his suasion upon his father, Chief Guanacante, whom he ardently wished to become the friend of his friend, Governor Vélez Cachupín.

The little *ranchería* remained unobtrusively camped near Taos from April 6 onward. Another small group arrived in July with pelts to sell. The newcomers numbered only thirty men, with ten tipis and some female captives, but included an unusually high proportion of chiefs. They were commissioned to pay respects to Governor Vélez Cachupín on behalf of all the chiefs who commanded large *rancherías*. The governor promptly invited eight or ten of the leaders to Santa Fe, where he entertained them in his home for two days and gave them presents. They assured him that all the chiefs had gathered to smoke the tobacco he had sent them the previous winter and that the whole nation firmly intended to maintain constant friendship and cordial relations with the Spaniards and the Pueblos. Many chiefs who had not yet seen the governor would visit him at Taos after the aspen leaves fell. Part of the delay in concluding peace arrangements stemmed from a scarcity that summer of pelts and captives. The Comanches needed now to campaign against enemy tribes for booty to trade at the Taos autumn fair.

Vélez Cachupín sent the delegates home with presents signifying his friendship for their chiefs; he also sent a firm warning that he would ruin them if they should attack his province. Little more than

---

nation. See Juan Joseph Lobato to Vélez Cachupín, San Juan de los Cavalleros, August 17, 1752, in Thomas, *Plains Indians*, pp. 114–117.

a week passed before he received four more Comanche visitors, including chiefs sent by El Oso himself. They had come to ask Vélez Cachupín for tobacco and to deliver El Oso's promise that he would bring his *ranchería* to Taos that fall.

A few incidents marred the truce that summer. Vélez Cachupín had found it necessary to punish some Comanches who attacked Galisteo. El Oso's messengers assured him that the chief was glad that the governor had dealt severely with the culprits, who had defied his will; he thought the warning example would be salutary for the rest.

Before El Oso's messengers left Taos, five more Comanches stole horses from Spaniards of the Rio Arriba district. Pursuing settlers recovered the horses, killed two of the Comanches, and wounded a third; the other two escaped. One settler died in the skirmish. His friends carried his corpse back to Taos for burial.

El Oso's four messengers bewailed the settler's death, regretted that any of the thieves had escaped death, and begged the Spaniards not to blame all Comanches or their chiefs for the bad deed of five. They explained that some Comanches were so deceitful that their chiefs' warning and counsel could not deter them from such crimes. Taos' *alcalde mayor* assured them that the New Mexicans understood their problem and would not break off the peace negotiations. Taoseños then escorted the Comanche party safely past any possibility of Apache attack in the valley of La Jicarilla, and their appreciation seemed boundless.

The chiefs made good their promise that fall. The Comanche peace with New Mexico endured as long as Governor Vélez Cachupín managed its complexities. He attended all trade fairs that Comanches attended, making certain that neither settlers nor Pueblos injured them. He patrolled their camps personally to protect them from theft and extortion, and promptly adjudicated disputes. His careful attention to appeals for justice and his solemn fairness pleased the Comanches, who developed great confidence in him. To avoid awkward confrontations, the governor banned proscribed goods from the vicinity of Comanche fairs. Most sensitive of the proscribed items were mares and studs. Vélez Cachupín kept breeding stock out of sight rather than insult some Comanche by denying him the right to buy an animal he fancied.

Governor Vélez Cachupín extended many practical courtesies to Comanche visitors. He always stationed an officer with a presidial squad in their camp to prevent anyone from entering it at any time other than the formal fair attended by the governor himself. The soldiers guarded the Comanches' horse herds, and relief from that chore especially pleased the visitors. Perhaps most important of all were the flattering ceremonial courtesies which the governor always observed. He welcomed the chiefs promptly, sat down and smoked with them, and made a formal speech expressing his affection and respect, always with the air of gravity and serenity that Comanches expected of great peace chiefs.

So completely did Vélez Cachupín win the Comanches' confidence and control the trade fairs that he even managed to avoid disruption when Utes and Apaches traded at Taos during Comanche visits. Realizing that Utes and Apaches would subordinate their old hatreds for each other to league against their principal enemy, Governor Vélez Cachupín stood alert to prevent them from injuring the Comanches. He kept their encounters harmonious, helped Apaches to ransom their people from Comanches, and even supervised peaceful exchanges of horses and arms among them. If haggling over prices grew acrimonious, the governor intervened to set a fair price. Because they trusted his impartiality among the tribes, all accepted his arbitration with good grace.

If the Comanche peace was the crowning achievement of Vélez Cachupín's administration, it was no isolated success. He managed an extraordinary set of alliances with disparate and, in many cases, mutually hostile Indian peoples.[27] His first emphasis was scrupulous executive protection and justice for the Pueblos, with close attention to their legal rights. He found them completely responsive to fairness and kindness, saw no tendency to subversion among them, and found their warriors always prompt to meet their obligations as vassals of the king.

Vélez Cachupín hoped that an example of well-being and prosperity in the pueblos would attract the *bárbaros* to the faith. He worked vigorously to establish friendly communications with all whom he could reach. Among most, there were years of hostility and well-founded grievances to overcome.

Vélez Cachupín inherited from his predecessor a bitter Ute war. Ute depredations had been an intermittent problem in northern New Mexi-

[27] The overall picture of Vélez Cachupín's Indian relations derives principally from Vélez Cachupín to Revilla Gigedo, Santa Fe, September 29, 1752, ibid., pp. 118–125, and Vélez Cachupín's Instruction to his Successor, Don Francisco Marín del Valle, Santa Fe, August 12, 1754, ibid., pp. 129–143.

co ever since the northward expansion of Spanish settlements, particularly Abiquiú, encroached upon their winter ranges. Ute horse thefts had frequently strained the patience of Spaniards and Pueblos. The Utes had suffered both insult and injury when changing Spanish trade regulations had restricted and occasionally even prohibited the *bárbaros'* trade with New Mexico. However, the Utes had sought new rapprochement with the Spaniards and their allies as their war with the Comanches grew, and the early 1740's had brought new cooperation against the common enemy.

Then occurred the awful episode when Utes who thought themselves allied with the Spaniards against the Comanches were surprised by a New Mexican force that destroyed a camp of a hundred tipis, capturing or killing all its occupants. The New Mexicans apparently had reacted against horse thefts by a few Utes and rampaged northward to punish any Utes they could find. Ute campaigns to avenge the atrocity devastated the northern frontier.

Vélez Cachupín recognized the Utes' just grievances and somehow managed to pacify them by 1750. He dealt with them just as carefully as with Comanches, protecting their interests and paying great respect to their chiefs. If Utes stole horses, the governor courteously notified their leaders, never suggesting any general threat against their nation. The chiefs responded satisfactorily, returning the property and handling the culprits according to their own customs.

The Utes so prized their good relations with Vélez Cachupín that they let themselves be tricked into giving unwonted quarter to their Navajo enemies, who were also friends and allies of the Spaniards. In 1752 they were fighting, and besting, Navajos, who suddenly stacked their arms and brandished a wooden cross and a Franciscan almanac on a pole. They told the Utes that the great chief of the Spaniards had sent them the cross and the "letter," commanding the Utes to be kind to the Navajos. Awed, the Utes decided they should grant their gracious pardon to the Navajos; they knew Governor Vélez Cachupín had pardoned some Comanches who had sued for peace bearing a cross. That was a handsome gesture by the Utes, in view of their profound old enmity with the Navajos.

The principal Ute chief rode to San Juan to report their action to Vélez Cachupín, who was quite touched and pleased. He promptly paid a two-day good will visit to their camp, forty miles north of the pueblo, and there supervised the big annual exchange of pelts so important to the economies of New Mexicans and Utes. The governor deemed it politic to go along with the Navajos' roguish deception, but he guessed that the peace between the two nations would endure only as long as the Navajos would refrain from stealing from the Utes.

Some Navajos soon took advantage of the Utes' naive confidence in the peace to surprise a Ute *ranchería*, killing or capturing all the inhabitants and stealing all their possessions. The Utes' relentless campaign for vengeance then drove those Navajos to abandon much of their accustomed range and seek refuge in La Cebolleta, near Laguna pueblo, and in the mountains near Zuñi. Vélez Cachupín thought the Utes entirely justified, so he took no steps to protect the Navajos. He did suggest that they move to the area of the abandoned pueblos and missions ranging from Socorro southward, well beyond Ute reach, and offered to help them relocate. Although the distance would have afforded them sorely needed protection from the Utes, the Navajos rejected his proposal. Vélez Cachupín left them alone to suffer well-deserved punishment.

Vélez Cachupín also restored amicable relations with the northernmost Apache groups—Carlanas, Palomas, and Cuartelejos—who had communicated little with the province since the 1730's and had shown signs of enmity. The governor encouraged them to trade in the province, and he soon won their confidence so completely that most of them came to live near Pecos. They often left their women and children in the pueblo for safety when they rode out to hunt buffalo.

Vélez Cachupín found the Carlanas and their associates invaluable scouts. Extraordinarily active and astute, they could reconnoiter three hundred miles with confidence, an accomplishment very rare and risky for Pueblos. He was confident that he could rely upon them as allies in case Comanches should attack the province.

The governor encouraged the Carlanas of Pecos to maintain cordial relations with Carlanas on the plains, whom they frequently visited. He also tried to foster the Carlanas' independence from the Natagés and Faraones farther south. Natagés rode northward regularly with horses and mules stolen from Nueva Vizcaya and El Paso to trade them to the Carlanas for buffalo meat, hides, and the tipis in which Carlana craftsmen excelled. That trade, exactly suited to their respective needs, was inevitable, but Spanish interests forbade that it lead to alliance or merger. To forestall such a development, Vélez Cachupín cultivated close Carlana ties with New Mexico. He also courted the friendship of the Natagés and Faraones whenever possible, but he assumed that New Mexico's security would require occasional campaigns to punish Faraon raiders in their home territory.

The Faraones, then living in the Manzanos and the Siete Ríos ranges, roved along the Rio Grande from Albuquerque to El Paso. Their incursions in those two districts and their plundering along the connecting caravan route hindered development of the province for many years. Yet, in the time of Governor Vélez Cachupín, the Faraones did their best to conciliate him, holding their raids to a minimum and offending very little around Albuquerque. They reported to the governor faithfully, as agreed, and twice refused Gila invitations to join in attacks on El Paso. They even fought the Gilas, who grew so disgusted that they left the Rio Grande area for a while. Vélez Cachupín worked hard to maintain good relations with the Faraones, but he saw less hope for a stable peace with those Indians than with any others on his frontiers.

Never did Vélez Cachupín take peace so much for granted as to relax his vigilance: his forces systematically patrolled every entry point into the province. He expected the Indians to test the qualities of his successor, and he predicted disaster if they should think the new governor not brave or vigorous enough to go to war if necessary or should find him a lax administrator of the trade fairs.

The Comanche peace was just two years old when Vélez Cachupín left the governorship. His departure in 1754 was as much an unfortunate mishap in the viceroyalty as his appointment five years earlier had been a lucky accident. Viceroy Revilla Gigedo, who posted the promising young officer to the Santa Fe presidio as captain of cavalry, made him governor ad interim in April 1749 for want of a proper appointee. Vélez Cachupín's work soon won the admiration of authorities in Mexico City, who recommended his permanent appointment. However, by the time authorities in Mexico discerned his worth, the Crown had already appointed Francisco Marín del Valle to the post. The disappointed viceroy asked Vélez Cachupín to write detailed instructions for his successor and prayed that the extraordinary network of amicable relations would survive the change.

Governor Marín del Valle tried to imitate his predecessor's supervision of the Indian trade. He proclaimed severe penalties for any failure to treat Indians fairly, explaining to the settlers that infractions would surely precipitate robberies and murders in the province. He regulated prices and banned the sale of arms, horses, mules, and burros to *indios bárbaros*. However, he could not control the situation as firmly as had Vélez Cachupín, and old antagonisms between Comanches and some Pueblos soon resurged. Again it grew commonplace that some Comanches traded peacefully at Taos even while others attacked pueblos. Those who valued peace and trade often warned Governor Marín del Valle not to be too trusting, because there were rogues among Comanches just as among Spaniards. They urged him to hang any whom he caught.

Such trusted allies as the Carlana and Jicarilla Apaches warned the governor when Comanches approached, so Marín del Valle managed to hold the balance of trading and raiding at a tolerable level until the last summer of his term.[28] Then, in 1760, the Taoseños maliciously provoked the Comanches to tribal war.

Early that summer the Taos Indians entertained Comanche visitors with a scalp dance, then gleefully announced that they had danced with Comanche scalps. Their tribal honor outraged, the Comanches reacted accordingly. On August 4, 1760, three thousand Comanche warriors swept into the Valley of Taos to avenge the insult by finishing off the pueblo and ranches. The twin fortresses of Taos pueblo withstood the onslaught relatively well, but the Comanches captured fifty-six Spanish women. Many ranches were abandoned in the wake of the attack. Governor Marín del Valle mustered a large force of Spaniards, Pueblos, and Utes to pursue the Comanches, but they rode five hundred miles in vain.[29]

Perhaps their triumphant sweep satisfied the tribal honor; perhaps the Comanches had second thoughts about sustaining a general war that would cost them access to the Taos trade. At any rate, after Marín del Valle relinquished his office to an ad interim successor, some three hundred Comanches rode to Taos in December 1761 to negotiate a peace with Governor Manuel del Portillo y Urrisola. In their camp were seven Spanish captives whom they hoped to use as bargaining stock.

When fourteen Comanche leaders presented their peace proposals, Portillo threatened to gun them down and thus got six captive women returned. However, the seventh captive was a nine-year-old lad who

[28] Eleanor B. Adams, "Bishop Tamarón's Visitation of New Mexico, 1760," *New Mexico Historical Review* 28 (1953): 215–216.

[29] Francisco Atanasio Domínguez, *The Missions of New Mexico, 1776: A Description, with Other Contemporary Documents*, ed. Eleanor B. Adams and Angelico Chávez, p. 251; Isidro Armijo, ed., "Information Communicated by Juan Candelaria, Resident of This Villa de San Francisco Xavier de Alburquerque, Born 1692—Age 84," *New Mexico Historical Review* 4 (1929): 290–292.

refused to leave the Comanche camp. When the Comanches upheld the child's refusal, Governor Portillo had the child forcibly seized and the Comanche camp surrounded by a combined force of Utes, Pueblos, and Spaniards. Three days later all two hundred Comanche men lay dead; their surviving women and children were captives.

After that, Governor Portillo refused to speak with any Comanche envoys. By the spring of 1762, the Comanches resigned all hope of negotiating either peace or the return of their people and started preparing for a general war against New Mexico. Then Vélez Cachupín arrived for his second term as governor, barely in time to avert disaster.[30]

As soon as Vélez Cachupín heard the sorry tale of Portillo's slaughter of the Comanches at Taos, he moved to placate the Comanches. He sent six of the captured Comanche women home as his emissaries and distributed the other captive women and children among Spanish families, enjoining utmost kindness in their care.

When the six Comanche women reached their *rancherías* with the governor's message, the chiefs and elders of the tribe were in council, planning a war to avenge their people for Portillo's massacre. They needed first to know beyond doubt whether the newly arrived governor was indeed, as their women reported and as his message declared, that same Vélez Cachupín whom they had known favorably in the previous decade. Nine emissaries rode to Taos to find out, taking along four women and sixty warriors, who awaited them discreetly short of the pueblo. Two of the delegates were chiefs in their own right and kinsmen of two others of much greater importance; two were elders who spoke with authoritative voice in the council. All four had known Vélez Cachupín during his first term. They approached Taos bearing a tall cross as their sign of peace; a small cross dangled from each delegate's neck. Nonetheless, they rode well armed, with French rifles, two pounds of powder in each man's flask, lances, and tomahawks.

The corporal of the Taos garrison, alerted by Vélez Cachupín to expect Comanche visitors, welcomed them cordially and notified the governor at once. Vélez Cachupín promptly invited the delegation to ride to Santa Fe with fourteen Pueblo escorts. *Alcaldes mayores* of districts along the route were advised to entertain the Comanche visitors and to give them presents if they could manage any, in order to

<hr />

[30] Armijo, "Information Communicated by Juan Candelaria," pp. 292–294; Vélez Cachupín to Marqués de Cruillas, Santa Fe, June 27, 1762, in Thomas, *Plains Indians*, pp. 148–154.

demonstrate each community's general kindness and good faith toward them. All the pueblos and settlements complied. The Comanches reached Santa Fe aglow with confidence and satisfaction. At the Governor's Palace they enjoyed an affectionate reunion with Vélez Cachupín. They welcomed him back to the province on behalf of their nation and gave him their arms for safekeeping during their visit. The governor accorded them Santa Fe's best hospitality, as befitted distinguished men of high rank in their nation.

Solemn preliminary smokes and long discussions occupied the governor and his guests for several days. When they described their dreadful loss at Portillo's hands, he acknowledged the justice of their complaint and shared their sorrow. He mentioned their breaches of the peace in the time of Governor Marín del Valle, but, when he heard their side of the matter, he recognized that the blame had not been solely theirs. Agreeing that both Spaniards and Comanches had acted insanely, they talked of ways to restore their friendship.

First must come mutual restoration of prisoners, then resumption of commerce. Governor Vélez Cachupín urged the Comanches to come often, without fear of the Spaniards, whom his orders would guide in accordance with the king's loving intentions. The governor reiterated his own friendship for the Comanches and promised to punish any of his subjects, Spanish or Indian, who should injure them. In turn, he asked the Comanches for similar guarantees: the chiefs and elders must punish those who came to steal the Spaniards' horses or did other harm, for peace could endure only if delinquents on both sides were corrected or rooted out.

The Comanche delegates promised to carry the matter back for consideration by all their chiefs and principal men, the only possible way to bind all Comanches. They also promised to search for all Spaniards captured since 1760 and to bring them back when three moons had passed. They had little hope of restoring all captives, for some would have died and others would have been traded to Frenchmen or Wichitas. They would negotiate to repurchase the latter, but they could guarantee no results.

Governor Vélez Cachupín saw the delegates off, well fed and heavily laden with presents: articles of Spanish clothing they particularly liked, personal ornaments, and, most important of all, many bundles of tobacco. Much smoke would rise from the leaders' pipes before their councils could make such a serious commitment, but generous supplies of the governor's good tobacco would keep them mindful of his affection and his power.

The delegates reported to the council: the newly arrived governor at Santa Fe was truly the same chief of the Spaniards whom they had known in former years. At once, the band chiefs summoned all *rancherías*, both to confer on the proposed peace terms and to facilitate return of Spanish captives. They planned to take the captives to the governor in July, as their envoys had promised, but the two most distinguished chiefs decided not to risk any lapse of communications with Santa Fe in the interval. They sent new messengers to Vélez Cachupín.

The very make-up of that delegation expressed confidence: just seven men, five women, and three children, traveling with three tipis. When they reached Taos on June 10, the corporal of the garrison sent their four leading men on to Santa Fe. The families camped at the pueblo to await their return.

Governor Vélez Cachupín, well versed in Indian courtesies, welcomed them graciously, furnished tobacco to smoke while they rested, and considerately waited a day to ask why they had come. Through his interpreter, they explained their errand: to confirm on behalf of the two most distinguished chiefs the agreements made by the commissioners in April and to take back still further assurances that this governor was indeed the same Vélez Cachupín and was maintaining his former good policies. The good treatment of this small party, with its women and children, would help the leaders to reassure their nation that they need not fear repetition of last December's slaughter of their people at Taos.

The governor sympathized with their fears, approved their precautions, and vowed again and again his absolute sincerity. Then, sensing that words could not suffice, he asked what sign they would like him to give. That pleased them. The eldest man answered that they wished to see some of their people who were held prisoner, and that each of the men would like to take back some close relative, perhaps even his own woman, if he should find her. Such a concession would leave no possible doubt of the Spaniards' good faith.

Since Vélez Cachupín had already compiled lists of the prisoners, he could immediately order them brought to Santa Fe by the settlers to whom he had assigned them. In short order, he produced thirty-one women and children and knew boundless relief when each delegate found his own relative. Delighted, the Comanche commissioners hugged Vélez Cachupín, thanked him, and assured him that their nation now would have no reason to fear the Spaniards or to follow any path but that of firm peace and alliance.

The governor saw them off with plenty of tobacco for the return journey and more for their leaders. To guard against any untoward encounter with Utes en route to Taos, he arranged an escort of thirty Pueblos. In good time, the delegates rejoined their families at Taos and trekked back to the Comanchería with their recovered kin and their good news.

Still Governor Vélez Cachupín took no result for granted. Knowing the depth of their grievances and the difficulty of binding the entire nation to peace, he hedged against Comanche vengeance: garrisoned the frontier settlements, kept scouts active on approaches to the province, and looked into legal justifications in case a Comanche onslaught should make war necessary, even while he prayed earnestly for peace.

The Comanche leaders did not disappoint him. They affirmed the peace and kept it as well as their difficult circumstances permitted throughout Vélez Cachupín's five-year term. Comanches annually attended the Taos fair. Unruly individuals of both Comanche and New Mexican communities sometimes caused trouble, but the moderation and understanding of leaders on both sides prevented general hostilities. Vélez Cachupín never deluded himself that he had reached a final solution to relations with Comanches or any other *bárbaros*. Frequent contacts of Comanches with New Mexicans would revive rather than heal their grievances unless they should regularly experience at the settlements the treatment Vélez Cachupín tried to foster: "good faith, equity, entertainment, and the measures which the rules of religion, respect for humanity, and rights of peoples dictate."[31]

The Comanche peace did not survive by many months Vélez Cachupín's second departure in 1767, but the achievements of his two terms had lasting and important effects. His voluminous reports clarified the Comanche problem for the first time and placed on record in Mexico City both his admiration for their excellent qualities and his conviction that they were more often sinned against than sinners. He had demonstrated the superior results attainable by affection and equitable treatment of Indians, had pointed out the limitations of force as an instrument of policy, and had bluntly expounded the guilt of Spaniards, including some governors, in provoking hostilities.

31 Thomas, *Plains Indians*, p. 153.

The achievements and advice of Vélez Cachupín won respect and admiration at the viceregal court. As a result, the viceroy began in the 1750's to consider alliance with the Comanches as a potential key to peace with many less powerful nations, none of which would dare oppose the Spaniards if they were effectively allied with the Comanches. At the same time, he realized the necessity of dealing individually with the various groups of the Comanches, comprehending at last the autonomy of their countless bands and the likelihood that the nation would never be truly unanimous either in hostility or in friendship toward the Spaniards.[32] Those were important perspectives to have on record at high levels as Comanches moved toward confrontation with another Spanish frontier, this time in Texas.

[32] Marqués de Altamira, Opinion, Mexico, April 26, 1752, ibid., pp. 76–80.

CHAPTER 9

Texas, 1752-1760

Comanches ventured upon the Texas frontier during the eight-year interval between the terms of Vélez Cachupín. Their Wichita and French allies on the Arkansas suffered changes of fortune that prompted a southward shift of activities. Some Comanches followed the trade to the Red River.

The New Mexican governor's own vigorous, uncompromising rejection of French trade overtures in 1751 and 1752 helped to precipitate the shift. The confiscation of goods and extended imprisonment inflicted upon all authorized French traders who reached Santa Fe, plus stiff official protests from Madrid to Paris, convinced Louisiana authorities that they would never be allowed commercial entrée to neighboring provinces of New Spain, Family Compact notwithstanding. Infuriated by the rebuff, Governor Louis Billouart de Kerlérec projected a vast new network of Indian alliances to bring the Spaniards to heel. So far as he knew, the Spanish flag was not established in the Apachería, so he proposed to bring the Apaches into the French imperium.

Kerlérec's grand design[1] called for French alliance with the Apaches and thus for reconciliation of the Apaches with all the Indian allies of France. It was a formidable list of old enemies that he proposed to bring into accord with the Apaches: the several Caddo groups, the Comanches, the Kichais, the Tawakonis and the Iscanis, the Osages, the Arkansas, the Missouris, and the Illinois. Kerlérec boasted that all of them were so devoted to the governor of Louisiana that they would not repudiate his desires, particularly if he should make an intelligent appeal to their common interests and should sweeten his proposition with nice presents. He would need only to explain that he wished to open and cleanse the roads because he could no longer bear to see them stained red with the blood of his children. In Kerlérec's own experience, it was a rare man who did not at heart prefer the advantages of peace to the horrors of war: certainly all tribes wished to hunt buffalo without fear of fatal encounter with enemies. Happiest of all would be the Apaches, who would gain access to French trade goods and no longer have to envy other tribes in that respect.

Most affected would be Louisiana's Indian allies on the Red River: it was they who risked encounter with hostile Apaches on every buffalo hunt. Governor Kerlérec proposed to send a person well known to them and familiar with their customs to explain his plan for general peace. Then, using the Kichais' village as the most convenient base, that agent would proceed into the unknown Apachería in autumn with a party so large and well armed that he need fear no surprise. He would bring from Louisiana an Apache slave competent enough in French to interpret, to be sent ahead to notify the Apaches that a French chief had come to see them, that he had brought them a present and a flag, and that he meant to procure for them peace with their enemies. Kerlérec had no doubt that Apaches would flock to meet his agent and that all the Indians would soon dance to celebrate a general peace.

The consequences for the Spaniards would be devastating. Kerlérec confidently predicted that they would have to abandon Los Adaes, probably the whole of Texas, perhaps even more, because Apaches armed with guns would pillage the province to get booty for the Louisiana trade. The French would occupy the resulting vacuum and from their dominant position in Texas would command commerce with New Mexico or Coahuila or any other Spanish province they might choose.

[1] Louis Billouart de Kerlérec, "Projet de Paix et d'Alliance avec les Cannecis . . .," *Journal de la Société des Américanistes de Paris*, n.s., III (1906): 67–76.

Allied with the Apaches, they could order peace or war with New Spain at their convenience. Louisiana traders could absorb as many horses and mules as Apaches could steal from the Spanish provinces and ship them to Santo Domingo at 800 to 900 percent profit over the New Orleans price.

Kerlérec never had a chance to test his grandiose scheme. Before it could be considered in Paris, France and Great Britain launched the final round of their contest for North American dominion. France could not then afford to alienate her Spanish ally. Furthermore, the French and Indian War disrupted the flow of trade goods to Louisiana, so that Louisiana could hardly sustain existing commitments for trade and tribute, much less enlarge them.

The Indians who depended upon French trade in the Arkansas Valley and in the Illinois country soon felt the pinch, for Britain's Chickasaw allies preyed upon the river commerce from New Orleans to the Arkansas and Illinois posts. The Wichitan bands on the upper Arkansas found their trade boom interrupted and their annual gifts uncertain; the impact of their disappointment and inconvenience reached far into the Comanchería.

It was a poor time for the Wichitas to suffer a breakdown in supplies of guns and ammunition. Their great victory over the Grand Osages in 1751 had sharpened the long-standing feud with that tribe. The Osage quest for vengeance naturally hit the fixed Wichitan villages more than the shifting Comanche camps. The pressures grew insupportable when French guns and munitions ceased to reach the Wichitas while the Osages could look to British traders for firearms. About 1756 or 1757, the last of the Wichitan bands gave up the struggle to survive on the Arkansas and fell back to the Red River. There they gained both safer distance from the Osages and more convenient access to the Natchitoches trade sphere, which was less affected by the war than those farther upstream because the Red River traffic to Natchitoches suffered little Chickasaw interference.

Dominant among the Wichitan bands that moved southward in the 1750's were the Taovayas. The much smaller Wichita band settled beside them and lived in close association with them through most of the century. The Iscanis divided: one segment located just a little way east of the Taovayas and Wichitas; the others settled five days southeastward, beside the Tawakonis on the Sabine River.[2]

2 The relationships of the bands are derived from the report of Antonio Treviño, a prisoner of the Taovayas in 1765; descriptions of the village location rely upon

Choice of a new location was the regular responsibility of the *okonitsa* ("one-who-locates"), second in rank only to the head chief of a village. It was his duty to look constantly for better village sites and, on the occasion of a move, to superintend the moving process, the laying out of the new village, and every detail pertinent to the location.[3] The *okonitsa* of the Taovayas acquitted himself with distinction in the mid-1750's. He chose an extraordinarily fine location on the Red River, at the western edge of the Cross Timbers,[4] eastern margin of the plains range of their Comanche allies and western limit of easy access for Natchitoches traders. The Red River ran four or five feet deep at the site, but a narrow ford gave the villagers access to both banks of the stream. The springs were excellent, the land fertile and arable. Buffalo and deer abounded in the vicinity; bears and wild boars were plentiful in the nearby woods. The Cross Timbers yielded all the firewood they needed and timber for construction, too; the lush prairies provided thatch for their houses and superior pastures for their horses. Conveniently near were quarries to meet certain important needs: *manos* and *metates*, points for arrows and lances, whetstones, and flints to strike fire. Nature constantly replenished a good salt bank in the middle of the river. The climate was pleasantly milder than they had known farther north. In short, it was a most agreeable place, a prize gained by ousting Apaches from the Red River Valley.

The Taovayas' occupation of former Apache territories angered and alarmed their old enemies. Lipan raiders harried the new villages, then scurried south to take refuge in the shadow of the Spanish frontier. Their certain expectation of vengeful pursuit made the Lipans reluctant to settle at the San Sabá mission when it was established for them in 1757, and their fears proved quite justified. In 1758, the Taovayas figured prominently in the northern nations' joint campaign for revenge

---

Treviño and upon Athanase de Mézières' account of his visit there in 1778. See Antonio Treviño, Interrogation, Nacogdoches, April 13, 1765, BA; Athanase de Mézières to Teodoro de Croix, Taovayas, April 18, 1778 (no. 2), in Herbert Eugene Bolton, ed., *Athanase de Mézières and the Louisiana-Texas Frontier, 1768–1780,* II, 201–203.

[3] The discussions of Wichita culture rely primarily on George A. Dorsey, *Mythology of the Wichita,* and W. W. Newcomb, Jr., *The Indians of Texas,* chapter 10. Some additional light is shed in Harold E. Driver, *Indians of North America,* and Gene Weltfish, "The Question of Ethnic Indentity: An Ethnohistorical Approach," *Ethnohistory* 6 (1959): 321–346.

[4] The Wichitan settlements ranged along the Red River in the vicinity of present Spanish Fort in Montague County, Texas, and across the stream in Jefferson County, Oklahoma.

against the Apaches, and they brought their Comanche friends with them.

Comanches already had a formidable reputation in Texas, thanks to the frank terror in which Apaches held them and tales of their wars in New Mexico. Comprehension of the Taovayas' impact on the balance of power among the Indians of Texas came more gradually. It was 1765 before the Spaniards had any reliable account of their village and 1778 before a responsible official saw at first hand and reported the significant potential of the Taovayas for the stabilization of the northern frontier. The lag cost both Taovayas and Spaniards needless years of war and suffering.

The Taovayas, like the other three surviving Wichitan bands, probably represented a fusion of several of the territorial-political kinship units that had comprised the Wichita world in centuries past. Although industrious and successful farmers and hunters, theirs was a society preoccupied with war. Accomplishment in war and wealth were the principal bases of distinction in rank. The leading warriors virtually controlled the village: they chose the head chief for his proven ability and generalship. Formal war records, painted on buffalo robes and tipis, preserved details of such feats as stealing horses, counting coup, stabbing, scalping, and killing enemies. That kept the record straight on long winter evenings when tales of war were recited in the grass lodges.

Shamans also ranked high in Wichitan society. One served as village crier. A vigorous ceremonial life kept the villagers in tune with the complex spiritual forces that they understood to govern their universe. A supreme creator, Kinnikasus, above the power of human understanding, headed their pantheon and figured in every invocation of the gods. Below him ranked deities whom they saw in the skies—the sun, the moon, the morning star, certain constellations—all believed to play vital roles in Wichitan destinies. Lesser spirits animated every object or being in their universe; some could become powerful guardians of individuals. A Taovayas gained his spiritual knowledge first through purposeful childhood instruction in the traditional beliefs of his people. For the rest of his life he sought revelation to enlarge his comprehension and effectiveness as a spiritual being. He looked forward to another life and expected to fare in eternity in just proportion to his accomplishments on earth.

Private and family observances punctuated his life cycle, and even his daily routine, with sober attention to the spiritual dimensions of the universe. Collectively, the villagers danced and chanted the major invocations of the people to the gods for their general concerns, usually under the auspices of particular dance societies. Some specific matters, like curing sickness, required the magic of shamans who owned the appropriate rites.

The quest for glory impelled Wichitan men to war as surely as Comanches or Apaches or Navajos, though raids figured less importantly in their more stable agricultural economy. War expeditions were meant to diminish the enemy by death or capture. Old traditions among both Wichitan and Caddoan peoples encouraged them to mutilate and eat captured enemies, as a magic way to wreak utmost damage on the enemy people and to enhance their own strength as a people. The cannibalism and the frenzied tortures inflicted upon some captives in the Taovayas-Wichita settlements horrified and sickened their Comanche allies as well as European visitors. Fortunately, the growing advantages of slave ownership in the expanding economy of the eighteenth century improved the lot of captives.

Occasional male captives might be pressed into service as scouts. Conspicuously brave fighters might be saved to bolster the fighting forces of the village. More generally useful and more numerous were captive women and children: as slaves, they enhanced the productivity of the villages and the prosperity of their owners' households. Some were eventually adopted into Wichitan families; some captive women became wives or concubines and bore children to swell the ranks of the nation.

The tempo of Wichita warfare depended upon individual discretion or impulse. Any man could initiate an expedition. He had only to call his friends to his lodge and explain his plan, then designate a subhead leader and two assistants who would serve as scouts. The return of a victorious party was a glorious time for a village. The leader announced their good news from the top of a nearby height set aside for that purpose, and there followed jubilant days of scalp and victory dances. Proud families sometimes gave away their possessions to celebrate the return of their warriors with enemy scalps.

Just as the whole village rejoiced with victors, all joined to mourn a warrior's death in battle. Vociferous general mourning lasted four days. Then a brave man voluntarily brought gifts to the bereaved family, telling them to cease their mourning and promising to lead a war party to avenge the death. If he could take a scalp, he would present it to the mourners. The dead warrior's family then mourned silently in their lodge until they received a scalp from a war party.

As surely as the loss of a Taovayas warrior impelled his people to avenge him, his successes evoked the vengeance of the enemy people he injured. The Taovayas and their associates escaped an insupportable level of Osage vengeance in the Arkansas Valley, only to be caught up in livelier pursuit of their old feud with the Apaches whom they had ousted from the Red River. Thus, prudence dictated that their new Red River village be fortified against enemy attack, as had been their settlements on the Arkansas. The importance of fortification grew when pursuit of Apaches carried the Taovayas and their friends into conflict with the Spaniards at San Sabá in 1758.

The Taovayas and their neighbors met the challenge well. Around the center of the Taovayas settlement they erected a stockade of split logs, spaced to allow for musket fire from within. They encircled the stockade with an earthen breastwork four feet high and in front of that dug a deep moat, four paces wide, to prevent any approach on horseback. Within the fortress, they excavated four large subterranean chambers to shelter all inhabitants not actively defending against an attack. How much their fortification derived from aboriginal tradition, and how much from example or advice of French traders, is uncertain. Over their fortress flew the French flag, which Wichitan peoples had cherished for four decades. When Spaniards saw that shocking banner in 1759, they leapt to the conclusion that unscrupulous French authorities had sparked the Norteños' attack on San Sabá and then masterminded their defense. That was an ill-considered judgment, inconsistent with the Texans' experience of the Natchitoches traders through several decades.

For more than a quarter-century, the respect and affection of the Caddo groups and neighboring nations had centered upon Commandant St. Denis of Natchitoches, regardless of international boundary. St. Denis had never hesitated to trade with Indians across the border, ignoring Spain's rigid, unrealistic proscriptions. Had he wished, St. Denis could have incited the Indians of the region to destroy the weak Spanish establishments of East Texas, but he wielded his power responsibly, fostering peace throughout the region as the basis for stable commerce and the general welfare of the peoples within his sphere of influence.

While the rivalries of their sovereigns waxed and waned over the decades, the frontier communities of Natchitoches and Los Adaes evolved a rather cordial, mutually supportive relationship. When Natchez warriors besieged Natchitoches in 1731, Spaniards from Los Adaes joined the Tejas and Atakapan warriors who rushed to help St. Denis and his Indian allies rout the aggressors. When French official-dom left Natchitoches priestless, friars from the Spanish missions ministered to its people.

On the other hand, the poor little Spanish community depended upon Natchitoches for its very subsistence, as well as its security amid the Indians. Supplies from Mexico and even from San Antonio were never adequate or reliable. To survive, even missionaries ignored the ban on trade with Louisiana. Annually, the friars traded a few hides at Natchitoches for the small quantity of powder and balls that they would barter to the Indians for their year's supply of bear fat.[5] Some Texas governors and some settlers exceeded necessity and ran con-traband trade operations for personal profit. The corruption and the weakness of Los Adaes varied in degree as successive governors varied in honesty and ability, but the dismal little presidio never became more than a travesty of a provincial capital. The two missions were mockeries, too, devoid of neophytes, able to count as saved only an occasional Indian presented for deathbed baptism. The Spanish es-tablishments contrasted poorly with Louisiana's bustling hub of trade and plantations at Natchitoches.

Because St. Denis left able successors, the stability of the Natchi-toches trade sphere survived his death in 1744, in his sixty-eighth year. His half-Spanish son, Louis Juchereau de St. Denis *fils*, had his father's flair with Indians and had inherited his authoritative mantle of respect and affection. Unfortunately, he paid a grave penalty for the frontier upbringing that so admirably equipped him to manage Indians and foster the post's economy: unable to read or write well enough to qualify for his father's job, St. Denis *fils* never rose above the rank of lieutenant in the Natchitoches garrison. The Indians gave him their devotion without regard to rank and frequented his plantation home to deal with him as they had once dealt with his father. French

---

[5] Certified copy of proceedings held by Martos y Navarrete to investigate charges against St. Denis for inciting Indians against the Spaniards and against Barrios y Jáuregui for trading with the Indians, Los Adaes, January 22, 1761–May 28, 1761, BA.

authorities realized the value of his special relationship with the Indians: standing orders forbade any Natchitoches commandant to tamper with it.

Happily, the post of commandant remained with the St. Denis family. Two of the four surviving daughters of Louis and Manuela married able men from France, who proved well qualified to succeed their remarkable father-in-law. Césaire de Blanc de Neuveville held the post from 1744 to 1763. Meanwhile, in 1746, Marie Petronille Feliciones Juchereau de St. Denis married a promising cadet, Athanase de Mézières, who had joined the Natchitoches garrison a year before her father's death. Marie died only two years later, but her widower remained a close associate of his brothers-in-law, de Blanc and St. Denis *fils*, and rapidly climbed both military and economic ladders. As soldier, as planter, and as Indian trader in charge of the Kadohadacho Post, he prospered. After de Blanc died in 1763, de Mézières took command, and he proved as able a frontier statesman as St. Denis père himself.

It was to that well-established trade sphere of the little St. Denis dynasty that the Wichitan bands gravitated southward from the Arkansas. The trivial Spanish capital within whose province the Tawakonis chanced to settle in the 1740's probably inspired little respect, but it provoked no antagonism until Los Adaes officials rashly tried to enforce the Crown's laws against the Louisiana traffic.

Early in his term Governor Jacinto de Barrios y Jáuregui heard of an extensive, voluminous French trade among the Tejas and Tawakoni settlements and of fine French regalia presented to the chiefs to woo their friendship. He sent his second-in-command, Don Manuel Antonio de Soto Bermúdez, to investigate in autumn 1752.[6] The Nacogdoches leaders welcomed Bermúdez and his party to their village, readily described the French trade, and indicated that Spaniards would be welcome to live with them if they would supply trade goods as satisfactorily as the Frenchmen they wished to supplant.

Bermúdez rode on to the Nasoni village, only to find his way blocked by the Nadote chief whose settlement lay next on his route. The Nadote chief had heard that the Spaniards meant to arrest all French traders and cut off trade with Louisiana. The idea was intolerable: the Indians depended upon that trade for their well-being. The Na-

---

[6] The documents covering the investigation appear in Charles Wilson Hackett, ed., *Pichardo's Treatise on the Limits of Louisiana and Texas*, IV, 54 ff.

dote chief told Bermúdez to hurry back to Los Adaes if he valued his life. The officer took him at his word.

The Nadotes pursued the matter vigorously, summoning to their village all Indians affected by Spanish trade policy in the area, Tawakonis as well as western Caddo groups. The assembly decided to exterminate the Spaniards and to invite St. Denis to become regional overlord. When they invited him to the Nadote village to hear their scheme, St. Denis objected angrily. He explained the close alliance between the French and Spanish kings and warned that, if the Indians should attack the Spaniards as proposed, French soldiers would have to defend the Spaniards. Convinced that he spoke the truth, some five hundred excited warriors calmed themselves and left the Spaniards alone.

The Nacogdoches chief told the story to Fray Calahorra, who informed the governor. Governor Barrios gratefully acknowledged that he and his compatriots in East Texas owed their lives to St. Denis. The other side of the coin was obvious, not only to Governor Barrios, but also to authorities in Mexico City: if St. Denis had enough authority to calm turbulent warriors, he could also incite them at his convenience. Here indeed was proof that Indian loyalties lay with France, thanks to the generous trade and presents and the freedom of religion that nation permitted natives within its colonial sphere.[7]

Governor Barrios appealed for relaxation of the trade laws to meet the emergency. He realized now that he could not control the Indians unless he could give them presents, but few goods that reached Los Adaes from the legal port at Veracruz pleased them. What they wanted were the powder, shot, muskets, cloth, blankets, razors, and knives that French traders sold them at prices lower than freight costs from Veracruz to Los Adaes. Barrios' sole chance to compete for the Indians' loyalty lay in buying goods from Natchitoches, which he vowed he could do without spending any money or trading off horses and saddles from his presidio. French merchants would gladly accept deer skins, on which they made excellent profits.

Although the *auditor* noted the gravity of the "silent conquest" the French trade was carving among the Indians of New Spain's northeasternmost corner, the viceroy and his council stood pat on the trade laws. They also insisted that Governor Barrios must, with all due caution and courtesy, demand that St. Denis cease his activities among the Indians of Texas and that the French interpreters withdraw from

[7] Reply of the Auditor, Mexico, 1753, *ibid.*, p. 90.

all the villages in which they were stationed. In due course, the king confirmed that instruction.[8] From the perspectives of Mexico City and Madrid, French trade activity inside Texas seemed a corollary to the intrusions of French traders at Santa Fe: all part of a master strategy to erode the Spanish frontier, all to be met with the same uncompromising stance.

Governor Barrios risked no new confrontation with St. Denis and his Tejas friends, but he did bestir himself to check other French traders among the Atakapan peoples of the lower Trinity Valley. His new show of toughness toward French traders, coupled with the Spaniards' total failure to meet the Indians' need for trade, riled the Indians of the region. Mindful of St. Denis' firm stand against violence toward the Spaniards, they tried talk. In the autumn of 1755, Indian leaders visited Governor Barrios at Los Adaes to state their case.[9]

They were an impressive lot: the leaders of such principal Tejas groups as Nabedaches, Adaes, and Ais; some Bidais headmen; "others," not further identified by Barrios, who, in light of other records, must have included at least the Tawakoni spokesmen of the Wichitan bands. Frankly and firmly, they explained that they depended upon the chase for their food and clothing and needed trade in guns, munitions, and other necessities. If the Spaniards would not accommodate them, they would trade with Frenchmen.

That challenge could not be ignored. Since Governor Barrios dared not risk an open breach with the tribes of that sensitive frontier, he bowed to their demand and licensed two Los Adaes settlers to trade with them. To hasten appeasement of all the Indians, he dispatched Lieutenant Domingo del Río to carry gifts to the chiefs and leading men at every village on the Texas side of the frontier. Henceforth, Los Adaes was actively, even openly, involved in the forbidden Indian trade, and governors included gunpowder in their gifts to keep the tribes friendly.[10] Barrios and his successor, Ángel Martos y Navarrete, defended their breach of the law as necessary to the survival of Spanish occupation in East Texas, but the irregularity shocked officials

[8] The King to the Viceroy, the Marqués de las Amarillas, Aranjuez, June 30, 1755; "Instrucción Reservada que trjo El Marqués de las Amarillas: Recibida del Exmo. Sr. D. Julián de Arriaga, Ministro de Indios," in *Instrucciones que los virreyes de Nueva España dejaron a sus sucesores*, pp. 94–103.

[9] Jacinto de Barrios, Deposition, October 29, 1755, in Certified Copy of Proceedings held by Martos y Navarrete to investigate charges . . . Los Adaes, January 22, 1761–May 28, 1761, BA.

[10] Martos y Navarrete, Statement of gunpowder used in 1763, Los Adaes, January 2, 1764, BA.

remote from the critical realities of the frontier, and the governors' own profitable participation in the trade cast a shadow of corruption.

Governor Barrios' desperate, dubious venture into trade and tribute was not the sole response to the Indian leaders' frank ultimatum in the fall of 1755. When they displayed such firm unity of purpose on behalf of such diverse Indian peoples, they made it clear that Spain could no longer hope to hold that frontier with its limited presence in the Tejas settlements. Within a year, a new presidio and mission were founded among the Atakapan peoples of the lower Trinity. The Crown extended Governor Barrios' term to 1759 to let him see the new establishments through the critical first years.

French traders had long collected hides at Atakapan *rancherías*; for neary as long, Spaniards had fretted about it. Since the mid-1740's, Spanish counter-agents had also visited those Indians in the guise of traders, while authorities debated endlessly about ways to counter French influence among them. The ill-starred missions on the San Gabriel were intended partly to attract the Atakapan groups away from the French traders. As that venture collapsed, there had emerged the idea of a mission and presidio to woo the Atakapans in their home territory. That project might have foundered in another decade of debate had not some Atakapan leaders taken part in the confrontation at Los Adaes.

There were four principal groups of the Atakapan-speaking peoples, probably never more than three thousand persons altogether: the Bidais, the Akokisas, the Deadoses, and the Atakapas proper.[11] Although there were some variations among them, and the Bidais perhaps had a more sophisticated culture by virtue of their closer proximity to the more advanced Caddo peoples, all were principally hunters and gatherers, living in scattered *rancherías*. They were, on the whole, amiable people, very responsive to trade, but their territories would never yield many converts to the faith or repay costs of occupation. Only fear prompted the Spanish occupation: fear that the French would consolidate control of the trade by settling in the region, then make it a base for expanded arms trade with the interior nations.

In the summer of 1756, Presidio San Agustín de Ahumada was established among the Akokisas, on the left bank of the Trinity not far upstream from its mouth on Trinity Bay. Mission Nuestra Señora de la Luz followed nearby in the autumn. The founding authorities envisioned a civil settlement around that nucleus. While the larger intent

11 Newcomb, *Indians of Texas*, pp. 315–329.

was to hold the whole Atakapan region, the immediate purpose of the new establishment was to serve the four segments of the Akokisas and all the Bidais, perhaps eventually congregating all Akokisas and Bidais in a single settlement. The Indians welcomed the presidio, which became a center for Barrios' trade enterprises and also for distribution of presents. The missionaries never made enough headway toward reduction and Hispanization to cause much friction.

The new presidio was hardly established before a French entrepreneur sought to make it his own base of operations.[12] M. Masse, who had already established a ranch among the Atakapas in Louisiana, petitioned to settle near Spain's new presidio in the Akokisa territory. He and his partner, the Abbé Disdier, would bring to the new settlement considerable holdings: twenty Negro slaves, whom they proposed to emancipate; seven hundred cattle; one hundred horses. Furthermore, M. Masse promised to secure for the new establishment the allegiance of all the Atakapas and the friendly assistance of the Nations of the North. Governor Barrios affirmed that the petitioner was influential enough among those tribes to make good his promise. Among the northern nations whose alliance he promised were some not mentioned earlier in that region: the Taovayas, Iscanis, and Wichitas; the Ietan and Paduca divisions of the Comanches.

Of course, the viceroy rejected the petition of M. Masse. Did not the impudent fellow seek to establish under Spanish sanction the very commerce and French influence that San Agustín was meant to prevent? Preoccupied with old rivalries, Spanish officialdom missed the significant thrust of the Masse petition: there were important newcomers in the northern interior, ripe for commerce and for alliance, and in 1756 M. Masse thought he could attract them to trade at San Agustín.

The opportunity slipped by. No Spanish agent ventured northwestward to examine the new villages on the Red River or to woo the newcomers with speeches and presents. Possibly Taovayas or Wichita or Iscani visitors, perhaps with Comanche companions, met Governor Barrios' clandestine traders at the Tawakoni village on the Sabine. There was no official recognition of their existence until they presented themselves so rudely at Mission San Sabá in the spring of 1758.

Virtually no information about the Taovayas and their associates figured in deciding Spain's response to the attack, and that ignorance

[12] Herbert Eugene Bolton, *Texas in the Middle Eighteenth Century*, pp. 359–360.

shaped the outcome. Of the dozen-odd nations involved in the San Sabá atrocity, the council targeted for the punitive campaign only the virtually unknown Wichitan and Tonkawan bands. Tejas had undoubtedly played a major role, but war against those long-time vassals of the Crown was unthinkable. Comanches had attacked, too, but their formidable reputation and their roving existence ruled out a campaign against them. It remained for Colonel Parrilla to discover for himself why the Taovayas were no easy target either.

The Spaniards were warned from Natchitoches against the folly of warring with the Norteños. Although deeply offended by charges that his traders had incited the attack at San Sabá, Commandant Césaire de Blanc offered to mediate peace with the Norteños.[13] Important considerations led him to prefer tranquil conditions on the frontier: the massacre of the priests and the desecrations at San Sabá horrified him as a faithful Catholic; trade thrived best under peaceful circumstances; Indian wars were hard to contain, and no one could guarantee that a general Indian war in Texas would not soon involve neighboring tribes within French jurisdiction. Thus, de Blanc offered the Spaniards all they lacked to negotiate an accord with the *bárbaros*: knowledge of their customs and modes of thought; well-established contacts and the services of interpreters; and the weight of French prestige on the side of peace.

De Blanc did not wait for the Spaniards to respond to his generous offers. Upon learning that the Tawakonis had participated in the San Sabá affair, he withdrew the French squad stationed in their village at their request for more than a decade, so as to dramatize his displeasure. Through his traders, he recovered some articles stolen from Mission San Sabá and restored them to Spanish authorities. Even more usefully, he relayed intelligence about the *bárbaros'* activities gathered from his traders, and counseled prudence.

The Comanches, Taovayas, Iscanis, and Tonkawas were said to be planning another concerted attack at San Sabá at the time of the winter buffalo hunt. Trouble brewed also in East Texas, where Tejas Indians were joining in some turbulent talking and dancing at the Tawakoni village. If their excitement were not quickly cooled, Mission Nacogdoches could suffer the same fate as that of San Sabá. Since there was no practicable hope of conquering the many Indian nations

---

[13] Césaire de Blanc to Governor Jacinto de Barrios y Jáuregui, Natchitoches, August 16, 1758, Archivo General de Indias (cited hereafter as AGI), Audiencia de México [Cunningham Transcripts, University of Texas Archives].

scattered over the vast, little-known northern interior, de Blanc urged the Spaniards to seek peace as the alternative to certain disaster.

His advice had no effect. Spanish honor demanded punitive action against the culprits or a carefully selected fraction thereof. Besides, how could Spanish officials trust a Frenchman?

De Blanc's warnings were a year old when Colonel Parrilla's motley command left San Antonio in mid-August 1759. They rode to the San Saba to pick up every man who could be spared from Presidio de San Luis de las Amarillas, then headed north-northeast in search of the enemy. Abandoned campsites and trail signs abounded, some obviously recent, but no Indians were sighted until October 2, when scouts spotted Yojuanes camped on the Clear Fork of the Brazos. With Apache warriors taking a vigorous lead, Parrilla surprised the camp and wiped out the Yojuanes in an hour. Fifty-five died in the battle; 149 were captured; the rest fled to the Tonkawas.[14]

It appeared a total and justified triumph. In the ruined camp the Spaniards found articles from San Sabá, including scraps from the robe of a martyred priest; among captured livestock were horses and mules with the presidio's brand. Parrilla could have turned back then, counting honor satisfied. Instead, he continued northward to confront the Taovayas and Iscanis, whom de Blanc had reported scheming with Comanches and Tonkawas to attack San Sabá. Some Yojuane prisoners offered to guide him to the Taovayas village, so Parrilla rode on to the Red River with 149 prisoners.

On October 7, sixty or seventy mounted Indians charged Parrilla's vanguard. A counter-charge seemed to disperse them readily. They fled into a forest, with cavalry pursuing closely. The woods stopped abruptly at a clear plain beside the Red River. The pursuing Spaniards emerged just in time to see the warriors ride into the fortified Taovayas village. Safe within the stockade, they laughed at the Spaniards and challenged them to enter if they could.

[14] The identity of the camp and the subsequent fate of the survivors are clarified in the Cabello Ynforme, San Antonio de Béxar, September 30, 1784, AGN, Provincias Internas, vol. 64. Parrilla's account of the campaign appears in his Testimonio de Campaña contra Indios Norteños, October 7, 1759, and his Carta Consultiva, San Antonio, November 18, 1759, both in AGI, Audiencia de México [Dunn Transcripts, UT Archives]. The standard secondary account is Henry Easton Allen, "The Parrilla Expedition to the Red River," *Southwestern Historical Quarterly* 43 (1939): 53–71; a more recent analysis appears in Robert S. Weddle, *The San Sabá Mission.* The archaeological problems of the battle site are discussed in Lathel F. Duffield, "The Taovayas Village of 1759: In Texas or Oklahoma?" *Great Plains Journal* 4 (1965): 39–48.

Parrilla paused to assess the problem. He had never anticipated such an enemy stronghold, and he had always doubted the military capabilities of the untrained, unruly militia that composed most of his force. As he wondered how to attack that moated palisade, bristling with muskets, the Taovayas seized the initiative. While men behind the walls maintained a deadly fire, mounted warriors made repeated sallies from the fort. Two men on foot carried spare muskets and ammunition for each man on horseback and kept them supplied with freshly loaded guns. Their disciplined offensive never flagged, even when the principal Taovayas leader died in the fray.

The battle lasted four hours, and Parrilla's force never managed to approach the stockade. Salvos from their two field cannons only evoked mocking laughter. All the while, a steady cadence of fife and drum rose from the fort, and the flag of France waved over it. Indian scouts reported fourteen Europeans, presumably French, inside the fort helping direct the action. The Indians obviously had so much ammunition that they felt no need to stint. The battle ceased only when darkness fell.

That night, while Taovayas danced and sang their triumph around great fires inside the stockade, Parrilla fell back to appraise his unhappy situation. His Apache allies reported that they had scouted every inch of the area and could find no way to approach that stockade. Many of Parrilla's men had fled in panic; he would certainly lose more if he should order his raw militia back to face that murderous gunfire on the morrow. The enemy, better disciplined in battle than most of his own men, far outnumbered his force. Scouts reported reinforcements arriving steadily at the stockade. His Apache allies and the Yojuane prisoners told Parrilla that he faced Comanches, Iscanis, Tawakonis, and perhaps several more nations, as well as Taovayas. Campaign tents visible beyond the village were assumed to belong to Comanches but could have belonged to any visiting nation, since they were standard equipment for the buffalo hunt or other extended travel. Most worrisome of all was the damning look of French involvement: the plentiful firearms, the sophisticated, disciplined offensive, the nerve-shattering din of fife and drum.

Parrilla decided to declare his objectives won and go home. After all, his force could take back 149 Yojuane prisoners and count their souls saved. He had eradicated an enemy camp and recovered some stolen property; he had campaigned deep into enemy territory and had carefully noted the terrain so that any future campaign could be planned on an informed basis. He estimated more than a hundred enemy dead, including the foremost Taovayas warrior. His own casualties appeared to be nineteen dead and fourteen wounded, though desertions made it hard to tally exactly. He would have preferred to achieve more and was game to try again at the earliest opportunity, but he could argue that Spanish arms had suffered no disgrace.

Colonel Parrilla gathered up his demoralized force as quickly as possible and began his orderly withdrawal, marching as rapidly as consideration of the wounded allowed. To expedite travel, he abandoned the two field cannons, which the Taovayas hauled into their fort as souvenirs of their triumph. Enemy warriors harassed Parrilla's retreating force but inflicted little damage. He reached San Sabá with most of his command and all the prisoners intact on October 25.

The colonel wanted to campaign immediately against the Tonkawas, but the other officers balked. They and their soldiers had acquitted themselves competently and honorably, but they had seen the poor odds for New Spain's untrained, ill-equipped militiamen against the skillful, well-armed Norteño warriors. Reluctantly, Parrilla accompanied the visiting squads to San Antonio, whence they dispersed to their home stations as soon as they and their mounts were rested.

His Apache allies dispersed, too, as soon as they marketed ninety-seven captives at San Antonio. In the camps of their waiting families, they danced with their fine collection of enemy scalps, celebrated their destruction of the Yojuanes, and mourned their one lost warrior. Parrilla's report praised their performance: throughout the campaign, the Apaches had faithfully rendered the best services of which they were capable. The colonel hoped that someday they would feel secure enough to settle down to mission life, but he thought them not unreasonable to fear life at San Sabá. For his own part, he resolved to hold that spot and someday to campaign against the Norteños again, with Apache warriors, to secure that frontier against the French and their Indian allies.

The next spring Parrilla won permission to travel to Mexico City to expound his view of the problems and potentials of the northern frontier. There he met the newly arrived Marqués de Cruillas, first viceregal appointee of Carlos III. Cruillas invited Parrilla to brief him extensively on the northern frontier situation and paid him the compliment of careful attention. Then, to his dismay, Parrilla learned that he would have no chance to pursue his carefully formulated plans. Captain Felipe de Rábago y Terán had somehow beaten the murder and adultery charges that had cost him the command of the defunct presidio on the San Gabriel; now the law entitled him to resume command of that company, though it had since been enlarged and transferred to the San Saba. The able Colonel Parrilla drew the governorship of Coahuila instead, and the unfortunate Captain Rábago rode off to San Sabá to try somehow to redeem his sordid reputation.

In vain the missionaries at San Antonio protested appointment of such a disreputable character to the San Sabá command; equally wasted was Governor Barrios' unfavorable report on Rábago's character. The viceroy also ignored warnings that the unfortunate change would alienate Apaches who had grown attached to Parrilla. After Rábago took command in the fall of 1760, San Sabá grew more isolated than ever, cut off from San Antonio by the missionaries' open contempt for Rábago and from every other quarter by his temperamental inability to work with any authority. Actually, Rábago did his best to protect the Apaches, even detailing presidial soldiers to escort their hunting parties. He thereby assured that San Sabá would be the constant target of angry Norteños.

Before Rábago took command at San Sabá, there was good reason to believe that the Norteños bore the Spaniards no deep enmity and had no desire to continue the war. In the spring of 1760, Tawakoni leaders visited Mission Nacogdoches several times to express their desire for peace. They met little response at first, for a paralysis of anger and suspicion gripped the Texas frontier. Tejas involvement in the San Sabá affair had undermined the Spaniards' confidence in all Indians, and Parrilla's reports of French complicity with the Taovayas had freshly strained relations between Texas and Louisiana.

Unfortunately, a new governor had to deal with the rising tensions: Ángel Martos y Navarrete replaced Governor Barrios in 1759. The change of administrations aggravated difficulties with the Indians, for Martos had first to investigate charges concerning his predecessor's trade with the Indians. Until the new governor comprehended the practical necessities to which Barrios had bent the law, Indians in East Texas suffered an annoying interruption of the Los Adaes trade. It was also hard for Martos to comprehend and accept the extra-legal accommodations with Natchitoches that made life in East Texas possible for Spaniards.

Just when the post–San Sabá tensions were at their worst and the governor was still green, two Bidais experimented with stirring up a little war. Exiled from their own village for mischievous lying, they

had gone to live at the plantation of St. Denis. Apparently unaware
of their bad habits, St. Denis asked them to invite the Akokisas to visit
him at Natchitoches to receive presents, an amenity he observed with
many tribes of the region. The two outcasts embroidered the invitation
with their own puckish invention: that St. Denis wished the Indians to
kill all the Spaniards and destroy Presidio San Agustín. Both the
Akokisas and the Bidais rebuffed them sharply. A little later they
sheepishly returned to confess their lie, explaining that they had
merely wished to test the devotion of the Bidais and the Akokisas to
the Spaniards.[15]

The slander against St. Denis quickly reached the ear of Governor
Martos; the retraction did not. He dashed off an indignant protest to
Governor Kerlérec and for good measure relayed Parrilla's suggestions
of French responsibility for arming the Taovayas and their cohorts.

In response, Kerlérec chided the Spaniards for blaming all Indians'
firearms on Frenchmen, pointing out that Barrios had sold all kinds of
goods to the Tawakonis and other *bárbaros* and that the three Spanish
missions regularly obtained from Natchitoches proscribed trade articles
to distribute to their Indian communities. It was fatuous to suppose
that circulation of goods among the several nations could be controlled.
The accusation against St. Denis raised graver questions. If false, it
was an intolerable slander against the scion of an excellent family; if
true, a vicious crime against the peace of the frontier and the honor of
France. Kerlérec promised a thorough investigation. He urged Governor Martos meanwhile to maintain good relations with de Blanc
of Natchitoches and to remember the high value of Indian allies.[16]

French investigators hurried to the Bidai country: St. Denis himself, understandably annoyed and eager to expose the lie; and Athanase
de Mézières, then commander of the Natchitoches garrison, gravely
concerned about the slur upon the reputation of his brother-in-law and
upon the honor of France. They accomplished their errand quickly,
for the Bidais and Akokisas gladly exposed the mischief-makers. Another problem engaged St. Denis and de Mézières: the plight of the
friars at Mission Nacogdoches, who suffered from the bullying, in-
sulting, thieving behavior of Indians caught up in sullen unrest since

[15] Certified copy of proceedings held by Martos y Navarrete to investigate
charges . . . , Los Adaes, January 1, 1761–May 28, 1761, BA.

[16] Kerlérec to Martos y Navarrete, New Orleans, March 13, 1760, translated in
a certified copy of an *expediente* dealing with the problem of French efforts to
influence the natives against the Spaniards, March 3, 1760–May 5, 1760, BA.

San Sabá. Concerned for the safety of the friars and the tranquillity of the frontier, the two French officers rode to the Nacogdoches village to intervene. They summoned the chiefs and leading men of the region and, with practiced skill, harangued them into a state of repentance. The Tejas leaders then prevailed upon the two Frenchmen to help them restore good relations with the mission friars and to solicit peace on behalf of the Tawakonis and their allies.[17]

Although suspicious of the French officers and their Indian friends, Fray Calahorra promised to relay their peace proposals to Governor Martos, and he was amazed to see how his promise delighted the Indians. To prove their sincerity, some voluntarily returned horses they had stolen from the missions. The Tawakonis' principal chief hurried to the Nacogdoches settlement for the negotiations and, in the presence of St. Denis and de Mézières, accepted peace terms formulated by the council. In the future, the nations would hand over to the governor any offender against the missions or against any Spaniards; they would return the two field cannons left by Parrilla; and they would not commit hostilities against any Apaches who were under Spanish protection and in good standing with Spanish authorities.

The Tawakoni chief urged Fray Calahorra to visit his village the next month to help to impress the peace agreement upon all the people. The old priest promised to try, but it was mid-September before he received the necessary permission from Governor Martos, with provisions, presents, and escorts. During the interval, he begged the government not to campaign against the Norteños.

The summer of 1760 passed peacefully. When Parrilla helped the viceroy review policy toward the Apaches and the Norteños, Fray Calahorra's reports and recommendations supplied a countervailing perspective. The viceroy authorized no further campaigns against the Norteños and apparently did authorize Martos to accept their peace overtures. For their part, the Norteños refrained from attacking the Spanish frontier, to the surprise and relief of the worried populace of San Antonio.[18]

---

[17] De Mézières' account of the affair appears in El Cavallero Macarty to Martos y Navarrete, Natchitos, September 10, 1763, BA; Fray Calahorra to Martos y Navarrete, Nacogdoches, May 27, 1760, AGI, Audiencia de México [Dunn Transcripts, UT Archives], is published in translation in Leroy Johnson, Jr., and Edward B. Jelks, "The Tawakoni-Yscani Village, 1760: A Study in Archaeological Site Identification," *Texas Journal of Science* 10 (1958): 409–410.

[18] Martos y Navarrete to the Alcaldes and Regidores of San Fernando, Los Adaes, October 10, 1760, BA.

That autumn Fray Calahorra journeyed to the Tawakonis with half a dozen soldiers from Los Adaes and an interpreter supplied by the French at his request. En route, he visited the Ainai village twenty miles from his mission and from that point had another hundred traveling companions from the Tejas and other nations. Six days later, they reached the Tawakoni village on the Sabine,[19] for a memorable experience of Indian hospitality.

A greeting party from the village escorted them the last ten miles, and all the men, women, and children turned out to welcome them. The four principal chiefs, presumably two Tawakonis and two Iscanis, showed the entire retinue to campaign tents prepared to accommodate them. The lavish welcoming banquet was just the first of eight that the four chiefs provided in turn, each in his own home, during the eight-day visit. After the stringent economy of mission life, Fray Calahorra found their unstinting hospitality almost overwhelming.

With ample time to observe the villages and the people, Fray Calahorra liked everything he saw. The Tawakonis and Iscanis had built their villages side by side on a beautiful meadow beside the Sabine. Only a village street separated the two, and each was handsomely arranged in an orderly pattern of streets and gardens. The *okonitsas* had performed admirably. Abundant pastures nearby supported a herd of excellent horses; less than three miles from the village the people farmed rich blacklands that they jealously guarded against encroachment. They regularly marketed crop surpluses to nearby tribes. The orderly efficiency of their agriculture and the quantity and quality of their harvest were unmatched in the Spanish settlements.

Fray Calahorra quickly concluded that these peoples and lands should be embraced within the realms of both Majesties. They were not numerous, just 47 big grass houses altogether, with a dozen families to each, and only 250 warriors. In order to defend themselves against the Spaniards or any other foe, they were building fortifications and underground shelters, presumably like those which had served the Taovayas so well when Parrilla invaded their land.

Peace ceremonies were delayed until the Taovayas delegation could arrive from their village, five days distant. A chief brought twenty men and six women to convey the peaceful greetings of all their people.

[19] Fray Calahorra, Diario del Viage, Nacogdoches, September 16, 1760–October 24, 1760, AGI, Audiencia de México [Dunn Transcripts, UT Archives]. The diary is translated in Johnson and Jelks, "The Tawakoni-Yscani Village, 1760," pp. 411–414, along with their analysis of his route and identification of the village site.

They offered to turn over Parrilla's two cannons if Fray Calahorra would visit them the following summer. The priest gladly agreed to attempt the onerous journey, for they promised to escort him to New Mexico, fifteen days from their village, and also to take him to the intervening land of the Seauttos, or Apaches Pelones, with whom they were presently at war. Those were heady prospects for a frontier friar: to open communication between the provinces of Texas and New Mexico and then to carry his peace-making mission into the heartland of the Apaches Pelones, who had in their time threatened New Mexico and Coahuila as well as Texas.

Toward the end of his visit, Fray Calahorra distributed the presents sent by Governor Martos. The grateful Indians insisted upon giving the travelers provisions of corn, pinole, and meat for their homeward journey. Fray Calahorra promised to return the next year. In spite of advancing years and uncertain health, he was determined to keep his promise if God would let him.

During Fray Calahorra's first sojourn with the Tawakonis and Iscanis, Captain Rábago took command at San Sabá. Not long afterward, he launched his own vigorous program of protection for the Apaches. Despite that untoward development, the Wichitan bands kept their promises of friendship with the Spaniards. In the spring of 1761, they held aloof from horse raids made by the Tonkawas, Yojuanes, and Mayeyes around San Antonio, and so informed Fray Calahorra. Chief Canos, of the Tejas, escorted Taovayas and Tawakoni leaders to Mission Nacogdoches to help them report.[20] Annoyed because they suspected the Tonkawas were trying to cast the blame on the Tawakonis, they had sent envoys to demand the stolen property; when the Tonkawas refused, they declared their intention of going to war against them. The Tawakonis offered yet more proof of their friendship for the Spaniards: they had rescued three captive New Mexican Spaniards from Apaches Pelones and would turn them over to Fray Calahorra on his next visit.

Again, Fray Calahorra had to postpone his intended summer visit until autumn, but his reception was even warmer than before.[21] He

[20] Fray Calahorra to Martos y Navarrete, Nacogdoches, May 6, 1761, in AGI, Audiencia de México [Dunn Transcripts, UT Archives].

[21] Fray Calahorra to Martos y Navarrete, Nacogdoches, October 18, 1761, in AGI, Audiencia de México [Dunn Transcripts, UT Archives]; Marqués de Cruillas to Martos y Navarrete, Veracruz, October 1, 1762, BA; Martos y Navarrete, Report on investigation of the Tawakoni mission proposal of Fray Calahorra, Los Adaes, May 7, 1763, BA.

bore three certificates of captaincy for the principal chiefs, appropriate
canes of office, and Spanish flags, one each for the Tawakonis, Iscanis,
and Taovayas. While all the villagers watched, Fray Calahorra and his
interpreter explained the solemn obligations of the office and of vassalage to the king of Spain, then gravely bestowed the symbols upon
El Flechado en la Cara of the Tawakonis and Llaso (Zurdo) of the
Iscanis. The ceremony ended joyously with the distribution of presents
from Governor Martos to all the Tawakonis and Iscanis. The Tawakonis and Iscanis took splendid care of their Spanish guests through
eight days of dancing and singing.

Fray Calahorra's health would not permit him to journey to the
Taovayas as he had hoped. He left with the Tawakonis the presents
and honors intended for the Taovayas and returned to Nacogdoches
with the two New Mexican women and one child whom the Tawakonis
had rescued from the Apaches Pelones.

That departure was not easy. The Tawakonis and Iscanis had grown
so fiercely determined to have Spaniards come to live with them and
to have their own mission that their insistence burgeoned into riotous
demonstrations. They threatened to detain Fray Calahorra forcibly and
make him establish a mission for them. To the considerable relief of
Lieutenant Pedro de Sierra and the half-dozen soldiers of the escort,
Fray Calahorra bargained his way out of the village by promising to
return to found a mission and stay with them permanently.

Expediency dictated the promise, but Fray Calahorra truly wished
to keep his word. The conspicuously able and good-hearted Tawakonis
and Iscanis would make splendid converts; with their rich lands and
agricultural skills, a mission would prosper. Galled to see such people
neglected while public resources and private philanthropy supported
the continuing fiasco at San Sabá, Fray Calahorra proposed that the
Apache project be abandoned and those resources reallocated to a
Tawakoni mission.

Governor Martos forwarded that recommendation to the viceroy with
his own favorable endorsement. The next autumn, when the Tawakonis
expected Fray Calahorra back, his proposal for their mission was in
the viceregal mill in Mexico City. On October 1, 1762, the viceroy
asked Governor Martos to make a thorough investigation, obtaining
more information from Fray Calahorra and interrogating the soldiers
who had escorted him. Priests sometimes let zeal and piety blur their
factual judgment; New Spain could not afford such a blunder now.
However, if Fray Calahorra were correct, the interests of both Majes-

ties demanded support of his proposition. At the same time, the viceroy also asked the priests at new, unauthorized Apache missions on the Nueces River to report their progress and make recommendations for their future.

Governor Martos' investigations, completed in spring 1763, completely supported Fray Calahorra. Even more extravagantly than the priest, the soldiers praised the Tawakonis' hospitality, their zeal for missions, and their superb lands.

Unfortunately, in the year and a half since Fray Calahorra's proposal, new developments had strained the friendship of the Wichitan bands for the Spaniards and even for each other. In the autumn of 1761, when Fray Calahorra proposed transferring the San Sabá resources to a Tawakoni project, Captain Rábago brought to a climax his own efforts to shore up the ill-starred venture.[22] By November 1761, he had nearly completed construction of an improved stone fort. As he hoped, the better defenses encouraged some Apaches to camp nearby on the San Saba River. Two big Norteño war parties pursued them there that fall, but left without attempting any damage. Thus encouraged, Rábago plied the Lipans with presents and hospitality and pressed the argument that their best interests lay in settled mission life, now that they had lost most of their territories to the Comanches and other Norteños and feared to hunt buffalo on the plains.

His comments gave the Lipan leaders a convenient opening: they asked him to detail soldiers to escort them on buffalo hunts. By the end of 1761, Rábago had supplied escorts on five hunts. He congratulated himself on having obligated the Lipans to the Spaniards.

Lipan leaders did bargain for those escorts. The first time, several chiefs promised to bring their people to live in a mission after one last buffalo hunt. All autumn, Rábago received more promises, but never any Apache neophytes. In mid-October El Gran Cabezón, a particularly distinguished band chief, promised to bring his people. Delighted with that apparent breakthrough, Captain Rábago summoned Fray Diego Jiménez, president of the Rio Grande missions, to meet with the prospective neophytes. Early in November, El Gran Cabezón brought ten other Lipan chiefs, all of whom testified that their people wished to take up mission life. They agreed to recognize El Gran

---

[22] The story of Rábago's relations with the Apaches and their record at El Cañon is developed in detail in Curtis D. Tunnell and W. W. Newcomb, Jr., *A Lipan Apache Mission*, pp. 162 ff.

Cabezón as their head chief and authorized spokesman, a commitment they did not long honor.

To the dismay of Rábago and Fray Jiménez, El Gran Cabezón flatly refused to settle on the San Saba. The earlier tragedy there, the alarming proximity of Comanches and Norteños, and their continual horse thefts from the presidio convinced the chief that the area would never be safe for Apaches, even in the shadow of Rábago's stone fort. He would consider settling on the upper Nueces River, halfway between the San Saba and the Rio Grande, a rugged area well known to Apaches but not yet penetrated by Comanches and Norteños. Besides dictating a new location, El Gran Cabezón set three conditions: more soldiers than ever before must be detailed for a big buffalo hunt; the daughter of his kinsman, the big chief of the Natagés, must be returned to her people from captivity somewhere in Nuevo León; and soldiers must accompany the Apaches on their campaigns against the Comanches during the prickly-pear season.

Rábago balked at the third point. For all his impulsiveness and indiscretion, he would not go looking for a war with the Comanches. The first two conditions seemed sensible enough to both Rábago and Fray Jiménez. It would be helpful if the Apaches could bring plenty of meat to the new mission so that the friars would not have to feed them at first. Coahuila needed relief from the robberies committed there by Mescaleros, and the Natagé chief had promised to make them desist if his daughter were returned to him. If Mescaleros should persist in raiding, the Natagé chief would take the horses from them and deliver them to Rábago for restoration to their owners. He would also take away from the Mescaleros all their horses, women, and children. That too appeared a good bargain. Captain Rábago agreed, and El Gran Cabezón led his people off on their big fall hunt with much of the San Sabá garrison.

Meanwhile, Fray Jiménez hurried back to the Rio Grande to secure supplies for the new mission from the established missions of San Juan Bautista and San Bernardo. Given the ephemeral nature of Lipan enthusiasm for mission life, he dared not wait for the customary viceregal and collegial authorizations. Although doubtful of the Lipans' sincerity and persistence, Fray Jiménez did respect Rábago's enthusiasm for the project, and personal inspection had persuaded him that the proposed location on the Nueces would accommodate three missions.[23]

---

[23] Robert S. Weddle, *San Juan Bautista*, pp. 268 ff.

Late in December 1761, El Gran Cabezón led his band back to San Sabá and demanded to be taken to the Nueces at once. Rábago sent a courier for Fray Jiménez, then, early in January, personally led thirty soldiers south to the Nueces with El Gran Cabezón and his people, a week-long trek. Within another week, Fray Jiménez joined them with Fray Joaquín Baños, a load of provisions and tools, and Indians from Mission San Bernardo to help build an irrigation ditch so that corn could be planted that spring.

Everyone agreed that the resources of the valley, which they called El Cañon, would support the proposed missions: abundant water of good quality, plenty of irrigable land, lush pastures, plentiful and varied timber. On January 23, 1762, the Spanish officers and priests and the Lipan leaders ceremoniously founded Mission San Lorenzo de la Santa Cruz (at present Camp Wood, Texas). On a flat knoll above a spring stood a hut with a cross before it, the temporary chapel. Some three hundred of El Gran Cabezón's band attended the service; so did other Indians not yet committed to mission life. After the Mass, Captain Rábago made a speech about the spiritual and material advantages enjoyed by faithful vassals of the two Majesties. El Gran Cabezón courteously assured the captain that his people indeed desired the protection and governance of the Spanish king; right now, they wished to be given possession of the spring and the land. Rábago agreed. As they walked together across the land, El Gran Cabezón uprooted some grass, scooped up water, and watered some stones he had gathered. The Lipan interpreter, who had learned Spanish during a long captivity, explained that these acts symbolized their possession of the land. Rábago appointed El Gran Cabezón captain of the settlement of Santa Cruz, but he postponed other appointments until the Lipans could learn more about Spanish civil government.

Captain Rábago had already exceeded his authority by founding a new mission a hundred miles from his presidio; now Fray Jiménez pressed him to a greater indiscretion. He demanded a sizable squad of soldiers to protect the new mission against the Lipans, whose reliability he doubted, and to secure both priests and neophytes against enemy Indians. Rábago gave him twenty soldiers, not only illegally but also imprudently, in view of the precarious condition of Presidio San Luis.

The outlook for Santa Cruz seemed promising enough, if only its provisions would hold out and the Spaniards could appear strong enough to intimidate and to protect the Lipans. Many more Lipans visited the new settlement, and several band chiefs expressed interest in making similar arrangements sometime soon. El Turnio, whose band numbered four or five hundred, chose a site ten miles downstream and demanded a mission for his people before Mission San Lorenzo was two weeks old. Rábago demurred: he had neither soldiers nor missionaries to spare for another foundation. El Turnio insisted, in a manner suggesting that everyone would suffer if he were not given equal treatment with El Gran Cabezón. Thus, on February 6, 1762, Mission Nuestra Señora de la Candelaria was born. Rábago gave El Turnio possession of the spring and the lands, showed him where the village should be laid out in the Spanish pattern, and appointed him governor of the village. El Turnio sulked when Rábago allotted only ten soldiers to guard Mission Candelaria. He envied the twenty at El Gran Cabezón's mission and doubted that ten soldiers would suffice if Comanches should find El Cañon. Captain Rábago also had reason to be glum. He had weakened San Sabá by detaching thirty men from its garrison without permission, and he had no assurance that either segment could survive a determined onslaught by well-armed Norteños and Comanches.

The Lipans' enemies were not slow to find them. In March 1762, Comanches destroyed a Lipan *ranchería* in a canyon near San Lorenzo; in May, they killed forty persons when they attacked another. Fourteen more Lipans died in a July raid. The raiders never approached the missions where the soldiers stood guard; the soldiers were too few to pursue the aggressors. The Lipans stuck close to Spanish protection. When the men left in June to hunt buffalo, their women and children stayed at the missions for safety. Then, and on subsequent hunts, most parties courteously obtained written consent from Fray Jiménez. He knew they would go anyway, but he liked them to carry his permission lest someone from San Sabá should meet them and think them deserters or hostiles.

As many as a dozen bands established some tie with the missions at El Cañon, though the stable core was limited to the four bands of El Gran Cabezón, El Turnio, Teja, and Boruca. More promised to settle there permanently as soon as there were more soldiers to protect them, and the mission fathers thought that reasonable. After all, they could hardly support more Indians unless the viceroy would sanction the new missions and provide a budget.

By early summer, the Taovayas knew of the new favors to Apaches at San Sabá and El Cañon, and their tolerance was exhausted. In

June 1762, they made several raids on the horse herd at San Sabá, killing three Spaniards and stealing seventy horses. The Tawakonis objected so strongly to the breach of peace with the Spaniards that they went to war over the matter before the year ended.[24] If the Taovayas suffered any untoward consequences from the raids, Tawakonis inflicted them. The divided San Sabá garrison had too few men to pursue raiders.

Throughout the summer of 1762, the Norteños pursued their vendetta with the Lipans and surely observed Rábago's deepening involvement with their enemies. Yet, they tried to avoid war with the Spaniards. On June 12, just thirty miles out of Béxar, a big party of Norteños fell upon a pack train bound for San Sabá. Four Tejas identified the train as Spanish and persuaded their associates to check the attack. They rode up for an amicable chat with the Spaniards, and for the rest of the summer the Norteños let the monthly supply trains move unmolested between the two presidios.[25] They also refrained from attacking San Antonio, although they were blamed for the death of one Indian from Mission San Antonio.

Norteños scored heavily against the Lipans in the San Antonio sphere that summer. They attacked a *ranchería* on the Frio River, where their captives included the sister of Chief Bigotes, destroyed another on the Guadalupe River, on the road to San Sabá, and killed more than forty Apache hunters on the Colorado River.

As their situation worsened, many Apaches fell back south of San Antonio. Since they dared not venture to the plains for buffalo, they found their meat in the livestock herds of San Antonio; as they lost mounts to the enemy, they replaced them also from San Antonio herds. The mounting toll exasperated the community, but Captain Urrutia lacked the manpower to protect their property. Twenty-two Béxar soldiers had been seconded to San Sabá. It took most of the remaining soldiers to guard the five missions and patrol approaches to the settlement. On a normal day, only five soldiers and one sergeant remained available for duty in the presidio. The Apaches knew the weakness of Béxar; Captain Urrutia feared the Norteños would soon find out.[26]

In mid-August Norteños were reported gathering on the San Antonio River to pursue Apaches. Aware that some had suffered injury from

[24] Fray Calahorra to Martos y Navarrete, Nacogdoches Mission, July 6, 1763, BA.

[25] Martos y Navarrete, Villa of San Fernando, September 15, 1762, BA.

[26] Toribio de Urrutia to Martos y Navarrete, Béxar, August 14, 1762, BA.

Parrilla's campaign, Captain Urrutia feared they might be tempted to wreak vengeance on Béxar if they should see it so ill-manned, even if they entered the area with peaceful intent.

Governor Martos could not give Urrutia the reinforcements he wanted, but he rushed from Los Adaes to Béxar to manage the situation personally. He did not believe there were any real grounds to fear this Norteño party, led by the Tejas chiefs Sanches, Canos, and Nason, all long-standing friends of the Spaniards. They had explained their current campaign to Governor Martos: they believed the Apaches had deliberately incited them to attack San Sabá in order to rid themselves of the friars, and they were very angry about the deception. Martos thought the Apaches deserved any punishment the Norteños could inflict. For his part, if war had to break out in the province, he would rather fight the Apaches than the numerous, well-armed Norteños.

Still, vigilance was in order. Big aggregations of Indians were volatile, and Martos realized that, except for the Tejas, they could easily turn hostile. Some unreliable elements were mixed up in the party: Sautos, Tonkawas, Hierbipiames, Yojuanes, Mayeyes.[27] Gentleness, discretion, conciliatory manner, all were necessary to their safe entertainment at San Antonio, and Martos hurried westward to make certain Urrutia understood that. He also insisted that the Béxar commander control the flow of guns and ammunition from his settlement to the Apaches. The settlers' irresponsible sales not only made Apaches more dangerous; they could provoke the Norteños to hostilities against the Spaniards.

The test that Captain Urrutia dreaded came on September 13, 1762, when four hundred warriors of ten interior nations visited San Antonio to convey their peaceful greetings. They scattered through the settlement and certainly could have destroyed it if they had wished, but they offered no harm. Even so, Captain Urrutia kept pleading for reinforcements. Dismayed that they had seen Béxar presidio with so few men, he feared they would sometime return in anger to take advantage of its weakness. He also suspected that the Norteños' visit had irritated the Apaches and that increased depredations would follow from that quarter.[28]

[27] The four latter were Tonkawan bands, some of whom were now merging as a result of their heavy casualties. More curious is the inclusion of the Sautos, a name generally equated with Apaches Pelones by East Texas sources in the 1760's. This may indicate that the Norteños had, at least temporarily, drawn that group into war against the Lipans.

[28] Toribio de Urrutia, Béxar, September 13, 1762, BA.

The infant missions at El Cañon soon felt the Lipans' reaction. The Indians asked Fray Jiménez for permission to go foraging for food, and they made it clear that they would leave with or without his consent because Comanches and Norteños were planning an attack. Since the thirty soldiers at El Cañon were unequal to such an emergency, Fray Jiménez made little effort to detain his charges, though he did tell them that the Comanches had promised on their visit to San Antonio not to attack any Lipans in missions. The priest found that just as hard to believe as did the Lipans. Anyway, he was running too short of supplies to support so many people.[29]

Soon after the Lipans left El Cañon, Fray Jiménez heard that Comanches had indeed attacked one *ranchería*, killing people and stealing horses, but he could not learn immediately which band had suffered the loss. He remained reasonably confident that the Lipans would come back to El Cañon. The mission buildings were well on the way to completion in the autumn of 1762, and the stout adobe structures had excited the Lipans' interest. They particularly admired the big warehouse then under construction, potentially a marvelous place to hide from enemies, and had asked to have similarly built houses. Fray Jiménez had promised them. Many did return that winter to the cluster of adobe buildings. Their behavior convinced the priests that they were now seriously interested in becoming true converts to mission life.

While the Lipans enjoyed their two new missions at El Cañon and exploited to the hilt the escort privileges that Captain Rábago granted their hunters, the Tawakonis and Iscanis waited in vain for some response to their own appeal for missions. After more than a year's wait, they sent three of their leaders to Mission Nacogdoches to fetch Fray Calahorra in December 1762. When he learned they were at war with the Taovayas because the latter had offended Spanish interests at San Sabá, he agonized over his government's failure to cultivate their friendship, but his hands were tied. Tawakoni and Iscani emissaries begged him again and again that spring to come, but not until mid-summer of 1763 could Fray Calahorra obtain the governor's permission for the trip and the necessary escort and supplies.[30]

Though he had yet to hear from the viceroy, Governor Martos dared wait no longer to conciliate the Indian peoples of his jurisdiction. He

---

[29] Tunnell and Newcomb, *A Lipan Apache Mission*, pp. 169–170.

[30] Fray Calahorra to Martos y Navarrete, Nacogdoches Mission, June 6, 1763, BA; Martos y Navarrete to Calahorra, Los Adaes, July 9, 1763, BA.

gathered up the best presents available at Los Adaes for Fray Calahorra to carry to the Tawakonis and Iscanis and also gave him special
gifts to present to the Tejas leaders en route. With the same soldiers
who had escorted him earlier and had testified in support of his
Tawakoni mission proposal, Fray Calahorra hurried to the Tawakoni-
Iscani settlement in July. He found them as eager as ever to have a
mission.

Much less cordial were the twenty-two Taovayas delegates who confronted him to demand a mission for their people and removal of
San Sabá presidio to their own territory. The Taovayas spokesman
minced no words: "The harm we cause is your fault, Father, because
you and the Big Captain are liars. You could already have placed
a mission and the Presidio of San Sabá between us and the Tawakonis
and we would have been peaceful."[31]

The Taovayas had had three years of promises, but their village
had yet to see a priest or any other Spanish visitor. Now they promised
to behave better than the Tawakonis if the Spaniards would live with
them and give them a mission. The delegates had brought horses to
carry Fray Calahorra back to their village, but he had to disappoint
them for want of authorization to extend his trip. He promised to
support their request, then hurried back to report it to the governor,
with still more disconcerting news.[32]

To the friar's utter consternation, French flags flew over the Tawakoni and Iscani villages, just below the rightful Spanish flags. They
were gifts from the commandant of Natchitoches, delivered by a
Frenchman who had also brought a captain's commission for Cuernitos.

Outraged that Frenchmen dared fly their flag over Indians in his
jurisdiction, Governor Martos protested to Natchitoches, demanding
that both the flag and Cuernitos' French commission be withdrawn.
Promptly came back the refusal of Athanase de Mézières, who had
taken charge of Natchitoches upon the death of Césaire de Blanc.[33]

De Mézières had not the slightest intention of sending anyone to the
Tawakoni-Iscani settlement to recall the French flags: they would
surely kill the messengers. They had venerated that flag nearly half
a century, ever since the time of La Harpe. De Mézières acidly noted
that it would go very hard with the Spaniards if he should have to

[31] Calahorra to Martos y Navarrete, Nacogdoches Mission, August 20, 1763, BA.
[32] Ibid.; also Governor Martos y Navarrete, Interrogation of the soldiers who
escorted Fray Calahorra to the Tawakonis, Los Adaes, May 19, 1763, BA.
[33] El Cavallero Macarty to Martos y Navarrete, Natchitos, September 10, 1763,
BA.

explain to the Tawakonis that he had to take the flag back because of Spanish enmity toward the Frenchmen. Reviewing the long history of Franco-Tawakoni relations and the several occasions on which St. Denis *père* and *fils* and their associates had intervened with Indians on behalf of the Spaniards, de Mézières reminded Governor Martos that the Tawakonis had only made peace with the Spaniards in the first place because the Frenchmen had persuaded them on grounds of friendship between Spain and France.

Governor Martos could only swallow his pride and anger and step up his competition for the friendship of the Indians in the region. At the end of 1763, his accounts showed that he had distributed powder to the Tawakonis, Iscanis, Bidais, Adaes, Ais, Nacogdoches, and unspecified "other" Indians.[34] He also grew more deeply involved in the Indian trade, relying heavily on merchandise procured from Natchitoches, and thus grew more vulnerable to criticism and disgrace as damning rumors reached Mexico City.

While Governor Martos and Fray Calahorra tried to conciliate the Norteños with promises and presents, events at San Antonio, San Sabá, and El Cañon continued to erode their good will. It was impossible for the Norteños to keep their promise not to attack Lipans under Spanish protection while Lipan warriors seized every opportunity to lash out from that sanctuary against their enemies. In the fall of 1763, some angry Norteños perpetrated damages in the San Antonio settlement and promised to pursue their vengeance further in spring. Perhaps their ruffled feelings could have been soothed by the veteran Captain Urrutia, who had dealt with them successfully the year before and understood Governor Martos' policies for their treatment. Unfortunately, the old captain died in the winter of 1762.

His successor, Captain Luis Antonio Menchaca, more fighter than diplomat, took a very skeptical view of Governor Martos' desire to cultivate the Norteños. Thus, after Norteños struck at San Antonio on October 2, Captain Menchaca appealed directly to the viceroy for reinforcements to prepare Béxar presidio against the promised spring hostilities. Adopting the captain's view that a vigorous defense would teach the enemy a needed lesson, Viceroy Cruillas seconded eighty soldiers to Béxar for the duration of the emergency, twenty-five to come at once from Los Adaes, twenty-five more from the new colony on the Gulf of Mexico, and thirty to be drawn from the presidios of

[34] Martos y Navarrete, Statement of gunpowder used in 1763, Los Adaes, January 2, 1764, BA.

Monclova and Santa Rosa.[35] Thoroughly dismayed, Governor Martos had no choice but to dispatch the twenty-five soldiers under the capable command of Los Adaes' Lieutenant Pedro de Sierra.

Perhaps the new concentration of troops warded the Norteños away from San Antonio; perhaps raiders from the Lipan camps around San Sabá and El Cañon drew more vengeful pursuit upon those areas. At any rate, the principal targets of Norteño and Comanche warriors in 1764 were those westerly outposts rather than Béxar. Captain Rábago called for help in the summer of 1764, pleading that his presidio could not survive the enemy onslaught without reinforcements. Viceroy Cruillas ordered troops there from Béxar, including the Los Adaes detachment whose return to home base Governor Martos had urgently requested.[36]

The strain of mounting hostilities told heavily upon the Lipans. The outlook for those in the missions worsened when other Apaches intensified raids in Coahuila and Texas. The consequent toll of lives and property seemed to support the contention that it was folly to trust Apaches, and even worse to try to convert them. Fray Jiménez and Captain Rábago pleaded that justice required distinctions among various Apaches, but even they painted a picture clouded with confusion.

Rábago reported that Apaches distinguished three divisions: Mescaleros, Natagés, and Lipans. Fray Jiménez emphasized the great difference between Lipan and Mescalero life styles, noting that the enemy onslaught had driven the Lipans to give up their fixed agricultural *rancherías*. He thought that in earlier times some Lipans had intermarried with Mescaleros and with Apaches,[37] but that practice had died; a bit of trade was their sole remaining connection. The friar attributed the weakening of ties among the groups to the Lipans' growing rapprochement with the Spaniards, which provoked resentment among the other groups. The Mescaleros had stolen half a dozen horses from the Lipans since the missions were founded at El Cañon, and they had twice urged the Lipans to join with them to fight the Spaniards. After the Lipans had rejected those propositions, Fray Jiménez thought they had grown more united among themselves.

[35] Marqués de Cruillas to Martos y Navarrete, Mexico, January 6, 1764, BA.

[36] Marqués de Cruillas to Martos y Navarrete, Mexico, September 10, 1764, BA.

[37] Apparently Fray Jiménez applies the name Apache to the Natagé division in this instance, but later in the same document he says that Lipans apply the term Apache to the same Indians whom Spaniards know as Mescaleros.

Some other Apaches had joined the Lipans after that, apparently preferring the Lipans' strategy of friendship with the Spaniards to continual warfare.[38]

Even as he defended the Lipans' cause, the missionary documented the difficulties of living with Apache "friends" who had horses and guns and who lived in their own territory. They often were truculent toward the priests; they dictated the terms on which they lived at the missions. The missionaries feared there would never be any true discipline or order at El Cañon without a strong military garrison to impose it.

Late in 1764 a smallpox epidemic swept the Lipans at El Cañon. Of the forty-five children and twenty-nine adults whom the priests baptized in *articulo mortis*, most died; there is no record of those who died unbaptized. The Lipans' nativist response to their new tragedy bewildered Fray Jiménez. Many had recurring visions of an old man, often in battle, and spread his message: fight a continuing war with neighboring nations and Spaniards; avoid baptism, on pain of prompt death. Those who died fighting at his behest were promised resurrection and reunion with their kinsmen in some Lipan paradise. Some shamans became vigorous exponents of his movement. Fray Jiménez had good reason to fear for the continued existence of the missions.[39]

El Cañon still had some value to the Lipans as a refuge: for another two years their enemies honored their promise not to attack Lipans in missions. No Lipan camp away from the mission sites was secure from attack. Around San Sabá, Norteños no longer hesitated to attack hunting parties escorted by Spanish soldiers. Indeed, they seemed to turn a special fury upon the Spaniards, as though to destroy those who shielded their enemies.

The Los Adaes detachment, sent to San Sabá from Béxar for emergency duty in the fall of 1764, found themselves assigned to the escort duty that rarely failed to provoke Norteño retaliation. Three of their number fell to the enemy before they were permitted late that winter to return home, guarding a horse herd consigned to Los Adaes.

Heavy rains and swollen rivers slowed their progress so badly that they ran out of supplies before they reached Mission Nacogdoches. Lieutenant Sierra halted his men and stock there to rest and await the

[38] Fray Jiménez, September 9, 1763, quoted in Tunnell and Newcomb, *A Lipan Apache Mission*, p. 170.

[39] Ibid., pp. 171–172.

supplies he had requested from Governor Martos.[40] To his sympathetic old friend, Fray Calahorra, he confided his disgust with the San Sabá fiasco.

Lieutenant Sierra despised the Apaches as much as he admired the Tawakonis, to whose village he had twice escorted Fray Calahorra. He considered the Apaches incorrigible thieves, driven by mortal hatred of the Norteños. They would venture as far north as the Taovayas village to steal horses. Pursuing Taovayas saw them arrive with the horses at San Sabá and naturally assumed that the Spaniards had sent them to raid, or at least had consented to the deed. The Norteños saw more evidence of Spanish enmity every time soldiers escorted Apache hunters. The Spanish soldiers' heavy equipment limited their ability to maneuver on horseback, making them so vulnerable to mounted Indians that Lieutenant Sierra believed their casualty rate would run high as long as Rábago pursued his reckless policy. The officer especially resented the sacrifice of three of his own men, whom he believed had been killed by Comanches while on escort duty.

Lieutenant Sierra reckoned without the toughness of one of his soldiers and without the shrewdness of the enemy, whose identity he also mistook. Antonio Treviño, a soldier of the Los Adaes detachment, was last seen by his comrades escorting Apache hunters from San Sabá on the winter buffalo hunt. Taovayas attacked. The odds looked so hopeless that Treviño's comrades gave him up for dead, but he resolved to sell his life as dearly as possible. Standing alone, surrounded by forty-seven hostile Indians, with four bullet wounds and two lance wounds, he fought so fiercely that the Taovayas chief, Eyasiquiche, intervened to save his life. Treviño had displayed a bravery and skill in battle highly honored among the Taovayas. Eyasiquiche wanted such a fighter to help him campaign against the Osages. He called off the attacking warriors and persuaded Treviño that he would not be harmed if he would lay down his arms. The chief had Treviño's wounds tended, then bore him back to the Red River, sending ahead news of his great feat and warning the people that this was an honored addition to their forces, not to be torn apart like an ordinary captive.

Treviño lived six months with the Taovayas, winning their friendship as well as their admiration. Eyasiquiche had guessed that Treviño was not one of those San Sabá Spaniards; after all, he did not flee the moment he saw Indians. As they penetrated the communications bar-

---

[40] Pedro de Sierra to Martos y Navarrete, Nacogdoches Mission, March 20, 1765, BA.

rier, the chief was pleased to learn that Treviño hailed from East Texas, whence Fray Calahorra had come to talk with the Tawakonis and Taovayas. Although he desired Treviño's service for his pending campaign against the Osages, Eyasiquiche decided that he would do better to send Treviño home in order to prove his good will toward those Spaniards and to demonstrate the desire of his people to live at peace with them. Hurrying to accomplish the errand before time to head for Osage country, he took Treviño to the Tawakoni–Iscani settlement, whence two Iscanis escorted them to Mission Nacogdoches.

It was an amazing visitation for that stagnant little mission compound: the breechclouted apparition Treviño, his distinguished patron, and their Iscani escorts, on stumbling mounts pressed too far and too fast in the dank July heat. Astonished, grateful Fray Calahorra had in his poor mission no resources equal to the occasion. He begged Eyasiquiche to go with him to Los Adaes to meet Governor Martos and receive his personal thanks. Eyasiquiche courteously refused. He had summoned warriors of several nations to campaign against the Osages and was anxious to be off for their rendezvous. The priest could only send a runner to inform the governor of the extraordinary event, begging him to send an appropriate gift for the chief and to provide good replacements for his exhausted horses.

Restoring Treviño was not Eyasiquiche's only overture. He offered to turn over to someone who would fetch them at his village five captive women and the two cannons that the Taovayas had been offering ever since Fray Calahorra's first visit to the Tawakonis nearly five years earlier. Once more, almost miraculously, there loomed a chance to cement the peace that Fray Calahorra had sought since 1760. The priest begged the governor not to muff it.[41]

Governor Martos did his best. Just five days after Fray Calahorra penned his urgent notice, Lieutenant Sierra left Los Adaes with the governor's reply, the nicest presents available on short notice, and authority to give the visitors three horses from the governor's own stock at Mission Nacogdoches.

Governor Martos desired Fray Calahorra to tell Eyasiquiche that he would do everything he could to preserve the peace but to explain that the Spaniards of San Sabá were one people with those of East

---

[41] Calahorra to Martos y Navarrete, Nacogdoches Mission, July 16, 1765, BA; Martos y Navarrete to Calahorra, Los Adaes, July 21, 1765, BA; Calahorra to Martos y Navarrete, Nacogdoches Mission, July 30, 1765, BA; Fray Calahorra, Certified Interrogation of Taovayas Chief Eyasiquiche, Nacogdoches Mission, July 30, 1765, BA.

Texas. It would be necessary to keep peace with San Sabá in order to be friends with those of Los Adaes and Nacogdoches, because the people of Los Adaes had to defend those of San Sabá when they were attacked. The governor also needed to know how this chief felt about settling in a mission so that he could take appropriate steps to fulfill his wishes.

July was nearly over when Lieutenant Sierra reached Mission Nacogdoches with the governor's gifts and messages. Meanwhile, Apaches surprised the Tawakoni–Iscani settlement, killing and capturing people and stealing all the horses they could find. Fray Calahorra and Eyasiquiche therefore held their formal talk on July 30 freshly reminded of Apache perfidy and Norteño grievances.

Fray Calahorra invited Tejas chiefs Sanches and Canos to interpret. He understood their Caddo language; they understood the Wichita tongue of the Taovayas. Lieutenant Sierra and Treviño witnessed the proceedings. Uncertain how to apportion the gifts, the priest presented the lot to Eyasiquiche, who gave his Iscani escorts what he thought proper and kept the rest. He seemed pleased and grateful and truly sorry that his pending campaign against the Osages ruled out a visit to Los Adaes.

The formal discussions were long. An articulate man with much on his mind, Eyasiquiche first detailed the story of Treviño's capture and his reasons for rescuing him and then for restoring him to his people. Only then did he answer Fray Calahorra's questions about why the Taovayas would not keep the peace at San Sabá after having promised at the Tawakoni village to keep peace with all Spaniards. Then he was blunt: the Taovayas had to attack the Spaniards at San Sabá at every chance because they protected and defended the Apaches so much, escorting them when they went out to hunt for meat, although they knew full well that the Apaches were the mortal enemies of the Norteños and stole horses at their villages. As a case in point, he cited the recent Apache attack on the Tawakoni–Iscani settlement. Eyasiquiche vowed that his people would not cease their hostilities at San Sabá until those Spaniards stopped helping and escorting the Apaches.

Would Eyasiquiche and his people settle in a mission now if the Spaniards would let him choose the location? He would not say without consulting all his people, but he hinted that they had cooled toward mission life because they had never received the promised visit of Fray Calahorra or any other Spaniard.

The company parted cordially. Eyasiquiche hurried off to lead the allied warriors against the Osages, while Fray Calahorra reported their talks to the governor and pleaded for concessions to their demands. Probably the hostilities at San Sabá would worsen now to avenge the Apache raid on the Tawakonis and Iscanis. Fray Calahorra deplored the waste of men's lives in the hopeless cause of converting Apaches, and he grieved to see such excellent Indians as the Taovayas and Tawakonis neglected and antagonized. At the very least, the missionary urged, the governor should respond to the Taovayas' invitation by sending someone to take presents to their village and to bring back the captive women and cannons.

Treviño, then about thirty-four years old, resumed his duties at Los Adaes and supplied the first detailed information about the Taovayas ever available to Spanish authorities.[42] Everything he said underlined the vital importance of cultivating the Taovayas, who were much more formidable than any other Norteño group. With the contiguous small villages of Wichitas and Iscanis, they could muster more than five hundred warriors. They maintained in excellent condition the fortifications that had repulsed Parrilla, and some Frenchman had taught them how to handle the two field cannons. Treviño had seen the pieces lying on the floors of two houses beside the fortress.

During his half-year in their village, Treviño had observed a lively trade with Frenchmen. The Taovayas bartered to the French traders skins of buffalo and deer, captive Apache women and children, and the horses and mules that they now stole from Spaniards as well as Apaches. In return, they acquired muskets, powder and shot, cloth, shirts, and most other articles of clothing that they used.

Although Spaniards had first seen Taovayas pursuing their retreating Apache enemies, Treviño noted that they had been themselves a people in flight. He thought it had been just about eight years since Osages had driven the Taovayas southward to the Red River. He knew that they still lived in dread of the Osages, whom they feared as superior gunmen. On the other hand, guns were only now coming into general use among their numerous Comanche allies. Treviño warned that Texas and New Mexico could expect serious troubles if they should fail to win over the Comanches before that numerous nation could consolidate their skills with firearms. Important enough within themselves, the Taovayas–Wichita villages also held the entrée

[42] Antonio Treviño, Testimonio, Los Adaes, August 13, 1765, BA.

to the Comanchería and thus the key to communications between Texas and New Mexico. From the Spanish point of view, it was a poor place to let French traders entrench.

Perhaps Governor Martos appreciated all the implications of Treviño's report, but he was on his way out of office by the time it came to hand, and his departure heralded a complete breakdown of relations with the Taovayas. In August 1765, Viceroy Cruillas dispatched Hugo O'Conor to Texas on a special assignment: to clean up the scandals at the eastern presidios and to investigate smuggling charges against Governor Martos. Unable to take any new initiatives, Governor Martos endured painful investigations in 1766; then in May 1767 he departed for Mexico City to stand trial on charges drawn by O'Conor. At his own request, O'Conor became governor ad interim of Texas, pledged to reform its rotten administration and to bring all its hostile Indians to heel.[43]

Eyasiquiche's masterly stroke of diplomacy had been in vain. No appropriate response ever reached his village. Before a year had passed, his people were actively raiding around San Antonio as well as San Sabá and were prime targets of O'Conor's wrath. To their mutual misfortune, the Taovayas had proffered their friendship when the Spanish government could not respond.

[43] David M. Vigness, "Don Hugo O'Conor and New Spain's Northeastern Frontier, 1764–1776," *Journal of the West* 6 (1967): 27–40.

CHAPTER 10

Texas,1759-1771

Momentous changes stalked the Spanish as well as the Wichitan world when their fortunes meshed in 1759. In mid-August, as Parrilla's force sallied forth from San Antonio to punish Norteños, the bells of Spain knelled the death of King Fernando VI. In mid-September, as Parrilla scoured the prairies for his Indian quarry, the fall of Quebec spelled the expulsion of France from America. In mid-October, as Parrilla's demoralized troops retreated from the Red River scene of Taovayas triumph, King Carlos III landed in Barcelona, home from Naples to succeed his late half-brother on their father's throne.

Carlos III would be Spain's exemplar of the enlightened despot, his three-decade reign one of Spain's most constructive. Building on foundations of domestic reform laid by his father and half-brother, he promptly undertook an extensive program of administrative and economic reform, long overdue throughout the decaying empire. The caliber of administrators assigned to colonial posts quickly improved, but prerequisite to fundamental reforms were accurate, comprehensive analyses of the empire's manifold problems. The process of study and decision consumed the first decade of the reign. While the Crown pursued its laudable long-range purpose, administrators cautiously marked time, eschewing new initiatives and postponing policy decisions. Thus, the question of relations with the Taovayas and Tawakonis came to the fore just when decision making was virtually suspended in New Spain.

Even without great changes in the offing, no viceroy would have found the problem simple. A jumble of conflicting reports and opinions concerning the Wichitan bands and the Apaches greeted the Marqués de Cruillas, whom Carlos III made viceroy of New Spain in 1760. From Los Adaes and Mission Nacogdoches, Governor Martos and Fray Calahorra urged missions for the Tawakonis and Taovayas and abandonment of the San Sabá project. Colonel Parrilla, reporting in person to the viceroy, advised an opposite course; the maverick Captain Rábago soon translated his own advocacy of the Apache cause into reckless new concessions to the Lipans. From San Antonio, Cruillas first had Captain Urrutia's temperate reports about Norteño behavior there; then followed the angry, alarmist views of Captain Menchaca. Fray Jiménez wrote that his unauthorized missions at El Cañon were viable if only the viceroy would allocate sufficient men and materials. Fray Jiménez and Captain Rábago praised the Lipans' favorable disposition, which assorted oddly with complaints about Apache raiders filed by governors of every province within their striking range. Puzzled, the viceroy sought further clarification from each source. Meanwhile, he temporized.

When Eyasiquiche restored Antonio Treviño to his people in 1765, there was even less likelihood of any satisfactory Spanish response to his grand gesture. José de Gálvez had just reached New Spain as visitador general, with powers exceeding those of the viceroy. The Marqués de Cruillas soon relinquished the office to the Marqués de Croix, a complaisant friend of the visitador, who was content to be caretaker while Gálvez tackled his tremendous task.

Gálvez attached high priority to the northern frontier. *Indios bárbaros* seemed to threaten the very existence of the northern provinces, from the Gila River Valley to Louisiana. In some places the frontier had actually receded before the onslaught. The toll of lives and livestock was nearly incalculable, but one fact stood out clearly: the Crown spent hundreds of thousands of pesos annually on the military budget for the northern provinces and had in return neither order nor security nor prospect of improvement. Why?

Gálvez himself examined beleaguered Sonora. To inspect the entire northern line of defense, he appointed a distinguished veteran officer, the Marqués de Rubí, particularly to evaluate the military establishments and recommend improvements. Since Rubí's duties would take him to Texas, the viceroy asked him to look into the dispute about the relative merits of alliance with Norteños or with Apaches and about the viability of San Sabá and the missions at El Cañon.

If Carlos III could count a decade well spent in orderly quest for reform in New Spain, he could afford no such deliberation in ordering affairs on its northeastern boundaries. When he ascended the throne in 1759, France was floundering badly in the fifth year of the Seven Years' War against Great Britain. Facing the unhappy prospect of a contest for the New World narrowed to Spain and its arch foe, Great Britain, Carlos tried to shore up the faltering French cause. In 1761, he renewed the Family Compact linking the two Bourbon thrones; in 1762, Spain joined France in the war against Britain. That venture cost Carlos Florida and Minorca and a few months' humiliating British occupation of Havana, all in vain: Great Britain virtually ousted France from the western hemisphere.

By way of compensation, France proffered New Orleans and western Louisiana to Spain. That was a dubious prize for Carlos III, already burdened with more territory than he could control, but the alternative was a British Louisiana bordering on New Spain, an unacceptable hazard to the northern mining provinces. Late in 1762, Carlos accepted the French gift. The Treaty of Paris, 1763, confirmed the Mississippi River boundary between the possessions of Spain and Great Britain.

Carlos III moved cautiously toward his new possession, well aware that it presented problems quite unlike those of his older colonies. Rather than attach Louisiana to the unwieldy, poorly functioning viceroyalty of New Spain, he assigned it to the captaincy general of Cuba, under the jurisdiction of the Ministry of State instead of the Ministry of the Indies. In order to cultivate the French inhabitants and the various Indian populations, the king directed his ministers to make no drastic changes in Louisiana's accustomed administrative procedures, regardless of conflict with Spanish principles and practices.

His conciliatory approach availed the king little. Although the French government tried to expedite the change and agreed to transfer its Louisiana militia to Spanish service, the French soldiery balked. Citizens of New Orleans proved so antagonistic that the first Spanish governor could govern only with the help of his French predecessor. Antonio de Ulloa, a distinguished scientist and naval officer with administrative experience in Peru, reached New Orleans in March 1766 and took formal possession of the colony in January 1767. With only ninety soldiers, not even enough for police duty, he could exert no real authority. In October 1768, the New Orleans citizenry ousted him, then appealed for restoration to French sovereignty. Versailles ignored them.

The Spanish Crown handed its Louisiana problem to Irish expatriate Alejandro O'Reilly, a noted veteran of European wars, widely considered Spain's finest general. He landed in Louisiana in the summer of 1769 with 2,056 Spanish soldiers and readily subdued the colonists, who could muster 1,800 men at most. He occupied New Orleans in August and established a real Spanish government.

Although Ulloa had been unable to govern New Orleans, he had laid foundations for Spanish policy on Indian affairs.[1] Since France had sustained friendship and alliance with many Indian peoples through trade and annual presents, there was no hope of substituting Spain's normal mission-presidio approach. Given British traders on the east bank of the Mississippi, poised to exploit any discontent among the Indians, Spanish officials in Louisiana dared not attempt any radical deviation from the French system, no matter how it clashed with Spain's established practices in the neighboring provinces of Texas and New Mexico.

Soon after Ulloa reached New Orleans, Indian delegations visited him, some from two hundred miles away, seeking assurances that the new regime would meet their needs. With the generous assistance of Philippe Aubry, the last French governor, Ulloa did his utmost to ingratiate the Spaniards with the Indians. He spent the summer of 1766 touring lower Louisiana with Aubry, cultivating friendships with the natives and collecting first-hand information on which to base management of Indian affairs. He conferred with Indian leaders, examined existing and potential sites of fortifications, and inquired into trade potential. At Natchitoches, he studied the extraordinarily complex Indian relationships in that old arena of Franco-Spanish rivalry and investigated possibilities for communications with Texas and New Mexico.

Ulloa retained veteran French personnel at the three major Indian

---

[1] The details of the transition and of Indian policy development by Ulloa and O'Reilly are drawn from John W. Caughey, *Bernardo de Gálvez in Louisiana, 1776–1783*, pp. 8 ff, and Lawrence Kinnaird, ed., *Spain in the Mississippi Valley, 1765–1794*, I, xv ff.

trade centers, Natchitoches, St. Louis, and the Arkansas Post. Unlike New Orleans' sullen citizenry, they served him well. Balthazar de Villiers commanded the Natchitoches Post; licensed traders served their established clientele; St. Denis *fils* remained the acknowledged leader, better able than any other man to guarantee the peace of the region. Ulloa accepted tacitly the customs of traders and Indians who crossed the provincial boundary between Louisiana and Texas as casually as they had always crossed international bounds. Unfortunately for the peace of the area, the governorship of Texas soon fell to a less tolerant officer.

Governor Martos spent 1766 in Los Adaes under the cloud of Hugo O'Conor's special investigation, which must have inhibited his Indian trade. Nevertheless, Indians in that jurisdiction remained peaceful and law-abiding through the spring of 1767, when Martos left to stand trial in Mexico City, and the summer, when O'Conor assumed command as governor ad interim. A few months later O'Conor moved to eradicate all contraband trade, barring all French traders from the Indian villages of East Texas.

St. Denis had once again to dissuade angry Indians from massacring all the Spaniards because a new governor had tried to deny them trade with Louisiana. For all his influence, St. Denis had no easy task. Dismayed to learn of the incident, Ulloa tried to convince O'Conor that sudden disruption of trade only invited disastrous uprisings and that the Indians would get all the goods they wanted from the British frontier if the Spaniards should fail them. He urged O'Conor to copy the Louisiana system, always giving presents when Indians came to talk and promising to continue trade as in the past.[2]

Even had O'Conor been informed and flexible enough to accept Ulloa's advice, practical difficulties would have compromised the worth of such promises to Indians of the Louisiana-Texas frontier. Confusion about mercantile regulations applicable to Louisiana checked the flow of goods from France to New Orleans for several years after the transfer. Supplies grew uncertain even for licensed traders operating out of Natchitoches. Governors Barrios and Martos had used Natchitoches goods for the illegal Indian trade that had purchased Spanish survival in East Texas and ruined their own careers. O'Conor would have found it hard to obtain merchandise enough to satisfy his predecessors' established clientele, even had he not scorned their expedient

---

[2] Antonio de Ulloa to Hugo O'Conor, 1768, in Herbert Eugene Bolton, ed., *Athanase de Mézières and the Louisiana-Texas Frontier, 1768–1780,* I, 127–130.

as criminal corruption. To Indians already inconvenienced by merchandise shortages, O'Conor's abrupt stoppage of the Los Adaes trade and his efforts to bar access to the French traders constituted outrageous provocations.

The incident dramatized inherent dangers in the contradictions of Indian policy between Spain's neighboring provinces of Louisiana and Texas, but it sparked no effort to resolve the conflict. The saving intervention of St. Denis averted the general massacre that might have alerted the Crown to the dangers, and events removed the two opposing governors from the border arena before they could pursue their argument further. Louisiana experienced nearly a year's hiatus in Spanish authority after the citizens of New Orleans drove Ulloa from the province in the autumn of 1768. Meanwhile, O'Conor moved his headquarters from Los Adaes to San Antonio to take personal charge of defending that area.

Indian depredations accelerated alarmingly around San Antonio in the summer of 1768. Countless horses and cattle were stolen; several herders were killed or captured. Some crimes were attributed to Apaches, some to Norteños, but the latter especially frightened the San Antonians. They had adjusted over many years to the livestock thefts that seemed an inevitable condition of peace with the Apaches, but they knew little of the Norteños, and they remembered too well the terrifying numbers those nations had once hurled against Mission San Sabá.

They had newer reasons to dread the Norteños. For the first time, in the autumn of 1766, Norteños had directly attacked Spanish soldiers guarding the missions at El Cañon, to avenge losses sustained by their own people. Pursuing Spanish soldiers had killed some Norteño raiders who had first struck Lipans congregated at El Cañon and then had stolen the horse herd from Mission San José. The series of vengeance parties did not wipe out Mission San Lorenzo and its thirty-man garrison as was apparently intended, but they did destroy its usefulness as a sanctuary for the Lipans. By the summer of 1767 the missions at El Cañon had neither Lipan residents nor visitors.[3] Norteños then intensified their vigilance against Apaches in the San Sabá area, keeping the presidio in a virtual state of siege.

By the spring of 1768, the San Sabá garrison was so ravaged by hunger and disease that those who did not desert were on the brink of

[3] Curtis D. Tunnell and W. W. Newcomb, Jr., *A Lipan Apache Mission*, pp. 172–173.

mutiny. Captain Rábago, now convinced that the viceroy would send no succor, abandoned the post and led his soldiers with their wives and children to Mission San Lorenzo at El Cañon. He never obeyed the viceroy's indignant order to reoccupy the fort lest the enemy occupy it.[4]

The Norteños felt no need to occupy the San Sabá presidio. They had destroyed its usefulness to the Lipans, which had been their purpose all along. Their triumphant warriors preferred relentless pursuit of the prime enemy. More than ever, eastern Apaches were driven back upon the Spanish frontier to find their meat in the livestock herds of the missions and ranches and to replace their lost horses with Spaniards' mounts.

Throughout the 1760's, mounting losses of livestock at San Antonio reflected Lipan misfortunes. Thus, tensions were already running high when large parties of Norteños appeared in the area in the summer of 1768. A new wave of murders and thefts swept outlying ranches. Captain Menchaca reckoned that between Apaches and Norteños there remained no safe road or place in all Texas. The *cabildo* joined his appeal to Governor O'Conor for protection.[5]

Rushing from Los Adaes to San Antonio to take charge, O'Conor decided hastily that the situation demanded active war against four nations suspected of recent depredations: Comanches, Tonkawas, Taovayas, and Tawakonis. On August 31 he asked the viceroy to authorize and support his proposed campaign. While he awaited the viceroy's reply, O'Conor intensified his efforts to bar French goods to the Indians of East Texas, lest guns and ammunition reach the nations he hoped to attack in the coming spring and summer. Naturally, he spurned Ulloa's urgent advice to encourage the Indian trade in East Texas.

Though O'Conor's position on the question of Indian trade needed no stiffening, a new argument came to hand that autumn with a dispatch from the viceroy. New Mexico's Governor Pedro Fermín de Mendinueta had reported that Jumanos were supplying arms and munitions to Comanches on his frontier. He understood the Jumanos to live at the junction of the Arkansas and Canadian rivers, some five hundred miles southeast of Santa Fe, where they enjoyed access to

---

[4] Robert S. Weddle, *The San Sabá Mission*, pp. 177–180.
[5] Luis Antonio Menchaca to O'Conor, Béxar, August 18, 1768, BA; David M. Vigness, "Don Hugo O'Conor and New Spain's Northeastern Frontier, 1764–1776," *Journal of the West* 6 (1967): 27–40.

British traders via the Mississippi River. The viceroy desired O'Conor to take the steps necessary to cut off that traffic and to report who the Jumanos were and just what trade they were receiving via the Mississippi.[6] A more open-minded officer might have seen in the viceroy's letter an echo of Governor Ulloa's warning against leaving a vacuum for British traders to fill, but O'Conor only found more reason to stop any flow of arms to Indians. It is unlikely that O'Conor realized that the Jumanos of the New Mexican report were the same Indians whom the Texans called Taovayas and Wichitas.

O'Conor counted on making war to solve the problems of Texas, until spring 1769 brought the viceroy's disappointing reply. The Marqués de Croix sympathized with the problems of the San Antonians and appreciated O'Conor's zeal for their protection, but he could not support an offensive campaign with the resources at his disposal. O'Conor and the people of San Antonio would have to make the best possible defense on their home grounds. By way of encouragement, the viceroy did authorize O'Conor to take back from the San Sabá garrison the twenty-one soldiers transferred there from Béxar a dozen years before and to take all the men he wished from the garrisons of Los Adaes and San Agustín. As a result of Rubí's report, those two presidios were destined to be closed soon and San Sabá to be moved elsewhere; Béxar and La Bahía would remain the only presidios in Texas. The viceroy promised to send all possible arms and ammunitions if O'Conor would submit an estimate of his needs.[7]

A defensive command in a dwindling province ill matched that young Irishman's energies and ambitions. He asked to be relieved of his post, then marked time in Texas for a year until Juan María, Barón de Ripperdá, reached San Antonio in the spring of 1770 to assume the governorship. Back to Mexico City for more suitable reassignment, O'Conor carried his convictions about Indian affairs in Texas with him. That boded ill for the Norteños and for the peace of Texas when O'Conor gained top military command of the whole northern frontier in 1772.

Ripperdá was an able, conscientious administrator, in the best Bourbon tradition. Unfortunately, his term began during that time of near paralysis when New Spain awaited the Crown's decisions upon the recommendations of Rubí and Gálvez. In those circumstances, Rip-

[6] Marqués de Croix to O'Conor, Mexico, September 3, 1768, BA.
[7] Marqués de Croix to O'Conor, Mexico, February 7, 1769, BA.

perdá could be little more than caretaker, frequently the victim, but never the shaper, of events. Meanwhile, a vigorous new initiative in Indian affairs emerged in Louisiana.

General O'Reilly swiftly ended the insurrection in New Orleans in August 1769, then energetically sought Louisiana's economic and political revitalization. Although Spanish mercantile laws applied to the province, O'Reilly won the Crown's permission for Louisiana to trade freely with Havana and all ports of Spain. Since the earlier experiment in retaining the French political system had ended in revolt, the Crown reversed that policy. O'Reilly reorganized the government from top to bottom in orthodox Spanish fashion. He drew upon the local French population to fill many civil offices and enlisted many in the colonial militia. He designated lieutenant governors for the districts of Natchitoches and Illinois, both critically important in Indian affairs. For the lieutenant governorship of Natchitoches, O'Reilly chose Athanase de Mézières, connected by marriage to the influential St. Denis family and in his own right experienced in the arts of trade, diplomacy, and war on the Louisiana-Texas frontier.

The Indians were so numerous and the colonists so few that Governor O'Reilly paid particular attention to Indian affairs, deviating from traditional French practices only with respect to Indian slavery. War captives had long been common barter in the Indian trade network in the Mississippi Valley; hence French traders had always encountered some pressures to buy war captives. La Salle had hit upon the idea of purchasing captives for resale to their own tribes, who gratefully paid high prices to recover their people. The system easily lent itself to abuse. By 1720 French *voyageurs* on the Arkansas and Missouri rivers were alleged to have incited Indian wars just to secure more captives for the slave traffic. The government ordered such criminals seized and their merchandise confiscated and finally condemned the principle of Indian slavery. In 1728, Governor Périer proclaimed Indian slavery detrimental to the progress of the province, although he did not forbid it. Besides the government's express disapproval, there was the practical consideration that Indian slaves escaped too easily to be good investments.[8] The 1726 census had

---

[8] Some entrepreneurs proposed to solve that difficulty by shipping Indian slaves from Louisiana to the West Indies in exchange for Negroes, arguing that Indians could not escape in the islands and Negroes would be too scared of wild Indians to run away on the mainland. The Crown rejected the scheme, and only a few clandestine transactions tested the theory.

shown 229 Indian slaves owned by settlers in Louisiana; by 1744 the number dwindled to 122.[9]

However small the number of Indian slaves in Louisiana by the 1760's, the principle loomed large in Spanish thought. On December 7, 1769, O'Reilly outlawed any purchase of Indian slaves after that date.[10] Slave owners could now dispose of them only by freeing them and had to declare the name, nation, and appraised value of each slave. O'Reilly ordered each post commandant to submit an exact, detailed census of Indian slaves within the bounds of his district. All details would be forwarded to the king for subsequent disposition as he should see fit, a rather pointed hint that emancipation, perhaps with some compensation, was in the offing.

In all other respects O'Reilly, like Ulloa, adopted French practices in Indian relations: annual presents, no attempt to missionize, reliance upon veteran French agents and traders. He invited to council at New Orleans the leaders of all Indian tribes within 175 miles of the capital so that he could personally promise them presents, to be delivered promptly each year, with no return expected beyond constant loyalty to the king of Spain. Like other vassals, they would enjoy the right to protection by the king's arms. With the help of French interpreters, O'Reilly delivered a stylish harangue, then hung medals upon the breasts of nineteen chiefs. As he had hoped, the chiefs went away deeply impressed.

Governor O'Reilly assumed that it would be particularly difficult to win the friendship of the Indians in the Red River Valley. There, many held a deep-rooted antagonism toward Spaniards as well as a staunch attachment to French traders, some of whom did not scruple to incite them against Spaniards. The governor also realized that temptations for contraband trade with New Spain were rife in the Natchitoches district. He banked heavily on the integrity and talents of de Mézières "to obtain for the presidios of Mexico a quietude which they have not hitherto enjoyed, and to make it very difficult for anyone to introduce illicit trade at these posts."[11] Somehow de Mézières would have to enforce the laws of Spain, yet convince the aborigines that the Spanish

[9] N. M. Miller Surrey, *The Commerce of Louisiana during the French Régime, 1699–1763*, pp. 97, 227–230.

[10] Alejandro O'Reilly, Proclamation, December 7, 1769, in Kinnaird, *Spain in the Mississippi Valley*, I, 125–126.

[11] O'Reilly to Arriaga, New Orleans, December 10, 1769, quoted in Caughey, *Bernardo de Gálvez*, p. 38; see also O'Reilly to Grimaldi, New Orleans, December 10, 1769, in Kinnaird, *Spain in the Mississippi Valley*, I, 129–130.

regime would not erode the friendship and mutual interest of the Louisianans and their Indian neighbors.

O'Reilly promised to furnish annually all the goods that de Mézières should think necessary for the Indians. He ratified the appointments of traders for the Indians if de Mézières certified their zeal, intelligence, and good character.[12] With that support, de Mézières confidently set about winning the Indians of the Red River to Spanish allegiance. Unfortunately for his purpose, O'Reilly's strong backing and confidence disappeared only a few months after de Mézières took office. Deeming Spain's authority established in Louisiana, O'Reilly turned the governorship over to Luis de Unzaga and sailed for Havana in March 1770. If de Mézières could have foreseen how the meddlesome Governor Unzaga would obstruct his management of Indian affairs, he would probably have resigned that spring to attend to his private interests.

De Mézières looked to his old trade connections to restore the tranquillity of the Red River nations. His friendship with the Kadohadachos dated back to the 1740's, when he had held the trade concession in the village of the Grand Caddos; both as a merchant and as an officer of the Natchitoches Post, he had long been on good terms with both the Natchitoches and the Yatasís. In the spring of 1770 he called to council at Natchitoches the leaders of those groups and won their promises of allegiance to the Spanish king. He promised them protection and fair treatment forever, annual presents, and licensed traders. He designated as medal chiefs both the Kadohadacho and the Yatasí headmen, a distinction both flattering and practical.[13] Both were able men of high prestige and integrity who would be invaluable representatives of Spanish authority among their own people and intermediaries to other Norteños.

What of the hostile Indians then marauding in Texas: the Ietan Comanches, Taovayas, Tawakonis, Iscanis, Kichais, and Tonkawas? Reckoning that economic pressure could bring them to terms, de Mézières moved to cut off their access to trade goods. At the same time, he hastened to restore the advantages of trade to the friendly nations, licensing two resident traders for the Kadohadachos and one for the Yatasís.

As in the French era, the resident traders' responsibilities transcended

---

[12] O'Reilly to de Mézières, New Orleans, January 22, 1770, and January 23, 1770, in Bolton, *Athanase de Mézières*, I, 132–134.

[13] De Mézières to Unzaga, Natchitoches, February 1, 1770, ibid., pp. 142–143.

business. They were expected to encourage the Indians to work so that they would not be dangerously idle. At all times, they listened for news and promptly sent runners with any information of interest to the Crown's service. It was their duty to function as peacemakers, conciliating quarrels within or between villages. If they found any Indian in danger of dying, they had to try to arrange for his baptism. The licensed traders were charged to watch out for vagabonds, to arrest them, confiscate their goods, and bring them into Natchitoches, by force if necessary. Under no circumstances were they to sell the Indians any British merchandise or intoxicating beverages. Although forbidden to sell goods to hostile Indians, under penalty of treason, they were expected to seize every opportunity to propagandize the hostiles about the costs of resistance and the rewards of cooperation. By their deeds and their daily conversation they were expected to show the Indians that Frenchmen really liked being subjects of the Spanish king.[14] The job demanded an extraordinary mixture of character, energy, ability, and courage.

While de Mézières laid for Spain the foundations of trade and alliance among his old friends, he sent messengers to the hostile bands to explain that the French and the Spanish people were now one and that to injure one would offend the other. De Mézières was taking firm measures to cut off all trade with the hostiles: if they should continue their depredations, he would have to come and punish them. On the other hand, if they would come to make peace and pledge their loyalty to the Spanish king, he would guarantee them trade, protection, and presents.

The friendly chiefs, who helped spread the message to the Norteños, held the key to the success of the boycott. They had given their word not to let goods from their villages reach the hostiles. De Mézières trusted the friendly nations to stand by him because their chiefs' honor was involved. Furthermore, restoration of tranquillity in the area was important to their own security and prosperity.[15] Each band making peace would mean potential customers for their trade centers. Confident of early success in his economic maneuver, de Mézières asked the governor's permission to escort Indian peace delegates to San Antonio to negotiate treaties with Texas. Only thus could he banish Indian doubts about the unity of Texans and Louisianans.

[14] De Mézières, Instructions for the traders of the Cadaux d'Acquioux and Hiatasses Nations, Natchitoches, February 4, 1770, ibid., pp. 148–149.
[15] De Mézières to Unzaga, Natchitoches, February 1, 1770, ibid., pp. 140–142.

Among the hostile groups, the Taovayas seemed to de Mézières most important. Of all the villages, theirs was said to be largest; their territory was rumored to be rich in metals as well as beautiful. Their triumph over Colonel Parrilla's force a decade before and their subsequent successes against San Sabá had left them arrogant and the Texans terrified. Tranquillity in Texas would be unlikely until the Taovayas would celebrate peace at San Antonio.

Luckily, de Mézières discovered a Taovayas who shared his concern for peace. San Yago had been captured from his Taovayas village in boyhood and sold; after years as a slave in Illinois, he had escaped to the Arkansas River, then found his way home to his own people on the Red River. He was dismayed to discover their bitter enmity toward the Spaniards of Texas and dreaded the consequences that their raids might bring upon the village. Reared as a Catholic, he also worried about his inability to perform his religious duties, and he sought a community of Catholics. That quest took him to Natchitoches.[16]

What better envoy to the Taovayas? De Mézières sent San Yago to New Orleans in February 1770 with the merchant going to fetch the annual consignment of goods for Indian presents. At de Mézières' behest, Governor Unzaga entertained San Yago generously, trying to impress upon him the Spaniards' desire for friendship and justice for all Indians. Besides the governor's flattering personal attention, the visit to New Orleans gave San Yago impressive glimpses of Spain's power and wealth and dramatized the oneness of the French and Spanish people in Louisiana. In mid-March San Yago rode back to Natchitoches in a convoy of canoes laden with a year's supply of presents for the friendly nations, tangible evidence of the advantages of peace. He himself was legally free, by special decree of Governor Unzaga. Good results were expected to follow as San Yago traveled among the Norteños and described his generous treatment by the new Spanish regime.

How much influence San Yago had is uncertain, but by mid-May leaders of all the hostile nations agreed to attend an August council in the village of the widely respected and trusted Kadohadacho medal chief, Tinhioüen, for peace talks with de Mézières. The lieutenant governor hoped to bring them to Natchitoches, then to Los Adaes to formalize with Governor Ripperdá their peace with Texas. He ex-

[16] De Mézières to Unzaga, Natchitoches, February 1, 1770, ibid., pp. 137–139; Unzaga to de Mézières, New Orleans, March 15, 1770, ibid., p. 152.

pected next to escort each delegation home to its respective camp or village, to take formal possession for Spain and to raise the king's flag, and to bring back from the Taovayas village the two cannons that Parrilla had abandoned in 1759.

Generous presents would be needed to compensate the Indian leaders for the long, onerous journey. Since there was no appropriate budgetary provision, de Mézières volunteered his own June salary to cover the cost. In the same mail that carried news of the forthcoming council, dated May 20, 1770, he ordered the goods that he would need for presents to the chiefs of the Comanches, Taovayas, Tawakonis, Iscanis, Tonkawas, and Kichais. Oddly enough, Governor Unzaga never vouchsafed any answer.[17]

De Mézières had powerful, albeit undesirable, assistance in his campaign to bring the hostile Norteños to a truce. Though the hostile nations were surely inconvenienced by de Mézières' tough boycott and impressed by the good offices of Tinhioüen, Osage warriors shoved them hardest toward the peace council. The Norteños' traditional enmity with the Osages had amounted mostly to talk in recent years because of the great distances between their territories. The Osages had been busy hunting to pay the Illinois traders; their enemies had been similarly busy in the Natchitoches trade sphere. But conditions changed once Spain acquired Louisiana: many traders who would not obey the Spanish laws flocked to the Arkansas River to live as contrabandists, peddling British merchandise smuggled across the Mississippi. The Arkansas outlaws incited the Osages to raid their old enemies in the Red River area for women and children and horses and mules to trade to the contrabandists, who peddled to British entrepreneurs those in excess of their own needs or desires.

The deadly Osage onslaught drove many Indians to retreat in despair. The Tawakonis, Iscanis, Tonkawas, and Kichais fell back toward the presidios of Béxar and La Bahía, where they recouped the Osage toll of their horse herds by stealing from the Spaniards.[18] Even the Taovayas abandoned their fortified village on the Red River for a while, caching their souvenir cannons while they sought refuge somewhere between the Red and the Arkansas. They also levied replacements from Spanish sources.

Not surprisingly, the Spaniards in Texas feared that the Norteños' raids foreshadowed a concerted effort to destroy the province. Since

---

[17] De Mézières to Unzaga, Natchitoches, May 20, 1770, ibid., pp. 199–200.
[18] De Mézières to Unzaga, Natchitoches, May 20, 1770, ibid., pp. 166–168.

the Spaniards' sponsorship of the Lipans had wrecked all possible lines of communication from Texas to the Norteños and since the viceroy would not support any military response to the thefts, the Texans could only appeal through higher channels for help from Louisiana. O'Reilly had therefore charged de Mézières to prevent the Norteños from destroying Texas. When O'Conor turned Texas over to Ripperdá in the spring of 1770, the new governor could only hope for some successful intercession by de Mézières.

De Mézières explained to Governor Unzaga in May 1770 the dangerous Osage factor in the Texas problem and urged expulsion of contrabandists from the Arkansas. With outlaws eliminated, the commandant of the Illinois district could be held responsible for restraining the Osages from depredations in Texas and Louisiana. In view of the importance of Illinois to the Osages as their trade center, de Mézières had no doubt that they could be controlled from that quarter.

Confused and confusing reports of turbulence among Indians in Texas reached de Mézières. Nacogdoches Indians reported that the Taovayas had recently been joined by the numerous Panismahas from the Missouri River; if so, their warrior strength had been doubled. The same Nacogdoches informants said that the Taovayas and Panismahas had gone along with the Tawakonis, Xaranames, and Mayeyes whom Comanches had recruited to attack Governor Ripperdá on his forthcoming journey from Béxar to Los Adaes. The Kadohadachos insisted that was nonsense; the big Norteño war party only wanted to fight Osages. De Mézières had more confidence in the Kadohadachos, but he alerted the Los Adaes commandant to take due precautions for the governor's safety.[19]

Considering the dangerously volatile conditions among the Indians, de Mézières grew loath to wait until August to meet the Norteño leaders. Bound not to leave his post without permission, he urged Governor Unzaga to send him at once to the Indian villages to negotiate a peace, arguing that his personal visit could help counteract the influence of intruding contrabandists from the Arkansas and Illinois districts. Governor Unzaga ignored that appeal, as he had ignored earlier messages regarding the peace council. On August 21, 1770, when the Indian leaders reached the village of Tinhioüen, de Mézières was still at Natchitoches, awaiting permission to leave his post to meet with them.

[19] De Mézières to Unzaga, Natchitoches, June 27, 1770, ibid., pp. 202–203.

The Indian delegates, fewer than expected, had come at considerable risk to themselves and their people. The Comanches had decided against peace talks. When their allies had persisted in going to the meeting, the Comanches had turned on them in anger and declared a state of war. Seven leaders of the Taovayas, Tawakonis, Iscanis, and Kichais actually reached the Kadohadacho village. Many companions who had ridden with them, including Tonkawas and Xaranames, had turned back at the Sabine, fearful that the council was merely a trick to slaughter them in retaliation for their crimes in Texas.

Tinhioüen played the role of host nobly. He grew uneasy as weeks passed without any sign of de Mézières and sent three of his leading men to fetch him. They persuaded de Mézières that he must wait no longer for the governor's permission and instructions, regardless of Spanish law. He had already risked affronting the visiting chiefs by keeping them waiting so long. In this prime season for Indian wars, he thought it not unlikely that the offended leaders would ride off to vent their anger against the Spanish frontier. Dashing off an apologetic note of explanation to the governor, with his promise to return within the month, de Mézières hastened to the Kadohadachos.[20]

Even in his hurry de Mézières did not forget to dramatize the new union of Spaniards and Frenchmen: his party included as many of the former as of his own compatriots. From Natchitoches he took one militia officer and five residents experienced in dealing with Indians. The Spanish contingent included a sergeant and five soldiers from Los Adaes and Fray Miguel Santa María y Silva, the aged, ailing president of that mission district. De Mézières hoped that he and his French companions could make such an impressive show of respect for the priest that they would prevent any more tragedies like the martyrdom of two Franciscans at San Sabá.[21]

The route to the Kadohadacho village took the party through the villages of the Adaes, the Yatasís, and the Petit Caddos. The chiefs and leading men of each village joined the procession to the Kadohadachos. De Mézières led an impressive retinue into Tinhioüen's village on the Red River in mid-October 1770.

Tinhioüen welcomed them with appropriate ceremony and announced for the next day a council of the chiefs and leading men of his jurisdiction. To that council he expressly invited the seven Tao-

[20] De Mézières to Unzaga, Natchitoches, September 27, 1770, ibid., pp. 204–206.
[21] De Mézières to Unzaga, Natchitoches, October 29, 1770, ibid., pp. 206–220.

vayas, Tawakonis, Iscanis, and Kichais who had braved the journey and endured the regrettable wait.

As host and initiator of the meeting, Tinhioüen presided. He invited de Mézières to speak first. Remaining seated at his prominent place in the council circle, de Mézières expressed his pleasure at talking personally with the dissident nations of the matters that he had earlier communicated to them through the friendly nations. He explained his new role as agent of the governor of Louisiana, who was now his own chief as well as father and protector of the Indians.[22]

Getting down to specific issues, de Mézières pointed out how times had changed since they had been able to rely upon Natchitoches for all the goods and guns they needed and reminded them that their awful misdeed at San Sabá had led to suspension of their privileges. He assured them that the generous king of Spain would grant them peace and pardon if they would desist from raids and wars and that he would punish them severely with his armies if they did not. He recommended the example of the faithful, friendly Kadohadachos, who had won the Crown's eternal gratitude.

Warming to his task, de Mézières reminded the visitors that they were surrounded by Osages on the north, Comanches on the west, Apaches on the south, and Spaniards of Louisiana on the east, all enemies who would consume them like four great fires racing across dry meadows to their villages. Since there were no longer any Frenchmen to help them, they would have to make peace on Spanish terms or suffer the awful vengeance of all those enemies.

In dramatic climax, the practiced orator reverently introduced the venerable Fray Santa María, noting that his gray habit marked him as a brother of the two helpless priests whom the hostile nations had hacked down at San Sabá. He had come, with great compassion, to offer them pardon in return for true repentance. To demonstrate the unity among Frenchmen and Spaniards, de Mézières then rose and affectionately took the hand of each Spaniard present.

Cocay, the Yatasí medal chief, and Tinhioüen then made well-reasoned, persuasive speeches supporting the lieutenant governor. The seven visiting chiefs sat nearly motionless, gazing at the ground throughout the speeches, then conferred among themselves. When they agreed, the man best versed in the language of the Kadohadachos spoke for the group.

---

[22] De Mézières' own summary of his harangue, *ibid.*, pp. 209–210.

With calm assurance, he pointed out that his people and their friends had never attacked the Spaniards until provoked by their protection of the Apaches at San Sabá, although they had always known where to find the Spanish settlements, ranches, and forts. They had begun to hate the Spaniards only when the Spaniards helped their Apache enemies; their enmity had hardened when Apache warriors helped the Spanish army attack the Taovayas village.

Despite those grave provocations, their peoples no longer hated the Spaniards, and they would do everything possible to live in friendship with them. Indeed, the Tawakonis and Iscanis had recently abandoned their establishment in the vicinity of San Antonio and San Sabá upon learning the wish of the Great Captain of Louisiana. Now they lived near San Pedro,[23] where they would remain.

They desired peace so greatly that they would even leave the Apaches alone rather than risk misunderstanding. Their decision to seek peace had cost them the wrath of their former allies, the Comanches, who now waged cruel war upon them in retaliation. Even so, they would stand firm upon their promise. They begged their ancient protectors, the French, to help them fight the Comanche peril.

De Mézières rose to remind the delegates that there were no longer any Frenchmen in the land: all now were Spaniards. He praised the rest of their response and promised to report their promises to his chief, the governor of Louisiana, who would surely be pleased to receive them as subjects of the king. Meanwhile, de Mézières wished them to travel to San Antonio to make a treaty with the governor of Texas, in whose jurisdiction they actually lived. De Mézières would furnish them an interpreter, and two Spanish escorts would carry the flag to protect them.

The seven leaders declined for many reasons: they had not enough horses; the trip involved too much danger from Apaches; they needed to build houses quickly; it was too late in the season, nearly time for winter storms. They would not even ride with de Mézières to Los Adaes to treat with the Spanish captain there. All the excuses they offered were valid enough, but de Mézières sensed a deeper reason: they feared that entering a Spanish settlement would expose them to some awful revenge. Only years of constant good treatment could allay that fear.

---

[23] San Pedro de los Nabedaches, the name Spaniards had given the Nabedache village of the Tejas.

De Mézières responded in sorrow rather than anger, protesting his own sincerity and that of his Spanish chiefs and predicting that time would prove their good faith. He would keep the presents meant to celebrate a peace treaty and would explain their case to the governor so as not to arouse his anger at their stubbornness. The departing Indians were equally civil, promising to meet him again in the spring and meanwhile to endure their poverty and confine their activities to hunting.

Whatever progress de Mézières made toward conciliating the Indians at Tinhioüen's meeting, he failed to convince the Spaniards whom he had so carefully included in his party. Offended by the Indians' affectionate reception of the Frenchmen and their relative indifference to the Spaniards, the Spanish delegation sat bewildered through the long harangues and the dramatic performances of the interpreters, not even certain of the identities of all the Indian nations represented. They were thoroughly alarmed when the meeting broke up abruptly and de Mézières loaded the intended presents back into the canoes for return to his warehouse. That seemed to the Spanish witnesses a certain provocation to further hostilities, and they had no doubt that the Indians would get all the guns and ammunition they needed for war through the French traders in the Kadohadacho and Petit Caddo villages. They saw no sign that any peace would result from the meeting.

Sergeant Domingo Chirinas and Christóbal Carbaxal, members of the squad from Los Adaes, filed depositions against de Mézières on October 30. Fray Santa María gave his general verbal confirmation of the soldiers' report, although he made no detailed deposition at that time. Captain Joseph González sent copies of the report to the governors of both Louisiana and Texas.

Oblivious of the mischief afoot at Los Adaes, de Mézières dispatched his own reports to Governor Unzaga from Natchitoches, predicting the conclusion of peace in the coming spring. The voluntary movement of the Tawakonis and Iscanis away from Béxar toward Los Adaes proved their sincere wish to cease depredations. The Taovayas had expressed the hope of coming back from their northerly refuge to the Red River to live near the Kadohadachos. The Kichais had always been docile and well intentioned; they had fallen accidentally into the great San Sabá attack, had been appalled by the results, and had ever since refused to join in hostilities planned by the other groups. All of them sorely needed arms, munitions, and agricultural implements. Worse, they were surrounded by enemies. Already drawing together for defense, they must soon realize that they needed Spanish protection to survive.

The marauders whose chiefs had shunned Tinhioüen's council constituted three completely different problems. The Tonkawas were said to be basically well disposed. The only real problem lay in their wandering way of life. Having no crops, they were constantly on the move hunting and gathering; they could never have afforded the five-week wait that farming Indians could brook in the post-harvest season. The Tonkawas had meant to talk with de Mézières, but they were off gathering wild fruits when he reached Tinhioüen's village. It had been impossible to locate them and allow them time to ride to the Red River. De Mézières had no doubt that the Tonkawas would subscribe to a general peace if he could meet with them.

The Xaraname problem was more complex. They were apostates who had fled the Mission of La Bahía del Espíritu Santo and settled near the Tawakonis. Their grievances, borne of abuses at La Bahía, made them dangerous. They tirelessly incited Norteños against the Spaniards and guided raiders straight to vulnerable targets. It would be safest, and probably easy, to induce the Tawakonis to destroy the Xaranames, but responsibility for their souls ruled out that expedient. The alternative was to bring them back promptly to the mission fold, both to save their souls and to end their mischief.

That would leave only Comanches hostile. De Mézières saw so little hope of peace in that quarter that he meant to spur the Wichitan bands to active pursuit of their quarrel. So numerous and so arrogant were the Comanches said to be, and so vast their range from the Missouri River to the frontiers of New Spain, that the costs and difficulties of subduing them would be incalculable. Since Comanches marauded regularly in New Mexico as well as in Texas and the provinces immediately southward, de Mézières proposed to encourage other Indians to destroy them.

Just after Tinhioüen's council, de Mézières learned that Los Adaes presidio would be abandoned and its troops transferred to Béxar. That undermined his plan to impress the Indians with parties of Spaniards and Frenchmen working together and cast doubt upon his assurances of the Spanish king's loving concern for the Indians' welfare.

Far more worrisome were reports that authorities at Béxar planned to campaign against the same Indians with whom he had talked peace. Why deal them new grievances while they debated their stand for next spring's council? De Mézières begged Governor Unzaga to forestall any attack upon them and to let him visit their villages. He was confident that they would keep their promises to live at peace until the spring meeting unless they should suffer some new injury.

Not until February 1771 did de Mézières learn that Unzaga had decided not to let him honor his own promise to meet the Indians that spring for further peace talks. On the basis of the reports filed by the soldiers at Los Adaes, the governor doubted that de Mézières' harangue could have convinced any Indians of the good faith of the peace proposals. Indeed, he suspected that those Indians were too fierce to be peaceful and the Crown's agents too much given to words without deeds. Unless de Mézières could produce convincing counterarguments, Governor Unzaga would deny him permission to attend the spring council.[24]

The personal affront was shocking. Even worse were the possible consequences of failure to keep the promises already given the Indians in the name of the Spanish Crown. All that spring de Mézières struggled to ward off disaster. He refuted the Spaniards' accusations, citing several months of unusual quiet at San Antonio just when his critics had predicted his actions must provoke war. The Kadohadachos confirmed that the Taovayas, Tawakonis, Iscanis, and Kichais were keeping the peace. De Mézières reiterated his own willingness to visit their villages any time Governor Unzaga would permit, and he warned that the Indians would feel deceived and angry if he should fail to meet them in the spring. He could not answer for the consequences.

When Governor Unzaga ignored two appeals in that vein, de Mézières begged for permission to send a courier to let the Tawakonis and Taovayas know they were not forgotten and to feel out their mood. If favorable, perhaps they could be encouraged to visit San Antonio to negotiate with Governor Ripperdá. Governor Unzaga would only have to send a small flag for the Indians to carry to San Antonio, a leaden passport, and a letter introducing them to Governor Ripperdá.

Late in the spring de Mézières learned that Unzaga would allow him neither to meet with the hostile nations nor to send them messengers nor to invite them to visit San Antonio. After months of obstruction, the governor of Louisiana virtually abdicated responsibility at a crucial point in the negotiations for peace with the Wichitan bands. He made just one concession: since de Mézières insisted the matter was vital to

---

[24] Unzaga to de Mézières, New Orleans, November 29, 1770, in Bolton, *Athanase de Mézières*, pp. 232–233.

Texas, Governor Unzaga would consult on the matter with Governor Ripperdá.[25]

On April 30, 1771, the governor of Louisiana wrote to the viceroy of New Spain, requesting his opinion and that of the governor of Texas. Noting reports of Taovayas and Tawakoni incursions at Béxar, he reported de Mézières' claim that he could reduce them to peace if allowed to meet with them again and his prediction of bad consequences if he should fail to keep his promises. Unwilling to judge at the distance of New Orleans, Governor Unzaga deferred to the advice of the viceroy and, through his courtesy, to the governor of Texas. On June 2 the Marqués de Croix wrote to Ripperdá; on August 26 Ripperdá replied; in the second week of October his reply reached Mexico City, to be considered by a new viceroy, Antonio María de Bucareli y Ursúa.[26]

Governor Ripperdá, who had suffered a very trying first year at Béxar, urged that de Mézières mediate as soon as possible in any way conducive to the tranquillity of Texas. Viceroy Bucareli assented, too swamped by his new job to accord the northern frontier more than a despairing glance.[27] Even so, it was winter before Unzaga could receive in New Orleans that and subsequent expressions from New Spain of confidence in de Mézières.

Meanwhile, the momentum of events among the Nations of the North outran the processes of the Spanish bureaucracy. Indian leaders took up the peace negotiations on which de Mézières had been forced to default and bridged the artificial, crippling communications gap between Lieutenant Governor de Mézières at Natchitoches and Governor Ripperdá at San Antonio.

Early in his term Governor Ripperdá had proposed to recruit some three hundred veteran French traders and hunters from Louisiana to control the Norteños, relying upon enlightened management rather than force. The viceroy demurred: it would be too costly; Louisiana would not let Texas have so many men anyway; the effort would

---

[25] De Mézières to Unzaga, Natchitoches, February 28, 1771, ibid., pp. 240 ff; de Mézières to Unzaga, Natchitoches, March 14, 1771, ibid., p. 245; de Mézières to Unzaga, Natchitoches, March 20, 1771, ibid., pp. 245–247; Unzaga to de Mézières, New Orleans, April 6, 1771, ibid., p. 248.

[26] Marqués de Croix to Barón de Ripperdá, Mexico, June 2, 1771, BA; Bucareli to Ripperdá, Mexico, October 12, 1771, BA.

[27] Bucareli to O'Reilly, October 27, 1771, cited in Bernard E. Bobb, *The Viceregency of Antonio María Bucareli in New Spain, 1771–1779*, p. 30.

probably provoke the Norteños to greater depredations and ultimate destruction of Texas.

Of course the Norteños' attacks around Béxar had to be checked, but the Marqués de Croix could conceive of no solution outside the conventional patterns of military force. He had no extra moneys at his disposal, but he could reassign to Béxar soldiers from the three Texas presidios condemned by Rubí: fifty men from Los Adaes, thirty-one from San Agustín, fifty from San Sabá. As the viceroy saw it, those reinforcements, plus ten Indians from each of the five San Antonio missions and a shipment of rifles to arm San Antonio's citizenry, would bring Béxar's fighting strength up to 303. That was no trivial complement for a garrison that had long survived with a mere twenty-two soldiers. The Marqués de Croix reasoned that Ripperdá should be able not only to defend San Antonio, but also to punish the Norteños in their home territories and to mete out punishment for the robberies and murders committed by Apaches in Texas.[28]

That program of heavy reinforcements for Béxar sparked rumors of a big offensive against the Norteños and thus alarmed de Mézières in the fall of 1770. Fortunately, the transfers could not be effected in time to mount campaigns that year, and the winter passed in relative quiet.

Ripperdá was in no hurry to take the offensive against the Norteños. He knew that even three hundred men had small chance to subdue countless mounted Indians scattered over the vast interior of Texas; he also preferred the principle of peaceful diplomacy with the Indians. Unhappily for the governor's moderate inclinations, Texas began to suffer Indian depredations unusually early in the spring of 1771. La Bahía fared worst, due to injuries suffered by Indians at the missions there. Some who had fled, especially Xaranames, rallied other Indians to help them avenge their grievances against the Spaniards. Raiders' identities were often subject to guesswork, but it seemed early that spring that Xaranames brought Tonkawas and Bidais to raid around La Bahía and Béxar. Other Norteños appeared to be involved, but there was doubt about the role of the Tawakonis and Taovayas. By the latter part of April it looked as though Comanches were marauding around San Antonio.

Indignant to hear of depredations in Texas after his generous reinforcements, the viceroy ordered the governor to deploy his forces

---

[28] Marqués de Croix to Ripperdá, Mexico, July 24, 1770, BA.

more effectively to protect exposed areas.[29] Ripperdá sent fifty men to La Bahía to help pursue raiders there and established a small post of ten to twenty men at Arroyo del Cíbolo (about forty-five miles southeast of San Antonio on Cíbolo Creek at Tawakoni Crossing), a step Rubí had suggested would be useful to check enemy incursions on the route between Béxar and La Bahía. At no time did the governor show any enthusiasm for the viceroy's recurring theme of punitive campaigns into Norteño territories. When he learned that the Norteño leaders had promised to meet de Mézières for more peace talks that spring, he pinned his hopes on the Frenchman's diplomacy. Late in April he sent de Mézières a warm note of appreciation and hopes for his success and urged him also to bring the Comanches into a peace pact.[30] Of course, the governor of Texas had no idea that the governor of Louisiana had suspended de Mézières' authority to negotiate.

Ripperdá did wonder about the worth of de Mézières' peace talks when his troops, pursuing Bidais and Tawakonis who had stolen horses, killed the same Tawakoni chief whom de Mézières had thought so peacefully disposed. Anxious to find out discreetly just what was going on among the Indians, Governor Ripperdá appealed to the Franciscans. Mission President Fray Pedro Ramírez promptly made a reconnaissance with Fray Francisco Zedano.

The missionaries found the Bidais plotting to avenge the men killed by the pursuing Spanish soldiers. More happily, they discovered that the prominent Tejas Chief Bigotes intended to mediate with the four nations whom de Mézières had offered a peace treaty in the previous autumn. The two missionaries attended some of Bigotes' meetings with the leaders of the four nations and through his good offices received from them two buffalo skins. One, pure white, signified that the roads should be open and free from blood; the other skin bore four crosses, attesting the desire of each of the four nations for a peace treaty.

Late in the spring the missionaries rode with Bigotes and his Indian retinue to Los Adaes, where the lieutenant of the garrison joined their party, and thence to Natchitoches. There Bigotes presented the skins to de Mézières and explained his errand as the deputy for peace from the Kichais, Iscanis, Tawakonis, and Taovayas. In Indian usage, those skins had the force of a contract, and de Mézières honored them ac-

---

[29] Marqués de Croix to Ripperdá, Mexico, March 12, 1771, and June 22, 1771, BA.

[30] De Mézières to Unzaga, Natchitoches, July 3, 1771, in Bolton, *Athanase de Mézières*, I, 252–254.

cordingly. He summoned the leading citizens of Natchitoches to witness the proceedings, presented handsome gifts to Bigotes and his Indian companions, and made a powerful speech about the importance of the occasion. Fray Ramírez admired the skill and care with which de Mézières harangued the gathering; his favorable impression later helped offset the damning reports of old Fray Santa María.

The peace overture that Bigotes brought from the four nations was a much better outcome than de Mézières had dared hope for when he reluctantly broke his promise to go to a peace council that spring. Now it was urgent for him to respond with visits to the four nations, but Unzaga's rigid prohibition made it impossible for him to leave his post. He could only arrange an unofficial embassy to convince the four nations that their decision was welcomed by the governors of both Louisiana and Texas. To the great relief of de Mézières and the pleasure of Bigotes, Paul Louis Le Blanc de Villeneufve, a gifted interpreter then living in Natchitoches, volunteered to make the trip at his own expense. Another Frenchman well versed in Indian languages, Fray Francisco Zedano, and two Spanish settlers accompanied him. Bigotes himself led the considerable cortege of friendly Indians who rallied to support the important peace negotiations. The envoys were to persuade the erstwhile enemies not to fear any retaliation for past misdeeds and to invite their chiefs to Natchitoches to be entertained by de Mézières. If they would come, de Mézières hoped to persuade them to ride to San Antonio to celebrate peace with Governor Ripperdá.

Before Le Blanc and Bigotes could visit the four nations, more peace feelers reached de Mézières. On July 2, 1771, couriers arrived from the Tawakonis to report their decision for peace. Meanwhile, the Taovayas chief visited the Kadohadacho village to tell the resident trader that he wanted to live in harmony with the Spaniards. He offered to attack any other tribes who disturbed the peace, and he left two hostages at the village to guarantee his good faith.[31]

De Mézières had no illusions about the sudden surge of peaceful sentiment. Although the lieutenant governor and the persuasive medal chiefs had surely made some progress toward pacifying the Wichitan bands since 1770, Comanche and Osage warriors impelled them to seek protection in 1771. Comanches had not only terrorized San Antonio that spring but had also waged war against their recent allies and had cut off their access to San Antonio. The four nations found them-

---

[31] Ripperdá to Unzaga, Béxar, December 31, 1771, ibid., pp. 262–269; de Mézières to Unzaga, Natchitoches, July 3, 1771, ibid., pp. 249–251.

selves sorely disadvantaged, losing many horses to the Comanches and the Osages, and now unable to count on seizing replacements from Spanish herds. Simultaneously, de Mézières' boycott had reduced the hostile Indians to the use of bows and arrows, which also inhibited their raiding and warfare. De Mézières considered it logical that the Wichitan bands should now seek peace, with the concomitant advantages of trade and protection, and should find it in their interest to honor their peace commitments. That peace was also in the interest of the several Caddo villages, not only to foster commerce but also to keep at a safe distance the formidable warriors of the Comanche nation. As de Mézières had hoped, war with the Comanches had helped to unify and pacify the Nations of the North. It was disconcerting that Ripperdá now asked him to pacify the Comanches, too, but de Mézières promised to try.

Late that summer Bigotes and Le Blanc escorted to Natchitoches four chiefs of the Kichais, Iscanis, Tawakonis, and Cainiones,[32] who claimed that they also had authority to speak for the Tonkawas. They promised to keep the peace and live as loyal vassals of the king of Spain. De Mézières gave the new friends generous presents, and they seemed well pleased when they left. They excused themselves from going to San Antonio to ratify the treaty on the grounds of excessive distance and of prior commitment to campaign against the Osages.

Bigotes, who enjoyed the political role, decided to accompany the two missionaries to San Antonio anyway. More than forty of his people joined him. On the trail to San Antonio four Bidais fell in with the party. All the Indian visitors stayed several days as guests at Béxar and at Mission San José, where Fray Ramírez made his headquarters. Bigotes announced that all the peaceful nations would visit the governor during the good travel season next year and that he had come to represent them in the meantime. He ratified the treaties on behalf of the absent nations.

Ripperdá gave appropriate presents to all his Indian guests and outfitted the Tejas chief with a fine new uniform. In recognition of his valuable services to the Crown, he designated Bigotes head chief of all the Nations of the North and gave him a new name: Sauto. Ripperdá staged the ceremony with all the pomp and glory he could

---

32 Subsequent events suggest that this was the Wichita group that had parted from the Taovayas to live on the upper Brazos rather than join in the retreat northward from the Red River.

manage in San Antonio. With the troops of the presidio drawn up in the background and the principal religious and civil leaders of the San Antonio community standing witness, he invested Sauto before a portrait of the king.

The visit had some worrisome aspects. The Bidais foursome tried to influence the Tejas in favor of the Apaches and against the Spaniards. Nevertheless, Sauto recommended that Ripperdá name Gorgoritos captain of the Bidais. The governor honored that request and bestowed upon the new appointee the name of Melchor.[33]

When Sauto and his retinue were ready to depart in mid-October, Governor Ripperdá provided an escort of thirty soldiers and an officer of the presidio to ride with the party as far as Sauto wished. A little way out of San Antonio, the group met an Apache chief with more than a hundred men, an encounter the Spaniards suspected the Bidais had arranged. Sauto alerted the captain of the escort, who sent for reinforcements and had them within twenty-four hours. The Spanish soldiers stood by as neutral observers while the Apaches persuaded the Tejas to make treaties with them. Once the treaties were concluded, the Indians spent a whole night trading; then the parties went their several ways.

Some of the Tejas remained with the Apaches, who now gave the Spaniards more trouble than in all the years since the peace of 1749. They omitted their usual courtesy call at Béxar when they passed nearby, and for the rest of that year they preyed upon the cattle more persistently and more insolently than ever. The rate of horse theft also shot up, and, most worrying, all the Apaches who had been living at the missions ran away. There could be no stronger hint that their people contemplated war. That winter Ripperdá heard rumors that Apaches were summoning the Tejas, the Bidais, and some other nations to the Béxar region. He feared they would combine to destroy the presidios in Texas and Coahuila. The key to the Apaches' new intransigence was their alliance with the Bidais, who purveyed guns and ammunition from contraband traders on the coast.

Governor Ripperdá believed that the Tejas had been pressured by overwhelming numbers into reluctant alliance with the Apaches and that they would gladly dispose of them if the Apaches could be cut off from the Bidais and thus from gun supplies. Reckoning that de Mézières was the man most likely to achieve the necessary control

[33] Ripperdá to de Mézières, Béxar, October 7, 1771, ibid., pp. 255–256.

among the interior nations, he again urged Governor Unzaga to send de Mézières to the interior to negotiate peace treaties.

Though still captive at Natchitoches to Governor Unzaga's distrust, de Mézières had already taken another important step toward pacification of the Norteños. In October 1771, Tinhioüen escorted from his village to Natchitoches three Taovayas chiefs who wished to accept the offer of peace for their own people and for their Comanche allies as well. The leading citizens of Natchitoches and Los Adaes turned out on October 27 to see the Taovayas chiefs and Tinhioüen mark their crosses on the treaty.[34]

The treaty bound the Taovayas to try to prevent other Indians, especially their Comanche allies, from committing hostilities and to regard them as enemies if they should continue their depredations. The Taovayas agreed cheerfully, explaining that they were confident that the Comanches would not go to war because they had already gone to New Mexico to make peace treaties that they valued highly.[35] The Taovayas also promised that, for appropriate pay, they would aid any presidios the king might choose to establish in their territory. They were eager to have one as soon as possible.

No one knew better than de Mézières that the treaty was no final achievement, but rather a hopeful step toward secure peace on the northern frontier. Its value would depend largely upon the effectiveness with which the Spaniards cultivated the loyalties of the Taovayas. Their emissaries insisted more vehemently than ever that de Mézières visit them: the Taovayas needed to see that tangible evidence in order to believe that the Spaniards truly meant to be their friends and brothers. The repeated failures to visit them and to accept their offer to return the two cannons had rankled deeply among Taovayas since the 1760's. To affront them again would only invite new raids by their proud young men, whom the village elders would be unable to control.

Far more than the alignment of the Taovayas was at stake. The numerous Panismahas were their friends and potential allies. Insofar as any people held the key to communication and friendship with the Comanches, it must be the Taovayas. What Comanches, if any, they bound by their proxy to the October treaty was any man's guess, but

34 Treaty with the Taovayas, Natchitoches, October 27, 1771, *ibid.*, pp. 256–260.
35 Charles Edward Chapman, *The Founding of Spanish California*, pp. 143–144, citing Hubert Howe Bancroft, *History of Arizona and New Mexico*, p. 259, notes that Mendinueta announced conclusion of a treaty with the Comanches on February 3, 1771. Then, citing AGI materials, Chapman goes on to say that the peace of 1771 was little more than a lull.

it was a beginning. De Mézières needed now to negotiate directly with Comanches, whom he could reach from a base in the Taovayas village.

Above all, de Mézières wished to go in person to persuade the Taovayas to settle permanently in a favorable location upstream from the Kadohadachos on the Red River, where traders could reach them by canoe and effective 'communication with Natchitoches could be maintained. It was not in the Crown's interest to have the six hundred Taovayas warriors brooding in isolation in that distant, rugged country where they had retreated in recent years. Only a lively trade and joint action against their mutual enemies could cement the sturdy alliance that de Mézières desired for the Taovayas and the Spaniards. All his hopes hinged upon his personal visit, but he could only explain to the importunate Taovayas envoys that he would go to see them as soon as his own chief would let him. Again he begged Governor Unzaga to let him get on with his crucial diplomacy.[36]

While de Mézières waited for Unzaga to relent, a new peace initiative emerged from a totally unexpected quarter. Gorgoritos, alias Melchor, the Bidai leader whom Ripperdá had honored with a medal at San Antonio in October, visited de Mézières on behalf of the Apaches whose chiefs had made peace with the Bidais that fall.[37] The Apache leaders wanted to be included in the general peace that the Spaniards were negotiating with the Norteños. Therefore, they had asked Gorgoritos to assure the Spanish commanders at both Natchitoches and Los Adaes that they would never harm either the Spaniards or their Indian allies. If the response were favorable, the Apache chiefs would soon visit those two posts.

Assuming that the Spanish king never denied peace to truly repentant Indians and that some general good might well come of it, de Mézières assured Gorgoritos that the Apaches would be welcome to visit him to make peace. He then asked Gorgoritos' help in dealing with the coastal Indians with whom the Bidais had some communication.

Ever since the sixteenth century, most shipwreck victims washed onto the Gulf coast had been slaughtered by such coastal peoples as

[36] De Mézières to Unzaga, Natchitoches, October 1, 1771, AGI, Papeles Procedentes de Cuba, Legajo 110, transcribed by courtesy of Professor Max L. Moorhead from the unpublished doctoral dissertation of Dr. Vicenta Cortés Alonso, "Historia de los indios del sureste de los Estados Unidos durante la segunda mitad del siglo XVII."

[37] Declaration of Gorgoritos, Bidai Chief, Natchitoches, December 21, 1770 (*sic*), in Bolton, *Athanase de Mézières*, I, 260–262.

the Karankawas and the Cocos. De Mézières commissioned Gorgoritos to persuade them to succor rather than murder shipwreck victims and to promise them generous rewards for escorting to settlements any people whom they could rescue. Gorgoritos promised to enlist the cooperation of his maritime friends and also to persuade them to re- mand to the missions any apostates seeking refuge in their camps.

Perhaps the Bidai medal chief could have proven as valuable an ambassador to roving nations as were the several Caddo medal chiefs among the village Indians of the Texan frontier. His efficacy with the Apaches was never tested, nor was their sincerity in seeking a place in the general accord, because Ripperdá balked at the idea. He had long feared that the new peace with the Norteños would somehow lead to their rapprochement with the Apaches and that all the Indians might then unite to oust the Spaniards from Texas. Since the Indians were more numerous and probably better armed than the Spaniards, that was a nightmarish prospect. Governor Ripperdá confided his worries to Viceroy Bucareli when he reported the peace agreements in October. Judging the risk to be less than the probable advantages of the peace treaties, the viceroy merely cautioned the governor to guard against the formation of friendships between Apaches and Norteños, lest guns begin to reach Apaches too easily.[38] In order to maintain that vigilance, he authorized Ripperdá to reside permanently at San Antonio instead of Los Adaes.

Certainly the Apaches' insolent behavior around San Antonio did nothing to reassure the governor. When de Mézières notified him of Gorgoritos' embassy to Natchitoches and suggested that it might be advantageous to reconcile the old Apache-Norteño enmities, Ripperdá objected sharply. De Mézières readily deferred to his opinion, promis- ing to thwart the Apaches' effort to gain new allies. Since he hoped to take many friendly Indians to San Antonio to celebrate peace with Governor Ripperdá, he could easily encourage them to attack the Apaches in that area during the visit and thus intensify the old enmities.[39]

Whatever his own inclinations toward the Apaches, de Mézières was in no mood to argue peripheral issues or to offend the governor of Texas. Ripperdá's urgent recommendations, endorsed by Viceroy Bu-

---

[38] Bucareli to Ripperdá, Mexico, October 31, 1771, BA.

[39] De Mézières to Unzaga, Natchitoches, February 25, 1772, in Bolton, *Atha- nase de Mézières*, I, 283–284.

careli, had at last moved Governor Unzaga to authorize de Mézières' journey to the interior nations and thence to San Antonio. At the end of February, 1772, de Mézières rode from Natchitoches with eight French associates and one Spaniard from Los Adaes to make the rounds of the interior nations. Upon his mission rested all hope of peace in Texas.

CHAPTER 11

Texas, 1772-1774

        While de Mézières canvassed the northern frontier nations through the spring of 1772, at San Antonio sundry Indians tested the wit and endurance of Governor Ripperdá. Even more embarrassing than the growing truculence of San Antonio's Apache "friends and brothers" were the wiles of Comanche women.

In mid-February, Governor Ripperdá sent a squad from Béxar to escort a party of hunters and woodcutters from the settlement to the Guadalupe and San Marcos rivers. Before the end of the month they returned with three women and one young girl who said they were Comanches from Chief Povea's band. Their friendly manner seemed consistent with reports from Natchitoches that the Comanches had indicated to the Taovayas and Kadohadachos their interest in peace. Governor Ripperdá therefore entertained them graciously, gave them presents to take to Chief Povea, and assigned soldiers to escort them homeward for five days. He hoped briefly that those courtesies would inspire some meaningful response from the Comanche leader, but his actual reward was an increased rate of Comanche depredations. The women divided his presents among their own camp, then led their tribesmen back to steal in the Béxar area.¹

Other Comanche women soon came to test the Spaniards' gullibility. Early in the spring of 1772, three turned up to stay at one of the San Antonio missions and made such convincing professions of faith that they were soon baptized. The implications were both exciting and alarming. A wonderful harvest of souls could result from a Comanche peace; however, if the converts should revert to paganism, their souls would be in grave jeopardy.²

The hopeful view did not survive the spring. In May a Comanche woman, carrying a flag of truce, led seven of her tribesmen into the settlement. They connived at the flight of the three baptized women from the mission and rustled about four hundred pack animals from nearby pastures. Their triumph was short-lived: Apaches attacked the Comanches on their way home, killed the seven men, and captured the women. The Spaniards recovered the three baptized women and shipped them off to the safer distance of Coahuila, lest their souls be jeopardized again.³

Those discouraging experiences did not kill Ripperdá's hope that de Mézières could solidify the peace, perhaps even including the Comanches, on his current trip to the interior. Unfortunately, the reports did feed the viceroy's growing skepticism about the possibility of true peace with the Indians.

Ripperdá saw evidence that spring that de Mézières' achievements of the autumn had not been altogether illusory. On April 7, Chief Quirotaches and four other Taovayas delegates rode into Béxar, bearing the flag of the Cross of Burgundy. They had come to ratify the treaty made at Natchitoches the previous October. One, called Jacob, knew enough French to interpret for the delegation during talks with Governor Ripperdá. On the twentieth day of their visit, the five Taovayas ceremoniously ratified the peace, burying the war hatchet in the presence of Governor Ripperdá and other witnessing dignitaries. They rode homeward with appropriate presents the next day.⁴

Neither side entertained any illusions that the Comanche peace provisions of the treaty had been effective. The Taovayas delegates

---

¹ Bucareli to Ripperdá, Mexico, April 28, 1772, BA.
² Ripperdá to Unzaga, Béxar, May 26, 1772, in Herbert Eugene Bolton, ed., *Athanase de Mézières and the Louisiana-Texas Frontier, 1768–1780*, I, 272–276.
³ Bucareli to Ripperdá, Mexico, June 16, 1772, BA.
⁴ Ratification of Taovayas Treaty, San Antonio de Béxar, April 27, 1772, in Bolton, *Athanase de Mézières*, I, 260.

themselves told Ripperdá how his first Comanche visitors had disposed of the presents he had given them for Chief Povea.

After Governor Ripperdá bade his Taovayas guests goodbye, he settled himself at his desk to inform the viceroy of important new conclusions that he had drawn about Indian policy.[5] He had now two years of personal observations in Texas on which to draw, had corresponded with de Mézières, had consulted with veteran Spanish personnel in the province, and had come to know Apaches who frequented Béxar. In recent months he had conferred with Chief Sauto and his Tejas delegation, with Chief Gorgoritos of the Bidais, and now, for three weeks, with the Taovayas delegation of Chief Quirotaches. Governor Ripperdá now concluded that lasting peace with the Norteños hinged upon radical departure from the traditional principles of Spanish Indian policy.

Not only must there be annual gifts to the Indians, but they must also be supplied trade in guns and ammunition. He wanted the system legally structured to operate independently of the governor, so as to obviate those unfortunate accusations that had destroyed more than one governor in Texas. Why this startling conclusion? These Norteños had grown accustomed to annual presents during the French era in Louisiana, and they saw the Kadohadachos still receiving them. They had also grown so used to trading pelts for guns and ammunition, knives, clothing, and ornaments that they now depended on trade goods and would surely despise any neighbors who could not provide them. If the Spaniards should fail to do so, the Norteños would be tempted to raid the Spanish frontier in order to steal horses to trade to the British traders or French contrabandists. Since the interior nations must, at all costs, be kept loyal to the Spaniards and hostile to the British, Ripperdá saw no practicable alternative to supplying all the goods they needed in abundance, including firearms.

Although pleased that the Taovayas had come to ratify the treaty, the viceroy rejected the governor's conclusions. Assuming that habitual caprice and treachery would lead the Indians to break peace as easily as they made it, he doubted that the peace could last. He objected to fixed annual gifts to buy peace and wanted presents given only as reward on occasions when Indians had demonstrated their loyalty and devotion to the king.[6] Accordingly, Viceroy Bucareli forbade Governor Ripperdá in the summer of 1772 the one course of action that would

[5] Ripperdá to Viceroy, Béxar, April 28, 1772, ibid., pp. 269–271.
[6] Bucareli to Ripperdá, Mexico, June 16, 1772, BA.

have enabled him to capitalize on the new accomplishments of de Mézières.

Throughout his journey, de Mézières strove not only to win the Indians' allegiance to Spain but also to devise strategies for their cooperation with the Spaniards to hold the line against Osage and British incursions. His proposals to the Crown took shape as he surveyed at first hand the problems that beset the interior nations.[7]

First on the itinerary were the most peaceful of all nations, the Kichais, who were closely allied with the neighboring Kadohadachos and Tejas as well as with the Iscanis, Tawakonis, Taovayas, and Wichitas. Certainly the Kichais needed all the friends they could win: they had only thirty households, with a total of eighty men. The women farmed industriously, gathered wild nuts and fruits, prepared the skins their husbands brought home from the hunt, and bore children prolifically. Like their Wichitan allies, the Kichais often left their village in winter to hunt the buffalo. They had long bartered skins to the Natchitoches traders for firearms and other necessities. The outlook for such a small group would be bleak indeed if the Osage onslaught should go unchecked or if angry Comanches should carry their wars to the easterly villages.

Twenty miles beyond the Kichais dwelled the Iscanis in an even more vulnerable condition: only sixty warriors and an astonishing number of women and children. To the dismay of de Mézières, they were not concentrated in a village that they might hope to defend but lived scattered about on their farms. He explained his worry and won their promise to build a compact village around their chief's house right after their harvest.

The Tawakonis' situation also distressed de Mézières. They had split into two villages, one whose chief favored peace with the Spaniards, the other whose chief adamantly opposed that policy. The pro-Spanish faction lived about eighteen miles west of the Iscanis, across the Trinity River. They had 36 houses, 120 warriors, a proportionate number of women, and countless children. They desperately wanted a presidio in their territory, even more than they had in Fray Calahorra's time, and vowed they would always respect the wishes of its commandant.

De Mézières assured his hosts that he would do his best to get them a presidio, and he hurried on to the dissident Tawakonis, seventy-five

[7] De Mézières, Report of Journey to the Interior Nations, Béxar, July 4, 1772, in Bolton, *Athanase de Mézières*, I, 284–306.

miles away on the Brazos River. In the interests of peace and mutual safety, he urged them to rejoin their fellows. After he harangued them about Osages on the north, Comanches on the west, and Apaches on the south, they promised to move to the other Tawakoni village just as soon as they could harvest their corn. Since there were thirty families in the dissident band, with many children, the reunion would improve all Tawakonis' chances for survival.

De Mézières did not intend to waste the dissidents' fine site on the Brazos. He hoped to persuade the Taovayas and Wichitas to occupy it, because he wanted those bands nearer the Spanish frontier. He also thought it a likely spot for the presidio that these nations desired and that he would recommend: a practical vantage point from which to encourage good behavior and punish wrongdoing among the Indians, a useful base for communications with New Mexico, and a strategic outpost to check incursions. Best of all, it would be a headquarters from which to chastise both Osages and Apaches. De Mézières felt increasingly determined to do just that.

While visiting the Tawakonis, de Mézières also contacted the Tonkawas, who ranged between the Trinity and Brazos rivers. By 1772 they had absorbed the kindred Yojuanes and Mayeyes but still could muster only 150 warriors. The settled Norteños detested them as irresponsible vagabonds, too much disposed to thievery. They lived solely by the hunt and marketed many buffalo and deer skins at the Tawakoni villages. Since they too had a long-established stake in the commerce of the region, the Tonkawa chief and his retinue responded readily when de Mézières summoned them to a meeting at the Tawakoni village.

While the chiefs of the Kichais, Iscanis, and Tawakonis watched approvingly, de Mézières scolded the Tonkawas for their thieving ways and threatened to ask the other nations to punish them. The chief apologized humbly and promised to do better in the future. He also agreed to accompany de Mézières and the other chiefs to San Antonio to visit Governor Ripperdá, but the Tonkawas trooped off instead with the other nations' warriors on an abortive campaign against the Apaches. De Mézières philosophically deferred until some other time a more formal agreement with the Tonkawas, confident that their fear of the other nations would bring them into line.

The Tawakonis had attracted other hangers-on, less easy to dismiss. Xaranames from Mission Espíritu Santo had taken refuge with the

Tawakonis until they gathered enough of their people to take up a separate, vagabond life. Their malevolent influence had incited and guided many Norteño marauders against Spanish establishments. When de Mézières summoned the Xaranames, he found that most of them knew Spanish and had some craft skills. Although baptized Christians, they had chosen the life of apostasy and now lived in barren poverty. De Mézières did not suggest their return to Mission Espíritu Santo, but he did urge them to go with him to San Antonio to choose any mission there. Since he could not override the strenuous opposition of the two men who had emerged as the group's leaders, he prevailed upon them to settle at a site that he designated nearby, with the Tawakonis' consent. They agreed to cease their depredations. Some protective arrangement was imperative if the Xaranames were to be spared violent death and, consequent to their apostasy, certain damnation, for they had somehow incurred the wrath of the Bidais. With only 46 Xaraname warriors to protect their numerous women and children from 150 Bidais warriors, their survival was doubtful.

De Mézières rode on toward the most critical objective of his mission: the westernmost Wichitan bands, with some six hundred warriors altogether, and their sometime Comanche allies. They too had divided forces after the Osage war drove them from their Red River villages at the western edge of the Cross Timbers. The Taovayas had fled into broken country farther upstream on the Red River, where they camped at the foot of a ridge said to furnish the river its principal supply of water. The Wichitas had retreated instead to the Brazos River, 150 miles southwest of the Taovayas refuge and 275 miles upstream from the Tawakoni dissidents. De Mézières went to the Wichitas and invited the Taovayas to meet him there. They came promptly. So did more than five hundred Comanches, whose chiefs apologized for not bringing all their people, explaining that they feared their excessive numbers would inconvenience the hosts.

That was a sound precaution. The Wichitas' flight had carried them to a dismal site on the treeless plain, too poor and arid for their agriculture and so bare of timber that they had to build wretched sod huts instead of their customary grass lodges. Its only advantages were superb year-round access to buffalo and safe distance from Osages. The Wichitas and Taovayas readily agreed when de Mézières urged them to reunite and live nearer the Spanish frontier in order to bolster the new Spanish–Indian alliance. Both bands promised to move at the year's end to a place designated by the governor of Texas. De Mézières meant that to be the Brazos River site that the dissident Tawakonis promised to relinquish.

It was especially urgent to relocate the Taovayas, whose isolated northerly location exposed them to disruptive influences that could easily spread to their kinsmen and allies. In their village lived an Indian called Joseph, sometime resident of Quebec where he had become both Christian and fluent in French. He had seen Quebec fall and had informed the Taovayas and their friends that the British now occupied most former French territories. Well acquainted with the Mississippi and its tributaries, Joseph had also explained to the Norteños how easy it would be to trade with the British, whom he touted as kind and generous. Joseph had lately taken droves of horses northward from the Taovayas village to the Panismahas on the Missouri and had brought back guns and ammunition of foreign make. Accompanying him to de Mézières' council at the Wichita village were two visiting Panismahas, who busily advertised the liberal advantages of British trade. De Mézières invited the trio to ride with him to San Antonio so he could show Ripperdá the immediacy of the British threat among the interior nations.

De Mézières liked much that he learned of the Wichitas and thought they would readily become civilized, given opportunity to associate with Spaniards. They recognized a supreme creator and believed in an afterlife in which the good would be rewarded and the wicked would suffer, which suggested to the Frenchman a superior intelligence. He noted many virtues among them: their carefulness to keep promises, their respect for the elderly, their gentleness toward women, their indulgence toward children, their charitable care of the sick, their generosity to strangers, their civil obedience to their chief. Their sexual mores shocked de Mézières, as did their appalling tortures of captives, but on the whole he deemed the Taovayas and Wichitas the most promising of the Norteño allies.

De Mézières particularly appreciated his first opportunity to observe Comanches. Although impressed by their numbers, he noted with interest the fragmented character of their society, divided into bands ruled by chiefs. He learned that most of those present belonged to the large divisions called Naitanes and Yarambicas.[8] Chief Povea[9]

[8] More often rendered *Ietan* and *Yamparica*.
[9] Usually rendered *Evea* in French documents. Apparently Spaniards discerned an initial P, which Frenchmen did not.

seemed the recognized leader among all Comanche chiefs present, but de Mézières had no illusion that Povea or any other chief could really control the behavior of Comanche individuals. Because practical necessities of the buffalo hunt and of pasture for their horses required Comanches to live dispersed in countless small groups, individuals were governed by their own whims. Chiefs could neither prevent marauding nor punish for offenses that came to their attention.

While de Mézières found no authority within the Comanche nation to enforce treaty commitments, he reasoned that practical considerations would impel the Comanches to honor peace treaties with Spaniards. They needed to purchase supplies at the villages of the Wichitan bands and would be loath to commit crimes that cost them access to those valuable market places. De Mézières saw the Comanches hemmed in by Osages and other enemies on the north, by Spaniards and Apaches on the south, by Norteños on the east, and by impassable mountains on the west.[10] Although the very name Comanche evoked terror in New Mexico and Texas, de Mézières guessed that they would not be terribly dangerous as long as their roving, pastoral life kept them from uniting to exploit their huge numbers. In a crisis they had either to remain dispersed, and thus vulnerable to conquest, or to come together and risk starving to death.

Like most Europeans who had an opportunity to know Comanches in the eighteenth century, de Mézières found them a people of superior quality. Notably brave, they asked no quarter and preferred loss of life to loss of liberty. Those were virtues much admired in western European societies, and Comanches had other attitudes very like those of Europeans. Their Norteño allies' cannibalism disgusted Comanches as it did Europeans. They condemned adultery and punished guilty parties so harshly as to dismay the most censorious European. De Mézières commended other Comanche traits: keen intellects, happy natures, personal modesty in dress, phenomenal skills as horsemen and men-at-arms. Indeed, he thought them potentially the most useful and satisfactory of all Indian allies if ever they would abandon the roving life to make fixed settlements. He hoped to foster that transformation by allotting the Comanches desirable townsites and trading them farm tools for the hides they brought to market.

[10] De Mézières erred, of course, in his assumption that the Comanches found the Rocky Mountains an impassable barrier, but their wars in New Mexico did impair their trade access in that province and thus increased their dependence upon Wichitan village marts.

Chief Povea accepted de Mézières' peace proposals and joined the Indian leaders committed to ride with him to San Antonio to ratify treaties with Governor Ripperdá. More than four hundred miles of often difficult terrain lay between the Wichita village and San Antonio, but none of the chiefs or their retinues boggled at the inconvenience. On June 10, 1772, de Mézières rode into San Antonio with chiefs of the Kichais, Iscanis, Tawakonis, Taovayas, Wichitas, and Comanches, and some seventy other Indian men and women.

They found San Antonio in a state of turmoil and uncertainty. For the past two weeks the community had suffered continual depredations, apparently the work of Apaches up in arms against the rapprochement of Spaniards and Norteños. Worse still, on the eve of de Mézières' arrival Indians stole a hundred horses and mules from Mission La Concepción, and the signs pointed to Taovayas and Comanche guilt. Ripperdá greeted his guests with that news, to the surprise and discomfort of the visiting chiefs. De Mézières firmly assured the governor that no Indians of his party were involved.

Concerned that the incident cast doubt on the value of the peace they hoped to celebrate, everyone cooperated to clarify the matter. Ripperdá, who was sending an officer with thirty soldiers and thirty mission Indians to pursue the thieves, furnished horses to permit the Taovayas chief and two Comanches to witness the outcome. De Mézières sent four of his Natchitoches men to keep an eye on the proceedings.

The pursuit party failed to recover the horses, but in three days they captured the thieves, who were indeed Comanches and Taovayas. Ripperdá had ordered the thieves put to death, and the chiefs of the other nations had approved the principle. Although embarrassed by the theft, Chief Povea argued so persuasively against the death sentence that the other chiefs reversed their stand and asked the governor to revoke the sentence. Ripperdá relented and turned the prisoners over to the Indian leaders. Povea and the rest punished the thieves in their own way and promised to declare war against them if they should continue their depredations.

The judicious restraint shown on all sides and their cooperation to resolve the incident fairly augered well for the negotiations. The visitors rested; then, through a series of talks with the governor, they agreed upon terms. All the dignitaries of San Antonio assembled on the plaza to see the Indians solemnize the peace with their feather dance, while the governor sat in the central place of honor. To symbolize recognition of Ripperdá as their absolute chief, the Indians wrapped him in buffalo skins; at the ceremony's end, they presented him with the feathers and skins that had figured in the ritual.

Taovayas and Tawakoni chiefs harangued the supreme creator and ruling spirit without whose approval they believed no enterprise could flourish. The orators also treated earthly matters, exhorting their own people to keep their promises, and pledging not only to oversee the Comanches' compliance but also to declare war on them if they should break the peace.

After the Tawakoni and Taovayas leaders pointed threatening remarks at their erratic allies, Governor Ripperdá embarrassed the Comanches by displaying the white flag used in their compatriots' false truce caper at San Antonio a month earlier. That tangible evidence of Comanche perfidy so embarrassed their delegates that they did not request the return of the women held as prisoners in Coahuila since the incident. Ripperdá made no move to offer their restoration before the Comanches' peace promises could stand the test of time.[11]

Chief Povea, an honorable man, had been sorely humiliated by the robbery episode at the time of his arrival and by the report of the false truce maneuver, but he weathered the reproaches at the ceremony with unruffled poise. He explicitly agreed that every Comanche aggressor should be put to death. However, he specified that his own acceptance of the peace treaty could bind no Comanches except his own people. He promised to recommend to other Comanche chiefs that they too become the friends and brothers of the Spaniards, but he could not predict whether they would agree. More than a dozen years would pass before the rest of his nation chose the path of peace, but Chief Povea honored his own peace commitment from the summer of 1772 onward, despite grave Spanish offenses against his people.[12]

The Wichitan leaders spoke for more cohesive groups, but they also knew that enforcing the peace would be no easy task. They urgently desired a presidio in their country to help them to guarantee the new peace as well as to protect them against the Apaches and Osages. Pending establishment of a permanent fort, they wanted Spanish soldiers stationed in their villages to witness their fidelity to their treaty commitments. The Taovayas chiefs particularly feared misunder-

[11] Ripperdá to the Viceroy, San Antonio, July 4, 1772, in Bolton, *Athanase de Mézières*, I, 314–317; Ripperdá to the Viceroy, San Antonio, July 5, 1772, BA.

[12] Cabello, Ynforme, San Antonio de Béxar, September 30, 1784, AGN, Provincias Internas, vol. 64.

standings for want of communication, so they urged that four or five Spanish soldiers live in their village for a while. That would dramatize for all Taovayas the friendship and alliance to which their chiefs had pledged them and also witness their good behavior in observing the truce.[13] No Indian people could be unaware that Spaniards had difficulty identifying marauders on their frontier, that mistaken identifications could spark wars, and that Apaches sometimes planted incriminating evidence to discredit their enemies with the Spaniards.

Since a new presidio required viceregal action, Ripperdá and de Mézières speedily prepared documents urging the importance of a prompt establishment among the Wichitan bands. Meanwhile, for the Indians' satisfaction, Ripperdá ordered five Los Adaes soldiers to visit the Wichita and Taovayas villages, with two mule loads of presents and a veteran Natchitoches trader as a guide. De Mézières helped by dispatching traders to the villages of the new allies, some as residents, some as itinerants. Both the visiting soldiers and the traders were joyously received at all villages.[14]

Meanwhile, Ripperdá strove to ingratiate the head chief of the Taovayas, whose wife had been captured by Apaches a few months before the peace talks. A fellow captive, who had escaped, informed the chief that the Apaches had sold his wife to a Spaniard in Coahuila. The chief and their two little children grieved for her, and at the San Antonio conference he begged Governor Ripperdá to help him to recover his wife. Ripperdá, who had heard of the woman's presence in Coahuila, promised to do his best and appealed to the governor of Coahuila. Whatever the price required to obtain the wife of the Taovayas chief, Ripperdá wanted her returned, lest the Taovayas take the warpath. The governor of Coahuila shipped the woman to San Antonio with the next supply train. Less than two months after her husband's plea, the missing wife was a guest in the home of Governor Ripperdá, to be presented to the Taovayas chief at the earliest opportunity. The governor hoped that her husband's gratitude would cement a lasting friendship between their nations.[15]

The peacemakers sorely needed such positive results to offset the many strains upon the peace, especially those inflicted by Apaches.

[13] De Mézières to Bucareli, Béxar, July 4, 1772, in Bolton, *Athanase de Mézières*, I, 310–312; Ripperdá to Viceroy, July 6, 1772, ibid., pp. 329–333.
[14] Ripperdá to Viceroy, July 6, 1772, ibid., pp. 329–333; de la Peña to Unzaga, Natchitoches, September 14, 1772, ibid., II, 22–24. See also ibid., I, 102–104.
[15] Ripperdá to the Viceroy, Béxar, July 5, 1772, ibid., pp. 320–322; Ripperdá to the Viceroy, Béxar, August 2, 1772, ibid., pp. 333–335.

Since the autumn of 1771, Apache raiders had vented around San Antonio and La Bahía their anger at the Spaniards' friendliness toward the Norteños. Their alarm was not groundless. Both Governor Ripperdá and Viceroy Bucareli had expressed hope that Texas could be protected by inciting the Norteños to war against the Apaches.[16]

De Mézières' approach with his big Norteño delegation in May 1772 spurred the Apaches to worse mischief all around San Antonio. An Apache apostate, Joseph Miguel, reared at Mission San Antonio, emerged as the most dangerous ringleader. He and his cohorts killed three of the Comanche peace delegates and captured three women and a girl from that nation. They also killed the Taovayas Chief Quirotaches and snatched the Spanish flag that had been given him at the treaty ratification in April. They insolently flaunted their souvenir to any Spaniards who ventured among them.

When those insults failed to disrupt the peace conference in San Antonio by late June, Joseph Miguel and a single Apache companion boldly entered the presidio, despite the presence of the large Norteño delegation. Certain that Joseph Miguel wanted to learn whether the Spaniards had decided to help their new friends make war on his people, Ripperdá jailed the pair as fugitives from the mission, then asked the viceroy's permission to sentence the dangerous Joseph Miguel to the mines.[17]

Mission President Fray Juan Joseph Gumiel protested. He had labored all year to recover the Apaches who had fled from Mission San Antonio. Now Joseph Miguel claimed in his jail cell that he and his friend had actually sought the mission and, if freed, would bring in the rest of the apostates. Fray Gumiel wanted the pair released to his custody. Governor Ripperdá balked. In view of Joseph Miguel's responsibility for the murders of Comanche and Taovayas leaders, the friendly nations would doubt the Spaniards' good faith if they let him go.

Even in jail, Joseph Miguel strove to divide the enemies of his people. A Kichai chief, one of two Norteño leaders who stayed a while at San Antonio to observe the Comanches' behavior, visited the prisoner. Joseph Miguel proposed alliance between the Kichais and Apaches and offered the Kichais many horses. He also asked his Kichai visitor to convey his promise of many horses to Chief Sauto, due soon

---

[16] Bucareli to Ripperdá, Mexico, June 30, 1772, BA.

[17] Ripperdá to the Viceroy, Béxar, July 4, 1772, in Bolton, *Athanase de Mézières,* I, 314–317; Ripperdá to the Viceroy, Béxar, July 4, 1772, ibid., pp. 317–320.

to visit San Antonio with his Tejas people. The astonished Kichai chief reported the conversation to Ripperdá, reinforcing the governor's determination not to release Joseph Miguel and somehow to isolate Apaches from the gun trade among the border tribes. The logical agent would be de Mézières, who could handle that and other errands on his journey home to Natchitoches.

Only half a year earlier, de Mézières had thought it not unreasonable to encourage a general peace among Apaches and Norteños. Courtesy rather than conviction had made him defer to Governor Ripperdá's objections. Now, after that summer's experience of Apaches at San Antonio, de Mézières, too, thought the Apaches incorrigible. Convinced that their depredations would only worsen, de Mézières proposed to lead Norteño warriors on a grand campaign against the Apaches in the following spring. If they could devastate the Apaches' home territories, destroy their crops, raze their *rancherías*, and seize their horses and mules, the Apaches would have either to take refuge in the missions or flee to some remote region whence they could not bother San Antonio. The joint campaign would also help to cement the alliance with and among the Norteños. Best of all from de Mézières' point of view, once the Norteños were rid of the Apache nuisance, they would be able to focus their energies against the worse Osage menace.[18]

De Mézières volunteered to pay for the necessary munitions for the Indians: this campaign was too important to run afoul of Spanish parsimony. He would ask San Antonio only to give the Indian allies provisions for their return home and to let them market their captives there. Humane considerations required that the Norteños be encouraged to sell their captives, lest they torture and eat all whom they did not choose to keep as slaves. A profitable outcome would probably encourage them to campaign again and again, until the enemy's final destruction.

Governor Ripperdá forwarded de Mézières' proposal to the viceroy with his own enthusiastic endorsement, volunteering to invade the Apachería from another direction with one hundred fifty or two hundred soldiers, militiamen, and mission Indians from San Antonio.[19] Neither man could prepare a campaign until the viceroy consented, but meanwhile they undermined the Apaches' capacity to fight back.

De Mézières left San Antonio in mid-July 1772, responsible for four

---

[18] De Mézières to Ripperdá, Béxar, July 4, 1772, ibid., pp. 312–314; Ripperdá to Viceroy, Béxar, July 6, 1772, ibid., pp. 326–327.

[19] Ripperdá to Viceroy, Béxar, July 6, 1772, ibid., pp. 327–329.

important errands en route to Natchitoches: to send the Tonkawas to San Antonio to ratify a peace treaty; to recover the apostate Xaranames from the Tawakoni village; to break up the Bidais alliance with the Apaches; to prevent affirmation of the tentative accord between the Tejas and Apaches. Fray José Abad de Jesús María, of Mission Espíritu Santo, went along to fetch the Xaranames, with half a dozen Spanish soldiers to help him to escort the apostates back to the mission. The rest of the party were Frenchmen whom de Mézières had brought from Natchitoches five months earlier.

They rode together to the Tejas village of Chief Sauto. Visiting him was Gorgoritos, the Bidais chief whom de Mézières needed to see. Ripperdá had sent strong messages to both chiefs: the Spaniards would call their Indian allies to war against the Bidais if the Bidais would not join the ranks of the Apaches' enemies; the Tejas must not visit San Antonio without bringing enough allies to destroy any Apaches whom they might encounter. Ripperdá did not intend them ever again to be intimidated by superior Apache numbers, as in the previous fall. Knowing that he would need all his diplomatic skills and unlimited time and patience to convey such orders without offending Sauto and Gorgoritos and their people, de Mézières decided to remain at Sauto's village for long talks with the two chiefs.

To expedite recovery of the Xaranames, de Mézières sent Fray Abad and the six Spanish soldiers on to the Tawakoni village with his nephew, Nicholas Layssard, and his own interpreter of the Tawakonis' language. Unfortunately, zeal overcame judgment when Fray Abad saw his strayed flock. Giving a marathon series of harangues, interspersed with Masses, he tried to repair with a week's hard preaching the damages of ten years' apostasy. The result was disastrous. The Xaranames rejected his appeals and threatened to kidnap or kill any Xaranames who should remain in his mission. The priest just kept talking, until the exasperated Xaranames sought respite in the other Tawakoni village upstream on the Brazos.[20]

Fray Abad could not doubt the devil's ultimate responsibility, but he cast immediate blame upon the Tawakonis and the Frenchmen. He demanded that the Tawakonis coerce the Xaranames back to the mission, to fulfill their earlier promise to deliver the apostates from their village. When the Tawakonis refused, Fray Abad dismissed their

[20] De Mézières to Unzaga, Natchitoches, August 20, 1772, ibid., pp. 336–337; Ripperdá to Viceroy, Béxar, August 25, 1772, ibid., p. 339; Ripperdá to Unzaga, Béxar, September 8, 1772, ibid., pp. 344–349.

recent peace treaties, and indeed those of all the Norteños, as worthless. He brooded over the trade, particularly in guns and ammunition, between the Norteños and Louisiana, then accused de Mézières of corrupt personal interest in the Indian trade. He demanded the right to travel to New Orleans to inform Governor Unzaga.

Governor Ripperdá faced a tough dilemma: he hardly dared stop the priest, lest he, too, be accused, but he was confident of de Mézières' integrity. He recalled the unfair manner in which the inaccurate reports of soldiers and priest at Los Adaes had undermined the lieutenant governor's peace talks in 1770, and he knew that Texas could not afford to jeopardize again de Mézières' crucial negotiations with the Indians. He begged the priest not to judge the Frenchman without opportunity to explain what he had done and why. De Mézières offered to escort Fray Abad back to the Brazos for another try at the Xaraname apostates just as soon as the lieutenant governor could recuperate from the bout of malaria that felled him that summer. A little mollified, the priest agreed to wait for him at Mission Nacogdoches instead of going down to New Orleans to complain to Governor Unzaga.

Certainly impressive results followed de Mézières' mission to the Bidais and Tejas: he obtained their chiefs' promise to kill any Apaches who made overtures to them. Shortly thereafter Ripperdá's courier brought word that four Apache chiefs were leading many of their people to the Bidais and Tejas villages to celebrate treaties with them and to trade for firearms. De Mézières promptly called upon Sauto and Gorgoritos to keep their promise to slaughter the Apaches.[21] The Tejas and Bidais invited the warriors of neighboring villages to come and help.

Most of the Apaches stopped to hunt about halfway from San Antonio to the Tejas, while seven of their leaders rode on to Sauto's village to parley. True to his word to de Mézières, Sauto arranged an attack upon the guests in his house. Three Apaches died in the fracas; four escaped to cry vengeance.[22] The Bidais danced with the Tejas over the fallen Apaches and were thenceforth deemed at war against the Apaches. Since the Bidais had been the prime source of guns for the Apaches, de Mézières' coup was a signal contribution to the security of Texas.

21 De Mézières to Unzaga, Natchitoches, August 20, 1772, ibid., pp. 337–338.
22 De la Peña to Unzaga, Natchitoches, September 14, 1772, ibid., II, 22–24; Ripperdá to Unzaga, Béxar, February 11, 1773, ibid., pp. 27–28.

Zealous Sauto sent a runner to ask if Governor Ripperdá wished him to attack the Apaches hunting buffalo on the Colorado.[23] His offer fitted the agreed strategy of Ripperdá and de Mézières: to encourage the Norteños to finish off the Apaches. Unfortunately for their purpose, Crown policy forbade the governor to authorize an offensive against any Indians without specific permission from the viceroy. Since authorities in Mexico City had yet to act upon his July recommendations, Ripperdá dared not accept Sauto's offer. Sauto lost his great chance to catch the Apaches off balance and perhaps wondered at the improvidence of his Spanish allies.

While Ripperdá waited anxiously at San Antonio for consent to measures he deemed necessary to a stable peace, the ponderous viceregal machinery in Mexico City ground out its negation of the governor's plans and hopes. Ripperdá had challenged one of the oldest assumptions of Spanish Indian policy in the spring of 1772 when he reported that ample trade and regular presents, including guns and munitions, were essential to peace with the Norteños. The viceroy referred his heretical proposition to the *fiscal*, who vigorously questioned its propriety and suggested that the interior nations should instead be given agricultural implements, maize, and grain, in order to encourage them to settle in villages and take up agriculture.[24] Since most of those people had been from time immemorial both village dwellers and successful farmers, the *fiscal's* idea was startlingly irrelevant. Unfortunately, it proved a harbinger of the standard of debate upon which hinged the fate of Norteños and Apaches and the province of Texas for years to come. The whole issue was referred, as usual, to a council.

The odds lay heavily against the propositions of Ripperdá and de Mézières. For more than a dozen years the viceregal councils had operated under the dread assumption that hostile nations of the interior, armed and incited by French traders, might at any time destroy Texas. Now, one of those same Frenchmen proposed to settle the strongest of the *bárbaros* much nearer the frontier of Spanish settlement in order to consolidate the frontier from Louisiana to New Mexico against penetration by the British and their Indian allies.

De Mézières would exploit the large numbers of the Norteño warriors and their skills with horses and guns, which had so dismayed the Spaniards in Texas, in order to defend their mutual frontiers against

[23] Ripperdá to Viceroy, Béxar, August 25, 1772, ibid., I, 339.
[24] Areche (*Fiscal*) to Viceroy, Mexico, July 31, 1772, ibid., pp. 277–282.

the Osages and Britons and to solve the Apache problem in Texas. He proposed a defensive cordon based on the villages of the Wichitan bands, with a new presidio in their midst to protect them and channel their energies. Westward extension of the cordon to New Mexico would depend upon Comanche settlements that de Mézières believed he could foster. The eastward anchor of the line would be the villages of the Tejas and Kadohadachos, stable allies of long standing, who could contribute three hundred warriors to the campaigns of the alliance without leaving their own villages unprotected. Commerce and their common need to protect their territories against mutual enemies would bind together the Spanish and Indian allies.[25]

In San Antonio, de Mézières had the good fortune to deal with two pragmatic Spaniards. Governor Ripperdá consulted Mission President Fray Pedro Ramírez about de Mézières' proposal; together they endorsed his plan with an important elaboration. Both men were steeped in the Spanish tradition of concern for the conversion of the Indians and were aware of the weight given the natives' spiritual condition in debates at high levels. Since de Mézières had suggested that the Wichitan bands would readily convert to Christianity from their aboriginal belief in a supreme being, both conscience and expediency forbade neglect of those numerous souls. Governor Ripperdá and Fray Ramírez proposed to transfer two priests from the languishing missions of Nacogdoches and Los Ais to the new presidio on the Brazos. At least they could minister to the soldiers and settlers at the presidio, and perhaps they could convert some of the new allies. A few souls would be reaped if the priests could only baptize the infants who died, as they had done for years among the Tejas. The missionary embellishment lent de Mézières' presidio proposal a respectable aura of Spanish tradition.

They planned in vain. Skeptical of all opinions and proposals of de Mézières, Viceroy Bucareli ordered Ripperdá to send the fellow back to Natchitoches to report henceforth through his own governor.[26] The viceroy thought the new treaties with the Norteños of dubious value, but he ordered them observed scrupulously, so that any infractions would clearly be the fault of the Indians, not the Spaniards. For

[25] De Mézières to Ripperdá, Béxar, July 4, 1772, ibid., pp. 284–306; de Mézières to Viceroy, Béxar, July 4, 1772, ibid., pp. 310–312; Ripperdá to Viceroy, Béxar, July 5, 1772, ibid., pp. 323–326.
[26] Bucareli to Ripperdá, Mexico, September 16, 1772, BA (appears also in Bolton, *Athanase de Mézières*, pp. 349–351).

the time being, Viceroy Bucareli expected Governor Ripperdá to eschew new initiatives and to inflict prompt punishment upon any Indians guilty of violating the peace in Texas, whether they were Apaches or Norteños. While the viceroy conceded that a presidio among the Norteños might be useful to police the peace, he postponed any authorization until his council could complete its analysis and come to some agreement. The *fiscal* was not alone in his misapprehensions about the semisedentary farming Indians of the interior: Bucareli also desired the governor to induce the Norteños to settle in formal villages and enter upon a semicivilized life.[27]

Stymied by the viceroy's delays and his obvious incomprehension, Governor Ripperdá could only dread the outcome. If de Mézières were not allowed to lead the Norteño warriors against the Apaches next spring, would there ever be another chance to mount a concerted offensive against them? If the Wichitan bands were denied that long-desired presidio, would their disappointment spur them to war against the Spaniards? How could Texas survive an onslaught of Comanches and Taovayas armed with British guns?

Late in 1772 the governor's dilemma worsened, as the viceroy spelled out his rigid adherence to the old restrictions on trade and presents. Bucareli reprimanded Ripperdá for presenting guns and knives to the Norteño chiefs, contrary to the king's intentions and orders. Ripperdá's consternation was complete when he received the viceroy's command to stop all trade with Natchitoches. The laws of New Spain permitted Texas to receive only goods imported through the two authorized ports of Veracruz and Acapulco.[28] Responsibility for the total observation and enforcement of the ban on trade with Louisiana rested with Governor Ripperdá.

Since the good will of the Norteños depended primarily upon their access to de Mézières' traders from Natchitoches and secondarily on their presents from San Antonio, the viceroy's policy virtually assured collapse of the accord with the Norteños. Having doubted the validity of the peace treaties all along, Bucareli was unlikely to perceive any connection between his own orders and the disastrous results that must surely follow. Ripperdá could anticipate blame for personal incompetence at best and would be lucky to escape accusations of malfeasance.

[27] Bucareli to Ripperdá, Mexico, October 7, 1772, BA.
[28] Bucareli to Ripperdá, Mexico, November 18, 1772, and December 9, 1772, BA.

The Norteños had actually displayed remarkable patience and fidelity since their peace treaties in June. Comanches kept stealing horses, but Chief Povea had specified from the beginning that his own adherence to the treaty could not bind the entire nation. By late summer the Wichitas and Taovayas were growing restive; in September they sent the governor a specific warning that they must have trade if they were to keep the peace.[29] When Ripperdá relayed that warning to the viceroy, Bucareli answered blandly that Ripperdá would have to calm the Indians by persuasion until he could command more force. No relaxation of the trade ban would be countenanced.[30]

Ripperdá kept trying to explain to Bucareli the vital importance to the Indians of trade, offering every possible evidence of the Norteños' good faith and expounding upon the dire consequences that would surely attend breakdown of the peace. Once, in mid-winter, he moved the viceroy to observe that the governor must keep both the Norteños and the Apaches calm until that happy time when Divine Providence should move all of them to adopt the Holy Catholic faith,[31] but that serene response was exceptional. More and more, the viceroy reacted irascibly, even irrationally, to the Indian problems in the north. Somehow Apaches and Norteños blended into one terrible specter in the viceregal mind: *indios bárbaros*, bearing guns in defiance of all the laws of New Spain. He assumed that the fault lay chiefly with the governor of Texas, who must willfully have neglected to enforce the laws against the Natchitoches traffic.[32]

The Norteño leaders had hoped to have their treaties ratified in Mexico City with the viceroy himself. The principal chief of the Tawakonis and two others volunteered to ride to Mexico City with Antonio Treviño, the brave former captive of the Taovayas whom all Norteños admired. The grumpy viceroy accorded their wishes scant courtesy. When Governor Ripperdá respectfully asked permission to send them, Bucareli asked peevishly why he should bother to receive them and told the governor to put them off while he pondered the question. When the viceroy handed down his negative decision several months later, the Tawakoni chief and his associates were deeply offended.[33]

[29] Ripperdá to Viceroy, Béxar, August 2, 1772, in Bolton, *Athanase de Mézières*, I, 333–335; Ripperdá to Unzaga, Béxar, September 8, 1772, ibid., pp. 344–349.
[30] Bucareli to Ripperdá, Mexico, November 18, 1772, BA.
[31] Bucareli to Ripperdá, Mexico, January 6, 1773, BA.
[32] Bucareli to Ripperdá, Mexico, December 9, 1772, BA.
[33] Bucareli to Ripperdá, Mexico, May 25, 1773, BA.

Meanwhile, Bucareli's strictures wrecked Ripperdá's best hope of winning over the Taovayas. Late in February 1773, the Taovayas chief rode to Béxar to fetch his wife, who had lived seven months in Ripperdá's household since being rescued from slavery in Coahuila. The governor's invitation had reached the chief through the good offices of the trader du Chenne, one of five whom de Mézières had stationed with the Tawakonis to maintain liaison with the Wichitan bands and to report on their conduct. Another French trader came with the chief and his eight associates to serve as their interpreter.[34]

Ripperdá not only restored the wife to the chief, but he also gave the visitors handsome presents, including three horses and six mares. Nothing sufficed to overcome their disgust at his failure to supply munitions, and the tone of their discussions made it clear that the visit was not a success. The Taovayas wanted trade. They could not be the friends of a nation that would not meet their needs. Ripperdá had counted in vain upon the chief's gratitude for his wife as a foundation for lasting friendship with the Taovayas.

The governor did his best to patch up the matter. With them as escorts on their return journey rode an officer and twenty-two soldiers including Antonio Treviño, the Spaniard best known and respected among Norteños, laden with presents. As the governor's representative, he made the rounds of the Tawakoni, Taovayas,[35] and Wichita villages, presenting to their leaders the best gifts the law allowed Governor Ripperdá to make. Neither Treviño nor Ripperdá deluded himself that the gesture would suffice to save the peace, but perhaps it could buy a little more time in which to educate the viceroy.

Despite the governor's anxieties, Texas enjoyed a welcome lull in depredations through the fall of 1772 and the spring of 1773. The Norteños had yet to vent their grievances forcibly, and the Apaches behaved better in Texas than they had done for more than a year. Perhaps sobered by Sauto's treachery and by the Bidais' repudiation

---

[34] Ripperdá to Bucareli, Béxar, March 3, 1773, BA.

[35] The Taovayas village was located two days from the Wichitas and two days from the Tawakonis; de Mézières had yet to reunite and relocate the two former groups as he had hoped. The chief in question was earlier called by Ripperdá the Taovayas head chief; at this point, Ripperdá refers to him first as principal chief of the Taovayas and Wichitas and subsequently as "this Wichita chief." Ripperdá speaks also of appointing Treviño to visit the two Taovayas villages and one Tawakoni village. This suggests confusion among the Spaniards about distinctions between Wichitas and Taovayas or perhaps the presence of a considerable number of Taovayas in the Wichita village at that time.

of their friendship, they scrupulously avoided offending against either settlers or presidios in Texas all that fall.[36]

The Apaches' chronic fears welled to panic in late March and early April when Comanche horse thieves made a spectacular sweep through the San Antonio area. Ripperdá could not check the raiders, and the Apaches had every reason to fear that the episode heralded a lively season of raids and warfare. By mid-April they had abandoned the field, discreetly retiring southward into Coahuila and Nueva Vizcaya.

Viceroy Bucareli, terribly worried about incursions into the second tier of the northern provinces, took comfort in the thought that Hugo O'Conor would soon mete out punishment to any Indians who might need it.[37] The impatient young Irishman had risen steadily in the king's service since leaving the ad interim governorship of Texas in 1770. First he had taken command of the San Sabá presidio, recently relocated just below the Rio Grande at San Fernando de Austria; there he was promoted to lieutenant colonel. In 1771 he became commandant general of the troops of Chihuahua; early in January 1772 he became commandant of troops for the entire northern frontier. Later that year, O'Conor gained the rank of commandant inspector, with responsibility for implementing Rubí's recommendations for improvement of the frontier defenses. The speedy rise gave him little time to learn and less humility. His ascendancy boded ill for Ripperdá and de Mézières and for the Norteños: O'Conor remembered those Indians with profound distrust, and he abhorred the Louisiana trade.

O'Conor served as commandant inspector until 1776. Most of that time he was Viceroy Bucareli's principal advisor and agent on Indian and military matters in the north. Governor Ripperdá soon found the viceroy awaiting O'Conor's opinion as he had formerly awaited a council's advice, and O'Conor proved less amenable to reason than any council, especially with regard to Texas.

The commandant inspector, busy shuffling presidios in Nueva Vizcaya, Coahuila, and Sonora, initially delegated much of his work in Texas to Governor Ripperdá. Luckily, no conspicuous difficulties arose in the summer of 1773 to stir the viceroy's anxieties about Texas. Although San Antonio experienced increasing thefts and an occasional murder or kidnapping, apparently by Comanches, the Norteños kept their peace treaties far better than Ripperdá had dared hope without satisfactory trade arrangements.

[36] Bucareli to Ripperdá, Mexico, January 6, 1773, BA.
[37] Bucareli to Ripperdá, Mexico, May 25, 1773, BA.

Suddenly the Tonkawas decided to join in the accords. In August 1773, a French interpreter rode into Béxar to announce that two elderly chiefs were bringing thirty-five Tonkawas to accept the peace treaties de Mézières had proposed to them two years earlier. They wished permission to enter the presidio. Ripperdá, who chanced to have three Taovayas guests at the time, welcomed the Tonkawas to the presidio with a nineteen-gun salute. His scrupulous care to honor all his Indian visitors equally pleased and reassured the Tonkawas, who were conscious of having come late to the alliance.[38]

The new treaty with the Tonkawas marked another encouraging success for the diplomacy of de Mézières and Ripperdá, but the governor doubted its long-term worth. His experience of Comanches had made him painfully cognizant of the problems of binding all the individuals of a roving nation. He found some consolation in recalling that the Tonkawas were much fewer than the Comanches and that de Mézières believed they could be controlled through their fear of the other nations.

The autumn of 1773 brought a dramatic surge of Comanche raids, on the largest scale yet known in Texas. Despite Ripperdá's precautions, they stole 100 animals from the horse herd at Béxar and another 272 horses in the vicinity of Villa de Laredo. The Spaniards suffered human casualties, too: four dead, one wounded.[39]

The Comanche depredations completely wrecked Viceroy Bucareli's confidence in the peace treaties with the Norteños. Explanations that Comanche chiefs had little power to control the activities of their young men led the viceroy to conclude that no interior nation could make meaningful treaties. O'Conor apparently encouraged the viceroy's misapprehension and, indeed, probably shared it.

Bucareli looked to O'Conor to remedy the situation and thenceforth judged Ripperdá largely by the fidelity and enthusiasm with which he followed O'Conor's orders. Since Ripperdá considered O'Conor's blind opposition to trade with the Indians and his vehement distrust of Norteños disastrous for Texas, the governor was in a miserable predicament.

De Mézières luckily escaped the early stages of the ordeal to which Bucareli and O'Conor reduced Indian affairs in Texas. His own foray into Texas in 1772 had been a succession of triumphs: peace treaties with the key village Indians of the interior; San Antonio's first successful

---

[38] Bucareli to Ripperdá, Mexico, January 4, 1774, BA.
[39] Bucareli to Ripperdá, Mexico, February 9, 1774, BA.

negotiations with any segment of the Comanche nation; and disruption of the dangerous Apache accord with the Tejas and Bidais. He probably did not know of the serious difficulties that Ripperdá encountered with Viceroy Bucareli in succeeding months. The governor, appalled by the viceroy's aspersions upon de Mézières' judgment and integrity, was more disposed to refute than to repeat them.

De Mézières was fully absorbed in the problems of his own jurisdiction, where a long-dreaded general Indian war now seemed imminent. Arkansas Indians had invaded Kadohadacho territory in August 1771, perpetrating some thefts and murders. Since war between those two key groups would have destroyed the peace of lower Louisiana, de Mézières strove to calm the Kadohadachos and, through Governor Unzaga, called upon the commandant of the Arkansas Post to restrain the Arkansas.[40] That proved inadequate. In October 1771, while de Mézières was away for Tinhioüen's peace council, Arkansas Indians ventured near Natchitoches, omitted the courtesy of reporting to the post, and stole a dozen horses. Angry citizens gave chase but failed to catch the culprits. Upon his return, de Mézières complained directly to the commandant of the Arkansas Post, asking that he convene the Indians of his jurisdiction, identify the thieves, administer a public reprimand, and make them pay for one horse they had wounded and return the dozen they had stolen.

Twelve Natchitoches Indians volunteered their good offices to help prevent a war. De Mézières gratefully accepted, hoping that a solemn ceremonial approach to the problem would sober the Arkansas and make them more respectful of the new regime. The Natchitoches envoys rode with de Mézières' messenger to the Arkansas Post, carrying their calumet and a Spanish flag. That commandant and the Indians of his jurisdiction cooperated fully. The Natchitoches emissaries brought home the twelve horses, to the entire satisfaction of the injured parties.[41] The Kadohadachos and the Arkansas subsequently composed their differences and pledged to avenge each other against their common enemy, the Osages.

That made war with the Osages an even more pressing threat to the Natchitoches district. De Mézières proposed that Governor Unzaga designate the Arkansas River an absolute boundary, which both

---

[40] De Mézières to Unzaga, Natchitoches, August 21, 1770, in Bolton, *Athanase de Mézières*, I, 182; Unzaga to de Mézières, New Orleans, September 20, 1770, ibid., pp. 184–185.
[41] De Mézières to Unzaga, Natchitoches, October 21, 1770, ibid., pp. 180–181.

Osages and Kadohadachos would be forbidden to cross. Confident that he could trust the Kadohadachos to honor such an arrangement, de Mézières saw no reason why the Illinois commandant should not similarly control the Osages.[42] Unfortunately, his proposal coincided with the breakdown of Governor Unzaga's confidence in him in the autumn of 1771, and the boundary was never effected. When Osages launched a very lively war against the Arkansas Indians in the winter of 1772–1773 and also raided in the Red River Valley, de Mézières concluded that the safety of the Norteños in the Natchitoches district and in Texas required decisive defeat or even extermination of the Osages.[43]

De Mézières thought the Osages vulnerable to a well-directed summer campaign of the allies. As he understood it, their reed houses stood close together in the middle of a plain, far from their only spring. In summer, cornfields encircled the settlement. A large attacking party could surround the Osage village, live on the grain in their fields, and cut off their access to corn and water until they were starved out. The Crown's only cost would be powder and balls for the Indians and provisions for a few Natchitoches militiamen to stabilize the Indian force. De Mézières anticipated no difficulty in recruiting warriors from his own district and from the northern frontier of Texas, since all of those nations had suffered grievously at the hands of Osages.

Because major campaigns by Indians often foundered for lack of discipline or direction, de Mézières suggested that the governor of Louisiana designate one Indian chief to command the expedition, or perhaps two to allow for some emergency. Given his own experience of cooperation with Indian leaders, he anticipated a successful collaboration to end the Osage menace.

When de Mézières submitted that proposal for a campaign against the Osages, he already had pending an application for permission to visit France on personal business. Late in the spring of 1773 he received the leave of absence and the necessary passport[44] and promptly left for a year. He returned to find his achievements among the Indians of Texas virtually undone through the intransigence of O'Conor and Bucareli, his friend Ripperdá reduced to a state of help-

[42] De Mézières to Unzaga, Natchitoches, November 29, 1770, ibid., pp. 193–195; Unzaga to de Mézières, New Orleans, December 1, 1770, ibid., p. 195.

[43] De Mézières to Unzaga, Natchitoches, February 10, 1773, ibid., II, 24–27.

[44] Unzaga to de Mézières, Passport, New Orleans, April 23, 1773, ibid., pp. 31–32.

less resignation, and himself so discredited that he was forbidden to communicate with the governor of Texas.

The impasse inflicted incalculable damage upon the long-range interests of the Spanish Crown, upon the careers of the able, dedicated officials, Ripperdá and de Mézières, and, saddest of all, upon Indians who had no way of comprehending the remote circumstances to which they fell victim. Most directly and regrettably affected were the Wichitan bands, whose first efforts at friendship with the Spaniards had foundered upon administrative paralysis in the 1760's.

The Tawakonis and Iscanis, the Taovayas and Wichitas had never had any way of knowing why, in spite of the evident good will and interest of Fray Calahorra, their overtures had won no tangible response from the Spaniards. New Spain had deferred its response to the point of failure in the 1760's, awaiting the outcome of the Rubí inspection and the Crown's comprehensive review of policy. By 1770, Rubí had submitted a report much in accord with the desires of the Wichitan bands, recommending alliance with the Norteños and the Comanches against the Apaches as the key to security on the northern frontier. Half a dozen more years passed before the Crown found officers to implement the new Indian policy in the northern provinces. In that unlucky interval, the Wichitan bands had even more discouraging experience of the Spaniards.

Responding to the peace initiative of de Mézières in spite of all the injuries they had suffered from the Spaniards, they negotiated treaties of friendship and alliance with Spain and ratified them before the Spanish governor in San Antonio in 1772. Once again they hopefully awaited a presidio in their territory and looked forward to the healthy commerce upon which hinged their prosperity and their security. But all the fair words and tokens of friendship at San Antonio depreciated because the distant viceroy and his commandant inspector did not know or understand and would not trust the Norteños. Small wonder that bewilderment and sullen disillusion clouded the Wichitan villages in the mid-1770's.

CHAPTER 12

Provincias Internas, 1766-1776

Pathetically plain in retrospect is the dilemma of Indian leaders buffeted by forces beyond their ken. Less obvious is the dilemma of Spanish leaders, obliged to decide matters of security and justice, even of survival, for which they had little basis of comprehension. No monarch tried harder to remedy that difficulty than did Carlos III in his exhaustive attack on the problems of New Spain. For his inquiry, he dispatched the most able and conscientious officials, already distinguished in his service in Europe and Africa, and allowed them time and resources to investigate the problems. Unfortunately, the quest for fresh, disinterested perspectives led the Crown to rely upon men ignorant of the New World natives, Hispanic as well as Indian, whose lives and fortunes hinged upon their conclusions.

A conspicuous case in point was the Marqués de Rubí, assigned to the northern frontier to inspect and recommend improvements of its defenses and thus necessarily to make judgments about the Indians who affected its security. Rubí did not shirk the duty. He spent two years, mostly in the saddle, inspecting presidios from Sonora to East Texas with the technical assistance of an able, articulate engineer,

Nicolás de Lafora. But he could spend very little time in even the most important posts. What he saw depended upon the conditions that chanced to prevail at the time of his visit. His impressions of Indians hinged almost entirely upon the attitudes and information of the few Spaniards who seemed to him knowledgeable.

Time played unkind tricks upon the earnest marqués. Some of the conditions on which he founded his judgments changed radically after his visit, so that his final report rested upon some assumptions already outdated. The result was perhaps less remarkable for its manifold shortcomings than for its kernels of sound advice.

Rubí attended first to the central sector of the frontier, proceeding northward to Santa Fe and back to El Paso del Norte, inspecting the presidios en route. He then rode the long trail westward through Sonora and afterward doubled back to inspect the easternmost presidios in Texas.[1] He thus visited Santa Fe early in his journey, from August 19 to September 15, 1766, and met Vélez Cachupín, the one governor who had achieved a substantial understanding of the Comanches and had dealt with them successfully.

In that last year of his second term, New Mexico was practically at peace with the Comanches, barring occasional horse thefts, which Vélez Cachupín accepted as unavoidable incidents of their way of life. Comanches traded regularly at the Taos fair. Vélez Cachupín emphasized to Rubí that the Comanches carried guns obtained through their Taovayas allies from French traders in Louisiana. In fact, the Comanches appeared better armed than the Spaniards in New Mexico. Rubí particularly noted two facts: in both his terms Vélez Cachupín had found the formidable Comanches able to honor peace commitments, and the Comanches had not tried to exploit their superiority in numbers and weapons to destroy the province.

The Comanche relationship was not the sole success of Governor Vélez Cachupín, who also maintained peaceful relations with Utes, Navajos, and some Apaches. The only really hostile Indians with whom New Mexico had to contend at the time of the Rubí visit were the Gila and Faraon Apaches, whose capacity to make and keep peace the able governor doubted. Thus, Rubí departed from Santa Fe convinced of the practicability of peaceful cooperation with Comanches and the

[1] Nicolás de Lafora, *Relación del viaje que hizo a los presidios internas, situados en la frontera de la América septentrional, perteneciente al rey de España*, ed. Vito Alessio Robles; idem, *The Frontiers of New Spain: Nicolás de Lafora's Description, 1766–1768*, ed. Lawrence Kinnaird.

utter incorrigibility of many Apaches. He could not have anticipated that, following Vélez Cachupín's departure the next year, Comanche warriors would ravage the New Mexican frontier for more than a decade.

The year's end found Rubí in Sonora, on a frontier terrorized by Gila Apaches since the turn of the century. He spent Christmas Day 1766 and New Year's Day at Sonora's northernmost presidio, Tubac, commanded by thirty-year-old Captain Juan Bautista de Anza, a native of Sonora. Rubí found Anza outstanding among presidial commandants, praising his personality and intelligence and officially commending his honesty and efficiency. Anza kept his accounts in excellent condition; his men testified that he treated them fairly and liberally. Indeed, the little settlement at Tubac had many settlers attracted by Anza's reputation as a just and able administrator. His father and grandfather, of the same name, had commanded presidios in Sonora before him and had died fighting Apaches. The third Juan Bautista de Anza had little reason to expect a better fate.

Captain Anza exercised constant vigilance, patrolling as frequently as possible between Tubac and the posts to its right and left. Pápago enemies threatened from the northwest, as well as the ubiquitous Apaches. Gila Apache raiders struck Tubac once during the visit of Rubí, and the inspector glimpsed the difficulties of fending them off.

Rubí collected as much information about the raiders as Anza and his associates could provide. Harking back to his African experiences,[2] he compared the social organization of the Gilas to Arab clans.[3] He understood that they congregated in *rancherías* or in migratory camps and that their annual mescal harvest brought them down from the mountains to camp on plains abutting the Sonoran frontier. Naturally, that convenient proximity to Spanish establishments sparked a high season of raids. Nothing that Rubí observed or that he could learn from Anza suggested that the western Apaches could ever be truly pacified. Anza's intelligence and his long experience in Sonora must have made him a particularly convincing informant on Indians. Unfortunately, his conversations with Rubí antedated by half a dozen years Anza's enlightening, formative acquaintance with remote Indians not yet driven to hate or fear Spaniards.

---

[2] Colonel Parrilla had compared the Norteños with Arabs. An interesting line of inquiry would be the extent to which impressions, accurate or inaccurate, of tribal societies in North Africa shaped Spaniards' perceptions of Indians.

[3] Rubí, Dictamen, quoted in Kinnaird, ed., *Frontiers of New Spain*, p. 24.

Rubí did not confine his inquiries to high-ranking officers, many of whom he found shockingly incompetent or corrupt. He observed carefully all the personnel he encountered, singling out for commendation those who impressed him, especially men capable of rising to more responsible jobs. That attentiveness to all ranks paid a useful dividend in the final, eastern third of his tour, when Antonio Treviño was among the enlisted men briefly assigned to his escort.

A less perceptive officer might have overlooked that illiterate soldier, the only Spaniard with first-hand knowledge of the Taovayas and Wichita villages and of their Comanche visitors. Treviño's experience as the Taovayas chief's captive was just two years behind him when he escorted Rubí. Furthermore, his few months of service at San Sabá had given him a look at Rábago's experiment in sponsoring Apaches; from his years of service at Los Adaes, he also knew the Indians of East Texas. In short, Rubí spotted in Treviño a uniquely valuable informant on Texas Indians, and he changed the man's orders to make the most of his services. Treviño agreed to return to Los Adaes to await the inspector. Rubí notified the governor to see to his subsistence there,[4] explaining that he wanted Treviño's help in matters on which he had to report to the viceroy after his visit to Los Adaes.

The viceroy had asked Rubí's advice on two issues in Texas: the viability of San Sabá presidio and the related missions at El Cañon, and the worth of the East Texas establishments now that Spain owned Louisiana. In addition, the Crown's charge to Rubí required judgments on broad Indian policies. It was of no small moment that the inspector found in Treviño an informant whose experience had made him a friend and partisan of Norteños and a distrustful critic of Apaches.

Rubí himself saw little to recommend cooperation with the Apaches in Texas, where his first destination was forlorn San Sabá presidio, on July 25, 1767. En route he saw the missions at El Cañon, both devoid of Indians. Thirty-one soldiers from San Sabá guarded San Lorenzo de la Santa Cruz, whose only other residents were two Franciscans. The waste shocked Rubí.

He judged San Sabá no better: a presidio with neither mission nor settlement to guard. Captain Rábago begged permission to move the presidio, but Rubí told him to maintain the status quo, pending receipt of a viceregal directive. Privately, Rubí decided to recommend either extinction or removal of the presidio, but not continuation of Captain

---

[4] Rubí to Martos, Villa de San Fernando de Austria, July 12, 1767, BA.

Rábago, whose presidial administration ranked among the worst he had seen.

The inspector next saw San Antonio, flourishing by comparison with everything else in Texas. Besides Béxar presidio, which he evaluated, there were five well-developed missions and Villa de San Fernando. San Antonio had its share of Indian problems. Nominal peace with the Lipans carried a price of continual livestock thefts; since 1763 the area had suffered sporadic small raids by Norteños. Rubí assumed that pursuit of Apaches would lead Norteños and Comanches to increased activity around San Antonio, and he wanted its defenses stiffened against that hazard.

Rubí found the easternmost outposts of New Spain mere travesties of empire. The Nacogdoches mission had one missionary and no neophytes; Los Ais had two Franciscans but no Indians; Los Adaes was no better. Presidio Los Adaes, nominal capital of Texas, was decadent, but Rubí saw little point in improving it to guard an international boundary that no longer existed. The local Indians seemed perfectly docile but not susceptible to propagation of the faith; Rubí judged that the natives warranted neither presidios nor missions.

Of course, Rubí saw Los Adaes at a low ebb. Governor Martos, after a year's investigation by O'Conor, had lately been shipped to Mexico City to face charges of contraband trade and fiscal malfeasance. Ad interim Governor O'Conor had not had time, nor perhaps inclination, to grow well acquainted with the local Indians, but he distrusted their keen interest in trade. Given no experienced commandant on whom to rely, Rubí had all the more cause to value the services of the common soldier, Antonio Treviño, whose return to Los Adaes he had providentially arranged. Treviño had every confidence in the peaceful disposition of the local Indians. Neither he nor Rubí could anticipate that O'Conor would soon provoke those friendly Indians to such a fury that only the good offices of St. Denis would prevent a general massacre of Spaniards.

Convinced that Los Adaes and its neighboring missions were superfluous, Rubí led his party back toward the Rio Grande. Just two more Texas presidios awaited his inspection: San Agustín de Ahumada, often called El Orcoquisac, and La Bahía del Espíritu Santo, which had been moved inland from the coast to a San Antonio River site near present Goliad in 1749.

San Agustín and the companion Mission Nuestra Señora de la Luz, founded on the Trinity in the late 1750's to forestall the intrusions of

French traders among the Indians, had never thrived. Indeed, unsavory events at San Agustín had damaged Spanish prestige and authority among Indians in the area.[5] Captain Rafael Martínez Pacheco, who took command in May 1764, so abused Spanish personnel that the missionary abandoned his station, many soldiers deserted, and the remainder threatened to decamp if there were not swift remedy. Governor Martos decided to suspend Martínez Pacheco from the command and sent Lieutenant Marcos Ruiz from Los Adaes to take over as acting commander. Aware of the threat to his command, Martínez Pacheco distributed swords, muskets, powder, and shot from the presidial arsenal to the Akokisas and Atakapas in the vicinity, calling upon them to defend him against the soldiers coming from Los Adaes to effect his removal. Martínez Pacheco barricaded himself in his house with some servants and defied all comers.

Since the captain had wooed the Indians with rations of beef that summer, they responded to his call. Loath to antagonize the Indians, Lieutenant Ruiz retired from the presidio until the resident interpreter, Lieutenant Domingo del Río, could visit their chiefs to explain the situation and ask them not to help the captain defy his own chief.

Lieutenant del Río visited the nearby Akokisa village, where he also found Atakapa Chief Canos and his people. When the officer convinced the Indians that Captain Martínez Pacheco truly exceeded the bounds of propriety, they promised to stay out of the quarrel. The host chief, Calzones, offered his own services for three days to persuade the captain to leave. If Martínez Pacheco should refuse to go after that, Calzones would let the Spaniards do whatever they wished with him. Lieutenant del Río gratefully accepted Calzones' offer and promised to come daily to learn of his results.

When Chief Calzones first called upon the captain, Martínez Pacheco not only refused to leave but also vowed to resist to the death. His bravado amused the chief. When Calzones visited the captain's quarters the second day, only to find him still intransigent, the chief warned him not to expect any help from the Akokisas or from the Atakapas or from the Bidai chief who had just arrived with many of his people. When Martínez Pacheco shrugged off his advice, Cal-

<hr />

[5] Testimonio of proceedings instituted by Lieutenant Don Marcos Ruiz against Captain Don Rafael Martínez Pacheco, 1764, BA; an account of the affair of San Agustín appears in Herbert Eugene Bolton, *Texas in the Middle Eighteenth Century*, pp. 365–374.

zones left, annoyed at the captain's folly, and reported the matter as hopeless.

Lieutenant Ruiz then resumed responsibility for dealing with the recalcitrant captain, and for two days he threatened to burn the house down if Martínez Pacheco would not submit. He was loath to proceed, not only because he lacked authorization to burn the presidio, but also because Martínez Pacheco and his two servants had barricaded themselves with enough armaments to assure some casualties. The Indians began openly ridiculing the cowardice of all those Spaniards against a mere three in the captain's house.

Unwilling to expose Spanish authority to Indian contempt, Ruiz called his final warning to Martínez Pacheco on the third day of their impasse. The captain fired a cannon in reply and called for the Akokisas and Bidais to help him. They prudently refrained. Only when a musket shot from the captain's quarters killed a soldier did Lieutenant Ruiz set the house afire. Rising wind fanned the flames, which devoured the house and contents, an old empty barrack, and part of the church. Martínez Pacheco and a henchman escaped unhurt through a back exit and fled to La Bahía, thence to San Antonio, and eventually stood trial in Mexico. A year later Inspector O'Conor arrested Ruiz for setting the fire, but afterward blamed Governor Martos. Burning the presidio figured importantly among O'Conor's charges against the hapless governor.

Sordid by any standard, the episode was particularly unfortunate in a presidio intended primarily to stabilize a loyal Indian population in a strategic location. The Akokisas occupied their villages only in spring and summer and spent the rest of the year away hunting bear. The Atakapas, whom the Spaniards knew as kinsmen and allies of the Akokisas, customarily paid long visits in the warm season. To keep all of them in the presidio area and reasonably content, the Spaniards had promised weekly rations of beef and corn. Fiscal difficulties and transport problems had made the rations so erratic that the program often generated more resentment among the Indians for failure to receive goods than friendly gratitude for rations. Martínez Pacheco's improvement of the rations after a lag in distribution had been the key to his friendship with the Indians. Lieutenant Ruiz strove to stabilize and increase the rations and to restore dignity to Spanish authority in the area, but the usual paucity of resources hampered his work.

Rubí saw San Agustín only three years after the disgraceful Martínez Pacheco episode: a garrison of thirty-one, lately driven to a temporary encampment when a hurricane destroyed the charred remnants of the presidio, a mission with two Franciscans and no Indians. The whole enterprise looked useless. Presuming French incursion no longer a factor, Rubí resolved to eliminate San Agustín. That he saw no Indians was surely due to their autumn departure for the bear hunt, probably hastened that year by the hurricane, but they were so few and so docile that he would not have thought they warranted a presidio anyway. With so little time to study the area, Rubí could not anticipate the consequences of withdrawing the Spanish presence on the lower Trinity. Within a year Akokisas, Atakapas, and Bidais would be purveying guns from French contrabandists to Lipan Apaches.

By contrast with San Agustín, Presidio La Bahía del Espíritu Santo looked viable. The soldiers and settlers suffered badly from malaria, which Rubí attributed to a swampy, unhealthful site. The missions were not flourishing, but each could claim some converts among the Indians. Ninety-three then lived at Mission Espíritu Santo, just across the San Antonio River from the presidio; 101 Indians lived at Nuestra Señora del Rosario, about five miles upstream. Rubí decided to leave La Bahía there as the easternmost post in a line of fortifications that he proposed to extend from Altar in Sonora to the Gulf of Mexico.

It seemed a safe, convenient anchor, just 175 miles east of San Juan Bautista. Apaches rarely came that far below San Antonio; Rubí thought the coastal Indians[6] too cowardly to be dangerous and easily amenable to management by Franciscans.

Lest Indian depredations in the area between La Bahía and San Antonio cut off their communications, he suggested a new subsidiary post on the Arroyo del Cíbolo, manned by an officer and twenty men seconded from Béxar, expressly to protect the road between the two presidios and the ranches south of San Antonio.

His responsibilities in Texas discharged, Rubí left La Bahía in mid-November 1767 on his way back to civilization at last. He crossed the Rio Grande at Laredo, a scattering of sixty huts on both sides of the stream, where settlers formed their own defense as militiamen under a resident captain. Though Laredo was increasingly important as a point of entry to Texas, Rubí hurried on to inspect the last presidio on his list: San Juan Bautista, earliest gateway to Texas, now of

---

6 Sometimes lumped under the general term "Borrados."

dwindling importance. Its garrison of thirty-three pursued Lipan and Mescalero marauders actively, to better effect than most other companies Rubí had seen. It fitted admirably into his concept of a systematically spaced defensive cordon.

Upon completion of his presidial tour, Rubí boldly reported to the Crown that much of its empire in the north was a sham. Over a vast territory Spain claimed dominion that it could not hope to realize with its available forces. With rare exceptions, the northern frontier presidios were military mockeries: crumbling structures, incompetently and corruptly managed; garrisons of untrained soldiers short of basic equipment, skills, and morale; each outpost so entangled in the mechanics of its own survival as to be nearly useless against the swift-moving *indios bárbaros*. Each garrison lived braced against a siege that never came because that was not the Indian style of warfare, while Indian raiders plundered settlements and missions, mines and ranches, and for good measure stole most of the presidial horse herds.

Rubí proposed a radical remedy: give up the expansion of empire; draw a realistic frontier line from the Gulf of California to El Paso del Norte, thence roughly along the Rio Grande to the Gulf of Mexico; and keep the hostile Indians north of it. Garrison that line with fifteen presidios spaced at regular intervals, each with fifty men and officers, competently trained and properly equipped.

Some realities would not mesh with that tough, systematic approach. For instance, in the two provinces north of the line, where Rubí found the Spanish Empire largely imaginary, lay two communities impossible to abandon: Santa Fe and San Antonio. In terms of people, property, and responsibilities to converted Indian populations, there were too many obligations to write off. To secure those important outposts and the supporting stations that he proposed at Robledo and Arroyo del Cíbolo, the Marqués de Rubí suggested a total of 160 officers and men for Texas and New Mexico.

Only three existing presidios fitted into Rubí's orderly cordon of defense. Many would be extinguished; others would be relocated, at enormous cost of time, money, and labor. Rubí slated six new presidio sites in areas that he had not personally inspected, some of which proved quite unsuitable.

Much of the difficulty centered upon the Bolsón de Mapimí, a rugged mountain and desert badlands running southward from the Rio Grande between the Sierra Madre Occidental of Coahuila on the east and the Conchos Valley on the west. The northward-moving Spanish frontier had surged around it, leaving it a sanctuary of *indios bárbaros,* now chiefly Mescalero and Natagé Apaches, who made it their base for raids into Nueva Vizcaya, Coahuila, and even southward into Nueva Galicia. Rubí now proposed that Spain draw its line of authority along the Rio Grande, north of the Bolsón, and drive the *bárbaros* north of that frontier or exterminate them. Unfortunately, he never saw that forbidding stretch of the Rio Grande on which he proposed new presidios.

Relocation of some existing presidios and extinction of others threatened the frontier populations. Most presidios had been founded to guard nearby missions; civil settlements had sprung up around many of them. Rubí's fetish of orderly spacing would strip the defenses from mission and civil settlements, save what they could muster from local militiamen and mission Indians.

In sum, Rubí proposed to guard the actual (as opposed to the imaginary) frontier of New Spain with a total of 960 soldiers, at an estimated annual cost of 373,575 pesos, a projected saving of 79,929 pesos over the current annual costs, disregarding the substantial expenses of founding new presidios and relocating old ones. So far as anyone could judge in Mexico City or Madrid, Rubí had rendered the efficient professional judgment that the enlightened Bourbon monarch sought.

Less predictable was Rubí's stand on Indian policy on the northern frontier, where he urged fundamental changes. For more than a century and a half the northern provinces had experimented off and on with "peace" with various Apaches, only to know a rising tide of depredations in most areas. Except for Jicarillas and Carlanas, who had taken refuge from Comanches in the shadows of the easternmost pueblos of New Mexico, no Apaches had ever sustained the obligations of vassals to the king. Long experience suggested that they were incapable of doing so. Such veterans as Anza in Sonora, Vélez Cachupín in New Mexico, and Treviño in Texas saw no hope of true pacification of Apaches. On the other hand, Comanches in New Mexico and Norteños in Texas seemed able to make and honor commitments if properly cultivated, while their greater numbers and their mastery of firearms made them potentially more dangerous enemies than the Apaches. Rubí suggested that the Spaniards abandon all commitments to the Apaches, which only invited the hostility of their enemies in the interior, and ally instead with the Comanches and Norteños, either to subdue or to exterminate the Apaches.

To dump the Apache pests and make common cause with the Norteños! That was precisely what Fray Calahorra had urged since the beginning of the decade: the unresolved issue that had frustrated all response to the overtures of the Tawakonis and Taovayas. But the Norteños never knew that in 1768 a high official had at last found in their favor or that he recommended extinction of both San Sabá presidio and the missions at El Cañon. By the time Rubí reported to the king, Norteño and Comanche warriors had already destroyed, for all practical purposes, those hated symbols of Spanish favor to the Lipans. Perhaps it was just as well that the Norteños had no inkling that they had scored a triumph in principle in 1768; another decade's wait lay in store before the Crown could effect the machinery for new policies in the northernmost reaches of the empire.

The Rubí recommendations on presidios were readily accepted in Mexico City and in Madrid as the considered judgment of a professional soldier. With little modification, they were promulgated in the Regulation of 1772.[7]

The inspector's harshly expedient plan to solve the Apache problem fared worse. The Crown recognized the unsatisfactory record of Apache performance, but the humane Christian tradition of Spanish Indian policy forbade exclusion of any people from peace and salvation. Therefore, the Regulation of 1772 proclaimed the prime objectives of the king on the northern frontier to be peace, the welfare and conversion of the pagan tribes, and the tranquillity of the northern provinces. Even Apaches were entitled to peaceful coexistence if they sincerely wished it.

The new regulation made some concession to the discouraging realities that Rubí had pinpointed. It authorized active, unceasing war on hostile tribes, right into their homelands. No general peace could be extended to any whole nation, especially to Apaches, without the viceroy's specific approval. Provincial and local commanders could only grant truce, and that only to specific groups.

The Crown required that necessary wars be managed as humanely as possible, rejecting the extermination that Rubí recommended for Apaches. Prisoners were not to be abused. Anyone killing a prisoner in cold blood would incur the death penalty. Captured warriors would be shipped, with suitable rations, to the interior, to be managed as the viceroy saw fit. Women and children would be kindly treated, with

[7] See translation in Sidney B. Brinckerhoff and Odie B. Faulk, *Lancers for the King*.

every effort to convert and educate them. Since a truce would require exchange of prisoners on both sides, a commander who believed a truce imminent should hold his captives available nearby for restoration to their people.

The new regulation enjoined forbearance and persuasion as the keys to good relations with peaceful or neutral tribes. In case of horse thefts or other crimes that could not be overlooked, they should be given the chance to make restitution; only as a last resort should force be employed against them, and even then with great care to inflict the least possible injury. In no case was corporal punishment to be administered or anyone arrested to be sentenced to servitude. The same standards of humane, generous treatment applied to prisoners of war would apply to any Indians subject to punitive action. Women or children taken in such action should be promptly restored to their families to prove that the arrests had stemmed from considerations of law and justice rather than hatred or greed.

The royal intent was clear enough, but what of implementation? What authority would realign presidios, pursue authorized wars against hostile Indians, and cultivate peaceful relations with the friendly and neutral Indians? Historical precedent argued that the overburdened viceregal administration could not manage the northern provinces. Visitador General Gálvez had already suggested a possible solution: a separate Comandancia General for the interior provinces, directly responsible to the Crown.[8]

Gálvez worried particularly about the stability of the northern frontier, for he intended its boldest expansion yet: colonization of Alta California. That conflicted with the contemporaneous recommendation of the Marqués de Rubí that New Spain forswear expansion and contract its responsibilities to match its resources. Gálvez prevailed, arguing that if Spain should any longer fail to occupy Alta California, Russia or Great Britain would surely preempt that strategic ground.

Separate governance for the northern provinces hung fire for several years while the visitador general pursued more immediately pressing matters. In 1768 he founded the new port of San Blas to serve as a base of supplies for the projected California colonies and beleaguered Sonora. The founding of San Diego in 1769 launched the extraordinary burst of expansion climaxed just seven years later by the founding of San Francisco. Meanwhile, in spite of grave illness, Gálvez spent much

---

[8] Charles Edward Chapman, *The Founding of Spanish California*, pp. 73 ff.

of his time in Sonora, directing campaigns against insurgent Seris and Pimas who again threatened its very existence. His suggestions of fundamental structural reforms still awaited action in Spain when the visitador general sailed homeward early in 1772.

Meanwhile, tentative steps had been taken to effect some of the Rubí recommendations. As ordered by the Minister of the Indies in 1770, Viceroy Croix issued in the summer of 1771 a detailed instruction for the formation of Rubí's presidial line from Sonora to Texas, effective January 1, 1772. Little was achieved under that order before the new Regulation of 1772 superseded it, effective January 1, 1773. Meanwhile, as if to compound the uncertainties, a new viceroy took over the government in Mexico City and adopted a thoroughly jaundiced view of the entire problem of the northern frontier.

Viceroy Antonio María Bucareli y Ursúa succeeded the Marqués de Croix on September 23, 1771. Within a few months, the visitador general departed, leaving Bucareli with sole responsibility for New Spain. A man of distinguished lineage, he had amassed a superb record of service to his king in both military and civil capacities, most recently as governor and captain general of Cuba. Bucareli had hoped to retire from that post to Spain; he was feeling his years heavily and his health had deteriorated badly in the punishing climate of Havana. Instead, the Crown handed the old man the toughest challenge of his entire career, the viceroyalty of New Spain, with all the problems attending a time of reappraisal and reorganization. A meticulous administrator with a keen sense of personal responsibility for every facet of his job, Bucareli was aghast to discover very early that the affairs of the viceroyalty were in such acute disarray that it was extraordinarily difficult to get any information about actual conditions. He confided his dismay to his good friend, General O'Reilly, singling out the northern provinces as the worst headache of all, marvels of fiscal and political chaos and plagued by Indian wars. The crowning blow was the new regulation, requiring expensive juggling of presidial locations and large reserves of supplies for which the treasury had no means: all that expenditure, with bills for the northern frontier already two years in arrears, and no funds in sight to meet the bills.[9]

No small factor in Bucareli's uneasiness about the Indian wars on the northern frontier was the visitador general's young nephew, who commanded troops for Nueva Vizcaya and Sonora. Even if Bernardo

[9] Bucareli to O'Reilly, Mexico, October 27, 1771, quoted in Bernard E. Bobb, *The Viceregency of Antonio María Bucareli in New Spain, 1771–1779*, p. 30.

de Gálvez were as promising as reported, Bucareli thought him entirely too young to have had any experience. Similar misgivings had occurred to the lad's distinguished uncle, but the visitador general did not countermand the "excess of kindness" shown the young officer, and Captain Gálvez led several major expeditions against the Apaches, beginning in the fall of 1770.[10]

The first two campaigns of young Gálvez were extraordinarily successful. On the autumn campaign he led about 135 frontier soldiers and Indian allies from Chihuahua to the Pecos River, where he surprised an Apache camp. At a cost of only one Spaniard wounded, they killed twenty-eight Apaches and captured thirty-six; only three were believed to have escaped. The booty included 204 horses and mules, divided among the Indian allies, and buffalo hides and antelope hides worth 2,000 pesos.

The most unusual aspect of the affair was the result Gálvez obtained by good treatment of the Apache captives: six months later, some of them accompanied the Spanish troops as guides and auxiliaries. Other Apaches heard of his kindness to the captives and proposed to Gálvez a general cessation of hostilities.

His "general peace" in 1771 proved illusory. Gálvez soon had to take the field again in the fall of 1771, when Gila Apaches stole a whole herd of horses and mules from Chihuahua. The raiders inflicted heavy losses on the pursuing Spanish troops; Gálvez himself was severely wounded. He tried to lead another expedition into Apache territory in November, only to be incapacitated by a fall from his horse.

The adversities that Captain Gálvez had to report to the new viceroy in the latter's first months in Mexico City assorted badly with his boy-wonder reputation and confirmed Bucareli's doubts. Fortunately for the viceroy's peace of mind, the visitador general had already arranged for his nephew to accompany him home to Spain. By the year's end Bucareli happily sent his own man to replace Captain Gálvez.

Bucareli had confided his doubts about the visitador general's nephew to General O'Reilly, who perhaps was thus moved to recommend his own kinsman, Hugo O'Conor. At any rate, Bucareli did appoint O'Conor to the job and thenceforth relied heavily upon his advice in matters concerning the interior provinces.

Captain Gálvez left New Spain on an inglorious note. When O'Conor reached Chihuahua to take command in December 1771, the vigorous young captain was off on a last campaign against the Apaches, netting just one horse. Another embarrassing failure marred his record. Still, Gálvez did not give up his experiment in conciliating Apaches, whom he admired for their fortitude and skill. When he rode south to Mexico City in February 1772, he took fourteen Apache captives whom he enrolled in the Colegio de San Gregorio. The captain sailed home from Veracruz with his uncle, and in Spain he found his extraordinary successes with the Apaches better remembered than his failures.

The radical experiments of Captain Gálvez were less kindly remembered in America by men whose attitudes could shape policies. General O'Reilly suggested that young Gálvez had "emboldened and incited" the Indians unduly and that it would now be necessary to mete out severe punishments to regain their eventual friendship.[11] He confidently expected his cousin O'Conor to achieve more effective control of the Apaches, an assumption easy enough at the comfortable distance of Havana but difficult even for the vigorous O'Conor to realize in the interior provinces.

O'Conor barely settled into his new command before Bucareli found another opportunity to promote him. The Regulation of 1772 provided for a commandant inspector for the interior presidios, at least of the rank of colonel, who for the time being would report directly to the viceroy; if the king should later find it convenient to appoint a commandant general for the interior provinces, the commandant inspector would immediately come under the orders of the commandant general. Meanwhile, the commandant inspector would enjoy extraordinary powers. He must not himself govern a province or command a presidio, but he would be responsible for overseeing all governors and captains and could reside wherever he thought necessary for the performance of his duties. His prime responsibility would be to oversee observance of the Regulation of 1772, reviewing the presidios annually and reporting to the viceroy on the conduct of the officers. It was a splendid opportunity for an ambitious career officer. O'Conor tackled his duties energetically, according to the viceroy's instructions.

Bucareli, who had floundered uncomfortably with the problem of the northern frontier ever since he took office, found in the Regulation of 1772 a definitive guide to management of the interior provinces. At last he felt in command of an active, coordinated effort to subjugate the Indians, from which might follow peace and security throughout

[11] Ibid., p. 66 (quoting O'Reilly).

the interior provinces. Swallowing his misgivings about the fiscal soundness of Rubí's program, Bucareli gave O'Conor a hundred veteran dragoon regulars for the recommended flying companies and defined his priorities. First, oust the Mescalero raiders from their sanctuary in the Bolsón de Mapimí; second, realign and reform the presidios as projected by the Marqués de Rubí. The reforms relating to New Mexico and Texas were delegated to their respective governors. Other governors and presidial captains were required to cooperate with O'Conor in realigning the presidios within their provinces, to the open disgust of some who questioned the worth of the program.[12]

The Regulation of 1772 specified that the presidios should be relocated with due attention to appropriate terrain and abundance of water and pasture, but in no case should they vary much from the sites indicated on Lafora's map. Those two provisions were not always compatible, especially in the regions never seen by Rubí and Lafora. O'Conor himself thought some of the new locations unwise, but wherever possible he effected the Rubí plan. He had not built his meteoric career by contradicting powerful superiors.

Keen to carry war into the Apache sanctuaries, O'Conor combined his drive into the Bolsón de Mapimí with a search for new sites on the Rio Grande for the presidios of San Sabá and Cerro Gordo. In April 1773 he launched a campaign from Santa Rosa presidio in Coahuila and congratulated himself that he had temporarily forced the Apaches out of the Bolsón. He next rushed to Nueva Vizcaya to strike against Tarahumaras who had allied with Apaches and were raiding southward to Durango. That summer O'Conor found it necessary to put a temporary defense line south of the Bolsón to check Apache and Tarahumara incursions until he could make the Rio Grande cordon a reality. Bucareli approved his improvisation, enormously relieved to have in action an officer who appeared competent to check the *bárbaros*.

By autumn 1773, O'Conor was ready to attack Apaches north of the Rio Grande. In November he campaigned in the Guadalupe and Organos mountains against Mescalero and Natagé Apaches who were raiding northward into New Mexico and southward into Nueva Vizcaya from that base. He surprised a large *ranchería*, killed forty-five,

---

[12] See Max L. Moorhead, *The Apache Frontier: Jacobo Ugarte and Spanish Indian Relations in Northern New Spain, 1769–1791*, pp. 33–34.

and wounded many before the survivors fled.[13] The unusual success improved Spanish morale and perhaps sobered some Apaches. Lipan Apaches who had raided heavily in Coahuila and Nueva Vizcaya in 1772 found it expedient in 1773 to make peace with O'Conor, whose instructions were to drive them back across the Rio Grande. The commandant inspector, never a charitable judge of Indian behavior, thought that the Lipans honored their peace commitment tolerably well, although some individuals occasionally joined Mescalero raiders.[14]

After the successful offensive campaigns of 1773, O'Conor spent most of 1774 on his other major task, establishment of the new presidial cordon, and on his supervisory duties throughout the interior provinces. Unhappily for Governor Ripperdá, O'Conor soon turned his attention to Texas.

Confrontation over Indian affairs in Texas had been shaping in widely separate arenas since the beginning of the decade. In 1770, while the new Governor Ripperdá grappled with the intricacies of Indian problems in Texas, young Captain Gálvez scored his important successes with, as well as against, Apaches on the Nueva Vizcaya-Sonora frontier. By 1772, when Governor Ripperdá reached his radical conclusion that unrestricted commerce was necessary to peace with the Norteños, the open-minded experiments of Gálvez had been discredited in important quarters. Viceroy Bucareli agreed with General O'Reilly that a naive show of trust in *indios bárbaros* only invited new injuries and that decisive military victories alone could tame such savages. The time was singularly unripe for the innovative proposals of Ripperdá and de Mézières.

O'Conor's ascendancy worsened their prospects. It was natural that Bucareli should rely upon O'Conor's judgment regarding Texas, oblivious to the peculiar bias inherent in his two-year experience there. O'Conor had gone to Texas as a special investigator. In that role he probed a wide range of possible deviations from the law but never grappled with the practical day-to-day problems of survival that beset any governor on that frontier. His investigations of commercial irregularities had made him deeply suspicious of Indian trade and particularly distrustful of Frenchmen and Norteños. As governor ad

---

[13] Paige W. Christiansen, "Hugo O'Conor's Inspection of Nueva Vizcaya and Coahuila, 1773," *Louisiana Studies* 2 (1963): 157–175.

[14] Hugo de O'Conor, *Informe de Hugo de O'Conor sobre el estado de las Provincias Internas del Norte, 1771–76*, ed. Francisco R. Almada, pp. 79–80.

interim, O'Conor had suffered one frustration after another. He had been unable to wipe out illegal trade across the Louisiana-Texas border and had been chided for his efforts by Governor Ulloa. In addition, he had been denied permission for a campaign to subdue forever all Norteños and Comanches. Those experiences inevitably influenced his response when Bucareli asked O'Conor's advice about Texas. They boded even worse for Ripperdá and de Mézières and the Norteños when Commandant Inspector O'Conor acquired jurisdiction over that province.

In May 1773, Governor Ripperdá received O'Conor's orders to implement the Rubí plans for Texas. He had no responsibility for San Sabá. Since Captain Rábago's abandonment of the original site in 1768, that presidio had been relocated below the Rio Grande. Ripperdá was expected to extinguish the presidios of Los Adaes and San Agustín, to close down the three missions in East Texas and the one on the Trinity, and to relocate at Béxar all settlers from those places, as well as the garrisons and their equipment. After those tasks, he would have to reform and enlarge the presidial garrisons at Béxar and La Bahía del Espíritu Santo and plant a new post on the Arroyo del Cíbolo.[15]

San Agustín had in fact been abandoned for nearly two years. Captain Martínez Pacheco, reinstated in that command in 1769, had led part of his garrison to San Antonio in the summer of 1770 when Governor Ripperdá called for help against the Apaches. The rest of the soldiers from San Agustín had answered a similar call from Béxar in February 1771; the missionaries had then abandoned their station at Mission Nuestra Señora de la Luz. Since Rubí had meant San Agustín's soldiers to shore up the Béxar garrison, events had only anticipated the order.

Much of the Los Adaes garrison had also been transferred to Béxar a year earlier, in response to *bárbaros'* depredations there and in anticipation of Rubí's known intent. Still, withdrawal from East Texas proved difficult because Indians and settlers objected. Governor Ripperdá hastily visited the area in May 1773 to launch the removal, but he had to return to Béxar after just eight days and left the actual work to Lieutenant González of Los Adaes.

During the governor's brief call at Mission Nacogdoches, the Tejas medal chief Sauto brought before him a large Indian delegation

---

[15] Bolton, *Texas in the Middle Eighteenth Century*, pp. 385 ff.

protesting the departure of the Spaniards. Sauto felt so strongly about the matter that he had suspended a campaign against the Osages in order to talk with Ripperdá. He had good reason to object: rumor had it that the Lipans planned to invade Tejas territories to avenge the murders of their three envoys at Sauto's house in the preceding fall. Sauto demanded the supporting presence of Spanish allies in his territory.

None of the Indians relished the loss of the Spanish settlements as sources of trade and presents, however unsatisfactory their quality and quantity. Even closing the missions distressed them. Though they had never taken to mission life, baptism at death had grown important to some of the Indians. They also appreciated, as Rubí had not, the missionaries' value as liaisons between Spanish and Indian communities.

Ripperdá sympathized with the Indian delegates, but he had no authority to yield to their protest. The governor could only hope that de Mézières would soothe their hurt feelings and help the Indians of East Texas to see that the withdrawal signified the new unity of the French and Spanish people rather than any loss of interest in those important friendly nations. Ripperdá had no idea that de Mézières was actually on his way to France and that his services would be unavailable for a year.

The settlers of Los Adaes were at least as indignant as the Indians, and with good cause. There, as in several other places, conditions had changed a great deal since Rubí collected his information. The inspector general had counted there in 1767 about thirty families, estimated at two hundred persons, but apparently there had been some influx across the Louisiana border once the two provinces had a common sovereign. Less than six years later, Governor Ripperdá found more than five hundred living near the presidio and on ranches around Los Adaes and Los Ais, a heterogeneous populace, primarily Spanish, French, Indian, and Negro. Their leading spokesman was a prosperous rancher and trader, Antonio Gil Ybarbo, a native of Los Adaes, then in his mid-forties.

Upon reaching Los Adaes early in June 1773, Governor Ripperdá notified the citizenry to be ready to depart for Béxar within five days. Their protests won a two-week extension, but they still felt aggrieved. Many were wrenched from the only home they had ever known and some from family ties in neighboring French and Indian communities. They lost all the property they could not move, and the short notice made it impossible even to load all their movable goods. There was not

time to round up all their scattered livestock, and they had to abandon
crops not quite ready for harvest.

The three-month trek from Los Adaes to Béxar, June 25 to September
26, became a nightmare of starvation and illness. Many died, especially
children and old folk. Old Lieutenant González survived only as far
as Mission Nacogdoches; the sergeant of the garrison led the rest of the
way. Some dropped out along the way. Of those who reached Béxar
in September, more than thirty died within the next three months,
victims of the health-breaking ordeal.

Some stragglers stole back to El Lobanillo, Gil Ybarbo's ranch between the Sabine River and Los Ais, where some sick people had been
left under the care of Gil Ybarbo's kinsmen. The clandestine community lived as best they could, smuggling goods, especially liquor,
from Natchitoches to trade to Indians. They had plenty of competition:
at the departure of the Spanish garrison, Frenchmen from the Natchitoches area flocked across the border to live among the Indians and
trade relatively free from supervision. Before the year was over,
developments in East Texas, as on the lower Trinity, cast doubt upon
Rubí's judgment that the dismal little Spanish establishments were
superfluous.

The Adaeseños soon brought to a head the differences between Ripperdá and O'Conor. When they reached Béxar, the governor invited
them to choose lands for homes, fields, and pastures anywhere within
the area, barring encroachment upon prior rights of any settlers or
mission Indians. A few families who had halted at Arroyo del Cíbolo
were offered the same privilege there. The Adaeseños soon declared
that no suitable lands were available. Seventy-five petitioned Governor
Ripperdá for permission to move back east to form a new settlement at
Los Ais.

Ripperdá, who had always doubted the wisdom of eliminating
Spanish presence from Norteño territories, promised to let their
leaders carry the issue to the viceroy if a reasonable search should
truly fail to turn up appropriate lands. To no one's surprise, two months
later the Adaeseños had yet to find lands to their liking. They were
desperately homesick for the well-watered, forested lands they had
left, and they were anxious to recover what they could of their
abandoned possessions. The best lands around San Antonio were long
since preempted by earlier comers; Apaches and Comanches preyed
upon outlying districts. The Adaeseños, in most cases bankrupted by
their forced removal, had neither the resources to develop new home-

steads nor the will to confront *indios bárbaros* after generations of peaceful coexistence with settled Indians in East Texas.

In December 1773, Gil Ybarbo and Gil Flores, with an Indian associate from East Texas,[16] left Béxar to carry the Adaeseños' petition to the viceroy. Governor Ripperdá gave them passports and his own supporting letters to the viceroy and the commandant inspector, advocating Spanish presence among the Norteños to keep the old friendships and strengthen the new ones. The only plausible counterargument was that proximity to Natchitoches would tempt settlers to contraband trade, but the Natchitoches trade was now reported to flourish more briskly than ever among all Indians of the interior. Efforts to eradicate the illegal trade would only antagonize the Indians and drive them to a greater evil, the British traders now easily accessible to them.

On the last day of February 1774, Gil Ybarbo and Flores personally presented their group's petition to the viceroy, describing the appalling human suffering that the removal had entailed. Moved by the urgent need of the Adaeseños, Bucareli decided not to await consultation with Commandant Inspector O'Conor, then busy in Chihuahua, and consulted instead Fiscal Areche, who speedily found for the petitioners. Ten days later a special council concurred; only six days later, on March 23, the viceroy authorized the Adaeseños to settle as they wished at Los Ais. The touching plight of the displaced settlers had wrought a near miracle of speedy action in the highest echelons of the viceroyalty.

The Adaeseños' triumph proved short-lived. O'Conor had received a letter dispatched to him by Gil Ybarbo en route to the capital and the governor's supporting letter. Gil Ybarbo's account of the hardships of his people left the commandant inspector unmoved. In fact, their presumption infuriated him. He fired off to Governor Ripperdá an order to make the Adaeseños settle at Béxar whether they liked it or not, and he dispatched to the viceroy his vehement objections to any new settlement in East Texas. Recalling that he had once arrested Gil Ybarbo for selling horses to Louisiana, O'Conor guessed that the petitioners only wanted to open a base for contraband trade at Los Ais. Outraged that Governor Ripperdá had supported the petition, he darkly predicted that disaster would follow because Ripperdá had let

---

[16] Presumably the Captain Texita who headed a Tejas delegation to San Antonio in 1779. See below, p. 537.

a Tejas Indian see the route into Coahuila and the state of defenses in that province.

O'Conor's letter reached Mexico City too late to figure in the council's decision, but four days later Bucareli referred the document to Areche. Oddly enough, the viceroy then validated the council's recommendation. The next week Areche recommended that the viceroy rescind his order of March 23 and call a new council to reconsider the matter in the light of O'Conor's objection. Instead of making a decision, on May 5 the new council referred the entire question to O'Conor, with authority to dispose of the petition as he should see fit. Given his vigorously stated objections to the project, there seemed no doubt that the Adaeseños had lost their case.

Deeply discouraged, Gil Ybarbo and Flores begged the viceroy to let them take their families temporarily to Natchitoches, from which base they might recoup some of their property losses. The viceroy absolutely forbade Governor Ripperdá to let them go to Natchitoches but directed him to help Gil Ybarbo and Flores settle their community of exiles in "a suitable place" more than 250 miles from Natchitoches. At the same time, Bucareli notified O'Conor of the council's decision to let him dispose of the Adaeseños' case.

Before O'Conor attended to the matter in 1775, Gil Ybarbo and Ripperdá established the Adaeseños in a new place quite unacceptable to O'Conor. Although the governor acted on the viceroy's instructions, the incident confirmed O'Conor's suspicion that Ripperdá was insubordinate and probably corrupt.

In the autumn of 1774, Ripperdá let the exiles settle as far east as the viceroy's 250-mile limit allowed, on the right bank of the Trinity where the route from Béxar to the Nacogdoches crossed the stream,[17] just five miles from the main Bidais village. The spot was an ideal base for Ripperdá's declared purposes: communications with the interior nations and vigilance against French and British contrabandists among Akokisas and Atakapas on the lower Trinity. Nevertheless, his aid to Gil Ybarbo in founding the settlement combined with his well-known association with de Mézières to expose the governor to charges of corrupt personal interest in the Indian trade that soon developed at the settlement.

---

[17] Bolton, in *Texas in the Middle Eighteenth Century*, p. 406, suggests that was the crossing called Robbin's Ferry, at the old village of Randolph in present Madison County, Texas.

In a hopeful appeal to the viceroy's personal patronage, the exiles called their new settlement Nuestra Señora del Pilar de Bucareli, shortened to Bucareli. Ripperdá confirmed Gil Ybarbo's leadership by appointing him *justicia mayor* and captain of the militia. Though Bucareli began with only seventy adult males, they formed a militia company of fifty to defend the settlement. Under Gil Ybarbo's leadership, they laid out a plaza around which they built houses, mostly jacals at first, then more of hewn wood as time allowed. The community gave first priority to construction of a wooden stockade all around the settlement.

Bucareli lived out its brief existence under a cloud of ambiguity. O'Conor, never reconciled to its existence, persistently demanded its extinction. Trade in horses and hides, natural pursuits in that locality, kept the community under constant suspicion of contraband enterprise, and there is little doubt that some charges were true. Given the heavy demand for horses in neighboring Louisiana and the great market for trade goods among the Indians, enterprising settlers were hardly content to eke their subsistence from fields along the Trinity.

Ripperdá counted on friendly Indians to help Bucareli, and they did not disappoint him. Its location was chosen partly because the Wichitan bands stood as buffers against Comanches. The Tawakonis gave unstintingly of their own food to see the settlement through lean times. As soon as the settlement was founded, Ripperdá invited the Bidais, Tejas, Kichais, Iscanis, and even more distant nations to live around Bucareli. Some did gravitate in that direction. Bucareli waxed important as a center for trade and presents to the interior nations. Unfortunately, success in that controversial business only exposed Gil Ybarbo and Ripperdá to stronger suspicions of corrupt practice.

Viceroy Bucareli countenanced that one major deviation from the wishes of the commandant inspector, apparently through compassion for the suffering exiles from East Texas, but he generally abided by O'Conor's vehement views. Once Ripperdá antagonized O'Conor by supporting the Adaeseños, he received only abusive dispatches from both viceroy and commandant and lost all hope of permission to cultivate the Norteños as he thought necessary.

O'Conor quickly built his case against the governor. On February 21, 1774, his aide, Captain Roque de Medina, reached Béxar on a tour of inspection, only to find the governor absent. Ripperdá had led a force of 130 soldiers, settlers, and mission Indians in fruitless pursuit of Comanches who had taken most of the horse herd from San Antonio.

They rode back into Béxar on March 2, several horses poorer after the strenuous chase.

Captain Medina had meanwhile turned up damning accusations that Norteños persistently stole horses to peddle to French traders and that Governor Ripperdá let Norteños and French traders come and go freely at Béxar, ignoring the residents' protests against his folly.[18] Captain Luis Menchaca filed a written charge that Ripperdá persistently ignored crimes of Norteños who came and went freely under the guise of peace and hinted that both Ripperdá and de Mézières were personally involved in the Indian trade.

O'Conor had suspected just that. He hurried to the new presidio of San Antonio Bucareli de la Babía to seek supporting testimony from Captain Martínez Pacheco, once the picaresque commander of San Agustín and more recently stationed at Béxar. He confirmed Menchaca's accusations against Ripperdá and expounded on the role of de Mézières in the Indian trade in the 1750's. O'Conor forwarded the reports to the viceroy in April with his own conclusions: that Ripperdá refused to obey orders and managed Béxar carelessly and that, with ample forces to prevent depredations, he clearly did not choose to do so. No more damaging report could have entered the governor's service record.

At the same time, O'Conor fired off new orders to Ripperdá that, if followed, would virtually paralyze his relations with the interior nations. The commandant inspector criticized the free access to Béxar permitted the "hostile nations, which your Lordship ranks as friendly." He warned the governor to punish all outrages impartially and to supply no firearms to any Indians, and he forbade him to promise any presidios, settlements, or peace without specific permission from O'Conor. In no case should he interfere in the war between Norteños, which O'Conor deemed advantageous to the Spanish settlements, no matter who should win.

The commandant inspector lingered several weeks at La Babía, enjoying a chance to discuss the troublesome matter of Texas with a host whose own convictions dovetailed so neatly with his own. By mid-May, O'Conor filed with the viceroy a whole new set of criticisms and charges

18 Medina to O'Conor, Béxar, March 8, 1774; Luis Menchaca to O'Conor, Béxar, March 9, 1774; Rafael Martínez Pacheco to O'Conor, Royal Presidio of San Antonio Bucareli de la Babía, April 20, 1774; O'Conor to Bucareli, Royal Presidio of San Antonio Bucareli de la Babía, April 20, 1774; O'Conor to Ripperdá, Royal Presidio of San Antonio Bucareli de la Babía, April 21, 1774, all in Herbert Eugene Bolton, ed., *Athanase de Mézières and the Louisiana-Texas Frontier, 1768–1780*, II, 32–49.

against Ripperdá and de Mézières.[19] He claimed that the truce with the Norteños was only imaginary, that Ripperdá had naively let himself be deceived by the malicious flatteries of de Mézières, and that Ripperdá himself understood nothing of the deceitful practices and twisted mental processes of Indians. O'Conor suggested that the viceroy seek the testimony of fathers Santa María and Abad, who had themselves been to Norteño villages with de Mézières and had both been sharply critical of the Frenchman. He omitted any similar call for the opinion of Fray President Pedro Ramírez, who had been so favorably impressed by de Mézières and St. Denis.

O'Conor concluded his diatribe by observing that he was considering operations against the Norteños but feared Ripperdá would charge that O'Conor's campaign had provoked an uprising of peaceful nations. The idea of a campaign against the Norteños, which O'Conor had promoted since 1768, was hardly consistent with either the recommendations of Rubí or the intent of the Crown. Perhaps the adventurous commandant was launching a trial balloon to see what support he could expect from the viceroy.

On the whole, Bucareli concurred in O'Conor's evaluation of the Norteños, of de Mézières, and of Ripperdá. Even before O'Conor lodged his most serious charges, the viceroy chided the governor for being too good-hearted in extending trade and confidence to the Norteños. Citing constant hostilities in Texas as evidence of the bad faith of the Norteños and the ineffectiveness of Ripperdá's policies, Bucareli charged him anew to follow to the letter the Regulation of 1772 and the orders of O'Conor.[20]

Once the viceroy received the reports of Medina's inspection and the consequent charges, Ripperdá was indeed in serious difficulty. The viceroy accused him of failure to follow orders from both Bucareli and O'Conor and deplored his lenience toward the Norteños, whom the viceroy deemed false friends. Recalling that in 1772 and 1773 Ripperdá had urged a flow of guns and ammunition to the Norteños, he informed the governor of the charge that the trade was now continued at Béxar by Frenchmen permitted to live there in the guise of interpreters. He forbade the governor to allow any Frenchman into Béxar and ordered him to cut off all communication with the lieutenant governor of Natch-

---

[19] O'Conor to Bucareli, Royal Presidio of San Antonio Bucareli, May 13, 1774, ibid., pp. 51–53.

[20] Bucareli to Ripperdá, Mexico, April 6, 1774, BA; see also Bucareli to Ripperdá, Mexico, July 6, 1774, BA.

itoches and all other Frenchmen. In a closing round, the viceroy asserted that Ripperdá had ample forces to defend Texas and contain the *bárbaros*; failure to do so must be attributed to his persistent failure to follow orders.[21]

Ripperdá, badly shaken, could only deny the charges and appeal for modification of orders obviously based on misinformation. Most crucial was the mistake of lumping all the interior nations together with the Comanches under the category of Norteños. Ripperdá protested that he did not trust the Comanches as friends but that the rest of the nations had kept their promises admirably.[22]

As to Frenchmen, only three had come to live at Béxar during Ripperdá's term: an interpreter of the Taovayas and Tejas languages, retained at the governor's own expense as necessary to maintenance of the peace; another who had come with the Tonkawa peace delegation and remained as a shoemaker; and a third who had come with de Mézières and had since left with the governor's permission. Several others had lived at Béxar for many years, but none engaged in commerce with Indians or with Natchitoches.

If Ripperdá could not afford to lose the services of his interpreter, he could afford even less to cut off communications with de Mézières. That officer, just returned to Natchitoches from a triumphant tour abroad, with honors at the courts of Paris and Madrid, had already invited the chiefs of the friendly nations to visit him. Ripperdá begged the viceroy either to permit communications with de Mézières or to send Béxar someone else to cultivate the friendly nations. Serious consequences would follow if the interior nations should perceive a breach between San Antonio and Natchitoches.

Ripperdá could not move the viceroy. As 1774 ended, he not only reiterated his ban on communication between Ripperdá and de Mézières but he also forbade admission of any Frenchman to Texas for any reason. Bucareli even asked the governor of Louisiana to prevent de Mézières from writing to Ripperdá, to preclude any excuse for disobedience.[23]

Bucareli possessed an overwhelming weight of testimony against

21 Bucareli to Ripperdá, Mexico, May 8, 1774, BA; also in Bolton, *Athanase de Mézières*, II, 50–51.

22 Ripperdá to Bucareli, Béxar, June 28, 1774, in Bolton, *Athanase de Mézières*, II, 57–61.

23 Bucareli to Ripperdá, Mexico, December 21, 1774, BA.

Ripperdá: the word of his own highly trusted, experienced commandant inspector, the assistant inspector, and two captains who had served
under Ripperdá at Béxar. Furthermore, he had followed O'Conor's suggestion that he seek the opinion of priests who had seen de Mézières at
work among the Norteños and had obtained the statement of Fray
Miguel Santa María, now retired from the mission frontier to the
Colegio de Zacatecas.[24]

When stationed at Mission Los Adaes, Fray Santa María had defied
old age and illness to accompany de Mézières to the Kadohadacho village for the first peace council with the hostile nations in 1770. Returning bewildered and upset, he had lent his verbal support to the critical
depositions filed by Spanish soldiers who made the journey. Four years
later, Fray Santa María was no clearer about what had happened, since
he knew neither the Indians nor the languages involved, but he had
formed some very harsh conclusions. In retrospect, he believed that the
Indians were really ready for conversion, but that callous, sinful
Frenchmen starved their souls in order to ply them with guns and
munitions. Searching his memory, Fray Santa María attributed to de
Mézières the surprising statement that the only possible end of the
matter was for O'Conor to wipe out the Indians with fire and blood.
The commandant inspector had indeed found an inspired supporter for
his point of view, though a critical analyst might have thought such an
allusion to O'Conor by de Mézières in the fall of 1770 an anachronism.

Fray Abad, who had suspected de Mézières of improper interest in
the Indian trade ever since his own abortive visit to the Xaraname
apostates at the Tawakoni village in 1772, also obliged with a statement
suggesting that Ripperdá and de Mézières were conspirators in contraband trade. He vowed his own conviction that the apostates could
never be recovered until the evil trade could be suppressed.

In all New Spain, no advocates stepped forward to support Ripperdá.
The unsympathetic climate cost him dearly when he found his resources sorely overtaxed in early autumn of 1774. Comanches raiding
from the northwest and Karankawas raiding from the southeast kept
his men constantly in action at Béxar, La Bahía, and Fuerte del Cíbolo.
Exhausted by incessant calls for their services, militiamen ceased to

[24] Fray Miguel Santa María y Silva to the Viceroy, Apostolic College of Nuestra
Señora de Guadalupe of the City of Zacatecas, July 21, 1774, in Bolton, *Athanase
de Mézières*, II, 68; Fray Joseph Abad to the Viceroy, College of Guadalupe, July
15, 1774, ibid., pp. 66–67.

answer the governor's summons to action. Without militia help, Béxar's troops could not guard all points of ingress, protect lives and property in the settlements, and pursue marauders. The governor's appeal for help only moved the viceroy to observe that militiamen always tried to slack off and that O'Conor would surely find some remedy.[25]

While Ripperdá suffered his helpless frustration at San Antonio and de Mézières enjoyed his year's leave in Europe, conditions worsened steadily for the interior nations. In the autumn of 1773, the Taovayas medal chief rode to the Kadohadacho Post to urge that traders and hunters be barred from the Arkansas. Some were peddling munitions to the Osages, and the Wichitan bands were suffering very heavy casualties. Though he obtained little satisfaction there, he agreed to escort two Frenchmen back to his village: de Mézières' nephew, Layssard, ready to settle in for a winter's trading, and an emissary to the Comanches from the acting lieutenant governor at Natchitoches.[26]

Balthazar de Villiers, acting for de Mézières, had heard late in 1773 that Comanche horse thieves were disrupting the peace in Texas. Eager to help, he called for some trader in his district to carry a flag to the Comanches and persuade them to make peace with Texas. Trader J. Gaignard volunteered, hoping thereby to win the post of captain of militia at Natchitoches. His month-long winter journey from the Kadohadachos to the Taovayas village proved an ordeal because the disgruntled chief under whose protection he traveled extorted a considerable quantity of goods to guarantee his safety.

The Taovayas leadership sat in council with Gaignard in mid-February, shortly after he reached their village. Their great chief spoke in favor of peace with the Spaniards as well as with the Frenchmen but insisted that he would need a small present to persuade his young men. Gaignard satisfied him enough to win expressions of peace around the council circle, but it was hardly a substantial agreement. Within a week, Gaignard heard rumors of plans for two parties of young warriors to go on the warpath in Texas. When he inquired, they made the excuse that de Mézières had lied: no Spaniard had come to see them and bring presents as he had promised. Gaignard insisted that the young men be

25 Bucareli to Ripperdá, Mexico, December 21, 1774, BA.
26 J. Gaignard to Unzaga, Village of the Grand Cadaux, January 6, 1774, in Bolton, *Athanase de Mézières*, II, 81–82; J. Gaignard, Journal of journey to the Panis and Naytane, begun at Natchitoches on October 1, 1773, dated at Village of the Chacto, November 10, 1777, ibid., pp. 83–100.

stopped. The head chief did so, on the condition that Gaignard write a letter to his commandant at Natchitoches, telling that officer to notify the governor at San Antonio to send plenty of presents as a reward for stopping the warriors. They wanted horses, bridles, sabers, and sundry other goods.

Gaignard stayed on uneasily with the Taovayas, awaiting a chance to contact Comanches, since no one would agree to guide him to the Comanche camps. Meanwhile, he observed life in the village. Like many Frenchmen, he called all the Wichitan bands "Panis," but he understood them to consist of four villages—Taovayas, Wichitas, Iscanis, and Tawakonis—able to muster about a thousand warriors in all. He found them preoccupied with stealing horses and capturing slaves but still inclined to cook and eat a captive capable of returning to his people. Their visitors included the Panismahas, who had moved south to join them after disturbances in their home territories on the Missouri. Layssard, who had seen them the year before, estimated Panismahas strength at six hundred warriors, an important new component in the northern frontier scene.

All spring the village bustled with coming and going. Early in March a group that had been separated from the rest for a long time returned to a joyous welcome. Ten days later more than four hundred warriors left to follow an Osage trail. They found their quarry in a week and killed an Osage with a gun that they had forced Gaignard to lend them. They brought that scalp back to him and made him pay for it, on the grounds that the Osages were also enemies of the French.

Two Arkansas River contrabandists visited the village in April to buy horses and slaves. Three weeks later, Layssard learned that a Taovayas party had gone to the Arkansas to pillage French hunters. Gaignard and Layssard feared that if some Frenchman, resisting attack, should kill one of the Taovayas the villagers might very well avenge the loss by killing every Frenchman within reach. They were sorry to be so handy. Fortunately, the adventurers returned unscathed. Within the month another half-dozen Frenchmen came from the Arkansas to trade for horses. Since they had no passports, Gaignard wanted to arrest them, but the Taovayas declared that they preferred the Frenchmen from the Arkansas River to the licensed Natchitoches traders, who now bought only deer skins. The Arkansas free-booters would take horses, mules, and slaves, so that the Taovayas could buy their goods much more easily.

At last, Gaignard prevailed upon three visiting Comanches to carry to their great chief an invitation to come to the Taovayas village for a parley. Little more than a month later, a secondary chief brought the great chief's friendly reply. He wished Gaignard to come to meet him and sent him a small slave as a present. He was quite willing to make peace with the Spaniards.

Gaignard wanted to ride back to the Comanche camp with the messenger, but the Taovayas chief would not let him leave. Gaignard's position in the village had deteriorated badly since three Comanches had stopped on their way back from fighting Apaches to report that Spaniards had furnished guns to their enemies. The Taovayas angrily concluded that de Mézières and all Frenchmen had betrayed them, demanded booty to compensate, and held Gaignard hostage against their demand. In mid-April, the Comanche messenger left without him.

At the same time, eleven more Comanches of a band Gaignard called Manharics (presumably Yamparicas) paid him a friendly call. They were delighted to see Frenchmen after a lapse of more than eight years. After that cordial visit, the worried envoy saw no more Comanches until June 11, when forty Comanche horsemen brought their great chief's new message. He had gone to war against the Apaches but would visit the Frenchman upon his return. They rode off the next day with Gaignard's admonition to be good to the Spaniards.

On June 20 a minor Comanche chief notified Gaignard that the great chief was back from the war. He had established a camp of three hundred tipis and wished Gaignard to visit him. It would be thirteen days' journey to his camp and another thirteen beyond that to Santa Fe, where the chief wished Gaignard to take him to make peace. To Gaignard's dismay, the Taovayas would not let him go.

The Taovayas were freshly aggrieved. A strong war party had left the village in mid-June to fight the Apaches. They had soon returned, outraged, to report that they had lost a man to the enemy and that the blame lay with Spaniards who had armed all the enemy with guns.[27] The whole village clamored for revenge. Gaignard denied the charge against the Spaniards and insisted that the Apaches must have acquired the guns by killing some friendly nation and stealing their weapons.

To Gaignard's relief, the great chief of the Comanches arrived on

---

[27] Although inconsistent with Spanish policy, the suspicions of the Taovayas and Comanches were not groundless. The next summer the commandant at San Juan Bautista asked Governor Ripperdá to arrest two Spaniards accused of illegal trade with Lipans. French powder and balls the pair had brought from Béxar to

July 3 with such an enormous entourage that the trader guessed the chief had brought his entire nation. They camped for more than a month, less than three miles from the Taovayas, and came to the village to hold council. All the chiefs and assorted French traders witnessed their agreement with Gaignard. The chief promised to fly the Spanish flag over his lodge and to make a speech that would persuade all his people to keep the peace with the Spaniards. Any Comanches going to war against the Spaniards would not be from his band. He would forcibly stop the three bad men in his band who sometimes stole horses from the Tawakonis, Taovayas, and Spaniards.

Late in July the great chief agreed to ride to Natchitoches with Gaignard to visit the lieutenant governor, but, before they could complete their travel arrangements, the chief's peace pact suffered a hard test. On August 7, five Comanches arrived from San Antonio to report that Spaniards had caught them stealing horses and had killed five of their comrades. The people of the camp began to wail and weep, but the chief sternly stopped them. Those men would not be mourned in his camp, because the Spaniards had been right to kill them after they broke their word to keep the peace. The whole camp obeyed him at once.

Perhaps the Comanche chief decided that he must remain to oversee his followers' observance of the peace. At any rate, Gaignard and Layssard had to make their way independently back to the Kadohadachos, with considerable hardship. They reported at last to de Mézières at Natchitoches late in November 1774. Gaignard thought his reception hardly commensurate with his services. Several years later he hinted that de Mézières resented reports that cast doubt upon his own peace with the Taovayas.[28]

De Mézières had had no reason to worry about his relations with the Norteños since his return home in March 1774. His own district had been at peace all year except for a few Osage incursions. Ripperdá had reported only Comanche offenses in Texas.[29] By the end of June, chiefs

---

some Lipans were thought to have sparked an uprising against Monclova. Ripperdá complained in the summer and fall of 1775 that he had been unable to prevent Lipans from entering in force at San Antonio, where they traded with unscrupulous settlers for arms and munitions. (See, in the Bexar Archives, Vicente Rodríguez to Ripperdá, San Juan Bautista, June 6, 1775; Bucareli to Ripperdá, Mexico, February 28, 1776.)

[28] J. Gaignard to Bernardo de Gálvez, Village of the Chacto, November 10, 1777, in Bolton, *Athanase de Mézières*, II, 101–102.

[29] De Mézières to Unzaga, Natchitoches, March 24, 1774, ibid., p. 103.

of all the friendly nations called at Natchitoches to welcome him home and renew assurances of peace; of the nations that had made peace in 1772, only the Comanches were not represented.[30] As Ripperdá had hoped, de Mézières harangued the visiting chiefs about the importance of avenging the Comanche robberies in Texas and won their unanimous promise to help.

Contrabandists posed the principal threat to the tranquillity of de Mézières' jurisdiction. With Kadohadacho help, de Mézières cleaned out an infestation of outlaw traders, including some Britons, who had set up shop on the Ouachita River. A more difficult problem was posed by a nest of contrabandists at the mouth of the Trinity River, who had attracted some Coco and Karankawa apostates from the missions at La Bahía. They had stirred up unrest among such interior nations as the Bidais and Tejas. De Mézières considered that his most pressing problem in the summer of 1774. He regretted that the Spanish withdrawal from East Texas had left such a wide "desert" between Natchitoches and San Antonio, but he expected to maintain communications through Indian couriers. Not until a year after his return did de Mézières learn that the viceroy had banned communication between himself and Ripperdá or between their respective jurisdictions.

In October the Tawakonis found occasion to honor their promise to punish Comanche raiders. A Tawakoni party encountered a dozen Comanche men and two women coming from Béxar with a scalp and killed them all. De Mézières' intelligence network informed him that now all the Wichitan villages were prepared to go to war against the Comanches and to treat the enemies of the Spaniards as their own enemies. He dispatched the news to Ripperdá, confident it would delight him.

When a courier reached San Antonio in March 1775 with the packet of letters from de Mézières, Governor Ripperdá faced a dilemma. To send them on to the viceroy would invite a rebuke for being in communication with Louisiana, but it could be even worse to risk some later charge that he had concealed correspondence from Natchitoches. Afraid to gamble, Ripperdá forwarded de Mézières' letters to Bucareli with a covering letter. The viceroy was fair enough to assume that de Mézières had written the letters before hearing from Governor Unzaga of the viceregal ban on any contact with Texas. His reply to Ripperdá late in July 1775 made no reproach, but he reiterated his absolute pro-

---

[30] De Mézières to Unzaga, Natchitoches, June 30, 1774, *ibid.*, pp. 104–107; de Mézières to Unzaga, Natchitoches, December 16, 1774, *ibid.*, p. 115.

hibition against communication with Louisiana and ignored the substance of de Mézières' letters.[31]

The viceroy guessed correctly. It was March 1775 when Governor Unzaga notified his lieutenant governor that the viceroy did not find it convenient to permit any correspondence between de Mézières and Governor Ripperdá. He also reminded him of the prohibition against exportation of any goods from Natchitoches to the presidios of New Spain.[32] Unzaga told him to honor the request, perhaps without understanding all its implications. In a few weeks, a startled Unzaga found himself the victim of the viceroy's obsessive objection to any intercourse between Texas and Louisiana.

Late in the spring of 1775, anticipating only courteous cooperation from the neighboring province, Governor Unzaga sent a few soldiers from Louisiana into Texas to purchase horses and mules urgently needed for both military and civilian use. As required by law, Governor Ripperdá had Unzaga's agents arrested at the new settlement of Bucareli, then requested the viceroy's instructions for disposing of them. Bucareli firmly reiterated his ban against permitting any Louisiana citizens to trade in Texas for any reason, even if sent by their own governor for official purposes. The unlucky agents had to be shipped back to Louisiana; their assets were confiscated and sold to cover costs. The same procedure would apply in every case, regardless of circumstances.[33]

The strange impasse continued as long as Bucareli had jurisdiction over Texas. Ripperdá sadly accommodated himself to the frustrating circumstances. The controversial settlement of Bucareli helped a bit to offset the restrictions that crippled Ripperdá's official relations with the Indians of the interior. The trading operations of Gil Ybarbo and his long-time partner, Nicolás de La Mathe, provided informal liaison with the nations of the interior, serving both to inform Ripperdá of conditions among them and to diminish the Indians' impression that the Spaniards had forgotten them.

If Governor Ripperdá enjoyed any real luck in the unhappy years after 1773, it was that both O'Conor and Bucareli grew too preoccupied with more threatened areas to sustain their angry focus on Texas. Hav-

[31] Bucareli to Ripperdá, Mexico, July 27, 1775, BA.

[32] Unzaga to de Mézières, New Orleans, March 13, 1775 (certified copy made in Mexico, June 26, 1775), BA.

[33] Bucareli to Ripperdá, Mexico, August 30, 1775, BA; Bucareli to Ripperdá, Mexico, January 17, 1776, BA.

ing spent most of 1774 realigning presidios, the commandant inspector devoted most of 1775 and 1776 to campaigning against Apaches. In the same period, New Mexico came so near destruction at the hands of *indios bárbaros* that it absorbed most of the attention that the over-burdened viceroy could give to the northern frontier.

CHAPTER 13

New Mexico, 1767-1776

Viceroy Bucareli had ample reason to worry about New Mexico. The province tottered on the brink of destruction by the same *indios bárbaros* whom Rubí had seen at peace with Governor Vélez Cachupín in 1766. Don Pedro Fermín de Mendinueta succeeded Vélez Cachupín early in 1767, and for some unknown reason he found it necessary to campaign against the Comanches before the year ended.[1] Unlike his predecessor, Mendinueta did not bother to distinguish among Comanche groups. Late in December he expressed some hope of peace with the Comanches, but he doubted their reliability.

Apaches were first to suffer Comanche raids in the spring of 1768. Comanches struck the Natagés just about the time that Apaches heard that Nueva Vizcaya was sending an army against them.[2] Seeing peace

---

[1] Alfred Barnaby Thomas, ed., in *The Plains Indians and New Mexico, 1751–1778*, p. 38. Note also that Mendinueta in 1774 attested that he had campaigned against Comanches in 1767 and 1768. See Mendinueta, Service Record, Santa Fe, December 31, 1774, in Alfred Barnaby Thomas, ed., "Governor Mendinueta's Proposals for the Defense of New Mexico, 1772–1778," *New Mexico Historical Review* 6 (1931): 25.

[2] Mendinueta to Marqués de Croix, Santa Fe, June 18, 1768, in Thomas, *Plains*

in New Mexico as a possible means of sanctuary, the Natagés and Sierra Blanca Apaches sent forty delegates to Albuquerque on May 24, 1768, with two captives whom they had taken from that settlement in 1767. They exchanged the pair for an Apache held prisoner there and promised to keep the peace faithfully. The law required Governor Mendinueta to agree, though he doubted their sincerity.

Less than two weeks later, other emissaries sought peace on behalf of Gila Chief Chafalote, an old foe whose *ranchería* had been destroyed by a punitive force of Zuñis and Spaniards fourteen years before. The Spanish officials treated them cordially, then awaited results. To their considerable surprise, the Natagés and Sierra Blancas honored their peace commitments well throughout the summer and fall. Only when a Christian Indian woman escaped captivity in an Apache camp did the New Mexicans learn that they were indebted to Comanches for the new Apache concord. By that time, the province had stumbled into a new Comanche war, probably of its own making.

Governor Mendinueta's doubts about Comanche intentions led him, in May 1768, to station fifty men on the hill of San Antonio, about fifteen miles north of Abiquiú, to guard the ford on the Rio Grande. Comanches used that route to Ojo Caliente, a frontier sector the governor thought especially vulnerable.

About five o'clock on the afternoon of May 31, six Comanche braves rode into Taos carrying a white flag. They announced that they were coming to ask for peace and that their *ranchería* would arrive at Taos on June 2 with a young man from the pueblo whom they held captive. They were traveling rapidly and would stay only long enough to market the goods they were bringing.

When the news reached the Governor's Palace at Santa Fe just twenty-three hours later, Mendinueta hastily called up the horse herd and set out with the troops and Santa Fe militia on a forced march to Taos. At midnight on June 2, he received another courier with the report that the Comanches had declared war just before dawn that morning. Mendinueta pressed on to Taos to learn the details.

The story he picked up there was that the Comanches had sent a hundred men to attack Ojo Caliente, confident that news of peace and trade would have attracted the men to Taos and left the settlement de-

Indians, pp. 159–162; Mendinueta to Marqués de Croix, Report of New Mexico events from September 17 to November 9, 1768, extracted from Croix to Arriaga, Mexico, January 30, 1769, ibid., p. 167.

fenseless. Meanwhile, more than four hundred Comanches arrived at Taos with guns, munitions, and standard trade items.

Atop San Antonio hill, Mendinueta's fifty presidials, Pueblos, and militiamen saw Comanches approaching Ojo Caliente and sallied forth to meet them. The Comanches did not join battle but fled precipitately. Some drowned in the river; the rest galloped on to inform those in Taos.

In the Comanche visitors' camp that night were five settlers and one Taos Indian, defying the regulations to do a bit of unsupervised trading. In the uproar that followed the arrival of the party from Ojo Caliente, the six clandestine traders paid for their greed with their lives; they took four Comanche lives with them. The Comanches fled, their trail marked by dead horses, supplies, saddles, buffalo skins, and bits of clothing.

Mendinueta, who reached Taos later that day, could not pursue them. His poor, range-fed horses, exhausted by the forced march to Taos, needed three days' rest even to return to Santa Fe. Back at headquarters, the governor did all that he could to reinforce the frontier, and he prepared to campaign against those Comanches.

As guide to the homelands of the offending Comanches, Mendinueta used the young Taoseño whom the Comanches had let the *alcalde mayor* ransom before the irruption. The lad had already produced one useful piece of intelligence: the Comanches were getting plenty of firearms from the "Jumanos," who had recently brought them seventeen packhorses laden with guns and ammunition.[3] That was grim news for the ill-armed New Mexicans poised to invade the Comanchería to punish the marauders.

On July 18, 1768, Mendinueta rode northeastward with 546 militiamen, presidial troops, and Indians. They found no trail until August 7, when their scouts sighted two Comanches with seven horses near a small tributary of the Arkansas River. Mendinueta hoped to surprise their camp, but his overexcited Ute and Apache allies rushed too soon. The two Comanches escaped and alerted the rest of their people to

[3] Mendinueta's information was that the Jumanos were "a tribe which lives in pueblos located at the junction of the Napestle and Colorado River," that is, at the junction of the Arkansas and Canadian rivers. Evidently the New Mexicans were unaware that the Wichitan bands had moved to the Red River more than a decade earlier. He assumed the guns to be from English sources "as there are no French to trade with the Jumanos," apparently ignorant of the problems of trade on the Louisiana-Texas border. His report to the viceroy prompted the latter's query to ad interim Governor O'Conor that bolstered O'Conor's adamant opposition to the Indian trade, whether or not he realized that Jumanos were actually the Wichitan bands of whose good faith he was so skeptical.

scatter. Mendinueta, sure that surprise was now impossible, gave up and led his men home.

Certainly the campaign was unsuccessful. Perhaps it was also unwarranted. The only report is that of Mendinueta, who assumed hostile intent by the Comanches, and it prompts several questions. Why did Mendinueta head for Taos with all the forces he could muster as soon as he heard of a Comanche peace overture there? Did the Comanche party approaching Ojo Caliente show hostile intent, or did the waiting New Mexican force simply charge at the sight of them, without waiting to learn the purpose of their visit? Why would the leaders of the *rancheria* encamped at Taos endanger the lives and property of their people by plotting an attack on Ojo Caliente to coincide with their days of talking and trading at Taos? If they had really meant to launch a war, why did four months pass before they resumed the offensive?

While there is reason to doubt that the Comanches intended war in early June, there is no question that some were truly at war by the autumn of 1768. The vehemence of their reaction suggests that they felt themselves truly aggrieved. A powerful new chief emerged to lead them in the crisis. Rumor had it that he commanded all the Comanche nation and employed all the panoply and ceremony of a king.

The Comanches' fall campaign commenced on September 26, when two dozen warriors struck Ojo Caliente and killed one unarmed settler. They fired just five shots at the settlement, with no effect. Mendinueta's garrison joined sixteen local settlers and some Utes in pursuing the raiders, with unusual success. They killed twenty-one Comanches and took two prisoners; only one escaped to cry vengeance. One of the prisoners died two days later, duly baptized.

Though first encouraged by their success against the invaders, the defenders soon learned that they had won a dangerous victory. Each fallen Comanche warrior had to be avenged by some friend or relative, who had to collect a compensating scalp from the New Mexicans. To make matters worse, one of the dead had been a principal associate of the new great chief. His loss thus transcended the level of personal vengeance by family and friends. It was an injury to all Comanches counting themselves followers of the great chief, who undertook personally a campaign to avenge his dead friend with many scalps and horses.

The first incident in October was not particularly alarming or even necessarily related: fifteen Comanches raided Picurís, where they killed one Indian; the pursuing force gave up the chase a dozen miles from the pueblo. The real impact of the drive for tribal vengeance hit at the end of the month, when five hundred Comanches encircled Ojo Caliente before dawn and tried to break in.

After the besieged townsmen repelled the first assault, the enemy retired to a nearby hill to keep the settlement under fire. Then a group of Comanches charged, conspicuously led by a chief whose leather headdress bore a green horn. He fell before the settlers' fire, to the obvious consternation of his warriors, who braved every danger to carry away his body. Once they recovered it, they retreated in disarray.

Watching Spaniards guessed that the loss of that chief pained the Comanches far more than their numerous other casualties and wondered if the fallen leader were that same "King of the Comanches" whose rise had been gossiped about at Taos and confirmed by interrogation of a Comanche prisoner. The next decade's history suggests that the speculation was correct: that the fallen chief left a son who dedicated his own life and those of his followers to vengeance for his father. Wearing his honored father's emblem, Cuerno Verde would scourge New Mexico until he died.

Comanche vengeance was not new to the people of New Mexico, but the horrors of the first two years of that war surpassed any previous ordeal. They too lost important leaders. Lieutenant General Don Nicolás Ortiz, second in rank only to the governor, died August 31, 1769, leading the New Mexican forces against Comanches in yet another battle at the hill of San Antonio.[4]

The northern and eastern frontiers bore the brunt. Comanche raiders struck impartially at Spaniards and Pueblos, for they had plenty of grievances against both. The compact, fortress-like pueblos protected their inhabitants well, and Spaniards soon learned to take refuge in them. In 1769, after Comanche raiders sacked the mission convent at Picurís, Governor Mendinueta conceded that he could not hope to prevent attacks against that isolated pueblo. He ordered the mission razed and another begun next to a large block of Picurís dwellings, whose people generously gave the priest three rooms for his convent. The new church was designed as a veritable fortress, with very thick walls and a connecting cloister to make it part of the Picurís block that housed the convent. During its construction, the priest made the best of his three

---

[4] Francisco Atanasio Domínguez, *The Missions of New Mexico, 1776*, trans. and ed. Eleanor B. Adams and Angelico Chávez, p. 240.

rooms a chapel and continued his ministry within the sanctuary of the traditional Pueblo structure.[5]

Taos pueblo's ancient fortress also gave Spaniards refuge. The Spanish community in the valley dwelled around a plaza about two musket shots west of the pueblo, though they farmed principally on better lands in a well-watered cañada about eight miles south (present Ranchos de Taos area). When the Comanches launched their intensive war, the pueblo of Taos and the settlement were too far apart to be defended as a unit, and the great communal dwelling blocks at the pueblo afforded better protection than the little Spanish town of separate buildings. By 1770 the Comanche raiders had taken such a toll that the settlers sought and received the consent of the Taoseños to move into their pueblo.[6]

Just across the stream from the south block of the pueblo, with a connecting wall across the stream from their new structure to that block, the Spaniards built a small block of dwellings back to back. Some faced eastward onto the pueblo's plaza and others faced westward away from it, but for safety's sake the only entrances gave onto the plaza side. That block of settlers' dwellings stood on the south flank of the pueblo's main, westward-facing gate; another block with a fortified tower flanked the gate on the north and ran clear to the gate of the mission complex, which stood just west of the pueblo's north block. Within the plaza they built corrals for their cattle.

It was a useful arrangement for the mutual defense of the two populations, but it was never meant to be permanent. When Governor Mendinueta sanctioned their move and ordered their old plaza razed, he also ordered construction of a new, defensible plaza for the Spanish settlers in the cañada where they farmed. Its construction was underway by 1776, and they were expected to occupy it upon its completion. If the emergency of the Comanche war warranted a temporary exception, it did not nullify the well-established rule against encroachment into the pueblos by Spanish settlers.

While their compatriots to the north sought physical refuge in pueblo compounds, Spaniards of Santa Fe sought spiritual refuge. Bemoaning the lives lost to the enemy and the inadequacy of their means to resist the onslaught, citizens of Santa Fe longed for a powerful patron saint to hear their supplications for divine succor. They turned to the Virgin Mary, whose image as Our Lady of the

[5] Ibid., p. 92.
[6] Ibid., pp. 111–113.

Rosary had adorned the local parish church for more than a century. That image, which had been rescued by the fleeing Spaniards in 1680 and brought back by Vargas at the time of the reconquest, was revered as "La Conquistadora," already of key importance in the spiritual life of the community. The idea of claiming her as special patron saint caught on as soon as the idea was mentioned in 1770. Governor Mendinueta, himself a devout man, encouraged the movement. Half a dozen leaders of the community founded a confraternity to foster special devotions and arrange the grand ceremonial in her honor every autumn.[7] The irregularity, indeed the presumption, of claiming a patron saint without due formal agreements with authorities of Church and State boggled some official minds, but the cult flourished from the start. By 1776, the October festival honoring La Conquistadora had burgeoned to three full days of all the pomp that New Mexico could produce.

It seemed to the people of New Mexico in the spring of 1771 that La Conquistadora had indeed interceded on their behalf. On April 25, Governor Mendinueta announced that he had concluded a peace treaty with the Comanches on February 7, and he urged the entire populace to observe all its provisions with scrupulous care.[8]

Taovayas reports to de Mézières in the fall of 1771 indicate that their associates, the Ietan Comanches, were sincere participants in that peace and perhaps had taken the initiative to establish it.[9] Ietan interests were ill-served by a war that disrupted the Taos trade at the same time that Wichitan markets deteriorated under de Mézières' boycott of hostile nations. Perhaps they persuaded their northern compatriots, the Yupes and Yamparicas, to abandon their vendetta; perhaps two and a half years of war had slaked the vengeful zeal of all but the son of the fallen chief.

If the peace of 1771 marked an end to the live war, it could not relax the overriding pressures for Comanche men to obtain horses. The next year Comanche raiders again stalked horse herds throughout New Mexico. Apaches, similarly compelled, also preyed upon the herds. In the spring of 1772 Mendinueta counted Comanches and

---

[7] For slightly differing contemporary accounts, see ibid., pp. 240–241; and Isidro Armijo, ed., "Information Communicated by Juan Candelaria, Resident of This Villa de San Francisco Xavier de Alburquerque, Born 1692—Age 84," *New Mexico Historical Review* 4 (1929): 294–297.

[8] Hubert Howe Bancroft, *History of Arizona and New Mexico*, p. 259.

[9] See above, p. 402.

Apaches as the two principal enemies of his province, attempting no distinctions among the divisions of either.[10]

Given the myriad raiders, how could Mendinueta protect settlers stubbornly scattered out on separate farmsteads? The governor appealed to the viceroy to order them to follow the sensible Pueblo example of dwelling around compact, defensible plazas. He also requested a new presidio at Taos, to protect the northern districts against Comanche incursions and thus to permit deployment of Santa Fe's eighty presidials for maximum protection of the southern districts.

Mendinueta's proposal for a new presidio at Taos had no chance, for it coincided with the Crown's new commitment to presidial retrenchment along the lines recommended by Rubí. His superiors did authorize him to concentrate the settlers at strategically valuable locations to facilitate their own defense. That authorization implied no immediate expenditures for the Crown and held some hope for eventual savings in defense expenditures. However, they enjoined him to employ only suave and mild measures, thus virtually ruling out any hope of success in relocating those nearly ungovernable folk.

At that gloomy juncture, New Mexico suffered the untoward impact of the Rubí recommendations. Predicated upon Vélez Cachupín's network of Indian friendships observed in 1766, the Regulation of 1772 reflected more the Crown's hopes than the current realities of New Mexico. "The presidio farthest north, and which forms a separate frontier, is that of New Mexico. That remote province is isolated and alone, but has sufficient strength in its many towns and in the good quality of its inhabitants. . . ."[11]

Rubí compounded that isolation by finding unnecessary the nearest presidio, at El Paso. That settlement, at the gateway to New Mexico, had prospered so that it comprised the largest population that Rubí saw beyond Durango. The inspector general concluded that El Paso's more than 5,000 inhabitants should assume responsibility for defending themselves with a local militia company, letting the established garrison be moved southward to Carrizal to form one of the presidios in his projected line of defense. To ameliorate Santa Fe's dangerous

---

[10] Mendinueta to Bucareli, Santa Fe, March 26, 1772, in Thomas, "Governor Mendinueta's Proposals," p. 27; see also Charles Edward Chapman, *The Founding of Spanish California*, p. 144.

[11] Regulation of 1772, in *Lancers for the King*, by Sidney B. Brinckerhoff and Odie B. Faulk, p. 62.

isolation, Rubí proposed a small post at Robledo, with one officer and thirty soldiers to be detached from the presidio at Santa Fe and thirty auxiliaries recruited from El Paso's citizenry. He predicted that in ten years Robledo could be a self-sustaining community, forming an effective barrier against incursions of the Natagés and Gilas.

Removal of the presidio from El Paso to Carrizal, a part of the presidial realignment entrusted to O'Conor, occurred promptly. The compensating post at Robledo never materialized.[12] Neither did the other provision of the Regulation of 1772 that Viceroy Bucareli delegated to Governor Mendinueta: revival of the ruined towns of Socorro, Senecú, Alamillo, and Sevilleta to shorten the gap between the settlements of the New Mexican heartland and the provincial gateway at El Paso. The immediate struggle for survival absorbed all the energies and resources at Mendinueta's command throughout his administration. Grand strategies for the long run were hardly germane from the perspective of Santa Fe.

Even in the optimism of 1766, Rubí had judged the province weak. His engineer, Lafora, had urged that the population and economy be strengthened to make New Mexico "an impenetrable barrier" against the Indians who threatened destruction of New Spain's interior provinces.[13] It was a modest base for such an ambitious purpose. There was a total population in all the province of 20,104, of whom 9,580 were Spaniards and 10,524 were Pueblo or *genízaro* Indians. With only 2,324 persons, including the eighty soldiers of the presidio, Santa Fe appeared not to be defensible. Lafora urged immediate construction of a new fortification to safeguard persons and property in case of a general uprising. Lack of a proper bastion seemed to invite disaster and ultimate loss of the province.

The primitive state of the settlers' arms worried the professional soldier even more. Most depended upon the lance, which they handled well. Even men with guns in working order hardly used them because powder was so scarce and costly. Settlers called to militia duty usually carried very small charges because they had to furnish powder at their own expense. To his dismay, Lafora realized that the New Mexicans

---

[12] Kinnaird, ed., in *The Frontiers of New Spain*, p. 17, points out that the United States government located Fort Selden there in 1865 to control Apaches.

[13] Nicolás de Lafora, *Relación del viaje que hizo a los presidios internos, situados en la frontera de la América septentrional, perteneciente al rey de España*, p. 105.

lost the advantage of firearms, so important to offset the disadvantage of the few Spaniards against the countless *indios bárbaros* upon their frontiers.

Poor beleaguered province! Added now to the problems Rubí had reported were those he had created, and meanwhile Mendinueta had blundered into a Comanche war. Then the region's oldest and worst enemy, drought, compounded the woes of all. The dry cycle began early in the 1770's, lasted through the decade, and spared no one, neither prudent Pueblos nor improvident settlers nor *bárbaros* ranging beyond the frontiers. Crops failed in all fields except those under irrigation. Pueblos had no surplus produce to sell to *bárbaros*. The drought played havoc with pastures and thus with livestock, the cornerstone of the provincial economy.

The drought afflicted *bárbaros*, too. It diminished the wild plants and game by which the hunters and gatherers lived and wrecked the crops of Navajos and of those Apaches who still planted little fields in hidden valleys. Now, more than ever, they needed corn from the irrigated fields of their settled neighbors, but the shortage of game left them little to barter for food, and they found Pueblos loath to sell from their dwindling stores. Inevitably, trade slumped; *bárbaros* raided for what they needed. Livestock was their principal quarry, for it could be eaten, and horses facilitated the raiding by which the people now had to live. The raiders did not intend war, but every raid was fraught with potential war. Of course, Spaniards and Pueblos fought to protect the property upon which their own lives depended, and casualties occurred. Each dead raider imposed a duty of vengeance upon his kinsmen; each loss among vassals of the Spanish Crown intensified pressures to campaign against the offenders.

The drought's repercussions first hit the Albuquerque district, where Gilas grabbed so much livestock that despairing settlers abandoned the settlements of Carnué and Las Nutrias. Gila raids for livestock continued through 1773 and 1774, principally around Albuquerque and Laguna pueblo. Worse still, the long-peaceful Navajos also began raiding in 1774. When settlers in the Rio Puerco district, northwest of Albuquerque, complained to Governor Mendinueta about mounting losses of livestock, he called upon Navajo leaders for restitution. Instead of cooperating to maintain the peace as the governor expected, they fled. Soon Navajos raided so openly and often that the Spaniards deemed them at war, too. Spaniards shortly abandoned ranches in the districts of Rio Puerco and nearby Navajo, where settlement impinged most closely upon Navajo ranges. By autumn 1774, Navajo raids extended to Laguna and neighboring ranches.

Determined to carry the war home to the Navajos, Governor Mendinueta sent two expeditions into their territory in 1774. Because Mendinueta could spare none of his eighty presidials from Santa Fe and the various frontier stations to which he deployed small squads, the entire burden of the Navajo campaigns fell upon militiamen and Pueblos of the Albuquerque, Laguna, and Keres jurisdictions. They killed twenty-one Navajos and captured forty-six, but it cost them four dead and thirty-one wounded.[14] The next year Navajos seized cattle and horses at Jémez, Cochití, Santa Clara, Zía, San Ildefonso, Abiquiú, and Albuquerque. Settlers and Pueblos joined to pursue the marauders on each of those occasions, with some modest success.

The cumulative effects of drought and of Gila and Navajo raids exacted a heavy toll of lives and property from both Spanish and Pueblo communities on the southern and western frontiers in the mid-1770's. Less palpable, but no less real, was the drain upon energies and hopes of peoples always living and working under threat of raids and too often forced to field their menfolk against the enemy. Yet, those troubles paled by comparison with the terrors of Comanche war that beset New Mexico on the north and east by 1774.

Troubles with Comanches resurged in the summer of 1772. An estimated five hundred Comanches joined to raid Pecos; Picurís suffered five raids; Galisteo four. Mendinueta never grasped the distinction between a war party attacking and a raiding party after horses, but the pattern of events suggests the latter. Which Comanches had raided was unknown, and neither side assumed any general breakdown of the peace. Comanches came as usual that year to Taos to trade skins, meat, captives, and horses for the goods of the Taoseños and settlers. Not until the last of the raids against Galisteo could Mendinueta mount a pursuit party. They overtook the invaders, killed some, and recovered about sixty animals.[15]

In July 1773, five hundred Comanches raided Cochití, whence their trail led northward toward the rugged San Juan range. Mendinueta's pursuit party chased them as far as the Rio Conejos.[16] They overtook fifteen Comanches on that stream and captured their horses, but all

[14] Mendinueta to Bucareli, Santa Fe, September 30, 1775, in Thomas, *Plains Indians*, p. 173.
[15] Thomas, *Plains Indians*, p. 43.
[16] Ibid., n. 70, p. 169.

fifteen escaped on foot.[17] A little mollified and thoroughly exhausted, the New Mexicans rode back home. Whether the fifteen Comanches whom they had despoiled were actually part of the group who had raided Cochití, or whether Mendinueta had only inflicted fresh injury on some entirely different group, is moot.

By mid-summer 1774, New Mexicans could not doubt that their province was the target of all-out Comanche war rather than occasional horse thefts. First to suffer were Pueblos. On June 23, Comanches killed two Picurís farmers whom they surprised in their cornfields. The next day Comanches ran off the entire horse herd from Nambé pueblo. Yet, on June 27, sixty Comanche groups peacefully entered Taos pueblo to trade, and no incident marred the market days.[18] The Comanches collected ransom for half a dozen Indian captives and bartered some 140 horses, two guns, and a large quantity of meat and salt.[19]

Only a month later, on July 27, a Comanche war party estimated at more than a thousand swept down the Chama to strike at Santa Clara and San Juan pueblos and three Spanish settlements in La Cañada district. The Indians of Santa Clara and San Juan repelled the Comanches who tried to seize their horse herds, but San Juan lost three men. The main Comanche attack focused upon settlers of La Cañada, bunched in a fenced field behind a house. A large Comanche force stormed their defenses again and again, until their leader fell under the settlers' gunfire. Several Comanches sacrificed their lives in a vain attempt to recover their chief's body; at last they galloped off with three hundred of the settlers' horses and mules. The Spaniards and Pueblos lost seven dead, three captured, and six wounded, the three hundred stolen horses, and twenty-five head of cattle killed by the invaders. They guessed that twenty-three Comanches were dead. Pursuit was impossible. Most of the settlers were now afoot; the soldiers and militiamen whom Mendinueta hastily dispatched from Santa Fe were too few and too late to be useful.

Pecos was the next target. In mid-afternoon on August 15, a hundred Comanches surprised Pecos Indians at work in their cornfields, killed nine, captured seven, and seized the horse herd. The next day Governor

---

[17] Armijo, "Information Communicated by Juan Candelaria," p. 294, mentioned this and five other efforts by Mendinueta against the Comanches.

[18] Recall that at this time a principal Ietan chief desired Gaignard, the envoy from Natchitoches, to escort him to Santa Fe to make peace. (See above, p. 460).

[19] Mendinueta to Bucareli, Santa Fe, September 30, 1774, in Thomas, *Plains Indians*, pp. 169–173.

Mendinueta dispatched a pursuit party of 114 soldiers, militiamen, and Indians.

The trail led them 175 miles from Santa Fe, to a big Comanche camp with tipis ranged so far along the banks of a stream that the scouts could not count them or even see the far end of the camp. The people of the camp were so absorbed in preparing a victory celebration that the New Mexicans scored a surprise attack. They rescued a Pecos woman, the only one of the seven captives not yet slaughtered, and killed many Comanches before the enemy realized how few they were and organized a counterattack. The Spaniards and Pueblos abandoned their horse herd to form a square formation from which they maintained fire on all sides and thus held their ground all day. They retired in good order at twilight, with twenty-two wounded and one soldier dead.

The Comanches were tricked into flight that night by a soldier who had spent a dozen years as a captive and spoke their language fluently. He warned them that these few Spaniards were just the scouts and that the rest of the army would arrive at any moment. The Comanches, whose heavy casualties had included seven chiefs, were too demoralized to stand against that threat. Wailing for their dead, they withdrew that night, abandoning tipis, horses, and even corpses, and traveled two days and nights before they stopped.

Meanwhile, another hundred Comanche warriors had struck Albuquerque on August 18, killing two Spaniards and three Indians, capturing four sheepherders, killing four hundred sheep, and stealing a herd of horses. Pursuit was impossible. The militia of that jurisdiction was off on campaign against the Navajos, and Mendinueta had already sent every man he could spare from Santa Fe to pursue the Comanches who had attacked Pecos.

News of the August 20 triumph over the Comanches proved a great tonic for the flagging spirits of New Mexicans. Governor Mendinueta seized upon the new mood to rally all the forces of the province to campaign against the Comanches, though he realized that few settlers could be properly equipped and that even the best-outfitted would have no more than three horses.[20] By mid-September they were ready, six hundred soldiers, militiamen, and Indians, led by the aged veteran Don Carlos Fernández.

Hopeful of surprising the Comanches again, the governor took extra-

[20] Mendinueta to Bucareli, Santa Fe, October 20, 1774, ibid., pp. 173–177.

ordinary precautions against disclosure of plans. In case the defeat on August 20 should have moved some Comanches to talk peace at Taos in order to spy out Spanish intentions, Mendinueta ordered the *alcalde mayor* to seize any Comanches reaching Taos on or after September 15 and ship them to Santa Fe. The *alcalde mayor* had occasion to act on September 19, the very day that the expeditionary force departed the capital. He arrested eight Comanche men and eleven women upon their arrival at Taos and set them, under guard, on the trail to Santa Fe.

The guards halted for the night at Las Truchas and quartered the Comanches in the town tower. When a pair of guards entered to build them a fire against the September evening chill, the prisoners killed the guards with their own weapons, then seized the arms stored in the tower and staked out a position in the entrance. The local settlers rallied to reclaim their tower; many were wounded during the night-long siege. The Comanches rejected all demands for surrender, insisting that they would rather die fighting. At dawn the Spaniards set fire to the tower and smoked out the besieged prisoners. The Comanches came out fully armed and fought to the death. Governor Mendinueta noted complacently that they had carried no news to their tribe.

Meanwhile, the New Mexican forces picked up the trail of a Comanche group more than eighty tipis strong, overtook them on September 28 in a wood about 125 miles from Santa Fe, and promptly attacked. Eighteen Comanche men escaped on swift horses. The rest of the men gathered the families behind a makeshift breastwork of logs, with a deep pond for defense on one side. The vassals of the Crown fired relentlessly for two hours, until only 115 Comanche women and children remained alive, most wounded. Many were dragged from the pond, half-drowned. The Spanish chaplain baptized ten dying Comanche children; more wounded died within the next three weeks. The rest fell under a proviso of the Regulation of 1772 that captive women and children be turned over to the religious for instruction.

The victors guessed that more than a hundred Comanches had been killed or captured. Only twenty-eight New Mexicans were wounded and one Indian killed. They divided the rich booty among themselves: about a thousand horses and mules, the eighty-odd tipis, and all the enemies' possessions. The Spanish populace would perpetuate their glee in the ringing verses of the folk play, "Los Comanches."

> Let them die, the more the better,
> There will be more spoils for me.

Soft tanned skins of elk and beaver,
What a comfort they will be.
Meat of buffalo in abundance,
Everything that one might need,
I will fill my larder plenty,
I have many mouths to feed.
My good wife shall want for nothing,
She shall cook a gorgeous meal.

. . .

Ah, at last I've reached their treasure,
There is plenty here indeed.
Sugars, fruits, and meats, and jellies,
What a life these heathens lead.
Everything to tempt the palate,
What a feast, fit for a king.
I shall eat and then I'll gather,
I'll not leave a single thing.[21]

Governor Mendinueta exulted that the Comanches had at last seen the king's arms destroy a *ranchería* and should be duly sobered. Apparently he did not consider the possibility that Don Carlos' force had attacked a peaceable camp of Comanches en route to trade, thus inviting a disastrous surge of hostile sentiment among their nation.

Viceroy Bucareli worried. What if the extreme punishment had only outraged the Comanches and rallied them to concerted vengeance? Though he commended the governor's zeal and efficiency, he offered to send arms to be sold to the settlers at cost and suggested that O'Conor reinforce New Mexico with troops from one of his flying companies in Nueva Vizcaya.[22]

The viceroy guessed better than the governor. The year 1775 brought the fiercest Comanche depredations ever. On May 1 Comanches attacked Pecos Indians planting their fields, killed three, and stole three horses. The Pecoseños gamely fought back, killed three Comanches, and wounded more.[23] Another big Comanche war party circled around Pecos on June 25, firing into the pueblo, and killed one resident. The Comanches retreated after the defenders killed three, but the

---

[21] These verses are from the translation of "Los Comanches" published by Gilberto Espinosa in *The New Mexico Quarterly*, I (1931): 133–146. Quoted by permission of Gilberto Espinosa.

[22] Bucareli to Mendinueta, Mexico, February 8, 1775, in Thomas, *Plains Indians*, pp. 177–179.

[23] Mendinueta to Bucareli, Santa Fe, May 12, 1775, ibid., p. 179.

terrified Pecoseños did not doubt that the enemy would return. No one dared venture out to work the irrigated fields some way northeast of the pueblo, so they had that year only the yield of the dry fields beside the pueblo.

Though pueblos were the Comanches' principal targets, tribal vengeance thrust clear into Santa Fe. One May night four Comanches slipped into the outskirts of the capital and killed a youngster herding his oxen near his house. Pursuers sighted the culprits but could not overtake them when they abandoned their horses to flee afoot into rugged mountains.

On May 13 a Comanche chief appeared at Taos with seven *rancherías* and announced their desire to trade. Since the governor had ordered trade limited to those chiefs who had come to Santa Fe to make peace with him, the *alcalde mayor* refused. The next day Taoseños discovered an apparent plot by their Comanche visitors to make a surprise attack on the pueblo. They engaged a hundred Comanche warriors on the spot, forcing them to retreat with losses of three dead, some wounded, and some horses with full harness. The Taoseños had just one man wounded and lost half a dozen horses to the retreating enemy.[24]

A fortnight later, on May 27, sixty Comanches struck the fields at Nambé pueblo, killed four Indians and wounded two, then captured two girls and the horse herd of the pueblo. Though caught by surprise, the men of Nambé successfully defended their women and children, who were working in the gardens at the time of the attack, and even recovered the two captured girls. That night they followed the enemies' trail into the mountains and retrieved horses that the Comanches had abandoned in the forests.

On June 23 a big Comanche war party swept through the pueblos of Sandía and La Alameda. The men of Sandía bravely pursued the enemy on foot, only to see the fleeing Comanches suddenly wheel back and hack down thirty-three of the most exhausted pursuers. At La Alameda the Comanches killed three persons, destroyed part of the sheep and cattle, and stole one girl and some horses. The defenders managed to kill one Comanche and recovered twenty-three exhausted horses that the raiders abandoned.

Governor Mendinueta promptly dispatched from Santa Fe a pursuit force of soldiers, settlers, and Indians. Traveling rapidly over very rough terrain, the next afternoon they stumbled upon the enemy, en-

[24] Mendinueta to Bucareli, Santa Fe, August 18, 1775, *ibid.*, pp. 180–183.

camped by a water hole. The New Mexicans attacked, killed some Comanches, recovered the captive, and captured thirty horses, at the cost of the first sergeant's life and three wounded. They could not dislodge the Comanches from possession of the waterhole; the enemy were well entrenched and had plenty of guns and ammunition, which they used with telling effect. Since the next waterhole was fifty miles away, the New Mexicans bowed to circumstance and retired. The Comanches soon departed, leaving behind a disarray that suggested they were very unhappy and discouraged.

On the same day that the force from Santa Fe bowed to the impasse at the waterhole in the Sandías, Pecos suffered the terror of another big Comanche attack. With all available forces already pursuing the Comanches who had raided Sandía and La Alameda, Governor Mendinueta could offer Pecos no aid. Nor could he help Galisteo on August 10, when four hundred Comanches surrounded that pueblo, charged its defenses several times, then rode off with the last mare of the pueblo. In fact, on the anniversary of his first great triumph over Comanches, Mendinueta found his province helpless against all raiders, with no meaningful help in sight.

The viceroy sympathized better than he comprehended the plight of the New Mexicans. His notion of direct assistance was to make arms available to the settlers at cost, but the New Mexicans had no money. Commandant Inspector O'Conor ignored the viceroy's suggestion that he second troops from his own command to aid New Mexico. Instead, he called upon New Mexican forces to participate in his own grand campaign against the Apaches. Impossible, for the same reason that it was no longer possible to campaign against Gilas or Navajos or Comanches: almost no horses remained in New Mexico.

Mendinueta explained tactfully to the viceroy why the settlers could not accept his generous offer to get them guns wholesale and assured him of their access to weapons. Since the Regulation of 1772 provided for new, improved arms for the presidials, the members of the garrison would barter their old ones to the settlers for local produce. The governor guessed there would be in the entire province about six hundred guns and one hundred fifty pairs of pistols in fair condition, plenty indeed for settlers too poor to buy enough powder and shot to make guns count for much.

New Mexico's critical problem was the lack of horses, impossible to resolve without outside help because raids and drought had wiped out the breeding stock. Since the destitute New Mexicans lacked means

to buy new stock, Governor Mendinueta appealed for a Crown gift
of 1,500 horses to save the province. Without it, he expected to lose
New Mexico; given it, he would try to quell all the enemies without
asking for any other reinforcement.[25]

The governor made such a persuasive case that, when his letter
reached Mexico City, two months after he wrote it, the viceregal
machinery ground out full approval in just two weeks. On the last
day of October 1775, the viceroy ordered Commandant Inspector
O'Conor to purchase 1,500 horses and ship them north to Santa Fe
as quickly as possible. Despite the viceroy's prompt, favorable response, a year passed before the required number of horses could be
purchased in Nuevo León and Nuevo Santander, then driven north
to Santa Fe. Meanwhile, Governor Mendinueta tried every measure
he could conceive to stave off disaster.

Since the New Mexicans could not quell the Navajos, the governor
sought Ute help. He had only to suggest that a campaign would be
appropriate punishment for Navajo breaches of peace against the
vassals of the king; Utes zestfully went after the horses and scalps
of their old enemies. One Ute campaign sufficed to chasten the Navajos and send their leaders to the Governor's Palace at Santa Fe to
make peace.

Mendinueta was a little muddled about his accomplishment. He
boasted that he had skillfully broken up an old Ute-Navajo friendship,
apparently unaware of their old enmity, only tempered in recent years
by mutual alliance with the Spaniards. He did appreciate the importance of conserving the Utes' friendship at all costs, and he tried to
protect them from exploitative New Mexicans. A gubernatorial order
in 1775 forbade any settler or friendly Indian to go to the Ute country
to trade, in order that all Ute trade occur under proper supervision
of provincial authorities. Since the wars and drought had made Ute
trade more important than ever to the northern settlements, the order
was much honored in the breach, often with the collusion of local
officials responsible for enforcing it, but no disastrous rift occurred.[26]
Perhaps the New Mexican traders operated more fairly or the Utes
proved more tolerant of abuse than Mendinueta had anticipated; perhaps the Comanche menace kept the Utes faithful to the New Mexican

[25] Mendinueta to Bucareli, Santa Fe, August 19, 1775, ibid., p. 183; approval
proceedings follow, pp. 184–189.
[26] Governor Francisco Trebol Navarro, Bando, Santa Fe, September 13, 1778,
SANM, no. 740.

alliance at all costs. The Navajos also honored their peace treaty, though Governor Mendinueta suspected that some maintained communications and perhaps even cooperated with Gila raiders on the southern and western frontiers.

The end of the Navajo war eased pressures on the western frontier pueblos, but Governor Mendinueta could do little for the beleaguered northern and eastern frontiers, short of ending the Comanche war. There his imagination fell as short as the military resources of his province. Assuming all Comanches committed to the war against New Mexico, he kept the Taos trade closed to all except those whose chiefs would come to Santa Fe to make peace with him. No Comanche leaders would risk that invitation, in view of the fate of the last nineteen Comanches on the road to Santa Fe in September 1774. Many Comanches wearied of the costly war against New Mexico, and some leaders desired peace. Only a fraction of the nation, apparently Yupes and Yamparicas, sustained a whole-hearted commitment to the relentless vendetta of Cuerno Verde. Yet, the breakdown of their customary contacts at Taos left moderate leaders within the Comanchería no safe avenue to negotiate with the governor. Thus, mutual mistrust, deeply rooted in experience on both sides, and misunderstanding needlessly prolonged the war between Comanches and New Mexicans.

The saddest results were at Pecos and Galisteo. The starving Tanos of Galisteo, reduced to just 41 families (152 persons) and plundered of all their cattle and horses, talked of quitting their pueblo altogether and dispersing among the best-supplied pueblos that would receive them. In an effort to keep that strategic spot occupied, Governor Mendinueta lent the people of Galisteo seven yoke of oxen so that they could plant their crops in the spring of 1776. Some of the population hung on for a few more years.[27]

Pecos fared little better. Once the biggest and richest pueblo, by spring 1776 it had only 100 families (269 persons). Most of their personal possessions had been sold for food. Comanche raiders and drought had reduced Pecos herds to just eight old cows and a dozen sorry horses. Governor Mendinueta sympathized, but the best help he could muster was a gift of twelve cows, hardly enough to arrest the pueblo's decline.[28]

[27] Galisteo still had some population in October 1780, but by 1792 it was extinct, and the remnants of its people lived at Santo Domingo (Adams and Chávez, eds., in Domínguez, *Missions of New Mexico*, p. 217).

[28] Domínguez, *Missions of New Mexico*, pp. 213–214, 217.

Knowing that the coming summer threatened worse Comanche depredations than ever, the governor tried to shore up New Mexico's defenses. The old pueblos left little to be desired in terms of defensive layout or of routine precautions against raiders; their people had come to grips with the *bárbaros* centuries before they saw either a Spaniard or a horse. Sandía was an exception. It had been abandoned during the turmoils of the 1680's, then reoccupied in 1748 by Tiwas who forsook exile among the Hopis to return to their ancestral homeland in the Rio Grande Valley, bringing a few Hopis with them. The two groups had maintained separate identities at Sandía, the Tiwa majority in a conventional pueblo arrangement of three blocks of communal dwellings around two plazas, the Hopi minority some way apart in small, casually placed houses, virtually impossible to defend. After Comanches swept the heart of the province and killed thirty-three men at Sandía in the summer of 1775, Governor Mendinueta ordered the Hopi minority into the more defensible structures of their Tiwa neighbors.[29] With just 92 families (275 persons) altogether, the people of Sandía readily cooperated.

The Pueblos' sensible examples left the Spanish populace quite unmoved. They balked all of the governor's efforts to consolidate them in defensible settlements. When raids and drought made life unbearable, some defied the law to flee to El Paso and points south; others moved to the straggling capital villa. Many clung to their scattered homesteads and, under the awful pressures of that time, grew all the more impoverished, embittered, and ungovernable.

Although ultimate disaster always loomed, the New Mexicans hung on. When their new horse herd arrived in the summer of 1776, they rallied 250 men for O'Conor's campaign against Apaches in the southeastern mountains of the province. Thus, they shared in the modest success of Spanish arms and contributed to a great Comanche triumph over the Apaches. That was a mixed result for the New Mexicans, who had long suffered much more from Comanches than Apaches. None dared guess what new flights of arrogance the victory might inspire among Comanche warriors.

New Mexico was not the only source of doubts about O'Conor's results and about the validity of his entire management of the northern frontier. O'Conor had spent most of 1774 realigning presidios according to the Rubí plan. With that task largely accomplished, he felt free

29 Ibid., p. 143.

in 1775 and 1776 to take the field against the Apaches to drive them
north of the frontier line. The contrast between his sweeping objectives
and his minimal results gave rise to questions about O'Conor's competence just as administrative reforms removed his office from the
friendly jurisdiction of Viceroy Bucareli.

O'Conor planned initially to launch a sweeping offensive against
Apaches all along the line in 1775, using two thousand men from four
provinces. His grand design broke down because the New Mexicans
had not enough horses to participate and Sonora required all its troops
to support a colonization effort in California. Thus, the campaign was
largely the work of forces from Nueva Vizcaya, directed by O'Conor
himself, and those of Coahuila, commanded by Governor Jacobo
Ugarte. O'Conor claimed fifteen victories over the Apaches and two
thousand horses and mules recovered. He counted 138 Apache warriors dead and 104 Apaches captured. In their second concerted offensive, in the fall of 1776, Spanish forces tallied fewer successes but
sparked a general flight that brought many Apaches to disaster. Fleeing
northward from the Rio Grande and eastward from the mountains
of southeastern New Mexico, Apaches blundered into a Comanche
horde on the Colorado River. The Comanches slaughtered three hundred families; only one Apache and a Spanish captive escaped to tell
the tale.[30]

Because Apaches suffered more in 1775 and 1776, it did not follow
that the people of the interior provinces suffered any less. While
O'Conor's vaunted campaigns engaged some Apaches, many others
marauded against unguarded settlements below the line of defense. As
Rubí's critics had always warned, the expensive, time-consuming realignment of the presidios had stripped the settled areas of protection.[31]
Apache warriors easily slipped through the hundred-mile spaces between the frontier presidios, then raided at will throughout the
provinces with little fear of opposition or pursuit.

Reports of continuing losses in the interior provinces routinely
flowed to Commandant Inspector O'Conor, but his own reports to
the viceroy dwelt on his successes against the *bárbaros* and his progress

[30] Analyses of the O'Conor campaigns appear in Alfred Barnaby Thomas, ed.,
Forgotten Frontiers, pp. 10–13 and 63–64, and in Donald E. Worcester, ed.,
Instructions for Governing the Interior Provinces of New Spain, pp. 8-12.

[31] Max L. Moorhead, *The Apache Frontier*, pp. 34–35; Al B. Nelson, "Juan de
Ugalde and the Rio Grande Frontier, 1779–1790," pp. 53–54; Fray Francisco
Garcés and Fray Juan Díaz to Viceroy Antonio de Bucareli, Ures, March 21, 1775,
in Herbert Eugene Bolton, ed., *Anza's California Expeditions*, V, 282.

in relocating presidios. Not until a new, independent commandant general took charge of the newly created Provincias Internas did the viceroy learn that the vigorous efforts of his trusted commandant inspector had produced very little security for the interior provinces. At the request of the new commandant general, Governor Felipe Barri of Nueva Vizcaya submitted a résumé of losses his people had suffered from Indian raiders in the years 1771 to 1776: 1,674 persons killed and 154 captured; 116 haciendas abandoned; 68,256 head of livestock stolen. Those totals did not include military losses or certain other losses in special categories.

O'Conor could hardly be presumed ignorant of the plight of the province that had been his principal residence as commandant inspector. Bucareli, much surprised, demanded an explanation from O'Conor and forwarded copies of the whole file to Minister of the Indies José de Gálvez in Spain.[32]

By timely departure, O'Conor largely escaped the embarrassing questions about his competence and integrity that the commandant general raised. The rigorous campaigns of 1775 and 1776, climaxing a decade's strenuous service on the northern frontier, broke his health. He requested transfer on that ground and was promptly promoted to the rank of brigadier general and the governorship of Yucatán. He died at Mérida in 1779, aged forty-five, unaware of a transformation on the northern frontier, wrought by new men and new policies of a kind he had always opposed.

[32] Croix to Bucareli, September 27, 1777 (enclosure no. 1 in Bucareli to Gálvez, October 27, 1777), cited in Bernard E. Bobb, *The Viceregency of Antonio María Bucareli in New Spain, 1771–1779,* p. 152; see also the analysis of Alfred Barnaby Thomas, ed., in *Teodoro de Croix and the Northern Frontier of New Spain, 1776–1783,* pp. 29–35.

CHAPTER 14

Provincias Internas, 1776-1779

Though life in 1776 seemed as bleak and precarious as ever for inhabitants of New Spain's northern frontier, the year marked a turning point in their fortunes. At last the Crown acknowledged that factors of distance and overwork made it impossible for the viceroy to govern satisfactorily the northern frontier provinces and detached them to form a separate jurisdiction.

The Comandancia General of the Provincias Internas first included the provinces of New Mexico, Texas, the Californias, Coahuila, Nueva Vizcaya, Sonora, and Sinaloa; Nuevo Santander and Nuevo León were later added. Its commandant general reported directly to the king rather than the viceroy and possessed both civil and military jurisdiction. However, the Provincias Internas was never wholly autonomous: its judiciary bodies remained attached to the Audiencia of Guadalajara; worse, it remained financially dependent upon the viceroyalty of New Spain.

The first commandant general was Teodoro de Croix, forty-six–year–old nephew of former viceroy Marqués de Croix. A native of France, he had enlisted in the Spanish army at seventeen and had served with distinction in Italy and Flanders before going to New Spain with his uncle in 1766. While his uncle was viceroy, Don Teodoro served first as governor of Acapulco, then as inspector of troops for New Spain. In both capacities he won the approval of Visitador General Gálvez. He also campaigned with the Gálvez nephew, Bernardo, in Nueva Vizcaya, where the two promising young officers formed a friendship that continued when both returned to Spain with their uncles in 1772. Each enjoyed the encouraging support of both distinguished uncles, and their careers mark two of history's happier instances of nepotism. Their staunch friendship and secure personal access to high authorities in Spain augured well for the territories that they came to govern in North America.[1]

Both nephews returned to America in 1776. Teodoro de Croix, eighteen years the older, sailed to much the greater office. In December 1776, he reported to Mexico City as commandant general of the Provincias Internas. Bernardo de Gálvez reported to Louisiana as colonel of the regiment, but, on January 1, 1777, he became acting governor of the province.

The implications for the frontier populations, Spanish and Indian, were extraordinarily hopeful. Both Croix and Gálvez had personal experience of Indian campaigns in the northern provinces, where Gálvez had proved open-minded and sympathetic toward *indios bárbaros*. The two good friends took for granted the desirability of cooperation for the mutual good of their jurisdictions and of the empire. They could expect from Minister of the Indies José de Gálvez informed support for enlightened approaches to the problems of the frontier.

Many months passed before Croix could effect working machinery and implement new programs, but frontier officials soon recognized pleasing currents of change eddying from Spain, Mexico City, and New Orleans. Earliest and best benefited by the new order were Ripperdá at San Antonio and de Mézières at Natchitoches and the Indians with

[1] John W. Caughey, in *Bernardo de Gálvez in Louisiana, 1776–1783*, points out the important friendship of the Croix and Gálvez families. The period of the establishment of the Provincias Internas is an area of considerable controversy, due in large part to the sharp differences that arose between Teodoro de Croix and Bucareli. Charles Edward Chapman, in *The Founding of Spanish California*, devotes Chapter 17 to "The Incompetent Rule of Croix, 1776–1783," pp. 386 ff.; Alfred Barnaby Thomas, ed., in *Teodoro de Croix and the Northern Frontier of New Spain, 1776–1783*, champions Croix and excoriates Bucareli; Bernard E. Bobb, in *The Viceregency of Antonio María Bucareli in New Spain, 1771–1779*, pp. 143–155, defends Bucareli against Thomas.

whom they dealt. Long forbidden to communicate with each other, the two officials were now encouraged, indeed expected, to cooperate in every useful way. After years of capricious interference from Governor Unzaga, de Mézières had in Gálvez a superior who admired the French style in Indian relations and gave him all possible support. Best of all, Ripperdá's long ordeal of vituperation and restriction by Bucareli and O'Conor was over. At last he could treat the Indians of his jurisdiction in a manner consistent with his convictions and his promises.

Ripperdá had regrettably little time to enjoy his triumph. Early in 1776 Viceroy Bucareli grew so convinced of the Texas governor's wrongful interest in contraband trade and alleged insubordination that he persuaded the Crown to remove him from the post.[2] Since no charges had been proved against him, the Crown appointed him to a distant post that could even be deemed a promotion. By autumn 1776, Ripperdá knew of his transfer to Comayagua, Honduras, in the captaincy general of Guatemala, and had no illusions about the reason for it.[3] His orders required him to await his replacement, Don Domingo Cabello, transferred to Texas from the governorship of Nicaragua. It was mid-autumn 1778 before Cabello reached San Antonio. Meanwhile, though impatient to move on to his new job, Ripperdá had in twenty months under Croix's jurisdiction his happiest experience of Texas.

Those same months were neither easy nor encouraging for the new commandant general. The king had set Croix two formidable objectives: defense and extension of the vast territories included in his command, within the terms of the Regulation of 1772, and conversion of the countless *indios bárbaros* in and beyond the provinces of his jurisdiction. Traditional ideas of expansion and of conversion still prevailed at court. Although the Crown had adopted his specific recommendations concerning the frontier presidios, the practical, ruthless spirit of Rubí's advice had not prevailed. The contradiction typified the philosophical and practical incongruities that dogged Spanish programs on the northern frontier.

---

[2] Bucareli also demanded removal of Governor Ugarte of Coahuila, who was loath to cooperate with Commandant Inspector O'Conor. Both Ugarte and Ripperdá were convinced that O'Conor was quite wrong, and events tended to vindicate their judgments, but Bucareli placed his entire confidence in O'Conor and was determined to have provincial governors faithful to the letter and spirit of his commands.

[3] Herbert Eugene Bolton, *Texas in the Middle Eighteenth Century*, p. 124.

Great Salt Lake

Utah Lake

ALTA CALIFORNIA

Monterey

HAVASUPAIS

Colorado R.

San Juan R.

UTES

YAMPARICA

Grand Canyon

JICARILLAS

Taos

San Juan

San Gabriel

HOPI

NAVAJOS

ZUÑI

Jémez
Pojoaque
Zía
Laguna
Ácoma

Santa Fe
Pecos
Sandia
Albuquerque
Isleta
Tomé

YUPES

CUCHA

San Diego
Concepción
Bicuñer

YUMAS

Gila R.

PIMAS

NUEVO
MEXICO

Socorro
Sabinal
Fray
Cristóbal

GILEÑOS
MIMBREÑOS

TE.

APACHERIA

Tucson

San Xavier
del Bac
Altar
Terrenato
Fronteras
Arispe

Tubac
Las
Nutrias
Janos

Robledo
El Paso

NATAGÉS

Carrizal

BAJA CALIFORNIA

SONORA

NUEVA
VIZCAYA

Rio Grande

MESCALEROS

El Norte
San Carlos
Chihuahua

Aqua
L

San
Vicente

0   80   160

Miles

Conchos

Parral

Bolsón
de
Mapimí

San

COA

PROVINCIAS INTERNAS
after 1776

LEGEND

- Spanish Settlements
- Spanish Missions
- Spanish Presidios
- Mission & Presidio
- French Settlements
- Pueblo Settlements
- Indian Settlements

SINALOA

PIMAS, YUPES, etc.– Ranges of Roving Indian Groups

GHW

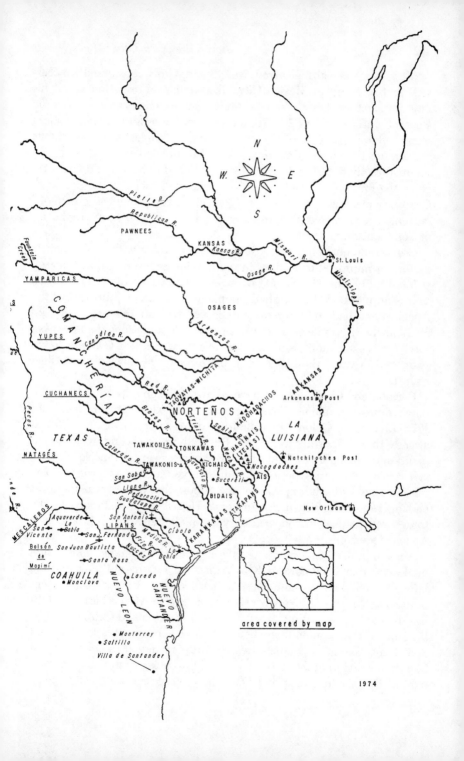

area covered by map

1974

After five years' absence from New Spain, Croix considered it necessary first to study in Mexico City all available information about his new jurisdiction. Only when he presented his credentials to Viceroy Bucareli on December 22, 1776, did the viceroy order a financial statement and a map prepared for Croix, as well as copies of all documents concerning the affected provinces. He also directed their governors to report directly to Croix. Not until the end of March 1777 did Croix receive the first set of archival copies, papers pertinent to the period of O'Conor's command. Meanwhile, he received the provincial governors' current reports of relentless Indian raids, laced with gloomy prophecies of imminent ruin.

Croix could not reconcile those current dispatches with the optimistic picture of improved conditions in the Provincias Internas that Bucareli painted for him or with the O'Conor reports on which the viceroy based his assumptions. If O'Conor had campaigned so successfully against the Apaches and had so enormously improved frontier defenses, why did most northern provinces now suffer greater depredations than ever before? Croix's question dismayed the viceroy, who asked O'Conor to explain and dreaded the blot of possible error on his own distinguished record.

Fortunately, Croix did not have to await documents to analyze Sonora's critical problems. When he reached Mexico City in December 1776, Lieutenant Colonel Juan Bautista de Anza of Tubac presidio was already there, reporting to Viceroy Bucareli on his second overland expedition from Sonora to California. Shortly afterward, Francisco Crespo arrived from Sonora, where he had just served a term as governor. Extensive talks with both men convinced Croix that Sonora was the most endangered of the Provincias Internas. He asked Anza to specify the forces and plan of action necessary to quell the insurgents and halt Apache incursions.

Anza impressed Croix so favorably that the commandant wanted him made governor of Sonora, but his request in February 1777 came too late. Bucareli had proposed a year earlier that Anza succeed Mendinueta as governor of New Mexico, so as to give Anza a base to establish direct communications from Santa Fe to Sonora and California. The king made that appointment before Croix's recommendation reached Spain, and change was impracticable. Croix managed to keep Anza in Sonora for one valuable year. He sent him back as military commandant of the province in spring 1777, then found its state of emergency sufficient excuse to delay Anza's departure for New Mexico until summer 1778.[4]

From consultations with Anza and Crespo, documents delivered by Bucareli, and current frontier reports, Croix drew conclusions odious to the viceroy. By the end of March 1777, Croix believed that the presidial alignment had been a disastrous mistake and that the troops remained just as untrained, ill-equipped, and exploited as Rubí had found them a decade earlier. Recognizing that he could not scrap the new presidial line, Croix suggested a string of fortified towns behind the presidial line to bolster the defenses of the provinces. Certain that the existing garrisons of less than two thousand soldiers could not defend the 1,500-mile frontier, he also asked Gálvez for at least two thousand reinforcements.

Although Croix repudiated the Rubí program with respect to presidios and manpower, he revived the most radical and least attended of the inspector general's ideas: alliance with Indians of the north against the eastern Apaches. If the eastern Apaches could be subdued or exterminated by a pincers movement of Norteño warriors and Spanish forces, even such troublesome western Apaches as the Gileños should be much weakened and relatively easy to conquer.

Current news appeared to vindicate Rubí's judgment of Apaches and Norteños. No province lacked Apache problems. Lipans were so troublesome in Coahuila that Governor Ugarte insisted the only remedy would be to deport all of them overseas.[5] In contrast, Governor Ripperdá reported that the Norteños had been remarkably faithful to their peace commitments in Texas, despite severe strains imposed upon their loyalty by Bucareli's policies. Lipans were doing considerable damage in Texas, taking advantage of their nominal peace to live near the presidios and prey upon livestock herds. They were increasingly insolent in the spring of 1777. Ripperdá guessed that Lipan boldness grew as Norteño visits to Béxar dwindled.[6]

The cessation of Norteño visits showed that those proud people did not visit people who would not return their visits. Governor Ripperdá had taken great care to send them visitors until local citizens' accusations against him and the orders of Bucareli and O'Conor forced him

---

[4] Alfred Barnaby Thomas, ed., *Forgotten Frontiers*, p. 19, n. 56; Croix, Report of 1781, in Thomas, *Teodoro de Croix*, pp. 133–134.

[5] Thomas, *Teodoro de Croix*, p. 26.

[6] Ripperdá to Croix, Béxar, April 27, 1777, in Herbert Eugene Bolton, *Athanase de Mézières and the Louisiana-Texas Frontier, 1768–1780*, II, 122–129.

to stop. Ripperdá wanted Croix to realize that the lapse in communications had cooled the friendship of those valuable nations, though they had yet to repudiate their peace treaties.

Ripperdá warned Croix of another chronic strain upon the Norteños' friendship: Spanish treaty commitments to the Lipans and the consequent Lipan advantage of sanctuary near the presidios. The old hatreds were as lively as ever, but Norteños no longer campaigned so relentlessly against the Lipans, lest they be mistaken for Comanches at the presidios. Comanches, whom Ripperdá then counted as the only recognized enemies of Texas, infested the hills just northwest of San Antonio and were as dangerous to other Indians as to Spaniards. The Norteños did not wish to be caught up in the Comanches' hostilities with the Texans.

Governor Ripperdá believed that all the difficulties dated back to San Sabá and Parrilla's initial error of campaigning with Apache allies against Norteños. The Norteños' resulting distrust of the Spaniards had never died, and now they suspected the Spaniards of giving the Lipans guns. Since they knew that the Lipans' gun trade with the Bidais and the Tejas had been checked, what else could they think when they met Lipans with firearms?

Governor Ripperdá could have wished no more encouraging response than Croix dispatched that summer.[7] The commandant general praised Ripperdá's zeal and competence, regretted the governor's scheduled departure, and congratulated him warmly upon the promotion. Chiding him for having trimmed his conduct toward the Norteños in response to slanders, Croix urged Ripperdá thenceforth to do all he thought necessary to conserve their friendship, including provision of frequent trade. He authorized him to use all the force he could muster against the Comanches and asked him to minimize Lipan damages by dissimulation until Croix could effect new approaches to the Indian problems of his jurisdiction.

Even before Ripperdá received Croix's heartening vote of confidence, he gambled that it would be forthcoming. When early summer brought new reports of the Norteños' growing disgust that they had not received the visits promised at the time of treaty making, Governor Ripperdá dispatched a Béxar lieutenant and twenty-eight soldiers to visit the Tawakonis and Iscanis. He also sought de Mézières' help. In a polite note congratulating Gálvez on his new position and offering his com-

---

[7] The Bexar Archives contain two letters from Croix to Ripperdá, Mexico, July 9, 1777, one of which appears also in Bolton, *Athanase de Mézières*, II, 133.

plete cooperation, Ripperdá asked Governor Gálvez to ask de Mézières to continue to watch the Indians whom he had brought to make peace in San Antonio and to bring the Panismahas into the concord. Ripperdá also requested that Louisiana officials watch their traders carefully to ensure that no goods reached the Comanches who still raided in Texas.[8]

Once assured of Croix's support for his efforts,[9] Ripperdá proposed stronger measures to control the effects upon Texas of the Indian trade. He had earlier stressed the value of the Adaeseños' controversial settlement of Bucareli as an outpost to maintain contact with the coastal tribes and forestall British intrusions in the Akokisas' area. By autumn 1777, he was emphasizing Bucareli's importance as a point of contact with Norteños, especially the Taovayas and Panismahas, who lived so far from San Antonio. Ripperdá hoped to centralize control of all traders by licensing them at Bucareli and putting Gil Ybarbo in charge of the trade, in a role much like that of de Mézières at Natchitoches. He wanted all the Indians to understand that they enjoyed trade through permission of Texas, even if the actual traders happened to come from Louisiana, and to understand the unity of Frenchmen and Spaniards. Ripperdá hoped to convey those two ideas also to the Comanches, who might thus be persuaded to join in the advantages of the general concord.[10] Ripperdá's idea seemed sensible to Croix. He relayed it to Governor Gálvez, asking his advice and cooperation in the matter of licensing traders through the governor of Texas.[11]

Both Gálvez and de Mézières were already alert to growing complexities among the Indians of the Red River Valley. Early in March 1777, when de Mézières reported general quiet and harmony in the Natchitoches area and among the Indians of its far-flung trade sphere, he noted that the Panismahas had migrated from the Missouri River to the Red.[12] He understood that they had come to enjoy the Natchitoches trade and to make common cause with the other Red River nations against their mutual enemy, the Osages. He was not aware that they had clashed with other Pawnees over trade from St. Louis and from British contrabandists.

[8] Ripperdá to Gálvez, Béxar, June 7, 1777, in Bolton, *Athanase de Mézières*, II, 131–132.

[9] Croix to Ripperdá, Zacatecas, September 11, 1777, BA.

[10] Ripperdá to Croix, Béxar, October 28, 1777, in Bolton, *Athanase de Mézières*, II, 135–136.

[11] Croix to Gálvez, Chihuahua, September 11, 1778, ibid., pp. 137–138.

[12] De Mézières to Gálvez, Natchitoches, March 4, 1777, AGI, Cuba, Legajo 112 (transcribed for the author by courtesy of Dr. Max L. Moorhead).

Whatever their reasons, Panismahas' movements affected the balance of power on the northern frontier because their three divisions could muster eight hundred warriors. They had chosen a fine location on the Red River between the Kadohadachos and the Taovayas, which de Mézières deemed advantageous to Spanish interests. Almost equally dependent upon hunting and upon agriculture, the Panismahas seemed very friendly. De Mézières heartily welcomed such strong new allies in the growing troubles with the Osages.

There had been a welcome lull in hostilities after 1773, when turbulence among Indians and traders in the St. Louis jurisdiction had led some Osages to abandon their old location in the Missouri basin.[13] Their long move and preparation of new homes and fields in the Arkansas Valley kept those Osage men too busy to raid much for several seasons, but by spring 1777 they marauded again in the Red River Valley. Given the disrepair of their trade relations at St. Louis and the inconvenient distance of that post from their new location, the Osages sought new trade connections at the Arkansas Post. To that end, early in the spring of 1777, they sued for peace with their old enemies, the Arkansas Indians, whose villages lay near the post.

Knowing their previous record of bad faith, neither Captain Balthazar de Villiers, then commandant of the Arkansas Post, nor Governor Gálvez expected the Osages to keep their new promises,[14] but Crown policy forbade them to deny any Indian nation's plea for peace. Governor Gálvez particularly welcomed the Panismahas' migration to the Red River because he anticipated worse behavior by the Osages and knew that the Red River nations would need all possible help.

First to suffer were those oldest and most faithful allies, the Kadohadachos. Tinhioüen visited Natchitoches early in May to report that Osages had killed five men and two women at his village and had stolen many horses. Both Tinhioüen and de Mézières feared that the incident marked the beginning of a war that might wipe out the Kadohadachos completely.[15]

Osage depredations cost Frenchmen dearly, too. No trader could transport his property safely. A Frenchman of Natchitoches, off to trade with the friendly nations, lost a herd of horses to Osage raiders. Grim atrocities occurred: a luckless young Frenchman found alone by Osages

[13] De Mézières to Unzaga, Natchitoches, September 4, 1774, in Bolton, *Athanase de Mézières*, II, 109–112.

[14] Bernardo de Gálvez to de Mézières, New Orleans, April 4, 1777, ibid., p. 122.

[15] De Mézières to Unzaga, Natchitoches, May 2, 1777, ibid., pp. 130–131.

who put him on a spit and roasted him alive; a French father decapitated by Osages who forced his son to carry the head countless miles to their village so they could dance the appropriate celebrations before the lad.

That was a poor time for de Mézières to learn from Gálvez of the Osage treaty with the Arkansas Indians under the reluctant aegis of the Arkansas Post commandant. De Mézières deplored unrealistic policies that required the forms of peace with peoples who deserved war. It was also a bad time to discover that the renegade trader Francisco Beaudoüin had skipped out of Natchitoches with a batch of stolen property, headed north to the Arkansas to trade with the Osages. News of Beaudoüin's activities came from the chiefs of the Kichais and Nacogdoches, who volunteered to confiscate his goods and arrest him. De Mézières gratefully accepted their offer.

Tinhioüen also helped to enforce the law on the Arkansas. Late in July he chanced upon four French hunters whom Osages had stripped of goods and clothing and abandoned to the Arkansas Valley wilderness. Infuriated, Tinhioüen followed the robbers' trail, killed five, and graciously restored their plunder to the owners. Then Tinhioüen notified de Mézières that Englishmen had built a blockhouse on the Arkansas, stocked with merchandise meant for Indians of the Natchitoches district. Tinhioüen wanted permission to oust the intruders. De Mézières agreed gladly, stipulating that the chief should bring him the Englishmen as prisoners.[16]

The Osages did not ignore Tinhioüen's attack on behalf of the French hunters. Captain Villiers reported from the Arkansas Post that Osages had killed seven licensed French traders in his jurisdiction; he guessed that vagabonds were suffering unreported casualties. Convinced that nothing short of a decisive victory over the Osages would secure the peace, de Mézières proposed to Gálvez a detailed plan for a combined assault of Norteños and Comanches upon the Osage village in late summer, preferably in the coming year.

De Mézières had been mulling over such a venture since 1773 and had perfected every detail. He proposed to leave Natchitoches the next spring with some Creoles skilled in Indian affairs and the French interpreters stationed in the Indian villages, canoe up the Red River to the Kadohadachos, then ride horses to the Taovayas village, where the fine plains would permit all the Indian allies to use their horses to good ad-

[16] De Mézières to Gálvez, Natchitoches, September 14, 1777, *ibid.*, pp. 141–143, with enclosed campaign proposal, pp. 143–147.

vantage. That would be the logical assembly point, conveniently accessible to all the allies and best supplied with pasturage, horses, mules, and trappings. The march to the Osage country would be shortest from the Taovayas, through uninhabited country where they could travel more easily and secretly, living off buffalo on the way.

How many Indians could he lead to war against the Osages without exposing their villages to undue danger? De Mézières' estimates reflected the sad decline of once-powerful Caddo villages: the Kadohadachos could spare just fifty men; the Nacogdoches and Nasonis together a mere twenty-five; the Nabedaches only thirty. He reckoned the Kichais could furnish twenty-five, the Tonkawas sixty, the Tawakonis sixty, and the Xaranames twenty. The real power lay westward with the Taovayas and the Panismahas, each able to contribute three hundred warriors, and the Comanches, from whom he figured four hundred. Since de Mézières deemed the Comanches superior to all the rest in breeding, strength, valor, and gallantry, he was prepared to gamble that he could win their friendship by inviting them to join his campaign. If he could draw them into a comrades-at-arms relationship with the campaign allies, de Mézières expected that sacred relationship to endure to the mutual advantage of all.

All the warriors would be mounted and skilled in the uses of gun and lance as well as bow and arrow. In view of their intense hatred of the Osages, no stipend would be necessary. Presents to the chiefs, including munitions, would be necessary, but de Mézières trusted them to use the munitions for the campaign against the Osages. Those presents would actually be his share of a ceremonial gift exchange rather than a payment. In return, he would receive provisions for his personnel and horses to carry the sick, the wounded, and the heaviest munitions.

Though de Mézières labeled the Osages cowards, his attack force would outnumber the eight hundred Osage warriors by half. He meant his men to take at once the horses, grain, wood, and water supply of the Osage village and then set afire their closely spaced houses. Any Osages fleeing the flames could be cut down by Norteño knives.

Again, as in 1773, outside forces spared the Osages a test of de Mézières' plan to exterminate them. Though Governor Gálvez promised to study the proposal, he ordered his lieutenant governor to go immediately to Texas in the service of Croix.[17]

That proved terribly difficult for de Mézières. A virulent epidemic

---

[17] Gálvez to de Mézières, New Orleans, October 28, 1777, ibid., pp. 138–139.

ravaged the populations of eastern Texas and western Louisiana in the late summer and fall of 1777. The Indian communities suffered first and most, for the epidemic not only decimated their numbers but also wiped out their leadership. Before August ended, the chiefs of the Bidais and of the Tejas villages of the Hainais and the Nabedaches all lay dead. Their mourning followers asked de Mézières to designate new chiefs, but he instructed them to go to San Antonio to elect their new leaders before Governor Ripperdá.[18] Gálvez found his action entirely proper.

Though Indian villages were especially vulnerable, San Antonio, Bucareli, and Natchitoches also suffered from the epidemic. Natchitoches, then grown to a thousand people, buried fifty in three months. In one December week the pestilence cost de Mézières his wife,[19] a son, and a daughter.[20]

De Mézières was vouchsafed little time either to mourn his own losses or to help his Indian friends. Commandant General Croix was on his way to Texas, where Gálvez had seconded de Mézières to help his friend solve the tangled Indian problems of the Provincias Internas.

Early in August 1777, the troubled commandant general left Mexico City to establish a new capital at Arispe, Sonora. He paused at Querétaro to take care of his mail, the most discouraging yet. Not only the late summer upsurge of Apache raids had occurred, but also the Seris and Opatas had rebelled in Sonora. The Opatas had a concrete grievance: O'Conor had not paid them for their services in his campaign of 1775.

That had been one affront too many for the Opatas, who already suffered, like most Sonora Indians, from an excess of work and discipline imposed by overzealous missionaries. What if the Opatas' example should inspire restive Pimas, Pápagos, Tiburones, and Gila Apaches to help them destroy the province? Croix ordered Sonora's military commandant, Anza, to pay the Opatas at once and do anything necessary to quell the Seris. Only the religious leaders could curb their missionaries, so Croix urged the Father Provincial at Jalisco to rectify abuses in the mission field. He also appealed to Viceroy Bucareli for an imme-

---

[18] Though the Crown's practice was to appoint chiefs chosen by the Indians, this and subsequent incidents suggest that years of wars and epidemics had disrupted the orderly hereditary succession to leadership among the Caddo peoples.

[19] His second wife, Dame Pelagie Fazendi, whom he married about 1760.

[20] Bolton, ed., in *Athanase de Mézières*, I, n. 104, p. 84; de Mézières to Croix, Natchitoches, November 15, 1778, ibid., II, 231–232.

diate two thousand reinforcements on the grounds of critical emergency in the northern provinces.

Bucareli demurred. Not until Croix could complete his personal inspection of the frontier could either viceroy or commandant general be sure that the situation was as bad as local officials claimed. Bucareli dared not risk any unnecessary commitments, because Spain stood on the brink of a new war with Great Britain. Even if the viceroy could find two thousand troops, which was not likely, they would cost 600,-000 pesos annually, plus the initial expense of outfitting them for frontier service.

Croix pressed northward to see for himself. Well briefed on Sonora and confident that Anza would make optimum use of any resources available there, the commandant general decided to inspect Coahuila, Texas, and Nueva Vizcaya before going to Sonora to establish permanent headquarters. Discouraging reports of deteriorating conditions dogged his route; he relayed them to the viceroy. By November, Bucareli was so impressed that he sent the Guadalajara fusiliers to aid Anza in Sonora and promised to help Croix raise two new flying companies. That was no trivial concession on the viceroy's part; fever was decimating his troops at Veracruz, and Spain could ill afford any deterioration of defenses at that key port while war with Britain loomed again.

Vital though it was for Croix to see the area of his command and to inspect his troops, it was perhaps most important of all for him to size up the provincial governors and presidial commanders upon whose competence so much of his success would hinge. Whether O'Conor was knave or fool or neither or both, there was good reason to think that excessive reliance upon his judgment had betrayed Bucareli into grave errors concerning the northern provinces. Which officials on the northern frontier really understood its problems? Which could Croix trust for honest reports and useful recommendations? Did any of the five provincial governors deserve O'Conor's nasty accusations? What did men with years of experience in the field think of the arguments concerning alliance or war with the Apaches or the Norteños? How much did they really know about the *indios bárbaros*? To find out, Croix called frontier officialdom to a series of three regional councils.

The first convened at Monclova, December 9 through 11, 1777. Senior man present was Colonel Jacobo Ugarte y Loyola, who had served since 1769 as governor of Coahuila and had turned the office over to Colonel Juan de Ugalde only two weeks earlier. He remained at Monclova for the council at the special request of Croix, who wished Ugarte to contribute his knowledge and experience to the deliberations in Coahuila before riding on to his next assignment as governor of Sonora. Half a dozen presidial commanders reported for the council with the new governor, Ugalde, and retiring governor, Ugarte.[21]

Croix, presiding, presented sixteen points for discussion; he would subsequently put the same issues to councils at San Antonio and Chihuahua. In their carefully recorded consensus, he would have the sum of available knowledge and judgment on which to base his decisions and recommendations. Just as important, copies of the proceedings would give the king and his council in Spain an unprecedented look at the problems of the northern frontier as they appeared to the leaders who grappled with them day by day. It was a formidable questionnaire.

1. How long has the Apache tribe of Indians been known on these frontiers, and since when have they made war on us?
2. What victories have we had over them, and especially in the last five years?
3. What, by prudent calculations, is the number of warriors composing each one of the branches or congregations which up to now we know as the Upper Lipan Apaches, Lower Lipan Apaches, Mescaleros, Natagés or Lipiyanes, Faraones, Navajos, and Gileños, and what friendship and bond of relations do these Indians have among themselves?
4. What arms do they use, where do they live, how do they support themselves, and how do they make war upon us and in what provinces and places?
5. What declared enemies do the Apaches have among the heathen nations bordering upon their lands, *rancherías*, and villages?
6. What interpretation does the peace which the Lipans have in this province merit; in what terms was it drawn up; what advantages have flowed from them; and what conveniences or inconveniences can the conservation of this peace or the declaring of war upon them produce?
7. What favorable or adverse results ought to be inferred from the delivery of five Mescalero Indians which the Lipan chief, Poca Ropa, made in the last general campaign to the detachment under the command of the retired lieutenant colonel, Don Vicente Rodríguez, and that which the Lipan chief, Xavierillo, has just made of the two *rancherías* of the same tribe to Captain Don Francisco Martínez?
8. Concerning the Comanches, Taovayases, Taguacanas, Texas, Vidais, Orcoquisacs, Atacapazes, and the rest of the Indians whom we know as the nations of the north, each one of the voters will state what he understands and may know and what may have come to his notice, distinguishing the reports and opinions in accord with the first six points.

[21] Max L. Moorhead, *The Apache Frontier*, p. 46; Bolton, *Texas in the Middle Eighteenth Century*, pp. 124–125.

9. Which nations of the north are nomadic and which live in settlements, plant crops, and so on.

10. What benefits will be achieved by making war upon these tribes, allying ourselves with the Lipans, or the opposite?

11. Whether the number of troops who at present guard our frontiers will be sufficient to undertake the hostile operations either against the Lipan and the rest of the divisions of the Apaches, or against the Indians of the north?

12. If an increase of forces is considered necessary, how much will be sufficient against the Apaches and how much against the Indians of the north?

13. If against the Apaches, especially of the east, the voters will state whether it will be possible to undertake one or several actions or particular ones; how, in what terms, at what seasons, places, or spots, supposing ourselves allies with the Indians of the north.

14 and 15. If against the Indians of the north, each one should state his opinion with regard to the lands they occupy, those of ours which they attack, and how to secure fortunate results from the operations; which Indians will be the ones most suitable to guarantee the good faith of the alliance of the Lipans against those of the north, or that of the latter against the former.

16. Finally, what measures ought to be taken with the present troops for the defense of each one of the provinces and what operations will be the most useful ones for this purpose and for the general pacification of the territory, if the proposed increase of forces comes about?

Except for Captain Rafael Martínez Pacheco, who had served several years in Texas, the officers convened at Monclova felt they could contribute nothing to a discussion of the Norteños, whom they had yet to encounter. However, they had much to say of Apaches, all unfavorable, and they did not hesitate to conclude that alliance with the Norteños against the Apaches would surely be the wiser course. They liked Croix's idea of a pincers movement against the eastern Apaches: Norteño warriors and Louisiana woodsmen led by Gálvez, attacking from north and east, and combined forces of the Provincias Internas led by Croix, attacking from south and west. All agreed that they would participate gladly, just as soon as the commandant general could increase his force to three thousand.[22]

The Monclova council's most important service was to clarify for the commandant general the puzzling question of the numbers and locations of the various eastern Apaches. If not entirely accurate, their consensus was the best information available to Europeans at that time.

---

[22] Report of the Council at Monclova, December 11, 1777, in Bolton, *Athanase de Mézières*, II, 152–163.

They knew Lipans now as residents on both sides of the Rio Grande, under shelter of the presidios of San Juan Bautista, Monclova, and Santa Rosa de Aguaverde, though part of them withdrew sometimes to the upper Nueces Valley. The Natagés sometimes camped with their Lipan relatives, but they tended to live on the plains near El Paso and New Mexico. The Mescaleros lived in the mountains in and near the Bolsón de Mapimí.

Though lacking personal experience of western Apaches, Coahuila's officers ventured opinions of them, too: the Gileños lived in the Gila and Mimbres mountain ranges and various other places between Nueva Vizcaya and Sonora, and the Navajos were another Apache tribe who lived in the neighborhood of New Mexico. Only Gileños raided in Sonora, but all Apaches raided unhappy Nueva Vizcaya. The Coahuila officers understood that the Apaches marauding in New Mexico were Navajos, Gileños, and Lipiyanes.[23] It was the eastern Apaches who raided in Coahuila, Nuevo León, Nuevo Santander, and occasionally in Texas, in addition to preying upon Nueva Vizcaya.

The assembled officers either knew nothing of Apache agriculture or dismissed it as insignificant. They understood all Apaches to subsist on deer and buffalo and, except for Lipans, on the flesh of horses and mules stolen from Spaniards. On the basis of observation and rumor, the council guessed that Apaches altogether numbered about five thousand men, but no one could really place much confidence in any estimate.

What of the value of peace treaties with the Lipans? Worthless, because they never kept them: witness their disregard of their recent treaty commitments to remain settled north of the Rio Grande. They had nearly ruined Coahuila and Nueva Vizcaya with their raids ever since. Nonetheless, it would pay to cultivate both Mescaleros and Lipans by giving them presents at the presidios. It might be feasible to make the Lipans, as intermediaries, stand guarantors of Mescalero peace promises, thus giving the Lipans reason to punish the Mescaleros when the inevitable violations should occur. If a general campaign could be made, the objective should be to drive the Mescaleros and Natagés to take refuge with the Lipans, then confine all eastern Apaches to a small district between Coahuila and the lands of the Norteños. Attacks by the Norteños should then drive the Apaches to seek asylum at the Rio Grande presidios, unless they should prefer

[23] Equated with the Natagés in a related document.

death to surrender. They would, of course, be legally entitled to the truce terms stipulated in the Regulation of 1772 and would have to be encouraged to settle down in formal pueblos to live as Christian vassals of the king. No one seriously anticipated that Apaches could live very long with that answer to their problems.

How realistic was talk of alliance with the Norteños? Croix hoped to find out at San Antonio. Northward with the commandant general rode Captain Rafael Martínez Pacheco of Presidio La Babía, the only officer in Coahuila who claimed any knowledge of the Indians of the north. He had gone berserk, defied all authority, and armed local Indians to help him attack Spanish soldiers when he commanded Presidio San Agustín; more recently, during his service at Béxar, he had accused Ripperdá of incompetence and corruption. Now he would contribute his judgment and experience to the deliberations at San Antonio.

Texas was not very impressive in 1778, even by the modest standards of the northern frontier. It had just the one straggling villa of San Antonio, the two remaining presidios of Béxar and La Bahía, and seven missions with congregations at low ebb. A 1778 census turned up a total population of 3,103. Croix conceded that it would be laughable to call Texas a province but for its excellent natural resources of soil, water, and minerals and the hope of converting its numerous *indios barbáros*. Now useful chiefly as a buffer to protect Coahuila and Nuevo Santander against Indians and Britons, Texas should eventually form a commercially and strategically valuable link with Louisiana.[24]

Governor Ripperdá and Captain Luis Cazorla of La Bahía, the two ranking officers in Texas, were the only new voices in the San Antonio council. General Antonio Bonilla (adjutant inspector and secretary of the Comandancia General), Captain Domingo Díaz (commander of the First Flying Squadron, which was escorting Croix), and Captain Martínez Pacheco had come from Monclova with Croix. Croix convened them on January 5, 1778, without the important presence of de Mézières, who was detained by pestilence and Osages in his own district. His knowledge and advice were sorely missed by the council at San Antonio. They reached only tentative conclusions, subject to review by de Mézières, and their recommendations presumed his subsequent availability as agent to the Norteños.[25]

Still, Governor Ripperdá could make an encouraging report. Since

---

24 Croix, Report of 1781, in Thomas, *Teodoro de Croix*, pp. 72 ff.
25 Report of Council at San Antonio de Béxar, January 5, 1778, in Bolton, *Athanase de Mézières*, II, 163-170.

Fray Ramírez and de Mézières had persuaded the Norteños to talk
peace in 1771, many chiefs had ridden to Béxar to ratify treaties with
Governor Ripperdá. He believed that all except the Comanches had
kept them very faithfully, and he counted their sporadic raids mere
nuisances as compared to the intensive Comanche warfare in New
Mexico. Other problems existed: thefts by Apaches, Karankawa depredations between the coast and La Bahía, and disruptive activities
among Xaranames. But some Karankawas were being brought to the
missions by force, and some Xaraname apostates were returning
voluntarily to missions.

What could the Texans tell Croix about the Norteños? They could
only guess their warrior strength, probably not taking into account the
recent epidemic: 300 Tejas, 70 Bidais, 500 Taovayas, 250 Tawakonis,
50 Iscanis, 90 Kichais, 300 Tonkawas, 50 Akokisas, 30 Ais, 600 Panismahas, 40 Xaranames. They understood Comanche to be a generic
term covering various groups of Indians whom they estimated at
5,000 warriors, without much basis for guessing that instead of any
other very large round number.

What else could they say about these Indian peoples who figured
so importantly in the history of the province? The only ones whom
they knew to live in settlements and plant crops were the Tejas, Ais,
Taovayas, Tawakonis, and Iscanis. They realized that the Tawakonis
were related to the Taovayas and Iscanis, and they recognized some
relationship between Bidais and Akokisas. The officers thought that
none of those nations recognized a superior, or head of government,
except when they went to war, but they knew that some chiefs had
been appointed by de Mézières or by the governors of Texas and
Louisiana. They had canes and medals symbolizing their ranks as officials of the Spanish Crown, and they flew the king's flag with the
Burgundian Cross.

Subject to de Mézières' approval, the Texas officials liked Croix's idea
of a campaign against the Apaches, using Norteño allies and Louisiana
hunters. Certainly the Norteños seemed promising allies. They were
skillful with both English and French guns, of which they usually had
a few to sell at Béxar. They were not yet solely dependent on firearms,
however. They fought competently with lances, bows and arrows,
and axes and were well protected with shields and leather jackets.
Their warriors had proved at San Sabá that they could mount a
concerted offensive, and they had recently joined forces against another
foe. Word had come to San Antonio of a war recently declared be-

tween a Comanche-Taovayas-Tawakoni coalition and the Osages, who lived much farther north and were hostile to all the nations in Texas.

No campaign would be feasible until Croix could get more troops. Meanwhile, de Mézières would be needed to keep the Norteños happy and ready to join the campaign against the Apaches when the Spaniards could be ready. The San Antonio council desired Governor Gálvez to assign de Mézières to that task and to send him to San Antonio to confer with the governor of Texas on techniques of managing Norteños. The council wished him to review their proceedings and give his opinions, particularly on the proposed campaign against the Apaches.

The council agreed that presents and favors for the Indians would be necessary, in due moderation, and that it would be appropriate to charge them to the Béxar company's fund. Unfortunately, no presidial budget allowed for enough visits and presents to sustain friendships with the diverse Indian peoples of Texas. With his own budget already strained, Croix happily spotted a new source of revenue to cover unusual expenses in Texas.

It seemed so simple and just to Croix at the time. Grazing the grasslands were countless cattle and horses, mostly unbranded, the natural increase of livestock introduced by Spaniards, largely at the Crown's expense. What could be fairer and more consistent with Spanish tradition than to claim all unmarked stock for the Crown and to collect fees for animals appropriated to private ownership? Croix issued a decree to that effect, established a brand register, and gave Texas livestock owners just four months to brand their stock. After that, the provincial governor would collect four reales for each wild cow captured and six reales[26] for each mustang, plus an export fee of two pesos per head of cattle.

The Mesteña Fund did produce revenues, though never as much as the Crown's auditors thought it should, and it did pay the bill for much of the hospitality and presents necessary to Indian diplomacy. But it proved burdensome to administer, and it antagonized the citizenry. The missionaries blamed the Mesteña Fund for the economic ruin of the Texas missions and their subsequent disintegration.[27]

[26] Subsequently lowered to two reales after citizens protested that capturing a mustang and breaking it for use was much more arduous than branding a cow.

[27] Fray José Franco López, Report on the Texas Missions, San Antonio de Valero, May 5, 1789, trans. J. Autrey Dabbs, in "The Texas Missions in 1785," *Mid-America* 22 (1940): 38–58. Odie B. Faulk, *The Last Years of Spanish Texas, 1778–1786*, p. 85, deals briefly with the Mesteña Fund.

The mission communities had long since given up the effort to brand all the increase of the vast herds that were their principal wealth. Now allowed only four months to brand unmarked stock, they had no hope of claiming all their rightful property. Recent epidemics had depleted their congregations and marauding *indios bárbaros* had nearly wiped out their horse herds. Given the resulting shortages of cowhands and horses and the dread of *indios bárbaros* that led many mission Indians to refuse to work outside the compounds, the missionaries could not prevent virtual confiscation of their congregations' chief resource.

Unaware of the bitterness and economic dislocation he had wrought, Commandant General Croix left San Antonio late in January 1778 to continue his inspection of presidios in Coahuila and Nueva Vizcaya, en route to Chihuahua. On March 1, 1778, in a canyon between presidios San Vicente and San Carlos, Croix and his party encountered a howling horde of six hundred Natagés, Mescaleros, and Lipans.[28] Only the good luck of spotting enemy scouts in time to avoid ambush saved Croix's retinue and horse herd from disaster. Croix had indeed a sobering welcome to Nueva Vizcaya and a convincing argument against trusting Apaches.

Urgent questions of Apache peace awaited Croix at Chihuahua in April 1778. Gilas had sued for peace at Janos in October; others had sought amnesty at Albuquerque but had balked at giving hostages to guarantee their good faith. An Apache had visited El Paso in mid-December to ask for truce on behalf of *rancherías* in the Sacramento, Petaca, and Organos ranges that had been recently driven by Comanches from their old homes in the Sierra Blanca. Croix ordered presidial commanders to concede no truces: they could accept nothing short of absolute surrender and Apache agreement to settle in formal pueblos wherever designated by the commandant general. The Apaches of the Organos rejected those terms at El Paso, but they promised not to raid any more. The first hint that Apaches might consider such stringent terms came at Janos, where some Gilas sued for peace and agreed to settle in a pueblo if they could be supplied food for a year, until they could harvest crops.[29]

Sure that the Comanche hordes would drive more and more Apaches to the Spanish frontier, Croix spelled out in detail the conditions upon which Apaches might live in the shelters of the Spanish frontier. They

[28] Domingo Cabello, Ynforme, San Antonio de Béxar, September 30, 1784, AGN, Provincias Internas, vol. 64.
[29] Thomas, ed., in *Forgotten Frontiers*, pp. 14–19.

must gather with their families near a designated presidio, on a site adequate for settlements, there to build houses and live in well-organized pueblos, and they must never leave without permission. They must obey the orders of the presidial captain or other officials appointed by Croix and must choose one of their own chiefs as governor. They must accept priests to instruct them. Adults would be encouraged, but not forced, to accept the faith; children would be required to live as faithful Catholics, observing all appropriate obligations.

Each Indian family head would be allotted a patch of ground for his garden and homesite, and the entire community must cultivate common fields. Necessary tools would be furnished them. For the first year each family would receive weekly subsistence rations. They would have to surrender their Spanish captives, but the Apaches would not have to relinquish the horses they had already stolen. Indeed, if they were short of horses, the Crown would give them enough animals for work and necessary travel.

Even with promises of a year's subsistence and important concessions about horses, Croix assumed that few Apaches could or would settle down soon. He cautioned his subordinates to extend the terms only to families who voluntarily presented themselves at the presidios and appeared eager to keep the bargain.

If Croix's peace terms had any effect in 1778, it was to inspire more Apache depredations and, by August, an actual declaration of war against the "Great Chief" in Chihuahua. Croix hardened his resolve to crush the eastern Apaches by alliance with the Norteños and envisioned for the future a complementary offensive against the Gilas, to be launched from two new presidios he meant to establish on the Gila River and in the Hopi country.

What of New Mexico's role in his plans? It would be crucial to definitive campaigns against either eastern or western Apaches. Furthermore, if the Comanche alliance should be realized, New Mexico would have to find a way for all its peoples to live at peace with those turbulent neighbors. The outlook was hardly favorable. All the records of the 1770's and current reports depicted a province at the point of destruction by *indios bárbaros*.

Croix dared not ride the long trail to Santa Fe to see for himself, because that would keep him too long out of touch with his own headquarters and with developments in Spain, New Spain, and Louisiana affecting the Provincias Internas. However, Croix had the detailed recommendations of retiring Governor Mendinueta for defense of the province,[30] and he planned personal consultations with Mendinueta, whose departure from New Mexico would bring him through Nueva Vizcaya. Furthermore, Croix had utmost confidence in Lieutenant Colonel Anza, slated to become governor of New Mexico as soon as Sonora could spare him.

Both the retiring and the prospective governors of New Mexico could attend the commandant general's third and final council, scheduled at Chihuahua that summer. So could Colonel Ugarte, recently governor of Coahuila and now on his way to the governorship of Sonora, and Governor Felipe Barri of Nueva Vizcaya. It would be an ideal opportunity to pool information and coordinate plans of action. Texas would lack representation, but Ripperdá and de Mézières appeared to have Norteño matters well in hand, and Croix already had the latter's helpful recommendations concerning the proposed campaign with Norteños against Apaches. It was regrettable that experienced, capable Ripperdá would soon be replaced by an officer fresh from Nicaragua, quite ignorant of the Provincias Internas and the peculiar problems of Texas, but the presence of de Mézières in San Antonio as Indian agent should forestall major errors.

De Mézières had reached San Antonio in mid-February 1778, a month after Croix's council there, to find the community enjoying an extraordinarily tranquil season. Comanches were giving no trouble, and the Lipans seemed responsive to the bland management enjoined by the council for the time being.[31]

As the council had requested, de Mézières reviewed its work and recommended procedures for the campaign against the Apaches. As he corrected and amplified the council's vague, inaccurate ideas of the Indians of Texas, the French visitor must have gained new insights into the Spaniards' basic difficulties with the *bárbaros*.

De Mézières explained that the Indian nations beyond Béxar fell into three categories.[32] First were the maritime, or southern, groups, such as the Atakapas and Akokisas at the mouths of the Nueces and Trinity rivers, and the Karankawas, who lived on the contiguous coastal area and sometimes allied with them. Second were the inland groups of the east: the Adaes, nearly wiped out by the last epidemic,

[30] Mendinueta to Croix, Santa Fe, November 3, 1777, in Alfred Barnaby Thomas, ed., "Governor Mendinueta's Proposals for the Defense of New Mexico, 1772–1778," *New Mexico Historical Review* 6 (1931): 35–39.

[31] Croix to Ripperdá, Chihuahua, April 29, 1778, BA.

[32] De Mézières to Croix, Béxar, February 20, 1778, in Bolton, *Athanase de Mézières*, II, 172–186.

now a pitiful drunken remnant; the Bidais, also hard hit by the 1777 epidemic, now reduced to a state of miserable vagabondage; and the Tejas, divided into several bands called Asinais, Nevadizoes, Nadacogs, and Nacogdoches. Still an admirable people, the Tejas were industrious farmers, living on good terms with the Spaniards.

Most important for Croix's purposes was the third category, frontier or northern nations: Tonkawas, Tawakonis, Xaranames, Kichais, and Taovayas, all of whom now maintained the peace they had made with Ripperdá, and the Panismahas, who had recently come from the Missouri River to join the Taovayas. There were also the Comanches, the only ones hostile to the Spaniards, whom de Mézières thought superior in such respects as modesty in dress, hospitality to guests, humanity to captives, and bravery. The Comanches' overwhelming propensity to theft obscured all those splendid virtues, but de Mézières attributed that failing to their wandering life rather than to innate perversity. Two possible correctives occurred to de Mézières: either to settle the Comanches in permanent locations and give them stable trade or to control them by force of arms. Neither seemed likely in 1778.

All the frontier nations except the Comanches and Tonkawas lived in villages and raised maize, beans, calabashes, and tobacco; all used the meat of the buffalo, deer, and bear. All of them were skillful with horses and carefully husbanded them.

Contrary to the council's impression, the Indians of Texas recognized chiefs, with whom they sallied forth to war, sometimes against Osages, sometimes against Apaches. All of them observed a kind of religion involving sacrifice of enemy scalps and their own first fruits to their gods. All the frontier nations visited each other and were at least nominal friends. Comanche friendships tended to be erratic, but breaches usually mended fast, so the Comanches could sell the horses that the other nations needed to recoup their own losses to Osages and Apaches.

De Mézières emphasized the importance of the Louisiana trade to all the Indians and explained why its advantage to settlers in Louisiana and Texas transcended any financial profit: Indians kept busy hunting in order to buy goods were less prone to such idle mischief as raiding. Each Indian village had its trader from Natchitoches, who watched over it and promptly reported any news to de Mézières. To assure efficient performance of those duties, de Mézières required his resident traders to be competent penmen as well as fluent in the local Indian languages and to maintain affectionate rapport with the host nation. He depended upon the traders to cultivate Indian loyalties to the Spanish regime and to impress upon the Indians the unity of Louisiana and Texas under one Crown.

De Mézières had long thought the loyal northern nations the best safeguard against Osage devastation of western Louisiana and against British incursions. The necessity of a Norteño campaign against the Osages remained uppermost in his mind, but he had no objection to a preliminary campaign against the Apaches. All northern nations so loathed the Apaches that they would be delighted to campaign against them, and, once they wiped out the Apaches, they could turn their total attention to the Osage war. With luck, the Apache campaign could be a useful dress rehearsal for the campaign against the Osages that de Mézières had long proposed to his superiors in Louisiana. Indeed, his most recent plan for the Osage campaign needed little modification to serve for the proposed Apache campaign.

The Taovayas village would still be the best rendezvous point for the Norteño warriors and the Louisiana woodsmen. The best time would be September, right after the Indians' harvest. All other seasons brought problems that could wreck a campaign: the troublesome rains of spring, the intense heat of summer, and the biting, unpredictable cold of winter. The troops from the Provincias Internas could camp well ahead of time at a rendezvous point between the Colorado and San Saba rivers, ostensibly to prevent Comanche incursions. However, they should refrain from using arms against any Comanches unless directly attacked, lest some rash soldier's blunder destroy progress toward alliance with the Comanches. The whole force could rally there, then form into two divisions to execute a pincers movement against the Apaches. Success would hinge upon faithful and intelligent guides supplied from Béxar.

De Mézières recommended certain precautions to assure persistence in the campaign. Ordinarily, Indians went to war without any supplies except their weapons. If they failed to find adequate supplies of buffalo, they readily turned back; on the other hand, if they found great herds, they were likely to abandon their campaign purpose for a lot of noisy, time-consuming hunting. De Mézières wanted the Spaniards to issue rations to the Indian allies so that they would have no reason to separate into little bands to hunt for food or to turn back home disgusted with the Spaniards' failure to provide. The most essential outlay would be a gift of ammunition and war supplies, which de Mézières promised to distribute economically and sensibly to the chiefs and leading men at the appropriate time. It would serve as pay for their services and would repay the king handsomely, both in Norteños' gratitude and in Apache lives.

De Mézières also recommended advance arrangements to protect captives from barbaric excesses. The San Antonio missions could purchase the captives, both to rebuild congregations decimated by epidemics, wars, and desertions and to serve the humane, Christian purpose of rescuing helpless captives. Such a display of magnanimity on the part of the Spaniards would favorably impress all the Indians.

De Mézières anticipated no great difficulty in conquering the Apaches if his program were followed, and he was eager to finish that job in order to concentrate on the Osage problem, which seemed to him far more serious. If the campaign should consolidate a new friendship with the Comanches, he also hoped to press immediate explorations toward the source of the Missouri River. Prompt action was imperative if the Spaniards were to beat the Britons of Canada to that territory. With Comanche friendship and help, there should be no major difficulty in reaching the source of the Missouri; if the Comanches should remain hostile, there was little hope of reaching that prize from Spanish territory.

The most urgent necessity that spring was to repair as speedily as possible the Norteño friendships damaged by years of neglect. Ripperdá and de Mézières decided that the latter should ride home from Béxar to Natchitoches via the villages of the frontier nations with whom Spain already had treaty relations. While pleasing those allies and collecting up-to-date information about them, he could also contact the Comanches and Panismahas whom he hoped to bring into the general accord. Though de Mézières felt perfectly safe with just the half-dozen Natchitoches militiamen who had ridden with him to Béxar, it seemed politic to add a conspicuous contingent from Béxar to compensate for years of neglect from that quarter and to re-emphasize the unity of Texans and Louisianans under the Spanish Crown. The obvious choice from Béxar was Lieutenant Antonio Treviño, who had enjoyed cordial rapport with the Norteños for the dozen years since his sojourn as captive hero in the Taovayas village. With him Ripperdá sent cavalry Lieutenant José Menchaca and twenty-two soldiers.[33]

---

[33] Croix to Ripperdá, Chihuahua, April 30, 1778, BA. The details of the ex-

The delegation enjoyed an extraordinarily pleasant, encouraging trip. They rode from Béxar to Bucareli early in March, across territory that de Mézières thought wonderfully rich in resources and healthful in climate. On neither the Guadalupe nor the Colorado nor the Brazos did they find any trace of Comanches. Bucareli had enjoyed more than a year's freedom from raids.

De Mézières liked Bucareli's controversial location on the Trinity River: equidistant from Béxar, Natchitoches, and the Norteños, an ideal center of communications. The community had its problems. The Bidais, cut in half by the last epidemic, down to a mere hundred warriors, hung around the settlement to beg. They were a pitiful nuisance to the settlers, who were themselves very poor. Indeed, the Bucareli settlers owed their lives to the generosity of the nearby Tawakonis, who helped so unstintingly that they did not even reserve enough food for their own use until the harvest.

Captain Gil Ybarbo and thirteen Bucareli militiamen joined de Mézières' party when he headed for the Norteño villages on March 18, 1778. Again, the purpose was less to protect than to show unity among the several European communities. Fray Francisco José de la Garza rode along from Bucareli to serve the company as chaplain and to help coax the Xaraname apostates back to the missions.

De Mézières found that several shifts had occurred among the Indian populations since his visit of 1772. The first whom he visited in 1778 were Kichais, only forty-five miles north of Bucareli. A broad, fertile valley with a saline nearby had attracted a little group of Kichais who had split off from the main body of their nation to settle there. They boasted only twenty warriors, but their cornfields and horse herds flourished, their hunters killed plenty of deer, and they marketed enough deer hides and salt to meet all their other needs.

From that Kichai village de Mézières' party rode westward toward the Tawakoni settlements on the Brazos. He hoped to treat en route with the Tonkawas, who camped between the Trinity and the Brazos, but their leaders were too widely scattered to assemble quickly. De Mézières asked the resident traders to convene them by the time he returned from the Taovayas so that he could address them in council. The Tonkawas, all of whose camps could muster just about three hundred warriors, had lately yielded to Tawakoni and Iscani pressures to

---

pedition are reported in a series of sixteen letters from de Mézières to Croix, March 18–May 2, 1778, which appear in Bolton, *Athanase de Mézières*, II, 185 ff.

restrain their depredations at the Spanish settlements. For more stable control of the Tonkawas, de Mézières hoped to persuade them to give up the apostates who exerted unsettling influences among them and to settle down in permanent villages to farm as peacefully as their Tawakoni neighbors. If they should refuse, he would threaten to cut off their trade, then give them time to ponder the risks of life without firearms in a world full of enemies with guns.

Early in April, welcoming Tawakonis helped the travelers cross the swollen Brazos to reach their village. On the next day the principal men of that Tawakoni settlement convened in the chief's house to hear de Mézières. He told them about Commandant General Croix, explained his superior authority over all other Spaniards whom they knew, and expounded on the protection they would enjoy from such a powerful leader. He praised the Tawakonis' well-known loyalty to the Spaniards and, in Croix's name, thanked them especially for their generous aid to the settlers of Bucareli. The leaders were pleased. De Mézières found them disposed to help him to solve his problems with the Xaranames and the Tonkawas.

The hundred-odd Xaranames apostates responded to neither de Mézières nor Fray Garza, so de Mézières asked the Tawakonis to pressure them to return to the missions. The Tawakonis promised to do so. The Tawakoni chief also sympathized with de Mézières' contention that the Tonkawas should settle down to agricultural village life. When a Tonkawa chief came to visit, the Tawakoni chief argued for de Mézières' proposal and urged his guest to persuade the rest of the Tonkawas.

The Tawakonis were suffering heavy losses of property to Comanches camped upstream on the Brazos in large numbers. Although the Tawakonis liked their fertile, well-watered plain, they were thinking of leaving because of the Comanches. Their only alternative would be alliance with neighboring villages to check Comanche depredations, because their 150 warriors could not alone challenge countless Comanches.

If Tawakonis calculated their odds prudently, they certainly had not forgotten how to fight. De Mézières was delighted to find them planning a new campaign against the Apaches, specifically to destroy the *rancherías* where the enemy planted crops.

Much the same attitudes and problems prevailed at the second Tawakoni village, twenty miles upstream from the first, where de Mézières visited next. It was a larger village than the first, with an even better site. The leaders welcomed the visitors joyously and got on so well with de Mézières and Treviño that they volunteered to ride with them to the other nations. One common bond was their loathing of Lipans, a prime theme of Tawakoni conversation. Like their compatriots downstream, these Tawakonis complained of Comanche thievery and speculated that war or withdrawal might become necessary. They raised new worries about Comanche intentions: three bands had lately gone into the interior, for purposes yet unknown.

Before the longer trek north to the Taovayas on the Red River, de Mézières reduced his force. The change implied no dissatisfaction with the Spaniards' performance. De Mézières warmly praised the work of Fray Garza and Treviño, Gil Ybarbo, and Menchaca, recommending all three officers as diligent and well qualified for command responsibilities. It seemed only prudent to send Gil Ybarbo and Fray Garza back to Bucareli with most of the ailing, ill-equipped militiamen from that settlement. Most of the Béxar contingent rode homeward with Lieutenant Menchaca, who carried de Mézières' dispatches for Ripperdá and Croix. De Mézières kept only Lieutenant Treviño with five Béxar soldiers and four militiamen each from Bucareli and Natchitoches. Ten Tawakonis rode with them.

Sometime during the week-long ride from the Tawakonis to the Taovayas, the party gained a Comanche. The young man had been wounded and captured near Béxar many months ago. During his convalescence, Ripperdá had treated the lad more as a son than as a prisoner and, when he was well, had freed him. The Comanche rode homeward alone, brimming with gratitude toward Spaniards. When he met de Mézières' party, he offered help. He would be their guide and interpreter and mediator if they should encounter Comanches, and he would help them in any way necessary against other enemies. De Mézières gladly accepted the extraordinary volunteer.

They actually needed little guidance as they followed the Cross Timbers at their right from the Brazos to the Red River, across two hundred miles of splendid lands, well watered and wooded, abounding in buffalo. As they neared the Taovayas village in mid-April, de Mézières sent advance notice. The leaders came out to greet the visitors, lifted de Mézières and Treviño off their horses, and carried them into the village on their shoulders. They were delighted to see Spaniards from Béxar at last, especially the well-loved Treviño. The men called all their women and children to welcome the visitors. Throughout their stay, the villagers lavished gifts of food upon them.

A few days later de Mézières invited the leaders to council with him. Giving them presents that Governor Ripperdá had sent in behalf of Croix, he assured them of the powerful aid and protection of the great chiefs of the Provincias Internas and Louisiana. Very pleased, the Taovayas ordered a large house built for the use of future Spanish visitors. They urged de Mézières to persuade Ripperdá to send Spaniards to settle among them, and they promised to give any aid needed for a settlement. De Mézières could only promise to report their loyalty and zeal.

De Mézières found the Taovayas settlements much more impressive than he had anticipated. He had meant to urge the Taovayas and Panismahas south to the Brazos or the San Gabriel to bolster the other nations against the Comanches. Once he saw their settlement, he dropped the idea of moving them and revised his plans around the location and the people, both of which he admired.

"Master key of the north," he called it, a base from which Spain could deal with the friendly nations through Taovayas mediation, could conquer such hostiles as Osages and Comanches, and could prevent invasion by Britons. It could also be the hub of communications for Natchitoches, St. Louis, Santa Fe, and San Antonio, because it was centrally located with reference to all those posts.

Occupation was undoubtedly urgent. Two British traders had come from the Arkansas River to trade with the Taovayas early that winter. The Taovayas claimed they had seized all their goods and expelled the intruders. They promised to arrest any subsequent intruders and deliver them to de Mézières, but he preferred a Spanish presence to rebuff all British adventurers.

There were actually two villages, one of 37 houses on the north bank and another of 123 houses on the south bank.[34] De Mézières named the larger San Teodoro, honoring Commandant General Croix, and the smaller San Bernardo, honoring Governor Gálvez. The Taovayas were obviously industrious and provident. Even late in April, each household had some twenty-five bushels of corn and plenty of dried beans and pumpkins. They never lacked meat: the river attracted many buffalo, and bear and wild boar abounded in the Cross Timbers. The Indians did not eat the fish teeming in the Red River, but Spaniards would find them another valuable resource. With its mild climate, perennially renewed salt deposits in the river, abundant timber in

---

[34] Some sources indicate that the smaller was actually the Wichita village.

adjacent woods, convenient quarries nearby, excellent springs, and fertile land that looked easily irrigable, the site met all criteria for Spanish establishments, whether presidio, mission, or pueblo.

De Mézières predicted an abundant spiritual harvest among the Taovayas, as well as economic and agricultural success. He thought their religion, which appeared to center about the veneration of fire, would be no great stumbling block to acceptance of Christianity, particularly if some exemplary Tlaxcaltecan families should settle nearby.

The Taovayas' invitation to Spanish settlers and their promises of assistance seemed as genuine as the troubles that prompted them. The Taovayas lived in constant dread of Osages who were then waging a bloody war against them, and they never felt entirely safe from Apache marauders. Comanches were problematic, too. They visited the Taovayas as friends, but their incorrigible thievery sorely tried their hosts. The Taovayas had to pretend not to notice because they could not afford to make more enemies.

De Mézières shared their annoyance with the Comanches. During his Taovayas sojourn, eight Comanches came from a camp on the Brazos, far upstream from the Tawakonis. They reported that a band of their people had recently raided on the road between Béxar and the Presidio del Río Grande and had returned without injuries, with lots of pack horses and a scalp that they thought had belonged to the lieutenant paymaster of the presidio. The visitors explained that they had quit raiding at San Antonio because the guard was too vigilant there, and they were now turning southward to the well-supplied, defenseless ranches of the Laredo area. De Mézières guessed that the same Comanches had been responsible for the murder of Béxar citizen Nepomuceno Trujillo, earlier attributed to Apaches. Chagrined to find that the respite at Bucareli and San Antonio had not signaled any change of Comanche hearts, he decided not to visit them as he had intended. The trip could be risky for his small party if the Comanches were excited over fresh successes in raiding, and he could emphasize his displeasure by avoiding their camps.

Fortunately, he had available an ideal messenger, the Comanche released by Ripperdá, still eager to repay Spanish kindnesses. De Mézières charged the lad to inform the Comanche chiefs that their robberies and hostilities had exceeded all tolerable limits and that de Mézières had come to offer them protection in the names of the Great Captains of Louisiana and the Provincias Internas, but, after seeing their misdeeds, he could not make that offer. He would await their final promise to keep the peace and would expect such proof as restoration of horses stolen from Spaniards. Breaches of the peace would henceforth be attributed to Comanches, whose abuses had already exhausted the patience of neighboring Indian nations. Unless there were speedy reform, the Spaniards would encourage all their Indian allies to war against the Comanches.

The Taovayas leaders approved both message and messenger. The Comanche brave started homeward, confidently predicting success. De Mézières was pessimistic about any Comanche response, but he thought he could get results by encouraging the Tejas, Nasonis, Tonkawas, Tawakonis, and Taovayas to avenge their own grievances. They had insisted they would need only munitions to make a fierce attack, and de Mézières thought that would be a worthwhile investment of powder, balls, and guns. A concerted Norteño offensive should rout the Comanches and cut them off from the Louisiana trade. Nevertheless, he had first to wait a reasonable time for some suitable response to his message.

One other disappointment marred de Mézières' visit. Governor Ripperdá had especially desired him to cultivate the recent Panismahas immigrants, but they had already withdrawn 175 miles northwest to establish a new village. De Mézières saw at the Taovayas village only ten Panismahas men, led by a nephew of the principal chief. To him de Mézières spoke regretfully about the Panismahas' departure from the Texas jurisdiction, persuaded him that the move had been a mistake, and suggested a site to which he wished they would return. It was a beautiful place, downstream on the south bank of the Red River, halfway from the Taovayas to the Kadohadachos, whence the stream was navigable all the way to Natchitoches. That would mean cheaper transportation for trade goods, and a Panismahas settlement there would also strengthen the cordon of villages against Osage incursions. The Taovayas also advocated the move. When the young leader promised to bring his people back to the Red River to settle where de Mézières wished, they praised his decision and promised him all the help due a brother. As a beginning, they gave him two good horses to speed his journey to his people. De Mézières felt truly hopeful of cooperation with the Panismahas.

By early May de Mézières' party returned to Bucareli, where they broke up. De Mézières bade goodbye to Don Antonio Treviño, and in his final dispatch to Croix he strongly recommended the old soldier for more important posts. The Béxar contingent headed homeward with dispatch bags marked for Croix's temporary headquarters at Chihuahua, while de Mézières hurried on to Natchitoches.

That proved a tragically premature departure. De Mézières could not know that his Comanche messenger had been well received and that Chief Povea's own son headed a peace delegation riding hard to overtake him. The Comanches came within sight of Bucareli soon after his departure, turned their horses loose to graze, and sat down to rest. Bucareli settlers spotted them, panicked, and drummed up a squad to chase them away. Surprised and scared, the Comanches fled, but the Spaniards pursued them across the Brazos and fired without stopping to ask their purpose. They killed several Comanches, wounded more, put the rest to flight, and triumphantly led back to Bucareli most of the Comanches' horses.[35] Povea's son led his angry, diminished delegation back to the Comanchería to report their calamity.

A grave question confronted the Comanches: did responsibility for vengeance belong solely to kinsmen of the dead, or did the unprovoked attack upon the delegation require tribal war against the offending people? If tribal war, must it be against Bucareli alone or against all Spaniards in Texas? Should it also involve Indian nations allied with the Spaniards? The aggrieved camps demanded war, but Povea and other elder statesmen suppressed their own natural anger to argue that war in Texas would ill serve their nation's interests. The issue raged in Comanche councils all that summer.

Far southward, in the villa of Chihuahua, Spanish leaders also spent the summer in council, oblivious of the issue before their Comanche counterparts. Early in June 1778, when Commandant General Croix convened the last of his series of councils, his latest dispatches from Texas were the spring reports of more than a year's tranquillity. He also had de Mézières' late February analysis of the proposed Apache campaign, with his optimistic suggestion of strong Comanche participation, to be followed by permanent alliance. It was autumn before Croix learned of new troubles with Comanches at Bucareli and yet another year before he knew the reason.

An impressive group reported to the commandant general's house at nine o'clock on the morning of June 9: Brigadier General Mendinueta, retiring after eleven years as governor of New Mexico; Colonel Ugarte, en route from the governorship of Coahuila to that of Sonora;

[35] De Mézières to Croix, Natchitoches, November 15, 1778, in Bolton, *Athanase de Mézières*, II, 232–233.

Lieutenant Colonel Anza, already distinguished for achievements in Sonora and California, now on his way to govern New Mexico; Lieutenant Colonel Felipe Barri, governor of the host province of Nueva Vizcaya; and Don Pedro Galindo y Navarro, auditor general of the Provincias Internas. Antonio Bonilla, who had survived a term as O'Conor's adjutant inspector to become principal adjutant to Croix, served the council as secretary. Croix himself presided, with the members sitting before him in order of rank and seniority.[36]

Croix explained that he wished them to examine all the information he had gathered from the archives, from the two earlier councils, and from the current reports of key officials of the provinces. At the end, they would be asked to state their opinions, beginning with the lowest-ranking officer and proceeding to the highest; a plurality of votes would decide the council's position on each question. Any man who dissented from the majority position should write out his reasons, so that all opinions could be forwarded to the king.

For two days the commandant general shared with his council all the information and advice available to him; on the next two he required them to share with him the responsibility for decision on the sixteen issues before them. They agreed with the Coahuila and Texas councils that the Apache wars had gone on for many years, that no Apaches had ever remained true to peace promises, and that the record of bad faith warranted the continuation of war with all Apaches. They attributed the worsening of Apache depredations in the last five years to the unwise relocations of the frontier presidios. Anza and Mendinueta challenged the Coahuila council's estimate of Apache strength at five thousand. It seemed obvious that there must be many more than that to permit Apaches to strike in all provinces at once, often in very large groups. They also thought it unrealistic to count the Apaches' strength solely in terms of men, because Apache women augmented war and raiding parties.

While the Chihuahua council concurred in the ultimate necessity of war against all Apaches, they also agreed with the earlier councils that a declaration of war against the Lipans would be impracticable until the troops of the Provincias Internas could be heavily reinforced. Even then, they would rely heavily upon the cooperation of Norteño warriors and of Louisianans. None of them knew enough about the Norteños to evaluate the report of the San Antonio council, but they

36 Council of War, Chihuahua, June 9–15, 1778, in Thomas, *Plains Indians*, pp. 193–211.

reasoned from their knowledge of Apaches that alliance with Norteños would surely be the lesser evil. They agreed that Croix should ask Governor Gálvez to transfer de Mézières from Natchitoches to Texas to help the new governor, Cabello, conserve the peace with the Norteños and win the friendship of the Comanches.

The council desired de Mézières and Cabello to avoid any premature revelations of purpose. The Norteño and Comanche warriors should not learn of the proposed campaign until time to carry it out, and the Lipans should be controlled meanwhile by cunning rather than by force. Texas officials would be responsible for preventing any flow of arms to the Lipans, either from the Bidais and Tejas or from unscrupulous settlers at Béxar.

The other provinces would coordinate their defenses as best they could until Croix could mount decisive campaigns, first against Apaches in the east and then against those in the west. If reinforcements were prompt, the council thought an additional 1,800 troops would suffice; if there were long delay, no conceivable force would serve to retrieve the imminent disaster. None denied that the program they proposed would be expensive; all argued that it would cost the Crown much more to let the Provincias Internas fall and to see *indios bárbaros* sweep the heartland of New Spain.

Croix reported the council's conclusions to Minister of the Indies Gálvez, with high hope that their well-reasoned consensus would prevail. The king had deferred action on his earlier request for two thousand additional troops until such time as the commandant general could report his personal knowledge of the frontier.[37] Now, given Croix's own comprehensive reports and the concurrence of all the ranking officials of the command, surely the Crown would support his program.

Even with the best of luck, it would be 1779 before the king's decision could reach Croix. Little more than holding operations against the Apaches could take place meanwhile in the southern tier of the Provincias Internas, but important initiatives could be pursued in the northern salients of Texas and New Mexico. Croix spent the rest of the summer of 1778 working on them.

Anza was assigned to New Mexico primarily to establish communications from Santa Fe to Sonora and California, which implied pacification of the Hopis. He would operate from a base continually

[37] José de Gálvez to Croix, El Pardo, January 20, 1778, in Bolton, *Athanase de Mézières*, II, 170–172.

jeopardized by Comanche warfare and intermittently plagued by Apaches, too. At the council's request, Mendinueta lingered at Chihuahua to formulate recommendations for defense of New Mexico.[38] Anza worked meanwhile on recommendations concerning Sonora and the proposed new establishments on the Colorado and Gila rivers. On August 8, 1778, Croix administered Anza's oath of office as governor of New Mexico. Anza soon rode north from Chihuahua to assume the command to which the king had appointed him on May 19, 1777.[39]

Confident that New Mexico gained in Anza the ablest and best informed of leaders, Croix looked again to Texas. Gálvez could not be spared from Louisiana to campaign against the Apaches as Croix had first hoped, but the Crown would let him second de Mézières to Texas and supply any other help against the Apaches that would not weaken Louisiana. The late August mail packet confirmed the importance of de Mézières' services, for it contained his detailed reports of the successful mission to the Norteños, the last dated May 2 at Bucareli, whence Antonio Treviño delivered them to Béxar. Ripperdá, writing before news of Bucareli's Comanche fiasco reached Béxar, reported continuing tranquillity in Texas.[40]

Though Ripperdá continued to govern Texas with laudable zeal, he was fretting about the long delay in departing for his new post in Honduras. Croix sympathized. He could not guarantee any arrival time for Domingo Cabello, but he could appoint a governor ad interim to relieve Ripperdá, and he had the ideal man available. Since the Crown and Gálvez had already agreed to transfer de Mézières to Texas, Croix asked him to proceed to Béxar immediately to take up his new duties. If Cabello should not arrive before de Mézières, Ripperdá could turn the province over to de Mézières ad interim and proceed to Honduras.[41]

Croix's dispatch to de Mézières included high praise for his excellent work and valuable reports. Enclosed was a copy of the resolutions of the Chihuahua council, so that de Mézières would reach Texas fully informed of the intended program. If he should find Cabello already in charge at Béxar and thus not be obliged to serve as governor ad interim, he was to await further orders from Croix, who hoped to be able to

[38] Mendinueta, Detail of Service for New Mexico, Chihuahua, June 22, 1778, in Thomas, *Plains Indians*, pp. 212–213.

[39] Croix to Gálvez, Chihuahua, August 24, 1778, and related documents of appointment in Thomas, *Forgotten Frontiers*, pp. 114–119.

[40] Croix to Ripperdá, Chihuahua, September 13, 1778, BA.

[41] Croix to Ripperdá, Chihuahua, September 11, 1778, BA.

give him a proprietary appointment, commensurate with his rank, merit, and services.[42]

Just what appointment Croix had in mind for de Mézières remained a mystery, but it probably related to the commandant general's excitement about possibilities opened by de Mézières' latest success with the Indians on the upper Red River. Croix now proposed a northward advance of the Spanish frontier, with establishments along the Red River from New Mexico to the Taovayas to form the main line of defense. Thus freed from invasions, the older frontier could prosper as never before.[43] Croix had high hopes for the development of Texas, and he knew that de Mézières shared his vision of its great economic potential.

De Mézières could hardly share either the excitement or the optimism of Croix when the order came late in the autumn of 1778. The dreadful epidemic that had taken such a heavy toll in 1777 had suddenly recurred late in the summer of 1778. From the Jotar, Kichai, and Nasoni villages it spread to the Tawakonis, Taovayas, and Kadohadachos. More than three hundred Kadohadachos died that fall, and their grieving friend de Mézières thought the loss as grave a blow to Spanish interests as to those loyal Indians. Worse still, Chief Tinhioüen and his close associate had died while visiting the governor at New Orleans, where they were buried with the full military honors due distinguished rank and years of service to the Crown. De Mézières heard that the Kadohadachos were bearing their tragedies with civilized resignation. They had suitable successors to the leadership, and they reaped an abundant harvest that fall. Still, he was loath to leave their district at such a crucial time. For the first time in more than half a century, there would be no stabilizing St. Denis influence among the Indians: the second Louis Juchereau de St. Denis had died in February, while de Mézières was en route to San Antonio.

De Mézières had still more distressing news not yet known to Croix. Indian friends had told him of the Comanche mishap at Bucareli, and he dreaded the awful consequences invited by the trigger-happy settlers. In October, Comanche vengeance began to take shape. Comanche raiders seized a herd of 240 horses being held at Bucareli for the trader Nicolás de La Mathe. The settlers pursued until they learned that the retreating Comanches had set up an ambush at the very spot

[42] Croix to de Mézières, Chihuahua, September 20, 1778, in Bolton, *Athanase de Mézières*, II, 216–217.
[43] Croix to José de Gálvez, Chihuahua, September 23, 1778, ibid., pp. 220–223.

across the Brazos where their compatriots had fallen the year before. The Spaniards turned back, but a party of Kichai and Tejas warriors took up their cause. Near the Taovayas village they found the horses with a seven-man guard; they attacked, killed three Comanches, and recovered the horses. The rest of the Comanches in turn pursued them, killed three Tejas, and recaptured the horses.[44]

On hearing that news, de Mézières feared more than ever that general war would blaze across the Texas frontier unless the Comanches were somehow placated. Given serious problems in his own district and the pressures to hurry to San Antonio, de Mézières dared not ride to the Comanchería. More than ever missing the good offices of Tinhioüen, he asked another trusted friend, the medal chief of the Nadacog village of the Tejas, to be his envoy to the Comanchería. Realizing the urgency of the mission, the Nadacog chief braved the rigors of winter travel to journey to the Taovayas village, whence Taovayas escorted him to the easternmost Comanche camps. He hoped at least to learn the Comanches' intentions. If lucky, he could propitiate them by explaining the error at Bucareli and promising that de Mézières would visit their camps as soon as possible.

The mission succeeded better than de Mézières had dared hope. Chief Povea received the envoy graciously and assured him that his nation would not go to war over the Bucareli incident. Of course, he had been offended by the violent reception given Comanche delegates by the settlers of Bucareli, but he readily accepted the Nadacog chief's assurance that it had been a mistake for which de Mézières sent sincere apologies. Some small bands had repudiated Povea's stand against a war of vengeance and had broken away to pursue an independent vendetta. Povea could not restrain them, but he knew they had already suffered substantial losses. Once they were destroyed, there would remain no ground for complaint between Comanches and Spaniards, barring some new affront.[45]

The Nadacog chief returned home to find new neighbors settling in among the pine forests. The citizens of Bucareli had persuaded newly arrived Governor Domingo Cabello that they lived in daily peril of annihilation by Comanches. From October onward, they

[44] De Mézières to Croix, Natchitoches, November 15, 1778, ibid., pp. 232–233; the Bucareli incident is discussed at length in Bolton, *Texas in the Middle Eighteenth Century*, pp. 434–446, relying largely upon Gil Ybarbo's reports, which conflict with those of de Mézières.

[45] De Mézières to Croix, Béxar, September 30, 1779, in Bolton, *Athanase de Mézières*, II, 289–291.

begged the governor either to send troops to protect Bucareli or to let them return to the Tejas territory from which the government had removed them in 1773.

Unable to grant either request, Cabello agonized over the piteous picture of a civil populace lying helpless before an onslaught of hostile savages. Early in 1779, on the twin excuses of the Comanche peril and February floods on the Trinity River, the colonists abandoned Bucareli to move as far eastward as they dared. Gil Ybarbo led them to a site near the old Mission Nacogdoches. Cabello, and eventually Croix, accepted their fait accompli.

Abandonment of Bucareli exasperated de Mézières, who had counted that settlement on the Trinity a valuable outpost for trade and communication with the most remote Norteños. He urged its prompt reoccupation. He saw no compensating merit in the new Nacogdoches location, and he denied that Comanche warfare necessitated the move. Governor Cabello rejected de Mézières' argument that the Comanches, wronged at Bucareli, had shown commendable forbearance on the whole.

The argument wore on for months, unfortunately straining relations between de Mézières and Cabello before they ever met. Sporadic Comanche attacks in the spring and summer of 1779 hardened the views of each. The slightest raids convinced Cabello that the Comanche nation was at war; the fact that no more than nine or ten raiders were ever sighted confirmed to de Mézières that a few hostiles acted independently. He knew that the war parties would have been far larger and the attacks much more frequent and devastating if their nation had indeed gone to war. A Comanche woman, captured that spring by Tawakonis and turned over to the Spaniards, said the same. Furthermore, neither the Taovayas nor traders residing at their village knew of any Comanche decision to go to war against the Spaniards. As Povea had said, the problem would last only until the marauding dissidents were killed by the people they raided, provided no new injury were inflicted upon the Comanche nation. Accordingly, de Mézières urged the Tawakonis and other Indians injured by Comanche raiders to limit their response to defensive warfare, and he so advised the Spaniards. A show of patience and understanding now could lead to that early pacification of the Comanches so essential to Croix's hopes and plans.

Undoubtedly, de Mézières could have made a stronger case if he had reported promptly to San Antonio in the autumn of 1778, but

Cabello awaited him at San Antonio for almost a year, with growing distrust of both the judgment and the sincerity of the noted Frenchman. De Mézières postponed his departure that winter on grounds of seasonal difficulties. High waters would make the rivers impassable; his Natchitoches militiamen were scattered into the wilderness for the winter hunt; it would be impossible to round up horses for the journey until the floods subsided. Meanwhile, he visited Gálvez at New Orleans in March.[46] He hoped to dissuade the governor from transferring him out of Louisiana, but he found Gálvez convinced that Croix must have de Mézières to solve the Indian problems of the Provincias Internas.

No small factor in the resolve of Gálvez was his own need for a trustworthy business agent in Texas. He needed Texas livestock, not only for Louisiana uses, but also to supply Spanish armed forces and to aid the American rebels against England. De Mézières agreed to purchase and ship herds for Gálvez upon his return to Texas.[47]

In turn, de Mézières needed the governor's full cooperation in his own business among the Indians. He wanted permission to visit key nations of the north on his way to San Antonio, instead of reporting directly to the Texas capital. He would also require a good supply of presents to take to the tribes, as well as an advance from the Louisiana treasury to equip and provision the escort of mounted militiamen who would accompany him from Natchitoches. Gálvez approved all his requests.[48]

De Mézières returned to Natchitoches late in April, his canoes laden with bales of presents that he meant to deliver in person to both Tawakoni villages, the Tonkawas, the Taovayas, the Panismahas, and the Comanches.[49]

[46] De Mézières to Gálvez, Río de los Caxizes, February 7, 1779, ibid., pp. 239–240.

[47] De Mézières to Gálvez, New Orleans, March 17, 1779, ibid., pp. 241–242. De Mézières prepared for Gálvez a memorandum of livestock prices prevailing at San Antonio in February 1778: four pesos for a fat cow; six pesos for a three-year-old sheep; three pesos for a breeding ewe; three pesos for a goat; six pesos for a half-broken horse. Mares could be purchased in droves at a peso a head, or even less; wild mules averaged eight pesos apiece. Shipping costs would be negligible because drovers could be hired cheaply; saddles, bridles, lassos, and halters also came cheaply in Texas.

[48] De Mézières to Gálvez, New Orleans, March 17, 1779, ibid., p. 241; Gálvez to de Mézières, New Orleans, March 22, 1779, ibid., p. 246; de Mézières to Gálvez, New Orleans, March 21, 1779, ibid., pp. 244–245; Gálvez to Croix, New Orleans, March 21, 1779, ibid., p. 243.

[49] The gifts consisted of 27 hatchets, 54 axes, 27 spades, 27 muskets, 135 pounds powder, 270 pounds balls, 67½ ounces Limbourg cloth, 54 staple shirts,

A fresh Kadohadacho crisis greeted him. The devastating toll taken over the last year by Osage raiders and by the epidemic had left that key nation terribly discouraged and divided. One faction wanted to abandon the great village, a move that de Mézières opposed because it would only expose the interior to Osage and British incursions. At that critical juncture, the new Kadohadacho chief announced that he would go to New Orleans to visit Governor Gálvez.

De Mézières tried to dissuade him. He knew how terribly busy the governor was; he also feared that Kadohadachos traveling to New Orleans might experience pernicious British contacts on the eastern banks of the Mississippi. However, when the chief remained adamant, de Mézières capitalized on the situation. He entrusted the chief and his three principal associates to the interpreter Jeanot, whom he charged to avoid the British on the way and to lose no opportunity to teach the Indians how perfidious and poisonous Britons were. To Gálvez he dispatched explanations of the importance of these Indians and, so far as he dared instruct a superior, told him how to treat them.[50]

It was vital that Gálvez comprehend that this was a loyal, friendly, courageous Indian, whose people were the principal defensive barrier against the Osages and whose high standing among other Indians helped to keep the rest loyal to Spain. It would be appropriate for the governor to turn out in full ceremonial regalia to receive this chief in a manner befitting a man who occupied one of the most important keys to the western country and who would influence his neighbors. No effort should be spared to make a grand ceremony of investing the chief with the large medal that he would wear as symbol of his office in the Spanish Empire.

There were certain policies to which de Mézières hoped the governor could persuade the chief. Hunters from the Arkansas River were now flocking to deal with the Kadohadachos. De Mézières wanted the chief to forbid the practice and to arrest all offenders and turn them in at Natchitoches. Gálvez would do well to speak of the king's great desire to preserve peace among the Kadohadachos, Arkansas, and other allies and to let the visitors know how abhorrent he found the Osages' awful deeds. However, it would be important not to imply so much

---

27 pounds vermilion, 27 dozen knives, 54 pounds glass beads, 27 dozen combs, and 54 rolls of tobacco.

[50] De Mézières to Gálvez, Natchitoches, May, 1779, in Bolton, *Athanase de Mézières*, II, 248, 252–253; Gálvez to de Mézières, New Orleans, June 1, 1779, ibid., p. 253.

support against the Osages that Kadohadachos would later have reason to think the Spaniards broke their word.

Gálvez rose to the occasion. The Kadohadachos were his guests through the latter part of May 1779, and their treatment left nothing to be desired in terms of ceremony or of time and attention lavished upon them by the governor. The medal chief and his principal associate returned to their people wearing medals hung upon their breasts by the governor himself, and all the delegates carried back important presents to help them remember the power and riches they had witnessed in New Orleans. Between them, Gálvez and de Mézières had done everything in their power to heal the crisis of authority among the Kadohadachos.

Meanwhile, de Mézières left for Texas in the last week of May 1779 with too few horses, all in bad condition because of the winter and spring floods. With him rode forty-three men. Twenty-seven were Natchitoches militiamen, including the lieutenant and sublieutenant of the local company; the rest were his own servants and a few travelers with business of their own in Texas. All traveled well armed, but de Mézières worried about the poor condition of the horses as he led his party into territory seething with tensions among the Indian nations.[51]

De Mézières hoped to prevent hostilities threatening in several quarters. Rumor had the Tonkawas and Tawakonis on the brink of war. De Mézières sent an invitation to the Tonkawas to meet him at the Tawakoni village so that he could mediate.

Most Indians in East Texas resented the Comanches, whose raids at Bucareli they blamed for disrupting trade in their region. De Mézières found the villages rife with talk of a general coalition to attack the Comanches. He wanted to calm them and persuade them to stay on the defensive, lest a general war among the Indians of the northern frontier wreck Croix's strategies. He therefore issued a general invitation to the nations to meet with him to discuss the Comanche problem.

As de Mézières rode westward from the Sabine River, a runner from Nacogdoches overtook him with Gil Ybarbo's appeal for help: the new settlement lay defenseless because all its militia were out chasing Tonkawa and Comanche marauders. Hurrying to respond, de Mézières fell from his horse. Shock, fever, and delirium ensued. After five painful days, de Mézières gave up hope of speedy recovery and let his servants bear him home to Natchitoches on a stretcher. He left his party, horse herd, and goods behind on the Atoyaque River, near the old site of Bucareli, partly to reassure the Indians that he would return and partly to let the horses grow strong on the lush pastures.[52] Not until August, after two months at home in bed, could de Mézières resume his journey; even then his limited recovery forced him to curtail his itinerary. The result was a summer of confusion and disappointment among Norteños and of rising chagrin for Governor Cabello, who had even less information than the Indians.

Commandant General Croix had a bad summer, too. Shortly before he was scheduled to move his headquarters from Chihuahua to the permanent capital at Arispe in May, a grave illness paralyzed his hands and arms. For weeks he lay at death's door.[53] During that gloomy time, one mail after another shattered his optimistic assumptions of 1778.

Reports from Texas were bad enough. The Comanches seemed nearer general war than peaceful accord with the Norteños and Spaniards; the novice Cabello grappled alone with the delicate, unfamiliar problems of Indian diplomacy while the indispensable de Mézières lay helpless in Natchitoches. Even worse was the mid-summer dispatch from Spain, notifying Croix that the king rejected general war against the Apaches.

That decision, promulgated on February 20, 1779, marked a convenient coincidence of principle and expediency.[54] Spain's pending entry into the war against Great Britain ruled out any new commitments of men and resources to the Provincias Internas. Furthermore, the Crown rejected on humanitarian grounds the forcible subjugation or extermination of any Indians, however misguided and unruly. In keeping with the longstanding principles, if not the consistent practice, of the Crown, peaceful persuasion and kind example would have to pacify the Apaches. Punitive expeditions would be permissible where such action might persuade the *bárbaros* to desist their raids or perhaps even to seek peace, but general offensives were absolutely forbidden.

The Crown also rejected as a deterrent to the civilizing process the stringent conditions that Croix had stipulated for Apaches seeking peace. The Indians must be allowed to live in their accustomed way

---

[52] De Mézières to Gálvez, Natchitoches, June 24, 1779, ibid., pp. 257–258; de Mézières to Croix, Natchitoches, Atoyaque, August 21, 1779, ibid., pp. 258–260.

[53] Thomas, ed., in *Teodoro de Croix*, p. 43.

[54] See Moorhead's discussion of the Royal Order of 1779 in *Apache Frontier*, pp. 120–123.

as long as they chose, but they should be plied with gifts of Spanish commodities to lead them eventually to appreciate the Spanish way of life and to wish to imitate it. They should even be given firearms for their hunting and defense, in the hope that they would lose their skills with their aboriginal weapons and thus be subject to control by the simple expedient of cutting off their gunpowder when necessary.

Unlike the king, Croix had seen Apache warriors at close range, and he knew they had learned to manufacture gunpowder. Therefore, he respectfully begged two thousand reinforcements to help him fend them off until kindly persuasion could work the desired miracle.

That hope vanished too in the autumn of 1779, when a courier overtook the commandant general en route to Arispe with the news that on June 21 Spain had declared war on Great Britain. Croix promptly withdrew his request for troops and notified the provincial governors of the discouraging new context within which they must all work.

CHAPTER 15

Texas, 1778-1779

      Nowhere did the reversal of plans pose greater dangers than in Texas. De Mézières' heady campfire oratory in the spring of 1778 had already roused the Norteño warriors' enthusiasm for big campaigns with the Spaniards against Apaches. Now their disappointment had somehow to be safely contained, and some means had to be found to manage the Lipans through kindness without alienating the Norteños. A welter of risks and contradictions engulfed the new governor of Texas. Contrary to Croix's expectations, he had little help from de Mézières.

      Colonel Domingo Cabello y Robles reached San Antonio late in October 1778 to succeed Governor Ripperdá. A Castilian, thirty-seven years an officer of the king, he had worked his way up from a lieutenancy; distinguished service at Havana during the Seven Years' War had gained him the governorship of Nicaragua. His unblemished reputation and particularly the fact that he was a stranger to New Spain's interior provinces had made him the ideal candidate for governor of Texas when Bucareli demanded replacement of Ripperdá in that remote post, too often tainted with suspicions of corruption. Ironically, the officer preferred by Bucareli for negative virtues arrived two years later when Commandant General Croix had tagged Texas for a very positive role in consolidation and development of the Provincias Internas.

Though the appointment was a tribute to his proven integrity and administrative skills, it must have been hard to consider it a promotion. As presidial commander, Cabello took command of the poor stockade of Béxar, with eighty soldiers and a few swivel guns better suited to ceremonial salvos than to battle. The civil populace was small and demoralized. Years of sporadic Indian raids had combined with inertia and excessive regulation to keep them always in poverty, and they had long suspected that their governors connived with Louisiana Frenchmen to countenance the raids. The once-flourishing missions were at a low ebb, thanks to raids and epidemics, and the Mesteña Fund had freshly embittered the friars' relations with the secular authorities.

Most discouraging for the new governor was the Indian problem. The success of Cabello's administration, even the survival of his province, would hinge upon a diversity of Indian peoples, all strangers to him, some covertly and some openly hostile to Spaniards. High strategy required manipulation of those Indians: alliance with some to subjugate or exterminate others. Though the ground rules varied from time to time, that practical necessity never really changed because the few Spaniards on the northern frontier never had any viable alternative.

At the beginning of Cabello's term, Croix's crucial objectives in Indian affairs depended largely upon the skills of de Mézières, borrowed from Louisiana for that purpose. Given his established leadership among Indians and Croix's expectation that Norteños and Spaniards would soon campaign together against the Lipans, reliance upon de Mézières made sense, but the situation exasperated Cabello. As governor, he would certainly pay the penalties for failure in his province, but any successes would surely be attributed to the Frenchman's skill with Indians. It was not at all clear that the lines of authority were to be at San Antonio, and de Mézières' long delay in reporting for duty aggravated Cabello's doubts. When de Mézières sent him letters of advice during the time he was detained in Natchitoches, the governor's irritation grew. He complained to the commandant general.[1]

Croix tried to reassure Cabello that de Mézières was in no way preferred over him but was transferred to San Antonio only to be of maximum assistance to the governor. That purpose could be served only if

[1] Cabello to Croix, San Antonio, June 20, 1779, BA.

the governor would accord de Mézières his friendship and support, in a manner consistent with his admirable character. Croix expected Cabello to overcome his petulance for love of the royal service but reminded him, in case he could not, that letters of resignation should be submitted in triplicate.[2] Recognizing that he had lost a round, the veteran public servant braced himself to work with de Mézières.

Northern frontier problems plagued Cabello from the outset. His arrival in October 1778 coincided with the first Comanche thrusts at Bucareli; he had to worry about protecting that settlement and then about awkward questions raised by its illegal move to Nacogdoches. Conflicting reports from Gil Ybarbo and from de Mézières compounded his difficulties. In his first year in Texas, Cabello boggled at the notion that savages rather than settlers could be the wronged parties and instinctively believed Gil Ybarbo's reports of misbehavior by Norteños and traders instead of de Mézières' reports of healthy commerce.[3] In the governor's mood of gloom and doubt, he naturally grew impatient for de Mézières to assume his assigned responsibilities for the Norteños and Comanches before some catastrophic outbreak should destroy the province, and with it Cabello's own career.

Though Cabello worried first and most about the northern nations, Apaches were the first with whom he had to deal directly. He found clear enough guidelines in the reports of the councils of 1778: ruptures with the Lipans must be avoided at all costs, unless and until a general offensive could be mounted against all Apaches. Cabello's responsibility to keep the Lipans in Texas calm and content was not easy to reconcile with Croix's order to cut off their access to the Tejas and Bidais and not at all compatible with his duty to cultivate the friendship of the Norteños.[4]

At first, Cabello tended to favor the Lipans, partly because his jealous resentment of de Mézières led him to reject the Frenchman's favorable attitudes toward Norteños and Comanches. In particular, de Mézières' pro-Comanche view of the Bucareli imbroglio so offended Cabello that he began arguing that many damages attributed to Apaches were actually wrought by Comanches intruding upon Apache ranges. Finding Lipan visitors at the presidio courteously attentive and respectful, the governor suggested that misleading reports from de Mézières had be-

[2] Croix to Cabello, Chihuahua, August 16, 1779, BA.
[3] Cabello to Croix, Béxar, August 31, 1779, BA.
[4] Croix to Cabello, Chihuahua, October 4, 1778, BA; Cabello to Croix, Béxar, March 9, 1779, BA.

trayed the officials of the Provincias Internas into wrong judgment of Apaches.

The Lipans noted the governor's sympathetic attitude and promptly tried to exploit it. On March 6, 1779, a delegation of some eighty Apaches[5] and Lipans requested an audience with the governor, saying that they had important things to tell him. Cabello granted the interview, and the chiefs entered the presidio on the usual condition that they come unarmed. El Joyoso was in charge; several other chiefs accompanied him, including Roque and Xavierillo, the son of Josecillo.[6]

El Joyoso told their story. A big Norteño war party, including Tonkawas, had attacked them, stealing many horses and killing or capturing more than three hundred persons of all ages and sexes. The Tonkawas were hunting now between the Colorado and the Guadalupe, and these Lipans and Apaches wished to exact vengeance from them. They called upon their friends the Spaniards to help them with men and ammunition.

Astounded by the bold request, Cabello answered that they asked the impossible: the Tonkawas were his friends, and he did not help attack friends who had given him no provocation. He distributed two candies and a box of cigars to each of the visitors and bade them goodbye. Apparently content, they left San Antonio the next day.

Ten days later the same chiefs rode back into Béxar, proud and happy. They had attacked a Tonkawa camp on the banks of the Colorado, killed four, captured four, and seized some horses. One of the captives was a Mayeye girl about ten years old, whom El Joyoso presented to his good friend Luis Menchaca, the son of Captain Menchaca.

Cabello tried to ransom the other three captives. Two were little boys, about seven or eight years old, whom he wished to rear as Christians. The other, a thirty-year-old Tonkawa woman, was probably too old to convert, but the governor thought it would be nice to give her back to the Tonkawas as a token of his friendship. Cabello offered eight horses for the trio. Chief Roque agreed, but the rest rejected the deal. They rode off later that day with the three captives and never indicated any further interest in Cabello's proposition.

Cabello had little more than a month after that to savor the thought of a stable modus vivendi with the Lipans. On April 23 an incredible

---

[5] Cabello appears to apply the term Apache to the Natagés; he always takes care to distinguish them from the Lipans.

[6] Cabello to Croix, Béxar, March 18, 1779, BA; Croix to Cabello, Chihuahua, May 14, 1779, BA.

rumor reached Béxar from Coahuila: the governor of Coahuila and all the officers in his province had met at Aguaverde presidio with the Mescaleros, made peace with them, and then joined them in a declaration of war on the Lipans and Apaches.[7]

Cabello, angry and alarmed, tried to suppress the news, lest it spark panic in his province. Everyone in his jurisdiction knew just as well as he that, if the Lipans and Apaches were driven back into Texas, the province would not have enough forces to resist them. He dispatched an indignant protest to Croix, asking how this squared with the decisions of the councils of 1778. Had there not been firm agreement that Apaches should not be attacked without reinforcements? What did the commandant general expect Cabello to do now?

Cabello could not know that, since the councils of 1778, Spanish officials in Nueva Vizcaya and Coahuila had dabbled in the dangerous game of playing Lipans and Mescaleros against each other, hoping that they would obviate the whole eastern Apache problem by destroying each other. Some Lipans had enthusiastically grabbed the opportunity to collaborate with Spaniards against Mescaleros. Thus, they were especially shocked in the spring of 1779 when Coahuila's Governor Ugalde joined with Mescaleros to wage war against Lipans. A climactic late spring battle destroyed countless Apache lives, both Lipan and Mescalero, and six hundred horses as well. It was a particularly grievous blow to the Lipans, following hard upon their recent heavy losses to the Norteños.[8]

Given the Mescaleros' new ascendancy in Spanish favor below the Rio Grande and the pressures of enemy nations to the north, the Lipans had to seek sanctuary in Texas. Croix hastened to warn Cabello that the Lipans had been driven back into his jurisdiction, where they might vent their anger upon San Antonio, but to no purpose. The Lipan fugitives reached Béxar two days before Croix penned the dispatch and two months before Cabello received it. Governor Cabello handled his first Indian crisis without prior warning and without any helpful briefing on the tangled Indian affairs of the Provincias Internas.

At the siesta hour on June 3 Chief Joyoso came with several other Lipans to the house of Captain Menchaca.[9] They told him of their calamity in Coahuila, then asked whether the Spaniards of San Antonio

[7] Cabello to Croix, Béxar, May 14, 1779, BA.

[8] Croix, General Report of 1781, in Alfred Barnaby Thomas, ed., *Teodoro de Croix and the Northern Frontier of New Spain, 1776–1783*, pp. 89 ff.

[9] Cabello to Croix, Béxar, August 19, 1779, BA.

were also against them. The other chiefs and the rest of their people were camped on the Arroyo del León, waiting to find out.

Captain Menchaca assured Joyoso that there would be no problem and led the delegation to the governor. Cabello summoned an interpreter but was pleased to find that he could understand much of the Lipans' story from their eloquent pantomime. They begged permission to settle in Texas under his protection. Cabello agreed, on condition of their good behavior, warning that, if they should do the slightest damage, he would declare war and gather up all his people to wipe out the Lipans.

Joyoso agreed to everything. Even when Cabello asked that the Lipans start their good behavior by returning the mules they had stolen in the province two days earlier, the chief agreed. Cabello passed out cigars and candies to signal the end of the conference. They left, apparently content. Mid-August found Cabello still waiting for some result, either in mules returned or further visits from the Lipan chiefs.

The movement of the Lipans cast new urgency upon relations with the Norteños, but Cabello had from the ailing de Mézières only a letter full of good advice and assurances that he would eventually reach San Antonio with his militia escort and seventy Indian delegates from the interior. De Mézières advised Cabello to deal moderately with the Indians and to learn and respect their customs in minute detail in order not to offend them. De Mézières had found the Indians' greed and ambition the keys to managing them, but he had also learned that exploiting those traits was a delicate, risky business.[10]

In view of de Mézières' failure to establish communications between San Antonio and the Norteños, Cabello found his advice more exasperating than useful. His impatience grew when he talked with Don Nicolás de La Mathe of Nacogdoches, who reached Béxar on June 20, just a day after de Mézières' letter. La Mathe reported frequent Comanche attacks and unrest among friendly nations about too little trade and too few visits and gifts from the Spaniards.[11] La Mathe sought Cabello's permission to travel to the interior in search of several hundred horses he had lost to Comanche raiders at Bucareli since the vendetta began. The governor readily consented and made the trader his emissary to the restive Norteños.

La Mathe failed to retrieve his horses, but he did visit some of the allies in mid-summer as Cabello's representative and assured them of

---

10 Cabello to Croix, Béxar, June 20, 1779, BA.
11 Cabello to Croix, Béxar, June 20, 1779, BA.

the new governor's good will toward them. He urged the chiefs of the Wichitas, Tawakonis, and Tonkawas to ride to San Antonio to meet Cabello and reiterated the Spaniards' appeal to the roving Tonkawas to settle down in a permanent village.[12]

Before La Mathe could report back to Cabello, five Tejas Indians presented themselves, unannounced, at the Governor's Palace on August 16. It was immediately obvious that these were distinguished men on an errand of importance. Their leader, Captain Texita, had been to Mexico City, where he had received from the viceroy himself a Spanish uniform and the cane of authority.[13] Cabello found him articulate, intelligent, and prudent. Communication presented no problem: many Béxar men had served at Los Adaes and spoke the language of the Tejas. Cabello called upon First Sergeant Pedro Granados to express the governor's pleasure at meeting the visitors and to inquire whether they were being properly looked after. After a brief preliminary exchange on the purpose of their visit, Sergeant Granados showed the Tejas envoys to quarters in a jacal and ordered food brought to them.[14]

Thus began Cabello's first experience of extended entertainment of Indian visitors, which he found both trying and, ultimately, rewarding. Their daily ration strained his poor budget: a quarter of beef; a bushel and a quarter each of beans and of corn ground for tortillas; roasting ears to the cost of one real; and a box of cigars apiece. Even worse for Cabello, they wanted to see him daily. That he found onerous because he felt miserably unwell in his first San Antonio August. However, remembering de Mézières' advice, he met all their expectations and took great care not to offend them in any detail. His effort paid good dividends. As he strove to establish a good reputation with the Indians, Cabello began to discover them as human beings and to respect them.

Texita's party had come on behalf of all the friendly nations of the interior. Their friend de Mézières, whom they called Captain Pintado, had told all the Norteños that the Great Captain in Chihuahua wished them to come together in Texas to make war on the Apaches. Everyone wanted to come, Tawakonis, Taovayas, Panismahas, Tonkawas, and others, more than a thousand warriors in all. They had expected Captain Pintado to join them with a cargo of gifts, thirty-five Creoles from

---

[12] Cabello to Croix, Béxar, August 30, 1779, BA.

[13] It seems likely that Captain Texita was the Indian companion of Gil Ybarbo and Gil Flores on their errand to Mexico City in 1774, for there appears no other record of an Indian leader sent from Texas to meet the viceroy.

[14] Cabello to Croix, Béxar, August 20, 1779, BA.

Natchitoches, and his own son, now a militia captain. But now they had heard that Captain Pintado was very ill with a great tumor on his thigh, lanced with a big incision. Uncertain when to come for the campaign, they had appointed Captain Texita to find out for them.

Cabello had to confess that he knew little more than they. A carpenter newly arrived from Natchitoches confirmed their report of de Mézières' ailment and his thirty-five escorts, hired at six pesos per diem. Embarrassed that he could give no adequate answer, Cabello asked Captain Texita to be his emissary to the Tawakoni and Taovayas villages, the two which de Mézières had called most important. When Texita pointed out that the Panismahas also were very loyal to the Spaniards and firmly allied with the friendly nations, Cabello expanded his commission to include their village, too.

Throughout his five days of talks with the governor, Texita emphasized most the shortage of traders and the clamor for them among all the nations. That same week a party of Akokisas, Bidais, Mayeyes, and Cocos visited La Bahía to declare their friendship and desire for trade. If Cabello had earlier wondered whether all the fuss about Indian trade was just traders' propaganda, he now had ample confirmation of its importance to the Indians.

The visit of Texita's delegation ended as unexpectedly as it began, on the morning of August 21. Early in the day, Cabello received the group for yet another conference, with Sergeant Granados interpreting. About nine o'clock, a runner appeared with a letter from Fray Juan García Botello, informing the governor that four Lipans had arrived at his mission. They were advance messengers for five Lipan chiefs bringing many of their people to make up their quarrel with the governor. Cabello dared not risk a Lipan encounter with the Tejas in the presidio, but neither did he wish to offend the Tejas.

The Tejas were immediately curious about the letter. Cabello showed it to Sergeant Granados and instructed him to tell the guests that five Apache chiefs were coming, looking for a fight with the nations of the interior. Cabello offered to give them a head start out of the presidio, with protection as far as the other side of the Guadalupe or the Colorado, and to detain the Lipans at Béxar until the Tejas had time to make a safe getaway. He also promised to warn the Lipans that the Tejas were under his protection and that he would kill the Lipans if they should damage the Tejas, even slightly.[15]

---

[15] Cabello to Croix, Béxar, September 3, 1779, BA.

Sergeant Granados interpreted the governor's words in fine haranguing style with plenty of gestures for emphasis. The astonished Indians left at once. Cabello provided a seven-man escort, as much to verify their departure as to protect them. The Tejas were out of the presidio by noon. When they bade the escort goodbye at the Guadalupe River, they expressed profuse gratitude for the hospitality they had received in San Antonio and for the presents they were taking home. They promised to visit all the friendly nations to report the good treatment and friendship they had enjoyed in San Antonio. Gil Ybarbo subsequently reported that the Tejas kept their promise and that they were particularly zealous for a big joint campaign against the Lipans.

Cabello had just five hours to compose his thoughts between the noon departure of his Tejas guests and the late afternoon arrival of the Lipans. While six hundred Lipans of all ages and sexes waited outside the presidio, five chiefs visited the Governor's Palace. To propitiate him, they presented sixteen of the thirty-eight mules recently stolen from Miguel de la Garza; Cabello responded with gifts of candy and cigars. Negotiations were off to an auspicious start. The next day all the Lipans were allowed to enter the presidio, unarmed. They brought in seventy mules and four horses that soldiers and settlers recognized as their property. The Lipans handed the animals over to the owners as asked, with no show of reluctance.

The chiefs were El Joyoso, who had come in June, and four others introduced to Cabello as Josef Grande, Josef Chiquito, El Manco Roque, and Manteca Mucho. They said they were going out to kill buffalo and acknowledged Cabello's warning not to kill any cattle while they were at it. To the governor's surprise, the Lipans expressed disappointment not to find the Tejas visitors, saying that they wished to be friends with them and had therefore meant to return to them four captives taken from that nation. Indeed, the Lipans now wished to be friends with all nations of the interior who were friends of the Spaniards. Only with the Comanches did they not wish to be friends.

Cabello acknowledged that the Tejas had visited him and pointed out that they were the Spaniards' friends, like all other Indians not doing anything wrong-headed. The Lipans proposed that Cabello arrange for them a meeting with the Tejas. Nothing could have been further from Spanish intentions, but Cabello glossed over that point, and his visitors departed amicably.

The week had been even more eventful than the exhausted governor realized. On August 21, as Cabello hustled the five Tejas emissaries out of Béxar just hours ahead of six hundred Lipans, de Mézières returned to the men and horses he had left two months before on the Atoyaque.[16] Although his recovery was far from complete and the horses were still not sound, de Mézières pressed on, eager to repair the damage of a summer's neglect among the peoples of the interior.

A visit to Nacogdoches on August 23 confirmed his opinion that the settlers' real problem was not so much Comanches as their own folly and cowardice. He thought them absurd to be so terrified of the Comanches, inasmuch as three of the raiders had died in the latest encounter. True, the success had been due largely to the bravery and zeal of Tawakonis who had helped the settlers repulse the raiders and had then overtaken the fleeing Comanches. The Tawakoni warriors recovered the scalp of the settler Mora, which Comanches had taken in May, and exacted a price of two Comanche lives for it. They had also captured a Comanche woman, whom they voluntarily turned over to the Spaniards. Her story agreed with that of Chief Povea: the marauders were a few die-hard hostiles, operating independently.

The Spaniards' withdrawal from the settlement on the Trinity had frightened and angered the Bidais, Nabedaches, and Tejas, who suddenly found themselves exposed to the dangers of frontier tribes. They were muttering about Spanish cowardice. To reassure those nations and to secure Spain's economic and military position in that area, de Mézières urged prompt, strong reoccupation of the Bucareli site. The Nacogdoches site appeared to him worthless, and events of spring and summer had proved that it lay well within the range of any Comanches who wished to attack that community.

At Nacogdoches, de Mézières heard that a great company of Panismahas awaited him at the Tawakoni villages. To expedite his progress, Gil Ybarbo lent him a militia sergeant who knew the road to San Antonio, and they hurried on through the Tejas country, camped overnight at deserted Bucareli, then headed for the nations of the north.

En route, de Mézières observed the pitiful condition to which recent epidemics had reduced the once populous, prosperous villages of the Tejas. He had seen in May that the Ais, near the Sabine, had dwindled to twenty families, existing in sad degradation. Now he reported that the Asinais had only eighty men left and the Nabedaches only forty. Their chiefs had died in the last epidemic. Only women greeted de

---

[16] The account of de Mézières' journey is drawn from the series of letters that he wrote to Croix en route, published in Herbert Eugene Bolton, ed., *Athanase de Mézières and the Louisiana-Texas Frontier, 1768–1780*, II, 258–285.

Mézières as he passed by their villages in late August; all their men were off hunting buffalo or visiting friendly tribes.

De Mézières soon had proof that the Tejas were still valuable friends. As he approached the Kichai village beyond the Trinity, a Tejas rider overtook him to warn of five Comanches sighted on his trail at the ford of the Trinity. They had fled when they realized they were observed, and de Mézières' scouts could find no trace of them. With due caution, he led his party on from the Kichais to the Tawakonis, accompanied by the friendly messenger. Within the week the Comanches had their revenge: they killed the Tejas messenger one night, almost within sight of the Tawakoni village he was visiting with de Mézières' party.

A big party of Tonkawas awaited de Mézières on the Brazos River, five miles below the Tawakoni village. As he approached, they sent runners and made smoke signals to summon others hunting in the vicinity. The Tonkawas had disconcerting news for de Mézières. The epidemic had left them only 150 men and had wiped out all their old leaders, including the chief to whom Ripperdá had given the cane and flag. Their new head chief was El Mocho, alias Tosche, an Apache captive adopted into the tribe.

Spaniards had recognized El Mocho and worried about him for two decades, ever since he distinguished himself by his fierce glee in sacking San Sabá mission. Eloquent and turbulent, El Mocho was diabolically skillful at stirring up an audience and bitterly hostile toward Spaniards. Governor Ripperdá had thought El Mocho such a malevolent influence that in the spring of 1778 he had asked de Mézières to get rid of him.

The Tonkawa camp held plenty of rivals glad of an excuse to dispatch the abrasive fellow. De Mézières easily arranged for three Tonkawa leaders to take El Mocho with them to Natchitoches, ostensibly to get presents, and to kill him en route in such a way that the death would appear natural. Unfortunately for his purpose, the epidemic intervened, killing the would-be assassins and leaving El Mocho in charge. De Mézières bowed to fate and greeted El Mocho as an honored friend.

El Mocho enjoyed the treatment due a distinguished leader: the ceremonial visit to his camp by de Mézières with troops and flag, and the role of honored guest at dinner in the Frenchman's own tent. He urged de Mézières to spend the night in his camp, where they talked through much of the night. De Mézières was pleased to find El Mocho friendly, reasonable, and apparently quite sincere.

De Mézières promised El Mocho Croix's affection and protection if he would gather his people into a village, grow crops, and live in harmony with the Tawakonis. El Mocho insisted that he would gladly establish a village. Indeed, he had ridden to the Trinity to agree with Gil Ybarbo on a site near Bucareli, so that the Tonkawas and the settlers could reap mutual advantages of trade and combined defense against Comanche incursions. He had found Bucareli deserted, but he still vowed he would settle down as soon as details could be worked out. More impressive, because subject to immediate test, was El Mocho's promise to do everything possible to make peace with the Tawakonis, even at his sacrifice of a private grievance.

Another encouraging development occurred at the Tonkawa camp. Several runaways from the San Antonio missions presented themselves to de Mézières and agreed to travel to San Antonio with his party. He carefully avoided talking about restoring them to the missions, lest he scare them away, but he hoped to influence them to return voluntarily to mission life.

With his augmented party, de Mézières rode on to the Tawakoni village headed by Chief Quiscat.[17] There, too, the epidemic had taken a heavy toll: only 250 Tawakoni men survived. The Taovayas and Panismahas had suffered much less, thanks to their remote location on the Red River, and the roving Comanches were said to have escaped the epidemic altogether. Quiscat was mourning a brother who had died just before de Mézières arrived, but he refused to let grief mar the long-awaited visit and turned out with all his people to give the guests a joyous welcome.

De Mézières hastened to tell Quiscat of the good feeling toward him that El Mocho had displayed, and the chief seemed very pleased. Soon El Mocho rode into the village to return de Mézières' visit to his camp. At the Frenchman's request, Quiscat and El Mocho shook hands and embraced. Then Quiscat directed the village crier to proclaim throughout the settlement that the Tonkawas must be affably treated there. Everyone respected the order. For the rest of the day the recent enemies celebrated their new accord with feasting, dancing, and revelry.

A major disappointment confronted de Mézières at the Tawakoni villages. Many Taovayas and Panismahas had awaited him there for six weeks, but they had gone home upon hearing of his serious illness.

---

[17] Apparently the same chief whose name Spaniards usually rendered as Siscat Gainon.

There was not time to summon them back. De Mézières sadly conceded that neither his own health nor that of his horses would permit the long ride to their villages. He could only hope they would come to Béxar for talks as soon as they heard of his arrival there. Quiscat said they had wanted to discuss important matters with him: quieting the Comanches, removing the hindrances to trade that they caused, and restoring the security of the roads.

De Mézières rested a week with the Tawakonis, waiting for many of their leading men to return from the buffalo hunt to complete the council circle. Meanwhile, he observed among the Tawakonis and the Tonkawas much agitation for a campaign against the Comanches. The Tawakonis had always considered the depredations at Bucareli an affront to their own territorial rights; now they also felt an urgent duty to avenge the Tejas man murdered that week by Comanches while a guest in their village. De Mézières quietly resolved to dissuade them, lest they worsen the Comanche problem beyond hope of resolution.

On September 13, 1779, in the spacious arbor that was the summer meeting place of Quiscat's village, de Mézières held council with the Tawakonis of both villages and the Tonkawas. He had first talked privately with the chiefs and now felt confident that he could win the general approval of their people. Once the village crier called them to silence and attention, de Mézières described to all the Tawakonis and Tonkawas Croix's affectionate concern for the friendly nations of Texas and his resolve to maintain harmonious alliance with them. To the Tonkawas he addressed a plea to settle down and farm as the means to a prosperous, tranquil existence. He mentioned Croix's displeasure with the erring Comanches, but he urged his listeners to conciliate rather than fight them, in order that peace should prevail in their lands. In closing, de Mézières announced that the Tonkawas had already agreed to ride with him to San Antonio and the Tawakonis had indicated they would come later with the Taovayas and Panismahas. He expressed his hope that they would indeed come and perhaps would persuade the Comanches to follow them to Béxar to hear the governor's expressions of good will.[18]

The assembly applauded his remarks and shouted their obedience and loyalty to the head chief of the Spaniards for whom de Mézières spoke. De Mézières thanked them for their devotion and loyalty, then distributed the presents, with scrupulous care to parcel out exactly

[18] De Mézières to Croix, Tuacanas, September 13, 1779, in Bolton, *Athanase de Mézières*, II, 275–276.

the same gift for each of the two Tawakoni villages and the Ton-kawas.[19] There remained a little more than half the goods he had picked up in New Orleans, intended for the Taovayas and Panismahas and, with luck, for the Comanches. Since he could not deliver them to the recipients as he had hoped, he loaded them back on his mules to be packed to San Antonio, there to be warehoused against the visit of Taovayas or Panismahas. They were never to understand or forgive his failure to deliver presents to them that September.

The generous Tawakonis saw de Mézières off with provisions for his troops and good replacements for his nearly useless horses. El Mocho and some of his people rode from Quiscat's village with De Mézières; more Tonkawas joined them the next day for the trip to San Antonio. The party had grown stronger by seventy-six: seven fugitives from the missions and sixty-nine Tonkawas, all well armed and most mounted.

De Mézières, who had known little of the Tonkawas, marveled at their disciplined competence on the trail. Indeed, he came to speculate that their apparently crude culture served their needs better than the complex European life styles that now impinged upon the wilderness.

Their offensive weapons are firearms, bows, and spears; their defensive armament, skins, shields, and leather helmets with horns and gaudy feathers. The country being dangerous, through its being frequented by the Apaches, they use great precaution; they explore the land, choose the most advantageous places to pitch camp, and post sentinels; they are exhorted morning and evening that their sleep be short and light; they arise at dawn to bathe; they give no chance by straying off from the march for being surprised by the enemy. . . .

No chief exerts himself to have a following; he knows that when there is no pay there is no obligation; . . . they are enlisted, freed, or privileged, without gratitude or ill feeling, without merit or note. One is caused to wonder at a liberty which keeps in harmony peoples seemingly irrational, but would cause the fall of those who flatter themselves that they are more prudent and wise!

The extreme neglect of the Indians to carry supplies would be criticized by one who did not know of their activity and sagacity in providing themselves with necessities; their temperance when these are lacking; their slight aversion to the most repugnant things. No longer are its rapid flights of avail to the turkey; to the deer, rabbit, and hare, their timidity and fleetness; to the turtle, its hole; to the skunk, its stink; to the viper, its deadly poison; I have seen them all buried in the stomachs of my friends, the Tancagues.

[19] Each gift consisted of 3 hatchets, 3 spades, 3 guns, 18 pounds powder, 36 pounds shot, 6 tomahawks, 8 ells cloth, 7 shirts, 3 pounds vermilion, 42 knives, 7 pounds glass beads, 48 combs, and 8 packages of tobacco.

Meanwhile, on my getting further away from the settlements, which drive the wild cattle from their neighborhood, they had better food, and their noisy glee in consequence was expressed in discordant songs.

In truth, one cannot exaggerate the inestimable benefits for which these natives are indebted to divine providence. The buffalo alone, besides its flesh, which takes first place among healthful and savory meats, supplies them liberally with whatever they desire in the way of conveniences. The brains they use to soften skins; the horns for spoons and drinking vessels; the shoulder bones to dig and to clear off the land; the tendons for thread and for bow-strings; the hoof, as glue for arrows; from the mane they make ropes and girths; from the wool, garters, belts, and various ornaments. The skin furnishes harness, lassos, shields, tents, shirts, leggins, shoes, and blankets for protection against the cold—truly valuable treasures, easily acquired, quietly possessed, and lightly missed, which liberally supply an infinite number of people, whom we consider poverty-stricken, with an excess of those necessities which perpetuate our struggles, anxieties, and discords.[20]

De Mézières also noted how abundantly providence had lavished upon Texas resources prized by Europeans as well as by Indians. The quantity and quality of wild grapes between the Brazos and the Trinity led him to speculate that the area held great potential for vineyards. He waxed even more enthusiastic about the economic potential of the San Gabriel River, whose clear waters he reported teeming with trout, carp, eels, and other savory fish. He envisioned those waters harnessed to irrigate the plain and then to grind its bounteous yield of grain. In his mind's eye he saw vast herds of cattle and horses, sheep and goats thriving on the lush grasslands. The bright carpet of wild flowers stirred visions of a domestic honey industry; the handsome live oaks suggested hogs fattened on acorns at no cost to the owners. He looked at the woods and saw lumber for building; he noted the splendid quarries and dreamed of substantial stone houses standing for grandchildren of the builders.

The Colorado River, then the San Marcos, and then the Guadalupe, all looked to de Mézières as richly promising as the San Gabriel. Apparent iron deposits along the Colorado seemed to foreshadow development of metal industries. As he progressed southward, de Mézières marveled at splendid springs gushing forth clear rivers and spectacular caves whose formations he thought rivaled the beauty and grandeur of Europe's great cathedrals. All those observations went into his reports for Croix, whom he knew to share both his interest in economic devel-

[20] De Mézières to Croix, San Xavier River, September 22, 1779, in Bolton, *Athanase de Mézières*, II, 278–280.

opment and his urge to comprehend the peoples and the land that comprised his vast responsibility.

On September 25 de Mézières pitched his last camp, on the Arroyo Salado, a little north of Béxar, and sent a courier to notify Cabello of their approach. Earlier that summer Cabello had complained to the commandant general about the trouble and expense that de Mézières would impose with his large escort and numerous Indian guests, only to be sharply rebuked. The escort was entirely proper and prudent; Indian diplomacy was de Mézières' principal charge. Croix expected Cabello to give him full support and to entertain the Indian guests as well as possible so that they would go home happy enough to influence others in favor of the Spaniards. The costs of entertainment could be charged to the Fondo de Gratificación.[21]

Since Croix's pointed reminder of procedures for resignation accompanied those instructions, Cabello spared no effort to be a gracious and generous host. Arrangements to feed and house more than a hundred visitors proved so difficult in the poor San Antonio community that Cabello claimed the effort cost him drops of blood, but within twenty-four hours he was ready to tender a proper reception.[22]

Perhaps the burden of arrangements for the Indian guests fell so heavily upon the governor because Béxar had just lost its oldest and best link with the Norteños. Antonio Treviño died at the presidio on September 24, 1779, an old man at forty-eight. By just two days, death cheated him of the opportunity to welcome his friend de Mézières, and only by hours of the knowledge that the commandant general had appointed him first *alférez* of the Béxar garrison. On the day of Treviño's death, the mail courier brought the appointment, Croix's response to de Mézières' advice that the fine old soldier deserved higher responsibilities commensurate with his abilities and experience. The choice dismayed Cabello, who thought Treviño's illiteracy disqualifying, regardless of his extraordinary rapport with the Norteños and his excellent character. Thus, when he notified Croix of Treviño's death and asked for another appointment, he specified a man who could read and write.[23] Experience had yet to teach Cabello to prize competence with Indians above all other qualities in his staff, but he would learn rapidly in the months following Treviño's death.

[21] Cabello to Croix, San Antonio, June 20, 1779, BA; Croix to Cabello, Chihuahua, August 16, 1779, BA.
[22] Cabello to Croix, Béxar, October 19, 1779, BA.
[23] Cabello to Croix, Béxar, October 9, 1779, BA.

Cabello welcomed de Mézières and his party with all due ceremony when they rode into the plaza on September 26, 1779. De Mézières publicly proclaimed the purpose of the visit: the Tonkawas had come to ask the governor to recognize El Mocho as chief of their nation. He also announced that they wished to fulfill their promises of last January. Thus, they had brought the Indian apostates in order that they should cease attacking the missions they had fled, and they intended to establish a village in a place designated by the Spaniards. The sixty-nine Tonkawas appeared content with his statements.

Cabello politely thanked de Mézières and the Tonkawas and deferred the formal investiture to a more suitable time, when the visitors should be rested and refreshed. He passed out boxes of cigars to the Indian guests and had them shown to their quarters in jacals. The Tonkawas found two men detailed to give them any assistance they might need and two enormous kettles that the governor had rented for their use. Each day the Spaniards gave them a beef and great baskets of squash and green corn, which they boiled together in the kettles. Delighted to find life in the presidio an endless feast, the Tonkawas kept fires blazing day and night by which to dance their happiness.

To Cabello's consternation, Tonkawas came to his house to talk with him for hours every day. As the talks wore on, the meticulous administrator fell woefully behind in his paperwork. Over and over they told him of their losses and of a thousand other things much on their minds. Communication flowed well, for the Indians were eloquent, and Cabello's ceremonious courtesy accorded nicely with their own proprieties. De Mézières had brought an exceptionally good interpreter, Andrés Courbière, who had worked several years for a Natchitoches firm of traders to the Tawakonis and Tonkawas and who was fully proficient in both those languages.

The governor also lavished time and attention on the seven apostates, hoping by affectionate persuasion to save their souls as well as to eliminate their threat to the missions. Since all seven spoke Castilian, Cabello could talk with them directly. He urged them to return without penalty to whichever mission they preferred; the Father President of the missions concurred heartily. Neither the missionary nor the governor even hinted at coercion, lest they frighten them back to the wilderness and jeopardize their souls.

The Tonkawas, reveling in Cabello's hospitality, seemed not to think of departure. Cabello worried about possible consequences if the Lipans should return to report to him on the promises they had given him in August, and within a week knew trouble loomed. On the night of October 3, First Alférez Joseph Antonio Curbelo spotted a Lipan prowling around the Tonkawa dance circle. Asked to explain his presence, the man said he had come to see those Indians. His own people were camped about twenty miles from the presidio, but they did not wish to come in to see the governor as long as those Indians remained. He asked when they would leave.

Alférez Curbelo explained that the Tonkawas had come with de Mézières and would presumably stay for the duration of his visit with the governor. The Lipan carried that news back to his camp, while Curbelo reported the incident to Cabello, who consulted de Mézières. They surmised that the Lipans hoped to even their score against the Tonkawas with a surprise attack on their return journey. The badly outnumbered Tonkawas would probably be slaughtered, with incalculable damage to relations with all the interior tribes. De Mézières remembered too well the experience of 1772, when Apaches had killed both Taovayas and Comanche delegates to the San Antonio peace talks. Cabello agreed that they must detain the Tonkawas until he could learn more about the Lipan situation.

They had not long to wait: Lipan chiefs Joyoso and Josef Chiquito entered the settlement the next night. Francisco Menchaca, one of the aides assigned to the Tonkawa visitors, found them waiting in his yard when he returned about midnight to his home across the river. They called him by name and told him not to be afraid. Since they were unarmed and he was carrying a good lance, he calmly and courteously asked whether they needed anything.

The chiefs wished Menchaca to take their message to Cabello. They had meant to report to the governor about the commitments they had made on their last visit, but now they did not wish to come in because of the Tonkawa presence. They wished to know when the Tonkawas would leave, so that they could come to see the governor.

Menchaca tried to put off the errand, arguing that the governor surely slept at that hour, but the two chiefs insisted until he complied. Cabello sent Menchaca back to tell them that the Tonkawas had accompanied Captain de Mézières, who had come to visit the governor; Cabello had no idea when they would leave. No Tonkawas had done him any damage, so the Tonkawas were his friends, as were the Lipans. If the Lipans should do them any harm, the Lipans could no longer be Cabello's friends, nor would they be permitted to enter Béxar again. Cabello carefully rehearsed Menchaca on answers to all likely questions and gave him cigars and candy to present to the visitors. The pair left, apparently satisfied.

When de Mézières arose on October 5, the governor told him what had happened in the small hours, and they worried together about ways to thwart Lipan vengeance. When El Mocho and several more Tonkawas arrived for their daily visit with the governor, they were included in the conference. De Mézières assured them that Cabello would furnish all possible protection to see them across the Colorado, beyond which they should be safe. When Cabello confirmed that promise, the Tonkawas declared they would leave on October 9. The governor agreed to invest El Mocho as chief a day earlier. Then he had to find and equip enough soldiers and settlers to deter the Lipans from intercepting the Tonkawas. He was humiliated to let de Mézières see Béxar's shortage of manpower and equipment.

The Tonkawas were not too badly worried to give El Mocho's investiture on October 8 a full celebration. They danced all afternoon in the plaza in front of the Governor's Palace. Cabello distributed the usual presents: for El Mocho, a fine uniform and a horse, as well as the cane of office, the medal, and the flag; for the second-ranking chief, a horse and less elegant clothing and trappings; for all the other Tonkawas, sundry trinkets, tobacco, sweets, and provisions for the road. The bill for the gifts, the entertainment costs, and the six-peso fee to interpreter Andrés Courbière totaled a little more than 278 pesos,[24] only the beginning of a serious drain on the provincial budget.

The final ceremonies came at departure time on October 9, just after breakfast, again in the presidial plaza. When El Mocho reported in his new uniform, Cabello hung upon his breast the large medal of a chief, then handed over the cane of office and the new flag emblazoned with the king's arms. There were embraces all around, and shouts of "Viva el Rey!" came from the crowd that had gathered to watch. Cabello handed out final parting gifts to all his guests, who expressed their great satisfaction through interpreter Courbière. Then they rode off with Lieutenant Menchaca and his squad of twenty-three soldiers and eighteen militiamen.

To the immeasurable relief of Cabello and de Mézières, that guard sufficed. Menchaca escorted the Tonkawas to the Colorado River without incident. When they said goodbye on the morning of October 15, the Tonkawas expressed warm appreciation for their excellent treat-

[24] Joseph Antonio de Bustillo y Zevallos, *Cuenta Formal* . . . , Béxar, October 19, 1779, BA.

ment by the Spaniards. El Mocho especially charged Lieutenant Menchaca to tell the governor that he would move all his people to the place designated for their new village. Now they would ride to all the nations to tell how well they had been treated at San Antonio, so that all the rest would also come to know Cabello.

The escort rode back into Béxar at noon on October 19. Menchaca saw no signs along the way that Lipans had followed, though he could not rule out the possibility that they had taken a higher route in the hill country to the west.

In another week, the Lipan situation grew a bit clearer. On October 26, Lipan chiefs Roque, El Joyoso, Josef Chiquito, and Manteca Mucho visited Cabello to announce that they had seriously considered fighting the Tonkawas but had refrained as a favor to Cabello. The manner of their declaration suggested that they expected reciprocal favors.[25]

Cabello inquired into the state of their relations with Apaches, Mescaleros, and Gileños, and they assured him that they hoped to convene all the Lipans to plan vengeance. They needed now to know whether he would help them as the Spaniards of Coahuila had helped the others.

The governor replied that he could help them only on two conditions. First, the Lipans must carry Cabello's letter to Croix to ask that highest of all captains to admit them to his protection. If they could convince Croix of their true hearts, then Cabello could help them as his commander should direct. Second, the Lipans must choose among themselves one great chief whom all would obey, because it was not good that so many chiefs had to be dealt with. Cabello would give the cane to the man of their choice and name him Great Chief of all the Lipans.

They seemed to think his answer reasonable on the whole, but they balked at going to Chihuahua, lest they meet enemies on the way. The second requirement appeared quite acceptable to them. They left in an affable mood for their camp on the Arroyo del León, about five miles from the presidio, where four hundred of their people waited.

The four chiefs returned the next day to say that they would all obey the chief selected by Cabello, but the governor refused to choose for them. Cabello would only confirm a head chief elected by all Lipans, not just by those of the group presently camped near San Antonio. Many other little chiefs led groups of Lipans; the agreement of all would be necessary for a valid choice of leader.

<hr/>

[25] Cabello to Croix, Béxar, November 2, 1779, BA.

The visitors raised no objection. The rest of the Lipans were camped at the Cañon de San Saba (probably the upper Sabinal); they could all gather soon to choose one great chief. These four pledged to arrange the gathering. Cabello signaled the end of the meeting with the usual gifts of cigars and candies.

Their cordial goodbyes were interrupted by two Lipan messengers from the Cañon de San Saba. Comanche raiders had stolen more than four hundred horses from the Lipans camped there; these men had come to alert their compatriots to danger. As the Lipans rushed off together, the chiefs hastily called back that they would gather all their people and that the governor would hear from them later. Actually, a long time passed before the Lipans resumed negotiations with Cabello.

Cabello could spare little time to wonder or worry about the Lipans at the moment, for he was caught up in a dizzying succession of crises of personnel and policy in the Spanish camp. Two weeks earlier, he had received dispatches from Croix transferring Cabello to the governorship of Coahuila and appointing de Mézières to succeed him in Texas, but de Mézières had fallen critically ill. Shadows of important business unfinished loomed ominously over the Governor's Palace in San Antonio.

The two officials had had so little time to work together. De Mézières had tactfully stayed in the background during the Tonkawas' visit in order to emphasize the governor's primacy and had given advice only when asked. His considerate behavior and his genuine helpfulness did much to allay Cabello's resentment. The two men worked together quite well when, after the Tonkawas left, they had time at last to confer on fundamental problems of the province.

During the fortnight that Tonkawa guests had taken most of Cabello's time, de Mézières worked on his dispatches to the commandant general. On the road he had written detailed reports of his journey; in the Governor's Palace, he addressed himself largely to general conclusions and recommendations. He praised the tremendous economic potential of Texas and deplored the failure to develop it, warning that the opportunity had better be seized before the British could appropriate it for themselves. He thought the key to development would be a coastal port, preferably on Matagorda Bay, and the fine river highways that flowed from the interior. He therefore urged immediate conquest and exploration of the coast by a seaborne expedition from New Orleans under Governor Gálvez. He thought the Karankawas, who had long plagued the coast, had only about 150 men and should be exterminated, especially the apostate Joseph María who had sparked so many infamous atrocities.[26] His view of the importance of coastal development dovetailed nicely with interests expressed by Croix during his tour of inspection the year before and with the program of Cabello, who had sent an expedition in April to explore the coast and to map the exact locations of the mouths of the Colorado and Brazos rivers.[27]

Cabello also found de Mézières helpful with regard to the problems of Béxar. The Frenchman was shocked to learn that, since Treviño's death, the presidio had no interpreter competent in the languages of the new Indian allies in the north. De Mézières' own party from Natchitoches included three excellent interpreters: Andrés Courbière, skilled in the languages of the Tonkawas and the Wichitan bands; Francisco Hughes, well versed in the speech of the Panismahas and in Tonkawa; and Julian Rondein, who could speak both the Caddo and Wichita tongues. Though French was their native tongue, all three understood Spanish; Courbière could also read and write. All three were so widely known and loved among Indians that they could travel anywhere with only a light escort, even into Comanche country. De Mézières begged permission to employ them at Béxar.[28]

Cabello liked the idea, but the only jobs at his disposition were in the garrison, where he had no vacancies unless the commandant general would issue a special authorization. He had already been much impressed by Courbière's excellent service during his talks with the Tonkawas, and he liked the look of Rondein and Hughes, both reputed to be good horsemen and brave. The governor urged Croix to issue the necessary order.

Until October 12, de Mézières and Cabello assumed that de Mézières was there temporarily to help Cabello manage the Indian nations of the province, but that day's mail changed everything. Croix had begun in May to work toward transferring Cabello to the governorship of Coahuila.[29] The commandant general had suspected from the time of Cabello's arrival that he would not work well with de Mézières and that he disliked the decision to favor Norteños and Comanches against Apaches; on the other hand, Cabello had coped nicely with the awkward problem of the Lipans. Croix had indicated all along that, if forced to

---

[26] De Mézières to Croix, Béxar, October 7, 1779, in Bolton, *Athanase de Mézières*, II, 291–303.

[27] Croix to Cabello, Chihuahua, August 16, 1779, BA.

[28] De Mézières to Croix, Béxar, October 7, 1779, in Bolton, *Athanase de Mézières*, II, 318.

[29] Croix to Cabello, Chihuahua, May 14, 1779, BA.

choose whether to support de Mézières or Cabello in Texas, he would back the Frenchman, but it was probably Coahuila's Governor Ugalde who brought matters to a head. Croix had no objection to playing off Mescaleros against Lipans and had indeed played that game himself. Nevertheless, Ugalde's rash open declaration of war against the Lipans, directly contrary to the councils' decisions and the Crown's standing policies, must have offended Croix almost as much as it incensed Cabello. He promptly asked the Crown's permission to move the more prudent and discreet Cabello, already on good terms with the Lipans, to Coahuila. With one happy move, he could give Cabello a more comfortable post, better suited to his advanced years and poor health, and give the able, experienced de Mézières a free hand in Texas. Just what the commandant general planned to do with the ubiquitous Ugalde is unclear.

The new development distressed de Mézières almost as much as it pleased Cabello. De Mézières had resisted transfer to Texas in the first place, and the job of governor seemed unthinkable.[30] He lacked knowledge of Spanish law; his limited experience of the Spanish administrative style had been largely unhappy. Even with respect to his own special competence, Indian affairs, he doubted his suitability. As governor of Texas, he would have to deal with the Lipans and thus jeopardize his friendship with the Norteños; when, following the strategy of the Provincias Internas, he should give the Norteños information and other assistance for campaigns against the Lipans, he would enrage the latter. De Mézières gloomily foresaw a time when he would enjoy no sound friendship with any Indian nation. Furthermore, his health was now so broken that he could no longer attempt the long journeys on horseback so vital to his relations with the interior nations.

De Mézières wanted most of all to go home to Natchitoches, to lead the Indians of that critical frontier through the imminent war with England. There he could contribute most effectively, and there his heart lay. However, he had no choice but to obey if Croix should insist over his objections. He had already asked Governor Gálvez to prevent his transfer from Louisiana and had lost the appeal. Therefore, he asked that, if Croix should require him to remain in spite of the drawbacks he listed, he be allowed an escort to bring his family from Natchitoches and that his four sons be given appropriate positions in the Béxar company.

[30] De Mézières to Croix, Béxar, October 13, 1779, in Bolton, *Athanase de Mézières*, II, 319–322.

Croix never had to settle the questions he raised. Within a week, de Mézières fell gravely ill. Cabello provided the best medical attention available in Béxar and sadly realized how inadequate it was. In the last week of October, the dying de Mézières wrote his last letters, appealing to Gálvez and Croix to protect his family. He had long neglected his private affairs in favor of public business: now the future of his motherless brood weighed heavily upon his mind.

De Mézières died at noon on November 2, 1779, and was buried the next day in the church with all the military honors the little garrison could manage. Cabello hastily approved a request that de Mézières had filed for 450 pesos to finance his escort party's return to Natchitoches, gambling that Croix would not object.[31] He thought it unnecessarily cruel to detain them at Béxar, especially since de Mézières' eldest son, captain of the squad, was so anxious to hurry home to his brothers and sisters. Cabello also gambled that Croix would approve his enlisting Julian Rondein and Francisco Hughes in the garrison to retain their services as interpreters. He hired the invaluable Courbière as his personal interpreter. Domingo Cabello knew well that he would need every bit of help he could get to maintain friendly relations with the nations of the interior.

Cabello had ample reason to worry. During de Mézières' illness the governor had received Croix's notice of the Royal Regulation of 1779, with all its far-reaching implications for Texas.[32] The Crown's decision was not inconsistent with Cabello's own views, thus far, about the Lipans, whom he had expected to cultivate from his new base in Coahuila. Any resulting tensions among the Norteños would have fallen to the management of the knowledgeable de Mézières in Texas. Cabello had hoped that news of the happy experience of the Tejas and Tonkawa delegations at San Antonio would soon move other nations of the interior to establish friendly relations at that capital.

The death of de Mézières wrecked all the governor's expectations. Cabello could not move on to Coahuila without a successor to take his place in Texas, and he knew that it would take months, or even years, for Croix to arrange his replacement. For the foreseeable future, the Norteños would be his problem. He was not at all sure how he could win their friendship. Convinced that much depended upon de Mézières' successor at Natchitoches, Cabello sent Governor Gálvez all available information on gifts for the Indians and urged him to have de Mézières'

[31] Cabello to Croix, Béxar, November 4, 1779, BA.
[32] Cabello to Croix, Béxar, October 20, 1779, BA.

procedures maintained at Natchitoches in every detail.[33] The governor of Texas would need maximum help from Natchitoches to maintain friendly relations with the Indians.

Any result of his appeal to Louisiana would take months. What could Cabello do at Béxar meanwhile? The presents for the Taovayas and Panismahas that de Mézières had warehoused at the presidio weighed heavily upon the governor's mind: the longer those powerful nations waited for presents and visits, the greater the risk of losing their friendship. Jealousies and resentments had surely stirred among the nations that the ailing de Mézières could not visit on his last trip to San Antonio. All year Gil Ybarbo had reported some key tribes restive because they needed more trade; Chief Texita had confirmed the seriousness of the problem. Now the Crown's rejection of the proposed offensive against the Apaches implied more disappointment and frustration among the interior nations. For months the projected campaign, with gifts from the Spaniards, booty from the Apaches, and glory for all, had been the talk around their campfires. How could the change of plans be explained to them? How were they to understand that the Spanish king now required his officers to give presents and assistance to any Apaches who would seek peace?

Cabello sorely missed Antonio Treviño, who could have conveyed to those nations the governor's high regard. Casting about for a substitute, Cabello hit upon Don Bernardo Portolán, who had lived at Béxar three years, spoke some Indian languages, and was said to understand the system of presents to the Indians. Cabello made him a sublieutenant of militia and sent him off to tell the Norteños how much Cabello valued their friendship and how much he wanted them to visit him. The overture failed. Cabello would have far longer to dread that the Norteños' sullenness would turn to belligerence.

Before the year's end, Cabello learned that he would have to solve his problems by himself with the meager resources already available. The mid-December mail brought Croix's notice of Spain's proclamation of war against Great Britain six months earlier.[34] There would be no more troops for the Provincias Internas, and little money to support existing forces. In Louisiana, Governor Gálvez could spare little attention to Indian affairs at Natchitoches. He had the Mississippi River to defend against the British and their Indian allies, as well as a chance to win Florida back for his king.

---

[33] Cabello to Croix, Béxar, November 12, 1779, BA.
[34] Cabello to Croix, Béxar, December 13, 1779, BA.

The financial prospect was worse than Cabello or even Croix could yet have realized. Viceroy Bucareli died in 1779, and there followed a decade of administrative chaos in the viceroyalty. Bucareli had often misjudged the problems of the northern provinces, and he had certainly been no friend to Croix after creation of the Provincias Internas. Nevertheless, he had been an extraordinarily able viceroy and had produced important support for the northern provinces when convinced of their needs. Since the Provincias Internas remained financially dependent upon the viceroyalty, the state of disarray in New Spain undermined the fortunes of the northern provinces just as surely as it penalized the provinces of the heartland.

Just one success alleviated the gloom that enveloped the Provincias Internas in 1779. Governor Anza had taken hold in New Mexico with his customary vigor, and within the year he had led its forces to decisive victory over the Comanches.

CHAPTER 16

New Mexico, 1778-1779

Lieutenant Colonel Juan Bautista de Anza brought to New Mexico at the age of forty-three a background of experience and distinguished achievement unparalleled in that or any other of the Provincias Internas. He had already served twenty-six years in the army in his native province of Sonora, where Apache wars had always been a condition of his life. His father and grandfather, both captains Juan Bautista de Anza, had died fighting Apaches in Sonora. The third Juan Bautista de Anza won his captaincy by distinguished performance against Apaches on the Gila River in 1759. The next year he took command of Sonora's northernmost presidio, Tubac, perennially plagued by Apache raiders. There he proved himself a just and able administrator as well as a military leader. The Tubac community thrived under his governance, and Inspector General Rubí commended him in glowing terms when he visited that presidio at Christmas 1766.

Captain Anza carried on his father's zeal for exploration and expansion as well as his military bent. In 1737 the elder Anza, then commandant at Fronteras, had volunteered to explore northward to the Colorado River, to found there a settlement as a base for further discoveries, and then to probe westward to determine once and for all whether California was indeed an island. The Council of the Indies approved Anza's proposal, but the venture was never carried out. Anza had later that year to subdue a Pima revolt, then was caught up in the quickening pace of war with Apache marauders, who took his life in 1739. His project died, too, but his idea did not.

The son broached the idea again soon after he became an officer in the 1750's, but he sparked no important response at that time. The possibility revived in 1769 after San Diego was founded to launch the colonization project in Alta California. Yuma Indians on the Colorado River heard of the Spaniards on the Pacific coast and told Pimas; they in turn told Captain Anza at Tubac. Anza reasoned that men could travel the route the news had traveled, informed his superiors in Sonora, and volunteered to open at his own expense an overland route from Tubac to the Spanish settlements on the California coast.

His offer was ill-timed. Sonora's very existence was threatened by Indian revolts within and Apache incursions from the north; no men or materials could be spared for explorations, however important. New initiatives had little better chance above the provincial level. The imperial machinery marked time, awaiting the results of the ambitious studies ordered by Carlos III and the reforms that were to follow.

Anza renewed his offer three years later under better conditions. He had now the vigorous support of Fray Francisco Garcés, who had traveled extensively among Indians north and west of Tubac since taking charge of Mission San Xavier del Bac in the summer of 1768. On the Colorado and Gila rivers he found numerous Indians who seemed ripe for conversion. Among them he heard excited talk of the Spaniards in California, saw shell ornaments of Pacific coast origin, and guessed that the route to California was less dangerously arid than was generally assumed. He also noted Hopi blankets, obtained by his hosts from neighboring people to the north who acquired them from the Hopis, and heard of friars like himself in New Mexico, only a week's journey away. All in all, Fray Garcés spotted on the Colorado and Gila rivers a happy opportunity to serve both Majesties: a promising mission field, plus a long-needed link between Sonora and Spain's remote outposts in California and New Mexico.

By 1772 Anza's California project also had a much better chance of approval at the higher echelons. The long administrative paralysis was ending; Rubí's reforms were getting underway on the northern frontier. Gálvez had persuaded the Crown to ignore Rubí's advice against expansion insofar as California was concerned and to expand the Spanish presence there. Viceroy Bucareli thought Alta California important as a barrier to Russian and British incursion, and he had in the Crown's Regulation of 1772 a clear directive to lend all possible support to the development of the Californias.

Meanwhile, experience proved the importance of overland connection between California and the main body of Spanish settlement. Baja California lacked the resources to sustain the supportive role that it played in the initial thrust northward. All foodstuffs had to be shipped to Alta California, because the local Indians were not agricultural and the missions could not yet produce enough to support themselves and the presidial communities. Supplies shipped from the port of San Blas reached California slowly, if at all, at exorbitant costs. The fragile new outposts weathered more than one starving time in those early years when supply ships failed them. Their woes multiplied when the Indians grew hostile. Fray Junípero Serra, who founded five missions by the end of 1773, concluded that neither his missions nor the presidios of San Diego and Monterey would ever be secure, nor would the planned expansion be possible, without full-scale colonization. To mount that effort and to sustain it, an overland supply route would be essential. Fray Serra wanted settlers: laborers, blacksmiths, carpenters, farmers, all to double as militiamen, and Christian Indian families to witness that Hispanic life style was good for Indians, too. To transport by sea so many people and goods to sustain them was totally impracticable.

On May 2, 1772, Captain Anza offered Viceroy Bucareli much the same proposition he had made to Gálvez in 1769: to seek at his own expense a route from Sonora to Monterey, preferably in October, with Fray Garcés and twenty-odd soldiers from Tubac. He promised not to neglect his primary duty to operate Tubac as a center of defense against Apaches.[1]

In August Bucareli sought opinions on which to base his decision. An engineer just returned from Monterey thought the project entirely feasible and suggested that two soldiers be brought by sea from San Diego to join Anza's party so that he would have competent guides as

---

[1] Anza to Bucareli, Tubac, May 2, 1772, in Herbert Eugene Bolton, ed., *Anza's California Expeditions*, V, 3–7. The account of Anza's California expeditions is drawn primarily from that five-volume collection of documents by Bolton, with supplementary reliance upon Charles Edward Chapman, *The Founding of Spanish California*.

he approached the Pacific coast. The *fiscal* also reported favorably, but he cautioned against leaving Tubac without replacements for the absent soldiers, lest Apaches exploit any temporary weakening of the garrison. In October the viceroy convened a council to decide the question. The council begged leave to defer a decision, pending further information.

Most of all, the council desired the diaries and the opinion of Fray Garcés, who responded with hearty advocacy of Anza's plan. He himself had already volunteered to seek a route from the Pimería Alta to Monterey and had caused a considerable stir by speculating that the distance from Monterey to New Mexico was probably very short. Since he had not won his own superiors' consent to explore to the Pacific, he was delighted to support Anza, in whom he had absolute confidence. Praising the Tubac commandant's well-proved zeal in the service of both Majesties, Fray Garcés added that "The said captain is exceedingly affable, patient, liberal, well-beloved by the Indians, punctilious in matters of the service, and with no improper habits of life."[2]

While Garcés labored over his response to the viceroy at San Xavier del Bac, Bucareli heard another decisive Franciscan voice in Mexico City. Fray Serra himself had come to tell the viceroy about the problems of California and to plead for improved support. Bucareli asked his opinion of Anza's proposal. Serra readily endorsed it: an overland supply route was essential to his own ambitions for California. Even more strongly, Serra urged the opening of a direct route from New Mexico to Monterey, arguing that the two mission provinces should be linked in order to consolidate the spiritual conquest.

The only dissenting voice was that of Sonora's Governor Sastre, who objected that Anza's venture would only stir up new Indian troubles for Sonora and Sinaloa. Garcés scoffed at that. He considered the Indians of the Colorado extremely docile and thought Anza much too diplomatic to offend them in any way. Anza also dismissed the suggestion that he would stumble into new hostilities. The only Indians he thought likely to hinder Spanish advance to the Gila and Colorado rivers were Apaches, but that very year he was taking part in O'Conor's first campaigns to obviate the Apache problem along the entire frontier. Given success in that undertaking, Anza anticipated no Indian problem on the route to California. Indeed, a Spanish presence should have

---

2 Garcés to Bucareli, San Xavier del Bac, March 8, 1773, quoted in Chapman, *Founding of Spanish California*, p. 165.

the virtuous effect of quelling the ubiquitous intertribal wars in that area.

Anza and Garcés only feared sabotage by self-seeking or jealous Spaniards. Fray Garcés cautioned the viceroy that, if he should approve the venture, he should send sealed orders to that effect and should forbid appeal by any objector. Anza stipulated that he must be responsible directly to the viceroy and must have the right to report in person at Mexico City upon his return from California. He thus hedged against interference and misrepresentation by Governor Sastre, already an open opponent, and by Commandant Inspector O'Conor, whose single-minded pursuit of his own objectives sometimes blinded him to the merits of other efforts.

In September 1773, Bucareli presented to the council the additional information it had requested, plus new reports of British and Russian activities on the northwest coast. Speedily the council approved, and Bucareli authorized the expedition. Anza could take twenty volunteer soldiers of his own choice; he should be accompanied by Fray Garcés and another missionary selected by Garcés. Kindness and moderation must govern the conduct of the expedition toward the Indians at all times, and arms must be used only if absolutely necessary for self-defense. No establishment should be made. Captain Anza must return promptly from Monterey to Tubac and from there to Mexico City to report to the viceroy.

It was early November by the time the authorization reached Tubac.[3] Captain Anza quickly notified Fray Garcés, and they agreed to start on December 15. They planned to aim for Monterey by the most northerly route possible, assuming that in case of difficulty they could fall back to the hospitable Yuma settlements at the juncture of the Colorado and Gila rivers, and thence proceed without difficulty to the coast.

Preparations proved more difficult and time-consuming than they had anticipated. They left Tubac three weeks later than they had planned, on quite a different route. Apaches caused the change in plan and very nearly managed to scuttle the venture at the outset. Apache raiders burst upon the Sonoran frontier with renewed vigor that winter. They scored a major triumph at Tubac on the night of December 2, when they stole 130 horses, many from the herd that

---

[3] The bearer was Juan Bautista Valdés, a soldier who had served in California with Gaspar de Portolá and who was now assigned to Anza's party in order to serve as guide once they should reach California.

Anza had assembled for his California expedition. No replacements were available in the vicinity. Anza decided not to wait at Tubac for new shipments of horses from the south, lest Apaches meanwhile grab the rest of his herd. Heading southwestward to Altar to get horses, he relinquished all hope of the northerly route in order to avoid Apaches. From Altar he would go to the juncture of the Gila and Colorado rivers, then to California by a route that would not in the future require protection from Apaches.

Such a route was now known to be feasible. Of five Indian runaways from Mission San Gabriel in Alta California, one, Sebastián Tarabal, survived the journey across the desert to the juncture of the Gila and the Colorado. A Yuma leader, Chief Palma, brought him to Altar to tell his story to the Spaniards and volunteered his own good opinion of that route to California.

The horses that Anza had expected to acquire at Altar were lacking, so he pressed on with too few animals. Sebastián Tarabal joined his party to serve as a guide from the Yuma country to the Pacific. A Pima interpreter and eight other Indians hired as muleteers, servants, and carpenter brought the party's strength up to thirty-four. Anza allowed provisions for four months, plus generous quantities of gifts for the Indians. His overloaded pack animals deteriorated rapidly.

Anza's first critical test was his reception in the Yuma country, for the ultimate usefulness of the route would hinge upon the attitude of those strategically placed Indians. A friendly Pápago warned that Chief Pablo was stirring up the Yumas to fight the approaching Spaniards, but he also reported that Chief Palma and two other powerful leaders were urging a peaceful reception, explaining the benefits of Spanish friendship and the dangers incurred by those who provoked Spanish vengeance. Anza sent an invitation to Palma to visit him, and they met on friendly terms at a Yuma settlement.

Palma's impressive welcoming address convinced Anza and the friars that this chief would indeed be a valuable friend. Anza formally asked the assembled Yuma men if they recognized Palma as their ruler. When they affirmed their obedience to him, Anza confirmed him "lord of everybody," in the name of Carlos III. The captain hung the medal of office about his neck, Palma vowed his loyalty to the Crown, and Anza embraced him. Chief Palma and his people were visibly moved by the ceremony.

Having fulfilled his duty to one Majesty, Anza turned to the service of the other and explained Christianity to the assembly. Anza, himself a devout lay brother of the Franciscan College of Querétaro, set forth the story in simple, direct fashion. God created all people and all things. All Spaniards were subjects of both God and the king. God gave the king these lands and many more, and countless Spaniards. The Spaniards had in return for their obedience to the king their many horses, fine clothing, iron implements, knives, and other riches. The king was even more generous to Indians than to Spaniards. He wanted their friendship, vassalage, and obedience. Most of all, he wanted them to stop warring among themselves. It grieved both God and the king to see their Indian children kill one another.

Palma followed the story intently, through the interpreter, and seemed much impressed. He then harangued his people for an hour and obviously stirred them with his earnest presentation.

From the very first, Palma's friendship proved invaluable. His men helped Anza's party cross the Gila River, not far from present Yuma; Anza then distributed beads and tobacco to the six hundred assembled Yumas. Chief Palma and his retinue of six hundred guided Anza the next day to a ford on the Colorado and marched with him three days down that stream. They camped with Anza's party at the village of Chief Pablo and by that confrontation overcame his hostility.

The whole episode was for Anza profoundly impressive and revealing. It was his first opportunity to know *indios bárbaros* who had not yet been given reason to hate the Spaniards. He found the Yumas and their neighbors merry, friendly, and generous; all in all, he liked them better than any Indians he had ever known. Before the spring was over, he had reason to appreciate them even more.

When Anza left the Colorado River to strike out across the desert, Palma and his people bade him goodbye. Ahead lay enemy territory into which they would not venture. The chief wept at parting from Anza. He promised to have rafts ready upon their return, for the river would then be at flood stage. Palma also promised to dispatch Anza's letters back to the Spanish frontier; within three weeks they reached Altar in perfect condition.

The route delighted Anza. After the first five days they found themselves in fertile lands with plenty of water. The Indians received them peacefully and the terrain appeared passable for wagons.

Anza's troubles were by no means over when he reached California. The missions, suffering grievous famine, could spare few animals or supplies for Anza. He therefore gave up hope of leading his party to Monterey and exploring from there a direct route back to Tubac or

Altar. Fray Garcés led most of the party back to the Colorado-Gila junction in April, while Anza made a hasty reconnaissance trip to Monterey with four of his men. Garcés reached the Colorado on April 26, 1774; Anza arrived two weeks later on May 10.

Palma had the promised rafts ready to help them cross the swollen river. To his great distress, the men whom Anza had left in his camp had returned to Altar after hearing a rumor that Anza's party had been killed by Indians. Chief Palma handed over to Anza all the provisions and the other livestock that had been entrusted to him, all in good condition and increased by several new calves.

More impressed than ever with Palma's reliability and his zeal for the king's service, Anza expressed his appreciation as best he could with words and gifts. When they parted, Palma assured the captain once more of his own life-long devotion and that of his people to the king of Spain. Anza reminded him again of the king's desire that all his Indian children live at peace with each other.

Anza rode back to Tubac by way of the Gila River, a more direct route along which he wished to work for peace among the warring tribes. He found residential patterns changing in response to increasing Apache raids. More and more the scattered farmers were drawing together in large villages to defend themselves against Apaches.

Anza reached Tubac on May 26, 1774. He had expected to proceed at once to Mexico City to report to the viceroy as his orders specified, but, to his dismay, the new jurisdiction of commandant inspector intervened. Adjutant Inspector Bonilla was at Tubac, making the required inspection for O'Conor. Finding the affairs of Tubac in their usual excellent order, he required its competent commander to proceed to Terrenate to take temporary charge of a presidio where mismanagement and abuse had driven the troops to riot. He forbade Anza to leave that post until the arrival of a replacement, regardless of the fact that Anza already had the viceroy's instruction to travel to the capital to report on his important discovery. When Bucareli discovered the situation in August, he was infuriated and demanded immediate relief for Anza. Even so, it was November before Anza could reach the capital and hand his diary to the viceroy.

The rewards were prompt and generous: for Anza, promotion to lieutenant colonel; for each of the soldiers who had accompanied him, a life-long bonus of one escudo of extra pay each month. Hoping that the example might stir other Spaniards to heroic contributions toward the consolidation and development of strategic frontiers, the viceroy ordered Commandant Inspector O'Conor to publicize the matter widely among the troops.

Bucareli had already decided that a successful exploration should be followed immediately by an overland colonization venture. Anza heartily concurred and within four days formulated a detailed plan of action. The viceroy desired Anza to explore the area around San Francisco Bay and to found there a presidial colony and two missions. He authorized Anza to take thirty married soldiers (ten veterans and twenty recruits) with their families to found the presidio at San Francisco. Anza suggested, and Bucareli appointed, Don José Joaquín Moraga, an officer of Fronteras with eighteen years' distinguished service behind him, to serve as second-in-command on the expedition and then as commandant of the new presidio. The colonists would be paid in equipment. Anza would be responsible for driving a herd of cattle and horses to provide foundation stock for the new settlements.

Anza proposed as his escort ten soldiers from Tubac, all veterans of his first expedition, so that he could be certain of knowledgeable, reliable soldiers to deal with the Indians. He would need tobacco and beads for gifts to the Indians and, for Chief Palma, a special suit, cloak, and hat.

Fray Pedro Font was appointed to accompany Anza all the way, in order to take scientific observations of latitudes. Fray Garcés would accompany the party as far as the Colorado and await them there, meanwhile cultivating friendship and peace among the Indians of that region. Bucareli, delighted that the Yumas had asked for missions, was eager to help Fray Garcés further that purpose.

Armed with assurances of the viceroy's fullest support, Anza hurried home to Sonora to recruit colonists and assemble supplies. He hoped to be ready by September 1775, but again Apache raiders spoiled his plans. Early in September, as Anza marshalled his colonists to depart from Horcasitas, Apaches ran off the entire Tubac horse herd, some five hundred animals all told, and left the garrison afoot. A stampede at Horcasitas cost Anza still more horses and mules. Anza had at last to set out from Tubac a month late, with too few, sadly inferior replacement mounts scrounged from every available source. Nevertheless, he led his entire group to Monterey with just one casualty: a soldier's wife died in childbirth on the first day out. Of the 240 persons, many were women and children of the soldiers' families; 8 babies were born along the way. A herd of 1,050 domestic animals further complicated the march.

Anza chose the Gila route, trusting that the Pimas would help in any necessary defense against the Apaches. As he approached the Pima lands, he issued an order forbidding every Spaniard to steal from the natives, molest their women, raise arms against them except in defense of life, or do anything whatsoever to diminish their loyalty to God or the king. Fray Font backed him up with a vigorous sermon on the same theme. Both the colonel and the missionary knew all too well how often Spaniards provoked trouble by thoughtless abuse of Indians.

Pima headmen greeted Anza with a gift: two fresh Apache scalps, taken just the day before. Fray Font, seeing the Pimas of the Gila River for the first time, agreed with Fray Garcés that they were prime mission prospects. Anza was loath to establish missions for them because of the Apache menace. Fray Font thought the missions very desirable but agreed that they would be a mistake unless a strong presidio could be established to protect them. The Pimas were a gentle people, already good farmers and accustomed to fixed settlements. They had seen little of Spaniards, but they had already adopted several Spanish imports besides horses. Wheat had become an important crop among them; they raised "Castilian hens" and sheep, and they spun and wove wool.

The expedition brought disappointment to Chief Palma, who had grown quite obsessed with the idea of having his people Christianized and bringing Spaniards and friars to live among them. When he heard of the approaching caravan, he hoped they had come to settle in his lands. When that hope proved false, Chief Palma insisted that he would go to Mexico City with Anza upon the colonel's return, to appeal in person to the viceroy. Fray Font counseled with the chief long and earnestly to make sure that Palma understood the obligations involved in conversion: to learn the catechism, masonry, carpentry, and farming; to live in fixed towns; and to build a church and a convent. Palma cheerfully agreed to all those conditions. Anza promised him all possible help to realize his dream.

The expedition crossed the Colorado on November 30; they rode into Mission San Gabriel in California on January 4, 1776. Anza immediately had to lead seventeen of his men to San Diego to help quell an Indian rebellion that threatened to destroy the province. The revolt was quickly suppressed, but afterward the commanding officer in California, Captain Fernando de Rivera y Moncada, refused to support Anza in his primary purpose at San Francisco Bay. Anza waited three weeks at San Diego for Rivera to act, then proceeded independently.

After moving his colonists from San Gabriel to Monterey, he took a dozen men north with him to explore around San Francisco Bay late in March. He pinpointed the presidio and mission sites and located timber and other necessary resources nearby. However, because of Captain Rivera's unwillingness to furnish support that spring, the actual establishment of the colony at San Francisco Bay was deferred until July 1776. Anza rode back to Monterey to bid the colonists goodbye, turned their command over to Moraga, and hurried home to Sonora. By early summer he was on his way to Mexico City.

The failure to establish the colony at San Francisco Bay exasperated Bucareli, who rebuked both Rivera and Anza for intransigence in failing to resolve their differences. The dispute left in its wake a residue of hostility toward Anza that would cost him heavily in the next decade.

As before, the success of Anza's trip had hinged upon the cooperation of the Yumas. He found the Colorado in late spring floodtide. Only Yuma rafts and swimmers, sometimes as many as two hundred men in the river at one time, made it possible for Anza and his escort party and their effects to cross the river. Anza emphasized the point in his report, though he had made it before: if the Indians who lived on the Colorado River were attached to Spaniards, the crossing would be possible without excessive labor; if they should ever be opposed, or even indifferent, the crossing would be virtually impossible. Chief Palma had earned any reward he desired, and his utmost desire was to visit the viceroy to request baptism for himself and missions for his people.

Anza asked what would happen among the Yumas if Palma should be gone for a year. He found that they favored the trip and that Palma had already designated two responsible men to lead them during his absence. Anza then agreed to take Chief Palma, his brother, and the son of Chief Pablo. He also took an adventurous Cajuenche lad, Pedro, who had long wanted to see Mexico City. The Yumas bade them a cheerful goodbye, urging them to return with friars and Spaniards.

The party reached Mexico City late in October 1776, after Bucareli knew of the creation of the Provincias Internas, but before Croix arrived to take command. The viceroy was delighted to receive Chief Palma and his company; he appreciated fully the Yumas' important role in the success of Anza's two expeditions and the necessity for their continued cooperation. Colonel Anza, true to his promise to Chief Palma, urged Bucareli to establish missions and a presidio among the Yumas. Palma himself asked the viceroy to let him be baptized in the capital city and to send missions to his people. Bucareli promptly arranged for the appropriate religious instruction for the four visitors.

For the next four months the viceroy entertained the quartet as his distinguished guests. Lieutenant Colonel Anza watched closely over their welfare all the while and stood sponsor and godfather when Chief Palma was baptized in the cathedral on February 13, 1777. Henceforth, he would be Salvador Carlos (for the king) Antonio (for the viceroy), called Salvador Palma. Anza called upon kinsmen to sponsor the other two Yumas. Don Marcelo de Ansa served by proxy as godfather to Joseph Antonio Marcelo; Don Pedro de Ansa stood godfather to Ygnacio Joseph. For young Pedro, Mexico City Regidor Don Juan Lucas Lasaga stood godfather. They had a splendid ceremony in the cathedral. The viceroy had fine new suits made at the king's expense for all four, justifying the outlay on grounds of the great benefits expected from their conversion.[4]

In the very week of the baptism, the king ruled favorably on the chief's petition.[5] No one could then have guessed how late and how little would be the action upon Salvador Palma's desires, or how far Spanish performance on his frontier would diverge from the benevolent intent of the king. Discussions of the proposed mission and presidio for the Yumas and another for the Gila Pimas had been underway for two years, and there was substantial agreement among those who knew the situation best. Garcés had suggested that the presidios of Horcasitas and Buenavista be moved to the Colorado and Gila rivers to guard the new mission enterprises. O'Conor had concurred. Now Anza endorsed the idea with detailed supporting arguments.

Anza recommended the village of Salvador Palma as the best site on the Colorado for one presidio and two large contiguous Pima settlements on the Gila as the place for the other. At both sites the lands were fertile, water plentiful, and irrigation readily feasible; scant pasture for livestock would be the sole problem. However, Anza warned that the Pimas were so close to the Apaches that they saw their smokes every day; he speculated that it might be safer to bypass the Pima locality in favor of another site farther up the Colorado toward the Hopis, among the Jalchedunes or the Jamajáes. Those he identified

---

[4] Bucareli to Gálvez, Mexico, February 24, 1777, in Bolton, *Anza's California Expeditions*, V, 411–412.
[5] Gálvez to Bucareli, Madrid, February 10, 1777, ibid., p. 401.

as Apache groups whom Palma had promised to win over to alliance
with the Spaniards. They had for some time been friends and allies of
the Yumas, and some of them had already requested a Spanish
presence.[6]

Palma had made that promise in a memorial that he presented, with
Anza's help, to the viceroy on November 11, 1776. He listed peoples
whom he could draw into alliance with the Spaniards if needed: Jalchedunes, Jamajáes or Soyopas, Pimas, Opas, Cocomarícopas, Cajuenes,
Jaliquamas, Cucupas, Comeías, Pápagos, and "part of the Apaches
who live on the opposite bank of the Colorado River and who do not
communicate with those of the other bank, some because of enmity,
others for the fear which my victories have inspired in them." Palma
went on to claim that "this alliance, together with the establishment in
my country, would not only keep the roads secure for the Spaniards, and
keep free mutual communication between California and Sonora, San
Francisco and New Mexico, because they will be situated in the center
of these provinces, but also, aided by the arms of the Spaniards, we
could serve to advantage in the pacification of the neighboring kingdoms."[7] Clearly, Colonel Anza stinted no effort to help Palma persuade
the viceroy to his cause.

Anza submitted good arguments to the viceroy over his own signature, too: the fertility of the land, the extraordinary docility and good
nature of the Yumas, and Palma's remarkable helpfulness. However,
he explicitly warned that the Spaniards must take great care to maintain that good disposition, and he particularly cautioned against certain
errors committed in earlier instances:

. . . the severity and force which has been used in other reductions, excessive
labor in the fields, and other tasks which are demanded of them at the
beginning of their conversion, causes sufficient to exasperate the first generation and make them inculcate in their children this feeling of exasperation,
which often becomes hereditary in all, when by opposite means we may win
them to this very thing that we wish, and especially by their Christian instruction in civil life. . . . extreme patience and compassion are necessary. Ordinarily
these are not possessed by men who do not understand their qualities, and it
so happens that for an indifferent word or deed an Indian is punished. He
does not fail to recognize our unreasonableness, and since he cannot avenge
himself alone he may suggest it to others, from which arises the loss of many
persons, or even a rebellion.[8]

[6] Anza to Bucareli, Mexico, November 20, 1776, ibid., p. 383.
[7] Palma's Memorial, Mexico, November 11, 1776, ibid., p. 375.
[8] Anza to Bucareli, Mexico, November 20, 1776, ibid., p. 385.

One of the common mistakes that Anza wished to avoid was immediate imposition upon prospective converts of the many unaccustomed labors required to establish a mission community. Why not take laborers from the Sonoran interior and rely upon them to instruct neophytes as well as to perform the necessary labors? Anza particularly recommended employment of Pápagos and other Indians of northerly origin who had for many years lived at the Spanish settlements, sometimes as slaves, sometimes as voluntary members of mission communities. Already Christian and Spanish-speaking, they could interpret religion and custom as well as language. Anza suggested that the viceroy free all of them to return to their own country and that he encourage Spanish families to volunteer for the Colorado and Gila projects.

Colonel Anza also warned against any dependence upon the natives' crops, another blunder that had estranged more than one Indian group. Even with fertile river lands and industrious Indians, primitive stick farming produced so little that the Spaniards ought to count themselves lucky if the Indians could support themselves. Anza wanted the Spaniards to take adequate supplies with them and promptly plant crops and build irrigation ditches. Not for one day should the Spaniards drain the Indians' limited subsistence.

Nor must the Colorado and Gila efforts be undermined by the lack of discipline among the Spaniards and the conflicts between the religious and secular leaders that so often undermined the interests of both Majesties. Anza urged viceregal consultation with and support of both the religious and secular commanders to prevent such difficulties.

Anza's recommendations involved no idle counsels of perfection. The qualifications that he specified for the religious and secular heads of the new establishments were obviously those of himself and Fray Garcés, already proved able to work together. Already established was the pattern of close consultation among Viceroy Bucareli, Colonel Anza, and Fray Garcés; each knew and admired Salvador Palma, whose zealous support augured so well for the venture. Anza had been promised generous rewards for his California exploits. Now he desired above all else a chance to bring to fruition all the splendid potential gains for both Majesties to which he had opened the way.

Anza hoped to create a hub of communications and commerce for a vast new surge of development. He proposed regular bimonthly overland mail service from Mexico City to Monterey and regular freight service, based on two droves of mules: one to ply the road from Sonora to the Colorado River, the other from the Colorado to Mission San Gabriel. The California market for Sonoran grain and fruit promised unprecedented prosperity for his native province. Anza wanted the Crown to let the Manila galleon stop at Monterey or San Francisco to take on supplies and unload some Oriental goods for Sonora and New Mexico. He did not doubt that the opening of commercial opportunity would attract many ambitious settlers to each of the provinces involved.

Not the least of Anza's concerns was the opportunity for Christian service. On his first two journeys he had made some headway toward curbing the frequent wars among the numerous Indian peoples of the Colorado and Gila valleys; he expected Salvador Palma's help to extend the king's peace over that vast frontier. With that peace, he hoped to see all the Indians converted. He had already discussed with Fray Francisco Palou at Mission Carmel a new chain of missions from Sonora to Mission San Gabriel. They had agreed that Fray Palou's College of San Francisco should be responsible for the missions west of the Sierra Nevada, and that those east of the Sierra should be the work of the College of Querétaro, to which Fray Garcés belonged and of which Anza was a lay brother. Anza meant to help Fray Garcés ensure that this mission frontier spread the benefits of the faith without the penalties too often inflicted by its overzealous, underinformed servants.

The very magnitude of Anza's success worked to thwart his aims. He had so completely engaged the friendship and cooperation of Salvador Palma that his superiors took for granted an easy success on the Colorado, ignoring Anza's detailed cautions to the contrary. On the other hand, full realization of the new commercial and spiritual opportunities would require both the linkage of New Mexico to Sonora and California and the solution of New Mexico's Hopi and Comanche problems. His renown as an explorer and his record of success in both war and diplomacy with Indians made Colonel Anza the obvious man for the crucial tasks in New Mexico. Sometime in 1776 Viceroy Bucareli proposed Anza for governor of New Mexico; the Crown appointed him on May 19, 1777.

The appointment of his friend and godfather to a post far distant was but one of several blows to the hopes of Salvador Palma. Viceroy Bucareli, who knew him and was so keenly interested in the mission and presidio for the Yumas and in the larger Alta California enterprise, lost jurisdiction over Palma's region in 1776. Quite understandably,

Commandant General Croix postponed new establishments among the friendly nations of the Colorado and Gila valleys to focus upon the urgent problem of *bárbaros* raiders and the imminent hazard of the British in the Mississippi Valley. Perhaps Salvador Palma and his people would have fared better if Croix could have made Anza governor of Sonora as he wished, but, even during the year that Croix kept Anza in the province as military commandant, the Seri and Opata rebellions and the incessant Apache raids kept the colonel too busy to visit the Colorado again. After that, Anza's extraordinary responsibilities in New Mexico never permitted him another chance to plead the Yumas' case.

Viceroy Bucareli had wished Anza to blaze the desired trail as he rode to New Mexico to take command of the province, going northward from Sonora as though toward Monterey, then branching northeastward at the appropriate juncture to pioneer the road to Santa Fe. Anza agreed that he could do it, but he would need sixty well-equipped soldiers for two months because the optimum route would lead right through the heart of the Apachería. Since Sonora could not spare sixty men in spring 1777, Croix adopted Anza's more practicable offer to go to Santa Fe by the usual route from Chihuahua through El Paso and subsequently organize a New Mexican expedition to Sonora.[9]

Corollary to the responsibility for opening the route from Santa Fe to Sonora and to California was that of reducing the Hopis. Tragic contradictions were no novelty in Spain's Indian policies, but none was ever more ironic than this: while his eager Yuma friends on the Colorado clamored for the benefits of vassalage to both Majesties, the Crown sent Anza to thrust those same benefits upon the reluctant Hopis.

The matter of the Hopis had loomed large throughout efforts to establish overland communications with Alta California. Fray Serra urged linkage of the two mission provinces of New Mexico and Alta California in order to consolidate the spiritual conquests of the Franciscan Order. The Hopi towns stood out as the obvious landmark and way station for such a route, just as the Hopis' long apostasy stood out as the missionaries' supreme failure.

Spanish secular authority had not intruded into the Hopi region since Governor Martínez ravaged their fields in 1716, but the missionaries had never given up entirely. Two Franciscans had visited Oraibi in

---

[9] Pedro Galindo Navarro to Croix, Arispe, July 28, 1780, in Alfred Barnaby Thomas, ed., *Forgotten Frontiers*, pp. 179–180.

the spring of 1724 in an effort to restore the Hopis to the faith, but the conspicuous breadth and depth of the Hopis' rejection of their appeal convinced the friars that there was no hope of success in the foreseeable future.[10]

The next flurry of missionary attention to the Hopis came in the 1740's, when Jesuits challenged Franciscan jurisdiction in that quarter.[11] Jesuit efforts to reach the Hopis from Sonora failed, but their attempt spurred the Franciscans of New Mexico to new activity among the Hopis. Frays Carlos Delgado and Ignacio Pino rode to the Hopi mesas in the summer of 1742 and were permitted to preach in all the towns. The Hopis themselves held fast to their leaders' rejection of the Spanish way, but the two missionaries scored a major success, bringing back to the Rio Grande 441 Indians of the groups who had fled the pueblos of Pajarito, Alameda, and Sandía during the 1680's. The friars reluctantly left behind the children and the aged members of the refugee group because they were not equipped to see them safely through the long journey, but they hoped to return later with the necessary help to harvest still more souls at those remote mesas.

Fray Delgado went back to the Hopis in the autumn of 1745 with two other missionaries and a small escort force. Again the Hopis peacefully allowed the friars to preach, but all was well in the mesatop towns that year, and there was not the new surge of conversions that Fray Delgado had anticipated. He blamed the Indians' refusal to journey back with him to the Rio Grande on the inadequate size of his military escort. Thenceforth, the missionaries eschewed efforts among the Hopis on the excuse that the governor would not give them the necessary support. When the Crown resolved the jurisdictional contest in favor of the Franciscans that year, the pressures to succeed among the Hopis receded. The New Mexican friars focused their hopes and energies instead upon a briefly promising mission field among the Navajos.

Missionaries found no further occasion to visit the Hopis until the

[10] Fray José Navares Valverde, Notes on New Mexico, Senecú, October 7, 1732, in Charles Wilson Hackett, ed., *Historical Documents Relating to New Mexico, Nueva Vizcaya, and Approaches Thereto, to 1773*, III, 385–387.

[11] Governor Gaspar Domingo de Mendoza to Fray Pedro Navarrete, Santa Fe, October 31, 1742, ibid., p. 388; Fray Ignacio Pino to Fray Pedro Navarrete, Mission of San Felipe de Albuquerque, November 16, 1742, ibid., pp. 388–389; Fray Cristóbal Yraete to Fray Pedro Navarrete, Paso del Río del Norte, November 24, 1742, ibid., pp. 389–390; Fray Carlos Delgado to Commissary General Fray Juan Fogueras, Isleta, November 15, 1745, ibid., pp. 414–415.

mid-1770's, when Viceroy Bucareli asked the Franciscan Order for all possible information about the territory between New Mexico and Sonora and California. The Order readily cooperated. Among the especially able friars asked to collect data was Fray Silvestre Vélez de Escalante, posted to the mission at Zuñi late in 1774.[12]

Opportunity to gather the desired information arose during Fray Escalante's first spring at Zuñi, when he entertained a Hopi trading party and won an invitation to visit them. Delighted, Fray Escalante hoped to win the Hopis back to the faith, then travel on to preach to the Havasupais, all the while collecting information about the Colorado River tribes and about the route to a rumored Spanish settlement far away.

Fray Escalante wanted no more company than a guide and an interpreter, but the Zuñis insisted the Hopis were untrustworthy. Seventeen Zuñis escorted him to the Hopi mesas in June 1775. A friendly reception at Walpi encouraged the friar, but he found at Oraibi a climate of chill aversion, rigorously enforced by the village headmen. He fared no better at Shongopovi, Mishongnovi, and Shipaulovi; then he returned to Walpi to find them too conforming to the policy set at Oraibi. He obtained little information from the Hopis because they were afraid to talk with him, but he managed to get some information about the lands beyond from Havasupais who visited him at Walpi despite Hopi efforts to dissuade them.

Fray Escalante's disappointment turned to horror when he saw masked kachina dancers beginning a summer ceremonial at Walpi. Convinced that he had seen the devil at work and that only forcible conquest could free the Hopis from Satan's thrall, Fray Escalante hurried back to Zuñi. Safely home on July 6, 1775, he forwarded his little bit of information about the Havasupais' territory and their speculations about possible routes to the Pacific.

That autumn Governor Mendinueta asked Fray Escalante's opinion of a scheme to conquer the Hopis and open a route between Santa Fe and Sonora. To the friar's dismay, Governor Mendinueta used his descriptive information about the Hopis but dismissed his conclusion that they could be managed only by force. Mendinueta reasoned that an unprovoked declaration of war against the peaceful Hopis would only inspire Utes and Navajos to fear a similar fate and would perhaps unite the three nations against the Spaniards. He wanted the task

[12] Eleanor B. Adams, "Fray Silvestre and the Obstinate Hopi," *New Mexico Historical Review* 38 (1963): 97–138.

of converting the Hopis and exploring the route to Monterey entrusted to three or four zealous, able missionaries, armed with presents for the Hopi leaders: precisely the approach that Escalante, having seen the Hopi villages, thought futile. Ironically, as the only recent visitor to the Hopis, Escalante seemed to authorities of Church and State an obvious choice for the job.

Mendinueta's idea that a handful of missionaries should open the route to the Pacific and subdue the Hopis appealed to higher authori-. ties on both humanitarian and economic grounds. Thus, when Fray Francisco Atanasio Domínguez rode to New Mexico to inspect the missions in the spring of 1776, he was also charged to explore the route to Monterey with Fray Escalante. In June 1776, the two missionaries met at Santa Fe to plan their probe northward and westward through Ute country, hoping thus to avoid confrontations with either Hopis or Apaches.

Before the prudent pair could mount their expedition, a more adventurous Franciscan blazed the trail from the west. Fray Garcés, dropped off at the Colorado River early in the preceding winter by Anza's California-bound caravan, had first explored extensively among the Indians of the lower Colorado, then pioneered another alternative route from the Gila-Colorado junction to Mission San Gabriel. When he inquired about routes from the Colorado River to the Hopis, Indians bound for the Hopi towns on business let him travel with them. They reached Oraibi on July 2, 1776.

The intrusion of Fray Garcés displeased the Hopis so much that they would neither talk with him nor accept his presents nor even sell him food and shelter. He had chanced upon the same ceremonial time that had so scandalized Fray Escalante a year earlier, and Hopi leaders plainly wanted him out of their pueblos. Though less shocked by pagan practice than his brother had been, Fray Garcés was thoroughly scared. The friar managed to talk with a few Zuñis and at least one Ácoma Indian whom he found visiting at Oraibi. They knew enough Spanish to tell him about the missionary at Zuñi, and one invited Fray Garcés to accompany him to Zuñi. His Yavapai guides refused to go to Zuñi, so Fray Garcés decided reluctantly that he must return with them to the Colorado. He gave one of the friendly Pueblos a letter for the missionary at Zuñi. Fray Escalante had already gone to Santa Fe to prepare for his trip with Fray Domínguez, but Zuñi runners quickly delivered the letter to the capital, where it produced something of a furor.

In effect, Fray Garcés had shown the way to link New Mexico to California and Sonora. His letter could have been an excuse to abandon the effort from Santa Fe, but Governor Mendinueta and frays Domínguez and Escalante decided that their project could still be useful. Fray Garcés' unfriendly reception at Oraibi confirmed Fray Escalante's opinion that the Hopis would not be helpful to Spaniards crossing their country; an alternative route was therefore desirable. Even if frays Domínguez and Escalante could not reach Monterey, they could collect valuable information about the lands and peoples to the north. They could return by way of the Havasupais to confirm that nation's interest in conversion, bypassing the Hopi interference that had so long barred extension of the New Mexican mission enterprise to the Havasupais.

Far less modest were the hopes of their companion, retired Captain Bernardo Miera y Pacheco of Santa Fe, a talented engineer and artist who volunteered his services as map maker and scientific observer. If the aging Captain Miera were ever to have a chance of fame and fortune, it lay in this trip to Monterey. He was not interested in results short of that goal, however pious.

The other seven members of the party had smaller ambitions: the chance to do a bit of profitable trading in the Ute country and perhaps a stake in any mineral or other valuable resources that the party might discover. Fray Escalante was annoyed to find them prepared to trade with the Indians and tried, unsuccessfully, to prevent it. He wanted the Indians to know Spaniards who did not live for material goals but only for the glory of God and the salvation of souls. He was also particularly concerned that the Indians not think this exploring party foreshadowed conquest.

Fray Domínguez headed the party; Fray Escalante served as diarist.[13] They left Santa Fe on July 29, 1776, several weeks later than they had hoped because Comanche raiders had struck the province in June. The Comanche menace shadowed their journey through the Ute territories. Sabuaguana Utes on the North Fork of the Gunnison River tried to persuade them that Comanches would make their journey impossible. The two friars shrugged off the advice, expressing serene confidence that their God would protect them against all enemies. The Utes were awed by the potent magic they seemed to possess.

[13] See the Escalante diary, translated in Herbert Eugene Bolton, *Pageant in the Wilderness*, with introductory analysis by Bolton.

The Sabuaguanas were at war that summer with the Yamparica Comanches whose territories lay beyond the Green River. A Ute just back from a horse-stealing foray against the Yamparicas said they had moved eastward, perhaps to the Arkansas River, but their raiders still struck westward into present Utah. Comanche pressures had lately forced many Utes westward from the Uintas Mountains to make new homes in the Utah Lake Valley, near present Provo. Those Utes urged the Spaniards to come live among them and make common cause with them against the Comanches.

The mission to the Utes got off to a shaky start because the friars relied upon the interpretive services of an old Spanish trader who was terrified by Comanche signs in Sabuaguana territory and did not want to court double jeopardy by antagonizing the Ute hosts. He trimmed the friars' message to his purpose: "The Father says that the Apaches, Navajos, and Cumanches who do not become baptized cannot enter Heaven, but go to Hell, where God punishes them, and where they will burn forever like wood in the fire."[14]

The Ute listeners were so manifestly delighted to hear a dire fate predicted for their enemies that the friars suspected the interpreter had failed to convey that Utes, too, must choose between baptism and eternal fire. Cross-examination confirmed their suspicions. A severe reprimand to the interpreter and utmost vigilance on their part kept the theology in a more conventional vein after that.

The prime mission potential lay in the Utah Valley, where the fugitive Utes so feared the Comanches that they no longer ventured forth to hunt buffalo. With their old patterns of life so badly disrupted, they liked the idea of Spaniards coming to live with them and teaching them to plant crops and raise cattle and build permanent houses. Fray Domínguez promised that the king would provide them all those things if they wished to be Christians because he would consider them his children.[15]

The Utes agreed: if the fathers would come to live with them and teach them, the Utes would let them build their houses wherever they pleased. They would watch out for Comanche intrusions, so that the Spaniards and Utes could all go out together to punish the invaders. The fathers promised to return soon with more Spaniards and missionaries and exacted the Utes' promise to be good meanwhile.

A. Ute emissary from the lake region volunteered to go to Santa Fe

[14] Escalante, Diary, ibid., p. 215.
[15] Ibid., p. 180.

with the friars to plead his people's case to the governor. The chiefs handed to the friars a buckskin painted with their message to the Spanish leaders. Earth and red ochre outlined the figures of the four leaders, with a cross above each to signify their desire for conversion. The figure with the most red symbolized the head chief, who had shed the most blood in encounters with the Comanches; two lesser chiefs were painted with less red; one with no red at all represented a leader who had won influence by some avenue other than war.

The two Franciscans, moved to see such zeal for Christianity, grieved over leaving those Utes without ministers or physical protection. They did their best for them by teaching them "Jesús María! Jesús María!" to invoke divine protection in case of trouble with sickness or enemies, and they resolved to hurry back to them within the year.

Anxiety for the Utes' welfare was a prime factor in the decision not to push on to Monterey. Having found among the Utes no knowledge of the Spaniards in California or of the visit of Fray Garcés to the Havasupais and Hopis, they concluded that those people had no communication with the Pacific coast. Snowstorms in late September reminded them of the grim risks of a winter attempt to cross the Sierra Nevada. Even if they should survive, their promised missions for the Utes would be intolerably delayed. The two friars were determined not to fail those "miserable little lambs of Christ who had strayed only for lack of The Light."[16]

Captain Miera contended furiously that the priests were robbing him by refusing to push on to Monterey and persuaded the other six laymen to that point of view. The friars stood firm through a chill week of argument and prayer, snow, hail, and rain. They would turn back to New Mexico by way of the Havasupais, Hopis, and Zuñi.

Bad weather plagued them much of the way. The party reached Oraibi in mid-November, hungry and exhausted, to face angry, suspicious Hopis. However, the headman ordered them lodged for the night and let them buy provisions, and he notified the other Hopi pueblos to extend the same courtesies. The Hopis now wished friendship with the Spaniards, but they would risk no involvement with Christianity.

Lacking an interpreter of Hopi, the Spaniards could not learn the reason for the friendlier attitude until they reached the Tano refugees at Walpi. Their leader, an elderly apostate from Galisteo called Pedro,

16 Ibid., p. 192.

had received Fray Escalante courteously the year before. Now he explained that the Hopis were suffering a fierce onslaught by Navajos, who had already killed and captured many of their people. They were glad to see Spanish visitors through whom they might beg the governor's intercession against the Navajos. Pedro himself offered to accompany the two friars to Santa Fe to negotiate an alliance on behalf of the Hopis and Tanos. Frays Domínguez and Escalante responded that they would gladly use their good offices with the governor but that each of the six pueblos must send an authorized spokesman to the governor.

Pedro called all the leaders to a kiva in his pueblo to talk with the friars. An apostate from Santa Clara, more fluent in Castilian, translated the friars' remarks into Tewa; Pedro then translated them into Hopi. At once they reached an impasse: the friars said the Indians could get help only by turning to Christianity; the Hopis balked. They advanced three arguments against conversion: they did not wish to submit to Spanish authority; heathen nations were much more numerous than Christian nations, and they wished to follow the path of the more numerous; and they lived in country very inconveniently placed for rendition of the obligations that Spaniards required of converted Indians. The friars remained adamant: no conversion, no help.

After long deliberation, the Hopi leaders decided they would rather suffer their current troubles than violate their ancestral traditions. They also decided not to send Pedro to Santa Fe, lest the governor forcibly detain him as an apostate. The friars, baffled, pushed on to Zuñi, where they rested three weeks. Then they rode on to the capital, pausing for Christmas at Isleta, and reported to Santa Fe on January 2, 1777. They introduced their Ute companion to the governor and handed over the buckskin petition of his compatriots.

Summarizing his observations of the Utes, Fray Escalante compared them to a kingdom divided into five provinces: Muhuachis, Payuchis, Tabehuachis, Sabuaguanis, and Cobardes. The last were further subdivided into Huascaris, Parusis, Yabuincariris, Ytampabichis, and Pagampachis. He had heard of, but had not seen, a Ute group called Payatammumis and others whose names he did not record. Most important was the fact that he and Fray Domínguez had found many Utes eager for baptism and that they had promised to return to the Ute territories. The friars did not doubt the feasibility of the project. Given the fertility of the land, the practicability of irrigation around the lake, and its abundance of fish, they believed the area could support at least as many pueblos as were in New Mexico. Neither man asked any better opportunity for service than to gather all those docile Utes into pueblos, thus saving their souls and warding off the earthly perils of Comanches and starvation.

Governor Mendinueta was taken aback to hear Franciscans talk of expanding mission commitments. Pueblo missions in New Mexico stood priestless because of the Order's alleged shortage of friars and material resources. The governor had no more authority to underwrite missions for the Utes than the zealous friars had to promise them. Nor was the winter of 1776–1777 any time for bold initiatives. Governor Mendinueta, long overdue for retirement, awaited his replacement; in Mexico City, Commandant General Croix was just assuming responsibility for the newly created Provincias Internas. The Franciscan Order had ample administrative work for both Fray Domínguez and Fray Escalante, and officials of the Provincias Internas soon required the scholarly services of Fray Escalante to investigate its historical roots. Far northwest of Santa Fe, the Utes saw the summer of 1777 pass, and the next, and the next, with no sign of the promised fathers and Spaniards.

The Ute project had just one persistent advocate. Captain Miera had not relinquished his ambitions, despite his anger and frustration at the friars' refusal to push on to California. He rode down to Chihuahua to propose three new settlements and three new presidios to consolidate Spanish control of the region between Sonora, New Mexico, and California, with a presidio and settlement at the lake of the Utes given first priority.[17] He wanted another presidio and settlement on the San Juan River in the present Four Corners area, long thought by Spanish explorers to have considerable mineral potential. To that location he proposed the forcible transplantation of the Hopis, whose notable industry and skills could form the basis of economic development. The third presidio and settlement that he deemed necessary would be at the junction of the Gila and Colorado rivers, to subdue the Gila Apaches, protect the converted tribes of the region, and serve as a way station on the route from Sonora to California and New Mexico. That was the command he asked for himself. He proposed to cooperate with forces in Sonora, New Mexico, and Nueva Vizcaya to drive the Gila Apaches eastward to the Buffalo Plains, there to let them grapple with Comanches in a war of mutual extermination.

[17] Miera y Pacheco to the King, Chihuahua, October 26, 1777, ibid., pp. 243–246.

It was as bold a plan as any frontier officer had ever advanced, and it had the unusual merit that its author had some first-hand acquaintance with all the lands and peoples involved. Its fate hinged first of all upon convincing Commandant General Croix. Captain Miera settled down at Chihuahua in the autumn of 1777 to await an opportunity to present his argument to Croix in person, quite unaware that better placed planners in Mexico City had preempted the topic earlier in the year.

Early in 1777, Governor Mendinueta had forwarded to the commandant general Fray Escalante's diary of the expedition, with its proposal for a vast new mission enterprise among the Utes. Croix, then engaged in his preliminary survey of all the problems of the Provincias Internas, requested the opinion of his secretary, the scholarly Franciscan Fray Juan Morfi. By mid-summer that priest submitted a detailed analysis that Croix found quite convincing.[18]

While Fray Morfi applauded the zeal of his colleagues, he thought they had exercised poor judgment in striking northwest rather than directly west toward Monterey and worse judgment in giving many strange Indians promises that had little practicable hope of fulfillment. For the foreseeable future, all available men and resources would be needed to pacify the northern frontier. Until the Comanche and Apache problems could be resolved, Fray Morfi suggested, the appropriate northern boundary line for the king's dominions would be the Colorado and Red rivers. The map submitted with Fray Escalante's diary indicated that the sources of the Colorado, Rio Grande, and Red rivers lay within forty miles of each other in the mountains north of Santa Fe. They appeared to embrace an area of great fertility, which Morfi thought should be colonized from the central base point of Chihuahua.

To pave the way for such a program, Morfi suggested that Anza route his forthcoming journey from Sonora to New Mexico along the north bank of the Colorado, to rendezvous with Fray Escalante at the territory of the Sabuaguana Utes. On his way to meet Anza, Fray Escalante should explore the upper reaches of the Colorado, Red, and Rio Grande rivers. They should then proceed together to Santa Fe by way of the Hopi and Navajo territories, making careful observations and noting good sites, with a view to ultimate conquest. Morfi thought a line of presidios along the Colorado would be necessary to protect the route from Santa Fe to Monterey.

[18] Morfi, Memorial (undated, but probably of July 1777), quoted in Chapman, *Founding of Spanish California*, pp. 398–402.

Morfi realized that expansion and development would never progress beyond speculation as long as Apaches and Comanches warred upon the Spanish frontier, but he hoped that Anza might win the Comanches to alliance with the Spaniards in order to wipe out the Apaches. A Comanche alliance would also open the way to exploration of the Red River, preferably by some religious so as to spare the Crown any expense. Morfi understood the Red to be a very large river near its source, so large that some Louisiana deserters to New Mexico claimed they had sailed on it. Perhaps it would become possible to implement the ambitious suggestion of Fray Garcés that supplies for Spanish establishments on the northern frontier from Santa Fe eastward be shipped by way of the Atlantic and the Red River and those for the western sector shipped by way of the Pacific and the Colorado.

Meanwhile, pending resolution of the Comanche and Apache problems, Fray Morfi thought it would be unnecessary to establish the proposed presidio and settlement at the junction of the Colorado and the Gila, regardless of the king's interest and the promises made to Salvador Palma. Salvador Palma would presumably lead most warriors in the region to participate in Croix's grand campaign against the Apaches, so few men would remain. Morfi expected that Fray Garcés and one other missionary would suffice to minister to the Yumas and their neighbors and to keep the numerous rival tribes at peace.

Croix, groping among a welter of unfamiliar problems, thought Morfi's analysis sensible, but he postponed any firm decision, pending consultation with Viceroy Bucareli, Colonel Anza, Governor Mendinueta, and frays Garcés, Escalante, and Domínguez. At best, there lay in store for both Utes and Yumas a long, incomprehensible wait before they could welcome the promised Spaniards to their homelands. If Morfi's recommendations should prevail, the Utes would never see them at all. Oddly, Morfi failed to apply to the Yuma problem the same principle by which he criticized the Domínguez-Escalante approach to the Utes: that serious consequences were apt to occur when nothing came of promises made to Indians about gifts and friendship.

Everything that Croix learned during his eight months of investigation at Mexico City, his subsequent tours of inspection, and his councils at Monclova, San Antonio, and Chihuahua supported Fray Morfi's conclusion that the best, perhaps the only, key to the health of the Provincias Internas lay in rapprochement with the Comanches. Thus, when Anza set out from Chihuahua late in the summer of 1778 to take command at Santa Fe, Croix's instructions to him emphasized first the importance of peace with the Comanches and, only second, the establishment of communication with Sonora and California and the reduction of the Hopis.

Fortunately, Croix had glimpsed the magnitude of New Mexico's problems through his consultations with retiring Governor Mendinueta. He gave Anza a set of minimum objectives as well as the ideal goals earlier adopted at Mexico City and Madrid. After a year on the frontier, a sadder and wiser Croix required only that Anza lessen the frequency of Comanche incursions in New Mexico, that he keep the Utes faithful to their alliance with the Spaniards, and that he deter the Navajos from siding openly with Apaches against Spaniards.[19]

Anza, for whom the northern frontier held few surprises, showed no sign of discouragement as he took command of the beleaguered province. En route to Santa Fe he reformed El Paso's four straggling militia companies into two with government equipment, placing forty-six Spaniards and thirty Indians in the one, forty-seven Spaniards and thirty Indians in the other. Continuing northward, Anza judged Socorro preferable to Robledo for the outpost recommended by Rubí, but Croix soon concluded that his limited resources ruled out any new establishment in New Mexico and that the province would be safer with the Santa Fe garrison and the El Paso militia undivided.[20]

That proved a good decision. Anza needed every man he could muster in the heart of the province. New Mexico's situation had deteriorated pitifully since Governor Mendinueta left in March. That summer Comanches had ravaged the province virtually unopposed by the scattered settlers; in one sweep they had killed or captured 127 persons.[21] The little village of Tomé, where Comanches had massacred 21 settlers on May 26, 1777, saw another 30 slaughtered when Comanches struck again on June 3, 1778.[22]

Anza lost no time compelling his constituents to the sensible concentration by which Pueblos had survived for centuries. Governor Mendinueta had long attributed much of New Mexico's suffering to the settlers' stubborn attachment to dispersed homesteads, but he had felt

[19] Croix, General Report of 1781, in Alfred Barnaby Thomas, ed., *Teodoro de Croix and the Northern Frontier of New Spain, 1776–1783*, p. 114.

[20] Alfred Barnaby Thomas, ed., "Antonio de Bonilla and Spanish Plans for the Defense of New Mexico," in *New Spain and the Anglo-American West*, I, 183–209; Croix, General Report of 1781, in Thomas, *Teodoro de Croix*, p. 107.

[21] Thomas, *Teodoro de Croix*, p. 111.

[22] Francisco Atanasio Domínguez, *The Missions of New Mexico, 1776*, trans. and ed. Eleanor B. Adams and Angelico Chávez, p. 154.

that only strong viceregal action could ever coerce the unruly New Mexicans into defensible compounds, even to save their lives. Governor Anza came armed with the agreement of Croix's Chihuahua council that the New Mexicans must bow to strategic necessities because there was an empire at stake as well as their own scalps. Brooking no nonsense, he methodically set about collecting the populace in walled towns with towers for their defense, and at least fifty families in each town. In 1779, the forceful governor consolidated around a plaza the straggling settlement of Albuquerque, now the frequent target of Comanche attacks as well as sporadic Apache raids, and he improved fortifications at Taos, closest of all to the Comanche frontier.[23]

Anza knew that improved defenses at New Mexican settlements were at best only half a solution to the problem of raids. He also needed to strike decisively into enemy territory during the raiding season, to make warriors think twice about leaving their own families unprotected to pursue glory and booty in New Mexico. Anza's wide renown as a great war captain helped him to rally forces. From the beginning of his term, Ute leaders begged him to let their warriors join any campaign he might wage against the Comanches. The settlers' enthusiasm revived, too, partly because improved protection for their families made it easier for militiamen to leave home during the raiding season and partly because the vigorous Anza simply would not brook the hopeless, helpless mood wrought by Cuerno Verde's vendetta.

Taos was the obvious, and therefore most often used, base for forays into the Comanchería; a north-northeasterly line from Taos to the Arkansas River was the obvious route. To surprise the Comanches, Anza avoided both. He rode from Santa Fe to Pojoaque on Sunday afternoon, August 15, 1779, and the next afternoon reviewed his assembled forces in a wood near San Juan pueblo.

They were a mixed lot. The hundred veteran soldiers of the Santa Fe garrison, adequately armed and provisioned for a forty-day campaign, had three horses per man. In contrast, the 203 militiamen and 259 Indians reflected the poverty and wretched helplessness of most New Mexicans. The best equipped turned up with two horses, but most of those were in such poor shape that they were practically useless. Their guns were as bad, and few had as many as three charges of powder.

---

[23] Morfi, Geographical Description of New Mexico . . . 1782, in Thomas, *Forgotten Frontiers*, p. 101; Anza, Diary of the expedition against the Comanche nation, Santa Fe, September 10, 1779, ibid., pp. 138–139.

Anza supplied the neediest with good horses from the presidial horse herd and issued working guns and ten ball cartridge belts to all. He formed three divisions of roughly 200 each, placing the vanguard under his own command and two others under the first and second lieutenants of the presidial garrison.

They crossed the Rio Grande a little after dawn on August 17, then rode north-northwest to camp overnight at Ojo Caliente, where the first great Cuerno Verde had fallen to settlers' bullets on October 30, 1768. That victory had proved costly: the settlement lay deserted now, testimony to the merciless vendetta that the second Cuerno Verde still waged for his dead father. That night, as Anza's forces camped among the ghosts of Ojo Caliente, Cuerno Verde camped far to the northeast with a big war party that he had summoned for a new attack upon Taos.

Two hundred Utes and Apaches, led by their principal chiefs, joined Anza's force on Conejos Creek, not far north of the present Colorado–New Mexico line. They readily accepted Anza's stipulation that they must obey his orders and divide equally with his men all spoils except personal captures.

The march had been northwest and north, but on August 21 Anza angled northeastward toward the Sangre de Cristo Mountains, moving by night lest the enemy spot the clouds of dust raised by more than a thousand horses. The force crossed the Rio Grande near present Alamosa on August 23, then skirted north around Pike's Peak. On August 24, the Utes proudly showed Anza the corpses of their dozen Comanche victims, rotting where they had fallen in July. Apparently their kinsmen had not discovered their fate, so the Utes had escaped vengeance. Anza wished much more to see live Comanches, but his many scouts found no sign until the last day of August.

That morning a large Comanche *ranchería* reached Fountain Creek. They began, not far upstream from present Pueblo, setting up camp at a spot reconnoitered at dawn by one of Anza's scouts, now manning a lookout post nearby. He sent a runner to Anza when dust clouds heralded several hundred enemy, so Anza knew of their approach by midmorning. Leaving two hundred guards with the horse herd and baggage train, he led the rest of his men as quietly and quickly as possible toward the enemy.

The banks of Fountain Creek hummed with the routine of pitching camp; before noon more than 120 tipi frames were up. The group happily claimed the choicest campsites, their prize for being the first *ran-*

chería at the stream to which Cuerno Verde had called his followers. All the rest were on the way to camp there, to welcome Cuerno Verde's war party back from New Mexico, and to help them celebrate a new triumph of vengeance.

Shortly after their arrival, four Comanches noticed the trail of Anza's scout, followed it almost to his lookout, then hurried back to warn their people that they were observed. They began at once to strike tipis and round up horses. The scout rushed to tell Anza that the enemy were about to flee.

There was neither time to surround the enemy as planned nor any way to approach stealthily on a plain blazing in noonday sun. Anza charged. The enemy were already mounted, even women and children, so they fled at once. The attackers pursued for eight miles, relentlessly gaining, until the rearguard wheeled to confront them. A running battle lasted another three miles. Eighteen of the bravest Comanches died; countless more were wounded; thirty-four women and children fell captive. The escaping Comanches lost all they owned except the horses they rode to safety.

Given the dust and confusion and the speed with which the Comanches scattered, it was impossible to know how many had escaped. Anza counted more than 120 tipi frames at the campsite and reckoned that six to eight warriors lived in each. (Half a dozen years would pass before he or any other Spaniard would learn that estimate to be twice the norm.) He spent five hours trying to learn from the thirty-four prisoners where to find the rest of their *rancherías*. The last two interrogated told him at nine o'clock that night that many other *rancherías* were converging upon the stream to meet Cuerno Verde. Since those who had escaped that day would warn all the rest, Anza relinquished all hope of finding other camps. He decided to turn back toward New Mexico and try to meet Cuerno Verde. With luck, he could administer swift retribution for any crimes committed in New Mexico and could perhaps rescue any captives whom the Comanches were carrying from the province.

Anza's party gladly turned back with their booty: more than five hundred horses and more goods than a hundred pack animals could carry, divided equally among all participants. After a night's vigilance against any possible return by the enemy, they started downstream early in the morning. By mid-morning they found the trail Cuerno Verde had ridden to New Mexico. Anza ordered advance scouts to cover the terrain to the right and left and thenceforth followed the trail of Cuerno Verde.

That same morning Cuerno Verde led his war party out of the Taos Valley, back toward the rendezvous on Fountain Creek, bearing sad news: the people gathered to celebrate victory would have to mourn instead. At twilight on August 31, just a few hours after his followers on Fountain Creek fled Anza's attack, Cuerno Verde suffered an unhappy surprise at Taos. Six days earlier Apaches had warned the *alcalde mayor* to expect a big Comanche raid. The *alcalde* sent runners to alert the rest of the province, stationed lookouts at all the usual Comanche routes, and organized the Taoseños to make the most of the defenses lately improved under Anza's prodding. The improvised seven-cornered compound of 1770 had been replaced by a square stockade with triangular towers on the corners. There all the people of Taos gathered on the night of August 30, when scouts' fires signaled the Comanches' approach.

Cuerno Verde led his 250 warriors in a twilight attack upon the pueblo and scored nothing. The war party fell back, obviously surprised by the new defenses. The *alcalde* then boldly sallied seventy yards from the walls with every armed man who could be spared from the stockade towers. The new turn of events so unnerved the Comanches that three were killed and many more were wounded before they retreated a safe distance to study the situation. Unable to devise a new tactic, Cuerno Verde attempted no further attack. His party vented their rage and frustration in an early morning rampage through the cornfields, then rode out of the valley on September 1.

The Comanche warriors paused that night on Culebra Creek, far north of Taos, to treat their wounded and to bury seven dead. They dug one grave for the seven, and over it they slew each man's favorite horse for his spirit to ride into the next world. Then Cuerno Verde led his men homeward over the Sangre de Cristos, straight toward confrontation with Anza.

On the morning of September 2, Anza crossed the Arkansas River and found horses identifiable as Comanche property, presumably owned by Cuerno Verde's men. Most of the Ute warriors left for home abruptly, perhaps content with the loot already won, perhaps loath to confront Cuerno Verde's big war party. Anza paused to rest his horses, then pressed southwestward toward the Sangre de Cristos.

Soon a scout reported a big Comanche force approaching, apparently unaware of the New Mexicans' presence. Anza concealed his force and waited to ambush Cuerno Verde. At sunset the Comanche vanguard rode into a narrow ravine that Anza had not had time to reconnoiter.

The Comanches met the attack of Anza's vanguard with no show of particular surprise or panic until they saw the other two columns moving to surround them; then they broke into headlong flight. Most escaped, because Anza's force bogged down in the valley in a swampy streambed of which they had not known, but eight Comanches died in the fray and many more were wounded. Anza counted himself lucky that the enemy did not regroup in the woods across the ravine while the New Mexicans floundered in the bog. He doubted that he could have gained the other side against a determined enemy stand. To the horror of his men, he camped that night beside the ravine, assuring them that he would be delighted to see the enemy return to attack. They spent a cold, rainy night under arms, without alarms. When a daylight reconnaissance turned up no sign of Comanche presence, Anza ordered his men to move out.

As the New Mexicans took the trail, fifty Comanches hove in sight. Anza deployed his forces to withstand possible attack and ordered them to continue forward. The Comanches rode toward them, firing their muskets, until they were almost within gunshot of the New Mexicans. Then a single rider burst ahead fearlessly, as though his fine pirouetting horse were winged and his elegant costume a suit of armor. His bearing announced his identity almost as plainly as the extraordinary helmet with the green horn: here was Cuerno Verde, ready for confrontation. Anza resolved to cut him down.

Perhaps Cuerno Verde was ready to end it all. A messenger had notified him of the disaster at the rendezvous on Fountain Creek, and he probably knew also of the eight killed in the previous day's action. In the last three days New Mexicans had killed no less than thirty-three of his men, captured thirty-four Comanche women and children, and seized hundreds of their horses and much of their other wealth. Many of his followers were wounded; most were scattered and demoralized.

To the colonel's astonished admiration, Cuerno Verde's fifty charged Anza's formation of six hundred. Anza strove to isolate Cuerno Verde and his closest associates from the rest and speedily trapped seventeen in the ravine where he had bogged down the day before. Springing down to make a last stand behind the bodies of their horses, they fought to the death in a manner which Anza deemed "as brave as it was glorious."[24]

With Cuerno Verde died his eldest son, his four leading war chiefs, the medicine man who had proclaimed him immortal, and ten warriors who defied overwhelming odds to go down fighting beside him. Anza's triumph was complete: none remained to carry on for Cuerno Verde a grand vendetta like the one he had waged for his father. The splendid green-horned headdress that had passed from father to son in 1768 was now Anza's trophy to ship to Croix at Chihuahua. So was the plumed headdress of Jumping Eagle, second only to Cuerno Verde himself.

The bloody episode ended, Anza waited for other Comanches to take up the fray, but his scouts could see only dust and smoke marking their retreat. At half past ten on the morning of September 3, 1779, Anza cheered victory in the names of King Carlos III and Commandant General Croix. Then his party hurried on to the Sangre de Cristos, anxious to reach Taos as soon as possible to see what damage Cuerno Verde had wrought.

The last of his Ute associates broke off on the morning of September 5 without the formality of goodbyes, bound homeward triumphant with rich booty and great news. Anza's day ended at Culebra Creek, where he found the carcasses of the seven horses slain by the retreating warriors three days before and signs that wounds had been treated there. Further investigation revealed the seven-man grave. Assuming those casualties had occurred at Taos, Anza grew more anxious than ever to know the outcome of that encounter. Less than forty-eight hours later his force rode into Taos, but they had not that long to wait for news. Anza sent a runner to notify the *alcalde* of their approach, and the *alcalde* himself rode out to tell the governor of his success. Anza was delighted to have his fortifications reform so dramatically vindicated.

More encouraging news awaited the governor at Santa Fe on Friday, September 10. The larger Ute contingent, which parted from the Spaniards at the Arkansas River crossing on September 2, had surprised a small Comanche family camp, seven men, and nine women and children. They slaughtered all but one child, who surrendered to the attacking Utes, and captured their forty saddle horses and all their goods.

In sum, for the week of August 31, known Comanche losses were

[24] Ibid., p. 135.

fifty-eight men, all dead, and sixty-three women and children, of whom thirty-four were now captive; no one knew how many wounded had since died or were seriously incapacitated. The Comanches had also lost more than six hundred horses and considerable goods and provisions, so that their prospects for the coming winter were grim. It seemed safe to assume that the nation would be demoralized as well as grief-stricken.

No mourning marred the jubilant mood of the New Mexicans. The cost of ending the terror of Cuerno Verde had been just one slight bullet wound received by a cavalryman.

As Anza had hoped, there arose in the Comanchería no new leader with the will to war against the Spaniards and the power to persuade other Comanches to follow him. Many Comanches had wearied of Cuerno Verde's compulsion to war and of the considerable penalties that it cost all their nation. All were appalled at the final price that he and his followers paid.

Anza did not rest on his laurels but worked all the harder to improve the defenses of the province. He took special pains to pursue and, when possible, punish the few Comanche raiders who ventured to try their luck in his province. The fall and winter passed with no hint of great vengeance in the offing. Spring, often a time of renewed Comanche depredations, brought instead in 1780 numerous Comanche peace overtures.[25]

Though pleased, Anza did not jump at the opportunity. He consistently told Comanche delegates who sought peace that the Spaniards wanted to treat with them but that negotiations would be feasible only when all their groups would unite to seek a peace binding all Comanches and all Spaniards. That was no easy condition for the far-flung Comanche nation with its fragmentary organization, but discussions of the governor's terms probably began in their camps that year.

Comanche leaders had good reason for somber reappraisal: difficulties now beset their nation on all sides. Cuerno Verde's war had cost his nation dearly in terms of years of disrupted trade relations in New Mexico. That had not mattered so critically as long as Comanches could market booty and buy French trade goods and Indian farm produce at the Wichitan and Pawnee villages, but the flow of trade goods to those villages had declined, and so had the Comanche friendships with those nations. Their thirty-year-old association with the Taovayas

25 Croix to Anza, Arispe, July 14, 1780, SANM, no. 799.

was now marred by occasional clashes, and relations were even worse with the Tawakonis and Kichais; their similar alliance with the Pawnees had crumbled into actual warfare.

The Pawnees were suffering intolerable pressures from tribes shifting westward and southward as a result of territorial changes engendered by the French and Indian War and the turmoils of the American Revolution. Pro-French tribes escaped British dominion after 1763 by moving across the Mississippi River, just as others pro-British would flee American dominion after 1783. Moving onto the plains, those woodland peoples tended to become equestrian and to challenge other tribes' control of the buffalo ranges. Those pressures upon Pawnees and Osages from north and east were reflected in turn by their pressures upon the ranges of Comanches and Norteños, who reflected those pressures still farther south against the Apaches and the northern frontier of Spanish settlement.

Their movement toward Texas had done the Comanches little commercial good, thanks to administrative chaos in Texas and to genuine shortages of trade goods, as well as to divided opinions among Comanches. Chief Povea of the easternmost Cuchanecs had long held that his people's best interest lay in peace and trade with the Spaniards in Texas, but his efforts had been largely thwarted, first by dissident Comanches and by breakdowns of communications at San Antonio and Natchitoches, then by the follies of the Bucareli settlers and a few Comanches' stubborn insistence upon vengeance against the Texans. The effect in Texas was much like that in New Mexico: the vendetta of the few denied all Comanches access to peaceful trade.

Raiders could still strike with relative impunity in New Mexico and Texas. Since the Spaniards could seldom pursue effectively, much of the Comanchería remained a safe haven from Spanish forces. But now, encircled by Indian nations who were either outright enemies or doubtful friends of the Comanches, all with easier access to trade, the Comanches needed friendships and commerce as never before. If some war leaders and the young men still gloried in attacking Spaniards, wiser leaders discerned a growing need for the benefits of stable peace and friendship with the Spaniards.

In the winter after Cuerno Verde died, a new threat loomed over the Comanche world. Just six days east of the site of Anza's triumph over Cuerno Verde, the Comanchería suffered invasion by uniformed strangers, few in number but excellent marksmen. They attacked the Comanches twice, killed many horses, and destroyed two *rancherías*.

When that story reached the Provincias Internas by way of New Mexico, the Spaniards first guessed the uniforms to be British, but further investigation indicated that the hard-fighting intruders were probably American soldiers from the frontier east of the Mississippi. Respected for their notable skill in frontier warfare, they had been invited across the Mississippi by the "A"[26] nation to help them fight the Comanches on the plains between Illinois and New Mexico.[27] That incursion, threat to Comanche and Spanish interests alike, gave thoughtful men of both nations new reason to seek rapprochement between their peoples.

Delighted to hear of Comanche overtures, Commandant General Croix encouraged Governor Anza to negotiate some arrangement that would content them to remain peacefully within the Comanchería. At the same time, Croix worried about Ute and Jicarilla Apache reactions to any rapprochement of Spaniards and Comanches. Those faithful allies of long standing meant so much to the security of New Mexico that Governor Anza would need to balance any Comanche negotiations with measures to reassure the Utes and Jicarillas. Croix anticipated the day when, Comanche problem solved, the Spaniards could concentrate all their forces against the Gila Apaches. He counted upon Ute and Jicarilla warriors to bolster New Mexico's thrust against the southwesterly reaches of the Apachería.

Anza could only wait to see the Comanches' ultimate response to their misfortunes of 1779. Would proponents of peace persuade all their nation to some meaningful treaty to end the wars, or would some successor to Cuerno Verde lead a massive assault upon the province as soon as his followers could recoup their losses of men and materials?

The governor could not ponder the Comanche problem at ease in Santa Fe. He returned from his triumph over Cuerno Verde to confront a critical emergency in the Hopi country. Though keeping his province braced against the possibility of a great Comanche raid, for the next year Anza focused most of his attention and resources westward upon a tragedy of drought, famine, and pestilence.

26 Probably a truncated rendition of the term Aguages, often applied to the Panismahas.
27 Croix to Cabello, Arispe, April 4, 1780, BA; Cabello to Croix, Bahía del Espíritu Santo, June 12, 1780, BA.

CHAPTER 17

New Mexico, 1779-1784

The rains failed in Hopi country in 1777, 1778, and 1779. So did the Hopis' crops and their supplies of potable water, their pastures, and their herds. When disease bred in the scant, stagnant water deposits, people weakened by hunger had little resistance to sickness. Nor could they offer much resistance to the Ute and Navajo enemies who increased their raids against the Hopis, partly because the Utes' and Navajos' own subsistence also suffered in the drought and partly because a traditional enemy's weakening posed irresistible temptation to prey.

Some Hopis sadly recalled the warning of Fray Garcés, whom they had treated so badly during his visit in 1776, that their persistent apostasy would invoke the biblical punishments of famine, pestilence, and war. Now, pondering his prophecy, some wished they had not refused to let him preach. Some wished to seek refuge in the Rio Grande pueblos, even at the price of renewed vassalage to the Spaniards and their God; some preferred to flee to distant woods and hills to gather some subsistence. Some threw themselves on the mercies of neighboring peoples, and not all of those lived to tell their story; some survived only as slaves. Some bartered their children to other nations for food in their desperation to hang on to life.

Word of the disaster reached New Mexico in the summer of 1779, when refugees from Hopi territory sought asylum at Sandía pueblo, most of whose residents or their forebears had once lived in Hopi country. They claimed that more would come if they could find means for the journey and could be protected against enemies en route. The missionary at Sandía reported the situation to Anza in August, as the governor rode north from Santa Fe to fight Comanches. Anza charged the friar to recruit some of the most reliable Indians at Sandía and ride with them to the Hopi towns to tell all who wished to be converted to go to Zuñi. There the governor would furnish transportation, supplies, and any other help they might need to move to Sandía or any other pueblo they wished. Anza meant to fulfill that promise immediately after his Comanche campaign. To his considerable chagrin, he returned home in September to find that the friar had shirked the errand.

Tales of trouble continued to reach Santa Fe. Hopis were trying to flee to New Mexico; Navajos were obstructing them by force and by strong propaganda against the Spaniards. Grimly noting that the friar at Sandía was not the first unworthy priest he had found in the mission field, Anza turned to the competent, zealous Fray Andrés García, fortunately stationed at Zuñi, the pueblo nearest the Hopis. The *alcalde* at Zuñi also proved very helpful, despite drought problems in his own district.

In early autumn the Hopis sent three apostates, long fugitives on their mesas, to Zuñi to seek the governor's forgiveness, and the *alcalde* escorted them to Santa Fe. There the three apostates vowed to return to the faith and promised to help convert the Hopis. Anza arranged for them to return to the Hopis with Fray García, bearing a generous offer to the stricken populace: the governor would bring them out if they wished; if they wished a separate pueblo, he would give them El Sabinal; he would give them any help they should need to reestablish themselves in New Mexico, without service obligations to any missionary or anyone else.[1]

As Fray García and the three apostates prepared to set out from Zuñi late in October, a group of Christian Zuñis returned from the Hopi country with thirty-three people of Oraibi who wanted to go to the Rio Grande pueblos. The *alcalde* of Zuñi took them to Sandía. The Zuñi

[1] The documents covering the Hopi emergency appear in Alfred Barnaby Thomas, ed., *Forgotten Frontiers*, pp. 142–171, 221–245.

emissaries told Fray García that all the people of Walpi were preparing to move to the site designated by Anza and that most of the rest would come out in the spring because all now believed starvation to be their only alternative. For the winter, the people would scatter to the wilds, to live on whatever they could gather. To the Zuñi emissaries, they had looked more dead than alive: how many would survive the rigors of winter in the wilderness? Fray García reckoned that he would accomplish nothing by traveling to the Hopis now that they were dispersing for the winter, but he resolved to go in the spring to see what survivors he could shepherd to New Mexico.

The dismal story reached Governor Anza in mid-November, too late in the season for him to mount a rescue expedition to Hopi country. He shipped supplies to Zuñi in the hope that they might somehow be conveyed to the Hopis. He also arranged to send back from the Rio Grande as soon as possible some of the recently converted refugees from the Hopi country, so that they could tell the rest how generously they had been helped.

What if the Hopis should not respond? Governor Anza discussed the problem with Fray Escalante, who had seen more of the Hopi pueblos than any other Spaniard of his time. Both agreed that they should somehow seize the opportunity for conversion created by the emergency in the Hopi country. Escalante argued that force should be used if necessary, that the Hopis were vassals in rebellion and thus not subject to the Crown's prohibition of force against peaceful neutral nations. Anza referred the legal question to Croix. More important in his view was the fact that he simply had not the means for forcible subjugation of the Hopis. However, he was game to attempt conquest if Croix should order it. What could be done with conquered Hopis? Anza wanted to resettle them, preferably on a voluntary basis, in New Mexico, where he could give them better protection without having to disperse too widely the scant forces at his command. If, as Escalante preferred, the Hopis should be maintained in their traditional homeland, then a very substantial Spanish garrison would be necessary to protect and control them.

What if the commandant general should reject all those approaches? Anza decided that in any case he should take some supplies to the Hopis at the earliest opportunity, in order to prevent their dispersal. The governor feared that, if the Hopis should grow accustomed to the wandering life, they would join their old Apache foes to form a permanent accretion to the ranks of New Spain's most troublesome enemies.

Anza dispatched the questions to Croix with the caravan in November and had decisions back with the returning caravan at the New Year. Croix held that the new Regulation of 1779 absolutely ruled out any use of force against the Hopis, even though they were rebels against both Majesties. Kindness and persuasion were the only permissible tactics. Croix authorized Anza to lead an expedition to the Hopis under the pretext of exploration or of a campaign against the Apaches, in company with two knowledgeable priests and one or two competent, reliable interpreters.

In order not to alarm or antagonize the Hopis, a priest should go ahead with the smallest possible guard to give notice of Anza's approach and of his desire to help. In the event of favorable response, Croix desired Anza to entertain the Hopis as kindly as possible and to offer them propositions with which he thought they would be willing to live for many years, long past the emergency. If they should decide, in good faith, to embrace the faith and vassalage to both Majesties, that would of course be the best possible outcome, but they must not be pressured to do so. They should be especially welcome to move to El Sabinal or to some other pueblo in New Mexico, where their skills and industry would be assets to the province, as would their numbers. On the other hand, if they should choose to stay in their homeland, Anza must give them all the support he could manage. Croix would be content to win their good opinion and to see them reunited in their pueblos, willing to accept help in their misfortunes and to trade with the Spanish dominions. Croix's stand completely reversed that which frays Domínguez and Escalante had proclaimed to the assembled Hopi leaders in November 1776: no Christianity, no help.

Now, in spring 1780, Governor Anza had to convince the Hopis that the change of policy was genuine. He sent them offers of his escort to pueblos in New Mexico. The smallpox epidemic now ravaging the Pueblos in New Mexico was reported also hitting the Hopis. Anza guessed that any survivors in the Hopi communities would be grateful to escape their ordeal on the mesas, and he expected that the diminished Pueblo communities on the Rio Grande would welcome the refugees to repair their numbers.

The first response came late in March, when Fray García delivered seventy-seven refugees to Santa Fe. Anza invited each to choose a pueblo in which to live, and he charged those pueblos to support the newcomers that year from community assets, because the increment would profit the community. The governor gave some of the refugees horses from the presidial herd and welcomed all with food, tobacco, and other gifts at his own expense. Conscious that neither his own purse nor the resources of the pueblos could stand the unusual expenses indefinitely, Anza asked the commandant general to authorize government expenditures in support of subsequent rescue and resettlement.

Fray García's March expedition brought to 150 the number rescued since autumn, but 20-odd had died after reaching sanctuary. All had been born in apostasy; all had requested baptism as soon as the danger to their souls had been explained. Fray García and Governor Anza counted their efforts well spent.

The number would have been larger but for murderous Navajo intervention. Two parties attempted the trek to New Mexico that winter and fell victim to Navajos, who slaughtered the men and enslaved the women and children. After that, others feared to attempt escape even more than they feared starvation at home. The atrocity outraged Anza, who called upon the Navajos to account for the deed and for their persistent thefts around the Spanish and Pueblo communities, in violation of their treaty agreements. Exasperated with their weak excuses, the governor resolved to campaign against both the Navajos and their Gila Apache friends as soon as he could. For the moment, he had to husband his men and materials for three greater priorities: defense against a possible big Comanche assault, the probable necessity of a Hopi rescue mission, and exploration of a route through the Apachería to Sonora.

The Hopis waited to see whether that year's ceremonials would bring rain. Late in the spring Anza heard that most of them were taking refuge with the Havasupais on the Colorado, where they hoped to harvest crops enough to start anew. If the rains should come, they would return to their mesas; if not, they would acknowledge the end of the Hopi world as they had known it. Some would go to pueblos in New Mexico; most would move permanently to the Havasupais. It would be a dispersal of the destitute. Even their precious seed corn was gone, and their herds, once counted in thousands, had dwindled to a scrawny few hundred.

Those who could muster the will and the means returned to the mesas in time to dance the July supplications for rain. By August they knew the gods had not relented. A Hopi messenger rode to Santa Fe to tell Anza that at least forty families wanted to move to New Mexico if the governor himself would come within a month to escort them from their homeland. As soon as Anza received that news on August 25, 1780, he began organizing the supplies, men, and horses necessary to feed the refugees and bring them safely to the Rio Grande. Only two weeks later, the supply train, with carts and mounts to carry the refugees, moved westward from Santa Fe.

On September 16, six days from Santa Fe, Anza pressed fifteen miles ahead of the caravan to Zuñi to study conditions there. The two-year drought had left few people in once-populous Zuñi. Some were camping far away with their flocks because pastures around Zuñi had failed; many more had taken refuge at more fortunate pueblos in the Rio Grande Valley. However, current crops looked promising. Barring some early frost to spoil their harvest, the Zuñis expected to resume the normal life of their community.

Governor Anza rejoined his rescue caravan as it reached Zuñi, and the entire party hastened on toward the Hopis. Anza sent ten Indian messengers ahead to notify the Hopis four days in advance of his arrival and to explain his peaceful purpose. He had come to fetch those who had requested his services, and he would gladly accept any others who wished to travel with him to New Mexico.

The emissaries reported back to Anza at the ruins of Aguatovi: they had been cordially received. The Hopi leaders were willing to welcome Governor Anza, but they begged that he not force any of their people to leave. Despite the present ordeal of war and hunger, most now on the mesas wished to end their lives there.

What of the forty families who had sent for him? They had left a fortnight earlier, thinking to meet Anza in Navajo territory. They had expected the Navajos to give them hospitable shelter, but the hosts chose instead to slaughter the men and capture the women and children. Two men who escaped the massacre had made their way back to the Hopis with the news. The grisly story had convinced most surviving Hopis that they would do better to endure the ills they had on their home mesas, but a few stepped forward to beg the messengers for Anza's help to escape to the Rio Grande pueblos.

Dismayed to learn that the Navajos had thwarted his principal purpose, Governor Anza decided to visit the Hopi pueblos anyway, to observe them at first hand and to see whether he could attract any more to his rescue train. In the early morning darkness, he dispatched Fray Fernández with four interpreters to announce at the two principal pueblos that the governor would visit them that afternoon, assuring the leaders that he would respect their wishes and explaining that his armed escort would be the smallest consistent with safety against their common enemy, the Apaches.

At daybreak Anza headed for Oraibi with another officer, twenty presidials, fifteen Indians, and Fray García. People came out of two pueblos on the way to greet them joyously and to accept gifts of food and small articles. Before noon the party reached Oraibi, where the headman greeted them in the presence of all his people.

Governor Anza announced that neither King Carlos III nor Commandant General Croix wanted anything of that chief or of any other apostate except voluntary recognition of both Majesties. There would be no compulsion. Neither that chief nor any other would lose his position of leadership if he should recognize those highest sovereignties. Whatever the Hopis might decide, Anza proffered them trade and friendship.

The old chief replied that he and all his people had always recognized the same lord and king as did the Spaniards. Although not baptized, they were turning to God in their present afflictions. He himself had resolved to die with most of his people, true to the Hopi way until death, but he would not impede any who might wish to go with Anza to become Christians, then or later. He appreciated the offer of trade and assured the governor that the Hopis would enjoy going to New Mexico if they should ever recover from their troubles, which he thought unlikely. Too many of his nation had died and too much of their substance had been lost, thanks to the failure of the rains and the pastures and continuous attacks by the Utes and Navajos.

The old man dwelt long and bitterly on the Ute and Navajo depredations. Governor Anza offered to mediate with both nations to stop the wars, but the old man asked him not to interfere. He had made up his mind to die at the hands of his enemies. Now Anza could believe all that he had heard of Hopi stubbornness, but he had more to learn. He offered in vain to give the emaciated old man a horse loaded with provisions. Lacking means to return the gift, the Hopi would accept nothing, even at the brink of starvation.

Anza chatted about less sensitive subjects, then reverted to the topic of religion and suggested that, if the chief wished to hear about the faith, frays García and Fernández could tell him very interesting things. Instant refusal: the chief did not find it agreeable to hear any friar.

Governor Anza knew a hopeless cause when he found one. He soon left, repeating that the chief and all his people would be welcomed any time to the protection of both Majesties. The crowd seemed impressed and their chief unmoved. The two leaders parted cordially, with mutual pledges of friendship.

Anza rode back to camp that night without Fray García, whom he had sent to Walpi to announce that any who wished to be converted and live in New Mexico should follow him back to join the governor's caravan. Anza had put in a nineteen-hour day, of which he had been twelve hours in the saddle. He was glad to spend the next day in camp at Aguatovi, awaiting decisions from the beleaguered mesa communities.

Many Hopis, most from Oraibi, visited the camp to trade. Anza saw to it that they enjoyed the most advantageous trade experiences of their lives, and many were so pleased that they stayed to visit with the Spaniards all day, long after the bargaining. From his own observations and from conversations with the Hopis, Governor Anza drew a picture of destitution tragically unlike the Escalante report of 1775, which he had studied carefully.

The 7 pueblos had dwindled to 5, none with more than 45 families. Oraibi, which had 800 families in 1775, had barely 40 in September 1779. Of 1,249 Hopi families four years before, only 133 remained. Escalante had calculated the population at 7,494, but few families now measured up to his 6-person estimate of family size; an estimate of 798 persons was probably much too high in autumn 1779. Of their once-thriving herds, there remained only 5 horses, no cattle, and just about 300 sheep, mostly at Walpi. The 1779 crops on which they had pinned their last hopes were drought-shriveled; Anza reckoned they could not harvest more than 500 bushels of all foodstuffs.

Though a native Sonoran used to desert life, the colonel marveled that the Hopis had ever managed to exist at all. Had they really attained the prosperity described by Escalante five years before? Nowhere did he see a spring sufficient to irrigate as many as ten plants of any kind. Their sandy fields appeared to need inordinate amounts of rainfall to prosper. The scant drinking water for both people and livestock was largely stagnant. Firewood and timber were equally scarce. Anza thought it small wonder that a few years' drought had destroyed their economy; he saw no hope of their recovery, even if he could make the Utes and Navajos stop preying upon their stricken neighbors.

While Anza pondered the Hopis' plight, the headman of Oraibi rode to Walpi to talk with that pueblo's headman about the governor's visit. The Walpi headman assured the Oraibi leader that he fully understood

Anza's proposition and that he personally was not inclined to accept any of the Rio Grande allotments mentioned by the governor. The stiff-necked old Oraibi conservative made a surprising reply: although he himself headed the foremost Hopi pueblo, he was prepared to go and live with the Walpi chief among the Spaniards if their misfortunes should continue, because, with all their subsistence gone, they could only die in their own land.

The Walpi headman had already proclaimed that any of his people who wished were free to join the governor's rescue party, and he had suggested that the Spaniards only desired their well-being. Even so, only thirty persons accepted rescue. The Walpi leader courteously escorted them and Fray García to their rendezvous with Anza. He greeted the governor affectionately and stayed the night in his camp to talk.

Governor Anza thanked him for his cooperation and expounded further the matters he had discussed at Oraibi, hoping that the chief and his people would reflect upon his propositions. He again offered to mediate with the Utes and Navajos to let the Hopis live in peace and assured the chief over and over that he and all the rest would always be welcome to New Mexico on the terms outlined. The Walpi chief gratefully accepted Anza's gift of a horse loaded with provisions and small articles. He bade a cordial goodbye when the governor rode off with the thirty fugitives next morning.

The party reached Zuñi on September 29. After a day's layover to attend to local matters at Zuñi, the governor hurried homeward. Back at Santa Fe a week later, he had little more than a month to settle the refugees in new homes, prepare his reports, and make final arrangements to explore the route from Santa Fe to Sonora.

The way to Sonora lay across rugged terrain in the heart of the western Apachería, but Anza found the New Mexican settlers his greatest impediment. His effort to consolidate the population in walled settlements had antagonized many. Even the stunning success of his new Taos fortifications against Cuerno Verde had failed to mollify his critics. None had actually rebelled, however, until the governor tried to reform the defenses of Santa Fe.

Soldiers and engineers had decried the poor location and design of Santa Fe almost since its founding, and the ease with which it fell in 1680 had tended to bear them out. Most recent and respected of the criticisms had been that of engineer Nicolás Lafora, incorporated in the Rubí report. Anza came to New Mexico instructed to implement the

Rubí report where feasible and to improve defenses. Neither Anza nor Croix heeded Mendinueta's warning that no mere governor could make those settlers conform and that the attempt might wreck his chance of ruling them in any matter. Mendinueta spoke from a decade's experience of that frontier community, when Anza and Croix had none.

The New Mexicans lived up to their reputation in 1779 when they learned of Anza's plans for Santa Fe. With Croix's approval, he meant to resettle the *genízaro* community of Barrio Analco on the frontier, then raze the presidio and plaza north of the river, and rebuild the presidio and villa south of the river on the Barrio Analco site. The settlers protested. When the governor rejected their protest, two dozen fled to Arispe to appeal to Croix. They won a restraining order early in 1780, the first legal triumph, though by no means the last, of citizens leagued to save Santa Fe from progress.

Anza gave up reconstruction of the villa altogether and proposed instead to move the presidio to a more central location on the Rio Grande, halfway between Santo Domingo and Cochití pueblos. Although Croix approved that plan and the presidial company voluntarily contributed 2,175 pesos toward the project, Anza was never able to implement it.[2]

Besides exasperating the governor, the most immediate effect of the settlers' flight and of the general antagonism toward Anza was to disrupt his Sonoran expedition. He had counted upon recruiting at least a hundred militiamen to make up a trade caravan for Sonora. He had eighty volunteers by the time the objectors fled, but after that recruiting was hard. So many backed out that by May 1780 he could count only sixty volunteers. No one would help make up a caravan, on the excuse of a rumor that came with the Chihuahua caravan in February: the big mines were playing out in Sonora, causing an economic decline that ruled out profitable trade with that province.

Anza gave up the notion of escorting a caravan to Sonora in 1780 and projected instead a combined exploration and campaign against Gila Apaches.[3] Able to recruit only fifty-five of the desired one hundred militiamen, he filled out his force with sixty presidials and thirty-six Indians. They rode south with the annual Chihuahua caravan, which

[2] Morfi, Geographical Description of New Mexico, ibid., p. 92; Croix, General Report of 1781, in Alfred Barnaby Thomas, ed., *Teodoro de Croix and the Northern Frontier of New Spain, 1776–1783*, pp. 107–108.

[3] The documents covering Anza's Sonora expedition appear in Thomas, *Forgotten Frontiers*, pp. 171–221.

left Santa Fe that year on November 9, doubling as caravan escort southward to the Sierra of Fray Cristóbal. There they parted on November 23. Anza had already arranged for El Paso militiamen to escort the caravan on to Chihuahua. He had also arranged, through Commandant General Croix, for forces from Nueva Vizcaya and Sonora to try to meet him in the Mimbres Mountains. All three forces would scour the area for Apaches and punish any whom they could find. Croix offered the men of Sonora and Nueva Vizcaya a bounty for captives or for a warrior's head or ears, giving them no incentive to bother to bring in captives when ears would bring as much.

Apache lookouts saw Anza's force turn toward the mountains and lighted fires to signal flight. A few deserted campsites were the only Apache signs visible to the invaders until they reached the Mimbres Mountains on November 27. There it was obvious that many Apaches had camped and that they had fled in haste only a little ahead of the New Mexican force. Anza ordered his men to scour the area for trails of escaped Apaches. They found a Spanish captive, apparently left in charge of a dozen pack animals. He seemed cooperative enough, assuring the Spaniards that the Apaches were few and not far ahead, in country favorable for attack. However, when asked to accompany a few Spaniards to attack the Apaches, he begged off, pleading that they were many and would surely kill him. Uncertain what to think of the enemy's numbers, Anza kept his camp alert that night.

In the early morning darkness the governor led thirty-six men in a surprise attack on an Apache camp of twenty-five or thirty households. In the fray there died three young men and three women of the Apache camp; one woman and six children were captured. The Spaniards freed another of their compatriots, held captive in the camp, and captured about two hundred pack animals, plus so much food and equipment that they could not haul all the spoils away. From the heights a few Apaches watched the Spaniards ride southwestward, guided toward a waterhole by the two liberated captives.

The New Mexicans crossed the path of a big Spanish party and guessed, correctly, that it was one of the forces sent by Croix to complement theirs, but they accomplished no rendezvous. They glimpsed a few Apaches but found no more opportunities to engage them. Ten days after the mountain skirmish, Anza found himself on the Camino Real from Nueva Vizcaya to Sonora, not far from the presidio of Janos, though he had hoped to strike Santa Cruz. He rode on to Arispe, where he reported to Commandant General Croix on December 18, 1780.

By the time Anza reached Arispe, Captain Francisco Martínez and Captain Joseph Antonio de Vildosola had returned to their respective bases at Carrizal and Las Nutrias, with the supporting forces that Anza had failed to meet in the Mimbres. They boasted an unprecedented penetration into the home territories of the Gila and Chiricahua Apaches. Captain Vildosola, with 172 Spaniards and 80 Opatas, and Captain Martínez, with 81 Spaniards and 48 Opatas, had left in their wake terror and consternation.

There had been no grand encounters from which to spin tales of military glory. The Apaches lived dispersed throughout the mountains in little family encampments, from which women and children scattered to gather the late autumn produce of the wilderness. The Spanish forces surprised two small family camps and slaughtered the inhabitants without discrimination as to age or sex; they also surprised and killed a few gatherers. Their spoils were substantial: all the worldly goods of the camps they attacked, goods abandoned by fleeing Apaches, and one rich cache of goods and produce sealed in a cave.

Some Apaches rallied to strike back, but, having only arrows, they had little effect. Some howled out to the Spaniards and the Opatas their rage and grief at the slaughter of their families, but Spaniards and Opatas had known too much grief and loss at the hands of Apaches to be much impressed. One large party of Apache warriors trailed the force of Captain Martínez and tried to lure them into a pursuit. Knowing they would be ambushed as soon as their mounts were exhausted, the Spaniards and Opatas spurned the challenge.

That three-pronged campaign into the Apachería was no statistical triumph. Three units, some 532 men altogether, in the field from early November to mid-December, tallied 31 Apaches killed and 25 captured, 4 captives rescued, and 315 head of livestock recaptured. Still, they had penetrated Apache homelands hitherto secure. Though they had surely invited vengeance for their deeds, they had also demonstrated that Apache men should look to the safety of their families at home. Never again would the innermost reaches of the western Apachería be absolute sanctuary, either for raiders or for those who stayed home to tend the little cornfields and gather fruits and seeds.

Anza's failure to find a direct route from New Mexico to Sonora was disappointing, of course, but not unduly discouraging. Both he and Croix hopefully assumed that the sum of the information gleaned by the three forces virtually assured success on the next try. Governor Anza spent a month in Arispe with Commandant General Croix, then rode back with the caravan to New Mexico late in January 1781, confident of his superior's informed support in his management of that complex province.

Certainly Anza needed that backing. Settlers still resented his insistence upon a disciplined, defensible pattern of settlement and his strict regulation of their trade practices, particularly with regard to the Utes. They showed remarkably little gratitude that he had won them a badly needed respite from hostilities.

In the spring of 1781 Anza alienated the missionaries, too. Since the previous year's smallpox epidemic had killed 5,025 of the missionized Pueblos, considerations of economy and safety prompted the governor to consolidate some missions, reducing the total to twenty. Though they had long lacked enough friars to man all their missions, the Franciscans objected vigorously. Some became virulent spokesmen for all of Anza's enemies in the province.

While antagonisms toward the governor fermented in the secular and religious communities of New Mexico, at the distant junction of the Colorado and Gila rivers there ripened the disaster that would pave the way for Anza's enemies to wreck his career. The protagonist was his old friend and godson, Salvador Palma.

Salvador Palma had ridden home to his people in the spring of 1777, resplendent in the uniform of a Spanish officer, the large medal of a principal chief gleaming upon his breast. He had wonderful tales and promises for the Yumas: tales of the grand hospitality he had enjoyed in Mexico City and of his baptism in the splendid cathedral; promises that the friars would soon come to make a mission and baptize all who wished it, and that the soldiers would come to build them a presidio, help them against their enemies, and bring them trade and presents. His expectations were well founded. The king had approved more than once the establishment of the mission and presidio that Salvador Palma wanted; Minister of the Indies Gálvez had emphasized the importance of those foundations in his instructions to Commandant General Croix. Viceroy Bucareli, himself keenly interested in the projects, had turned over to Croix complete files on the subject, and Croix had had the opportunity to discuss the matter fully with Anza in Mexico City during his first months in office.

To the dismay and bewilderment of Salvador Palma, two years passed without any sign of the promised establishments.[4] Croix, pre-

---

[4] Charles Edward Chapman, *The Founding of Spanish California*, pp. 403–416.

occupied with Apache and Comanche problems, postponed commitments to the peaceful frontier at the Colorado-Gila junction. The implications for Salvador Palma far outweighed mere personal disappointment: as time wore on with no Spanish action, he began to seem to his own people either a fool or a liar, perhaps both. He rode often to the frontier presidios in Sonora to petition for the friars and soldiers to come to his land. Croix finally paid the request some attention in February 1779, but his response fell far short of the Yumas' expectations and, indeed, short of the Crown's decisions two years before.

Croix decided to send only two missionaries with a small military escort. He left the escort up to the commandant at Altar. Croix specified that Fray Garcés must be one of the missionaries; the College of Querétaro assigned another old friend of the Yumas, Fray Juan Díaz, to accompany him. Fray Garcés requested at least a dozen married soldiers, all with their wives, and a carpenter, three months' provisions, and gifts for the Indians. To offset dangers from neighboring tribes, he also wanted settlers from Sonora encouraged to migrate to the new mission area. Fray Garcés stressed the importance of all the Spaniards having their own crops and domestic animals, so as not to impose any burden on the Yuma economy. He also requested authority over the whole community, except in military matters.

The earnest friar spent the spring and summer trying to organize the project, uncertain just which of his requests would be honored and handicapped by an insufficient budget for presents and provisions. He left for the Colorado River in August, badly underequipped, with just a dozen soldiers. Governor Corbalán had decided not to send the wives, lest the Indians covet them; therefore, the missionaries had to contend with the disruptive problem of lonely Spanish soldiers coveting Indians' wives. The journey proved so difficult that Garcés forged ahead to the Colorado with just two soldiers. Their provisions barely lasted the journey, and the friar's scant stock of presents was quickly exhausted. Salvador Palma welcomed him as cordially as ever, but one friar and two soldiers, no richer than themselves, were a poor substitute for the colony and the presents the Yumas had expected. The arrival of Fray Díaz with another ten soldiers a few weeks later hardly allayed their disappointment.

The consequences for Salvador Palma were indeed grave. True to his vows as a vassal of the king, he had persuaded the Yumas to refrain from their customary, often profitable, wars with neighboring tribes, on the grounds that the king of Spain wished all his children to live at peace and that they would prosper best as his loyal subjects. The long delay of the Spaniards, followed by their poor token effort, undermined Salvador Palma's leadership. Indeed, his influence waned so conspicuously that Fray Garcés feared dissident Yumas would conspire to kill the distinguished chief.

Fray Garcés wrote many letters that autumn to persuade Commandant General Croix that the Spanish enterprise on the Colorado must be quickly improved and expanded if it were not to spark disaster. More missions should be founded among neighboring tribes, lest jealousy over the Yuma mission provoke the rest to war. More Spaniards, especially muleteers and carpenters, were needed, and all should bring their wives in order to build a stable, self-sufficient community. It was out of the question for the first dozen Spaniards to survive alone among the disgruntled Yumas. When the letters brought no action, Fray Díaz rode to Arispe to appeal to Croix in person, warning that without more troops and more funds the friars could not keep the Indians at peace.

Croix acted on the petition that very week and did his best to meet the request, although earlier that year he had been inclined to cancel the whole enterprise. He provided for two Spanish mission settlements among the Yumas, one with eleven soldiers and the other with ten. Each was to have sixteen subsidized civilian settlers, among whom must be artisans and interpreters. Each mission would have two friars. All the soldiers were to be married men, required to bring their families. They were all to be allotted lands in accordance with the Laws of the Indies, with one tract reserved for usage in common and another for the benefit of the Church. He intended the Yumas to share in the land distribution, but he was uncertain whether they should be allotted individual plots or one large grant in common. Fray Díaz thought it desirable to assign individual plots to all who wished, on the grounds that the Yumas were used to agriculture and to individual proprietorship of fields. Assessor Pedro Galindo Navarro protested that the existing land-use patterns of the Indians should be left undisturbed until the Spaniards could gain a clearer understanding of their practices.

The soldiers and settlers were recruited that spring and summer, and the two settlements were founded on the west bank of the Colorado in the fall of 1780: Purísima Concepción near the Gila junction and San Pedro y San Pablo de Bicuñer a little farther downstream. There was trouble from the first. Spaniards as neighbors in residence came as an awful shock to the Yumas, who until that year had known Spaniards only as transient visitors given to generous distribution of presents. Sorely lacking among the newcomers were the careful courtesies of Anza and his hand-picked soldiers and the selfless spirit of frays Garcés and Díaz. Either from ignorance of Yuma customs or from indifference, the Spaniards paid scant respect to the rights of the natives when they allotted land. Worse still, their roving cattle wrecked the Yumas' crops.

Tensions between the Spanish and Yuma communities sharpened early that winter, when the Spaniards ran out of provisions and found that the Yumas would supply them only at prices the settlers deemed extortionate. The Yuma leaders, even Salvador Palma, joined their people in angry muttering against the settlers.

The final insult occurred early in the summer of 1781, when a wagon train of forty families of settlers crossed Yuma country en route to California. Captain Fernando de Rivera y Moncada, in charge of the escort force, saw his charges safely across the Colorado, then came back across the stream with a dozen soldiers and camped to let his animals rest and graze before moving them on to California. He had already made the mistake of distributing too few gifts. Now he made the additional, insufferable error of letting his cattle ravage the mesquite trees that played an important role in Yuma subsistence.

Captain Rivera's obstruction had thwarted Anza's effort to establish San Francisco in the spring of 1776, marring the colonel's otherwise superb service record. Now the same captain's carelessness drove the Yumas to the rebellion upon which Anza's distinguished career foundered. By mid-July the Yumas could brook no more. They revolted at both settlements, killed most of the men, including all four friars, and captured the women and children; the next day they massacred Rivera and all his soldiers. Spanish enterprise among the Yumas was ended forever. Croix had not even the forces to punish the rebels. Troops did venture into the region that year, but they could accomplish little more than to ransom the captives.

Few events in the long history of Spain's American empire shocked authorities from the king downward as profoundly as did the Yuma massacre. The Yumas controlled one of the most important strategic locations on the frontier of the empire. Their ardent desire to welcome the Spaniards had accorded happily with the Spaniards' need for a base of operations there. Salvador Palma was widely renowned as the very model of an enlightened chief, leading his people into the virtuous paths of vassalage to both Majesties. Salvador Palma was a baptized Christian, the godson of the noted Colonel Anza, who had vouched for his loyal disposition and for the importance and feasibility of the presidio and mission that the chief requested. Exhaustive inquiries into the cause of the disaster began immediately, with grave effects for Anza.

Croix, vulnerable to embarrassing charges of undue delay and inadequate support for the venture, found it expedient to attribute the fiasco to the early reports of Anza and Garcés, who were alleged to have exaggerated both the power and responsibility of Salvador Palma and the productivity of the Yuma lands. Although Anza had warned during the earliest discussions of the project that it would be disastrous to establish a colony without an ample garrison, had cautioned that the Spaniards must bring adequate provisions so as to impose no strain upon the fragile Yuma economy, and had insisted upon scrupulous respect for Indian rights, that record was ignored. The early reports of Fray Garcés suffered a share of the criticism, but a martyred priest was hardly a serviceable scapegoat: all the opprobrium fell upon Anza.

Croix's report blaming Anza for the fiasco was a grave enough setback for any officer's career, but it marked only the beginning of the colonel's ordeal. The next year, 1783, Croix became viceroy of Peru, and Commandant Inspector Felipe de Neve succeeded to command of the Provincias Internas. Perhaps Neve already disliked Anza. He had taken command of California soon after the impasse between Anza and Rivera delayed the founding of San Francisco. Bucareli had charged Neve to repair the damage; certainly he would have heard some angry recrimination against Anza at Monterey and San Diego. Whatever the reason, Neve no sooner took charge of the Provincias Internas than he launched a systematic campaign to oust Anza from the governorship of New Mexico and to wreck his career.

When the caravan arrived from Santa Fe in the first winter of his administration, Neve welcomed the testimony of some settlers and friars who had come to complain against Anza. It was just the support he needed for his request to have Anza relieved on grounds of incompetence and malfeasance. One Don Francisco Antonio de los Reyes testified that New Mexico was in a dreadful state due to abuses by Anza, whom he accused of scandalizing the missionaries, oppressing the civilized Indians, and catering to the wild Indians.[5]

---

[5] Felipe de Neve to José de Gálvez, Arispe, January 26, 1784, and Don Francisco Antonio de los Reyes to Neve, Arispe, January 23, 1784 (certified copy by Christó-

Months passed before the minister of the Indies could act upon Neve's request. Meanwhile Anza helplessly endured humiliation and interference at the hands of the commandant general. In response to settlers' complaints, Neve forbade Anza to restrict their trade with the Utes, thus opening the way for the exploitative trade tactics that could so easily turn friendly Indians into angry enemies of the province.[6] Even more shocking, Neve forbade Anza ever again to list on his service record his two greatest exploits: discovery of the overland route to California and defeat of Cuerno Verde. The Council of the Indies countermanded that absurd injustice, but the furor caused Gálvez to appoint another governor for New Mexico and to leave Anza's fate dangling.

Meanwhile, Neve tried to assure that Anza would have no opportunity to score another triumph, particularly in the critical matter of negotiating peace with the Comanches. He tried to transfer all responsibility for Comanches to Governor Cabello in Texas, on the excuse that Indian affairs in New Mexico would be too dangerously complex if Comanches were allowed to frequent that province.[7] Since Cabello had yet to establish any communication with Comanches, Neve had little chance of success in that particular effort to undercut Anza.

Governor Cabello could not know of Neve's malicious vendetta against Anza, but other veteran officers of the Provincias Internas knew and were appalled. Luckily for Anza, Neve died in the summer of 1784. Both his ad interim successor, Commandant Inspector Joseph Antonio Rengel, and his permanent successor, Colonel Ugarte, tried to undo the damage Neve had wrought. Ugarte pointed out that Anza never had a chance to answer his accusers and that Neve based his charges against the governor solely upon testimony of his known enemies, with no effort to secure balancing testimony. But Gálvez had already appointed another governor for New Mexico, and the action was for all practical purposes irreversible. Anza requested another, comparable post in the viceroyalty, with the warm endorsement of both Rengel and Ugarte. Ugarte tried in vain to have Anza appointed governor of Texas to succeed the aged, ailing Cabello, whose replacement was overdue, but to no avail. When Anza was at last relieved of the governorship

---

val Corvalán, Arispe, January 26, 1784), AGI, Audiencia de la Guadalajara [Dunn Transcripts, UT Archives].

[6] Neve to Anza, Arispe, January 20, 1784, AGI, Audiencia de la Guadalajara [Dunn Transcripts, UT Archives].

[7] Neve to Cabello, Arispe, January 9, 1784, BA.

of New Mexico, his next assignment was back to the provisional command of the armed forces of Sonora and the presidial command that he had held before his rise to fame in 1774.

Fortunately for the health of the Provincias Internas, more than four years elapsed between Neve's request for Anza's dismissal and the arrival of his replacement. Meanwhile, although Anza himself was in a miserable predicament, the Comanches had no way of knowing that his departure was imminent or that his standing in the Spanish government was precarious. Within the Comanchería they knew only that this governor was a very powerful war leader, firm and clear in the conditions he proclaimed for peace. Those Comanches who argued for peace in the 1780's gambled that Anza was also a just man and that he could truly speak for his king.

CHAPTER 18

Texas, 1779-1784

Anza's triumph over Cuerno Verde and subsequent Comanche peace feelers in New Mexico increased pressures for some Texas contribution to peace with the Comanches. That posed an awkward dilemma for Governor Cabello. The autumn of Cuerno Verde's death coincided with that of de Mézières. For several years afterward, Cabello could find no other agent to establish communication with Comanches or even with the Taovayas, whose village was the key listening post on the eastern fringe of the Comanchería.

The Comanche problem baffled Cabello from the outset of his term. Nothing in his previous experience had prepared him to evaluate the conflicting reports of the Comanche troubles kindled at Bucareli in 1778, but he naturally sympathized with Spanish settlers as opposed to unknown *indios bárbaros*. Perhaps, given more time with him at San Antonio, de Mézières could have convinced the governor that the Comanches had indeed been wronged and that their consequent depredations marked a fleeting episode of kinsmen's vengeance rather than tribal war. But de Mézières' death left Cabello solely dependent upon frontier intelligence from Gil Ybarbo, the Nacogdoches leader whom he appointed lieutenant governor of Texas in the fall of 1779.

Gil Ybarbo had a double stake in the argument that the Comanches had launched a war against his sector of the Texan frontier. If it were established that a peaceful Comanche delegation had indeed suffered unprovoked attack at Bucareli, then he and his colonists stood guilty of a grave breach of the king's law. Furthermore, Gil Ybarbo and his associates had exploited the alleged Comanche war to justify their long-desired move back to East Texas. It was unlikely that Governor Cabello would ever have objective, or even informed, reports about Comanches from Gil Ybarbo, or that Nacogdoches could become a viable base for communication with the Comanchería.

What of Comanche intentions toward San Antonio? Governor Cabello could only wonder whether their animosity toward the Spaniards of Bucareli would lead to attacks on the provincial capital as well. A big Comanche force did invade the area northwest of San Antonio in the autumn of 1779, but they bothered only Lipans. Two more major raids followed their great October triumph over the Lipans at Cañon de San Saba, and the Lipans never recovered any of the horses or people whom they lost to the raiders.

The badly crippled, demoralized Lipans fell back into the region between the presidios of Béxar, Rio Grande, and La Bahía, and the seacoast. Afraid to hunt on the Comanche-infested buffalo ranges, they ate cattle instead of buffalo that winter and thus ran afoul of the Spaniards. Either they poached upon herds belonging to missions or to individual owners or they preyed upon the vast wild herds claimed by the Crown.[1] In effect, hunger drove the Lipans to offend the Spaniards even as they sought the protective shadows of the presidios.

Their eastward flight from the Comanches carried the Lipans within easy reach of Cocos and Mayeyes. They soon established a trade pernicious to Spanish interests: guns and ammunition, which eastern nations obtained from Louisiana traders, in exchange for the horses and mules that Lipans stole so easily from Spaniards and mission Indians. Spanish authorities first spotted the new hazard when well-armed Lipans visited Monclova on their way home from a hunt. The governor of Coahuila ascertained the source of the guns and reported it to the commandant general, who ordered Cabello to stop the traffic.[2]

The order reached Governor Cabello at Presidio La Bahía, where

[1] Cabello to Croix, Bahía del Espíritu Santo, February 12, 1780, BA.
[2] Croix to Cabello, Arispe, February 1, 1780, BA.

he shifted his base of operations late in 1779. Texas had some unfinished business, initiated by Croix, Ripperdá, Gálvez, and de Mézières, that Cabello could better attend at La Bahía: the matter of a
campaign to subdue or exterminate the Karankawas in order to open
the province to coastal shipping, and the matter of shipping livestock
to Louisiana, for which Governor Gálvez had counted upon de Mézières. Both grew more urgent in December 1779, when Cabello had
Croix's dispatch announcing Spain's entry into the war against Great
Britain. The Gulf of Mexico would be an important war arena, and
Gálvez would need livestock from Texas, both for his own forces in
Louisiana and for the Americans whom he would assist. Cabello
hurried down to La Bahía before the New Year to meet the responsibilities of Texas in the new war. His errand happily afforded him a
chance to see that sector of his command, to get acquainted with the
Indians drifting in and out of the two missions there, and to examine
the administration of the presidio, where affairs were unevenly managed at best and damaging quarrels with the neighboring missionaries
were chronic.

The governor had hardly settled into his temporary headquarters at
La Bahía before San Antonians clashed with Comanches on the
Guadalupe River on New Year's Day 1780. No reason was recorded.
Perhaps the Comanches did invade the area to attack the Spaniards;
perhaps they were hunting buffalo on the Guadalupe or looking for
Lipans or Tonkawas, only to be attacked by frightened Spaniards
assuming they threatened San Antonio. Circumstances suggest the
latter, for the force of settlers, soldiers, and Indians from San Antonio,
led by Béxar's First Alférez Don Marcelo Valdés, killed nine or ten
Comanches and lost just one soldier. The trophies they bore home to
Béxar included a gun, three lances, eight heavily feathered headdresses, various bows and arrows, and an English hatchet.[3]

Lipans flocked to Béxar to exult over the Comanche losses, wailing
for the dead soldier and bidding any number of horses and mules
for the Comanche trophies. Valdés resented the proposition: the
principle annoyed him, and he suspected that the proffered horses and
mules were stolen from Spanish herds in the first place. When the
Lipans would not accept his refusal, the exasperated *alférez* sent them
down to La Bahía to appeal to the governor.

Cabello berated the Lipans as cowards, challenging them to take

---

[3] Cabello to Croix, Bahía del Espíritu Santo, February 12, 1780, BA.

Comanche trophies by fighting Comanches, as the Spaniards had done. Suffering his rebuke in silence, the Lipans fed Cabello's growing impression that they were as cowardly as the Comanches were daring. Certainly the Lipans never tried to conceal their overwhelming fear of the Comanches.

Inherent in the San Antonians' New Year's Day victory was the question of its ultimate cost to the community: how would the Comanches respond? If the Comanche party on the Guadalupe had not intended war that day, would the new injury provoke their tribe, or at least their kinsmen, to war against San Antonio? No speedy campaign for vengeance ensued. Early in February, eight San Antonio settlers encountered nine Comanches on the Guadalupe, but they assumed a defensive posture and shooed the Comanches away. When that news reached the governor, he dispatched a strong patrol to scout the area and try to scare the Comanches out of the region, though he realized that Comanches were less easily intimidated than Lipans. Cabello suspected that they were not afraid to venture anywhere.

All that spring Comanches were conspicuous only by their absence around Béxar. Governor Cabello had reason to wonder whether he had succeeded too well in scaring them away, once he received the late spring mail from Arispe. Croix, eager to capitalize on Anza's success against the Comanches in New Mexico, asked Cabello to find an agent to carry peace offers into the eastern Comanchería and to continue to Santa Fe in order to coordinate Texan and New Mexican negotiations with the Comanches.[4] After the tensions of that winter and spring, Governor Cabello found his province understandably short of men willing to seek out Comanches on their home grounds. Six months passed before he found veteran French personnel from Louisiana to undertake the assignment. Meanwhile, the summer brought Comanches to his jurisdiction in force.

Until mid-June Cabello had more trouble with ostensible friends than with the presumed enemy. Though Lipan cattle thefts were a nuisance, Governor Cabello found it expedient only to scold them and make them promise to do better, as long as they preyed chiefly upon wild herds toward the coast. Unfortunately, the dearth of Comanches that spring encouraged some Lipans to drift back west. In mid-May, a large group camped on the Medina River, out toward the Cañon de San Saba where they had suffered such grievous loss in the previous

[4] Cabello to Croix, Béxar, October 20, 1780, BA.

autumn. Still not confident enough to venture out for buffalo, the Lipans looked to the Atascoso ranch of Mission San José for meat. They killed sheep from the mission flocks and stole four horses and two mules.[5]

That infuriated the Father President of the missions, who called upon Governor Cabello to control the Lipans or bear the blame for their destruction of Mission San José. Cabello doubted that a little Lipan poaching seriously threatened the life of the mission, but, when forced to choose between a dispute with an angry missionary and a confrontation with the Lipans, he preferred the latter. He ordered Lieutenant Joseph Menchaca, an old hand with Apaches, to gather all available men from San Antonio and carry a tough message from the governor to the Lipan camp: get out immediately and move down to the Nueces. The governor did not wish them to visit San Antonio or to be friends with them, unless they would find out which Lipans had robbed the Rancho del Atascoso and deliver them to the governor. Cabello proposed to punish the Lipan thieves just as he had, before Lipan witnesses, punished Spaniards for stealing horses from Lipans.

Lieutenant Menchaca rode out to the Medina from Béxar on June 1 with eighty soldiers, settlers, and mission Indians, only to find the Lipans' campsite abandoned. He swept north to the Guadalupe to see whether the Lipans had moved there, but he saw no sign of them. Menchaca reported back to Béxar on June 5 and sent word of his failure to the governor at La Bahía.

The Lipans' hurried departure was ominous. Cabello and some officers at Béxar first guessed they had decamped to avoid answering for their crimes. The governor resolved to discover the culprits and make examples of them. Actually, the Lipans were fleeing a threat far worse than the governor's displeasure. A big Comanche war party crossed the Guadalupe in June and marauded widely through the area.[6] Woefully short of troops at both Béxar and La Bahía, Cabello could not pursue or punish the invaders. His helplessness encouraged the marauders and demoralized both Spanish and mission Indian communities.

The Comanche raiders speedily undid all that Cabello had accomplished toward shipping the livestock that Gálvez needed for Spanish and American forces. To meet the Louisiana governor's request for one or two thousand head of cattle, Cabello had negotiated a purchase

[5] Cabello to Croix, Bahía del Espíritu Santo, June 17, 1780, BA.
[6] Cabello to Croix, Bahía del Espíritu Santo, July 4, 1780, BA.

of two thousand head from the missions and had hired twenty men from San Antonio to drive them to Nacogdoches, whence Governor Gálvez could have them driven wherever he pleased. To facilitate the drive, Cabello had decided to ship two herds of a thousand each.[7]

Don Cristóbal Ylario de Córdoba and his crew headed east with the first thousand head late in June, but Comanches soon checked them. A hundred warriors struck the cow camp on the Arroyo de Nogales, killed one drover, wounded two others, destroyed some cattle, and dispersed the rest. When that news reached La Bahía on July 3, Cabello dispatched the dozen available soldiers to pursue the hundred Comanches. That mattered little. The raiders had retired beyond the Guadalupe, safe from any reckoning, and surely oblivious of their impact upon the contest for North America.

Though Texan livestock was vitally important to the Spanish and American forces, the Comanches had, in effect, made the animals unavailable. The terrified populace would not serve as drovers at any wage; the missionaries refused to gamble cattle on any more shipments. Indeed, they grew loath even to corral stock, lest the convenient target only invite raiders.

The Comanches camped the rest of the year on a ridge between the Guadalupe and the Colorado, from which they preyed so fiercely that the citizenry dubbed that height El Monte del Diablo.[8] Outlying ranches fared worst. Efforts to pursue the marauders produced one humiliating failure after another. When Indians stole horses from the ranches of San Bartolo and Las Mulas on the night of June 18, 1780, nine soldiers from the outpost of Cíbolo helped the rancher trail them to the Guadalupe. Across that stream they sighted so many Indians that they dared not risk a fight. In fact, they fled so precipitately that they lost ten horses, two guns, and a shield on their frantic ride home.[9]

Their apparent cowardice outraged Governor Cabello and Alférez Valdés. As interim commander of Béxar, Valdés mustered everyone available to attack the enemy: ninety-one men, of whom forty were settlers and ten were mission Indians. They too reached the Guadalupe only to see so many Indians across the stream that Valdés quickly ruled out attack. Entrenching his company in a mustang corral on the south bank, he sent appeals for reinforcements to Governor Cabello at

[7] Cabello to Croix, Bahía del Espíritu Santo, July 10, 1780, and July 17, 1780, BA.

[8] Cabello to Croix, Béxar, October 20, 1780, BA.

[9] Cabello to Croix, Bahía del Espíritu Santo, July 17, 1780, BA.

La Bahía and Lieutenant Menchaca at Béxar. Cabello sent a dozen men from La Bahía; Menchaca brought ten soldiers, sixteen settlers, and fourteen mission Indians from San Antonio. They reached Valdés at the corral on the Guadalupe on June 26, with their horses so worn out that they were in no condition to engage the enemy.

Valdés and Menchaca hoped at first to find a small party of the enemy and drub them so severely as to warn off the rest, but they scouted all along the lower Guadalupe without finding any Indians. They decided then to cross the Guadalupe to seek the enemy, and they soon found the wide trail of a very large party. They were just a day behind them when a courier summoned the force to the Arroyo de Nogales to help pursue the Comanches who had despoiled the cattle herd bound for Louisiana. They hurried back to join in that fruitless chase, while Comanches roved the lands beyond the Guadalupe unchallenged.

The fatigued men and horses were hardly back home before thirty Indians raided a supply train carrying corn from Béxar to La Bahía. They killed one muleteer, wounded another, and stole all the mules and some of the horses that belonged to the escort troop. A small pursuit force from La Bahía chased the raiders across the Guadalupe to the San Marcos River, about 125 miles from La Bahía, before giving up the chase in exhaustion. They reached La Bahía on the night of July 16, only to be called out again at noon the next day to rescue another eight-man camp of Spaniards ambushed by Indians. The travelers had managed to stand off the enemy but had lost all their mules to them. Cast-off harnesses, cut cinches, and wantonly destroyed mules conspicuously marked the trail, but the enemy had a good head-start, and pursuit was impracticable, as usual.

That same day Indians struck the Rancho de San Bartolo again. They killed two cowhands at the morning milking, carried off all the calves, broke down the door of the house, and smashed all the furniture. The wanton destruction of the household was such a puzzling, alarming new pattern that Valdés led a force out from Béxar in a particular effort to track the enemy and take a prisoner for interrogation. He glimpsed the enemy on the Guadalupe but won no prisoner. Veteran Sergeant Urrutia identified one arrow as Comanche, but they returned to Béxar none the wiser about the reasons for the virulent hostility. Ranches in every sector reported similar depredations. Governor Cabello gloomily concluded that the destruction and loss of his province were imminent.

Cabello's apprehension deepened after three Tejas Indians visited him at La Bahía in July. When the governor asked them about the new pattern of destruction at the ranches, they speculated that the broken doors and smashed furniture were the work of some Taovayas, Tawakonis, and Tonkawas working with the Comanche raiders. However, they confirmed the Spaniards' assumption that the main problem was Comanche hostility and that the extraordinary voracity of the summer's depredations was characteristic of Comanche warfare.

Cabello feared that, if the Comanches had indeed persuaded Taovayas and other Norteños to join in their war, there was no hope for Texas. He had neither the troops nor the horses to withstand a general onslaught; the nearly destitute settlers could contribute little to their own defense. In mid-July Cabello warned Croix that only substantial help from the south would give the province any chance to survive, but he knew the commandant general's problems too well to expect any useful support.

In August, another Tejas delegation painted a slightly less dismal picture for the governor. They came to La Bahía on an important errand: their village now lacked a chief, and they wished Cabello to appoint another. Cabello explained that he did not make such selections. Only the villagers could name the man whom they thought would be the best governor for them and the best friend of the Spaniards. Cabello would gladly confirm that man chief and give him the cane of office; then the rest would have to obey him. His answer appeared to satisfy the visitors.[10]

For a week Cabello entertained the four Tejas as well as the poor resources of La Bahía permitted, listening avidly to all they could tell him of Indian affairs in the interior. They stressed the Taovayas, Wichita, and Panismaha resentment of de Mézières' failure to bring them gifts on his journey to San Antonio the year before, when he had given presents to the Tonkawas, Tawakonis, and Cudeflechas.[11]

Discouraged to hear that same old complaint again, Cabello explained as simply and as patiently as he could that only nations closer to San Antonio had received gifts and that some had actually ridden to San Antonio to receive their presents and meet the governor. He assured them that the gifts for the Tejas, Taovayas, Wichitas, and

---

[10] Cabello to Croix, Bahía del Espíritu Santo, August 17, 1780, BA.

[11] Identified by Cabello as one division of the same Tawakonis, of larger number and greater valor.

Panismahas remained in his San Antonio storehouse and that he wished them to visit him to receive their gifts and get acquainted with him. Satisfied, the Tejas promised to explain to the rest.

Most immediately important to Cabello was the visitors' insistence that only Comanches were doing the heartless killing in Texas. Though some Comanches had urged the Taovayas, Tawakonis, and other interior nations to join in their war, none had accepted the invitation, despite their disenchantment with the Spaniards. The campaign was pursued only by two big camps of Comanches called Namboricas.[12] They meant to avenge members of their group who had been killed in the battle with the Spaniards, and they would not rest until they cost the Spaniards plenty of scalps and horses.

The Tejas visitors had been at La Bahía only two days when the son of Chief Casaca brought twenty Lipans to the presidio to talk with the governor's guests. Forewarned of the Lipans' approach, Cabello saw that the Tejas were in their quarters and refused to admit the Lipans to the presidio. Undaunted, the Lipans shouted propositions of trade and friendship over the walls to the Tejas. The Tejas assured the governor they would not assent. He praised their good judgment and reminded them that Apaches could be dangerously unreliable visitors in Tejas villages.

Cabello had ample cause to worry. Croix had warned him again to stop the arms traffic between Lipans and the East Texas nations, on the grounds that it endangered Coahuila.[13] Cabello was sure that the Lipans would proposition the Tejas on their way home. His worries multiplied when twenty-two Mayeyes, Cocos, Bidais, and Akokisas visited La Bahía. They had been camped together on the Brazos River eight days earlier, when Comanche raiders had fallen upon them, taking some of their horses. Having been swift enough to escape with their lives and liberty, the victims decided to report to the governor their encounter with the common enemy.

Cabello welcomed them cordially, distributing cigars and candy with a lavish hand. They stayed four days, amiably sharing in the talks and entertainment that Cabello had arranged for his four Tejas guests.

[12] Apparently Cabello's rendition of the Caddo enunciation of the Comanche division name usually written Yamparica. The deaths that they sought to avenge were apparently the ten suffered in the clash with the San Antonians on the Guadalupe, January 1, 1780. This raises the interesting possibility that the two big Yamparica camps had moved south through the Ietan range in reaction to the September disaster suffered by Cuerno Verde's followers.

[13] Croix to Cabello, Arispe, June 2, 1780, BA.

The governor urged all the visitors not to trade or be friends with the Apaches or the Karankawas because he was very angry with both those nations. They eagerly volunteered to go Karankawa-hunting with him, and Cabello agreed to do so at some suitable time in future. He saw his twenty-six guests off on August 16, with an especially nice parting gift to reward the Tejas for rebuffing the Lipan overtures.

A few days later Cabello himself departed from La Bahía for the capital. Whether Norteños were or were not involved in the hostilities, he could no longer doubt that some Comanches were engaged in a war of vengeance against his province. While that war lasted, he could accomplish neither of his two principal objectives at La Bahía. No herds of livestock could be driven to Louisiana. No troops could be spared for a campaign against the Karankawas, nor could settlers or mission Indians be expected to go off on a coastal campaign and leave their families and property exposed to the Comanche menace. Cabello's place now was at Béxar, his overriding task to secure Texas against the Comanche vendetta. By September he was back in residence at his adobe "palace" in Béxar, there to remain for the rest of his term.

After September 12, 1780, no day passed without Comanche tracks reported in the vicinity. Some seventy or eighty Comanches struck the outpost of Cíbolo on September 18, killed three soldiers, and stole some of the horse herd. Alférez Francisco Amangual had left at Cíbolo only twenty men, plus three detached from Béxar to carry the mail. Cabello dared not send him reinforcements from Béxar, which already had too few men to defend the presidio and villa and protect the outlying missions and ranches. It took thirty-three men just to guard the horse herd, necessarily pastured some distance from the presidio. The governor resigned himself to the prospect that the eighty Comanches would wipe out the presidio, villa, and missions.[14]

The assault on Béxar never occurred, either that September or on several subsequent occasions when it seemed to the governor inevitable. Like everyone else in Texas and his superiors in New Spain and Spain, Cabello gauged his expectations of the Comanches and other interior nations by that one awful episode at San Sabá mission a quarter-century past, in many ways a misleading precedent.

Thanks perhaps to the Lipans' special terror of the Comanches, that nation's role at San Sabá had been exaggerated from rather minor peripheral involvement to one of leadership, though the prime initia-

[14] Cabello to Croix, Béxar, September 19, 1780, BA.

tive came apparently from Taovayas and Tejas. That massed campaign by a concert of nations had been the extraordinary product of their overwhelming grievances against the Apaches. The massacre at the mission had been an accidental byproduct of the excitement and a matter of real regret to many of them afterward. Cabello could not know that aggrieved Comanches satisfied their lust for scalps and horses with scattered hit-and-run tactics and were unlikely to risk their own lives in a direct attack on a presidio. Nor did he comprehend that the other nations of the interior had suffered enough abuse from Comanches to make them unlikely to join any Comanche vendetta against the Spaniards.

Cabello knew only that Comanches and Norteños had once massed thousands of warriors—the numbers multiplied in memory with the passage of years—to destroy a Spanish mission and eventually a presidio. Assuming that it could happen again at San Antonio, he worried desperately about reports of disaffection among the interior nations. All that year Gil Ybarbo reported steady deterioration of the mood of the Norteños, insisted that some had indeed allied with the Comanches against the Spaniards, and complained particularly that Chief El Mocho of the Tonkawas was growing truculent. The crux of their discontent was the lack of trade and presents, which the French had always provided and the Spaniards had only promised.[15]

Cabello grimly realized the truth of the Norteños' complaint. He and Gil Ybarbo had agreed ever since de Mézières' death that they could maintain peace with the Norteños only by following the trade and gift pattern set by the Frenchman, but goods were so scarce and expensive that they had never been able to supply more than token quantities. In October 1780, the supply of goods at both Natchitoches and Nacogdoches ran out altogether. Tribes reporting to Natchitoches for their scheduled presents left disappointed and angry. Cabello received notice that a shipment of gifts for the Norteños had landed at New Orleans, but transportation upstream to Natchitoches could be a long, uncertain business, dependent upon seasonal vagaries of the Red River; even transshipment from Natchitoches to Nacogdoches hinged upon the mood of the Natchitoches commandant. In short, Cabello was saddled with promises to the Indians of both trade and

[15] Cabello to Croix, Bahía del Espíritu Santo, February 7, 1780, BA; Croix to Cabello, Arispe, June 2, 1780, BA; Cabello to Croix, Béxar, September 17, 1780, October 12, 1780, and October 20, 1780, BA.

presents that he lacked means to honor. He keenly resented the predicament.

The governor's discomfort worsened when Croix warned him that the king was now inclined to have the Norteños administered in Louisiana, regardless of their residence in Texas, and to have them given arms as in the days of the French regime. Cabello glumly predicted that, if the Crown should so dispose, the Norteños would soon be better armed than his troops in Texas.[16]

Actually, the only campaign that Norteños threatened to make in Texas that year was one ostensibly supporting the Spaniards against the Lipans. The odd situation developed in the spring, when a Xaraname Indian christened Basilio ran away from Mission del Espíritu Santo to the Tawakonis. The Tawakoni chief paid him a lot of attention and questioned him very closely about the Lipans. Basilio told him that the Lipans were thieves and that those around Béxar killed the mission cattle. The Tawakoni leader waxed very indignant and announced that he would arrange with the Tejas, Taovayas, and Tonkawas a campaign to punish those Lipans. He dispatched runners to invite the other three nations and sent Basilio to advise the governor of his plan. The Tawakonis and their friends were short of powder, balls, and guns and also loincloths, because they no longer went to the French traders. They hoped Cabello would give them all those things so they could drub those Apaches.[17]

Basilio dutifully returned to the mission in June and told his story to the friar, who promptly sent him to Cabello. The governor was able to question him closely without any interpreter because Basilio spoke Castilian very clearly. His answers, plus results of other inquiries, convinced Cabello of the truth of his story. It posed a curious dilemma.

The governor could not know whether the Norteño force was actually assembling. If he should supply them the desired guns and munitions, his own resources would be dangerously depleted. On the other hand, a refusal could antagonize them irreparably. If the proposed campaign should take place, the Lipans might retaliate by turning openly on San Antonio and wreaking extensive damages there. That would bring down upon the unhappy governor the wrath of all the leadership of San Antonio, civil, military, and, above all, religious. Cabello braced himself for the arrival of a cavalcade of Tawakonis,

[16] Cabello to Croix, Béxar, November 15, 1780, BA.
[17] Cabello to Croix, Bahía del Espíritu Santo, June 17, 1780, BA.

Tejas, Taovayas, and Tonkawas, armed at the very least with lances, and asked the commandant general for instructions to cover that contingency, though skeptical that any reply could arrive in time.

To his considerable relief, nothing came of the matter all summer. He concluded that Basilio had fabricated the whole yarn. However, in the autumn several Norteño leaders informed Gil Ybarbo that they were going to campaign against the Apaches and demanded that he give them powder, balls, arms, and all the other necessities for a good campaign. Gil Ybarbo scraped up some trinkets to give them instead, and they remained quiet in their villages.[18]

Cabello felt especially frustrated that he personally knew none of the interior nations except the Tonkawas and thus had no effective basis for communication with them. When he had Gil Ybarbo's adverse reports about El Mocho, he sent word of his displeasure to the Tonkawa camp and hoped that El Mocho would come to Béxar so that he could persuade him to settle down, even though he lacked force to back his suasion. He had no comparable personal acquaintance through which to deal with the other nations, which had vouchsafed no response to the embassy of Portolán. That autumn, even his limited staff of interpreters for the Norteño languages dwindled by a third: at Cíbolo in September 1780 the Comanches killed Julian Rondein, one of the three interpreters whom de Mézières had brought to Béxar. How could Cabello honor Croix's request to send an envoy to the Comanchería, and thence to Santa Fe, when he could not even establish communication with the interior nations nominally pledged to Spanish allegiance?

The veteran French trader Nicolás de La Mathe volunteered in October to attack both problems: to visit the Norteños and try to calm them, then to try to visit many Comanche camps and see whether he could win their friendship. With him would travel Juan Baptista Bousquet, another veteran of the French trade now residing in San Antonio, and Francisco Hughes, another of the interpreters whom de Mézières had brought from Natchitoches to join the Béxar staff. All three were proficient in the languages of the interior nations. If they should succeed in the errand to the Comanches, Bousquet and Hughes would attempt the journey to Santa Fe, while La Mathe would escort some Comanche and Norteño chiefs to Béxar to talk peace and receive presents.[19]

[18] Cabello to Croix, Béxar, November 15, 1780, BA.
[19] Cabello to Croix, Béxar, October 20, 1780, and November 17, 1780, BA.

Cabello saw La Mathe off from San Antonio at the beginning of November, with supporting letters bespeaking the assistance of Commandant Esteban de Vaugine at Natchitoches and of Governor Gálvez.[20] He also notified Croix, who in turn alerted Governor Anza to give all possible aid if Cabello's agents should reach New Mexico.[21]

By the time La Mathe left San Antonio, Gil Ybarbo had grown so pessimistic about the deteriorating relationship with the Norteños that he took the extraordinary step of appealing to Governor Gálvez to make Governor Cabello do something about it.[22] He blamed much of the trouble on de Mézières for having promised the Indians an annual present, a trader in every village, and a table of prices for every chief to show what the Indians should pay the traders for merchandise and what the traders should pay for skins. Gil Ybarbo contended that the arrangement had indeed pleased the Indians at first, because de Mézières' price list had treated them very favorably, but that the system had soon broken down because traders and suppliers could not stay in business at those price levels. The Indians had thus suffered two rude breaches of treaty promises that year: the French traders had left many villages, and the Spanish government had not supplied the annual presents. The disappointed Indians were finding neither Frenchmen nor Spaniards reliable. Gil Ybarbo claimed that they were tearing up the symbols of their Spanish allegiance—the flags, medals, and canes of office—to dramatize their inability to live on the luster of those emblems, and that they had issued a four-month ultimatum. If the promises of de Mézières were not fulfilled within that time, they would consider the Spaniards their enemies. Gil Ybarbo was not content to report the crisis to Governor Cabello and to Commandant Vaugine at Natchitoches. He also appealed to Governor Gálvez, complaining that Cabello would only forward his reports to Commandant General Croix and that Croix could surely not send any help in time, even if he should comprehend the need.

Gil Ybarbo fretted particularly about the Taovayas, whom he considered the most disaffected of the Norteños as well as the most numerous. He deemed their unrest especially dangerous because they had "some connection" with the Comanches. As was often the case,

[20] Cabello to Vaugine, San Antonio de Béxar, October 31, 1780, in Lawrence Kinnaird, ed., *Spain in the Mississippi Valley, 1765–1794*, I, 389–390.

[21] Croix to Anza, Arispe, March 25, 1780, SANM, no. 819.

[22] Gil Ybarbo to Gálvez, Natchitoches, November 1, 1780, in Kinnaird, *Spain in the Mississippi Valley*, I, 390–391.

Gil Ybarbo's report differed sharply from actual experience with the Indians. In the very week of his extraordinary appeal, the Taovayas graciously welcomed an agent of Governor Gálvez.[23] Far from repudiating his treaties with the Spaniards, Chief Qui Te Sain readily handed over five Spanish captives residing in his village, explaining that they had come from the Comanches "who happen to be our neighbors, but who shed our blood and steal our horses daily."[24]

Recovery of the Spanish captives, promised by the Taovayas ever since their first treaty with de Mézières, was the agent's principal errand. Qui Te Sain welcomed the occasion to show loyal obedience to Gálvez and to appeal for his help. He dictated a list of his troubles: the murders and horse thefts inflicted by Osages upon his own and neighboring people; the shortages of hardware and armaments in their villages; and the disrepair of their remaining rifles, hatchets, and picks. If the Great Father in New Orleans could not send them the goods they needed, could he not grant them a blacksmith to repair their worn implements? Though Qui Te Sain complained that de Mézières had deceived him on their trip to San Antonio in 1772, he sent a courteous, not a threatening, message to the Louisiana governor.

Neither the appeal of Qui Te Sain nor that of Gil Ybarbo stood much chance of attention in New Orleans that winter. Early in 1780, Governor Gálvez had captured Mobile from the British. By the end of the year he sailed to Havana to lead a campaign against Pensacola, another distinguished success: he captured all West Florida by May 1781. He attended briefly to the Red River tribes in the interval between the Mobile and Pensacola campaigns, for reasons born of the war. A British expedition, comprised chiefly of Indian allies, attacked St. Louis in May 1780. The Spaniards repelled the attack, but it dramatized the danger of British influence among the Indians and caused a new flurry of anxiety at New Orleans about foreign traders among the interior nations and about their temper.[25] Gálvez therefore intruded his own agent into the neighboring jurisdiction of Texas, but he neces-

[23] Probably the veteran Natchitoches trader Paul Louis Le Blanc de Villenuefve, for Cabello later complained of Gálvez's impropriety in permitting him to go to the Norteños. Certainly Le Blanc would have been the logical choice as emissary to the Taovayas, for he had helped to negotiate their first peace treaty in 1771.

[24] Qui Te Sain to Gálvez, Village of the Taovayas, November 4, 1780, in Kinnaird, *Spain in the Mississippi Valley*, I, 392.

[25] Kinnaird, ed., ibid., xxviii–xxx.

sarily turned his full attention to the Pensacola campaign long before his agent could report back to Louisiana.

While Qui Te Sain waited hopefully at his village for help from Governor Gálvez and Gil Ybarbo fumed at Nacogdoches, Nicolás de La Mathe pressed on to the interior nations. At San Antonio Governor Cabello awaited the results of his embassy, oblivious of the latest moves of Gálvez and Gil Ybarbo and optimistic about La Mathe's chances. Meanwhile, he had welcome reassurances about the mood of the Tonkawas.

Cabello's message of displeasure with El Mocho had reached the Tonkawa camp that fall, and the chief dutifully traveled to Béxar to repair the difficulty. At first, all his people meant to come with him to visit the governor, as so many had done the year before with de Mézières. After a good visit at San Antonio, they expected to raid the Lipans for a lot of horses. The whole camp happily set out, but on the way they heard rumors that some Akokisas, Bidais, and Mayeyes who had gone to Béxar from La Bahía had smallpox. The Tonkawas prudently stopped north of the Guadalupe, where El Mocho told them to wait while he went on to San Antonio, accompanied only by the son of his predecessor. Elegant in the feathered headdresses and buffalo robes appropriate for tribal spokesmen, each armed only with a lance, bow, and arrows, they traveled on foot by night to avoid detection and encountered neither Comanches nor Apaches. Before dawn on November 24, 1780, they rapped at the door of the Governor's Palace.

Fortunately, the staff recognized the pair from the previous year's visit and welcomed them. Chatting amiably with the servants in the kitchen and downing great quantities of meat and tortillas, the two Indians waited to see the governor. Cabello, quietly awakened to hear of the visitors, inquired about their demeanor and learned of their overnight walk. Despite Gil Ybarbo's unfavorable tales of El Mocho, he decided to receive the visitors cordially and to give them no cause for complaint.

With his indispensable interpreter, Courbière, Cabello welcomed the two Tonkawas in his salon at eight o'clock that morning. They embraced him with a great show of feeling. The governor passed the cigars necessary for a talk and, after an appropriate interval of smoking, asked why they had come.

El Mocho replied that he had come because he had heard that the governor was very angry with him. He had, therefore, traveled lightly armed, with just one companion, and had entered the governor's room naked of any defense. Cabello marveled, "How subtle and astute this wicked man is in this generous action!"[26]

Not to be outdone, the governor responded that of course he could not be angry. If he were, he would mount his horse and go with all his people to punish the chief. He observed, however, that he could not admire El Mocho as a truly rational Indian until he should keep his promise to settle all his people in a village and cease to roam from place to place.

El Mocho explained that, between Comanches on one side and Osages on the other, the harried Tonkawas hardly had horses to ride, much less time or opportunity to build a village. He expressed the hope that he could fulfill his promise in the coming spring. Cabello urged him to do so and pointed out that the proposed village could have been a fine base from which to exploit the Lipans' difficulties that autumn.

When the governor asked El Mocho which nations helped the Comanches against the province, the chief assured him that he knew of none. Indeed, those Comanches were so wrong-headed that they were inflicting heavy damages on other Indians as well as the Spaniards, and some people were retreating to the coast to escape their depredations. Well satisfied, Cabello told Courbière to take the guests to his house for the customary entertainment, with special emphasis on plenty to eat.

The next day Cabello grumbled that Lipans, like the devil, are found everywhere. Several turned up at Béxar to invite El Mocho and his companion to their camp, promising them horses and other inducements. Cabello accused the Lipan leader of scheming to lure his Tonkawa guests out to kill them and steal their horses; he denied it and left. Other Lipans came the next two days to press the invitation. Cabello offered to give each of the two Tonkawas a horse if they wished to make a night getaway. They accepted gratefully and rode off on the night of November 27, extolling the advantages of friendship with the Spaniards. In parting, El Mocho expressed his relief that the governor had not been angry as they had feared and promised again to establish a village and to avoid dealing with Apaches.

Cabello felt at least as relieved as El Mocho after their conversations. He had reckoned that, if the Tonkawas should join forces with

[26] Cabello to Croix, Béxar, November 20, 1780, BA.

the Comanches, the two nations could wipe out the province in just eight days. Now he was convinced that the Tonkawas would not join the Comanches, who were indeed their enemies, and that no Indians except Comanches were at war against Texas. With an experienced frontiersman already bound for the Comanchería with peace overtures, Cabello felt more hopeful than at any time since the death of de Mézières.

It was a badly needed glimmer of encouragement. That fall, while the Comanche attacks were at their worst, a smallpox epidemic swept the province. As in New Mexico, the disease decimated the Spanish population and wrought havoc among mission Indians. The sense of helplessness before the twin scourges of smallpox and Comanches and of virtual abandonment by a government preoccupied with war in other arenas had reduced morale to a low ebb everywhere in Texas, from the Governor's Palace to the presidial barracks, the mission compounds, and the settlers' jacals.

The smallpox spread to scattered Indian groups, and none suffered more than the Lipans. The epidemic dealt them a particularly cruel blow, coming hard upon their heavy losses at the hands of Comanches. To make matters worse, the Lipans fell victim to an appalling error by Laredo settlers. The Comanches, triumphantly pillaging from their base on El Monte del Diablo, extended their horse raids clear down to Laredo. Hastily blaming their losses on Lipans then encamped on the Nueces, 170 Spaniards of Laredo rode out for revenge. They surprised the Lipans, killed two men and one woman in the camp, and captured more than fifty horses and mules. Of course the Lipans vowed a terrible vengeance against Laredo and other settlements on the Rio Grande. They notified Governor Cabello that they were moving all their women and children to the Cañon de San Saba.[27] For the moment, the Lipans found the Comanche menace pale compared with Spanish vigilantes on the Rio Grande. Knowing the truth of the Lipans' grievance, Cabello could only deplore the misery that would flow from the gratuitous error of blaming the Lipans for Comanche deeds.

Meanwhile, La Mathe journeyed toward the Taovayas, slowed by the problems of winter travel and by his obligation to carry Cabello's greeting to any nation within practicable distance of his route. He called at the camps of the Akokisas, the Bidais, the joint camp of the Cocos and Mayeyes, and the principal Tejas village. He found the

[27] Cabello to Croix, Béxar, October 20, 1780, BA.

Kichai village empty, perhaps because its people had gone on the winter buffalo hunt, perhaps because they had fled the Comanche fury. La Mathe pressed on to visit the Tonkawa camp, then the main Tawakoni village, and the neighboring Flechazo village of that nation. Late in February 1781, he rode from the Tawakonis on the Brazos River to the Red River to visit the Taovayas and Panismahas.[28]

There the mission broke down. Perhaps the Taovayas and their associates could contain their exasperation no longer when La Mathe arrived with new promises and too few gifts to back up the old ones; perhaps the Norteños suffered some new affront, real or fancied. At any rate, in the spring of 1781 La Mathe sent word to San Antonio that he had failed to negotiate peace with the Comanches and that the Norteños were so dangerously sullen that there was no possibility of peaceful commerce with them. The personal safety of La Mathe and his two companions was in grave doubt.[29]

Governor Cabello notified Croix of La Mathe's failure and of continuing Comanche hostilities, as well as lesser depredations by Karankawas and Lipans. Croix could send no help. He recommended prayer for La Mathe's safety and authorized Cabello to take any other steps practicable and appropriate to bolster Providence. As to the future of Texas, the commandant general suggested that Cabello consolidate all forces at San Antonio de Béxar, where the presidio, villa, and missions together comprised an establishment of considerable size.

If that contraction should occur, the Bucareli settlers, newly established at Nacogdoches, would be recalled to the one defensible settlement in Texas. The ill-placed outpost at El Arroyo del Cíbolo and the nearly useless presidio of La Bahía would be abandoned, and their garrisons would be used to bolster the defenses of Béxar. Cabello did abandon El Cíbolo the next year, but he rejected the rest of Croix's suggestion because he considered the Nacogdoches settlement and La Bahía vital bases for contact with the Indian populations of their respective regions.

The Comanche vendetta raged on through most of 1781, and the beleaguered Spanish community never mounted effective opposition to the guerrilla tactics of the raiders. With Indian scouts, usually Lipans, informing him of enemy movements in the area, Cabello

[28] Croix, General Report of 1781, in Alfred Barnaby Thomas, ed., *Teodoro de Croix and the Northern Frontier of New Spain, 1776–1783*, pp. 80–87.
[29] Croix to Cabello, Arispe, June 13, 1781, BA.

minimized losses of life and property for those citizens who would cooperate in their own defense.

Cabello realized that the Comanches were unlikely to desist as long as they suffered no retaliation. By the year's end, he was ready to gamble everything to check the raiders. On December 5, when four of his Indian scouts sighted Comanches in the vicinity, Cabello decided to throw every available force against them. They numbered only 172: Alférez Valdés in command, 2 sergeants, 5 corporals, 49 soldiers, 59 settlers, 52 mission Indians, and the 4 scouts. Cabello ordered Valdés to lead an attack at daybreak the next morning, and late in the afternoon he dispatched a cavalry squad to cut off the enemy's retreat.[30]

When Valdés led his force out at dawn on December 6, the scouts put them on the enemy trail, leading to the Medina River. Cabello waited in the presidio with a fragment of the garrison: one sergeant in charge of the horse herd, three sick men, and two retired soldiers whom he put on guard duty. A few settlers, left behind for want of arms, manned the cannons. They corralled the horses inside the presidio because there was no one to guard them in the pasture. Cabello and his companions stayed awake all night, grimly conscious that a determined Comanche attack now could take the presidio and wipe out every defender.

The night passed without incident. Early the next morning, the sergeant and a dozen settlers herded the restless, hungry horses out to pasture. They weathered the day without encounters and drove the herd back into the presidio at dusk. Cabello and his men kept another all-night vigil, still without news of the troops. At sunrise, the sergeant led horse herd and herders back to pasture.

At noon shouts from the northwest signaled the return of the troops. The four Indian scouts galloped into the presidio waving Comanche trophies on their lances. The waiting community turned out to see its men ride into the presidio, unscathed except for one soldier with an arrow wound under his arm. Every man had acquitted himself bravely, and they had routed the enemy.

They had found the Comanches camped on a hill by the Medina, about sixty men, perhaps two dozen women and children, and a sizeable horse herd. The San Antonians tried to outflank them, but the Comanches saw that they were badly outnumbered, and many fled before Valdés could cut off their escape. Almost a third of the warriors and

[30] Cabello, Diary, Béxar, December 31, 1781, BA.

their chief died fighting while the rest escaped. The San Antonians rushed on to pursue the rest, who stood atop another hill and forced the Spaniards back with arrows and stones. The tired horses could not charge uphill against that barrage, so Valdés recalled his men to the initial battleground to assess their gains.

The survivors on the nearby hill shrilled their mourning cries while the San Antonians surveyed the carnage. Eighteen Comanche warriors lay dead. Their chief still clutched his heavily plumed lance, eight feet long. Buffalo horns adorned his headdress, and his splendid horse wore a matching buffalo-horned mask. Many scalps decorated his shirt: the San Antonians guessed that eighteen had belonged to mission Indians. No one knew his name, but this obviously had been an important war chief.

On the corpses were pitiful mementos of Spanish settlers killed in recent weeks: the cloak of Martín de la Garza; the wrought silver buttons of Marcos Montes; and trousers, shoes, and a silk kerchief, of unknown ownership. Also recovered were ten mules and seventy-four horses, all with trappings, many with well-made face covers.

Valdés could not pursue the sixty-odd survivors with such tired horses. He presented the Comanche souvenirs to the four Indian scouts who had made the victory possible, both to reward them for invaluable service and to inspire all scouts to still greater efforts in future. The men of San Antonio rode home the next day, happier than Texans had been for years.

Cabello greeted them with high praise, thanked them in the king's name, and promised to divide among them the booty of mules, horses, and saddles. The next day he solved the problem of dividing 84 animals among 171 men by converting the stock to a cash value of 445 pesos, which he divided among the fighters at 2 pesos and 4 reales each. The remaining seventeen pesos and four reales bought boxes of cigars for all. Everyone seemed as pleased with the settlement as with the grand victory. The Christmas season was off to a joyous start in San Antonio in 1781.

A week later, big smokes rose in the skies west of San Antonio. Cabello sent his four Indian scouts and a settler to investigate. They reconnoitered clear to the Guadalupe, and in three days reported that they had seen no enemy. They guessed that the smokes were Comanche signals, calling scattered raiders to count their losses and plan their response. Cabello assumed the Comanches would return in a month or two to revenge their dead chief and his seventeen warriors.

The governor was wrong. The forty-odd surviving warriors of the hostile group were either too few, or too bereft of leadership, or too disheartened to mount a new vendetta, and no other Comanches rallied to their cause. Unless the fallen chief had left a son who would grow up to avenge his father, as had the first Cuerno Verde, the San Antonio forces had finished that vendetta against their province. The tale of the disaster on the Medina surely made the rounds of Comanche camps in 1782, lending new force to the arguments of those chiefs who wanted peace with the Spaniards.

Cabello and his people dreaded Comanche vengeance for another four years, for they could not know how decisive their victory had been. The governor's real problems in 1782 developed among Apaches, Tonkawas, and Karankawas. As before, the bustling governor of Coahuila precipitated his difficulties with the Apaches.

Governor Ugalde campaigned vigorously against the Mescaleros and Natagés in 1781 and 1782, both in the Bolsón de Mapimí and in their mountain sanctuaries across the big bend of the Rio Grande. The first six months saw heavier casualties among Spanish soldiers than among Mescalero warriors and took such a toll of horses that critics later charged that every four animals Ugalde recaptured from the enemy cost the Crown twenty of its own. Even worse, while Ugalde and his troops chased the enemy in distant mountain ranges, Apache raiders took advantage of the troops' absence to inflict unusually heavy damages in Coahuila.

The fiasco so exasperated Commandant General Croix that he removed Ugalde in the spring of 1783, on grounds of insubordination and negligence. His replacement, Lieutenant Colonel Pedro de Tueros, assumed responsibility for repairing Coahuila's sagging defenses and morale and putting its troops into condition for a general offensive against the Apaches. Two influential *hacendados* in the areas of Saltillo and Parral had complained to the Crown that Croix protected their property from raiders less effectively than had O'Conor, thus precipitating late in 1782 a royal order to Croix to take the offensive against the Apaches. Croix respectfully went through the motions of making his troops ready, but the poor results achieved by Ugalde had confirmed Croix's earlier opinion that no effective general campaign could be made with the scant resources then available in the Provincias Internas.[31]

[31] Al B. Nelson, "Juan de Ugalde and the Rio Grande Frontier, 1779–1790," pp. 60–65; Thomas, ed., in *Teodoro de Croix*, pp. 61–62; Max L. Moorhead, *The*

Fortunately, a new peace overture from Mescaleros had given Croix an excuse not to proceed with the offensive. Perhaps because of Ugalde's incursions into Apache sanctuaries, one of the most notorious of the raiding chieftains rode into El Paso in July 1782 to sue for peace. When Croix agreed, on the condition that he and the others principally responsible for the recent raids in Coahuila would surrender, 137 Apaches, including 3 prominent chiefs, gave themselves up, a remarkable sacrifice to secure the safety of their people within the Apachería. Croix deported them to the interior under guard, and Coahuila and Nueva Vizcaya briefly enjoyed respite from raids.

Surrender to the Spaniards was not the only Apache reaction to Ugalde's offensive. To repair their shortages of warriors and guns, the Mescaleros and Natagés approached the Lipans to reconcile their two-year-old quarrel. The Lipans, battered by Comanches and by Laredo's trigger-happy settlers, responded gratefully. Late in 1781 or early in 1782, the hostile factions made peace, then sought guns.[32]

Apache envoys proposed alliance to the Tonkawas, who had access to firearms from Louisiana traders. When the Apaches offered to trade horses and skins for guns, the Tonkawas listened. Comanches and Osages had lately cost them many horses, and their treaty with the Spaniards inhibited raids on Texas herds. Skins were always good currency in the border trade, legal or illegal. Furthermore, El Mocho had not forgotten his Lipan origins. He persuaded the Tonkawas to consider the alliance, and he designated November and December 1782 as the time for a great trade fair for all the new friends.

Cabello heard of the deal. Angry and alarmed, he ordered the Tonkawas to cease dealing with the Lipans, whom he had already forbidden access to San Antonio. Several times that spring and summer Courbière harangued the Tonkawas about the obligations they had assumed when El Mocho became a medal chief; once he conveyed Cabello's threat to have El Mocho executed if the proposed gathering should occur. The Tonkawas ignored the messages.

Cabello asked Commandant General Croix for two hundred reinforcements for the Texan forces, so that the governor himself could punish the Tonkawas and make them an object lesson for all other nations tempted to traffic with Apaches. Croix could spare no troops.

Apache Frontier, pp. 205–206; Cabello, Ynforme, San Antonio de Béxar, September 30, 1784, AGN, Provincias Internas, vol. 64.

[32] Cabello, Ynforme.

Unable to prevent the meeting, Cabello determined at least to know what transpired and sent his interpreter to spy.

The governor had long esteemed Courbière as a man of extraordinary skill and daring. His performance on this mission more than vindicated that opinion. A native of Lyon, Courbière had gone to sea from his home city of Marseilles at thirteen.[33] He abandoned the ocean-going life at New Orleans to work on merchant boats plying the New Orleans-Natchitoches run, then spent five years in Natchitoches as a bookkeeper for a firm of traders catering principally to Tawakonis and Tonkawas. He became unusually proficient in the languages of those Indians and attracted the favorable notice of de Mézières. He accompanied the lieutenant governor to New Orleans, then served in his militia escort on his last trip to San Antonio. He proved an excellent interpreter for the Tonkawas who rode with de Mézières to San Antonio to establish treaty relations with Cabello. De Mézières recommended that Cabello retain Courbière permanently as an interpreter at Béxar, and Cabello was so favorably impressed that he did so, apparently at his own expense for two years. In November 1781, Cabello was able to award him a special post as soldier-interpreter in the Béxar garrison. Just a year later, Courbière donned Indian garb and rode alone from Béxar to spy on the assembly of Tonkawas and Apaches.

Courbière estimated more than four thousand Indians convened on the Guadalupe River in November and December 1782. About two thousand were Lipan, Mescalero, and Natagé warriors. Only six hundred Tonkawas came; the rest remained in their camps. Another assorted three hundred Tejas, Akokisas, Bidais, Cocos, and Mayeyes turned up. They traded about two hundred guns with powder and balls. The Tonkawas traded only seventy guns with ammunition. All gave the excuse that firearms were growing scarce because Spain's war with Great Britain had curtailed supplies in Louisiana. The Apaches were terribly disappointed. They had brought three thousand horses for a great trade, but they had to herd more than two thousand back home. The horses bore Spanish brands, evidence that they were stolen from private or presidial herds rather than captured mustangs.

Horses were not the only livestock involved. Courbière reckoned that the assembly ate more than four thousand cows, branded and

---

[33] Frederick C. Chabot, *With the Makers of San Antonio*, pp. 257–260, citing BA document of March 7, 1795.

unbranded. Great piles of bones marked the campsite when the gathering broke up, in haste and some discord, on Christmas Day 1782.

Although Apaches had initiated the meeting, El Mocho sought to turn it to his own purposes. Appealing to bonds of kinship, he proposed that the three Apache groups accept him as their principal chief: as leader of the Tonkawas and all the eastern Apaches, he would oust the Spaniards and all other Indians and control all the land. To push his claim, he sought out his Lipan kinsmen for a great sentimental reunion at the assembly, but in vain. Apache leaders were skeptical of El Mocho's grandiose scheme and loath to yield so much authority to such an ambitious man.

While the would-be allies wrangled over the scarcity of guns and the ambitions of El Mocho, old enemies brought them new woes. In mid-December, a big war party of Tawakonis, Taovayas, Wichitas, and Iscanis clashed with Lipans and Tonkawas on the Colorado River, perhaps catching them out hunting meat for the huge congregation on the Guadalupe.[34] The Apaches did not tarry long after that, lest the enemy return, reinforced, to fight another round. They abruptly pulled out of the assembly with their 270 new guns, their 2,000 surplus horses, and their disappointment, off to Coahuila and Nuevo Santander to rob and kill in one sector while Ugalde gave chase in another.

Courbière infiltrated the councils and celebrations without attracting notice, thanks to his extraordinary fluency in the languages and his successful disguise, and perhaps also to the cooperation of Tonkawas who disliked El Mocho. He did not dally long after the Apaches left. On New Year's Day 1783, he reported back to Béxar, rested a few days, then prepared a diary of the mission for the governor. Excited by its urgent importance, Cabello forwarded it to the commandant general on January 20.[35]

Croix promptly ordered him to have El Mocho killed. Spanish authorities could only regret the failure of de Mézières' arrangement to have him dispatched in 1778. Not until July 1784 was El Mocho's death

---

[34] Cabello to Don Pedro Piernas, Béxar, January 13, 1783, in Kinnaird, *Spain in the Mississippi Valley*, II, 70.

[35] Perhaps Cabello did not take time to have the customary copy made for his files; the Courbière diary is not in the Bexar Archives. Fortunately, a brief account of it occurs in Cabello's Ynforme on the Apaches, of which this author has used the Provincias Internas, AGN, copy. Presumably, copies of the diary were sent from Arispe to Mexico City and Seville. They would be well worth an extensive search, because Courbière was an extraordinarily intelligent, informed observer of Indians.

accomplished, and then less subtly than the Spaniards wished. They preferred not to kill him outright, especially as guest in a Spanish establishment, lest they incite the Tonkawas to revenge or shake the confidence of other chiefs whose visits the Spaniards desired. Ideally, they wanted El Mocho slain by Tonkawa malcontents. Courbière thought Yaculehen a likely assassin, and he was authorized to arrange it.[36]

While El Mocho and the Apaches experienced their failures at the meeting on the Guadalupe, Spain suffered a diplomatic reverse in Paris. The fighting on the American mainland had been virtually ended for a year, and the British ready to make peace with the Americans. Though nominally partner to victory, Spain was far from satisfied, despite her recapture of Florida from the British. At sea and at the conference table, Spaniards struggled on through 1782 for two prime objectives: to recover Gibraltar and to confine the new United States of America to the seaboard beyond the crest of the Appalachians. Gibraltar remained firmly in Great Britain's grip, and on November 30, 1782, the Americans signed preliminary peace terms with the British, designating the east bank of the Mississippi River their boundary. Regarding the new republic as a more threatening neighbor than even the British had been in North America, Spain began an urgent reassessment of Louisiana and the Provincias Internas vis-à-vis the United States.

Spain's best hope of containing American expansion was to solidify the loyalties of the Indian populations between the Spanish and American frontiers of settlement. Officials in Louisiana and the Floridas hastened to cement cordial relations with the tribes east of the Mississippi whose lands the Paris treaties would place under the American flag. New attention focused also upon the tribes of Texas and Louisiana, whose discontents invited penetration by British and American traders. More conspicuously dangerous than ever was the disarray that had marked Indian affairs west of Natchitoches ever since the death of de Mézières.

For all his earnest efforts, Cabello had never established diplomatic relations with any important interior nations except the Tejas and the Tonkawas, whose loyalty was now in serious doubt. Though he had meant to carry on the system of trade and presents established by de Mézières and to avoid any changes as potentially unsettling to the

---

[36] Neve to Cabello, Arispe, December 26, 1783, BA.

Indians, practical difficulties had foiled his purpose. By 1783 Cabello
was convinced that the system of gifts was, on the whole, pernicious
because it fostered the Indians' greed but not their gratitude and it
ensured their hostility when presents could not be obtained. He had
also come largely to oppose trade, arguing that frontier commerce
could not be effectively policed and that the traders' guns and liquor
tempted Indians to steal livestock from the Hispanic communities.
The toll of property and lives paid by the people of Texas seemed to
him the fault of contrabandists and of Louisiana officials indifferent to
suffering outside their own province.

Cabello's desire to abandon the system of trade and presents assorted
badly with the Crown's renewed interest in conciliating the interior
nations, and so his proposal was promptly squelched. That decision
was surely made easier at Arispe by the arrival in February 1783 of
the Louisiana trader La Mathe. Undaunted by the failure of his peace
mission in 1781, La Mathe proposed a new system of managing the
Norteños, with himself as commissioner. He offered to carry the appropriate present to each nation as soon as possible in the current year
and annually thereafter. Croix gratefully accepted La Mathe's offer
to act again as emissary to the interior nations and authorized the
financing of his mission from the Mesteña Fund.

La Mathe would try again to reach the Comanches as well as the
villagers of the interior. Croix felt so optimistic about the venture that
he urged Governor Anza to intensify his own efforts to negotiate peace
with the Comanches in order to complement the work of La Mathe.
The commandant general noted complacently that, if Comanches
should breach the peace, they would be deprived of their trade with
the Taovayas.[37] Obviously, he had not thought through the difficulties
of enforcing bans in the remote Red River villages or of protecting
from Comanche wrath Indians who would deny them trade.

In fact, the commandant general had not even guaranteed that the
project would take its intended form in Texas. To avoid any real or
fancied slight to Cabello, Croix granted the governor wide discretion
in implementing La Mathe's proposal. Cabello, who now trusted La
Mathe no more than any other Louisiana trader, dared not openly balk
a plan endorsed by Croix, but he modified it almost beyond recognition.

If Cabello were to be saddled permanently with the deplorable
system of presents, then he wanted at least to control distribution

[37] Neve to Cabello, Arispe, October 3, 1783, BA; Croix to Anza, Arispe, February 24, 1783, SANM, no. 858.

within his own province, the better to focus Indian loyalties upon Texas rather than Louisiana. Rather than transport presents to the Indians as La Mathe proposed, Cabello would have the Indians report for their gifts at a Nacogdoches warehouse that he would establish. That would leave no role for La Mathe, since Cabello meant for Lieutenant Governor Gil Ybarbo to administer the gifts at Nacogdoches, with Courbière seconded from Béxar to help at key distribution times.[38]

If Cabello could maneuver La Mathe out of the gift-distribution system, he had still to rely upon the governor of Louisiana for the required goods. The easiest and cheapest route for shipping goods was upstream from New Orleans, not overland from Veracruz. Cabello did try, however, to avoid dealing through the commandant at Natchitoches, who had an obvious stake in thwarting diversion of Indian traffic to Nacogdoches. The governor of Texas appealed directly to the governor of Louisiana for his cooperation in the procurement and shipment of goods for the interior nations. He forwarded La Mathe's estimates of the quantities needed, recommending certain increases and additions.

If the experiment had to be made, Cabello hoped that it would not founder on parsimony. The chiefs whom he had to conciliate counted great generosity an essential quality of leadership. For the Spanish king to show less than appropriate generosity in his gifts to them would be a grave error. Cabello found La Mathe's suggested annual presents for each chief almost insultingly small.[39] His list of general presents for the tribes seemed deficient, too. Welcoming the opportunity to show that he comprehended the Indians' desires better than did the Louisiana entrepreneur, Cabello recommended hats trimmed with imitation braid, small mirrors, awls, needles, scissors, steels, worm screws, and embroidered woolen braid with red edges. He requested ells of second-grade red cloth in addition to the usual blue limbourg, and braided as well as ordinary shirts. Cabello also objected that La Mathe's list allowed only for nations with whom the Spaniards already had treaty relations. If the desired peace were to be made with the Comanches

[38] Cabello to the Governor of Louisiana, San Antonio de Béxar, September 20, 1783, in Kinnaird, *Spain in the Mississippi Valley*, II, 80–85.

[39] La Mathe proposed to give each chief one axe, one hatchet, one gun, four pounds gunpowder, eight pounds bullets, one pair trousers, one fine trimmed shirt, one pair knitted stockings, one pair shoes with one pair common metal buckles, one-half pound vermilion, six large heavy knives, one pound beads, and one bundle of tobacco.

and if the Panismahas were to return to his jurisdiction, he would
need double quantities.

The arguments wore on interminably. What goods to which Indians?
In what quantities and at what cost? Under which provincial jurisdiction and from which distributing agent? Where? All the while, the Indians at issue suffered economic scarcities and uncertainties, growing
weaker, more demoralized, and more skeptical of the good faith of
either Spaniards or Frenchmen. Lacking either direct communication
or reliable information to help him to comprehend the plight of the
interior nations, and painfully conscious of the suffering of his own
constituents, Governor Cabello doggedly advocated the interests of
his province as he saw them. He would either control the livelihoods
and the loyalties of the interior nations or abandon all hope for the
survival of Texas.

While Cabello pursued the argument over the interior trade as
vigorously as slow communications allowed in 1783, he confronted
renewed difficulties with coastal Indians. Since the Comanche vendetta
had forced him to abandon the proposed campaign to exterminate
the Karankawas in 1780, their depredations had worsened considerably.
An apostate christened Joseph María emerged as a principal leader,
given to unusually persistent and damaging raids. He had a deep
grudge against Spaniards, rooted in his experiences at Mission Rosario,
and enough knowledge of Spanish ways to inflict cruelly telling blows.

The presidial garrison at La Bahía regularly tried to pursue the
offenders and just as regularly failed. Joseph María's Karankawas grew
so bold that their depredations extended westward, even to the San
Antonio area. Added to the dread of Comanche raids, the doubts about
the Norteños, and the vagaries of the Lipan "peace," the Karankawa
problem seemed intolerable by the end of 1782. Croix and Cabello
concluded that the Karankawas must be exterminated, as de Mézières
had contended in 1779. The principal thrust would be from La Bahía.[40]

Neither Croix nor Cabello had ever seen the stark, rattler-infested
barrier islands from which they now proposed to oust the Karankawas
in the interests of the Spanish Empire. Even if de Mézières had guessed
correctly that there were only 150 Karankawa warriors, it would be
dangerous to campaign against them in their coastal habitat. In addition to the usual difficulties of mustering men, horses, and supplies in

---

[40] Cuaderno regarding provisions for making war on the Carancaguazes in view
of their offenses, November 25, 1782, BA. See especially Croix to Cabello, Arispe,
November 25, 1782, and Cabello, Order, Béxar, April 4, 1783.

poor Texas, there was the problem of canoes to attack the coastal islands. The motley Texas forces would have to learn entirely new tactics even to survive the campaign, much less win. In short, a campaign to exterminate the Karankawas was a staggering responsibility for a province that had tottered on the brink of extinction for several years.

The Texans faced the spring of 1783 in the gloomy certainty that Comanches would resume any day their campaign for vengeance and loot. Daily Cabello sent patrols from Béxar to scout for signs of enemy approaches, especially on the north and west; not until May 26 did they find the dread indicators. Cabello sent out two Indian scouts to pursue the lead. By six o'clock that evening, one reported a big Comanche *ranchería* across the Guadalupe at Arroyo Blanco; the other returned three hours later with news of a big trail leading toward La Bahía. Governor Cabello effected security measures at Béxar, alerted the missionaries, and summoned all available mission Indians and armed settlers.[41]

Within thirty-six hours two squads were ready, one under Alférez Valdés, the other under Alférez Amangual. Of the total force of 122 men, 50 were members of the garrison, 40 were mission Indians, and 32 were settlers. To the governor's dismay, a dozen Lipans joined them. Casual visitors at the presidio, they saw the force assembling, guessed that it was going after Comanches, and insisted upon going along. Cabello emphatically preferred not to have Comanches see Lipans and Spaniards joined in battle against them, but at that moment he could not prevent it without provoking the Lipans. The San Antonians and Lipans rode out of the presidio together at noon on May 28, bound for Arroyo Blanco.

Cabello deployed his few remaining troops to protect the horses of the presidio and missions. He awaited the outcome in the nearly unmanned presidio, awake all night, using unarmed settlers as guards and cannoneers. Sentinels watched the countryside from the commanding viewpoint of the church tower. A week passed without news.

On the afternoon of June 6, Valdés and Amangual led their discouraged squads back into the presidio. The Comanches, forewarned, had fled the Blanco, abandoning poles of twenty tipis in their haste. The San Antonians followed their trail to the hills of the Pedernales, about eighty-five miles from Béxar, where the Comanches had erected another twenty tipis on a hilltop. Valdés and Amangual divided their force

[41] Cabello, Diary, Béxar, May 31, 1783, BA.

into several parties to head off the enemy; the largest headed for the Colorado River. They sighted the enemy, but their horses were too fatigued for effective pursuit, and the Comanches appeared uninterested in confrontation.

If the scouts' estimate of ten Indians to a tipi were valid, four hundred Comanches had invaded the area. A tense summer loomed ahead for Cabello and his constituents in 1783. However, June passed with only one more alarm, and that proved false. Missions San Juan and Espada reported ominous tracks in their vicinity, but Amangual's reconnaissance party found only a few Lipan hunters returning from the Guadalupe with ten or twelve horses, whose hoofs made the "big trail" that had scared the mission denizens.[42]

For several days in July, smokes rose northwest of Béxar, a sign that enemies were gathering again. Cabello sent Amangual out with twenty-five men to investigate. Shortly afterward, the lookout at Béxar reported eighteen Comanches. Cabello sent three of his best Indian scouts with twenty-one mounted Spaniards to give chase, but they failed to overtake the intruders. The next day settlers found the corpse of a Spaniard who had been so rash as to sleep in his house on the fringe of the settled area.[43]

Amangual returned in a week, again forced to give up pursuit of invaders because the mounts were in such poor condition, although each man had three horses. The trail had led to the headwaters of the Guadalupe, where a hastily vacated camp had accommodated perhaps eighty Comanches, who abandoned many mules as they fled. The San Antonians followed the trail on toward the hills of the Pedernales; on August 4 they reached the Llano River, more than 125 miles from Béxar. Dead horses marked the rugged trail. Many of the San Antonians were exhausted from crossing the rocky hills, and eight of their own horses dropped dead. They had to turn back.[44]

A week later, on August 13, Valdés rode out with twenty-five men to patrol the western approaches to San Antonio. Two Indian scouts helped them to scour the area of the Guadalupe's headwaters, but nowhere could they find any sign of the enemy. On the sixth day they rode back into the presidio. In turn, Amangual led out twenty-five men on August 24, with two Indian scouts well versed in Comanche ap-

[42] Cabello, Diary, Béxar, June 30, 1783, BA.
[43] Cabello, Diary, Béxar, July 31, 1783, BA.
[44] Cabello, Diary, Béxar, August 31, 1783, BA.

proaches. Four days later they too returned without having sighted an enemy.

Smokes rose southwest and west of Béxar on September 3. Again Amangual took twenty-five men out with two Indian scouts to check for signs of enemy presence. Cabello ordered them to head for the Medina River and from there to circle around to the hills of the Comal rising northwest of San Antonio. Amangual reported back on September 9: nothing.[45]

Friendly Indian visitors broke into Cabello's tense preoccupation with Comanches. On the night of September 13, three Tejas Indians rode into the presidio to ask permission for their chief and others of their nation to enter for a visit with the governor. Cabello readily assented and ordered the customary arrangements for hospitality. Interpreter Courbière rode out with a corporal and six soldiers to escort the visitors into Béxar. They reached the governor's house about ten o'clock next morning: thirty-one men and three women from the village of Bigotes. Cabello greeted all of the party, then had most of them shown to their quarters while he talked with the leader and two others.

A sad, important errand had brought them to the capital. Bigotes, or Sauto, the able chief long noted for exceptional loyalty to the Spaniards, was dead. This group had come to ask the governor to name Bigotes' brother, the leader of this delegation, to succeed the dead chief. They bore Gil Ybarbo's letter vouching for them. Courbière testified that he had known these Tejas Indians well for many years and that the man they named would be a very good chief. Accordingly, Cabello arranged to furnish him the usual uniform and flag.

The Tejas made a cordial eight-day visit. Cabello talked frequently with the new chief and other leading men of the party, earnestly counseling against involvement with Lipans. On September 21, 1783, Baltasar Bigotes, splendid in his new uniform, accepted from the governor the cane of office, the official patent, and the flag of the Cross of Burgundy to mark his formal investiture as chief of his small community of vassals of the Spanish Crown. Cabello presented one of his own horses to the new chief and distributed small gifts to all the party. Again he charged them to avoid trade and communication with the Lipans.

The next day they started homeward by way of La Bahía, traveling with a large party of Spaniards. Cabello entrusted to them papers for

[45] Cabello, Diary, Béxar, September 30, 1783, BA.

delivery at Nacogdoches, including important dispatches to the governor of Louisiana and the commandant of Natchitoches. The Tejas bade their Spanish companions a cordial goodbye at La Bahía, where El Mocho and some Tonkawas fell in with them, ostensibly to accompany them across the Guadalupe. Their promises notwithstanding, the Tejas soon paused to trade with Lipans. No Spaniard could be sure whether a superior force of Lipans waylaid and intimidated the Tejas or whether they chose to trade as a matter of convenience. El Mocho's presence suggested that he had set up the encounter, which strengthened the Spaniards' determination to dispose of him. With the approval of both Cabello and Commandant General Neve, Courbière pursued negotiations with Yaculehen, a Tonkawan rival of El Mocho.[46]

A day after the Tejas delegation left San Antonio, heavy equinoctial rains marked the beginning of the coldest, wettest autumn within Spanish memory of the region. Incessant rainstorms hampered the operations of the Béxar troops, but they also discouraged raiders. Cabello relied entirely upon Lipan scouts instead of his usual patrols, and they found no enemy signs in the whole province. One pair reported back on October 13. On a thirty-two-day sweep out past the abandoned San Sabá presidio and nearly as far north as the Taovayas villages, they had seen no signs of enemies.[47]

Cabello feared that the dearth of Comanches in the usual places simply meant that they were gathering elsewhere, perhaps concerting with other nations in a great war party to wipe out San Antonio. Most of his garrison fell sick as the heavy rains continued through October, and the governor wondered how his troop of invalids would defend the presidio against a Comanche assault.

Apprehension mounted with two disquieting incidents on the last day of October 1783.[48] A Jacame Indian called Francisco, from Mission Espada, was herding sheep at the junction of the Medina and San Antonio rivers when a man on foot hailed him. The stranger, dressed in Indian style and carrying bows and arrows, introduced himself as Miguel Jorge Menchaca, son of retired Captain Luis Menchaca, and explained that he had been living for more than two years among the Comanches. He asked where the king's horse herd was pastured. When Francisco said that it was on the Arroyo del León, west of the presidio,

[46] Neve to Cabello, Arispe, December 26, 1783, BA.
[47] Cabello, Diary, Béxar, October 31, 1783, BA.
[48] Cabello, Diary, Béxar, November 30, 1783, BA.

Menchaca protested that he had just been there with fifteen Indians and had seen no horses.

Just then two Indians on foot, one armed with a lance and one with a gun, came up to speak with Menchaca. Francisco, who claimed that he knew the speech of Comanches, Taovayas, Tawakonis, and Tonkawas, could not recognize the speech of those two. They had short hair, an important identifying characteristic, but Francisco had no idea of their tribe. Menchaca strode off with them. Francisco hurried back to Mission Espada to tell the missionary, who promptly sent him to the presidio to tell the governor.

Unidentified Indians looking for the king's horses with a renegade Spaniard to guide them! Cabello was gravely alarmed, but among his ailing soldiers he could find only ten fit for duty. He sent them after the intruders with fifty-five militiamen and Francisco as guide. They achieved nothing.

At dusk the settler Gaspar Flores reported another encounter with Menchaca. Flores and two other settlers had been about five miles northeast of Béxar to catch some horses when the same young man, dressed like a Comanche, approached them, riding a bay horse. Flores, who had been a servant in Captain Menchaca's household, recognized Miguel and, seeing him unarmed, paused to chat with him. Miguel asked about the health of his parents and his grandmother. Flores replied that the father and mother were both well, but the old grandmother had died nearly three weeks before. Miguel's eyes brimmed with tears, but he rejoined his Indian companions. Flores hurried back to Béxar to tell the governor, who surmised that young Menchaca had come to guide Comanche raiders.

Quite apart from the heartbreaking disgrace to his locally prominent family, Menchaca's presence suggested grave danger for San Antonio. With his intimate knowledge of the locality, he could sharpen the effectiveness of any raiders whom he guided. He had to be captured at all costs, both to avert immediate danger and to make an example to any potential renegades. Commandant General Neve shared the governor's concern. He issued a general alert and sent young Menchaca's description to Governor Anza. If Miguel should visit New Mexico with one of the Comanche groups seeking peace, he would be jailed at Santa Fe.[49]

[49] Neve to Cabello, Arispe, December 26, 1783, BA.

Neither Menchaca nor the Comanches fulfilled the Spaniards' gloomy forebodings, but reports of *bárbaros* roving the area kept tension high at San Antonio. On November 6, Cabello's four Lipan scouts reported some sixty Indian men and one woman across the Colorado, about 150 miles north of Béxar. Since they had short hair, they were presumed to be Taovayas and Tawakonis en route to San Antonio to meet Cabello, but no such visitors arrived.

The scouts had also spied a very large Comanche camp at the junction of the Llano and Colorado rivers. A tipi count suggested two hundred Comanches, but few horses were visible. That was ominous: surely those Comanches did not plan to walk back to the Comanchería. Cabello was not surprised when reports of horse thefts, seventy here, a dozen there, poured in from outlying ranches at dusk on the very day of his scouts' return; the puzzling thing was that most of the reports blamed Tonkawas. No matter who was guilty, Cabello could do little to investigate or pursue. Again he had only ten soldiers and some settlers available; most of the troops had gone to escort the caravan from Saltillo.

Again Cabello relied upon Apache scouts. They reported back in ten days. The trail of the stolen horses had led them to the Guadalupe; the signs seemed to indicate Tonkawas or Karankawas. There had been no other signs of enemy activity. On November 19, more scouts reported that the big Comanche *ranchería* sighted three weeks earlier at the Llano-Colorado junction had moved southward, perhaps driven away by the excessive rains plaguing San Antonio. Gone too was the big party of short-haired Indians reported earlier across the Colorado.

The Comanches' southward movement seemed confirmed on November 28, when two settlers from Laredo rode into Béxar. Fifteen Comanches had attacked them on the trail five days earlier. They had escaped with their lives, thanks to their good mounts, but had lost ten horses to the raiders.

The miserable year of 1783 blew out with a blizzard, a fitting climax to three dismal months of rain, cold, and suffering. With the few men whom he could find well at any given time, Cabello struggled against minor depredations and brooded upon the prospect of an ultimate fatal concert of Indians against his presidio. Given the uncertainty about the identities of most raiders, it appeared that any or all of the Indian populations might be turning hostile.

Weather dealt the community another heavy blow on the night of

January 7, 1784, when a fierce norther stampeded all the horse herds of San Antonio. The troops fanned out in all directions to recover the animals, but five days' hard work recovered only fifty-six horses belonging to either soldiers or settlers. The San Antonians suspected that some of their horses were appropriated by Lipans camped across the Medina at Atascoso.[50]

The feeling of helpless outrage in San Antonio swelled in mid-January, when silent raiders filched a dozen horses tied at the doors of their owners' homes within the settlement. Cabello's scouts said the signs indicated Tonkawas, and the governor grimly vowed to punish them when and if he could muster the strength. When the snowstorm finally ended on January 19, he sent Valdés and Amangual north to find the robbers, with orders to treat Tonkawas just like Comanches if found with stolen horses. The force to execute that order consisted of thirty-one soldiers, twenty settlers, and four Indian scouts. They returned to Béxar after a week's search revealed no trace of the stolen horses. They had trailed sixteen or twenty Indians afoot but could not identify them. Cabello assumed that those Indians, whoever they were, would not leave the area without horses to ride.

Although the beginning of 1784 found Cabello mired in a day-to-day struggle with petty raiders and weather problems, the new commandant general soon demanded more and better attention to the longer view.[51] Spain now needed more desperately than ever the loyalty of all interior nations; Neve wanted Cabello to discover at once how to win them to meaningful alliance. Most of all, he urged Cabello to try hard to pacify the Comanches and particularly to attract them to trade in the Taovayas and Tawakoni villages, so as to draw them away from New Mexico.

Cabello could not find an agent who would venture to the Comanchería or even to the Taovayas in that dismal, tense spring, but he did have a startling opportunity to learn more about the latter.[52] A big Taovayas-Wichita war party rode south in May 1784 to avenge four of their people killed by Lipans. Most of them headed for La Bahía, where half a dozen leaders and 102 warriors paid Captain Cazorla a

[50] Cabello, Diary, Béxar, January 31, 1784, BA.

[51] Neve to Cabello, Arispe, January 28, 1784, December 18, 1783, and January 9, 1784, BA.

[52] Cabello to Neve, Béxar, March 22, 1784, March 3, 1784, March 23, 1784, and March 31, 1784, BA.

courtesy call to notify him that their quarrel was with the Lipans, not the Spaniards. Since their purpose well suited Spanish policy, Cazorla extended his poor presidio's best hospitality.

Unfortunately for their serious tribal purpose, some adventurous young warriors split from the main party en route to La Bahía to look for excitement. One group tangled with twenty-five men from Béxar who had gone out with Luis Mariana Menchaca to round up wild cattle. The Taovayas not only disrupted their round-up but also roasted some of their herd and seized a horse from the Spaniards.[53]

Menchaca's party retreated unhappily, camping for the night down toward La Bahía. Lipans happened by, on their way to join three hundred more for a hunt beyond the Guadalupe. Menchaca aired his grievance, suggesting that the bullies had been Comanches. The Lipans rode off to investigate and clashed with five Taovayas, of whom they killed four and captured one. Under interrogation, the captive said that he had come with many others who had already gone to La Bahía and that Governor Cabello had invited the chiefs of the interior nations to come to Texas to make war on the Lipans.

Understandably annoyed, the Lipans carried the tale to their hunting assembly. A big Lipan force rode to La Bahía and chased the Taovayas visitors when they emerged from the presidio, much to the annoyance of Captain Cazorla, whose guests they had been. The Taovayas escaped by outmaneuvering their enemies. The Lipans returned to their old camp between the Nueces and the Rio Grande to dance and to eat their one captive. En route, Chief Casaca and a few more of the Lipan leaders best acquainted with Cabello stopped at Béxar to complain vociferously about his reported invitation to their enemies and about the entertainment and gifts accorded the Taovayas at La Bahía. Somehow Cabello soothed them for the moment, but he did not delude himself that he had solved the problem.

No Taovayas called upon the governor at Béxar. Cabello heard of scattered depredations in the area and, in the absence of Comanche signs, suspected the Taovayas. He was annoyed that Cazorla had not admonished them at La Bahía.

The situation took a graver turn on July 8, when fifteen Indians skewered and scalped two luckless Spanish plowmen in a field just south of San Antonio. Four of Cabello's Indian scouts trailed the marauders northwest to San Sabá, concluded there were fifteen or

[53] Cabello to Neve, Béxar, June 20, 1784, BA; Rengel to Cabello, Chihuahua, April 25, 1785, BA.

twenty Comanches, and turned back because they were too exposed to danger out there.[54]

The crowning insult occurred just a week later. On the night of July 15, Indians broke through the gates of the house just south of the Governor's Palace, then forced their way through barred windows and a padlock into the pen back of his house, and stole two of Cabello's own best horses and two that belonged to his servants. They also trampled the garden west of his house, wrecking all his melons, squashes, and corn.

The governor's servants awoke him at dawn on July 16 to report the outrage. He promptly dispatched Amangual with twenty soldiers and two scouts, but they had to turn back to Béxar after they followed the trail for fifteen miles, because they had only one horse apiece. Convinced that Comanches must have committed the daring crime, Cabello began organizing a major expedition to punish them wherever they might be found.

Two days later the governor learned that the culprits were actually fifty adventurous Taovayas and Wichita lads, who had tarried behind to seek excitement after the rest of the big vengeance party rode homeward. With them as a servant had been Francisco Xavier Chaves, a Spaniard captured from New Mexico by Comanches and subsequently sold to a Taovayas master. Chaves escaped on the morning of July 18, as the raiders hit the homeward trail, and that afternoon presented himself at Béxar. One brief talk with Chaves convinced Cabello that all the recent depredations should be blamed on the Taovayas and Wichitas, and he resolved to punish them. He resented particularly the apparent faithlessness of the Taovayas medal chief Gransot, whom La Mathe had praised.

Indignation overcame judgment. Cabello knew perfectly well the fate that Parrilla's large force had suffered on the Red River in 1759, but, on the morning of July 19, 1784, he directed a much smaller force toward the Taovayas and Wichita villages. Valdés and Amangual commanded only seventy-nine men: forty soldiers and two sergeants, twenty-eight settlers, and nine mission Indians. In their absence, the presidio stood nearly defenseless. Cabello set an all-night watch at each of the five gates and wondered whether the Tonkawas would choose this time to attack. While the force was gone, no one dared work in the fields because no protection was available.

[54] Cabello to Neve, Béxar, July 20, 1784, BA.

With five Indian scouts guiding them, Valdés and Amangual followed the Taovayas-Wichita trail easily enough across the Guadalupe. There they chanced upon another trail, apparently of about forty Comanches, on the route customarily used to raid Béxar. Duty was clear. They sought out the Comanches and engaged them in a day-long battle in the thick woods on the bank of the Guadalupe. The San Antonians killed ten Comanches, captured many more, and took all their horses. Valdés and Amangual congratulated themselves on the greatest success against the Comanches in three years.

They tried to pick up the Taovayas-Wichita trail again the next day, but the raiders now had a hopelessly long lead. With three soldiers and one Indian scout badly wounded, Amangual and Valdés turned back to Béxar.[55]

Cabello found their triumph a dubious blessing. Béxar garrison lost two of its best veterans when two of the wounded soldiers died.[56] To fill their places, Cabello speedily hired the two best young men whom he could recruit from the settlement, lest the Comanches come to avenge their losses and find a diminished garrison. He also worried that the Taovayas and Wichitas, having suffered no penalty for their escapade, would return to prey upon the settlement more arrogantly than ever.

At that gloomy juncture, a Béxar resident volunteered to visit the Taovayas village. Juan Baptista Bousquet, a veteran of the Louisiana trade, fluent in the languages of the Tonkawas, Taovayas, and some other Norteños, had accompanied La Mathe to the interior nations in 1781. At the Taovayas village he had heard of a silver deposit and had brought back ore samples that assayed well. Now he wanted to fetch a quantity of the ore.[57]

Cabello not only granted Bousquet a passport but also appointed him envoy to convey the governor's good will to the villages of the Iscanis, Flechazos, and Tawakonis en route. The governor ordered special attention to the great Tawakoni chief, Siscat Gainon, and a report on his mood. At the Taovayas, Cabello wanted particular courtesy shown the great chief, Gransot, and close observations made of the temper of his people. Above all, he wanted to find out why they had been raiding in Texas. Cabello wished the Iscanis, Flechazos, and Tawakonis invited to San Antonio for gifts, but he meant the

55 Cabello, Ynforme.
56 Cabello to Neve, Béxar, August 18, 1784, BA.
57 Cabello to Neve, Béxar, August 19, 1784, BA.

Taovayas and Wichitas to understand that they had sacrificed that privilege by their treachery and wrong-headedness. If the two disaffected groups should resent that message, Bousquet's lot would not be happy, but on July 31 he cheerfully set out.

Gransot died before Bousquet reached the Red River that autumn. His people counted it but the latest in a long series of misfortunes. Their friendship with the Comanches had fallen into grave disrepair when they negotiated peace with the Spaniards in the time of de Mézières, and they had suffered damage from that quarter ever since. Meanwhile, their economy, and thus their war potential, had eroded because trade had broken down under the Spanish regime. To crown their woes, rash young men had that summer jeopardized their peace with the Spaniards. While down south to look for Lipans, they had deviated from their purpose to commit crimes at San Antonio. They had even stolen the governor's own horses from his house.

To steal a picketed horse from the owner's lodge was usually counted a glorious coup in plains warfare, but in this instance the lads did not find themselves hailed as heroes. Their thoughtless exploit endangered the concord of their people with the Spaniards at a time when they needed support rather than new enmities. On their way home the young men stopped at the villages of the Tawakonis, Flechazos, and Iscanis to boast, only to be severely scolded by the elders. When the leading men of their own village learned of the theft, they were dismayed and wanted to make amends, but they were afraid to go to Béxar. Therefore, they welcomed Bousquet and gladly accepted his offer to mediate for them with the governor.

Gransot had bequeathed his cane of office and his medal to Guersec, stipulating that it was only an interim succession and that a proper new commission could be issued only by the Spanish Crown. The people of both villages affirmed their desire to have Guersec as permanent successor to Gransot, so Bousquet volunteered to escort their spokesmen to the governor to make the request. He also persuaded three Europeans then residing in the village to accompany him to San Antonio, promising them that the governor would pardon their offense of living illegally among the Indians and welcome them into the San Antonio community.

Unfortunately, the journey to Béxar took much longer than any of the party anticipated. Comanches stole their horses early in the trip, so they had to walk much of the way. It was February 1785 before they arrived at San Antonio, and much longer before anyone realized what a useful contribution Bousquet had made. One of the new residents whom he brought to San Antonio from the Taovayas village was the prodigious frontiersman Pedro Vial.[58]

Certainly Cabello had no indication during the fall of 1784 that Bousquet would achieve any great result. Bousquet himself was a hapless fellow whom Ripperdá had jailed on suspicion of trafficking with hostile Indians. Cabello had found the evidence against him unconvincing and had released him in 1779.[59] He had no reason to think that Bousquet would actually bring back any wealth from the Taovayas; indeed, Gil Ybarbo's reports indicated that he would be lucky just to get back with his scalp. Gil Ybarbo attributed to Tejas Indians a report that many Taovayas and Wichitas were gathering with the Comanches to mount a big September campaign against the Spaniards of Béxar and against any Apaches they could find.[60] As was often the case with Gil Ybarbo's reports, that story agreed very little with conditions found by observers in the Taovayas village and with the actual course of events, but it spawned much anxiety in San Antonio and Arispe.

Lacking that comforting knowledge, Cabello spent a gloomy September awaiting the grand assault. Most able-bodied settlers had gone to the Saltillo fair, leaving only seventy-four men at the governor's disposition. To make matters worse, a four-month drought had so completely ruined the pasture at Béxar that the horse herd had to be pastured nearly fifty miles from the presidio, with a heavy guard that absorbed most of the available manpower. If a large party of Comanches, Taovayas, and Wichitas should attack the presidio, Cabello could muster no force to defend it.

Cabello fretted even more about reports from La Bahía of a new rapprochement of Tejas and Lipans. That had occurred when rumors of a Comanche-Taovayas-Wichita thrust into the Béxar area deflected a party of Tejas from their intended visit to the governor. They turned instead to La Bahía, where a Lipan invited them to visit his camp at Atascoso. Cabello did not doubt that the affair would soon involve Bidais, Akokisas, Mayeyes, and Cocos and that a great volume of trade in guns, munitions, and stolen horses would follow. It was fearsomely reminiscent of the problems with the Tonkawas in 1782.

Now, in the autumn of 1784, the Tonkawas gave Cabello his one

---

[58] Cabello to Rengel, Béxar, February 18, 1785, BA.
[59] Cabello to Croix, Béxar, August 13, 1779, BA.
[60] Cabello to Neve, Béxar, September 30, 1784, BA.

ground for optimism. Through the spring and early summer they had been unusually troublesome. Cabello's intelligence network indicated that the root of the problem lay with Xaraname apostates from Mission Espíritu Santo, who incited and guided Tonkawa raiders to satisfy their own grudges,[61] but Tonkawa depredations reminded the Spaniards that El Mocho was dangerous. Since the plan to have him assassinated discreetly had never worked out, Captain Cazorla acted when the chief visited La Bahía in July 1784. El Mocho died in the presidio, obviously the victim of the Spaniards. Cabello spent some anxious weeks wondering about the outcome. Presumably the Tonkawas would now be less likely to consort with the Lipans and therefore easier to manage.[62] However, if they should decide to avenge their murdered chief, Spaniards and mission Indians would pay dearly.

It was thus an immeasurable relief when, in early autumn, the new chief of the Tonkawas led a delegation to Presidio La Bahía to assure the Spaniards that they held no resentment for the execution of El Mocho as ordered by the commandant general. They recognized the correctness of the decision.[63]

If the new chief of the Tonkawas proved as friendly toward the Spaniards as he first appeared, then the implications were as far-reaching as they were favorable. The Tonkawas had been the largest nation maintaining trade and communication with the Lipans. Once divorced from that connection, they could become a valuable buffer to cut off the Lipans' access to the Tejas, Cocos, Bidais, Mayeyes, and Akokisas. Cabello speculated that he might even be able to involve all those groups with the Taovayas, Wichitas, and Tawakonis in a grand alliance against the Lipans. For the time being, the Tonkawas would receive especially favorable treatment to cultivate their friendship and loyalty to the Spaniards.

Certainly a grand design to end the Lipan problem suited Cabello's mood that autumn. Lipans had sued for peace in Nuevo Santander, and Viceroy Matías de Gálvez desired Cabello's opinion of its merits. The question aroused all the indignation accumulated in six years of managing the anomalous peace with the Lipans in Texas. Cabello not only counseled against admitting them to peace in Nuevo Santander; he also argued forthrightly for their extermination.

Realizing that his stand laid him open to charges of inhumanity,

[61] Cabello to Neve, Béxar, March 20, 1784, BA.
[62] Cabello to Neve, Béxar, July 15, 1784, BA.
[63] Rengel to Cabello, Chihuahua, December 31, 1784, BA.

Cabello extracted from the Béxar archives a detailed history of Spanish relations with Apaches in Texas. After a scathing analysis of campaign methods hitherto employed against Apaches, especially by Ugalde, he advanced a detailed plan to conquer or exterminate them, openly preferring the latter. He cited Old Testament chronicles of tribal warfare to justify his moral position, arguing that the king of Spain had a duty to wipe out the Apaches even as God had ordered King Saul to kill the Amalekites. Cabello had come to see Apaches as incorrigible enemies of God and the king and the human race.[64]

While the governor brooded about grand biblical wrath, 1784 ended quite routinely, with no sign of great onslaught by any *bárbaros*. Minor Karankawa depredations continued, and Cabello pursued the problem of procuring men and canoes for the job of exterminating them. On Christmas Day a squad of twenty-six men from La Bahía made a gesture toward checking their depredations, but the Karankawas spotted them and simply withdrew. Comanches took horses from corrals in the San Antonio settlement and left plain tracks, but nothing could be done about it. Cabello had few soldiers available, and for those he had left just one horse apiece.[65] Fortunately for the governor, he was no longer under such great pressure to achieve some grand breakthrough on either front. The ambitious Commandant General Neve died in November, and his ad interim successor, Commandant Inspector Joseph Antonio Rengel, held more realistic expectations of his subordinates.

[64] Cabello, Ynforme.
[65] Cabello, Report for December 1784, Béxar, December 31, 1784, BA.

CHAPTER 19

Texas and New Mexico, 1785-1786

February 1785 marked an inconspicuous, but vitally important, turn in the fortunes of Texas. Sometime during the night of the thirteenth, Juan Bousquet walked into San Antonio with seven companions. He found lodgings for all of them in the presidio, and next morning he brought them to see the governor.[1]

Four were Taovayas and Wichita leaders, authorized by their people to seek a new medal chief and to repair their relations with the Spaniards. Pedro Vial and Alfonso Rey were Frenchmen who had lived for some time with the Taovayas; both spoke Spanish fluently. Antonio Mariano Valdés, a native of San Antonio, had lived eight years with the Taovayas. All three had broken the law by dwelling unauthorized among Indians, but, as Bousquet had promised, Governor Cabello readily pardoned them and bade them welcome to the community.

Most immediately important were the Taovayas and Wichita spokesmen. Bousquet urged Cabello to honor their choice of Guersec as their medal chief. The governor agreed and held formal council with the

[1] Cabello to Rengel, Béxar, February 18, 1785, BA.

four delegates. Andrés Courbière interpreted for the governor, as usual, assisted by Francisco Xavier de Chaves, who had lived at the presidio since his July escape from the Taovayas raiders. Captured in childhood from New Mexico by Comanches and later sold to Taovayas, he knew the speech and customs of both nations. The meeting of February 14, 1785, began his long, useful career as interpreter and intermediary with those key nations.

Observing quietly were three men whom Chaves must have known at the Taovayas village, Vial, Rey, and Valdés. Never before had Cabello enjoyed access to so much intimate knowledge of the interior nations or so many competent checks upon accuracy of interpretation. Nor was the advantage one-sided. These Taovayas and Wichita spokesmen had an unusually good chance to convey exactly what they intended to say. Bousquet first aired Governor Cabello's complaints about the escapades of the previous summer, particularly the theft of his own horses and the damage to his house and garden. The delegates explained apologetically that rash youngsters had acted without their leaders' knowledge and had been severely reprimanded for their folly. All their people were deeply sorry and wished to make amends. The young men had gotten out of hand during Gransot's declining years, but the vigorous Guersec would control the nation. If any more wrong-headed youngsters should breach the peace, he would make them pay with their lives. The four emissaries prayed the governor to confirm Guersec as grand chief of both villages and to let the Taovayas and Wichitas show what faithful friends they could be.

Bousquet, Chaves, Vial, Rey, and Valdés all vouched for their story and for the excellent qualities of Guersec. Satisfied, Cabello turned to his other great concern, urging the delegates not to let their villages make peace or trade with the Comanches. They responded that they were actually hard at war with them; indeed, they had lost all their horses to Comanches en route to Béxar. Guersec and his people hoped that the Spaniards would help them maintain a lively war against the Comanches. The Taovayas could point out the Comanche camps so that the Spanish soldiers could punish them well.

Cabello was astounded to see how enthusiastically the Taovayas and Wichita spokesmen bid for friendship with the Spaniards. They wanted so much traffic between their villages and San Antonio that no grass would grow on the road. Cabello obtained their promise to visit Nacogdoches in June for his annual distribution of gifts to the allied nations. He apologized for not having at Béxar gifts suitable to celebrate their new accord, but he did present them with four horses for their homeward journey and made sure they enjoyed the presidio's best hospitality throughout their visit.

The four delegates carried back home a chief's commission for Guersec, empowering him to govern the two villages in peace and in war. The document attested his reputation for bravery, his loyalty toward the Spaniards, and his command of a good following in the two villages; it also stipulated that Guersec have his people live as vassals of the king of Spain and take them to war only in defense against his enemies. It would be his duty to help all other vassals of the king and to join campaigns against the enemies of His Majesty. Over his village he would fly the royal flag, bestowed upon him with the medal of merit, the cane of office, and the hat and coat of a captain.[2] The four delegates accepted all those conditions in the name of Guersec and all his people. Bousquet, Vial, Rey, and Valdés affirmed that the people of the two villages truly understood and desired the arrangement.

After the Taovayas and Wichita envoys left, Cabello assessed the new members whom Bousquet had brought to the community. Two were extremely valuable. Pedro Vial, a native of Lyon, was a good blacksmith, able to make lances and repair guns, skills that Spaniards prized in their own communities and preferred not to see established in Indian communities. How and why and when Vial had come to ply his trade in the wilderness was never clear, but Spanish authorities had first noted and worried about him in 1779. During de Mézières' first attempt to travel to San Antonio that spring, Vial visited Natchitoches en route to New Orleans. He had redeemed a Spanish captive from the Indians and presumably claimed proper reimbursement from the authorities. Whatever Governor Gálvez learned about Vial prompted an order to prevent him from returning to live among the unfriendly nations. Not only did the fellow repair arms for Indians; it was said that he had even taught one the gunsmith's trade.[3]

Vial somehow evaded Spanish authorities to return to the wilderness, where he lived and worked among Indians for nearly six years before Bousquet found him at the Taovayas village and persuaded him to seek pardon in San Antonio. Vial again returned to civilization with

---

[2] Cabello, Commission appointing Guersec as Captain of the Taovayas Indians, Béxar, February 14, 1785 (copy), BA.

[3] Noel M. Loomis and Abraham P. Nasatir, *Pedro Vial and the Roads to Santa Fe*, pp. 264–265.

captives redeemed from the Indians, an act both humane and provident. He purchased them with goods or services valued in the Indian economy, then at San Antonio collected sixty pesos reimbursement to stake a new life in a money economy.

One of the captives whom he delivered was a six-year-old Apache girl, who would be reared in a local Christian household, either Spanish or Indian. The other was a Spanish girl, now eighteen, captured by Apaches in New Mexico a dozen years earlier, then captured by Comanches, who sometime later sold her to a Taovayas owner, who sold her to Vial. She was sure only that her name was María Teresa; she thought that her family name had sounded something like Santos. Cabello made inquiries to establish her identity, then arranged for her return to the settlement of Santa Cruz.[4]

With Vial's sixty pesos' stake, he and Alfonso Rey rented a little house and settled into the San Antonio community. Vial opened a smithy at the house and proved a skilled armorer, locksmith, and silversmith, as well as a good blacksmith and an unusually alert and intelligent citizen. Rey hung out his shingle as a barber, bloodletter, tooth puller, and surgeon early in March, just before Comanche raiders inflicted twenty-seven wounds on a soldier defending the horse herd. Everyone despaired of Antonio Baguera's life, but Rey vowed that he could pull him through, and he made good his promise. Other patients flocked to the new practitioner; more remarkable cures followed. The presidial company retained him to care for themselves and their families for a small monthly fee from each member of the garrison, plus the cost of medicines, to be borne by individuals.[5]

Antonio Mariano Valdés, unskilled, hired out as a servant in a local household. The fortunes of Bousquet, who had made it all possible, hung in doubt, pending analysis of his modicum of ore, lugged home on foot.

Governor Cabello found himself suddenly rich in interpreters for the nations that he had so long needed to conciliate. All four new residents spoke the language of the Taovayas; thus, they could talk with Tawakonis, too. Vial and Chaves also spoke Comanche. Cabello soon appreciated his gain, for the once-tenuous relations with the Taovayas suddenly became almost intensive.

Early on the morning of May 16, two Taovayas and two Wichita

[4] Cabello to Rengel, Béxar, February 20, 1785, BA.
[5] Cabello to Rengel, Béxar, May 19, 1785, BA; Rengel to Cabello, Chihuahua, April 30, 1785, BA.

messengers asked permission for a delegation from Guersec to enter the presidio to pay their respects. Cabello assented, of course, and hastily arranged housing and food for them.[6] Later that day, two dozen Taovayas and Wichita delegates called upon the governor with their calumet, which was their credential for the parley. They wanted it smoked to cement the new friendship. That appalled Cabello, who abhorred smoking, but he weathered the requisite puffs.

Only then did the delegation reveal its principal quest: help in war against the Panismahas, once their friends and close associates, but now their fierce enemies. Panismahas had invaded Taovayas territory in mid-April, killed two men, stolen most of their horses, and threatened to return to wipe out the Taovayas and Wichita villages. Lacking horses and ammunition to defend themselves properly, the Taovayas and Wichitas looked to Governor Cabello as their *padrone*, confident that he would supply all they needed. They also wanted him to prod Siscat Gainon to bring the Tawakonis, Flechazos, and Iscanis to their aid and to furnish all necessary support for their joint venture.

Cabello disappointed them with his answer: he could not help them because it took all his resources to fend off Comanche depredations at San Antonio and Nacogdoches. Blaming Comanches for disrupting the trade and leaving the interior villages in want, Cabello reminded the visitors of their solemn obligation to war against the Comanches. The visitors retired to their quarters to mull over the governor's words while they feasted on his meat and corn.

The next afternoon six more unexpected guests rode up to the Governor's Palace: Bidais, well mounted and well armed, calling as spokesmen for the Cocos, Mayeyes, and Akokisas as well as for their own people. All of them wished to pay their respects to the governor and to express their thanks for the gifts that Courbière had recently distributed at Nacogdoches. Surprised to see their enemies, the Taovayas and Wichitas, at the presidio, they had first hesitated to enter, but had staked their lives on Cabello's protection. Cabello assured them that their enemies would not attack them and carefully arranged for them hospitality of exactly the same quality as that given the Taovayas and Wichitas.

Cabello had a delicate matter to handle. He could not afford to upset the new accord with the Taovayas and Wichitas. If affronted, the Bidais might resume trade with the Lipans, to the grave detriment of

[6] Cabello to Rengel, Béxar, May 20, 1785, BA.

the province. As soon as the Bidais were shown to their quarters, the governor summoned the Taovayas leader and demanded that he and his people prove their sincerity as Spanish vassals by good conduct toward the Bidais. When he promised, Cabello escorted him and three more leading delegates to the quarters of the Bidais. Then and there they discussed and reconciled their differences, to the apparent satisfaction of all.

The erstwhile rivals harmoniously shared the governor's hospitality for five days. When the Bidais left, the Taovayas stayed on, happily eating and smoking and talking. On May 24, ten compatriots, just back from campaigning against the Osages, joined them. All thirty-eight rode off together on May 27, apparently content. Cabello had promised them no direct aid, but he had sent word to Tawakoni Chief Siscat Gainon to help the Taovayas against the Panismahas and had encouraged everyone to campaign against the Lipans. By the standards of both his settlement and theirs, he had entertained the delegates royally, furnishing all the tobacco they could smoke and more food than they could eat. In parting he gave trinkets to each, sent along a good horse for Chief Guersec, and reminded them to report to Nacogdoches for gifts in June.[7] As a final courtesy, the governor sent Amangual with twenty men to escort the delegation beyond the range of Lipan activity. As far as the hazards of Comanches, Osages, and Panismahas were concerned, they were on their own.

While his recent guests braved the hazards of the trail northward to the Red River, Governor Cabello found himself freshly challenged to extend the king's peace to all the nations of the northern frontier. The May courier brought dispatches from Bernardo de Gálvez, captain general at Havana since late 1784, now succeeding his late father as viceroy of New Spain. The extraordinary terms of the appointment showed the Crown's boundless confidence in the brilliant young officer. In addition to New Spain, he retained jurisdiction over Cuba, the Floridas, and Louisiana and acquired jurisdiction over the Provincias Internas as well. Somehow he must weld those far-flung dominions of Spanish North America into a united front against the ambitious Americans and Britons to the north and east.

Gálvez reasoned that the diverse Indian nations of the frontier held the key to his problem. Unlike any predecessor, he had some personal knowledge of the Indians of both the Provincias Internas and Louisi-

---

[7] Cabello to Rengel, Béxar, June 2, 1785, BA.

ana. He believed that fair and sensible treatment would make them valuable vassals of the Crown, able to consolidate the marches of empire against encroachment.

Thus, the new viceroy notified Governor Cabello of important postwar diplomatic successes with major tribes east of the Mississippi and demanded similar achievements in the western sector. Louisiana's Governor Estevan Miró had held great councils with the Indians at Pensacola in May 1784 and at Mobile in June. The Pensacola meeting had produced a treaty placing the Creeks under Spain's protection, excluding from Creek lands all white men without Spanish passports or trading licenses and binding the Creeks to fight under Spanish orders to defend the province whenever necessary. At Mobile the Choctaws, Alibamons, and Chickasaws had made similar commitments, although the Chickasaws were not bound to defend the Spaniards in case of war. Miró had negotiated the best possible repair for the mischief done Spanish interests at the Paris peace talks.[8]

Now, more than ever, the Crown's interests demanded an equivalent breakthrough on the northern frontier of the Provincias Internas, but the key to peace lay deep within the Comanchería. Five years after the first Comanche peace feelers, Governor Anza still waited at Santa Fe for that vast nation to coalesce its scattered desires for peace into some meaningful commitment of all Comanches. Across the Comanchería, in Texas, Governor Cabello had only obtained new Taovayas pledges to fight the Comanches. Although better than the prospect of Taovayas-Comanche alliance against the Spaniards, that really solved nothing. Spain could never stabilize the northern frontier against intrusion while there were wars among the tribes.

Desperate to convey peace overtures into the Comanchería, Cabello consulted Pedro Vial. To the governor's delight, Vial volunteered. He did not know the Comanches well enough to venture into their territory alone, but he was confident that his Taovayas friends would support the peace effort by introducing him into the camps of the more moderate eastern Comanche leaders. Speed was essential: the Taovayas would pick up their gifts at Nacogdoches in June; Vial needed to be there to ask their help. If they would consent, he would ride home to the Red River with them, then visit the Comanchería from that base.

Cabello readily agreed, gambling on the subsequent approval of

[8] Lawrence Kinnaird, ed., in *Spain in the Mississippi Valley, 1765–1794*, II, xv–xvi.

the commandant general. Vial chose as his companion Francisco Chaves, who had escaped captivity in the Taovayas village only a year earlier and who must have been his acquaintance during their years of common residence there.

On June 17, 1785,[9] Cabello issued his two envoys equipment for themselves and presents for Comanche chiefs in case they should be received in the Comanchería. The government provided only the gift articles; the equipment was charged to the personal expense of Vial and Chaves, as were the salaries of two servants hired to tend their packs and livestock.[10]

Vial and Chaves reached Nacogdoches in July and luckily found Taovayas and Wichita delegates there for the gift distribution. Vial sent word to Cabello that the Taovayas and Wichitas had offered to introduce the two envoys to the Comanche *rancherías*, and on July 23 the party headed back to the Red River villages from Nacogdoches.[11]

Within the Comanchería the time was exactly ripe for peace. In July 1785, while Vial and Chaves negotiated at Nacogdoches for Taovayas help in their peace mission to the easternmost Comanches, those farther west were making important new overtures in New Mexico.[12] On July 12, four hundred Comanches visited Taos pueblo to express their people's desire for friendship with the New Mexicans. They were welcomed cordially and assured that they would be accorded a peace treaty as soon as all Comanches would join to seek it, just as Governor Anza had promised since 1780.

On July 29, two chiefs led 120 warriors from 25 different *rancherías* to Taos to learn whether peace had been granted the first 400 and to affirm their own desire to participate. Meanwhile, their people camped about ninety miles from Taos, processing skins for the October trade fair that they all hoped to attend.

Not all Comanches were yet persuaded to peace. In the last week

[9] Loomis and Nasatir, in *Pedro Vial*, pp. 357–361, apparently relying on a defective copy rather than the original inventory in the Bexar Archives, assume a date of 1789 rather than 1785. The resulting four-year error leads to an inaccurate speculative account of Vial's activities in 1789 and an unfortunate failure to credit Vial and Chaves with the initial Comanche peace in 1785.

[10] Cabello, Inventory of goods and effects that I have provided to Pedro de Vial and Francisco Xavier de Chabes who have gone as emissaries to the *rancherías* of the Comanche Indians . . . , Béxar, June 17, 1785, BA.

[11] Rengel to Cabello, Presidio de San Eleceario, October 29, 1785, BA.

[12] Extract from the occurrences in New Mexico on the peace of the Comanches of the west, from July 12, 1785, when four hundred Comanche Indians presented themselves at the Pueblo of Taos, BA.

of August a fugitive Indian warned of Yupes and Yamparicas coming from north of the Arkansas River to attack the province. Governor Anza took appropriate precautions, and the invaders only killed twenty-three animals found without a shepherd.

That incident was hardly over before 30 Yupes and Yamparicas visited a friend at Taos on August 29 and swore to the governor that their own people, who lived on the lower reaches of the Arkansas, would faithfully keep the peace. On September 4, 110 more Comanches came to Taos to trade and warned the Spaniards that some of the earlier group would return to fight. Precautions were taken again, but the alarm proved false. In the second trade fair of the year, the visitors marketed a lot of buffalo meat and hides, some tanned skins, fifteen horses, and two guns. They left in a friendly fashion, offering to continue the peace and to join the Spaniards in a war against the Apaches.

The third trade fair occurred on October 28, as promised the 120 visitors in July. To prove their good will, the Comanches returned without ransom two New Mexican captives. Their foremost chief voluntarily left his own son as hostage to guarantee the peace.

Perhaps that chief was Ecueracapa, a prime mover among the Cuchanec chiefs who called all Comanches to the Arkansas River that fall to decide the question of tribal peace. More than six hundred *rancherías* came. The northernmost Yupes and Yamparicas, cut off by early snows, awaited news of the outcome with sympathetic interest. The easternmost Cuchanecs did not come either; they had already sent delegates to San Antonio to respond to peace overtures from the governor of Texas.

Vial and Chaves could have wished no better reception than the eastern Cuchanecs gave them in August 1785. They were glad of the chance to make peace with the Spaniards and with the Taovayas and Wichitas, too. Three chiefs and their wives rode back with Vial and Chaves, first to the Taovayas-Wichita villages to celebrate a new accord and to promise amends for past injuries, then on to San Antonio to negotiate a peace treaty with Governor Cabello.[13]

---

[13] Vial presented Cabello a diary of their mission. Cabello sent a copy of the diary to the commandant general on either October 12 or November 25, 1785, but neither that copy nor the original retained at Béxar has yet turned up. Thus, the events of the journey can only be sparsely derived from related documents. The observations of the knowledgeable Vial, the first European visitor received in the Comanchería since the 1740's, would surely constitute an ethnohistorical treasure. It is to be hoped that the diary will eventually be found among the still uncatalogued Spanish documents in various repositories.

Cabello had no inkling of the fate of Vial and Chaves from the time that they left Nacogdoches on July 23 until they rode into the presidio with the Comanche delegates on the afternoon of September 29.[14] He was nearly overwhelmed with gratitude and relief.

Cabello had spent much of the summer preparing for negotiations with the Comanches, just in case Vial and Chaves should succeed where other agents had failed him again and again over the last six years. As soon as he learned of their agreement with the Taovayas and Wichitas, the governor ordered Courbière to return from Nacogdoches with all the remaining presents. Cabello wanted plenty of gifts on hand for any Comanche chiefs who might respond to his peace overture, and he wanted the all-important annual presents administered thenceforth at Béxar under direct gubernatorial supervision. With the Taovayas and Wichitas already involved and with Comanche participation in the offing, he would risk no new follies by underlings at Nacogdoches.[15]

It was touch and go whether Cabello himself could see through any negotiations with the Comanches, for he was preparing to leave Texas. On May 20, 1785, he had petitioned for relief from his post on grounds of broken health.[16] By mid-July he was arranging his papers for an expected successor and urging the commandant general to empower the new governor to distribute the gifts from Béxar so as to avoid disruption of the peace effort.[17]

That a successor was on the way seemed certain in August: acting Commandant General Rengel ordered Cabello to prepare detailed information on the Indian presents and to remain at Béxar until the arrival of the new governor.[18] Cabello was provisionally slated for the governorship of Nueva Vizcaya, until Viceroy Bernardo de Gálvez assumed responsibility for the Provincias Internas and asserted strong new leadership in the matter of Indian policy. Gálvez, primarily concerned with the Comanche and Norteño peace, apparently would not risk moving the experienced Cabello from Texas at that juncture. Early in November 1785, Cabello received the viceroy's order not to transfer to Nueva Vizcaya, no reason given, no date for his relief indicated.[19]

<hr>

[14] Cabello to Rengel, Béxar, October 3, 1785, BA.
[15] Cabello to Rengel, Béxar, August 19, 1785, and September 20, 1785, BA.
[16] Cabello to Rengel, Béxar, May 20, 1785, BA.
[17] Cabello to Rengel, Béxar, July 20, 1785, BA.
[18] Rengel to Cabello, Chihuahua, August 27, 1785, BA.
[19] Cabello to Rengel, Béxar, November 10, 1785, BA.

Fortunately for the governor's health, the summer of 1785 proved the least strenuous he had known at San Antonio. Texas had suffered no fatal depredations since May, when Comanches killed two men in widely separated incidents.[20] One awkward episode occurred at La Bahía in June, when Comanches came in pursuit of Lipans. Two or three Lipan groups were camped in the vicinity, essentially taking refuge from their enemies, and they faced destruction if not protected by the Spaniards.[21] To let them be destroyed could call down the vengeance of all the Lipans and their kinsmen upon the Spanish settlements. On the other hand, the Lipans were a perpetual nuisance, disrupting relations with the Norteños by their illegal trading and making trouble when other Indians visited Béxar and La Bahía. Cabello had long thought extermination of the Lipans the only answer, but dared he countenance it in the very shadow of a Spanish presidio? Fortunately, the Comanche warriors did not test the issue.

Some other problems still plagued Cabello. The Taovayas and Tawakonis still held captives whom they glibly promised to return, but they always contended that they lacked horses to transport them to Béxar.[22] Some Norteños still found themselves irresistibly tempted to trade with Lipans and with contrabandists from the Arkansas River.[23] That meant horse thefts in Texas, guns among Apaches in Coahuila, and sometimes dangerously drunken Indians in the villages, for brandy was a prime commodity in illegal trade.

The great news of the summer had been the Tonkawas' village on the Navasota River, where at last they had kept their seven-year-old promise to settle down. The Spaniards felt the event vindicated their assassination of El Mocho, in whose lifetime they believed it could not have happened. Acting Commandant General Rengel urged the governor to encourage the Tonkawas and their new chief with every possible assistance to consolidate their new village and to neglect no precaution to keep them cut off from trade and communication with the Lipans.[24]

The crowning triumph of the year, indeed of Cabello's whole term, came on September 29, when Vial and Chaves rode into the presidio with three Cuchanec chiefs and their wives. Although the Comanches

---

[20] Rengel to Cabello, Presidio del Principe, October 21, 1785, BA.
[21] Cabello to Rengel, Béxar, June 4, 1785, BA.
[22] Cabello to Rengel, Béxar, September 20, 1785, BA.
[23] Cabello to Rengel, Béxar, September 19, 1785, BA.
[24] Rengel to Cabello, Chihuahua, August 25, 1785, BA.

had not designated a single head as the Spaniards would have liked, they had agreed among themselves about the desirability of peace. These three spokesmen committed the eastern Cuchanecs to a peace treaty that October 1785. It was observed to the end of the century, with only the minor deviations inevitable in a society that allowed individuals so much autonomy. Their leaders honored the agreement all those years and strove to enforce it, even among their most adventurous young men.[25]

With Vial and Chaves interpreting, negotiations went smoothly and quickly. Hostilities would cease; Spaniards and Comanches would treat each other as brothers and good friends wherever they should meet. Those terms applied to all vassals of the king. Thenceforth, Comanches would be friends of the Spaniards' friends and enemies of their enemies.

The Comanches particularly declared their enmity to the Lipan Apaches and promised to report the results to Béxar whenever they attacked Lipans. They pledged always to notify the governor of Texas when they planned to go to the Coahuila frontier to fight the Lipans and Mescaleros.

All Spaniards whom the Comanches had seized for ransom would be returned, and the Comanches would no longer kidnap any for ransom. They promised to admit no strangers to their camps, except traders buying hides. In return, the Spaniards promised an annual gift to the Comanche leaders to affirm their good friendship.

Such an important treaty required lavish celebration, with ceremonies for all the subscribing *rancherías* and fine presents for everyone. Cabello, terribly embarrassed, had to postpone the proper ceremonial ratification because he did not have suitable gifts on hand and could not hope to obtain them for another six months. He asked the Comanche envoys to come back with all their leaders in that time, and they obligingly agreed. Fortunately, Andrés Courbière had come from Nacogdoches just ten days ahead of Vial's party, with adequate presents for the three distinguished visitors and their wives.

The Comanches stayed nearly three weeks, enjoying the best entertainment that Cabello could provide and engaging in long talks with the governor. Cabello, who found them pleasant and interesting com-

---

[25] Pedro de Nava, Report on the Indian situation, Chihuahua, July 23, 1799, AGN, Provincias Internas, vol. 112. An excerpt from the Nava report, including the treaty terms, is published in translation in Marc Simmons, ed., *Border Comanches*, pp. 21–22.

pany, made the most of the opportunity to learn all that he could about their nation. Lipans, moving freely in and out of the presidio, noted the new accord and were not pleased. The governor heard of 158 Lipan warriors roaming the vicinity, incensed by the Comanches' presence and determined to attack them upon their departure. The maximum force that Cabello could spare was twenty soldiers and a sergeant, clearly inadequate for the case, so he hastily summoned an equal number from La Bahía for forty-five days of duty at Béxar. With luck, forty-two soldiers, with ten militiamen to guard the horse herd, could escort the three Comanche chiefs homeward without incident.

The Comanches left on October 19, 1785, in a grand climax of brotherhood. Each of the chiefs wore the full uniform of a captain of Spain. Their wives happily carried in their saddle bags sundry articles prized in Comanche households: mirrors, ribbons, needles, and knives. Alférez Amangual formed the escort on the plaza before the Governor's Palace, where the chiefs joined them. In parting speeches, Cabello stressed the obligations of fidelity and vassalage that went with those handsome Spanish uniforms, and the Comanches expressed their gratitude for his hospitality, vowing their eternal brotherhood to the Spaniards and promising to return soon. The most important chief bore the flag of Burgundy as they rode out, flanked by columns of soldiers. Last traveled the horse herd and the Comanche wives, guarded by ten militiamen.

Cabello expected some of the ubiquitous Lipans to see the Comanches depart under heavy escort and warn their big war party not to try interception. Apparently his strategy worked. Within the week the Lipans passed the Rancho de San Miguel, about twenty miles from Béxar, en route to their own area.

Amangual's escort party rode back into Béxar on November 6. They had escorted the Comanches beyond the Colorado, to a place three hundred miles from Béxar, considered a safe distance from Lipans. Chaves, whom the Comanches had asked to ride along with the escort as their interpreter, reported that they had expressed great satisfaction with the new peace and with the hospitable Spaniards.[26]

Governor Cabello promptly returned the Bahía contingent, probably none too soon for the tranquillity of Captain Cazorla. During their absence, 108 Taovayas, Wichitas, Tawakonis, and Flechazos had

---

[26] Cabello to Rengel, Béxar, November 25, 1785 (ms. incomplete), BA.

visited the presidio for four days.[27] It had been a completely cordial episode, but no captain liked his presidio exposed to Indian eyes in such weak condition.

Now, while San Antonio enjoyed the greatest peace in years, the Comanche envoys had weeks of work ahead. They had to visit all the camps they had represented, to report their happy visit at San Antonio, and to explain how they had made all Spaniards their brothers, especially Cabello. Everywhere they had to explain the terms of the peace treaty in exact detail; most important of all, they had to report back to the great chiefs Camisa de Fierro and Cabesa Rapada. Everywhere the news was well received. Many Comanches could hardly wait to go to San Antonio, but the three chiefs explained that they must wait five months for the grand ceremony.

While those three chiefs toured the eastern Cuchanec camps, the Cuchanecs of the west and many Yupes and Yamparicas held council on the banks of the Arkansas River, at a place called La Casa de Palo.[28] Some members of the peace faction had grown so fiercely determined to end the wars with the Spaniards that they conspired to assassinate Toroblanco, a leader of great influence among the Yupes and Yamparicas, whose boundless hatred of the Spaniards ruled out all possibility of peace. After Toroblanco's death, most of his followers peacefully joined the Cuchanecs. One small group of irreconcilables from his own camp split into a little band to wage an independent war and suffered in consequence a fatal ostracism.

More than six hundred *rancherías* participated in the great council. They understood Governor Anza's requirement that their nation speak with a single voice, and they reasoned that their single representative should confer with none other than the governor himself. Too often they had seen some New Mexicans fail to honor the commitments of others. Now they desired a precise understanding between their spokesman and the governor to forestall new tragedies of misunderstanding.

The council chose the Cuchanec chief Ecueracapa to negotiate a general peace and make new trade agreements with New Mexico. Long distinguished for exploits in war, he had won the name Contatanaca-

---

[27] Cabello to Rengel, Béxar, October 24, 1785, BA.

[28] Pedro Garrido y Durán, An Account of the Events which have occurred in the Provinces of New Mexico concerning Peace conceded to the Comanche nation and their reconciliation with the Utes, since November 17 of last year and July 15 of the current, Chihuahua, December 21, 1785, in Alfred Barnaby Thomas, ed., *Forgotten Frontiers*, pp. 294–321.

para, signifying one unequaled in military achievement; in his maturity, he had also emerged as an extraordinarily wise, able peace chief. New Mexicans already knew him as Cota de Malla, for the shirt of armor that he wore in battle, and it was probably he whom Cabello's interpreters called Camisa de Fierro. If the resulting confusion of names was never quite resolved, there was never the slightest confusion about the great chief's extraordinary ability and integrity, among either Comanches or Spaniards who were so fortunate as to know him.

Ecueracapa accepted the commission only on condition that none of the chiefs or their followers would betray his word and vowed to help the Spaniards destroy them if they should not honor their assurances to him. All six hundred *rancherías* swore their good faith. Then they cast about for some means to contact the governor at Santa Fe without undue risk to Ecueracapa.

They had not long to wait. On December 10 scouts from Ecueracapa's camp captured a New Mexican Indian, Joseph Chiquito, who had become separated from a party of Spanish buffalo hunters. Discovering that Joseph was associated with the Spaniards and that he spoke Comanche fairly well, the captors took him to the lodge of Ecueracapa, where he was fed, clothed, and treated with utmost generosity. The Comanches had found their messenger to Santa Fe.

Ecueracapa swiftly summoned chiefs from as many *rancherías* as he could reasonably contact and held four consecutive councils upon the best means of achieving a truly successful peace. He required Joseph to witness all their discussions and agreements. Once the chiefs deemed Joseph sufficiently informed, they dispatched him to Governor Anza with Chief Paraginanchi and one other Comanche. The three were to inform Anza of the full powers vested in Ecueracapa as Comanche peace commissioner, then request permission for him to ride via Pecos to Santa Fe to negotiate, with Anza's guarantee that the Jicarillas would not molest him.

The trio reached Santa Fe on December 30, 1785. Anza welcomed them with great delight and entertained them for four days. Two very pleased Comanches prepared to ride home on new horses presented them by the governor as marks of his esteem, carrying other smaller gifts. They asked that Joseph Chiquito accompany them, as the other chiefs had requested in case of a favorable reply. Anza not only agreed, but he also sent thirteen Pecos Indians and one Spaniard thought diplomat enough to win friends in the Comanche camps. The seventeen headed for the Comanchería on January 3, 1786.

Anza's agent had precise instructions: to give Ecueracapa the horse and the fine scarlet headdress sent him by the governor, then to answer his petition. In response to the Comanches' gesture of confidence in sending their emissaries over the Pecos route to Santa Fe without prior arrangement, Anza was sending back to the Comanchería fifteen of his own people. When it should please Ecueracapa to come to Santa Fe to negotiate the peace, those fifteen would escort him. Ecueracapa should ride confident that Anza desired the terms most beneficial to the Comanche nation. The Jicarillas would be warned not to interfere.

Before the envoys could reach their destination, news of pending peace talks with the Comanches spread through New Mexico, to the great encouragement of settlers and Pueblos who had suffered such heavy losses during the years of war. The reports provoked an opposite reaction among the Utes, whose two foremost chiefs hurried to Santa Fe to protest. When Moara and Pinto called at the Governor's Palace on January 7, they would neither smoke with Anza nor accept any presents. They harangued against the Comanche peace for four hours, indignantly charging that Spaniards preferred frequent, unfaithful rebels to obedient and faithful friends.

Anza heard them out patiently. He and his superiors had long realized that it would require great delicacy to make a Comanche alliance without jeopardizing the vital alliance with the Utes. Now the governor had to persuade the Ute chiefs that he could not accept their arguments.

Anza dwelt on the greatness and incomparable piety of the king, who extended grace to those who implored it, no matter how vicious their previous enmity. The king's piety also bound his vassals. That made sense to Indians who counted generosity and magnanimity essential attributes of a great chief. The Ute leaders therefore agreed not to oppose the king's wish or to obstruct Anza's implementation of it in New Mexico. They asked instead to be included in the peace arrangements. Gladly promising to mediate on their behalf with the Comanches, Anza invited them to be his guests at Santa Fe until the Comanche delegates should arrive, so as to witness his good offices. Moara and Pinto readily agreed.

They had less than a month's wait. Paraginanchi led his party swiftly back to the Comanchería, where an enthusiastic welcome awaited them. Chiefs and ordinary individuals alike lavished kind hospitality upon Anza's fifteen emissaries. Ecueracapa soon sent three of them back to Santa Fe with Chief Cuetaninabeni and two other Comanches, to thank the governor for his gracious response to the first Comanche deputation and to explain the first incident marring the peace. The small rebel band of Toroblanco's followers had killed a Pecos Indian. Outraged by the affront to his nation's honor and his own, Ecueracapa himself had killed the guilty leader. He wanted Governor Anza to know that the Comanches abhorred the crime and had destroyed the murderer.

Cuetaninabeni and his two compatriots were so confident of the Spaniards' good faith that they took their women with them to Santa Fe. They delivered Ecueracapa's message at the Governor's Palace on January 30. All six men, New Mexicans as well as Comanches, vouched for the widespread enthusiasm for peace in the Comanchería and the general disgust with the renegades' crime against Pecos. Anza thanked them for their assurances and again arranged for an equal number of New Mexicans to accompany the Comanche delegates home. To Ecueracapa Anza sent word that they would decide together in conference the best way to punish rebels against the peace. The recent incident would be overlooked because Ecueracapa had already given satisfaction.

On February 25, 1786, Ecueracapa approached Santa Fe with three of his own men and three of Anza's. Alerted in good time, the governor staged a handsome welcome. A party of footsoldiers and one mounted cavalryman went out to meet the chief, along with the most prominent settlers. A festive crowd cheered Ecueracapa as he reached the plaza with his impressive escort.

Obviously pleased, but unruffled, Ecueracapa dismounted at the Governor's Palace, embraced the waiting Anza, and made a ten-minute speech of greeting. Anza then led the chief into his house, congratulating him upon his successful journey and gratefully remarking upon Ecueracapa's show of confidence in the Spaniards.

Ecueracapa responded with a long discourse upon the problems of peace, then explained the terms that the council of Comanche leaders had in mind. He first reviewed the difficulties experienced in the past when some *rancherías* had sought peace at various frontier settlements and pueblos. He hoped now, with himself commissioned to negotiate for all the Comanches in the very capital once so terrifying to them, that they could all have mutual confidence in the peace terms. Ecueracapa had exacted a commitment that the peace would never be impaired by his people, especially with the knowledge of the chiefs and leading men. In return, they wished to be admitted to Spanish protection and allowed to settle and subsist near the Spanish settlements. The Comanche nation declared strongly against the common enemies, the Apaches, and offered to join Spanish expeditions against them, if on a route and within a range feasible for Comanches.

In order to foster friendship and commerce between the Comanches and the New Mexicans, Ecueracapa himself wanted free, safe passage through Pecos to visit the governor at Santa Fe whenever he should find it desirable. The rest of his nation desired free trade with Pecos pueblo and regular trade fairs there.

Ecueracapa asked Anza to postpone his reply to the proposed terms until they could meet in Pecos with other Comanche chiefs and authorized representatives then riding to the pueblo. If Anza would respond in the presence of all those witnesses and at the same time present some token of authority to Ecueracapa, it would be difficult for any segment of the nation ever to plead ignorance of the treaty.

The Comanche proposals seemed eminently sensible and realistic. Anza gladly agreed. Moving on to another pressing matter, the governor introduced Chief Moara and six authorized Ute representatives and called for a permanent reconciliation between Comanches and Utes. The negotiators from both nations exchanged charges, countercharges, and explanations until all were satisfied. Then they celebrated a peace agreement, exchanging clothes in the presence of Governor Anza, who stood guarantor for the observance of peace terms on both sides. All of them expressed their gratitude to the governor, and a substantial harmony seemed to prevail among the erstwhile enemies.

Their new accord stood the test of three days together in Santa Fe as guests in the Governor's Palace. Anza scrupulously treated Ecueracapa and Moara with equal distinction to avoid any upsetting jealousies. Reports of their new accord traveled to Taos, where the Ute chiefs Surdo and Yugopampe had arrived with three of their tribesmen. They promptly called upon two Comanche visitors in the pueblo. The seven affectionately embraced and smoked to cement the new friendship.

Meanwhile, Anza studied the reports of his own emissaries to the Comanches. They agreed that Ecueracapa exercised a natural authority well understood by all the Comanches, a product of the remarkable talent and judiciousness that Anza had also perceived in the man. Anza thus conceived that the chief should be more than peace commissioner and privately proposed to Ecueracapa that it would be desirable to formalize his leadership of the entire nation in all matters: in effect, to obtain a broad extension of the confidence already voted by his people. If he could achieve that, Anza could promise full support of his leadership and of the interests of the Comanche nation, provided that Ecueracapa always remain a faithful vassal of the king and lead his people along that road. Ecueracapa agreed to try to achieve such an arrangement and promised, whatever the outcome, to remain a loyal and obedient vassal. The fate of Anza's proposal could only be resolved over the coming months within the Comanchería.

Early on the last morning of February 1786, Governor Anza rode to Pecos with chiefs Ecueracapa and Moara and their associates. Some two hundred chiefs and authorized representatives of the Comanches had camped beside the pueblo to await the peace talks. When Anza dismounted at their camp, each individual embraced him. Ecueracapa delivered an appropriate oration, then led the governor to a large lodge already prepared for him. Most of the chiefs accompanied them, to celebrate their friendship by eating the midday meal with Anza.

The formal meeting convened at two o'clock that afternoon in Ecueracapa's lodge, with all the chiefs and thirty-one other persons present. These greatest Cuchanec leaders seated themselves in strict order of protocol. Ecueracapa, presiding, invited Anza to speak. The governor announced that he was ready to reply to the peace proposals stated by Ecueracapa, but that, if there were anything else on their minds, that should come first. The Comanches murmured approval and turned to the third-ranking chief, Tosapoy, as their spokesman.

Tosapoy rose and bared his breast for a formal harangue, well organized, logical, and dignified. First, he expressed the Comanches' appreciation of the generous reception of their peace proposals and urged entire, mutual forgetfulness of the wrongs committed on both sides over the long years of war. The Comanches proposed to behave thenceforth as the king's affectionate children. They wanted special attention to equity and justice in commerce, so that greed should not again cause the trade fairs to erupt in violence. Tosapoy confessed that he had himself offended in that respect a Spaniard now present, and he delivered, on his knees, Alejandro Martín, a native of Santa Fe who had been his captive for eleven years.

Anza rose to respond to their peace proposals. First, in the king's name, he conceded inviolable peace, on condition of their promise to commit no violence against His Majesty's dominion or vassals, especially with the knowledge or connivance of the chiefs. Second, he admitted them with all their subjects to the king's protection, with the right to live on his territories. Third, he granted Ecueracapa free access to Santa Fe by way of Pecos and free commerce to all Comanches, with protection against the abuses that they had heretofore suffered in trade. Fourth, Anza accepted their offer to maintain incessant, open war against Apache enemies, sometimes alone, sometimes with Spanish troops when the route and region of the campaign would be suitable for Comanches.

In conclusion, Anza formally presented to Ecueracapa a saber and banner symbolizing Spain's recognition of his authority as peace commissioner. To emphasize his high esteem, Anza presented his own staff to Ecueracapa, explaining that it was the very staff with which the king had conferred the governorship of New Mexico upon him.

Anza had done just the right things. The Comanches responded with their own ceremony, making and refilling a hole in which they symbolically buried the war. Ecueracapa accepted the tokens with thanks, but he asked that the staff be given to the second-ranking chief, Tosacondata, whom he would commission to display it in all the *rancherías* as evidence of the peace. Accordingly, Anza bestowed the staff upon Tosacondata, to the murmured approval of the gathering. Ecueracapa had pleased them by the high quality of the appointment and his willingness to share authority and responsibility.

One after another the chiefs rose to voice respect for Anza and appreciation of his willingness to honor all their requests. At the end, late that night, they asked the governor to open the first trade fair to them next day. Again, he agreed.

After breakfasting with the Comanche and Ute chiefs, Anza announced the fair, stipulating that everyone, Pueblos as well as Spaniards, must eschew the violences and excesses that had marred past fairs. He specified the trade procedures to be followed at all fairs and reestablished the old price list, adjusted for a recent rise in the value of buffalo hides and a drop in the cost of knives. The Comanches and Utes, thus favored, were delighted.

At the fair site, Anza drew two long lines with his sword. Traders of either side could line up with their wares outside the lines to show their goods and bargain; they could deliver goods in the space between the lines. Anza oversaw the trading, with troops positioned about the area and additional overseers appointed to help him. He was particularly alert to see that no one exacted from the *bárbaros* fees for the right to trade, an extortion that had often sparked trouble in the past.

The Comanches traded more than six hundred hides, much meat and tallow, fifteen horses, and three guns and were satisfied that they had fair bargains. They enthusiastically asked Anza to continue the new system, remarking that this display of justice proved the worth of peace with the Spaniards.

One more ceremonial requirement remained. On the day of the fair, the Comanche dignitaries reconvened to ratify their peace with the Utes. Both nations promised good behavior and exchanged symbolic acts of good faith.

Ecueracapa then tackled two subjects not resolved the day before. Now that the Comanches were pledged to obey the king, he desired the governor to prescribe penalties for any infractor of the peace and also to set a time and place to fight the Apaches, so that the Comanches could prove their friendship by sacrificing blood and lives in the service of the king.

Anza replied that he had no doubt of their good faith and would rely upon them to propagate their good attitudes throughout their nation. He would not advise that they put to death any infractors of the peace unless they should grow numerous enough to jeopardize its permanence. In that case, Anza would wish the chiefs to consult with him about an appropriate remedy.

Ardent, constant war against the Apaches would best serve the king's interests. For that purpose, Anza pledged the Comanches free access to Apache ranges beyond the Gallinas River and the right of residence and any necessary aid in the Spanish settlements. Anza promised them another trade fair at Pecos in July, when together they would choose an opportune time for Comanches to campaign with Spanish forces against the Apaches. Meanwhile, the governor would order the Jicarillas to leave the Comanches and their property alone and would punish them for any infractions reported to him.

Anza requested a monthly report of events among the Comanches, to which they agreed. Everything had gone to the Comanches' liking. They especially appreciated the offer of entry to the Spanish settlements and assistance in hunting the enemy.

The conference broke up on March 2, with long, cordial farewells among all the participants. One Comanche chose to return to Santa Fe with Anza. The rest of the Comanches and the Utes dispersed to their far-flung camps. Ecueracapa and Tosacondata had now to make the peace understood and respected in every Comanche *rancheria*, a matter of countless hours in the saddle and around the council fires. Ecueracapa had also to explore, discreetly, his nation's reaction to Anza's idea of a permanent head chieftainship and to direct the Comanche thrust against the Apaches.

Anza had no time to rest on his laurels as peacemaker. Just three weeks after the celebrations at Pecos, he culminated more than two years of intricate maneuvering with the Navajos. Thus, his Comanche guest saw the governor coax another nation into his framework of New Mexican alliances.

The Navajos had long kept a relative peace with New Mexico, but in recent years some had helped their Gila kinsmen raid the Sonoran frontier. A succession of punitive thrusts into the Gila sanctuaries by troops from Sonora and Nueva Vizcaya led the Gilas to look northward for Navajo help. By the end of 1783, the commandant general ordered Anza to break up the pernicious connection and ensure permanent hostility between the two groups by making the Navajos go to war against the Gilas, all without angering the Navajos and provoking them to war against New Mexico.[29]

Anza notified the Navajos that he would have to deny them the right to trade in New Mexico if they should fail to side with the Spaniards against the Gilas, and he threatened to loose the Utes upon their territories if they could not be faithful friends. The Navajos, dependent upon the New Mexican trade and scared of the Utes, promised in 1784 to do as he asked, but they could not bring themselves to any effective exertions against the Gilas. Quite apart from sentiment about ties of kinship, the Navajos had no stomach for Gila retaliation against their families and fields and flocks.

Early 1785 brought new complaints about the Navajos from the Comandancia General, so Anza pressed them harder. He forbade them to trade with New Mexican settlers and Pueblos and also forbade them to cross the Rio San José, traditional boundary between their lands and the Gilas, on pain of arrest. Forty men patrolled the river to back his order. By June, some Navajos bowed to the pressure. They announced at Laguna pueblo that they were going to campaign against the Gilas and invited the Pueblos to help them. Five influential headmen led 150 Navajos and 94 Laguna warriors into the Gilas' range in the Datil

---

[29] For documents covering Anza's attack upon the Navajo-Gila problem, see *ibid.*, pp. 245–272, 343–363.

Mountains, where they killed 40 Gilas. The Gilas, outraged to see the Navajos' perfidy, swore revenge and managed to kill two Navajos and wound several more as they withdrew.

Governor Anza promptly readmitted the Navajos to the New Mexican trade. They made two more independent campaigns that summer, and also promised that in the future a Navajo contingent would accompany each New Mexican force campaigning against the Gilas. Anza agreed to furnish corn meal and horses for each Navajo participant and two cattle for each contingent, so that war against the Gilas would not strain the lean Navajo economy.

Anza had never deluded himself that there was any Navajo polity, but in the summer of 1785 he could see four headmen emerging as principal spokesmen, at least for those families who desired alliance and trade with the New Mexicans. In order to define some Navajo authority with which Spaniards could deal, he proposed to recognize those four chiefs with silver-tipped canes and medals. Acting Commandant General Rengel agreed to send the tokens. More important, Rengel sent practical support for the New Mexicans whom he now expected to mount regular offensive campaigns against the Gilas: a thousand pesos for provisions, four hundred horses, twenty mules, two hundred guns with ammunition, all for use by Spanish, Pueblo, or Navajo participants. He also sent colorful cloth, knives, and bridles to reward Navajos for good service.

Despite that bonus, Navajo participation in the campaigns soon dwindled to a scant token effort. Anza suspected that the influential headman Antonio, one of the four whom he had planned to recognize with a silver-tipped cane, was subverting the alliance; he wondered whether he could somehow elevate a rival headman, Cotón Negro, to a countervailing position. Rengel authorized Anza to do so and to threaten to oust the Navajos from their homelands if their cooperation did not improve. The Navajos would realize just as well as the Spaniards that they had no place to go.

In the autumn of 1785 Anza found it difficult to judge the Navajos' frame of mind. They furnished scouts who proved extremely helpful to New Mexican forces campaigning against the Gilas, and some campaigned with Utes against the Gilas. Anza concluded that most Navajos wanted desperately to please the Spaniards but so dreaded Gila retaliation that they dared not be seen invading Gila lands with the New Mexican forces. Commandant General Rengel urged Anza not to relax the pressures for full-scale Navajo participation and to warehouse a substantial cache of guns and ammunition at Laguna pueblo, right on the Navajo marches, to underline their cruel choice. The Navajos could view that either as armament for a punitive New Mexican campaign into their own country or as Anza's guarantee to protect them against Gila retaliation for their services to the king.

Early in 1786, Rengel recommended that Governor Anza visit the Navajo communities in person if necessary to make an effective alliance with them, but Anza found that impracticable. Navajos were too scattered over a vast region for him to visit all or even most of them, and the governor could ill afford a long absence from Santa Fe with the Comanche negotiations reaching a climax and the Utes needing reassurance. Instead, he asked the *alcaldes* of Zuñi, Laguna, and Jémez to invite all Navajo leaders to meet with him late in March on the Rio Puerco, southwest of Zía pueblo.

To the dismay of the *alcaldes*, no Navajo leader would come or send any representative, even though the *alcaldes* volunteered to remain in their camps as hostages. Indeed, most Navajos fled to the hills as the *alcaldes* approached. Someone had spread the rumor that the commandant general had ordered Anza to kill all the Navajos and that he was arranging a gathering only to massacre those foolish enough to come. The *alcaldes* reported to Anza on the Rio Puerco on March 23, 1786, with just one Navajo, whom they had found on their way and had brought along, willy-nilly. Anza questioned the lone Navajo, who confirmed the *alcaldes'* report of panic among his people. Since the governor's small party was obviously not equipped to wage war, the Navajo readily accepted Anza's assurance that he truly wanted to negotiate arrangements helpful to Navajo as well as Spanish interests and agreed to inform his people. He left with Anza's interpreter, promising to return within two or three days, and he kept his word.

With him rode about eighty Navajos. Four were headmen; thirty-six were authorized spokesmen for their local groups. Anza welcomed them cordially, deplored their lack of confidence in him, and remarked sadly on their failure to declare openly against the Apaches. He reminded them of benefits they could enjoy by throwing in their lot with the Spaniards against the Apaches and of the sorrows they would reap if they should not.

The Navajo emissaries promised to be loyal friends and to bring the unruly members of their nation under control. They also agreed that their lack of any unified structure of government was a source of much of their difficulty. Their elders had lately counseled them to solve the problem by electing a single governor, as did the Pueblos, and to make that individual their agent to deal with the king and his ministers. In fact, they had already chosen two men, the sons of the two old men friendliest to the Spaniards, and they wished Governor Anza now to designate one the governor of all Navajos.

The interpreter, who had long known the Navajos and had lately visited their territory, testified that they spoke truly. Anza, enormously pleased, would not affront either powerful headman by rejecting his son for an official position. He suggested that the widely scattered Navajos would surely need a lieutenant governor as well as a governor to manage their affairs. The assembled Navajos promptly elected the two men to the new posts, and Anza recognized their new distinction with new Spanish names. To Don Carlos, now governor, he promised a large medal; to Don Joseph Antonio, now lieutenant governor, he promised a smaller medal. He suggested that they deal with nation-wide matters, but that they leave existing headmen in control of local affairs, excluding only those who should reject the authority of their new governor.

The recent, unnecessary panic over the rumor about his orders from Chihuahua had reminded Anza of the difficulties of maintaining reliable communication with distant Indian groups. He therefore proposed to station an interpreter with the Navajos, in order to facilitate their communication with Santa Fe and forestall misunderstandings. They approved and asked for the interpreter who had just visited them. Anza, who considered the man competent and reliable, hired him on the spot at a monthly salary of eight pesos, plus horses, arms, and other supplies.

That day the Navajos concluded a five-part agreement, most of which they kept reasonably well for several years. First, they would be obedient and faithful vassals of the king and would thus enjoy his protection. Second, in order to prove that they were really at war with the Gilas, either Don Carlos or Don Joseph Antonio would campaign against them in July with an all-Navajo force, accompanied only by an interpreter. Third, the Navajos would also furnish monthly thirty men to campaign with New Mexicans against Apaches, with horses and supplies provided by the Crown. Fourth, they would immediately go back home and plant their crops, and, because the governor would guarantee their safety against all enemies, they would proceed to build sod huts, rather than rove about with temporary housing. Fifth, they would be responsible for the life of the interpreter and would heed his advice.

Upon conclusion of the agreement, Anza's Comanche guest harangued the gathering. He threatened that, if the Navajos should break their promises, the Comanches would fulfill their responsibilities as the good allies and friends of the Spaniards by exterminating the Navajos. Terrified, the Navajos promised to give the Comanches no cause for complaint.

As the conference broke up, Anza asked the new governor and lieutenant governor to hurry home to inform all their people of the new arrangements and then come to Santa Fe for appropriate ceremonies of investiture in their new offices.

Don Carlos and the interpreter reported to Santa Fe with amazing speed, on March 30. Don Joseph Antonio could not come, because he had to pursue four Apaches who had stolen five horses from him. Don Carlos and the interpreter reported the Navajos well pleased with the new treaty and already making arrangements to plant, build, and campaign as they had promised. Anza presented the appropriate uniform and medal to Don Carlos, who rode homeward on April 2, commissioned to make an official visit to every Navajo community and to enlist the help of other leaders in taking a census of his people and their livestock as he traveled.

Gila horse thieves distracted the Navajos from immediate attention to their duties, but on May 25 the interpreter notified Anza that the Navajos had finished sowing their crops in their old lands and that all who had horses would join in the general campaign against the Gilas. Among those who would participate were the Ute *ranchería* of Captain Peechá, apparently residing then among the Navajos.

On June 8 the interpreter rode into Santa Fe with Don Carlos, Don Joseph Antonio, and seven other Navajos, prepared to report to the governor. Don Carlos vowed that he had visited every community and had everywhere been recognized and applauded; his people consented freely to all terms of the treaty. The headman Antonio had been deposed without difficulty, on suspicion that he fomented unrest. The interpreter made the census report. The Navajo nation had seven hundred families, more or less, with four or five persons in each; about a thousand men were able to bear arms. They lived in five regional divisions: San Mateo, Zebolleta or Cañon, Chusca, Hozo, and Chelli. Their livestock consisted of about five hundred tame horses, six hundred mares with corresponding stallions and young, seven hundred black ewes, and forty cows with bulls and calves, all managed with great care for their increase. Those who had never planted crops before were now doing so after the example of the others. The interpreter had seen only tranquil dispositions among the Navajos.

The Navajo leaders begged Anza to reopen the New Mexican trade to them. They had lost that privilege again during their lapse of the previous year and had suffered grave scarcities as a result. Anza granted that request and invited them to display their woven goods at the Comanche fair scheduled at Pecos in July. Delighted, they confirmed arrangements for the forthcoming campaign, then rode homeward on June 10.

Anza could not as easily know what was going on in the Comanchería, and he wondered how much he had actually achieved at Pecos on February 28. Although Yupes and Yamparicas had helped elect Ecueracapa in November, only Cuchanecs had participated in the Pecos meeting. Anza would not count on Yupe and Yamparica commitment to the peace until he could talk with some of their leaders. As long as winter snows cut their *rancherías* off from communication with the Cuchanecs, he could not even assume they knew the treaty terms.

There was uncertainty in the Comanchería, too. Several Yupe and Yamparica chiefs, with about three hundred tipis, were moving about in search of Ecueracapa that spring. They had supported his commission; now they wished to know whether the outcome had been favorable. In mid-April, Comanches of the two northern divisions visited Taos to trade. The *alcalde* notified the governor, who invited the leading men of the group to Santa Fe for a talk. The principal leaders declined. Having found no buffalo on their hunt, they had left their camps with very short meat supplies. As soon as they finished their transactions and had mounts rested enough to take the trail again, most of the party hurried homeward. Only a minor Yupe chief called Chamanada, a medicine man called Querenilla, and one other rode to Santa Fe to see the governor.

Disappointed not to talk with leaders of greater standing, Anza nevertheless strove to entertain the visitors handsomely. He would neglect no opportunity to cultivate the good will of the Yupes and Yamparicas. The tone of their reports was entirely encouraging. The three Comanches left on April 21, riding horses presented them by the governor, and carrying his letter to the governor of Texas, which they promised to carry at least as far as the Taovayas village. Anza had summarized for Cabello his detailed report of the peace to the commandant general, hoping thus to coordinate Spanish policy on the eastern and western margins of the Comanchería.

With Chamanada's party, Anza sent five New Mexicans commissioned to go as directly as possible to Ecueracapa. One was Francisco Xavier Ortiz, a literate man noted for his understanding of and rapport with Indians. Anza desired his assessment of conditions within the Comanchería. Juan Urbano went as interpreter.

Also with Chamanada's party rode the Comanche observer who had stayed with Anza since the Pecos meeting and had attended his Navajo conference on the Rio Puerco. He had witnessed the governor's review of the militia of three districts, thus gaining a new appreciation of the number of men whom the province of New Mexico could field; he had also seen that just three Navajo groups had more warriors than his people had known to exist in that entire nation. The Comanche visitor especially liked the idea of one superior chief for an entire nation and the institution of a resident Spanish interpreter to strengthen a tribe's communications with Santa Fe. Anza felt confident that he would advocate similar arrangements among his own people and that the new ideas would be wisely discussed in the Comanchería in the coming months.

The exchange of visitors fostered a healthy new respect by each of the new allies for the other. Just as the Comanche visitor had been impressed by the numbers of New Mexicans and Navajos, so Anza's emissaries to the Comanchería were astounded by the vast numbers of Comanches, who seemed to outnumber all the population of New Mexico. They brought back glowing reports of the Comanches' excellent disposition and enthusiasm for friendship with the Spaniards, as well as better comprehension of the problems of life within the Comanchería.

That there were indeed problems had become obvious when five Comanches stole two dozen horses from the presidial herd at Santa Fe. Anza wisely suspended judgment on the meaning of the act until his emissaries could report back from the Comanchería. It turned out that the thieves had acted in defiance of the will of their nation and had been punished by ostracism from all the *rancherías*. Pawnees had surprised their half-dozen tipis, killing all but one of the men and capturing their women, children, and horses. There survived only one child, minus his scalp, and a wounded man. The latter lived in disgrace in a

Comanche camp; he could atone only by voluntary suicide or by exceptional valor in war against enemies of the nation.[30]

The Comanches feared that their reckless fellows had wrecked the peace, but, to their great relief, Anza's representatives asked no explanation and accepted without question the information volunteered. Once they heard the story, they asked neither reparation for the horses, by then far away in some Pawnee camp, nor the life of the surviving thief. The Spaniards' just forbearance reassured the Comanches of a practicable chance for a working peace, and they responded gratefully. The peace was immeasurably strengthened.

Ortiz stayed as a guest in eight Cuchanec camps, comprising some 700 tipis altogether, and found everywhere generous hospitality and affectionate attitudes toward the Spaniards. Ecueracapa's camp of 157 tipis was largest; the smallest had just 30 tipis. Ortiz noticed countless other tipis scattered away from the main camps. There appeared to be three or four warriors in each tipi, with seven or eight women and children. At the little 30-tipi camp, Ortiz reported nine hundred pack animals and separate droves of branded mares, with young up to three years. He could not count the enormous horse herds at the larger camps or estimate the numerous horses wandering about in scattered herds.

Ortiz spent his longest and most pleasant sojourn in the camp of Ecueracapa, whom he called Captain Malla. Yamparica chiefs rode there from the north to pay courtesy calls. The Yupes were too far away to extend a similar courtesy, but Ortiz returned to Santa Fe in mid-May with no doubt of the Comanches' universal enthusiasm for the peace. All seemed truly convinced of their own words: now the Comanches are Spaniards, and Spaniards Comanches.

Much was done within the Comanchería during that spring of 1786 to honor the commitments made at Pecos. Ecueracapa sent four expeditions against the Apaches on the eastern periphery of New Mexico, driving them out of the eastern side of the Sierra Blanca and taking many horses. The Comanches killed seven Apaches and captured four without losing a man of their own. Meanwhile, Tosacondata made his rounds with the ceremonial staff, displaying it in all the Cuchanec *rancherías* and among many Yupes and Yamparicas. Everywhere the response was overwhelmingly favorable. The peace meant new security in the tipis of the Comanches and the opportunity to trade safely at

[30] Francisco Xavier Ortiz to Anza, Santa Fe, May 20, 1786, *ibid.*, p. 322.

Pecos, where many Comanches now journeyed, often in small groups with minimal weapons.

Anza had his first firm information on the progress of the peace at the end of April, when Ecueracapa sent his eldest son with two other lads to report to the governor. Presenting his father's sword as credential, the young man told the events of the last two months and conveyed Ecueracapa's promise to spend all of June with Anza if circumstances should permit. After resting four days at the Governor's Palace, the chief's son, escorted by seven Pecos Indians, carried back to his father's camp the governor's message of confidence and encouragement. Anza urged Ecueracapa to drive the enemy relentlessly southward until he could establish his own people on the banks of the Pecos River. That would place the Comanches conveniently near the New Mexican settlements and would bolster New Mexican security better than two new presidios. Ecueracapa would be welcome in Santa Fe at his own convenience. The two leaders could then decide together upon measures to prevent or punish breaches of the peace.

On May 9 Chief Tosacondata led an important delegation to Santa Fe to report his successful procession through the Comanchería with the official staff. His party included Cuchanec Chief Huanacoruco, slated to lead the second of three projected campaigns against the Apaches after Ecueracapa himself led the first. With him also came Yamparica chiefs Tosporua and Pasahuoques, which further reassured Anza about the attitude of that northern division. During the four days that Anza entertained the delegates, he frequently exhorted them to acknowledge the supreme command of Ecueracapa. He bade them goodbye with messages of affection for their nation and of appreciation for the Comanches' zeal in their new roles as vassals of the king. Chief Huanacoruco carried instructions for Comanche participation in at least one campaign with the Spaniards and a blank tally card on which Anza desired Ecueracapa to record his own forthcoming campaign.

Just three days after Tosacondata's delegation left, Chief Tosapoy arrived with his wife and three Yupe chiefs, Hisaquebera, Tuchubarua, and Encantime. With them rode three more Comanches, escorts assigned by Ecueracapa to the five Spaniards whom Anza had sent to his camp in April. Again Anza entertained the Comanche guests in a manner suitable for a distinguished delegation and touted the importance of vesting supreme authority in Ecueracapa. He also urged the Comanches to oust the Apaches from the Sierra Blanca before winter and supplied information to facilitate their pursuit of Apaches in the Mimbres and other ranges down toward El Paso. Assuring his guests that there were many more Apaches down there and thus much richer prospects for pillage, Anza promised to back Comanche war parties with aid from New Mexican villages and pueblos. The visitors appreciated both the information about Apache whereabouts and the routes to their territory and the governor's generous offers of assistance. Vowing to make the most of it, they left on May 18.

Anza then had a little time to study the report submitted by Ortiz. It confirmed in every respect Anza's own high opinion of the leadership and reliability of Ecueracapa and of the good faith of the lesser chiefs and the rank and file of the Comanche nation. The Pecos delegates who had gone to the Comanchería with Ecueracapa's son also reported enthusiastic hospitality and loyalty among the Comanches.

On May 28 Paraginanchi appeared at the Governor's Palace in Santa Fe with another son of Ecueracapa, a twenty-year-old called Tahuichimpia, whom the father wished instructed in the language and customs of the Spaniards as if he were Anza's own son. Anza readily agreed to do all that he could, although he cautioned that the lad's age and the short time available would limit possible achievement. The important thing was the extraordinary gesture of affection and confidence that Ecueracapa made by entrusting his son to the Spanish governor.

The chief remained preoccupied with Apache wars. In mid-May some of his people killed two Apaches and recaptured fifteen mules. Ecueracapa himself set forth on May 23 to lead an expedition against the Apaches on the route advised by Anza. He had already remarked to Ortiz that he would not visit Santa Fe until he had completed a campaign against the Apaches and had also visited the Taovayas on the easternmost periphery of the Comanchería. Anza had thus a considerable time to wait before he could learn whether Ecueracapa deemed feasible the supreme chieftainship in peace and war that the Spaniards desired him to establish.

Paraginanchi had brought to Pecos fifty-seven tipis of his own followers, who wished to trade, and three Yamparica chiefs who wished to know the governor. They wanted him to ride to Pecos, both to confer with the Yamparica leaders and to open a trade fair for the Cuchanec visitors. Anza rode back to Pecos with Paraginanchi on May 30 and held council with the assembled Comanches, hearing their reports of enthusiasm for the new peace among their people and complimenting

their faithfulness and their wisdom in deferring to the authority of
Ecueracapa. The trade fair on the next day, June 1, duplicated the
orderly procedures of March 1, producing similar satisfaction and good
will. The Comanches started home the next day, well pleased with the
outcome of their visit.

Anza had suggested that Ecueracapa send eight warriors just before
the full moon of July to campaign with Spanish troops against the
Apaches in the Mimbres Mountains. That invitation for eight brought
twenty-two promising young Comanche warriors to Santa Fe in mid-
July. Oxamaguea, a younger son of Ecueracapa, led them. Tomaneguena, another son of the chief, brought Ecueracapa's message that the
young men had been sent to shed their blood on a campaign with the
Spaniards in the service of the king and were instructed to obey to the
letter the orders of the governor and those of the commander of the
expedition.

Ecueracapa intended soon to bring a hundred tipis of people to
trade, and he would then tell Anza of his progress in establishing his
authority throughout the nation. In addition to all Cuchanecs, he had
drawn the Yupes into his sphere of authority, and some Yamparicas.
There remained only the larger part of the Yamparicas, whose distant
location had prevented consultation. He had invited them to council
in the coming autumn and was optimistic about achieving overall
command of the Comanchería at that time.

Because of the extraordinary vigilance of the quarry, Ecueracapa
had achieved disappointingly little in his thrust against the Apaches.
He had led 350 men in 5 parties, but they had killed only 6 Apaches,
captured 2, and seized 85 horses. One Comanche had died in action;
seven had been wounded. Ecueracapa himself had sustained two light
wounds.

Now his son would lead twenty-one of their best young Comanches
into action alongside the Spaniards. To give his charges the best possible care, Anza devised a buddy system. He assigned each Comanche
to a soldier of corresponding seniority, to be looked after with every
kindness and consideration. Each guardian gave his own name to his
charge, obviating difficulties with Comanche names and making it easy
to identify them with their assigned partners. Oxamaguea was accorded the rank of captain, a much appreciated gesture of respect to
his distinguished father.

Anza hoped, by incorporating the Comanche warriors directly into
the Spanish force, to prevent any confusion arising from their different

styles of warfare or any friction between the Comanches and the Navajos who were joining to honor that nation's commitment to campaign with New Mexicans against Apaches. To avoid possible confusion between friendly and enemy Indians in battle, the governor issued each Comanche a printed cotton shirt and a red badge, very like those furnished Navajos campaigning with Spaniards.

Alférez Salvador Rivera led the expedition out of Santa Fe on July 15: thirty-seven presidials, ninety militiamen, sixty Pueblos, twenty-six Navajos, and the twenty-two Comanches. They bore south to scour the mountain ranges for Apache *rancherías*, then continued to El Paso so Rivera could dispatch a report to the commandant general.

They first found action in the Socorro range, where sixty Spaniards probed with the twenty-two Comanches and twenty Navajos. They surprised four dwellings of Apache women and children, protected by just two men. The men fled, abandoning their charges. One woman was killed and the remaining thirteen Apaches captured. Rivera sent the prisoners back to Santa Fe with thirty militiamen and the Navajos.

The trivial nature of the first encounter disappointed both Navajos and Comanches. When the force continued southward along the Rio Grande, the Comanches volunteered to scout ahead. They found seven trails and in the San Mateo range discovered a large Apache *ranchería*. Reckless of their inferior numbers, the Comanche lads attacked, killed three of the enemy, and escaped with several horses, which they triumphantly presented to Alférez Rivera. Four Comanches were wounded. Lest those lads get themselves killed while he was responsible for them, Rivera sent all the Comanches back to Santa Fe with the remaining militiamen and the Pueblos. He rode on with his soldiers to El Paso to mail his report to Chihuahua on August 1.

Rivera's force had hardly left Santa Fe on July 15 when Ecueracapa and his retinue arrived for a cordial reunion of the two leaders. Ecueracapa reported his people willing to make him their Superior Chief in all things, saying as much as could be said about their affection and loyalty to him without exceeding the bounds of modesty.

The Comanches also liked Anza's proposal that they carry the war against the Apaches south to the Rio Grande. Ecueracapa expected to campaign in that region upon the return of his young warriors from their expedition with the Spaniards. From October through spring the buffalo would range west from the Pecos, a roving commissary available to Comanche invaders in the Apachería.

Anza, now completely confident of Ecueracapa's standing among

Comanches, bestowed upon the chief the trappings of high authority: a large medal with the king's likeness, a complete officer's uniform, and another colorful suit. Ecueracapa was very pleased. Anza rode with him the next day to open a trade fair for the many Comanches waiting at Pecos, then returned to Santa Fe to contemplate the year's achievements and to compose his reports to the commandant general.

Anza had tried to learn from Ecueracapa the state of the peace in the easternmost Comanchería and his relationship to the Comanche delegates who had negotiated the treaty at San Antonio. Apparently, Ecueracapa had not yet made his planned visit to the Taovayas, but he did have recent reports that the easternmost Cuchanecs were making peace in Texas. He knew that delegations had visited Governor Cabello on four different occasions and named some chiefs who had gone. Anza relayed that information to Chihuahua to facilitate coordination of reports from New Mexico and Texas.

That coordination proved so difficult that some questions were never resolved. Part of the problem lay in the Comanche practice of conferring new names upon individuals to celebrate important events or notable personal characteristics. Chiefs, with more eventful and distinguished careers, were especially likely to bear several names during a lifetime, sometimes in sequence and sometimes concurrently. Of course, duplications of names occurred among Comanches as among any other people.

When Spaniards attempted phonetic spelling of Comanche names, uttered in sounds so unlike Castilian, results varied widely. Often they gave up altogether on the Comanche name and either used its Spanish equivalent or applied some Spanish descriptive unrelated to the person's Comanche name.

A prime case in point was Ecueracapa, known also as Contatanacapara. Ortiz, Anza's emissary to the chief's own camp, knew him as Cota de Malla, presumably derived from a shirt of mail that he liked to wear in battle. The governor of Texas, through his interpreters Vial and Chaves, understood the eastern Cuchanecs to acknowledge as foremost leader a great chief called Camisa de Fierro. Commandant General Ugarte, given reports of Cota de Malla from New Mexico and Camisa de Fierro from Texas, assumed at first that those were simply two different Spanish expressions of the descriptive name of one great chief,[31] then grew to doubt it. Questioned by the governor in San Antonio, Vial

---

[31] Ugarte to Cabello, Chihuahua, August 17, 1786, BA.

and Chaves confirmed that Cota de Malla and Camisa de Fierro were indeed names applied to one Comanche chief, the greatest of them all.[32]

Cabello, who had expected to see no more of the Comanches for six months after negotiating the October peace treaty, reckoned without their enthusiastic conception of friendship and brotherhood. From November 1785 onward, he was the surprised host to a bewildering succession of Comanches. First a pair of Comanche lads appeared, well armed and well mounted, at San Pedro Springs, not far beyond the presidio, to the terror of half a dozen Spanish youngsters hunting there. The Indians kindly assured them that they were friendly Comanches, brothers of the Spaniards, and only wanted to see their Father, the Great Captain. After a cordial handshake with the six boys, the two young Comanches rode on into the settlement and searched the streets until they found Cabello's door. Greeting the governor with many enthusiastic hugs, they displayed their credential: the gun that Cabello had given the leader of the Comanches who had negotiated the treaty in October.[33]

Vial and Chaves heard of the visitors and hurried to the Governor's Palace to greet them and to help Cabello find out why they had come. They were from the first camp that the three chiefs had visited on their way home from San Antonio. They wanted to report the enthusiastic reception of the peace news by all their people and to convey the compliments of the chiefs.

Very pleased, Cabello arranged for them to stay at the home of Courbière with all they could eat and smoke. During their week's stay, Cabello talked with them several times and found them very polite, reasonable young men. They repeated their chiefs' promises to war unceasingly against the Lipans, even down into Coahuila. The pair left on December 2, very happy with Cabello's small parting gifts, expressing their gratitude and their surprise to find the Spaniards such good people. Cabello could only pray that the commandant general would approve the unauthorized expenses for entertainment and gifts and that the shipment of gifts for the entire nation would reach San Antonio during the five months before the promised return of the Comanches.

December was a great festival time, when celebrations honoring the Virgin of Guadalupe ran into those of the Christmas season. Thanks to

[32] Cabello to Ugarte, Béxar, September 24, 1786, BA.
[33] Cabello to Rengel, Béxar, December 9, 1785, BA.

the new peace, 1785 found San Antonians celebrating more joyously than in many years. On December 15 Cabello joined most of the populace on the plaza to watch the bullfight, a traditional part of the festivities. To his amazement, two Comanches, man and wife, rode into the gathering and embraced him, greeting him as "Fata." The bewildered governor gave them tobacco and sweets and called for Vial and Chaves. Before the two interpreters could arrive, the Comanche man drew the governor's attention to his white scarf, painted in red ochre with a well-formed cross, which the Indian indicated was the sign of being a Spaniard.

Vial and Chaves soon learned the purpose of the visit. This couple had been so impressed with the Comanche chiefs' reports of San Antonio's excellent hospitality that they had hurried to confirm their own loyalty to the peace with the Spaniards. They had simply felt too impatient to wait five months to come with the rest of their people at the designated time.[34]

Since the two interpreters vouched for their good character, Cabello felt it absolutely necessary to entertain them as well as he had entertained their predecessors. Again he called upon the hospitality of Courbière, now an experienced host to Comanche houseguests. During their visit the governor talked with the couple several times, both to learn about their *ranchería* and to assure that they would ride home happy with their San Antonio experience.

When Cabello inquired about the current state of Comanche relations with the Panismahas, the visitors explained that, when the Panismahas had been friends with their friends, the Taovayas, the Comanches had been their friends also. Once those two groups had separated and had fought, the Comanches had repudiated their own friendship with the Panismahas. However, this man expected no great difficulty if the Spaniards should desire a reconciliation among them. En route to San Antonio, the couple had traded with the Taovayas, Wichitas, Tawakonis, Iscanis, and Flechazos. The breach of recent years between the Comanches and those Wichitan groups was already healing nicely, although they would not celebrate their new accord until the next moon. Cabello cheerfully anticipated an early campaign by all those Indians against the Apaches.

The Comanche couple had been at San Antonio two weeks when a much larger delegation of their compatriots arrived. They ap-

34 Cabello to Rengel, Béxar, December 24, 1785, BA.

proached the settlement in mid-afternoon, firing their guns into the air to announce themselves as at their own *rancherías*. Cabello sent troops to escort them into the presidio, and a crowd gathered at the Governor's Palace to see them.

At the head of the party rode one of the three chiefs who had visited Béxar in October, dressed in his Spanish uniform, displaying the cane and medallion that symbolized his authority. He embraced Cabello and introduced him to the rest as the Great Captain. All twenty-two embraced the disconcerted governor. He could only wonder why they had come until Vial and Chaves arrived to interpret. After he and his interpreters smoked with the four chiefs, Cabello voiced his concern that they had come before he was in a position to present them gifts as he wished. The visitors assured him that gifts were not necessary. All of their people were very pleased with the peace, but the sixteen youngsters of this group could not wait to confirm it with their own experience. They had all been out pursuing horses and Apaches and were dropping by on their way home to express their affection for Cabello and their fidelity to the peace. The governor thanked them and enthusiastically discussed with them the joys of war against the Lipans.

This group also lodged with Courbière, where, as usual, Cabello furnished all they could eat and smoke. It was hard to keep accurate count of the guests. The first couple departed on January 2 but soon returned in order to travel with the other Comanches. Some of the young men left within ten days, but their chiefs stayed much longer.

The raiding party had two small Apache captives from Sonora, whom they sold at the market to the settler Francisco Xavier Rodrígues for three horses. The Comanches also bartered hides and meat for knives and sweets, all at regulated prices.

Cabello spent much time with the Comanche chiefs, both to honor them with his attention and to encourage an all-out effort to exterminate the Lipans. Vial and Chaves hammered home the same theme in their own conversations with the visitors.

The governor learned more of affairs within the Comanchería. The other two of the chiefs who had negotiated the October treaty had not yet returned from talks in the rest of the *rancherías* about the peace, but Camisa de Fierro and Cabesa Rapada were reported very pleased to be friends and brothers of the Spaniards and of the Taovayas, Tawakonis, and other nations with which the Spaniards were friends. The Comanches envied the Taovayas their trade with the Spaniards.

This delegation pleaded to have traders sent to Comanche camps, so that they would no longer have to beg trade goods from the Taovayas.

The visitors' height and robustness and their pleasant dispositions made a great impression on the governor. When he remarked upon their splendid physiques, the visiting Comanches proudly assured him that they were quite typical and in fact had many more powerful men among their people. Their size posed a problem, since none of the clothing on hand in the warehouse would fit those tall chiefs. Dismayed that he could not present them uniforms suitable for their rank, Cabello could only give the chiefs the same trinkets as all the rest of the party.[35]

Some of the Comanches were still at Béxar on January 10 when a Wichitan party arrived to see the governor. Most of the thirty-seven were Taovayas and Wichitas, but a few Tawakonis rode with them. The Taovayas and Wichita leaders had sent the delegation to announce that the Comanches had fulfilled all the promises they had made when they visited the Taovayas-Wichita villages with Cabello's envoys.[36] They reported everything going well with their people, unaware that Osages had inflicted severe damages on their villages soon after their departure.[37]

On the third day of their visit, Cabello invited the Taovayas and Wichita leaders, one Tawakoni, and the Comanche chiefs to a parley. The governor made a speech about the importance of unity among all of them and of incessant war upon the Lipans. All concurred, then discussed the problems of recovering captives from the Lipans and of carrying the war into their hunting grounds and *rancherías*. Their enthusiasm moved them to launch on January 16 a joint expedition against the Lipans to recover a Comanche woman captured in the San Antonio area five years earlier.[38] All the Taovayas and Wichitas went, as did one Tawakoni and most of the Comanches.

Four more Comanches arrived on the night of January 16, so seven of the prospective campaigners stayed at San Antonio to help the newcomers enjoy the food and tobacco at Courbière's house. Not until January 24 did Cabello set the rest of the Comanches on the road; then, within two days, four of them returned to enjoy another round

[35] Cabello to Rengel, Béxar, January 10, 1786, BA.
[36] Cabello, Diary, January, 1786, BA.
[37] Ugarte to Cabello, May 24, 1786, BA.
[38] Cabello to Rengel, Béxar, January 24, 1786, BA.

of Spanish hospitality.[39] There seemed no doubt that all the visitors liked their treatment by Cabello and the San Antonians. Cabello was sure that the Comanches had come just to satisfy themselves of the reality of the peace and to have a look at their new "brothers."[40]

San Antonio had seen only the beginning of the enthusiastic Comanche response to the new friendship. Late on the afternoon of February 7, a great burst of gunfire north of the settlement announced yet another Comanche party, twenty men and five women. Vial and Chaves again rushed to the Governor's Palace to help Cabello greet them.

At the head of the group rode the most impressive Comanche chief yet seen by Cabello, beautifully turned out in a fine robe and a grandly plumed headdress. He announced that he was the brother of Chief Cabesa Rapada, come to embrace the Great Captain, his father, and to assure him of his brother's pleasure at the peace. Cabesa Rapada knew how well the governor had received the Comanches at his presidio, and he looked forward to the time when the whole nation would ride to San Antonio to ratify the peace. This party were out to fight their enemies and had been charged to deliver the chief's message at San Antonio.

Apologetic about having so little to give the visitors, Cabello quartered them at Courbière's house. Apparently his hospitality satisfied them; they stayed eighteen days. Cabello talked often with the leader of the group, through whom he hoped to encourage Cabesa Rapada and Camisa de Fierro to wage continual war upon the Lipans. The governor complained at length about Lipan insolence and reported that they had recently won over to their side the Tonkawas, Cocos, Bidais, Mayeyes, Akokisas, and some of the Tejas, a conclusion based on recent reports from La Bahía. The visiting chief assured Cabello that he would persuade Cabesa Rapada and Camisa de Fierro to arrange a big campaign against those Lipans and to invite Taovayas and other Norteño warriors to help.

Since this appeared to be the most important Comanche visitor yet, Cabello managed to give him the uniform coat and trousers considered essential to proper recognition of distinguished rank. He had a hard time scraping up some small parting gifts for the rest of the party, and he began to worry very seriously that the expected gift shipment would

---

[39] Cabello, Diary, Béxar, January, 1786, BA.
[40] Cabello to Rengel, Béxar, January 25, 1786, BA.

not arrive before the whole Comanche nation should appear in April or May.[41]

Two days out of San Antonio the homeward-bound Comanches encountered three compatriots en route to visit the capital; two of the recent visitors obligingly turned back to keep the new trio company for another round of brotherliness. Cabello accommodated them graciously, of course, but the constant demands of hospitality were strenuous and the mounting costs of entertainment and gifts appalling. The governor apologized repeatedly to the commandant general for the unauthorized expenditures, justifying them as preferable to the cost of lives in times of war with the Comanches.

It had become clear that the new friendships would require frequent and often extended entertainment of Indian guests. Visits and unstinting hospitality were such integral parts of Indian life that Spaniards could not hope to hold their friendship if they should fail to measure up to that standard. Consulting with Courbière, Cabello decided that spring to build a big *jacalon* to house future visitors.[42]

Courbière and his wife must have been weary of the constant stream of houseguests, for the governor had relied upon them to lodge his Indian visitors ever since their marriage in 1780. Doña María Feliciana, born a Durán, had meanwhile produced several of the nine children that she bore Don Andrés. However dutiful and hospitable she was, and however pleasant the Indian guests, she must have welcomed, or perhaps even suggested, the construction of roomy separate quarters for the visitors. Don Andrés donated land next to their own home, so that he could continue to oversee entertainment of the guests.

It was an ideal location, outside the presidio in the district called the Potrero. There, in the horseshoe bend of the San Antonio River, between the presidio and Mission San Antonio de Valero, people pastured their horses because that area was least exposed to passing thieves. A main road ran through the Potrero, and Courbière's land lay on that well-traveled route, right by the river. Water ran in the river at all times, an important consideration to Indians who bathed daily in a stream. By the standards of the settlement, frequent baths were a barbaric eccentricity, but Courbière convinced Cabello of the necessity of accommodating it.

The *jacalon* was an impressive structure, about 144 feet long by 15 feet wide, partitioned into four 36-foot rooms, the better to lodge

[41] Cabello to Rengel, Béxar, February 28, 1786, BA.
[42] Cabello to Rengel, Béxar, March 14, 1786, BA.

visitors from different nations. Although the *jacalon* was built especially to accommodate Comanches during the anticipated convocation to ratify the peace, it housed visitors of all nations. As soon as the structure was completed, late in July 1786, friendly Norteños stayed there.[43]

While local settlers constructed the *jacalon*, Cabello tackled another task arising from the Comanche peace. Acting Commandant General Rengel, striving to correlate reports of Comanche negotiations reaching him from New Mexico and Texas, desired Cabello to submit all available information concerning the Comanches. What were their leaders' names? Did they rule by election or by inheritance? What manner of men were they? What were their customs? What was the nature of life in their *rancherías*? The more the Spaniards could learn of their new friends and brothers, the more successful the peace would be and the better the communications between the two peoples.[44]

Fortunately, Cabello had learned much from his Comanche visitors as he strove for rapport with them. He could also draw upon the knowledge of Vial and Chaves for his report to Chihuahua in April 1786.[45] Although he had yet to meet the great chiefs Camisa de Fierro (whom he understood also to be called Cota de Maya) and Cabesa Rapada, he believed them to have been elected to their superior posts by all their people, on the basis of esteem earned by valorous performance in war. He vouched for the affectionate dispositions of those Comanches whom he had met, and he named a few lesser chiefs of the Orientales whom he had met or had learned about from his visitors.

Cabello's report on the Comanches reached headquarters at a time of far-reaching change in the leadership of the Provincias Internas. A new commandant general, Jacobo Ugarte y Loyola, assumed command in April 1786; Rengel reverted to the position of commandant inspector. However, supreme command of the Provincias Internas now vested in the new viceroy, Bernardo de Gálvez; no longer would the commandant general report directly to Spain. Worse still, Gálvez divided the military command in thirds: Ugarte himself commanded the western division of Sonora and the two Californias; Rengel, the central division of New Mexico and Nueva Vizcaya; Comandante de

---

[43] Cabello to Ugarte, Béxar, July 31, 1786, BA.
[44] Rengel to Cabello, Chihuahua, January 27, 1786, BA.
[45] Cabello, Responses of the Governor of the Province of Texas to the questions which the Commander General raised in his order of January 27, 1786, on various circumstances of the Eastern Comanche Indians, Béxar, April 30, 1786, BA.

Armas Juan de Ugalde, the eastern division of Texas, Coahuila, Nuevo
León, and Nuevo Santander (the two latter not yet part of the Provincias Internas). Rengel and Ugalde, though nominally subordinate to
Ugarte, could report directly to the viceroy, and in their own jurisdictions they enjoyed wide discretion with regard to peace or war with
the Indians. They were subject to Ugarte's orders when they did not
conflict with those of the viceroy.[46]

The result was an administrative monstrosity that virtually defied
coordination and continuity of policy among its diverse elements. Good
working relationships among the officials might have eased the problem, but Ugarte and Ugalde were old rivals, often at odds. Gálvez had
devised the peculiar structure to facilitate his personal management
of the complex Indian affairs of the northern frontier. Perhaps he could
have made it serve that purpose, but he died in November 1786, soon
after issuing important new Indian policy guidelines.

Not only were there radical changes in the high command of the
Provincias Internas just as the Comanches came to terms with that
authority. The governors of New Mexico and Texas, who personified
Spanish authority to Comanches, anticipated their own replacements
even as they labored to establish strong working relationships with the
Comanche leaders. Cabello retired from Texas in 1786, and Anza
from New Mexico less than a year later.

The Spaniards had found it difficult to comprehend the Comanches'
leadership structure or to depend upon any continuity of relationships,
thanks to the high mortality rate of Comanche chiefs and their fluid
social-political structure. Given the jurisdictional complexities and the
rapid turnover among top officials, the Spanish structure must have
seemed to Comanches no more stable or geared to continuity than their
own. Indeed, Comanche leaders juggling peace negotiations with the
Spaniards of New Mexico on the west and those of Texas on the east
must have been just as puzzled and wary as were Spanish officials
striving to deal with the Comanches of the east and the west.

[46] Max L. Moorhead, *The Apache Frontier*, pp. 64–70.

CHAPTER 20

New Mexico and Texas, 1786-1788

Whatever the uncertainties about the Comanche peace, east and west, and the quirks of the Spanish chain of command, the earliest yardstick of the alliance would be Comanche performance against Apaches. Responsible for meshing Comanche thrusts with Crown purposes were the governors of New Mexico and Texas, who operated under very different circumstances.

Anza, with lifelong experience of Indian diplomacy and warfare on the northern frontier, enjoyed in New Mexico a more stable base of Indian alliances. The Pueblos, just as threatened by hostile *indios bárbaros* as the Spaniards, were staunch allies of proven capacity; the Utes and Jicarillas, generally reliable, kept closely in touch with Santa Fe. Although problems occurred with the Navajos, they valued trade with New Mexico too much to clash openly with Spanish purposes, and they could be nudged into cooperation by economic pressure and threats to unleash Utes or Comanches against them. Governor Anza spent much of his time in the field managing New Mexico's complex Indian alliances, with gratifying results.

Cabello, only half a dozen years acquainted with Indians in Texas, comprehended much less of their circumstances. He never saw a camp or village but stayed in his capital to receive Indian visitors. That provoked criticism, probably unfairly. Cabello was old and ailing throughout his term, never up to the rigors of long horseback journeys to the farflung Indian peoples of Texas, nor did he ever have all the affairs of the province controlled enough to risk long absence from headquarters. Essentially the captive of practices inherited from the French regime in Louisiana, predicating Indian relations on annual gifts to the friendly nations, he always doubted the soundness of the policy and never had the resources to carry it out properly. He was hampered by proximity to and frequent conflict with the jurisdiction of Louisiana, the old focus of Norteño loyalties, and by disruptive contrabandists roving the marches of lower Louisiana.

In contrast to New Mexico's well-established working alliances with most of its Indian populations, Cabello had to manage much newer alliances, based in part on loyalties uncertainly transferred from the old French regime. Trickiest of all was his Apache problem. Anza directed Comanches and Navajos against declared enemies of his province, the Apaches of the mountain ranges in southern New Mexico. Cabello had to direct Comanches and such Norteños as he could incite against the Lipans, who were nominally at peace with Texas and frequented both Béxar and La Bahía. If the Lipans should realize his double-dealing and grow so outraged as to resume open warfare, they might very well wipe out Spanish Texas.

From the inception of the Comanche alliance, both governors urged and abetted campaigns against Apaches in their respective jurisdictions. Their new friends and brothers responded promptly and vigorously, with disastrous impact upon the Apaches.

In Texas, the increasing pressure made the Lipans work harder than ever at trade with nations willing to sell them guns from contraband sources in Louisiana. Cabello moved to break up their friendship with the Tonkawas, whose location made them critical either as bridge or as barrier in the Lipan trade with more easterly groups. Cabello meant them to be a barrier.

To turn the Tonkawas against the Lipans, the governor employed a survivor of a Lipan raid a quarter-century past. Miguel Peres, of San Antonio, had been only eight years old when Lipans attacked his little Yojuane camp on the Rio del Fierro in 1759. Those Lipans, campaigning with Parrilla's force, surprised the Yojuanes, slaughtered about a third of them, and captured another third. The rest fled to join a Tonkawa camp.

Among those captured was the eight-year-old lad, whom the Lipans subsequently sold to a retired Béxar soldier, Don Baltasar Peres, who reared the lad in his home and gave him his own name. Miguel grew up thoroughly Hispanicized, married a young Indian girl from a local mission, and lived as a model resident of the settlement. Somehow Miguel discovered that his father and older brother had escaped to the Tonkawas, where they won such respect that the brother became chief after El Mocho died. Miguel often visited his father and brother, although he had no wish to return to the Indian life.

In February 1786, when Miguel applied for permission to visit his kinsmen, Cabello recognized the ideal messenger to the Tonkawas. With the desired passport, Miguel received Cabello's message expressing displeasure with the Tonkawas' Lipan connection and hinting that he could not, under those circumstances, distribute gifts to the Tonkawas.

Miguel informed his father and brother, who were utterly dismayed. Friendly relations with the Spaniards profited the Tonkawas far more than any dealing with Lipans, and of course this particular family had little cause to love Lipans. They expressed their concern to the other warriors and cast about for some positive means to conciliate the governor.

As they pondered the problem, the son of Siscat Gainon stopped by with a war party of about two hundred Tawakonis, Iscanis, and Flechazos, on their way to fight Lipans. He invited the Tonkawas to come along. Spotting a chance to show Cabello that they were no friends of the Lipans, 150 Tonkawas joined the war party.[1]

Swollen to more than 300, the war party found its target on the Colorado River: a big Lipan camp, including the followers of Chief Cuernitos and Chief Panocha, with about 160 warriors. A surprise attack at daybreak threw the Lipans into total consternation, especially when they recognized their erstwhile friends, the Tonkawas, attacking. The women, children, and old people fled to the hills while the warriors stood their ground at the camp. The battle raged until late afternoon, when the surviving Lipans had at last to flee. More than thirty Lipans lay dead, including chiefs Cuernitos and Panocha and the latter's son; two women were captured, and countless horses seized or

[1] Cabello to Ugarte, Béxar, July 3, 1786, BA.

stampeded. When the survivors carried their pitiful tale to other Lipan camps, the entire people retreated to the Nueces River to mourn their losses and gird themselves for revenge.

Although it was precisely the kind of attack that Cabello had urged, he too had cause for regret. Cuernitos, most rational of the Lipan leaders, had often restrained his people from depredations against the Spaniards.[2] Now, in lieu of his moderating influence, his people had in the spring of 1786 the overwhelming necessity to avenge his death.

Repercussions began almost at once. In April, forty-nine friendly Norteños visiting La Bahía were attacked by the Lipans, who would not ordinarily have been so bold.[3] Spanish authorities decided not to intervene for the time being in hostilities between the Lipans and Norteños but to hope for a better opportunity to punish the Lipans later. It seemed likely that the Lipans would also open hostilities against the Spaniards. Already they had stolen about forty horses that settlers, lulled by the new peace with the Comanches, had carelessly pastured near San Antonio. Five Comanche men and two women approaching Béxar clashed with Lipans. Fortunately, none were killed, but Cabello fretted about such a small party of Comanches braving an area rife with angry Lipans.[4]

Desperately preoccupied with the problem of gifts to celebrate the peace, the governor greeted his new Comanche visitors with assurances that their gifts would come just as soon as there should be enough water in the Red River. Actually, that was not their concern. They were scouting the area to ascertain the whereabouts of the Lipans while awaiting a planned gathering of forces in their *rancherías* and the Norteño villages to mount a great offensive against the Lipans. Running short of provisions, the scouting party dropped by to visit their Spanish brothers at Béxar. Cabello entertained them for a week, then saw them off with new provisions and personal gifts and with the fullest possible information on the location of the Lipans to share with the gathering allied forces.[5]

The Lipans were indeed in desperate straits. Very probably they had now been ousted forever from the area between the Colorado and Brazos rivers. That, plus the enmity of the Tonkawas, would gravely impair their access to the eastern Indians who had supplied them guns

---

[2] Cabello to Ugarte, Béxar, June 12, 1786, BA.
[3] Cabello to Rengel, Béxar, April 18, 1786, BA.
[4] Cabello to Rengel, Béxar, April 24, 1786, BA.
[5] Cabello to Rengel, Béxar, May 8, 1786, BA.

and ammunition in recent years.[6] Cabello resolved to arrest their coastward drift in order to complete their isolation.

The Lipans maneuvered desperately to retrieve their shattered fortunes. Regrouping and additional numbers were imperative. One possibility appeared to be a union of forces with the Jumanos and Joviales, also hard pressed in the Rio Grande area, under the overall chieftainship of the strongest surviving Lipan leader, Zapato Sas.

A month after their disaster on the Colorado, Zapato Sas requested and received permission to talk with Cabello as head of all the Lipans. Twenty Lipans accompanied him to Béxar on June 24. They asked Cabello to take them under his protection and name Zapato Sas Great Chief of all the Lipans, just as he had done for the chiefs of the friendly nations. Zapato Sas offered, in return, to locate the Lipans wherever the governor should choose and to restrain all of them from thefts or hostilities against the Spaniards. He would punish any offenders and would restore all the horses that had been stolen. It was clear that Zapato Sas was trying desperately to ward off a repetition of their beating by the Norteños or worse at the hands of the Comanches.

Cabello saw some merit in the leadership claims of Zapato Sas, who was reputed to be very brave and to have much the largest following among Lipans. Certainly the fallen chiefs Cuernitos and Panocha had been quite rational to deal with and had restrained many rash impulses of their people. Left without responsible leadership, the Lipans would be impossible to manage, and Zapato Sas probably could do more than anyone else to curb depredations against the Spaniards. Unfortunately, he would not forswear war against the Norteños and Comanches. Given the necessity of choice among warring Indians, Spanish interests unquestionably lay with the Lipans' enemies.[7]

Cabello rejected the petition, arguing that he had no assurance that all Lipans would obey Zapato Sas and keep the bargain. What of all the lesser chiefs? Cabello would need proofs of their fidelity, starting with restoration of the many horses Lipans had stolen from Spaniards. Only if they would do everything the governor asked of them would he ask his own Great Chief, Ugarte, to grant their request. Meanwhile, he wanted them clear away from all Spanish presidios. They must move their *rancherías* out west to the headwaters of the Frio River, there to await the decision of the commandant general.

---

[6] Cabello to Ugarte, Béxar, June 12, 1786, BA.
[7] Cabello to Ugarte, Béxar, June 12, 1786, nos. 271 and 231, BA.

In no position to argue, the Lipans agreed to return to their camp at Atascoso the next day and to begin the required removal of their *rancherías*. Aware that his conditions carried very harsh implications, Cabello tried to soften the blow with cigars and candies for all the delegates and a handsome red loincloth for Zapato Sas. They left as scheduled next day, ostensibly to begin the move. With a horse herd said to number a thousand, they would make a tempting target isolated out on the Frio. Cabello gloated that he now had the Lipans set up for a knock-out blow:[8] he was about to destroy his Amalekites.

The Lipans did not so tamely accept their death sentence. Tonkawas notwithstanding, they managed to visit the Bidais, presumably to trade for guns, after Cabello ordered them off to the west. That news only hardened the governor's resolve to see them perish on the Frio.[9]

The victorious Norteños had gone home to celebrate their great victory, but Cabello guessed their appetites were whetted for more successes to come. The Tonkawas' involvement especially pleased him. On the other hand, the Taovayas and Wichitas had not participated, despite their vows of friendship for the Spaniards and hatred of the Lipans. Annoyed, the governor sought to prod them into action.

The Taovayas and Wichitas were preoccupied with their own troubles throughout 1786. The Spanish commandant general had ordered them rewarded for their help to Vial and Chaves in negotiating the Comanche peace,[10] but, before anything could come of the reward, Osages struck their Red River villages. That devastating winter raid was a harsh blow to peoples already weakened by several years of losses. The period of strained relations with the Comanches had taken a considerable toll, as had the recent quarrel with their former neighbors and allies, the Panismahas. In no condition to risk more onslaughts by the Osages, the Taovayas and Wichitas adopted the advice of Camisa de Fierro to move from the Red River.

The Comanche chief wanted to strengthen and consolidate the grand alliance against the Lipans and to facilitate trade and communication with the Spaniards of Texas. He therefore persuaded the Taovayas and Wichitas to move to the Pedernales River, handily near their friends and kinsmen, the Tawakonis, Iscanis, and Flechazos, and convenient for Comanches who needed a base to deal with San Antonio. Guersec acceded to those arguments, all eminently sensible.

[8] Cabello to Ugarte, Béxar, July 3, 1786, BA.
[9] Cabello to Ugarte, Béxar, July 3, 1786, no. 232, BA.
[10] Rengel to Cabello, Chihuahua, January 27, 1786, BA.

Neither he nor Camisa de Fierro considered that the Comanche leader's renowned wisdom stopped short of matters agricultural and that the harsh caliche soils and the scant rainfall along the Pedernales would sorely try his farming allies.

Camisa de Fierro helped, as well as persuaded, the Taovayas and Wichitas to move. His people escorted them on the journey, presumably to safeguard the moving families from some Osage or Panismaha or Lipan assault. Tawakonis, Iscanis, and Flechazos came to help build the new houses, and the joint effort warmed friendships among the groups. They all meant to seal their brotherhood still more firmly by campaigning together against the Lipans.[11]

Guersec also reached out to reconcile the quarrel with the Panismahas. Cabello had urged conciliation of the Panismahas at midwinter, only to be rebuffed by Taovayas and Wichita spokesmen at San Antonio.[12] Now Osage raiders, perhaps reinforced by the moderating counsel of Camisa de Fierro, had persuaded Guersec that it would not, after all, be impossible or undesirable to heal the breach with the Panismahas. Eighteen Wichita and Taovayas delegates rode north to the Missouri River early in the spring of 1786 to offer the Panismahas new friendship and alliance.

The surprising move to the Pedernales was an accomplished fact when Cabello learned of it late in March. Guersec sent a lesser chief with ten men to San Antonio to notify the governor. The Spaniards approved. The action seemed to confirm the zeal of all those Indians for close cooperation with the Spaniards and with each other. Commandant General Ugarte ordered Cabello to keep up a good flow of trade to the village and to supply any assistance needed to solidify Taovayas-Wichita control on the Pedernales.

They stayed less than half a year. Perhaps one season's effort to farm on the Pedernales was enough. Perhaps they missed too much the trade, legal and illegal, that they had so long enjoyed on the Red River. San Antonio afforded no adequate substitute. Perhaps the move proved to be a premature thrust into territory too recently held by Lipans and the village unduly tempting to Lipans bent on revenging their March losses. Apparently the new villages were not secure enough to spare many men for war parties. Taovayas and Wichitas

[11] Cabello to Rengel, Béxar, April 16, 1786, BA; Ugarte to Cabello, Chihuahua, May 24, 1786, BA.
[12] Rengel to Cabello, Chihuahua, October 21, 1786, BA; Cabello to Rengel, Béxar, December 25, 1786, and January 23, 1786, BA.

participated in few of that year's allied campaigns against the Lipans, much to Cabello's disappointment. Perhaps the decisive factor was the death of Guersec, whose name abruptly ceased to figure in Spanish records that summer. By the summer's end they fell back to the Red River, with their young men again out of control. Perhaps the village elders decided to retreat to the old location in order to avoid punishment for the misdeeds of the lads. At any rate, the year of general success among the friendly nations was a disappointing one for the Taovayas and Wichitas and for Spanish hopes concerning them.

Cabello was too preoccupied that spring to fret much about the Taovayas and Wichitas. Six months had passed since the October agreement, and the Comanches were pledged to come en masse with their great chiefs for a ceremonial ratification. As April and May wore on without their appearance, Cabello worried about the Comanches' apparent indifference to the peace treaty. On the other hand, the shipment of gift goods also failed to arrive from Louisiana, and the governor dreaded the consequences if the Comanches should find him unable to present the promised gifts.

Not until the end of June 1786 did Cabello receive the explanation written by the governor of Louisiana in March. Although the gifts had reached New Orleans from Veracruz, the Red River was low; not until the spring rains should raise the level could goods be shipped to Natchitoches. The shipment involved the annual gifts for the twenty-one friendly nations as well as the Comanche peace presents, so the delay jeopardized most of Cabello's Indian alliances.[13]

Within a week of that discouraging dispatch, the outlook improved. On July 6 another messenger from Nacogdoches brought word that the goods had been shipped from New Orleans: seventy-five bundles for the Comanches and seventy-six for the friendly nations. There would also be 203 pounds of salt for the friendly nations. While Lieutenant Governor Gil Ybarbo began work at Nacogdoches on the necessary transportation arrangements, Cabello began to worry about warehousing the goods.[14]

Timely reassurance also came from the Comanchería. In mid-July three Comanche men and two women, one said to be the daughter of Camisa de Fierro, visited Béxar to explain why their people had not yet come to ratify the peace. Camisa de Fierro had gone to lead a great campaign to avenge the death of the other great chief Cabesa

[13] Cabello to Ugarte, Béxar, June 30, 1786, BA.
[14] Cabello to Ugarte, Béxar, July 11, 1786, BA.

Rapada, who with twenty other Comanches had fallen in action against Mescaleros and Lipans on the Pecos River. Much confusion had prevailed in their camps during the process of electing a successor to Cabesa Rapada, and there was also the problem of Camisa de Fierro's long absence. The people remaining in the *rancherías* had decided at the end of May to send these five to explain the delay, lest the governor of Texas think them lacking in integrity.[15]

Cabello thanked them for their courtesy, explained his own difficulty about the delayed gifts, and invited them to be his guests as long as they wished. An apartment in the new *jacalon* next to Courbière's house awaited their pleasure.

The Comanche guests had some cheerful news for the governor. En route to San Antonio they had passed the villages of the Tawakonis, Iscanis, and Flechazos. Many men were absent from those villages, off with Tonkawas to attack Lipans. A few weeks later Gil Ybarbo passed the same villages on his way to San Antonio and found no more than twenty Indians in residence. A summer buffalo hunt could have been a major factor, but Cabello hopefully envisioned them all involved in a decisive campaign against the Lipans.[16]

On the morning of August 22, Gil Ybarbo arrived from Nacogdoches with a pack train laden with all the goods for the twenty-one friendly nations as well as the Comanches: thirty-seven boxes of goods imported from Europe, plus 474 bundles of tobacco. At last Cabello could take personal charge of the all-important gift distributions. As soon as the impressive shipment was stacked in the warehouse, Cabello showed the bundles and boxes to his five Comanche guests and explained that they would be opened when Camisa de Fierro should come to ratify the peace. They were obviously pleased. The governor hoped they would soon carry the news to their *rancherías*.

Four days later the Comanche delegation announced that they wished to leave that afternoon to notify Camisa de Fierro and the rest of the Comanches that the gifts had arrived, although the three men were very ill. Cabello gave them some small presents and powder and balls, and they set out in mid-afternoon. Within twenty-four hours two of the men and one of the women returned with another Comanche couple and small boy whom they had met on the road, coming in to visit Cabello. The three had decided to come back with the newcomers to make better recovery from their illness. The remaining couple had pressed on toward the Comanchería. The new arrivals brought no news except that Camisa de Fierro had not yet returned from his errand of vengeance for Cabesa Rapada. All of them settled down to enjoy the hospitality at the *jacalon.*

About nine o'clock on the last morning of August 1786, gunfire in the north signaled the approach of a large Comanche party, which rode up to the Governor's Palace flourishing the flag bestowed during the first Comanche visit the previous October. Leading them were two of the chiefs who had come for the initial negotiations and an imposing young man introduced as the brother of Camisa de Fierro. They embraced Cabello and presented to him the flag, which they had meticulously preserved for the occasion of their return.

Cabello arranged for quarters for all the company, then asked the three leaders into his home to smoke their pipe. Interpreters Courbière, Vial, and Chaves joined in the occasion. After the smoke came speeches about the flag, and then an exchange of news. Camisa de Fierro had returned from his campaign against the Mescaleros and Lipans. He regretted that his sad duty of vengeance had prevented his visiting Cabello as he had intended, and he was sending his brother with this delegation to explain everything to the governor before the coming of cold weather.

An important part of their errand was to warn Cabello that some wrong-headed young Comanches were coming to inflict damages on their brothers the Spaniards. Incensed because the Spaniards had not kept their promises to visit the Comanches, they deemed them false friends. Camisa de Fierro himself thought the Spaniards' lapse regrettable: after all, they could have come in complete safety, nothing bad would have happened to them, and the Comanches would have been happy to return to San Antonio with them.

Cabello had committed a serious breach of courtesy by his failure to reciprocate the many visits of the Comanches. They had been given no opportunity to make the proper return for his lavish hospitality, and some were deeply offended. The governor explained in his most conciliatory manner that Spaniards could not travel the great distance on foot, as could Comanches. The San Antonians were very short of horses because Comanches had taken so many during the years of war and because Lipans continually stole horses now. The shortage of horses even kept the Spaniards from pursuing the Lipans and preventing their crimes. That reply produced some confusion among the Comanche leaders.

Turning the conversation into less delicate channels, Cabello inquired about the size of their party. They had brought nineteen men, with seventeen women to take care of their forty-two horses. Cabello, who already had some Comanche guests, reckoned that he now had twenty-two men and nineteen women of the nation to entertain. He ordered them amply provided with food and tobacco as long as they should wish to visit and showed them the hoard of gifts in the warehouse. The governor hoped they would carry back reports that would soon move their compatriots, especially Camisa de Fierro, to ride to San Antonio for the important ratification ceremony, now running nearly half a year late.[17]

Cabello held several more parleys with the Comanche chiefs, always paying special attention to the brother of Camisa de Fierro, to whom he showed the large medal awaiting the great chief. If the visitors knew that their leader had already received the large medal of a principal chief in Santa Fe six weeks earlier, they tactfully refrained from mentioning it.

At the last parley, on the eve of their departure, the Comanches urged Cabello to send some Spaniards with them on their return to their great chief. Cabello refused, feeling that the great distance and the very real shortage of horses would mean undue hardship for his people and that the lateness of the season would make the return journey unduly hazardous.[18]

Significantly, in his final report of the visit of this delegation, Cabello referred to the great chief as Cota de Malla. His information from these visitors, the first who had also been delegates to Santa Fe, apparently squared with the assurances of Vial and Chaves that the name applied to Camisa de Fierro. The visitors left promising that Cota de Malla would indeed come to ratify the peace, which they all wished to be permanent. They also promised to war more vigorously against the Lipans and to return those captives due the Spaniards.

The governor's hospitality, of which they were warmly appreciative, had not been entirely simple. Unable to outfit such a tall, robust man as Cota de Malla's brother, Cabello regretfully gave him only a fraction of the proper uniform for his rank. He tried to compensate for the deficient presents by having repairs made at the presidio on some of their guns and lances, which were in very bad condition. Fortunately, he hit upon one of the most valued services that the Spaniards

[17] Cabello, Diary, Béxar, August 31, 1786, BA.
[18] Cabello to Ugarte, Béxar, September 24, 1786, BA.

could render Indians. The governor also provided unstintingly the watermelons, roasting ears, and sweets so relished by Comanche visitors. They seemed quite content with his efforts. The delegation called at the Governor's Palace on the morning of September 13 to reclaim the Spanish flag that he had kept for them during their visit. The leader held it high as they rode out of the presidio, followed by a crowd of local residents who turned out to wish them Godspeed.[19]

That was Cabello's last important encounter with Comanche leaders. Both conditions within the Comanchería and policies decided in Mexico City and Chihuahua impelled them thenceforth toward Santa Fe rather than San Antonio. On August 26, 1786, as the three chiefs led their delegation toward the Texan capital, Viceroy Gálvez issued his landmark Instruction of 1786, governing the conduct of war and peace with the Indians of the northern frontier.[20] Although Gálvez focused primarily upon the Apache problem, his disparate provisions for New Mexico and Texas bore heavily upon Comanche fortunes. He wanted the Comanches and Norteños kept friendly at all costs: he needed them to solve the Lipan problem and to stand buffer against other powerful tribes now pressing toward the Spanish frontiers from north and east. Gálvez so dreaded gratuitous disruption of the alliances by some rash provincial officers that he reserved to himself alone the power to decide whether Spanish officers should punish infractions by the Norteños. The viceroy did well to take such a precaution, because he was giving command of the eastern sector to that notorious stormy petrel, Colonel Juan de Ugalde, and was about to send another, Captain Rafael Martínez Pacheco, to govern Texas until some qualified administrator could be found.

In contrast, Gálvez entrusted extraordinary discretion and responsibility to the governor of New Mexico, recognizing its extreme distance from higher authorities and the inordinate complexity of its Indian affairs. The viceroy wished El Paso made a center for treating and trading with those Apaches who should respond to his terms for peace; as to the rest, the governor was to war unceasingly against hostile Apaches as he should think most expedient, cooperating with the forces of Sonora and Nueva Vizcaya when feasible. Gálvez desired encouragement of Navajo hostilities against the Gilas and vigorous trade

---

[19] Cabello to Ugarte, Béxar, September 25, 1786, BA.
[20] Bernardo de Gálvez, *Instructions for Governing the Interior Provinces of New Spain*, ed. and trans. Donald E. Worcester.

to bind Navajo interests firmly to the Spaniards. He wanted the peace with the Jicarillas conserved, no effort spared to keep the Comanches happy, and the Utes carefully cultivated so that they could be used against the Comanches or Navajos if either should act in bad faith.

By the time the Instruction reached Chihuahua in mid-November 1786, the young viceroy had fallen victim to the epidemic fever that killed him that month. His program survived him: the document was already on its way to Spain, where the king gave it the force of a royal ordinance in February 1787. Meanwhile, Commandant General Ugarte had begun to implement its principles even before he received the formal document. Gálvez had summoned him to Mexico City for extensive consultations upon the topic early in 1786, before Ugarte took command in April. How much Ugarte contributed to formulation of the Instruction is uncertain, but its principles accorded so well with his convictions concerning Indian policy that he followed them from the moment he took command of the Provincias Internas.[21]

Certainly the commandant general acted within the viceroy's intentions when, in October 1786, he considered the Comanche and Navajo alliances.[22] Ugarte reversed Neve's earlier instruction that the principal focus of Comanche relations should be San Antonio and that the Comanches should be attracted away from New Mexico into Texas; instead, he ordered the alliance with the whole Comanche nation managed from Santa Fe. One reason was that all agreements in Texas involved distribution of annual presents, while the Comanches had never asked more than friendship and trade in New Mexico. Another factor was Santa Fe's better proximity to the Yupes and Yamparicas; another, the excellent working relationship between Governor Anza and Chief Ecueracapa. Unlike Neve, who had vindictively sought to destroy Anza's career, Ugarte esteemed the New Mexican governor and tried to redress the damage done him by Neve.[23] Perhaps Ugarte also took into account the failure to obtain a qualified replacement for the retiring governor of Texas.

Of course, no Comanches would ever be rebuffed at San Antonio, and the easternmost Cuchanecs would probably find it more conven-

[21] Max L. Moorhead, *The Apache Frontier*, pp. 132–133.
[22] Ugarte to Anza, Chihuahua, October 5, 1786, in Alfred Barnaby Thomas, ed., *Forgotten Frontiers*, pp. 332–342, 351–357.
[23] Ugarte to the Marqués de Sonora, Chihuahua, December 21, 1786, ibid., pp. 365–366.

ient to do business with the Texans. But even they were to be included in a grand convocation on the New Mexican frontier of all the Comanche nation, to ratify with Anza not only the general peace but also their allegiance to the Supreme Chief, Ecueracapa.

Given so much evidence of Ecueracapa's extraordinary character and abilities and of his high standing among the Comanches, Ugarte and Anza confidently anticipated his election to the new office of Supreme Chief, for which the Provincias Internas allocated a salary of 200 pesos annually. Ugarte desired the Comanches also to elect a second in command, to reside among the Yupes and Yamparicas, at a salary of 100 pesos. If Ecueracapa and Anza should think it desirable, Ugarte would also authorize another 100 pesos for another lieutenant commander for the eastern *rancherías* of the Cuchanecs, a matter that could be administered in Texas.

Ugarte considered Anza's establishment of a resident interpreter among the Navajos so useful that he wanted the practice regularized, expanded, and extended also to the Comanches. The commandant general therefore authorized two resident interpreters for the Navajos and four for the Comanches, two of whom he wished to reside with Ecueracapa and two with his lieutenant governor. The interpreters would draw the pay of presidial soldiers, on the roster of the Santa Fe company. Ugarte stipulated that the appointees must be highly qualified men, skilled in dealing with Indians, expert in the pertinent language, and able to write; he promised appropriate rewards for meritorious performance.

The commandant general assumed the Comanches ready for a giant step, of nearly revolutionary proportions, toward a national polity. He expected them not only to take the first steps toward a unified tribal government but also to curb the autonomy of the individual Comanche. Ugarte desired the chiefs to collect in their camps and immediate command all wandering and dispersed individuals, particularly the remaining dissidents from the camp of the late Toroblanco, or, failing that, forcibly to subdue or destroy them.

Ugarte required Anza to ask the chiefs in council to decide the penalties they would impose upon Comanches breaking the peace. Anza himself could only urge them to fix the penalties and to apply them rigorously and consistently. He was never to order punishments or help carry them out. Even intervention to grant clemency from Comanche punishments that seemed to Spaniards unduly harsh should be avoided.[24] He must act solely to support the tribal council's authority, never to supersede it.

Two considerations moved Ugarte: the immediate practical point that Indians generally accepted punishments imposed by their own people but rebelled against any levied by outsiders, even if more moderate; and the necessity for a stable authority administering a well-defined body of law among the Comanches, to pave the way for development of even more comprehensive political institutions. It was in Spain's interest to foster political institutions within the Comanchería, but experience had taught that such changes could not be imposed from outside a nation, no matter how virtuous the intent of those who intervened.

Some Comanches had shown a lively, sympathetic interest in Spanish language and customs, which augured well for the new friendship. Ugarte hoped to encourage that trend by offering to educate the sons of Comanche leaders in Mexico at royal expense. Relatives would be allowed to accompany the youths to witness their good treatment in the capital and to carry that reassurance, and tales of metropolitan splendors, back to the Comanchería. Instruction in Catholic dogma would be available to Comanche students in Mexico City, but none would be admitted to the Church until after their return home. Any decision to become Catholics must be their own, freely made in their home environment, away from the overawing grandeur of Mexico City. Again, experience dictated policy: Ugarte would court no repetition of the tragedy of Salvador Palma. Of course, true converts among the young men of leading Comanche families would be joyously welcomed, as the best and perhaps only possible means to propagate the faith within the Comanchería. Utes and Navajos could enjoy the same opportunities if they so desired.

Ugarte worried about the long-term quality of Spain's relationship with the Comanches. For the moment, their zeal for war was Spain's best hope to solve the Apache problem, but how could their warlike propensities be channeled once the Apaches were subdued? In the interests of all concerned, Spanish authorities ought to begin at once to woo the Comanches to peaceful, settled life. Since they had already

---

[24] A case in point was Anza's grant of asylum to a Comanche who reached Santa Fe on May 26, 1786, begging the governor to save him from chiefs planning to kill him for adultery, a capital crime in the Comanchería (Thomas, *Forgotten Frontiers*, p. 313).

asked permission to live near the Spanish settlements in New Mexico, Ugarte asked Anza to influence their chiefs toward an agricultural way of life. The game that they pursued so strenuously could not last forever, especially as more and more tribes came to contest hunting rights on the buffalo plains. Ugarte wanted the Comanches encouraged to supplement their hunters' subsistence with products of their own fields, to prepare them eventually to settle down entirely to civilized life as Spaniards understood it.

The farming-hunting transition stage that the commandant general proposed would hardly be a novel idea to Comanches, who had long observed such a dual subsistence pattern at the Wichitan villages. Nevertheless, the sum of Ugarte's proposal implied a gradual social and economic revolution among the Comanches to match the political revolution that he expected of them. Coercion would be eschewed as useless, but Spain would offer encouragement and hope. As a beginning, Ugarte offered to subsidize any Comanche attempts toward agricultural settlement. He authorized Anza to send Spanish settlers and Pueblo Indians to live near them to teach agricultural techniques: the plotting of fields, the construction of dams, the opening of irrigation ditches, and the management of crops. The government would equip both the Comanche volunteers and their exemplars with oxen, ploughs, and other necessities. Similar subsidies would be given Navajos who would organize formal settlements and increase their emphasis on farming. Encouraging the Navajos to do so would be another of Anza's responsibilities.

Was the scheme quixotic? Ugarte believed that it could work among Comanches because it was genuinely in their interest and because Spain could support it, both to protect imperial interests and to serve the obligations of piety. That it was not entirely far-fetched was shown when Comanches voluntarily tried the scheme.

While Ugarte anticipated a peaceful, settled future for Comanches in the long run, an immediate purpose of the alliance was war, and that, too, posed problems. How were frictions among the disparate allies to be avoided when they fought side by side, especially when they took captives, of whom different peoples disposed in conflicting ways?

To protect Apache captives, Ugarte proposed to guarantee a small ransom to the captors for each one under age fourteen. That would stimulate search and capture of the youngsters and thus contribute to the attrition of Apache numbers. The obligation to save souls would be served by rearing the youngsters in the faith, then incorporating them in the *genízaro* population of the province. Adults were not amenable to that treatment, so the Crown would not ransom Apaches older than fourteen, although they could assume that males' lives would be forfeit.

There was also the question of captives already held by Comanches. Some were Spaniards, some Christian Indians, some members of allied nations, such as the Utes. Ugarte proposed that the Comanches simply release all those whom they had captured in war. As to those whom they had purchased from other nations, they would be compensated for the purchase price in the case of all Christians and in the case of pagans wishing to return to their own people. Spain would in turn restore all Comanche prisoners, even those who had been shipped to the fortress of San Juan de Ulúa. Some, especially those who had been baptized, might prefer to remain with the Spaniards, but, if their nation should choose to reclaim them, the demand would be honored. Ugarte assumed that those returned would carry back to the Comanchería impressive tales of the cities of New Spain and the vast numbers and wealth of its peoples.

Since healthy commerce forged the most enduring links between peoples, Ugarte required that the final treaties include trade regulations, guaranteeing fair treatment of the Comanches and the Navajos by setting prices and restraining exploitation by the New Mexicans. Price fixing would run counter to the general liberalizing trend of Bourbon economics, but Ugarte thought it entirely justifiable in this particular situation: ". . . a bridle necessary for containing the greed of the more enlightened party until . . . our heathen neighbors may . . . understand their interests and . . . establish by themselves the equilibrium of values in their goods bought with what they need from our hand."[25]

Ute sensibilities were a prime concern, because that alliance was too old and too valuable to sacrifice even for the most important new connections. Ugarte wished Ute representatives to witness the ratification of the Comanche treaty and to understand its terms fully, in order to spare them any fear of collusion against themselves. He expected Anza to require the Utes and Comanches to draw up formal guarantees of their peace with each other, with very specific definitions of violations and procedures for redress of grievances. The governor of New Mexico would thenceforth stand guarantor for the enforcement of the agreements between the two nations.

[25] Ugarte to Anza, Chihuahua, October 5, 1786, ibid., p. 356.

All in all, Ugarte set for Anza an extraordinary task: to nurture a
political structure where almost none had existed before and to foster
social and economic revolution among an alien people; to prepare a
nation of warriors for peace, even while inciting them to war; to make
fast friends of tribes long hostile to one another; and, perhaps hardest
of all, to restrain his own people from abusing the interests of the new
allies. Having some inkling of the magnitude of the task, Ugarte allocated an extra six thousand pesos annually for unusual expenses New
Mexico would incur in the attempt. He also gave the governor of New
Mexico great discretion to alter orders when he should deem it desirable in view of local conditions, a privilege confirmed by the viceroy
and the Crown within the next few months.

Anza speedily set about fulfilling Ugarte's instruction, though it took
several months to achieve the necessary ratification of the peace by all
segments of the Comanche nation. The council of Comanches with
which he met in the fall of 1786, sometime after Ugarte's directive,
consisted largely of Cuchanecs. They elected Ecueracapa captain general of the nation and Tosacondata second in command. They also
ratified the articles of peace, as modified along the lines specified by
Ugarte.

When the annual caravan plodded from Santa Fe to Chihuahua in
November 1786, a dozen Comanches rode with it. Ecueracapa's eldest
son, Oxamaguea, carried the treaty, which they would ratify before
Ugarte once they confirmed that he did truly commit himself and his
superiors to its terms. With him rode Chief Tosacondata, who expected
to be invested by Ugarte with his new office of lieutenant general, and
Encantime, a Yupe war leader who was the son of a peace chief much
honored among Yupes and Yamparicas. Two of Ecueracapa's younger
sons, Tomaneguena and Tahuichimpia, went, too, as did five more
warriors and two wives of Tosacondata.[26]

Ugarte found the Comanche men pleasant to deal with and impressively handsome and robust. They handled themselves well at the lavish civic reception in their honor on December 30 and on several subsequent occasions when Ugarte entertained them in his own home.
The commandant general disappointed some of their expectations. He
did not ceremonially invest the chiefs or distribute any canes of office,
because tales from Texas had led him to fear that the planned procedures might run afoul of some obscure Comanche superstitions. He

---

[26] Moorhead, *Apache Frontier*, pp. 156–159.

also questioned whether so much distinction could be accorded the Cuchanecs without arousing jealousies in the other divisions. He did entertain the visitors generously and assured them of his full accord with Anza's commitments to them. They assured him of their own determination to keep the peace and promised to help bring the Yupes and Yamparicas into the concord.

Indeed, they parted so cordially that Ugarte feared he might suffer a constant stream of Comanche guests, as at San Antonio, once the twelve delegates reported their happy experience in Chihuahua. The commandant general decided that Anza should not deter any who might wish to make the same trip but that he should warn them that they must bring an interpreter and that they would be received only to market hides at the more favorable southern prices or to be recognized for participation in a campaign against the Apaches. He ordered presidial commanders to welcome Comanche visitors and to provide necessities for their return trip and for campaigns against the Apaches. No presents should be given them except cigars and candy and whatever food they should need. The Comandancia General could not afford endlessly to entertain all Comanches on the same generous scale as the first dozen representatives.

His conversations with the Comanche delegates convinced Ugarte that Ecueracapa and Camisa de Fierro were two different chiefs, the one powerful among western Cuchanecs and the other among eastern Cuchanecs. He had doubted the single identity since autumn, when he could not reconcile Anza's news of Ecueracapa with the reports about Camisa de Fierro that Cabello gleaned from Comanches at San Antonio. After questioning the three sons of Ecueracapa who visited him in January 1787, he concluded that the name Cota de Malla belonged to another chief of equally high standing among the easternmost Comanches in Texas, who had recently died in battle.[27]

That confirmed Ugarte's doubts about the real extent of Ecueracapa's power and his concern about the attitudes of other powerful Comanche leaders. The commandant general therefore turned entire responsibility for investing the medal chiefs back to Anza, admonishing him to resolve the problem in the light of Ugarte's new questions and in the spirit of his October instructions.

Ugarte might also have questioned the accuracy of his interpreter's service in the discussions with Ecueracapa's sons. In that same month

27 *Ibid.*, p. 154, n. 10.

of January 1787, Pedro Vial talked with Chief Camisa de Malla in the Comanchería and found him worried about the practical difficulties of commerce with San Antonio. Certainly Vial and Chaves, who had long known the Comanches in their home territory, believed Cota de Malla, Camisa de Fierro, and Ecueracapa to be one. Certainly Ortiz had returned to Santa Fe from Ecueracapa's own camp calling him Chief Malla, the name that appeared on the peace treaty ratified at Pecos in February 1786. Cabello received no report of the death of the great chief of the eastern Comanches in 1786, though followers of Camisa de Fierro did tell him in mid-summer that Cabesa Rapada had died that spring in action against Apaches. As late as September of that year, representatives of Camisa de Fierro promised that he would indeed come to San Antonio to ratify the treaty with Cabello. That he never did was surely not the result of carelessness about his word, but of Ugarte's specific decisions that autumn and Anza's resulting instructions to Ecueracapa.

In April 1787, the ranking chiefs of the Cuchanecs, Yupes, and Yamparicas convened in grand council within the Comanchería and concluded with Anza the definitive peace treaty binding all their nation. At their behest, the governor confirmed Ecueracapa as captain general of the entire nation, Tosacondata as lieutenant general for the Cuchanecs, and the Yupe chief Paruanarimuca as lieutenant general for his own people and the Yamparicas. Together the Comanche and Spanish leaders had triumphed over immeasurable barriers of time and distance and difference.

Their triumph boded disaster for the Apaches, whose lives dwindled to little more than a succession of defeats, both in war and in diplomacy. In mid-September 1786, Zapato Sas led fifteen Lipan delegates to Béxar to ask about the commandant general's answer to their June petition. Cabello pointed out that the Lipans had yet to meet his terms. They had stolen many horses, which had escaped the settlement in two or three stampedes started by Lipans. Also, in defiance of the governor's instructions, more than two hundred were camped only twenty-five miles from Béxar on the Arroyo del Atascoso, where they were killing many cattle. Cabello saw no evidence of good faith to support their requests.[28]

When Zapato Sas protested, Cabello told him to move all his people

<hr>

[28] Cabello to Ugarte, Béxar, September 25, 1786, BA.

out to the plains around the abandoned presidio of San Sabá and there prove his determination to control them and keep them away from Spanish settlements. The governor passed candies and cigars to end the conference and threw in for good measure two fine knives for butchering buffalo. All vowed once more their great desire to be friends. The Lipans assured Cabello that they had only been in the vicinity to hunt and that, since it meant so much to him, they would mount and move all their people.

That fall the discouraged Lipans launched peace overtures in New Mexico. Comanches heard of it and begged the governor not to consent: the Comanches had to have some enemies against whom to war, lest they become a nation of women! The commandant general did not necessarily subscribe to their reasoning, but he reckoned that such a peace would undermine the whole structure of the Indian alliances in New Mexico. He ordered the governor to entertain no peace feelers from any Apache source.[29]

Meanwhile, Cabello chipped away at the friends of the Lipans. When Tejas visited San Antonio for their annual gifts, Cabello criticized their friendship with the Lipans. He would not give them presents until they broke off the relationship completely, and he vowed to give the Bidais, Cocos, Mayeyes, and Akokisas the same treatment. That shook the Tejas, who were already dismayed by the Lipans' reverses. When another successful campaign against them by the Taovayas, Wichitas, Tawakonis, Iscanis, and Flechazos further demoralized the friends of the Lipans, Governor Cabello thought that he could soon complete the isolation of that troublesome people.[30]

The campaigns of the Wichitan bands were not an unmixed blessing in Texas, for it was hard for all members of a big war party to keep their minds on the Lipan objective. Early in September 1786, the son of Siscat Gainon led two hundred Taovayas, Wichitas, Tawakonis, Iscanis, and Flechazos in search of Lipan quarry on the Colorado and Guadalupe rivers. Instead, they found a party of San Antonio mustangers, who told the warriors that the Lipans were out on the Frio River and urged them to go after them. The Indians appreciated the information but seemed disinclined to ride the long distance to the Frio before touching home base again.[31] Most of the warriors headed

---

[29] Moorhead, *Apache Frontier*, pp. 160–161.
[30] Cabello to Ugarte, Béxar, September 10, 1786, and November 20, 1786, BA.
[31] Cabello to Ugarte, Béxar, September 29, 1786, BA.

homeward, but some Taovayas and Wichita lads broke off to raid the Béxar herd. Caught in the act, two were killed, one at the gates of the presidio and one on the road; the rest escaped with some horses.

By that time the Taovayas and Wichitas had abandoned their Pedernales experiment to return to the Red River, where again they lived across the stream from each other. Cabello had heard in August of shady French traders from the Arkansas River who urged the Taovayas to steal horses from the Spaniards to trade for contraband goods. He blamed the September escapade on that bad influence and worried about the implications for his entire fabric of Indian alliances. Fortunately, the governor had available an ideal emissary to express his concern to the Taovayas leaders.[32]

Pedro Vial had volunteered that summer to establish the long-desired communications link between San Antonio and Santa Fe, less than a year after his peace mission to the Comanchería. In the interval, Vial had posed a problem to Cabello. Unquestionably, he and Chaves merited great reward for their services in making the Comanche peace. Cabello had tried soon after their return to find out what he could do for them that they really wished. Chaves only wished an interpreter's salary. Cabello did not then have such a position, but he expected that he could soon employ Chaves, like Courbière, as a soldier of Béxar garrison, with special assignment as an interpreter. Chaves claimed competence in the speech of the Cocos, Bidais, Mayeyes, Akokisas, Tonkawas, Tejas, Taovayas, Wichitas, Tawakonis, Iscanis, and Flechazos, as well as the Comanches. Cabello could use such a man, not only to interpret, but also to distribute gifts and care for Béxar's Indian visitors.[33]

Vial, a more ambitious man and literate, wished a better position, but Cabello had none at his disposition. When the governor asked the commandant general's advice, Ugarte replied that he did not find it convenient to grant either man a position and suggested a lump sum to compensate each for his labors.[34]

Cabello then proposed 200 pesos for Chaves and 300 for Vial, who had been the leader and had written the diary of the mission. Cabello expected to call upon Vial again if he should need an emissary to the Comanches or to some other nation. He also hoped to send him to dis-

---

[32] Cabello to Ugarte, Béxar, November 20, 1786, BA; Cristóval Ylario de Córdova to Cabello, Nacogdoches, August 26, 1786, BA.
[33] Cabello to Rengel, Béxar, April 30, 1786, BA.
[34] Ugarte to Cabello, Chihuahua, June 7, 1786, BA.

cover a route from Béxar to Santa Fe and to prepare an itinerary for the guidance of future travelers.[35]

That sparked a prompt, favorable response from Ugarte, who agreed to the 500 pesos and set guidelines for Vial's trip to Santa Fe. Ugarte desired a direct route from the most convenient of the friendly Indian villages in the interior, and he expected the explorer to prepare an exact itinerary to guide future travelers. The Comandancia General had reports of various Spaniards who had lately ventured into the land between Chihuahua and the Taovayas and had been well received in Comanche *rancherías*, but Vial appeared the most intelligent and useful of the lot. Ugarte offered to compile all available information at Chihuahua, with the names of the chiefs of the camps already visited, and forward it all to help Vial determine a safe and accurate route.[36]

Vial had no desire to await further intelligence from Ugarte. Cabello checked with him as soon as he received Ugarte's approval and found that Vial wanted to leave immediately. He only needed time to buy three horses, three mules, and some supplies, but he was stymied until Cabello could obtain Ugarte's formal authorization to pay Vial and Chaves from the Mesteña Fund for their previous year's service as envoys to the Comanches. With his 300 pesos, Vial financed his next great service to the Spanish Crown, discovery of the route to Santa Fe. September wore into October before Vial could depart, and he had meanwhile plenty of time to ponder the self-defeating parsimony of his new sovereign, at least in his Texan realm.

Before Vial could complete his travel arrangements, the Taovayas and Wichita warriors made their horse raid at Béxar. Cabello called Vial to identify the dead, marked as Taovayas by their distinctive tattoos. Vial recognized one as a recent visitor to San Antonio.

Cabello then modified the earlier instruction to seek the most direct route and charged Vial instead to go via the Taovayas villages on his way to Santa Fe. He wished Vial to express to the Taovayas as forcefully as possible the governor's displeasure at their conduct. Cabello planned to follow through by displaying his anger when the Taovayas delegation reported to collect their annual gift, if that should occur before his relief arrived. Cabello hoped to have time to see the matter through. The episode could spark dangerous antagonisms, and an inexperienced successor might ruin it.[37]

[35] Cabello to Ugarte, Béxar, July 17, 1786, BA.
[36] Ugarte to Cabello, Chihuahua, August 17, 1786, BA.
[37] Cabello to Ugarte, Béxar, November 20, 1786, BA.

Thus, Vial had two missions when he set out early in October, and the errand to the Taovayas had first priority. He knew about the progress of the Comanche peace in New Mexico through mid-July, because Ugarte's summary of Anza's report reached San Antonio just before his departure. Neither Vial nor Chaves could recognize the names of the chiefs treating with Anza, either from the phonetic renditions of the Comanche names or the Castilian translations, but they and Cabello remained convinced that Cota de Malla, Ecueracapa, and Camisa de Fierro were one. Vial and Chaves did admit to less perfect mastery of Comanche than of Taovayas. Cabello surmised that much of the confusion arose from the difficulties in both Texas and New Mexico of hearing and rendering Comanche names and narratives with reliable precision.[38]

Cristóbal de los Santos of Béxar accompanied Vial as aide. Vial purchased his own animals and provisions; Cabello furnished a few effects for the journey. The king's bounty produced five bundles of tobacco for the indispensable smoking with the Indians and a small axe, five pounds of powder, and ten pounds of balls to sustain the pair across that vast plain, plus a few small items suitable for gifts to the Indians.[39]

Vial planned to rely on Comanche help after visiting the Taovayas. He bore Cabello's passport and his letter to Governor Anza, setting forth the purpose of the journey and bespeaking his assistance to Vial. Ugarte also notified Anza that Vial had volunteered to undertake the journey, "guiding by the villages of the friendly Indians of the North and Comanches, with whom he has lived and dealt for many years," although he was also committed to undertake the straightest feasible route and to record it for the benefit of future travelers. Ugarte urged Anza to pool his knowledge with that of Vial, in order to formulate a better understanding of the situation within the Comanchería. He also recommended that Anza send back with Vial over the same route someone from New Mexico, in order to acquaint men of both provinces with the way.[40]

The journey began badly. Crossing the Guadalupe River on the second day out, Vial and Santos lost their provisions, and one of their

[38] Cabello to Ugarte, Béxar, October 9, 1786, BA.
[39] Cabello to Ugarte, Béxar, October 8, 1786, BA.
[40] Cabello to Anza, Béxar, October 3, 1786, BA; Ugarte to Anza, Chihuahua, October 26, 1786 (certified copy by Pedro Garrido y Durán, October 26, 1786), BA; Cabello, Diary, Béxar, October 31, 1786, BA.

horses drowned. By the fifth day out, when they reached the Colorado River, Vial was ill. On the tenth day they found the trail of the Taovayas and Wichitas who had stolen the horses at Béxar, but the next day the ailing Vial fainted, fell off his horse, and lay unconscious for two hours. Santos, terrified lest Vial die and thus bring an accusation of murder upon his companion, begged for a paper certifying his innocence as soon as Vial regained his senses. Rejecting the notion of dying, Vial resolved to seek treatment at the Tawakoni village.[41]

They wandered for two miserable weeks, often stopping when Vial was too sick to ride. The site where he expected to find the Tawakonis was deserted because the group had gone deeper into the interior. Not until the afternoon of October 29 did Vial and Santos reach the village of Siscat Gainon. The Tawakonis greeted them with cordial surprise. Vial explained that he was on his way to the Comanches, from whom he expected to obtain information about the road to Santa Fe.

The village leaders gathered at the lodge of Siscat Gainon to talk with Vial. They asked whether there was now in San Antonio a certain Taovayas who had gone there to steal horses. Vial told them that a Taovayas-Wichita group had stolen several horses one night at San Antonio. Cabello, thinking them Apaches, had ordered his sentinels to shoot if they should return, and one was killed the next night.

Chief Siscat Gainon reported that the thieves had stopped at his village on their way home from San Antonio. He had scolded them for their theft and had taken some horses away from them, telling them they were fools to injure the Spaniards, with whom the Tawakonis were brothers. All of the Tawakoni leaders urged Vial not to think that the Taovayas and Wichita chiefs had sent those young men. Siscat Gainon reminded Vial how he had restrained his own people from war with the Spaniards ever since de Mézières had persuaded him to make peace with Governor Ripperdá. The Tawakonis had fared well ever since and had received a great deal of merchandise from the Spaniards. Vial advised him always to cherish that valuable friendship.

The discussions satisfactorily completed, Vial mentioned his illness and asked whether someone there could cure him. Siscat Gainon placed all their resources at his service and kept him in his own lodge

[41] Vial, Diary, Santa Fe, July 5, 1787. Copy by Manuel Merino, Chihuahua, September 12, 1793, in AGN, Historia, vol. 43. A translation of the diary based on another copy appears in Noel M. Loomis and Abraham P. Nasatir, *Pedro Vial and the Roads to Santa Fe*, pp. 268–285.

until he was well enough to set out again on December 15. Vial was indebted to the Tawakonis for nearly seven weeks of hospitable care and perhaps for his life.

While Vial recuperated at the lodge of Siscat Gainon, a major upheaval occurred at San Antonio. Only a week after his departure, Ugarte announced Cabello's long-awaited replacement.[42] The Crown had ignored his suggestion that Anza be given the job, and no other properly qualified administrator was immediately available. Ugarte therefore gave an interim appointment to Captain Rafael Martínez Pacheco, an aging veteran near retirement.

Nothing in the long career of Martínez Pacheco hinted any talent for civil administration; indeed, his was a singularly stormy record. He had gone berserk and called upon Indians to help him defy all Spanish authority at the ill-fated presidio of San Agustín de Ahumada, his first command. He had later been a major contributor to O'Conor's campaign to undermine Ripperdá as governor of Texas, apparently because he shared that Irishman's profound distrust of the Norteños and all who trafficked with them. He had since served as a presidial captain in Coahuila without revealing significantly better judgment than had characterized his earlier service in Texas. That he was appointed a provincial governor, even ad interim, underlines the appalling shortage of leadership material in the Comandancia General as the century waned.

Although Cabello had long pleaded for relief because of his failing health, he worried about yielding to an untried successor in the fall of 1786.[43] He had·at last established San Antonio as the distribution center for annual presents to the twenty-one friendly nations and the Comanches; he had even persuaded the viceroy to ship the goods from Saltillo to obviate the problems of shipment from Louisiana.[44] Though a valuable managerial tool for an experienced official, the gift distribution could be risky in the hands of an inept or inexperienced governor.

Unaware of Ugarte's decision to centralize management of the Comanche alliance in New Mexico, Cabello believed that he still had pending the ratification of the Comanche peace treaty with the principal chiefs. Also in progress was the mission of Vial, presumed to be somewhere in the Comanchería blazing the way to Santa Fe. Most delicate of all, there remained the responsibility to maneuver the

[42] Ugarte to Cabello, Chihuahua, October 11, 1786, BA.
[43] Cabello to Ugarte, Béxar, November 19, 1786, BA.
[44] Cabello to Ugarte, Béxar, November 6, 1786, BA.

Lipans into extermination by other Indians without making them so enraged and desperate as to attack San Antonio.

Most immediately urgent was the question of relations with the Taovayas and Wichitas. No one at San Antonio knew why they had broken the peace in September, and Vial had sent no word of success or failure in his mission to the Taovayas. Indian visitors at Nacogdoches had reported some of the Taovayas chiefs disposed to attack the Spanish presidios to avenge the pair killed at Béxar in September, and the issue of a vengeance campaign was said to be very hot in the Taovayas and Wichita villages that autumn.[45]

By any criterion, it was a poor time to change governors at San Antonio. Lacking a qualified appointee, the potential for disaster loomed large. Captain Martínez Pacheco presented his credentials to Cabello on November 30. Cabello spent the next two days briefing his successor, especially emphasizing the Comanche peace in New Mexico and his own expectation that the same great chief would soon come to ratify the peace terms in Texas. On December 3, 1786, Cabello turned the governorship over to Martínez Pacheco, with inventories of the documents and specific information on the Indian gifts, as directed by Commandant General Ugarte.[46]

Cabello, slated for a more comfortable post in Havana, lingered nearly four months in San Antonio getting his records in order, particularly the Mesteña Fund accounts. When he left on March 26, 1787, Cabello must have been terribly worried about the condition of the province where he had labored so long for tranquillity.[47]

Not only had a poorly qualified officer taken over the governorship of Texas at a very critical juncture in its Indian affairs; he reported to a new commanding officer who had no comprehension of Indians north of the Apaches and a dubious record with Apaches. With the accession of Comandante de Armas Juan de Ugalde, the new tripartite division of the Provincias Internas put Texas at the mercy of an uninformed commanding officer who placed strenuous demands for information and performance upon a new governor both ill-informed and ill-equipped to produce either written reports or judicious decisions.[48]

Martínez Pacheco found little time for the research and writing de-

[45] Gil Ybarbo to Martínez Pacheco, Nacogdoches, November 30, 1786, BA.

[46] Cabello to Ugarte, Béxar, December 4, 1786, BA.

[47] Martínez Pacheco to Ugalde, Béxar, April 23, 1787, BA.

[48] Ugarte to Cabello, Chihuahua, October 11, 1786, BA; Ugalde to Martínez Pacheco, Santa Rosa, December 19, 1786, BA.

manded by Ugalde. He had been in office only a week when Lipans warned him of two hundred Taovayas coming to steal horses at Béxar or La Bahía.[49] They meant to avenge their two compatriots killed at Béxar in September.

San Antonians, absorbed in the long fiesta honoring the Virgin of Guadalupe, took little interest in Martínez Pacheco's alarm, but he tried to alert them to a defensive posture and deployed troops as best he could to ward off attack. Amid the confusion of fiesta and defense alert, on December 13 the mule train arrived from Saltillo with the viceroy's shipment of gift goods for the friendly Indians. Martínez Pacheco paid the muleteer's freight bill from the Mesteña Fund and warehoused another stern test of his judgment.[50]

Having ingratiated themselves with the new governor by warning him of the approaching Taovayas, the hard-pressed Lipans made the most of the confusion at Béxar. The delighted and appreciative Martínez Pacheco entertained them lavishly in the presidio and gave them many presents, dipping into goods meant for the friendly nations and the Comanches. That impulse cost him 438 pesos, 6 reales, 8 granos, and the incredulous wrath of his superiors.[51]

The Lipans solemnized a new peace with Martínez Pacheco that December, promising to congregate at the San Antonio missions in return for the Crown's protection. The governor agreed that they could live off the produce of the mission congregations until they could harvest crops of their own.

For the next nine months, Martínez Pacheco repeatedly sent soldiers to escort the main body of Lipans to the missions or to retrieve small groups who had come to the missions and then speedily fled. Some were found camped at Atascoso, others on the Frio River, with endless excuses not to enter the missions: they had to finish hunting; they had to recover some lost horses; they needed to wait for better weather. Sometimes they were a bit truculent, but usually just evasive. Not until September 1787, when their old friend Manuel Urrutia rode to the Frio to ask them again to come to the missions, did they confess the truth. They wished to be friends with the Spaniards, but they simply could not adopt the settled life. By playing upon the naive hopes of Martínez

[49] Certified Copy of Cabildo's Affidavit of defensive measures taken by Martínez Pacheco against the Taovayas, San Fernando, December 14, 1786, BA; Martínez Pacheco to Ugalde, Béxar, December 17, 1786, BA.

[50] Martínez Pacheco to Cabello, Béxar, December 13, 1786, BA.

[51] Martínez Pacheco, List of Gifts, Béxar, February 23, 1787, BA; Ugarte to Martínez Pacheco, Chihuahua, February 1, 1787, BA.

Pacheco, they had won a badly needed respite and had obtained provisions intended to sustain them on the trek to San Antonio that never occurred.

Texan affairs now lay under the new jurisdiction of Ugalde, but that officer spent the early months of his tenure campaigning against Apaches instead of attending to administrative duties. Ugarte therefore intervened with a sharp reprimand to Martínez Pacheco. He pointed out that the unauthorized departure from Cabello's policies gravely jeopardized the peace with the Comanches and Norteños, who could hardly retain confidence in the Spaniards if they should see Lipans living in San Antonio missions. Ugarte thought the only remedy now would be to remove any Lipans in the San Antonio area to Coahuila. A few might wish to live in missions there for a while, but Ugarte expected Lipans in the long run to prefer settlements of their own near Spanish establishments in Coahuila or Nueva Vizcaya as sanctuary against their northern enemies.

Martínez Pacheco defended his extraordinary deviation on the grounds that Comanche peace commitments were no more plausible than those of Lipans, mentioning as a case in point Chief Povea's 1772 treaty, which the rest of the Comanche nation had never honored. When the Lipans had offered to settle down peacefully, Martínez Pacheco had thought it reasonable to accept. After all, the Spanish forces of all the eastern provinces had never been able to conquer the Lipans. He had directed them to the five San Antonio missions because there was no other establishment large enough to feed a numerous people until they could reap their own harvest. By March Martínez Pacheco piously counted one soul gained by his policy, one very old, very sick Lipan woman, baptized at the mission.[52]

Actually, Martínez Pacheco's aberration proved less disastrous than his superiors feared. Perhaps the Lipans' failure to congregate at the missions spared San Antonio a repetition of the San Sabá calamity. Perhaps equally important was Ugarte's October decision, focusing Comanche relations at Santa Fe and reducing San Antonio to a peripheral role. Also, despite his general clumsiness, Martínez Pacheco did not deal too badly with the Norteños.

His first test came with the Taovayas warriors who marauded around San Antonio in December and January. On the night of January 29, 1787, when seventeen made their first attempt on the capital

[52] Martínez Pacheco to Ugarte, Béxar, March 10, 1787, BA.

itself, Alférez Amangual's patrol managed to capture fifteen without taking any lives. Martínez Pacheco understood that killing Indians often provoked vengeance and prolonged hostilities. Therefore, he talked at length with his prisoners about the importance of reestablishing the peace, then sent a pair home to their chiefs in February. They bore Martínez Pacheco's letter urging the Taovayas and Wichita leaders to visit him to discuss their grievances and to satisfy themselves of the Spaniards' justice and good will.

His tactic worked. After a considerable delay, four men brought the Taovayas chiefs' friendly response. They were grateful that their young men had been treated well as prisoners when they deserved punishment. The chiefs themselves would come to verify the peace in two months: now there was too much rain and cold, and they had too few horses for the long ride to San Antonio.[53]

How did these events correlate with Pedro Vial's mission to the Taovayas? When he resumed his interrupted journey on December 15, 1786, he probably did not know of the big Taovayas-Wichita party marauding around Béxar and La Bahía, and he certainly could not have anticipated that Lipans would successfully woo a new governor. Pressing on as Cabello's messenger to the Red River villages he had once called home, Vial reached the Taovayas and Wichitas on December 28, 1786.

The village leaders, highly excited, gathered immediately at the lodge of Chief Corichi to talk with Vial. Knowing that the September raiders had been fired upon, they demanded to know whether the missing Taovayas had been captured or killed.

Vial answered that he was not afraid to tell them the truth, even though he had just one companion, and that they knew very well he was no liar. Vial himself had seen their man dead and had recognized him as a petty chief, one of five Taovayas who had lately visited San Antonio. The governor, loath to believe that Taovayas were making trouble, had first assumed the thieves were Apaches, but now he realized that the Taovayas peace was a sham and that they were a bad people. He had therefore sent Vial to warn them to do no more evil, lest all the Indians who frequented the presidio pursue and kill them, and to remind them that no Indians who injured any Spaniards could be recognized as friends.

Warming to the job, Vial delivered a formal harangue about the

[53] Martínez Pacheco to Ugarte, Béxar, October 12, 1787, BA.

material advantages of friendship with the Spaniards and the awful perils of living without guns and munitions and axes in a world of enemies so armed. He could only speculate that they must wish to see their villages destroyed and their families enslaved by other nations. He shamed them for breaking their promises to the governor, then taunted them with cowardice: ". . . if you wish to make war on the Spaniards, the men do not need to go; send the women, which will be the same. You have for enemies the Osages and Apaches, who are killing and taking your horses every day, while none of you has the courage to go take a scalp."[54]

In ringing climax, Vial urged the chiefs to open their eyes and rid themselves of those who were making mischief. He then announced that he was going to discover the road to Santa Fe in order that the Spaniards of San Antonio and those of Santa Fe could travel back and forth through the Comanchería, now that they were all friends. If he should find the Taovayas peaceful upon his return, he would take them to San Antonio to see the governor and discover his kindness for themselves.

Sobered by Vial's remarks, the chiefs abandoned their threatening, contentious stance, admitted the truth of his remarks, and promised to behave better in future. They disavowed the wrongdoers, whom they said had flaunted their advice and had left by night, ostensibly to campaign against Apaches. The chiefs wished to ride with Vial on his return from Santa Fe to San Antonio to make amends to the governor, but they feared to go any sooner without him. Meanwhile, they were arranging for a big visit to the Comanchería to dance and to trade.

Vial stayed eleven days with the Taovayas, resting and renewing friendships. Winter nights were times for talking in the grass lodges, a season when men recounted their war records and discussed the affairs of the nation. It was a good time for Vial to be present, to increase his knowledge of those troubled villagers, and to plead the case for friendship with the Spaniards and their allies. That he knew of the large party off to raid San Antonio is doubtful.

Many of the hosts kindly escorted Vial and Santos a considerable distance when they took the road on January 8, 1787. The next day brought the two explorers to a Comanche camp, where they had to wait two days to talk with the leaders. The camp's head chief, Zoquiné,

---

[54] Translated from Vial, Diary, Santa Fe, July 5, 1787, AGN, Historia, vol. 43.

had ridden to another camp to retrieve horses that Comanches had stolen from Taovayas, in order to restore them to the owners. He welcomed Vial graciously when he returned with the horses and summoned many chiefs to his lodge to smoke the pipe with him. Only after smoking did they ask the purpose of his visit.

Vial reminded them that the Spaniards looked upon the Comanches as brothers and that the governor regarded them as sons. He had therefore come to open the road from San Antonio to Santa Fe so that Spaniards and Comanches could travel from one part of the country to another. For that purpose, he bore a letter from the captain at San Antonio to the captain at Santa Fe.

Vial's speech pleased the chiefs, but they thought his project presently impracticable because of the extreme cold and heavy snow at Santa Fe. They invited him to pass the winter with them and promised to take him to Santa Fe in the spring. Vial did not accept their invitation, but he visited them for a week, learning much about the problems of enforcing the peace within the Comanchería.

Vial had been out of touch with San Antonio for more than three months, so Comanches who quizzed him about recent occurrences found themselves informing him instead. Spaniards had killed one of the Comanche chiefs who had gone to Santa Fe to make the peace.

Chief Pataurus had led a Comanche party out on the plains to campaign against the Apaches. They encountered a squad of Spanish soldiers from Aguaverde, led by Don José Menchaca, serving as escorts to a party of 226 Mescalero hunters. The Spaniards welcomed the Comanches at their camp in the usual friendly fashion, but the young men of the Comanche party decided it would be a good idea to steal the Spaniards' horses. Chief Pataurus demurred, asking why the lads should wish to injure their good friends. The youngsters taunted the older men as cowards and declared they would no longer recognize Pataurus as chief if he were determined to befriend the Spaniards. Pataurus angrily retorted that not all Comanches were fit to face danger before Spaniards.

At once the Comanches fired upon the Spaniards, who returned a heavy volley of gunfire. Pataurus and another chief fell; the rest of the Comanches fled. At their safe rendezvous, the remaining leaders reproved the young men for having fought. Then they raised the flag, and chiefs Guaquangas and Tanicón, the latter a brother of Zoquiné, surrendered to the Spaniards. Captain Menchaca embraced the two chiefs, and together the Comanches and the Spaniards buried the two dead chiefs, placing the Spanish flag at the head of Pataurus' grave. After a friendly conversation, both groups rode homeward, honor satisfied all around.[55]

In the camp of Zoquiné, Vial was surrounded by relatives of the dead men, but they assured him they would do him no harm because they recognized the fault of the dead men in letting themselves be goaded into firing on the Spaniards. Vial responded forgivingly and praised their friendship. A truly remarkable accommodation had occurred.

On the day before Vial's departure, the chiefs gathered again at the lodge of Zoquiné to smoke and talk with him. They asked him to send to Cabello for some tobacco that they needed, and Vial at once wrote a letter that the leaders dispatched with a minor chief and a fledgling warrior. They were to deliver the letter at Béxar, then try to learn which nation had killed a brother of Chief Taraquiqui. Two Comanches had died at the hands of unknown Indians, and tribal vengeance awaited identification of the culprits.

The chiefs complained that San Antonio was too far from the Comanchería and the road too fraught with danger from Apaches and Tonkawas. They wished the Spaniards either to reestablish the abandoned presidio of San Sabá or to place a settlement on the Pedernales River, so that Comanches could trade with them without going to San Antonio. If that were done, the young men could simply hunt within the Comanchería and avoid the temptations that beset them around San Antonio.

Among the chiefs who talked with Vial that day was Camisa de Malla, also called Guaquangas, who apparently concurred in the recommendations of the assembly. Perhaps he now sought a Spanish establishment on the Pedernales to substitute for the Taovayas-Wichita village that Comanches had helped to establish there for a short while

---

[55] Ugarte derived a very different version of the fray from his Comanche visitors that January, understanding them to say that the chief who was killed was Camisa de Hierro, also called Cota de Malla, the only chief inclined to attack the Spaniards in order to steal their horses. Vial's version, certainly more consistent with subsequent events, casts still further doubt upon the competence of Ugarte's interpreters at the Chihuahua meeting. See Luis Navarro García, *José de Gálvez y la Comandancia General de las Provincias Internas del Norte de Nueva España*, p. 468, citing Ugarte to Sonora, no. 56, Chihuahua, January 4, 1787, AGI Guadalajara, 286.

the year before. At the end of the conference, Camisa de Malla told Vial that he would accompany him on his return to San Antonio, taking many persons to see Governor Cabello.

Vial and Santos pushed on the next day, January 18, but they bowed to the weather on the nineteenth and established a winter camp on a stream. There they stayed until March 4.

They set out again with Zoquiné, who had promised to guide them to Santa Fe, and a party of Comanches just returning from San Antonio. Soon a Taovayas chief accosted the travelers to ask whether the Comanches had seen any of his people who had gone to rob the Spaniards. The Comanches reported sixteen Taovayas raiders jailed at San Antonio. Vial commented acidly upon the promises the Taovayas had made when he visited their village, and the chief expressed great shame for the incident. He promised that when the guilty ones returned to the village they would be made to stop their mischief.

Vial and Santos pressed on with Zoquiné's escort party. On the night of April 7, two Comanche visitors stirred up the camp, claiming that three Comanches had come from San Antonio to warn them that Vial was actually leading the Comanches to Santa Fe in order to kill them there and that the Spaniards would also kill all Comanches going to trade at San Antonio.

Vial defended himself and the Spaniards against the accusation and called the rumor mongers bad-hearted. Chief Zoquiné stood by Vial, promising not to leave him until he saw him safe in Santa Fe and telling the troublemakers he knew they lied. Tension subsided, to the boundless relief of Vial and Santos.

Except for the steadfast Zoquiné, the composition of the Comanche escort was fluid. As May began, Vial and Santos found themselves riding with four chiefs and two braves, all with their wives. On May 14 they reached a tributary of the Canadian River where Chief Paruanarimuco had established his great Yupe *ranchería*. The chief unfurled the Spanish flag to greet them and took them to his lodge.

Paruanarimuco had much to say of Anza: how very well pleased he was with that great captain of the Spaniards! Perhaps modesty forbade him to tell Vial of his own election at the great peace council, less than a month before, to the position of lieutenant general for the Yupes and Yamparicas, but the visitors realized their host was a very distinguished leader.

Vial's party moved on the next day to a Yamparica camp, where they enjoyed such a friendly reception that they stayed two days.

Eight more days of travel followed. On May 25, with flag unfurled, Vial triumphantly led the way into Pecos. The next day, May 26, 1787, marked the official end of his mission. When troops rode out from Santa Fe to welcome the explorers, Vial turned his flag over to their commanding officer, Captain Manuel Delgado.

For Spain, Vial's success fulfilled hopes dating back to the 1750's. Its encouraging implications were analyzed at every level from province to Crown. For the Frenchman Vial and his invaluable Comanche associate, it was only the first of a series of epic journeys across the plains in the service of Spain.

Vial spent a busy June in Santa Fe, preparing his diary and a map of his route and talking with Governor Anza. Already envisioning greater things to come, Vial volunteered to blaze the long-desired route from Santa Fe to Natchitoches. Anza forwarded Vial's proposal for the second exploration to Ugarte with the diary of the first.[56] The processes of decision and of preparation for the Natchitoches venture consumed a year. Meanwhile, Vial grew to prefer Santa Fe above San Antonio as a home. When he left the next year, he meant to return as a permanent resident.

It was hardly a surprising decision. Vial reached Santa Fe during one of the most interesting and successful eras of that capital, just a few weeks after ratification of the great Comanche treaty. Anza was adroitly managing active alliances with the Comanches, Navajos, Utes, and Jicarillas, as well as the settled Pueblos, and was directing wars against the Apaches with notable success. Thanks to the Gálvez Instruction of 1786 and the confidence of Commandant General Ugarte, New Mexico's governor enjoyed unusual discretion in running his province, and he had annually a 6,000 peso discretionary fund to back his judgment. He had jobs at his disposition, including four salaried positions for Comanche interpreters. That contrasted favorably with the sorry situation at San Antonio, where Governor Cabello could not find a job for Vial, had found it difficult to disburse any compensation for his Comanche peace mission, and had not even been able to underwrite Vial's journey of exploration to Santa Fe.

Anza acted promptly upon Ugarte's suggestion that he send New Mexicans to San Antonio to firm up their knowledge of the route, but he asked them to find a more direct way if possible. Vial, given Cabello's definite instruction to visit the Taovayas first and the difficulties

[56] Ugarte to Fernando de la Concha, Arispe, January 23, 1788, AGN, Provincias Internas, vol. 183.

imposed by his illness and the consequent delay into the winter season, did not claim that he had discovered an optimum route. His feat had been to prove that the journey could be made.

A retired corporal of the Santa Fe garrison, José Mares, led the return party that set out from Santa Fe on July 31, 1787.[57] With him rode the same Cristóbal de los Santos who had accompanied Vial from San Antonio and the interpreter Alejandro Martín, eleven years a Comanche captive before Tosapoy released him to Anza at Pecos in February 1786. Domingo Maese went as a servant. As Vial and Santos had done, the Mares party relied upon Comanche escorts to see them across the Comanchería and to their destination. They too traveled via the Taovayas village, but they rode into San Antonio in October 1787, little more than two months from Santa Fe.

Kind helpfulness to Spanish explorers and vigorous persecution of Apaches were not the Comanches' only manifestations of zeal for their new alliance. In mid-summer 1787, Paruanarimuco's enthusiasm for the Spanish way led him to ask Anza to help the Yupes build a permanent settlement on the Arkansas River. Anza duly forwarded the request to Ugarte on July 14, but within a fortnight Paruanarimuco returned to urge the project so strongly that the governor agreed without waiting for specific authorization. Meanwhile, Utes made a similar request for a permanent settlement three miles south of Abiquiú on the Chama River. They hoped to hear the governor's decision when they returned early in August from the Sabuaguanas, where they collected pelts annually for the Taos fair.

Paruanarimuco and Anza met at Taos on August 10, as agreed two weeks earlier in Santa Fe. Anza found suitable the chief's plan for the village, which they agreed to name San Carlos de los Jupes. The governor entrusted to Paruanarimuco tools, implements, and thirty laborers led by Manuel Segura. Anza recommended to Segura that he prefer a site with a spring and plenty of land with good agricultural potential. The first priority was to be given the construction of houses, according to the petitioners' most urgent desire.[58]

Paruanarimuco led the workers to the junction of the Arkansas and the San Carlos, where their work progressed well. By September 16

[57] Mares, Diary, San Antonio de Béxar, October 19, 1787. Copy by Manuel Merino, Chihuahua, September 12, 1793, in AGN, Historia, vol. 43. A translation based on another copy appears in Loomis and Nasatir, *Pedro Vial*, pp. 289–302.

[58] Alfred Barnaby Thomas, "San Carlos, A Comanche Pueblo on the Arkansas River, 1787," *The Colorado Magazine* 6 (1929): 79–91.

the Comanches occupied nineteen completed houses; many more were in various stages of construction. A temporary setback occurred in October, when the Comanches learned that Fernando de la Concha had come to Santa Fe to succeed Anza as governor. Assuming that the change of leaders nullified Anza's commitments, Paruanarimuco sadly but firmly turned the tools back to Segura and sent him home with all his laborers. Fortunately, Concha soon persuaded the Comanches that he and his commandant general fully supported Anza's program of friendship and aid. The interrupted project was resumed and flourished into mid-winter. Sheep, oxen, maize, and seed were transported to San Carlos de los Jupes at government expense.

Ugarte followed the experiment with keen interest. Financial support for the venture came logically enough from the 6,000 pesos allocated annually to the extraordinary expenses of New Mexican Indian affairs, but the commandant general was wary of giving too much aid, lest the Indians conclude that the Spaniards helped them only because their own nation's interests required reduction of the Comanches. Just as the initiative for the settlement had to rise out of the Indians' own felt needs, so must the principal investment of labor and resources be their own. Results too easily attained would be too readily abandoned for a return to the roving life. Ugarte instructed his governors to give the Indians only necessary supplies that they could get in no other way and to provide them models to imitate in the skills of civilization.

All the hopes invested in the experiment crumbled in January 1788 when a much-loved wife of Paruanarimuco died. As their custom dictated, his people moved far from San Carlos. They were not moved by a terror of the dead like that which plagued Navajos, but rather by a delicacy of feeling that sought to ease their chief's grief by leaving the painful reminders at the scene of death.

Spaniards, of course, considered it a barbarically irresponsible abandonment of property. Thoroughly taken aback by the news, Concha feared that protest could only antagonize the grieving chief, so he held his tongue and resolved not to gamble again on settling nomads. Ugarte was even more chagrined when Viceroy Manuel Antonio Flores gloated that he had always opposed the venture as lunatic. Casting about for consolation, Ugarte suggested that Spanish families occupy San Carlos. They would be able to observe the northern Comanchería from that vantage point, and, if the peace were ever broken, San Carlos could serve as a base for military expeditions against the

Comanches. It could also stand as an outpost against foreign encroachments on the northern frontier. Governor Concha objected: to place settlers in that exposed position without strong military protection would invite disaster; to provide protection at that distance would be inordinately expensive and would surely overtax New Mexico's limited resources.

In November 1788, nearly a year after their departure, there glimmered some hope that the Yupes themselves might reoccupy San Carlos. Concha wanted to encourage them. Ugarte consented, on condition that no further expenditure be made on that project, or on any of a similar nature, without the viceroy's express permission.

In effect, bitterness over the apparent loss incurred in the San Carlos experiment ruled out further ventures of that kind, but the investment hardly seems lost in retrospect. Those pesos circulated in a province desperately in need of economic stimulation and chronically short of money. Master Manuel Segura and his thirty laborers collected 282 pesos for their services. The pueblos of Cochití and Santo Domingo realized 58 pesos for maize and flour that they sold and transported to Santa Fe for the project. Sale of seed, sheep, and oxen for San Carlos brought 250 pesos to Don Antonio José Ortiz. Alcalde Don Juan Joseph Levata of Taos collected nine pesos for ten bushels of flour that he supplied the workers, and Vizente Sena collected three pesos' milling fee. Three settlers earned 106 pesos carting supplies and tools to San Carlos. Another freight bill of 70 pesos was paid Don Salvador García and Diego Montoya for delivering seed to the settlement. Presumably that money circulated in New Mexico for goods and services and eventually traveled to Chihuahua with the caravan to purchase goods there. Unfortunately, the 1780's produced no advocate of the proposition that moneys spent on Indians would foster economic development of the lagging frontier provinces.

The failure of the Comanche experiment with the settled village life was only an incidental disappointment, handsomely offset by the great successes born of the alliance. Both Spaniards and Comanches enjoyed greater safety in their homes and profited by the trade that flourished in both New Mexico and Texas. Those benefits were shared by all Spain's Indian allies: Norteños and mission Indians in Texas, and Pueblos, Utes, Jicarillas, and Navajos in New Mexico.

Anza, relieved of the governorship of New Mexico by Concha in the fall of 1787, became military commandant of Sonora, the post that he had held temporarily under Croix before his transfer to New Mexico in 1778. That appointment hardly fulfilled Anza's request for a chance to recover his health and repair his personal fortune with a governorship somewhere in the viceroyalty. It did mean a return to the province of his birth, scene of his first successes and of the military careers of his father and grandfather before him. It also marked a return to the Apache wars, an opportunity to finish from the south the subjugation of the Apaches toward which he had directed his alliances in New Mexico, and implied another chance to win his old objective of opening communications between Sonora and New Mexico. But years of strenuous campaigns had taken their toll: Anza did not live to complete his important agenda of unfinished business. He died at Arispe in December 1788, aged fifty-three, a veteran of thirty-six years in the service of the Spanish Crown.

The month of Anza's death was a fateful time for the Spanish Empire. The able Carlos III also died in December 1788; the son who succeeded him as Carlos IV was ludicrously weak and inept. Though Carlos III had allowed a miscarriage of justice to mangle Anza's career in the final half-dozen years, the enlightened monarch's zeal for reform and development had also made possible the distinguished contributions of the Creole officer who served him so well throughout the twenty-nine years of his reign.

Anza's crowning achievement had been the Comanche alliance, bringing that vast Indian nation, with all its exciting potential for war and peace, into the ranks of vassals of the Spanish Crown. Now there awaited the Comanches an experience grimly reminiscent of the Pueblos' calamity two centuries earlier. Pueblos had pledged themselves vassals of the Spanish Crown in 1598, just when the death of Felipe II marked the abrupt degeneration of the Hapsburg line, and had suffered a century as victims of a decaying regime. Now the Comanches had linked their fortunes to the Spanish Crown just as the last of the able Bourbon monarchs died. They too would suffer one painful disappointment after another as Spain's fortunes crumbled again.

CHAPTER 21

New Mexico and Texas, 1787-1795

The Comanche alliance miraculously survived the adversities of its first autumn. Anza's departure alone would have been a severe enough test. At the same time, unanticipated tensions developed in the much-heralded joint campaigns against the western Apaches. Worse still, 1787 saw the beginning of a cycle of drought, and therefore famine, that plagued the southern Comanchería for three seasons. Yet, through the extraordinary patience and tenacity of purpose of Ecueracapa, Anza, and Concha, the alliance weathered all those stresses and prospered.

Fortunately, Fernando de la Concha proved as skillful and patient in Indian diplomacy as his distinguished predecessor. He reached Santa Fe in August 1787 and worked nearly three months with Anza to master the complexities of the Indian alliances before taking charge of the province on November 10, 1787. Like Anza, Concha realized the limitations of force and believed "gentleness, affection, and a few gifts" the only viable means to manage any Indian people.[1] His interest

[1] Concha to Ugarte, Santa Fe, November 1, 1787, quoted in R. J. Benes, "Anza and Concha in New Mexico," *Journal of the West* 4 (1965): 63–76.

and understanding paid off. When he took command of the province in November, Concha reported that he had formalized continuation of the peace with the Comanches and had been able to continue uninterrupted the Ute and Navajo alliances.[2]

Continuation of the Comanche alliance represented Concha's first triumph over misfortune. During the period of gubernatorial transition, a force of Comanche warriors, Santa Fe presidials, New Mexican settlers, and Pueblos made a disastrous September campaign against the Apaches southwest of the Hopis. When the enemy gained the upper hand in battle, the New Mexicans fled the field, while the Comanches held fast and lost a man.[3]

The Comanche warriors were therefore skeptical of their allies' dependability when they were invited the next month to another campaign southwest of Zuñi. The expedition leader was Commandant Inspector Joseph Rengel, visiting New Mexico for the first outside inspection of its troops since that of Rubí in 1766. Ecueracapa himself answered Rengel's call with thirty-four Comanche warriors; New Mexican soldiers, militiamen, and Pueblos and five Jicarillas comprised the other three hundred of the force.

Rengel found the Comanches an undisciplined rabble, abusive of both their own horses and their Pueblo and Spanish allies. As they neared the Apache *rancherías*, it grew obvious that the Comanches suspected they would again lead the attack and that they had no confidence in their allies' support. Insulted, Rengel told Ecueracapa and eight war chiefs that they and their warriors were quite superfluous and that Spaniards would, of course, spearhead the assault, with Rengel himself leading. Thus challenged, most of the Comanches chose to participate in the November 5 attack that scattered the Apaches and, according to Rengel, reassured the Comanches as to the worth of Spanish troops.

Rengel finished that campaign almost equally scornful of Comanche warriors, New Mexican militiamen, and Pueblo warriors, none of whom met his professional standards. He recommended against further joint campaigns by Comanches and Spaniards, calling their styles of fighting incompatible. Rengel thought the Spaniards would do better to give the Comanches horses, guns, and ammunition and encourage them to

---

[2] Viceroy Manuel Antonio Flores to Concha, Mexico, January 2, 1788, SANM no. 981.

[3] Max L. Moorhead, *The Apache Frontier*, pp. 164–166; Oakah L. Jones, Jr., *Pueblo Warriors and Spanish Conquest*, pp. 160–161.

go after the enemy in their own fashion. Ecueracapa was happy to plan separate operations, provided he could count upon the assistance mentioned by Rengel.

The alliance survived Rengel's impatience and the tensions of two joint campaigns only to be tested by the oldest enemy of man in New Mexico. Drought seared the southern plains; by autumn 1787, it was clear that the great buffalo herds would not range there that season. The scarcity of game forced Comanche men to hunt intensively to feed their families instead of raiding against distant Apaches. They mounted few campaigns against the Gilas that season or the next. From November 1787 to June 1788 Cuchanecs did not ride to New Mexico for the trade fairs because they had no meat or buffalo robes to sell.

Concha helped as best he could, shipping supplies of corn into the Comanchería in both 1787 and 1788 in an effort to prevent starvation. Even so, some Comanches perished of hunger. Early in the summer of 1789 Ecueracapa brought 180 of his people to Santa Fe to appeal for more help. The community responded at once. Local citizens donated 160 bushels of corn; Concha furnished 200 bushels at the Crown's expense. When the governor forecast a need for larger relief shipments at shorter intervals until the return of the buffalo, the commandant general and the viceroy endorsed the program as proper use of the Crown's funds.[4]

Both Comanches and Spaniards scored well in the test of brotherhood imposed by the long drought. The relief shipments of New Mexican corn strengthened ties of friendship and gratitude. For their part, the Comanches did not make the drought an occasion to seize what they needed from the pueblos and settlements, as roving Indians had done from time immemorial. Their remarkable restraint attested both the powerful stabilizing influence of Ecueracapa and the Comanches' widespread commitment to their Spanish alliance.

Equally remarkable was the Comanches' continuing hospitality throughout the hard times. The drought did not disrupt the program of exploration underway when Anza turned the government of New Mexico over to Concha in 1787, just as the specter of famine began to stalk the camps of the Cuchanecs.

The Comanche alliance permitted Spain to make Santa Fe the hub of a landmark series of explorations designed to link the northernmost provinces of New Spain with each other and with seaports. In

[4] Ugarte to Concha, Chihuahua, November 21, 1789, SANM, no. 1067; Benes, "Anza and Concha"; Moorhead, *Apache Frontier*, pp. 167–168.

the fall of 1787, while Concha and Anza worked at Santa Fe on the problems of transition and Ecueracapa campaigned southwestward with Rengel, Vial marked time in the New Mexican capital, awaiting action on his proposal to show the way from Santa Fe to Natchitoches. That October Mares reached San Antonio, having largely retraced the trail Vial had blazed between the Texan and New Mexican capitals. There he waited for the Comanche Sojaís to declare the time ripe to fulfill his promise to guide Mares back to Santa Fe by a direct route, not detouring by the Taovayas villages on the Red River.

Commandant General Ugarte enthusiastically supported the explorations, reasoning that the time of peace with the Comanches must be seized as the opportunity to make those important discoveries. If ever the peace should be broken, the same objectives that now cost so little could be carried out only at frightful cost, if at all.[5] It thus seemed reasonable to underwrite Vial's Natchitoches venture with that elastic 6,000 pesos allocated annually to the extraordinary requirements of New Mexico's Indian affairs.

At the same time, Ugarte wished routes opened from Santa Fe to Sonora and from Santa Fe to Monterey, California.[6] Since Natchitoches was linked to New Orleans by river, in effect he postulated a system of routes linking the Spanish possessions across the country from New Orleans on the Gulf of Mexico to Monterey on the Pacific. Santa Fe would enjoy direct links, not only to Monterey and Natchitoches, but also to Sonora and San Antonio. With the end of the long Indian wars in sight, it was becoming possible to think of the economic development and the expansion of population that could make the northern provinces a true bulwark against the swarming Anglo-Americans. The initial explorations depended heavily upon the active help of the Indians whose territory they probed.

Although it was clearly understood that the new peace with the Comanches had made the explorations possible, Spanish officialdom scarcely comprehended the importance of the Indians' active assistance to expeditions in their territories. Not only did they guide visitors across the vast sameness of the plains, but they also furnished provisions, sometimes replaced exhausted horses, and sheltered travelers in their lodges. Rarely did Spain's agents lack protective Comanche com-

---

[5] Ugarte to Flores, Chihuahua, July 17, 1788, in AGN, Provincias Internas, vol. 183.

[6] Ugarte, Instruction, Chihuahua, May 5, 1789, AGN, Provincias Internas, vol. 183.

pany as they crossed the Comanchería: sometimes just a few obliging guides, sometimes a big party riding with them for joint safety and companionship.

Explorers' diaries tended to be laconic itineraries, emphasizing physical landmarks and making only passing references to the aid given by Indians. Officials who had never confronted the sheer physical problems of survival across the plains tended to overlook the importance of the Indians' support. Thus, Vial's first route via the Taovayas villages and Comanche camps had been much criticized, even though he had followed Cabello's specific orders to visit the Taovayas. Criticism worsened when Mares, sent from Santa Fe to learn the way to San Antonio and to improve upon it by coming directly across the shortest distance, also let himself be guided via Comanche *rancherías* and the Taovayas villages.

It was October 7, 1787, when Cristóbal de los Santos came home to Béxar, a year after he had set out for Santa Fe with Pedro Vial. Two Comanches rode with him. Mares arrived the next day with the rest of his party and a large contingent of eastern Comanches: four chiefs, ten leading men, thirty-eight warriors, twenty-three women, and six children. The Comanches stayed eight days, enjoying the presidio's best entertainment and receiving gifts for their devotion to the Spaniards. Especially fine presents were awarded three men who had also accompanied Vial and Santos to Santa Fe. The party departed happily, with twenty presidials to escort them a considerable way along their homeward trail.

The Comanches understood Martínez Pacheco's disappointment that Mares had come by the less direct route via the Taovayas village and readily agreed to rectify the matter. They would not start back to Santa Fe with him at once, lest heavy snows block their way. However, they promised to return in March to guide Mares and his two associates back home to Santa Fe by a direct route.[7]

The winter started off in such mild fashion that Sojaís decided it would not, after all, be necessary to delay the journey till March. Arming himself heavily in case of encounter with Lipans and taking only his wife for company, Sojaís made the ten-day ride from his camp to San Antonio. His unheralded arrival on New Year's Day 1788 and his announcement that he was ready to escort Mares, Martín, and Maese to Santa Fe surprised the Spaniards, but none was so impolitic

[7] Martínez Pacheco to Ugarte, Béxar, October 12, 1787, and October 27, 1787, BA.

as to dispute the guide's judgment.[8] Sojaís rested a little more than two weeks in San Antonio, enjoying the company of numerous Comanches who happened to be visiting at the same time and giving the Mares party time to complete their own travel preparations.

Sojaís and his wife left San Antonio with Mares, Martín, and Maese on January 18, 1788, with four chiefs and a good many other Comanches who were ready to go home. They hurried to overtake another large Comanche party escorted from the presidio by Lieutenant Curbelo's squad three days earlier, and joined forces with them on the Llano River four days later, just as Lieutenant Curbelo turned back toward Béxar. Mares' party pushed on with the Comanches. Rocky terrain punished the horses; dense woods sometimes slowed their progress.[9] Snow provided water where it was otherwise lacking, but it also created unpleasant travel conditions. On February 4 they reached the camp of Chief Sojaís, where they rested for a day before setting out again on February 6.

They stopped that night at a large Comanche camp in a canyon blessed with a permanent water supply, pushed on until February 11, then camped in another canyon for two and a half weeks, presumably to wait out bad weather or to rest their horses. They covered eighteen miles on February 29, then halted again until March 6. They made one more day's progress on March 6, another on March 9, then traveled almost daily from March 15 through March 24. On March 16 the trio from Santa Fe and three Comanches led by Sojaís parted from the band with which they had been traveling and struck northward. On March 24 they met a sizeable band of Cuchanecs led by chiefs Coniquitan, Paruamumpes, and Zanchaguare.

Mares, Martín, and Maese stayed in that camp two weeks, resting their worn-out horses. Sojaís and his companions turned back to their own homes; Chief Zanqueoyaran lent Mares two of his own sons as escorts for the rest of the journey to Santa Fe. They set out on April 6, traveling and resting on alternate days, perhaps to avoid pushing their horses too hard again. On April 27, 1788, they reached Santa Fe.

The Comanches had shown Mares a route from San Antonio to Santa Fe considerably shorter than that pioneered by Vial and repeated by

[8] Martínez Pacheco to Ugarte, Béxar, January 19, 1788, BA.
[9] José Mares, Diary. Copy of the original, Santa Fe, June 20, 1788, certified by Concha. Copy by Manuel Merino, Chihuahua, September 12, 1792, AGN, Historia, vol. 43. A translation based on another copy appears in Noel M. Loomis and Abraham P. Nasatir, *Pedro Vial and the Roads to Santa Fe*, pp. 306–315.

Mares. Not only the success of Mares' errand but also the survival of his party had lain in Comanche hands from January through April. The vows of friendship and brotherhood were being taken very seriously indeed within the Comanchería, surviving even such stern tests as encounters with Spanish soldiers defending Mescalero hunters against Comanche attacks. It was an auspicious time for Vial to try the road to Natchitoches.

Vial's second exploration was considerably more elaborate than the first. Four companions were assigned him for the trek to Natchitoches and thence to San Antonio. Appointed as official diarist was Francisco Xavier Fragoso, a literate native of Mexico City who had long served in the Santa Fe garrison. Three adventurous young men of Santa Fe volunteered for the trip: José María Romero, José Gregorio Leyva, and Juan Lucero. In addition, Concha sent a literate officer, Santiago Fernández, and four cavalrymen to escort Vial's party as far as the Taovayas, then report back to Santa Fe. He charged Fernández to keep a careful diary and to learn as much as possible about the route.[10]

Vial fared better financially than on his first expedition, when he had paid his own expenses out of the money earned on his Comanche peace mission. Concha outfitted the Natchitoches expedition with ten horses and two mules, the supplies needed for the trip, and gifts for the Indians whose lands they would cross. All of them expected to return to Santa Fe from San Antonio. Concha had already asked the commandant general to let Vial settle permanently in Santa Fe.[11] Santa Fe needed that Frenchman's gift for dealing with Indians and his knowledge of the lands that separated New Mexico from Texas and Louisiana.

The two groups set out separately on June 24, 1788, spent the night at Pecos, and rode on together the next day. They first encountered Comanches on July 1, when they were pleasantly welcomed at the camp of Chief Naisare. They paused there to smoke and eat and to discuss the purpose of their trip, then visited three more Comanche

---

[10] Santiago Fernández, Diary, Santa Fe, December 16, 1788. Copy certified by Concha, Santa Fe, June 20, 1789. Copy by Manuel Merino, Chihuahua, September 12, 1793, AGN, Historia, vol. 43; Francisco Xavier Fragoso, Diary, Santa Fe, August 2, 1789 (signed also by Pedro Vial). Copy by Manuel Merino, Chihuahua, September 12, 1793, AGN, Historia vol. 43. Translations of the Fernández and Fragoso diaries based on other copies appear in Loomis and Nasatir, *Pedro Vial*, pp. 318–367.

[11] Martínez Pacheco to Ugalde, Béxar, November 21, 1788, BA.

camps within a few leagues as they rode on. Part of the day Comanches rode along to assure them that they were indeed on the best route to the Taovayas.

The Spaniards again found Comanches on July 5, scattered in individual camps along a stream running through an area rich in good grass and timber. One Comanche graciously insisted on taking them to his lodge for the night. The travelers enjoyed supper with the host while their animals were cared for and pastured along with his. On July 9, Fernández' squad came upon another Comanche camp, some fourteen lodges headed by Pochinaquine, where again they were urged to stop. They smoked and ate with their hosts and with others who came to talk with them, then slept that night in the camp. The Fragoso-Vial contingent, who had gone afield to kill some buffalo, missed that pleasant interlude. Vial briefly veered north alone to seek some Yamparicas whom he hoped to find not too far away, but without success.

On the fifteenth and sixteenth of July the two parties came together again at a very big Comanche camp, where they were urged to visit. At the 372 lodges of the followers of chiefs Pisimape, Zoquacante, and Cochi,[12] they found the usual generous hospitality: food, shelter, and plenty of entertainment. The Fernández squad left their exhausted horses with the chiefs, who lent them replacements and promised good care to restore the Spaniards' horses for the return trip to Santa Fe.

The explorers rode on the next day guided by the indefatigable Sojaís and his wife. Sojaís had seen Vial to Santa Fe the year before and then had guided Mares across the plains to and from San Antonio; his wife had covered much of those distances with him. Now they courteously escorted the visitors to the Taovayas villages, four days' ride from the big Comanche camp.

The Taovayas turned out in enthusiastic welcome when the travelers reached their villages on July 20, 1788. Although running more than a year late, Vial had kept his promise to return. The many Spaniards with him and the announced purpose of their trip augured well for future trade at the Taovayas villages.

In that summer of 1788 the cluster on the Red River consisted of three villages, two on one side of the Red River and one on the other,

---

[12] So Fernández understood the names. Fragoso recorded them as Pisimanpit, Quibuniputimi, and Chocobante. The discrepancy between renditions of the three chiefs' names by two official diarists visiting their camps simultaneously illustrates the considerable difficulty Spaniards incurred in recording Comanche identities.

with about seventeen grass lodges in each. Their maize, beans, watermelons, and pumpkins were thriving. The travelers rested several days in that pleasant situation, then parted company on July 24.

Fernández and his squad rode back with Sojaís to his camp, which they reached the next day. There they exchanged the borrowed mounts for their own, now fit for the ride to Santa Fe, thanks to ten days' recuperation on good pastures. Fernández did not immediately begin to travel in earnest, but moved in leisurely fashion from one Comanche camp to another, visiting all who wished to talk with him. Then, with a Taovayas couple and a Comanche couple for company, he struck out at four o'clock on the morning of July 27. Traveling in early morning and late afternoon, pausing for long midday siestas, they progressed steadily across lush, well-watered, and wooded terrain, abounding in game, apparently well to the north of the drought area. At six o'clock on the evening of August 17, 1788, Fernández reported to Concha at the Governor's Palace in Santa Fe, after the shortest, fastest crossing yet and the least onerous.

Meanwhile, Vial pressed on toward Louisiana with Fragoso and the three young men of Santa Fe. Vial found it politic first to spend some time visiting in each of the three villages of the Taovayas and Wichitas, but on July 26 they said goodbye to the third village and crossed the river to continue their journey with an Indian guide. He was replaced the next day by a Taovayas called Bautista, who guided them thenceforth.

How remote the mountains and deserts of New Mexico must have seemed as the explorers rode eastward across increasingly lush vegetation, contending with the rains and swollen streams that were the price of verdure, observing alligators instead of buffalo. On August 12 they were hospitably welcomed to the Nadacos' village of thirteen grass lodges. Two days later they stopped at the home of a Bidai Indian, then on each succeeding night at the home of some Frenchman. At each stop they enjoyed the customary hospitality of the wilderness; at the second French home they rested two days. Resuming their march on August 19, they rested at another Frenchman's cabin at noon, passed three more French homesteads, then stopped overnight at the home of an Englishman. The host and guests could not understand each other, but he entertained them nonetheless cordially. The next day, August 20, they rode the last twenty-five miles into Natchitoches, just three days after Fernández reported home to Santa Fe.

They had ridden some nine hundred miles from Santa Fe and had not found the trip particularly grueling. After their second day out of Santa Fe, they had seen an abundance of horses and game of all kinds. Thanks to their Indian guides, they had been able to come quite directly, though skirting some badlands; assistance had been generously forthcoming whenever needed. The feasibility of the route from Santa Fe to Natchitoches via the Taovayas seemed incontestable.

Natchitoches looked good after that trek across the wilderness. Commandant Louis de Blanc, grandson of the settlement's founder and scion of the family that had nearly always governed the post, received them kindly. He assigned them lodgings at the home of a soldier, who entertained them well. The explorers turned over their official dispatches for de Blanc to send to Governor Miró of Louisiana, who forwarded them to Cuba for transshipment to Spain.

Vial's party rested ten days in Natchitoches before setting out for San Antonio. They found the settlement's size impressive and its dwellings almost splendid by northern frontier standards. Its inhabitants, whom they estimated at just under three thousand, were a mixed lot of French, English, and Negro; some of the latter were slaves. It was a bustling trade center. On the river lay countless canoes, large and small, that carried goods to and from New Orleans. Such an outlet might indeed stimulate commercial development of Santa Fe and its hinterland.

Louis de Blanc, an entrepreneur in the family tradition, readily envisioned a trade boom based on the new connection. While Vial and his associates rested in Natchitoches, their host wrote to Commandant General Ugarte to affirm the feasibility of commerce between Santa Fe and Natchitoches. He estimated the journey would take forty days, with loads, in spring and autumn. Experience now indicated that it would be safe enough to cross the Comanchería, but from the Taovayas to Natchitoches there would be danger of harassment by Indians, especially the ubiquitous Osages. De Blanc considered an escort of twenty-five men sufficient to protect a pack train on that leg of the trip.

De Blanc wanted the route secured by a fort at the Taovayas village, with an adequate garrison and an experienced commandant. Its garrison could also check the contraband trade from the Arkansas and White rivers, whence Englishmen still intruded to trade arms and ammunition, corrupting the Indians and making them unreliable allies. The abundant nature of the Taovayas country and the flourishing agriculture of the villages would make it easy to support a garrison there. The post would undoubtedly become a prosperous center of trading and trapping.[13]

Ugarte relayed de Blanc's ideas to Governor Concha, who saw even greater possibilities for commercial development. Because the port of New Orleans enjoyed free commerce with the West Indies and with many foreign countries, goods could be purchased there at relatively low prices. If shipped to Santa Fe via Natchitoches, they could be transshipped to Sonora and Nueva Vizcaya to undersell goods shipped from Veracruz via Mexico City and the intervening provinces of New Spain, each of which levied a tariff. Water transport from New Orleans to the Taovayas and seasonally abundant pasture and water for pack mules on to Santa Fe would make transportation relatively cheap; Comanche and Taovayas help would minimize costs of supplies for freighters.

Concha rejected the idea that a fort would be needed to protect the traffic, reasoning that the Indians' self-interest would guarantee the trade far better than any isolated fort. However, he did advocate a Spanish post at the Taovayas to discourage foreign traders who might be attracted by a surge of commerce on the Red River.[14]

Thus, hope glimmered briefly for the Spanish fort that the Taovayas had first demanded a quarter-century earlier. They needed it now more than ever. On it hinged not only the restoration of their once prosperous trade, but perhaps their very survival against Osage aggressions.

Meanwhile, after ten days' rest in Natchitoches, Vial and his companions headed westward on August 31, 1788. By the time they reached Nacogdoches on September 4, Fragoso, Romero, Lucero, and Leyva were so wracked with chills and fever that they could not resume travel until October 24.[15] Only partly recovered, they traveled at an invalid's pace and did not reach San Antonio until November 18. There they were ill most of the time until their departure the following June. Whether they had fallen victim to malaria or whether adjustment to the damp lowlands posed some other problem for men acclimated to high, dry Santa Fe is not clear. Whatever the difficulty, it did not affect Pedro Vial, who tried another adventure while waiting to return to Santa Fe. On February 5, 1789, he rode off with a French

[13] De Blanc to Ugarte, Natchitoches, August 26, 1788, quoted in Loomis and Nasatir, *Pedro Vial*, p. 350.

[14] Concha to Ugarte, Santa Fe, June 15, 1789, SANM, no. 1049.

[15] Gil Ybarbo to Martínez Pacheco, Nacogdoches, October 20, 1789, BA.

entrepreneur, Alexandre Dupont, a dozen helpers, and four Comanches to seek mineral ores in the lands of the Taovayas and Comanches.[16]

Meanwhile, the convalescing Fragoso and his three companions found the provincial capital San Antonio much less impressive than the trading center at Natchitoches. The villa seemed to number just about seven hundred Spanish persons. Some dwellings were stone "rubble work," but most were modest wooden structures. Béxar presidio stood in the center of the settlement. Within its walls was the parish church, which had its own clergyman. Across the river that surrounded the village lay the five missions. Fragoso observed some trade among the citizens in food and clothing, but little more commerce.

Governor Martínez Pacheco graciously welcomed the explorers and furnished them quarters and subsistence, pending completion of arrangements for their return to New Mexico. Unfortunately for his budget and their morale, the mills of government ground slowly. Officials wrangled about responsibility for expenses incurred by the various explorers in the three provinces; above all, they disagreed about Vial's future. The initial ruling denied his petition to establish himself in Santa Fe, on grounds that his knowledge of the Norteños would be more useful in Texas.[17] However, the matter rested ultimately with the viceroy. Ugalde directed that Vial be paid twenty pesos monthly until the viceroy should act and that Fragoso and his three companions return promptly to Santa Fe.[18]

Martínez Pacheco had that order by mid-March, but its implementation was delayed for nearly three months. The men of Santa Fe were too sick to start home, and Vial had taken their horses off on his prospecting excursion. Not until he returned and the horses (now half the number that had left Santa Fe) were sufficiently rested could the journey begin. Meanwhile, Martínez Pacheco faced the unhappy duty of telling Vial that he must remain at San Antonio against his own desires.[19]

[16] Martínez Pacheco, Diary, February 28, 1789, BA. The details of Dupont's expedition appear in a Texas State Archives Ms. labeled Hawkins, "The Adventures in Texas and Louisiana of Alexander Dupont," based largely on documents in Mexico. Roderick B. Patten analyzes the materials, though without identifying Vial as a participant, in "Miranda's Inspection of Los Almagres: His Journal, Report, and Petition," *Southwestern Historical Quarterly* 74 (1970): 223–254.

[17] Martínez Pacheco to Concha, Béxar, February 8, 1788, BA.

[18] Ugalde to Martínez Pacheco, Santa Rosa, February 28, 1789, BA.

[19] Martínez Pacheco to Ugalde, Béxar, March 14, 1789, BA.

Somehow, by summer, the decision was reversed, and the quintet straggled out of San Antonio. Fragoso and the three young men of Santa Fe headed north with four Comanche guides on June 25. The next day a pair of soldiers overtook them with dispatches that Martínez Pacheco had not completed in time for their departure. On June 25 they reached the Guadalupe River and paused to wait for Vial, who did not leave San Antonio until June 30. From the Guadalupe, the Comanches would lead the explorers to their *rancherías*, whence they could take the road to Santa Fe.[20]

Vial arrived with a corporal and eight soldiers, assigned to escort the travelers as far as the Colorado River. They crossed that stream on July 4, and the escort turned back toward San Antonio the next day. Vial's group pressed on with the four Comanches, following the Colorado upstream two more days before striking out across country.

On July 13 they met seventeen young Comanches, setting out without a chief to try their fortunes against the Lipans. One of the four guides found the opportunity irresistible and joined the adventurers. Vial gave them tobacco, food, and best wishes and pushed on northwestward. On the night of July 15 the party camped with some Taovayas at holes filled with rainwater.

Vial's party traveled without further encounter until August 2, when they met a lone Comanche who told them of a single Comanche lodge by a lake in the middle of the plain. He guided them to the lodge in two days' travel. There they spent the night and accepted their host's gift of meat to sustain them over the next leg of their trip.

The next day they reached the springs they deemed headwaters of the Red River, where they had camped on July 3 the previous year, and felt themselves back in home territory. They pointed straight toward Santa Fe, and their trail led to the camp of Ecueracapa (also called Chief Malla in the same diary entry), where they spent the night. That was a delightful climax to their journey, for the great chief entertained them with the highest honors he could accord distinguished guests.

At their request, Ecueracapa sent messengers to detain thirteen people from his camp who had lately left to trade at Pecos and Taos, so that the explorers could overtake them the next day and ride with them the rest of the way. They continued safely with the Comanche group to Pecos, then into Santa Fe at mid-afternoon on August 20,

20 Martínez Pacheco to Ugalde, Béxar, July 4, 1789, BA.

1789. The trail seemed so routine for the last few days that Fragoso no longer bothered to record details.

While Vial and Fragoso had led their party from Natchitoches to San Antonio, yet another step had been taken toward opening trade and communication among the northern provinces. Late in September 1788, a detachment left Sonora to discover the route to New Mexico. The operation differed substantially in kind from Vial's explorations, but it was part of the same plan to consolidate the northern provinces through improved trade and communication among them. Commandant General Ugarte, who had encouraged Vial, also fostered the Sonoran enterprise. The commanding officer of Sonoran troops was Colonel Anza, who had once made the effort himself in 1780 and who had lent his support when Vial first reached New Mexico in 1787.

In the fall of 1788 Anza ordered Captain Manuel de Echeagaray of the presidio of Tucson to reconnoiter the San Francisco River and the Mogollón Mountains.[21] Echeagaray led four hundred men right into the westernmost Apachería, as concerned to subdue the enemy as to explore. No route would be worth discovering unless the Apaches were sufficiently controlled to make it useable.

The campaign lasted well into November. Very early the Spaniards learned that some Apaches had left their families in the Santa Rita Mountains for safety while their raiders struck Altar or La Ciénega. Echeagaray's warning reached Arispe in time for Anza to frustrate the Apache attack. While runners alerted the targets, scouting parties scoured the Santa Ritas to wipe out the families left behind.

Early in his campaign Echeagaray captured some Apaches, who joined his force. They led him to some *rancherías*, and actively fought other Apaches. With their help, the campaign took forty-one Apache lives. Echeagaray's force then pushed on, late in October, through the mountains and onto the plains of New Mexico, finding Apaches very scarce as they rode through the sierras. Turning back toward Tucson, the Spaniards discovered the pass that would lead to Zuñi, but they refrained from going to the pueblo. Instead they returned to the Gila River to engage more Apaches. The final score for the expedition read 54 Apaches dead, 125 captured, and 55 enlisted as friends and allies, a total of 234 subtracted in one way or another from the

---

[21] George P. Hammond, ed., "The Zuñiga Journal, Tucson to Santa Fe: The Opening of a Spanish Trade Route, 1788–1795," *New Mexico Historical Review* 6 (1931): 40–65.

fighting forces of the Apaches. A further gain was 61 mounts recaptured.

Anza's reaction was mixed. Initially, he reprimanded Echeagaray for exceeding his authority and contravening established practice by enlisting the enemy in his own army. Ugarte rebuked Anza in turn, pointing out that Echeagaray's successful use of Apaches had furthered the Spaniards' aims and seemed to warrant suspension of the rules.

Certainly Anza was as pleased as Ugarte by the expedition's blows against the Apaches and its discovery of the pass leading from Sonora to New Mexico. Even though the New Mexican settlements had not been reached, the way had been shown. Anza believed that a few more expeditions like that of Echeagaray would soon overcome the Apaches and open the way to commerce with New Mexico. Unfortunately, Anza died in the month after Echeagaray's return, and the vigorous follow-up that he intended never occurred. Through 1790 New Mexico and Sonora were tranquil enough to permit such campaigns, and Ugarte urged Anza's successor to send Echeagaray out to finish the job. Grimarest dragged his feet, trying to persuade the viceroy to let him have the assignment instead. By the time that permission came through in 1791, renewed Apache hostilities required all the forces of Nueva Vizcaya and Sonora to stave off disaster. The New Mexican route had to be postponed another three years.

The troops of Sonora and Nueva Vizcaya were by no means uniformly successful in their campaigns northward against the Apaches, but the old security of the mountain sanctuaries was broken. Echeagaray's telling thrusts into the home territories of the Gilas had added yet another dimension to the growing terror and misery of life within the Apachería. The drought that temporarily blunted the southward drive of the Comanches probably affected also the subsistence of many Apaches. Worst of all their woes was the way the Spanish alliance sharpened the effectiveness of Comanche war parties.

Both Santa Fe and Béxar possessed widespread intelligence networks, partly based on Apaches in their employ and, especially in New Mexico, on information picked up from various Indians coming to trade or visit at the settlements. Information about the Apache ranges, often with exact locations of *rancherías*, was passed on to enemies of the Apaches. That rendered Comanche warriors immediately devastating in the southernmost reaches of New Mexico and Texas. They might otherwise have needed years to know that expanse well enough for effective campaigning. The Spanish alliance also expanded the striking range of the Apaches' enemies. Provisions, replacements for horses, places to rest and celebrate between forays against Apaches, all were available to Comanches in the villages and pueblos of New Mexico and at San Antonio. Booty, including captives, could be disposed of in those marketplaces, and the incentive of immediate profit further stimulated raids on the Apaches.

To make matters still worse for the Apaches, early in 1788 the Spaniards adopted a policy of shipping Apache captives in chains far south into New Spain, whether taken in war or purchased from other Indians.[22] No longer was it relatively easy for Apaches to recover lost kinsmen by claiming a truce and exchanging prisoners with the Spaniards.

Indians less warlike than Comanches were goaded into fighting more often and more zealously by pressures like those Cabello had focused upon Norteños. The Apaches' friendships had been systematically broken by the Spaniards. Lipans in Texas found themselves attacked by Tonkawas; Gila Apaches saw Navajos leading Spaniards into their home ranges to destroy their camps and cornfields. Spanish officials spared no effort to isolate the Apaches by cutting off their trade. Rarely were a people so beleaguered as were most Apaches by the end of the decade.

In the summer of 1789 some Gila and Sierra Blanca Apaches sought peace in New Mexico. Concha put them off while he inquired whether they still raided farther south, for he did not mean them to use peace with his province to secure a base for continued depredations south of the Rio Grande.[23] A year later, satisfied of their sincerity, Concha concluded a peace treaty with those same Apaches, identified as residents of the mountain ranges along New Mexico's southern frontier from Zuñi to El Paso.[24] He hoped the new peace would relieve some of the Apache pressures upon Sonora and Nueva Vizcaya.

Those Apaches made a formidable set of commitments: to keep a firm peace; to inform the Spaniards promptly of entrance by Natagés or any other Apaches not included in the peace, and to help to expel them; to turn in any of their own people who should steal horses or break the peace in any other way; to stand ready always to aid Governor Concha in campaigns against the Natagés or other hostile

---

[22] Ugarte to Concha, Arispe, January 23, 1788, SANM, no. 993.
[23] Concha to Flores, Santa Fe, July 6, 1789, SANM, no. 1052.
[24] Concha to Ugarte, Santa Fe, July 13, 1790, SANM, no. 1086.

Apaches; and to exhort their people not to commit hostilities against El Paso, Fronteras, or Nueva Vizcaya, to report to Concha any infractions, and to forbid their *rancherías* to any offenders. They also promised to settle down on the bank of the Rio Grande, twenty-five miles below Socorro, where they would try farming with tools furnished by the Spaniards. Concha counted upon the good example of Navajo and Jicarilla farmers to facilitate the "civilizing" of his new Gila friends.

The governor's optimism proved well founded. In November 1790, he reported that the Gila Apaches had scrupulously kept their July peace agreements in New Mexico.[25] By July 1791, there seemed no doubt of their sincerity. They had warned Concha of Natagé plans to raid New Mexico, enabling him to forestall damages. Even more important, they were settling down to the disciplines of the farmer's life on the Rio Grande. Already they were regularly cultivating three fields and tending livestock donated by local settlers as foundation stock for their herds. Concha was enormously pleased by their progress toward a settled agriculture, which he considered the only basis for a stable peace. As long as Apaches should live scattered in the mountains, dependent for subsistence upon natural products and the scant agriculture that they could manage under the pressure of Comanche raiders, they would need to rob in order to live.[26] Under those circumstances they could never dwell in peace with neighboring peoples, either Spaniards or Indians.

The durability of Concha's experiment in settling Gila Apaches surprised many skeptics. They stayed in their settlement at El Sabinal until the autumn of 1794, when they broke their treaty for the first time by withdrawing to the mountains, perhaps due to Concha's departure from New Mexico. The commandant general ordered them brought back if possible, with no particular punishment for that first offense, and charged the New Mexicans to exercise the greatest possible care to prevent a second withdrawal. The Apaches returned to their settlement before the year ended.[27]

While some Gila Apaches trod the path of peace at El Sabinal, many more marauded southward in Nueva Vizcaya and Sonora and north-

[25] Concha to Ugarte, Santa Fe, November 19, 1790, SANM, no. 1102.

[26] Concha to Revilla Gigedo, Santa Fe, July 12, 1791, SANM, no. 1132, and July 22, 1791, SANM, no. 1203.

[27] Nava to Governor Fernando Chacón, Chihuahua, October 11, 1794, SANM, no. 1290a, and December 31, 1794, SANM, no. 3030a.

ward against the Navajos and the New Mexicans of the Albuquerque, Laguna, and Zuñi districts. By the end of 1788 Governor Concha had found it necessary to erect ten stone fortifications in the Navajo country to protect that allied nation against the Gileños. He concluded that the Navajos could secure permanent peace only by congregating in formal pueblos near New Mexico's frontier settlements.[28]

Though the Navajos did not go that far toward Hispanicization, by the summer of 1791 Governor Concha happily noted that they were settling down nicely, in better houses than most of the *bárbaros*, and owned much livestock of all kinds. They were also holding their own against Gila raiders. In a recent campaign they had captured seventy-one Gileños, slaughtered most, and enslaved the rest.[29]

An especially helpful development was that the headman Antonio, alias El Pinto, once suspected of disruptive pro-Gila influence among the Navajos, emerged as a staunch ally of the Spaniards. In 1789 he succeeded Don Carlos as captain general of the Navajo nation and filled that office with distinction until November 1793, when he died of wounds received in battle against the Gileños.

All the Indian allies—Navajos, Utes, Jicarillas, and Comanches—maintained excellent relations with the Spaniards throughout Governor Concha's term,[30] but troubles occurred among them in spite of the governor's assiduous labors for tranquillity. Since the Jicarillas felt terribly threatened by the Comanche rapprochement with New Mexico, the governor strove to reassure them. At their request, he sent three interpreters fluent in Comanche to accompany the Jicarillas on their buffalo hunt in October 1787, as a precaution against some untoward encounter with Comanches. Later that year Concha sent several soldiers from Santa Fe with the Jicarillas when they campaigned against the Apaches in the Sierra Blanca, again to forestall any misunderstanding with Comanches. By the fall of 1789 the Jicarillas had relaxed enough to tell a Comanche war party the location of some hostile Apaches' *rancherías*,[31] but Jicarilla braves still too often conspired with Utes against Comanche interests.

Ute and Jicarilla leaders tried earnestly to cooperate with Governor

[28] Concha to Ugarte, Santa Fe, November 12, 1788, SANM, no. 1022.

[29] Concha to Revilla Gigedo, Santa Fe, July 12, 1791, SANM, no. 1132.

[30] Concha to Ugarte, Santa Fe, September 7, 1790, SANM, no. 1090; Concha to Nava, Santa Fe, July 12, 1791, SANM, no. 1131; Concha to Revilla Gigedo, Santa Fe, November 8, 1792, SANM, no. 1215, and May 6, 1793, SANM, no. 1234.

[31] Concha to Ugarte, Santa Fe, November 20, 1789, SANM, no. 1066; Benes, "Anza and Concha."

Concha to maintain the general peace, and Comanches patiently tried to live within the new rule of law. The Comanche leaders lodged complaints of horse theft with Governor Concha, who in turn notified the Ute and Jicarilla leaders, who saw to proper restitutions. At Concha's request, the Ute Chief Muguisacho once made his people return twenty-six horses stolen from Comanches.

Repeated incidents exhausted the patience of some Yupes and Yamparicas. In July 1789, a Comanche war party pursued Ute thieves to the *ranchería* of Chief Muguisacho, attacked, and slaughtered eighty Utes, including Muguisacho. Surviving Utes appealed to Governor Concha, who called in Chief Paruanarimuco and listened to both sides of the story. No one could deny the validity of the Comanches' grievance. Concha could only recognize a new Ute medal chief, Ysampampi, and exhort both nations to keep the peace.[32]

The lesson endured only three years. Early in the winter of 1792, Utes and Navajos held council together and resolved to attack the Comanches. Their joint war party set out immediately and found a Comanche camp left unguarded while its men were hunting buffalo. The Utes and Navajos easily destroyed the camp, capturing and killing the women and children and running off the horse herd. A Comanche vengeance party then invaded Ute territory and wiped out an entire Ute camp. The score between Comanches and Utes thus stood about even by the time Governor Concha heard of the turmoil, but the Comanches had yet to punish the Navajos. Concha was appalled to think of the possible consequences if a big Comanche vengeance party should pass through the center of New Mexico to strike the Navajos in their home territories. He moved to reconcile the two nations with all possible speed.[33]

Concha first notified Captain General Antonio that he must gather all Comanches being held captive by Navajos and bring them to Santa Fe, with the leading men of the Navajos, to render complete satisfaction to Captain General Ecueracapa and the other Comanche leaders. The governor informed the Comanches of his order to the Navajos, and they patiently deferred tribal vengeance to give Concha and Antonio time to work the matter out fairly.

Perhaps the Utes found it harder than any other allies to keep the

[32] Concha to Ugarte, Santa Fe, November 18, 1789, SANM, no. 1064; Benes, "Anza and Concha."

[33] Concha to Viceroy Conde de Revilla Gigedo, Santa Fe, May 6, 1793, SANM, no. 1234 (published in translation in Marc Simmons, ed., *Border Comanches*).

peace because they no longer had legitimate enemies within feasible striking range, while their young men still needed horses as badly as ever. Navajos had every encouragement, indeed pressure, to campaign against Gilas to the south. Comanches had not only the satisfying challenge of campaigns against Apaches to the south, but also the growing pressure of war with the Pawnees to the northeast. They could legitimately find more than enough booty and glory for every warrior in their nation.

In the fall of 1789 Ecueracapa pursued a very lively war against the Apaches, first striking southward into the Sierra Blanca, then increasingly into the Lipan and Mescalero ranges lying between San Antonio and El Paso.[34] The banks of the Nueces and San Saba rivers were ever more frequent battlegrounds. The aggressors reported regularly to Santa Fe, where Concha gave them guns and best wishes and praised their successes.

Occasionally Comanche warriors joined forces with Norteño warriors, and even with Spanish forces of Texas and Coahuila, to slaughter Apaches, and they used San Antonio as a convenient base of operations. However, they essayed no close working relationship with authorities at San Antonio like that which they enjoyed at Santa Fe. Governor ad interim Martínez Pacheco never earned, or merited, the confidence of the Indian allies, or his Spanish constituents, or his superiors. Even less attractive to the Indians was Juan de Ugalde, commandant general of the eastern Provincias Internas from 1788 to 1790. Flouting law and custom, Ugalde dealt so treacherously with the Lipans and Mescaleros that no Indian or Spaniard, save the gullible short-term Viceroy Flores, dared trust him in anything.[35]

The Comanches found no more reason to work with the Texas authorities designated by a new viceroy, Conde de Revillagigedo, who ousted Ugalde in 1790. Commandant General Ugarte then briefly regained jurisdiction over Texas and Coahuila, but Comanche leaders already communicated with him through New Mexico. Manuel Muñoz, the veteran presidial commander who became governor of Texas in the summer of 1790, was too old and ill to manage the province, but

---

[34] Concha to Ugarte, Santa Fe, November 20, 1789, SANM, no. 1066; Concha to Revilla Gigedo, Santa Fe, July 20, 1792, SANM, no. 1200; Nava to Concha, Chihuahua, August 6, 1792, SANM, no. 1205; Concha to Nava, Santa Fe, November 10, 1792, SANM, no. 1218.

[35] Moorhead, *Apache Frontier*, pp. 234 ff.; Luis Navarro García, *José de Gálvez y la Comandancia General de las Provincias Internas del Norte de Nueva España*, p. 476.

lack of a qualified successor kept him in office eight years. His slack grip permitted tensions among the Indian allies in Texas to run rife. Breaches of the peace grew commonplace. In the spring of 1791, Comanches killed five men at San Antonio, and the Wichitan bands were rumored on the brink of insurrection.[36] No real outbreak ensued, but throughout the decade some Comanches and Norteños committed petty depredations around San Antonio as they pursued Apaches southward.

No such deterioration occurred in New Mexico, where Governor Concha and chiefs Ecueracapa and Paruanarimuca cooperated vigorously to make their alliance work. In the summer of 1790 Paruanarimuca persuaded Concha that the Pawnees had grown so dangerous to the northern Comanches, and thus to New Mexico, that New Mexican soldiers should escort the Yupes and Yamparicas on their summer hunt in ranges contested with the Pawnees. Perhaps their suggestion stemmed from knowledge that Spanish soldiers often escorted hunting parties of Apaches counted peaceful at certain presidios south of the Rio Grande.

To the consternation of his superiors, Governor Concha not only furnished the Comanches a squad of soldiers for their hunt, but also lent them guns. They were in the field nearly two months without encountering Pawnees. Upon their return to Santa Fe, the Comanches dutifully returned the borrowed guns to the governor.[37]

Nevertheless, new Commandant General Pedro de Nava worried that Concha had rashly given cause for distant, little-known nations to penetrate the New Mexican frontiers in search of Comanches. The Comanches were of tremendous value to New Mexico as a barrier against the Pawnees. Nava feared that New Mexicans riding far afield in search of the Comanches' enemies could only erode that barrier.

Concha thought it absurd to call the Pawnees an unknown nation. He understood that they lived only four hundred miles northeast of Santa Fe and that their two villages could field seven hundred warriors. It seemed only sensible to support the Comanches against them. He assumed that the Pawnees' wars with the Sioux and Osages and several

[36] Luis de Blanc to Don Estevan Miró, Natchitoches, March 20, 1791, in Lawrence Kinnaird, ed., *Spain in the Mississippi Valley, 1765–1794*, II, 408–410.

[37] Juan de Dios Peña, Diary of Campaign with the Comanches against the Pananas, Santa Fe, June 12–August 8, 1790, SANM, no. 1089; Concha to Nava, Santa Fe, November 1, 1791, SANM, no. 1164 (appears in translation in Abraham P. Nasatir, ed., *Before Lewis and Clark*, I, 146–148); Nava to Concha, Chihuahua, December 17, 1791, SANM, no. 1178.

other nations kept them too busy to launch any grand invasion of New Mexico.

Even without Pawnee incursions into New Mexico, the rising tensions between Pawnees and Comanches worried Spanish authorities. The Comanches were such valuable allies and their interests were so closely identified with Spain's on the northern frontier that any injury to them in effect injured the Spaniards as well. Furthermore, the state of war between Pawnees and Comanches ruled out direct communication and commerce between Santa Fe and St. Louis, now deemed vital to the security and prosperity of the northernmost provinces.

Again, Pedro Vial offered a solution. The Illinois district had been an early arena of the Frenchman's far-ranging career, and he knew much of the geography and the natives north of the Arkansas. Vial believed that he could travel from Santa Fe to St. Louis in a month and that he could mediate an end to the war between the Pawnees and Comanches. In May 1792, Concha commissioned him to do so in the service of the king.

Vial's instructions were to blaze the trail to St. Louis on a southerly route via the Osage villages.[38] He was to return that autumn on a more northerly route through the territories of the Pawnees and the A's,[39] though not so far north as the Arikaras, thence down the northern reaches of the Comanchería in the Arkansas Valley and home to Santa Fe. An important part of his mission was to persuade the Pawnees to make peace with the Comanches.[40]

With two young companions from Santa Fe, Vicente Villanueva and Vicente Espinosa, Vial set out on May 21, 1792.[41] On the morning of May 25, a few miles beyond the Pecos River, Vial was surprised and delighted to meet his old friends Francisco Xavier Chaves and Sojaís. Chaves, who had joined the Béxar garrison with a special assignment as interpreter in 1788, had obtained three months' leave to visit his birthplace in the Albuquerque area.[42] There he hoped to see his relatives for the first time since his childhood capture by Comanches and

---

[38] Concha, Instrucción, Santa Fe, May 24, 1792. Certified copy by Manuel Merino, Chihuahua, August 9, 1792, AGN, Historia, vol. 43. Translations of the instructions, diary, and other relevant documents appear in Loomis and Nasatir, *Pedro Vial*, pp. 369 ff.

[39] Again, probably the Panismahas (Aguages).

[40] Trudeau to Carondelet, no. 84, St. Louis, June 16, 1793, quoted in Loomis and Nasatir, *Pedro Vial*, p. 393.

[41] Vial, Diary, San Luis de Ylinueces, October 7, 1792. Copy by Manuel Merino, Chihuahua, January 9, 1794, AGN, Historia, vol. 43.

[42] Frederick C. Chabot, *With the Makers of San Antonio*, pp. 183–191.

to collect affidavits establishing his origin in a family of considerable distinction in New Mexico.[43] Riding with him were seven Comanche couples, including the faithful Sojaís and his well-traveled wife. Vial and Chaves led their groups to the Pecos River to camp together overnight, so that the old friends could reminisce and exchange news of the three years since they had parted at San Antonio.

Vial also found old acquaintances at his next encounter, with even greater reason to rejoice. Illness cost him ten days in mid-June, so that his party was already behind schedule on June 28 when they encountered a hunting party on the Arkansas River. Thinking that the hunters were Osages and that the Osages were on good terms with the government of Louisiana, Vial hailed them. The Indians cordially crossed the stream to greet them and identified themselves as Kansas. Suddenly, some Kansas seized the horses and equipment of Vial and his two associates, stripped them naked, and set about beating them to death. Others protested that the travelers should not be killed. One brave who had known Vial during his years in the Louisiana trade pulled the explorer up onto his own horse, then fought off several Indians who rushed up to kill Vial; his brother sprang to help him defend the Frenchman. Another Kansas, who had once been a servant in St. Louis and spoke French very well, also recognized Vial from the old days. He yelled to the rest to hold off because he knew the fellow and could find out where he had come from and why. He rushed Vial off to his own tent and hastily made him eat, so as to invoke the law of hospitality that forbade Kansas to kill a man who had eaten with them. Not until the next day did Vial learn that kinder or less reckless Indians had also rescued his two companions, though not in time to prevent mauling of both men and severe wounds for Villanueva.

Soon after Vial gulped down a meal in his benefactor's tent, some Kansas chiefs came to ask why he had come. When he explained that the Great Chief of the Spaniards of Santa Fe had sent him to open the road to Illinois and that he carried letters to the Great Chief of the Spaniards at St. Louis, they left him alone.

The hunters camped on the Arkansas another six weeks, keeping their three captives naked all that time, apparently to discourage escape. On August 16 the hunters started homeward with their cap-

---

[43] Chaves reported back to Governor Muñoz at Béxar in October, 1792, still riding in the safe company of his Comanche friends. He presented credentials obtained through hearings at Isleta on July 12, 1792 (see the Muñoz record of his return in the Bexar Archives, October 24, 1792).

tives, to their village on the Kansas River ten days northeastward across the plains.

The lot of the captive trio did not improve until September 11, when a licensed French trader from St. Louis reached the village with a pirogue full of merchandise. On Vial's assurance that the commandant at St. Louis would settle the bill, the trader sold the three captives clothing, a musket with powder and balls, and the goods necessary to buy their way out of the village. On September 16 they embarked with him for St. Louis. Eight days later they reached the confluence of the Kansas and Missouri. Frequent stops to hunt along the banks of the stream slowed their progress, but on the night of October 3 they reached St. Louis at last.

Vial saw deserted now the Osage village and the Missouri village that he had once known on the Missouri River, their inhabitants driven out by Sacs and Iowas. Those Osages, from whom Vial had expected friendly greetings and assistance, now warred against the other tribes and especially against the Spaniards of Illinois, badly disrupting trade and travel on the Missouri. Though Concha expected Vial back at Santa Fe that very month, the three explorers were advised not to risk the journey back to Santa Fe until they could travel with a larger group in the coming spring. Commandant Zenon Trudeau accommodated them comfortably through the winter in St. Louis and outfitted them well for the homeward journey in June.

The trio headed from St. Louis for the Pawnee villages on June 14, 1793, with a pirogue and four oarsmen furnished by Trudeau.[44] For mutual protection, they traveled with a pirogue of five traders going to trade with the Pawnees. Constant precautions against discovery by Osages delayed them. So did the rough currents as they battled upstream on the high-running Missouri for more than two months. On August 24 they reached the junction of the Little Nemeha and the Missouri, a landing place traders used to reach the Pawnees because they found it safely remote from Osages. The traders dispatched two men to ask for guides, and a Pawnee party promptly came to escort them. On September 12, 1793, Vial and his companions started southwestward with the Pawnees.

The party marched about fourteen miles a day, southwest and west. As they started early on the morning of September 20, a Pawnee rode

44 Vial, Diary, Santa Fe, November 16, 1793. Copy by Manuel Merino, Chihuahua, January 9, 1794, AGN, Historia, vol. 43.

ahead to notify Chief Sarisere that they were approaching his village. The chief rode out with a greeting party, which met the visitors at noon. The travelers raised the Spanish flag when they saw him coming. Sarisere greeted them with apparent delight and kissed the flag, which he called the mantle of his father's heart. The chief's party then escorted the visitors back to his village, where they enjoyed two weeks of excellent Pawnee hospitality. Vial thought them a nation of fine character, very favorably disposed toward the Spaniards.

Certainly Sarisere reacted sympathetically to Vial's errand. In a formal council in his lodge with the visitors and the leading men of his village, the chief expressed pleasure that Vial had come to open a road between the Spaniards of the west and those of the east. The licensed trader had already brought Sarisere a flag and a medal from Trudeau, and the chief valued the connection. He had been telling his people that if it were not for the St. Louis commandant who sent them guns, powder, balls, and other goods, their enemies would destroy and enslave them. He would be delighted to have Spaniards of the west and the east pass freely through his territory. He was also glad to talk of peace with the Comanches. For the moment he himself could not ride to Santa Fe to meet Governor Concha, though he hoped to do so someday. However, he would send two lesser chiefs with some young men to visit the governor, and he would instruct them to ride on with the Spaniards to the Comanches to make peace.

The Pawnees were allies well worth courting. Vial reckoned that Sarisere's village could field three hundred warriors and that the other three Pawnee villages had perhaps a thousand. Their allies were the Panismahas, the Kansas, and the Otoes, whom he thought must have about 1,100 men altogether. The Pawnees were at war against the Osages, who had about a thousand warriors, the Taovayas, who had about four hundred, and the countless Comanches. If Vial could indeed cement a peace between the Pawnees and Comanches, it was reasonable to expect that the peace would also be extended to the allies of each nation. Then no barrier to safe passage would remain between St. Louis and Santa Fe, save the Osages.

On October 4, Vial distributed farewell gifts to the Pawnees, then set out with ten horses that he had purchased from them. With him and his two associates rode two chiefs and five younger Pawnees, Chief Sarisere's emissaries to Governor Concha and the Comanches. They rode without incident until the night of October 19, when fifty-six Pawnee warriors fell upon their camp and very nearly killed them before Sarisere's envoys managed to correct the attackers' assumption that they had found sleeping Comanches.

The two chiefs whom Sarisere had sent with Vial were annoyed to find other Pawnees out campaigning against the Comanches while they were attempting a peace settlement, but the leaders of the war party rejected their protest on grounds that the Comanches had already killed their relatives. The next morning Chief Sarisere's envoys turned back homeward without a word to Vial. The war party, at whose mercy they left the Santa Fe trio, assured Vial that they would not kill him, then asked him for powder, balls, and other goods. As soon as he gave them what they wanted, they rode away, too. Just one Pawnee remained, declaring himself so eager to see Governor Concha and the Comanches that he would have to come anyway, even though he feared it would cost him his life.

The four men rode on together for four days, taking every precaution against discovery. By the fourth night, Vial suspected that the Pawnee planned to steal the horses, so he gave him some small presents and suggested that he go home. After that incident, Vial's party saw only one other human being, a Comanche man, naked, unarmed, nearly dead of cold and hunger, whom they rescued on the Canadian River during a snowstorm on November 8 and brought home with them. They reached Pecos on November 13, rested a day, then rode on to Santa Fe on November 15, in weather so miserable that the trip lasted from dawn to dusk.

That night Vial presented Governor Concha his diary and a letter from Commandant Trudeau, then explained why he was home more than a year later than they had anticipated and why he had deviated from Concha's instructions. The accidents of his illness in June and the captivity among the Kansas had cost him three months of the good travel season. Then the Osage wars, of which they had not known in Santa Fe, had ruled out independent travel and had made it inadvisable to go directly overland to the Pawnees as planned. Vial had abandoned the planned visit to the A's in order to bring Sarisere's envoys directly to Santa Fe.

Vial remained convinced that geography posed no barrier to travel between Santa Fe and St. Louis in a month's time. Although his first effort to mediate peace between the Comanches and Pawnees had foundered upon dissension among Pawnees, Vial had every reason to believe that the principal leaders of the Pawnees sincerely wanted the peace, and he was quite willing to try again. Concha thanked him and tried to arrange a suitable reward for his services. He wanted to make Vial an *alférez* of the Santa Fe company, thus to accord him well-earned distinction and to have him available for new expeditions and new missions at all times.

Concha and Vial had little time to relish the partial success of their most recent venture or to anticipate better successes. The year 1793 proved another time of abrupt changes in the tides of fortune for Spaniards and Indians alike, a new ebb from which the northern frontier would never recover.

In the summer of 1793, as Vial paddled up the Missouri River to talk peace with the Pawnees, the Pawnee-Comanche rivalry peaked on the high plains. Until then Yupes and Yamparicas had borne the brunt of Pawnee incursions, while Ecueracapa had concentrated his own leadership and the energies of his Cuchanecs on the great southward push against the Apaches. By 1793 the Pawnees so threatened the northern reaches of the Comanchería that Ecueracapa himself led the campaign against them, with grave results. The Comanche Chief Hachaxas died in the campaign; Ecueracapa suffered terrible wounds.

News of the calamity reached Santa Fe late in July. Governor Concha at once dispatched to Ecueracapa's camp Santa Fe's best medical help, the apothecary, with his limited set of surgical implements and medicines. Neither Spanish nor Comanche medicine could save the great chief. Sometime in the late summer or early autumn of 1793, Ecueracapa died. Another question of life or death arose: had the new institution of Supreme Chief of the Comanches died with him?

The Comanche nation decided that it had not. The chiefs summoned all the nation to council that autumn on the Canadian River to elect Ecueracapa's successor. Only three days after Concha welcomed Vial back to Santa Fe, he prepared to ride to the Canadian for the great council of the Comanche nation.

The outcome was eminently satisfactory. Some 4,500 Comanches pitched their 800 tipis on the banks of the stream and conferred upon their nation's future. They unanimously chose Chief Encanaguané, whose character and ability Concha deemed entirely suitable for the head chieftainship. The governor enjoyed every possible courtesy and deference from the Comanches. Concha, in turn, made the most of the opportunity to show his own great respect, and that of the Crown, for Encanaguané and for the other Comanche leaders who took part in the council.[45] The alliance would not founder for lack of good will on

[45] Nava to Concha, Chihuahua, August 8, 1793, SANM, no. 1247, and Decem-

either side. Only time would tell whether it could really continue to work throughout the Comanchería without the personal force of Ecueracapa's leadership.

While Governor Concha labored to perpetuate the Comanche alliance, New Mexico's vital network of Indian alliances sustained another blow. The captain general of the Navajo nation, El Pinto, died in November 1793 of wounds received in battle against Gila Apaches.[46] His twenty-four-year-old nephew, Baquienagage, succeeded him, but there was grave doubt that the young man could effectively lead the nation. Both Governor Concha and Commandant General Nava mourned the deaths of the two ablest leaders of their Indian allies, well aware that Spanish interests, as well as those of the Comanches and Navajos, had suffered grievous reverse.

Time ran out for Concha, too. Six years of strenuous service in New Mexico had undermined his health. He rode south with the caravan in December 1793 to seek medical help at Chihuahua, and he was never able to return. The next summer Lieutenant Colonel Fernando Chacón rode north to Santa Fe as the new governor of New Mexico.

Governor Chacón served out the century in New Mexico without particular distinction, good or bad. Poor old Governor Muñoz of Texas remained a cipher, at least in the strenuously demanding business of Indian affairs. Once more the remotest provinces mirrored the dilemma of the mother country: Spain had in Carlos IV only a trivial king to pit against the explosive forces of the French Revolution and the swarming American republic.

Spain went to war against France in 1793, with results all too familiar in the long-suffering frontier provinces of New Spain. Money, men, and materials grew painfully scarce as the empire's resources were concentrated on the more important arenas of war. The old Francophobia flared up again during 1794 and 1795, with blanket interdictions against Frenchmen impairing the usefulness of such key Indian agents as Vial and Courbière.

The Indians of the northern frontier did not seize upon the weakness to repudiate their Spanish alliances. Indeed, they took new initiatives to bolster the cordon of alliances against growing pressures from north and east. In 1794, Chief Encanaguané prevailed upon Governor Chacón to send Pedro Vial again to the Pawnees to mediate a peace be-

---

ber 31, 1793, SANM, no. 1272. Translations of both documents are printed in Simmons, *Border Comanches*. See also Navarro García, *José de Gálvez*, p. 492.

[46] Benes, "Anza and Concha."

tween that nation and the Comanches. Vial accomplished the mission in the spring of 1795, riding in eight days from Santa Fe to the Pawnee village on the Kansas River. He presented to the Pawnee chief the medal and uniform appropriate to a leader of vassals of the Spanish Crown, then oversaw reconciliation of the two long-hostile nations.[47]

While Vial undertook his new mission to the Pawnees early in 1795, allies of those Pawnees looked to Texas for help against the westward-thrusting Americans. On February 15, 1795, a dozen Panismahas called upon Governor Muñoz at Béxar, accompanied by thirty-nine Wichitas and eighteen Taovayas.[48] They announced that they had fled their former home because of damages inflicted upon them by Americans and had come to live among the Wichitas and Taovayas. For that reason, their Chief Yrisac had sent them to establish friendship with the Spaniards at San Antonio. They claimed friendship with thirty-three other nations that would also be interested in friendship with the Spaniards.[49]

Thirty-three nations wishing to align themselves with the Spaniards against the Americans! That was the most exciting news heard at Provincias Internas headquarters in many years. Commandant General Nava demanded more details so that he could formulate an appropriate response.[50] To his utter frustration, Governor Muñoz did not even acknowledge his questions. By the end of July Nava was still trying to coax some response out of Muñoz and complaining angrily to the viceroy about the breakdown of responsibility at Béxar.[51]

Apparently the Panismahas also found Muñoz a less than satisfactory negotiator. When Chief Yrisac himself rode south from the Red River to negotiate for a Spanish alliance, he bypassed Béxar and called instead at Laredo. The astonished captain of the Laredo Company sent the delegation on to see his own provincial governor at his capital, the Villa de Santander.[52] Yrisac called upon the Conde de Sierra Gorda on

[47] Nava to Chacón, Chihuahua, December 31, 1794, SANM, no. 1303a; Trudeau to Carondelet, St. Louis, July 4, 1795, in Nasatir, *Before Lewis and Clark*, I, 329–330.

[48] Muñoz to Nava, Béxar, February 15, 1795. Copy by Manuel Merino, Chihuahua, July 30, 1795, AGN, Historia, vol. 430.

[49] The names of the thirty-three nations as recorded by Muñoz are analyzed and some identifications are ventured by Rudolph C. Troike in "A Pawnee Visit to San Antonio in 1795," *Ethnohistory* 11 (1964): 380–393.

[50] Nava to Muñoz, Chihuahua, March 13, 1795, BA.

[51] Nava to Muñoz, Chihuahua, July 30, 1795, BA; Nava to Marqués de Branciforte, Chihuahua, July 30, 1795, AGN, Historia, vol. 430.

[52] Capital of Nuevo Santander from 1750 to 1825; the town now is called Jiménez, Tamaulipas.

June 12, 1795, with a retinue whom he introduced as representatives of the thirty-three nations of the north that his envoys had mentioned at Béxar in February. At least, that is what the governor of Nuevo Santander understood from a conversation that must have depended upon very limited interpretive resources. He could only report the visit to Commandant General Nava, who grew even more bewildered and frustrated by his inability to find out what was going on.

Muñoz was not particularly embarrassed to learn that Chief Yrisac had bypassed him; in fact, he seemed not even to comprehend it. At the end of August he responded to Nava's repeated questions. The Panismahas had stayed four days at Béxar in February and had seemed glad to carry back to Yrisac word that the province of Texas would permit him to visit San Antonio to negotiate. Muñoz had heard nothing more since February, but he attributed that to Wichita and Taovayas campaigns against the Osages. His leisurely inquiries at San Antonio had turned up the information that the Panismahas had formerly lived in the jurisdiction of Texas with the Taovayas but that they had quarreled over some horse thefts; the Panismahas had then retreated to the area inhabited by the thirty-three nations they now reported interested in some Spanish connection.[53]

Nothing more came of the Panismahas overtures. Perhaps Yrisac and his friends were too completely discouraged when their overtures in Nuevo Santander brought them no more satisfactory response than they had received in Texas.

The capacity of Spanish authorities to generate, or even to respond to, important initiatives dwindled steadily as the eighteenth century dragged to a close. The autumn of 1795 saw Spain forced to make important concessions to the United States in the Treaty of San Lorenzo, thus intensifying American pressures upon the Indian populations of the former Spanish territories. Those pressures sparked new intrusions by those Indians upon the territories of Indians still under Spanish jurisdiction, but Spain could provide little support or encouragement to the Indians who had cast their lot with hers on the northern frontier. For the rest of the century Spain's shrinking energies and resources were fully absorbed in a disastrous new war with England and in the losing struggle to stem the tide of revolution threatening her empire.

Most Indians of the northern frontier stood remarkably faithful to their disappointing alliance through the century, perhaps for want of any real alternative. The more Spain failed to meet her commitments

53 Muñoz to Nava, Béxar, August 30, 1795, AGN, Historia, vol. 430.

for gifts and trade goods, the more often little raids breached the peace, but, of all the allied nations, only the Navajos resorted briefly to insurrection. The Comanche leaders tried particularly hard to honor their treaty commitments. Until the end of the century none of the Comanche leaders broke the peace, and they conscientiously made reparations when Spanish authorities notified them of transgressions by their young men.

Some rash officials in the eastern Provincias Internas grew impatient enough with the thefts to talk of campaigning against the Comanches to stop the raids, especially in 1799 when a smallpox epidemic ravaged the Cuchanecs and made them seem momentarily vulnerable. The experienced Commandant General Nava acidly pointed out the folly of sending Coahuila's five hundred and Texas' two hundred soldiers to war against an estimated two thousand Cuchanec warriors.[54] If attacked by Spaniards, the Cuchanecs could rally the Yupes and Yamparicas, thought to have more than four thousand warriors. Although Spanish settlers suffered much inconvenience and some heartbreak at the hands of erring Comanches, circumstances dictated that Spanish communities continue to tolerate small breaches and rely upon the good offices of Indian leaders committed to the new rule of law within their nation.

Of course the alliances could not survive when Spain's authority crumbled in New Spain during the first quarter of the nineteenth century. Those years brought to the Indians of the northern frontier bewildering new disappointments and frustrations, borne of political revolution and economic chaos among their Spanish allies.

With the Louisiana Purchase in 1803, new tides of change surged upon the Indians who had so slowly and painfully worked out their accommodations with the Spaniards. All those costly lessons that Comanches and Spaniards had learned in dealing with each other fell useless: in the swarming Anglo-Americans the Indians confronted a people of very different law and custom and cast of mind. The Americans understood nothing of Comanches or Norteños or nations farther west, and they would not learn in time to treat them wisely or well. A century of new tragedies loomed ahead.

[54] Nava to Viceroy Miguel José de Azanza, Chihuahua, July 23, 1799, AGN, Provincias Internas, vol. 12.

Afterword

A multiplicity of Indian peoples weathered the surging tides of Manifest Destiny. They survived not only wars of conquest, forced removals, confinement to reservations, and in many cases allotment of tribal lands in severalty, but the more insidious threats of misguided benevolence, of educational and economic programs aimed at the obliteration of Indianness. At mid-twentieth century the Indian populace stood triumphant over the old expectations of extinction and assimilation, resurgent not only in numbers but in pride of identity, and fiercely resistant to such new threats as corporate termination.

Not for the first time, there were pangs of national conscience about the Indian experience of this democratic republic and efforts in both governmental and private sectors to make amends. The hopeful new element was the dawning comprehension of surviving Indian cultures as enriching rather than burdening the national life, and a new perception that Indian societies can flourish only in partnership with a federal government that respects their fundamental rights to self-determination. That principle was articulated by President Lyndon B. Johnson in a special message to the Congress on Indian policy in March 1968; it was reiterated in a special message of President Richard M. Nixon in July 1970. At long last the executive leadership of the United States had reached the understanding voiced by Commandant General Ugarte in 1786: changes must not, indeed cannot, be simply imposed from without a nation, no matter how virtuous the intent of those who intervene. Tribal structures must be fostered as the key to stable development rather than discarded as impediments to speedy progress.

What does the United States' new wisdom imply for those Indian peoples through whose worlds Spanish authority marched to that same conclusion two centuries ago? Some who have managed to keep their lands in common and their communities functioning are in good position to grasp a "second chance." For others whose lands were dissipated and communities fragmented, prospects are far less encouraging.

In the vanguard are the Navajo, now some 130,000 strong,[1] with a reservation of nearly fourteen million acres. Their constitutional tribal government dates back to the 1920's, when they found it necessary to establish a central authority to cope with the discovery of oil on their lands. Navajo traditions of local autonomy survive in the chapter units of that government. A prime concern of the tribal government has been economic development, based on exploitation of their extensive mineral and timber resources, utilization of their sizeable labor pool, and the tourism potential of their extraordinarily beautiful homeland. Unless the burgeoning Navajo populace can find suitable livelihoods on or near the reservation, their cherished world erodes. Navajos concerned for the unique values of that world now demand that education on the reservation foster rather than obliterate the indigenous culture of their children, and some play active roles in curriculum development and school management. Their new Navajo Community College embodies their determination that Navajos have access in their own homeland to the skills necessary for their individual and collective prosperity.

The Hopi world endures, a dozen autonomous villages now atop their timeless mesas: more than 7,000 people on a 2,600,000 acre island surrounded by Navajo reservation lands. The questions of proper response to the pressures and the opportunities of the outside world

---

[1] The contemporary estimates of population are variously derived: from reports, often conflicting, of the federal bureaus of the Census, Indian Affairs, and Indian Health Service; from the Texas State Auditor's Report of 1972 (in the case of the Tiguas); and from Professor W. E. Bittle, whose personal communication of October 1971 helped with the enormously complicated question of reckoning Plains Indian group figures, particularly in Oklahoma.

remain profoundly divisive. Some Hopi villages recognize the authority of a tribal council established in 1955; those of the traditionalists remain aloof, wary of any change that might threaten the integrity of the Hopi Way. Progressives seek economic development to afford livelihoods to all tribal members. Old rivalries with the Navajos persist, exacerbated by Navajo occupation of much of the land to which the Hopis hold title. Judicial efforts to resolve the dispute have foundered upon the practical difficulties of enforcing any ouster of Navajo occupants and upon Hopi ambivalence toward exercise of the machinery of the United States government in their lands. Pending congressional efforts augur little more hope of resolving the difficulty.

Among the groups best equipped to seize upon improved opportunities are the Pueblos surviving in New Mexico.[2] Although many Pueblos are employed off their reservations, their lives remain deeply rooted in the old values. Despite some crippling factionalism, most of their nineteen communities still function on their home grounds, and their political institutions have long been geared to cope with outsiders. Defending their lands against encroachment in the 1920's, they rallied to form an All Pueblo Council, still a useful forum for communication and cooperative action among their autonomies and experienced in dealing with the vagaries of federal and state governments.

A landmark victory for Taos was an early product of the United States' new enlightenment. That pueblo had long contended for the return of sacred Blue Lake and its 48,000 acre watershed in the neighboring mountains, a place of vital importance in their ritual life, expropriated in 1906 for creation of a national forest. As recommended in President Nixon's July message, the Congress voted in December 1970 to restore those lands to Taos. The action was widely hailed as indicative of a new general willingness to respond to other just grievances of Indian peoples.

The new federal dispensation also focused upon Zuñi, whose government had initiated in the 1960's a notably purposeful attack upon its

---

[2] In 1971 their populations and land holdings were estimated as follows: Ácoma, 1,944 persons, 245,672 acres; Cochití, 490 persons, 28,779 acres; Isleta, 2,030 persons, 210,948 acres; Jémez, 1,449 persons, 88,867 acres; Laguna, 2,464 persons, 417,853 acres; Nambé, 171 persons, 19,075 acres; Picurís, 93 persons, 14,947 acres; Pojoaque, 65 persons, 11,599 acres; Sandía, 198 persons, 22,884 acres; San Felipe, 1,347 persons, 48,929 acres; San Ildefonso, 232 persons, 26,192 acres; San Juan, 870 persons, 12,235 acres; Santa Ana, 376 persons, 42,527 acres; Santa Clara, 493 persons, 45,748 acres; Santo Domingo, 1,851 persons, 69,259 acres; Taos, 961 persons, 95,341 acres; Tesuque, 167 persons, 16,813 acres; Zía, 464 persons, 112,511 acres; Zuñi, 4,952 persons, 407,247 acres.

depressed economy and poor living conditions. Chosen therefore as a pilot community to test the new principles of political and economic self-determination, Zuñi assumed in 1970 nearly all the managerial and administrative responsibilities customarily exercised by the Bureau of Indian Affairs.

Southern Ute peoples hold two enclaves in the southern Colorado mountains where their ancestors proved such valuable allies of Spain: 611 persons on the 307,110 acres of the Southern Ute Reservation; 1,143 on the 567,377 acres of the Ute Mountain Reservation. On each, constitutional tribal governments established in the 1930's direct economic development programs, based upon proceeds from their natural resources and upon substantial awards won in their claims cases against the United States government.

Who survived the manifold trials of the diverse, beleaguered Apache peoples? The 1970 Census enumerates 22,993 Apaches, of whom 11,735 live on identified reservations. Western Apaches occupy the two reservations in Arizona on which their forebears were concentrated, willy-nilly, in the 1880's: 5,903 at Fort Apache; 4,525 at San Carlos. Their nineteenth-century ordeals of war and displacement, even more severe than they experienced in the eighteenth, splintered many group identities almost beyond possibility of historical reconstruction. Contemporary tribal governments on the reservations have faced the challenge of creating new functioning communities on the basis of emerging pan-Apache consciousness and common economic concerns.

Luckier in terms of historical continuity are the 1,797 Jicarillas, whose grandfathers accepted in 1880 a 460,384 acre reservation in the mountains of northern New Mexico. An oil strike on their lands in 1940 set them on the path from paupery to economic security. Their constitutional tribal government directs a sophisticated program of investment and development, with emphasis on education, designed to improve the quality of life on the reservation and to secure a sound economic base for their people in perpetuity.

Other eastern Apache peoples survive on the 460,384 acre Mescalero reservation in the mountains of southeastern New Mexico. Of that reservation's population of 1,695, perhaps 600 conceive of themselves as Mescaleros, and some forty as Lipans. Some are Chiricahuas, survivors of Geronimo's band, shipped there after their exile in Florida.[3] The

---

[3] Some 135 more survivors of Geronimo's band, now called Fort Sill Apaches,

constitutional government of the reservation is run by the ten elected members of the tribal business committee, which fosters their established cattle industry and seeks increasingly to exploit the timber and tourist potential of their forested domain.

The surviving Lipans figure importantly in a grave dilemma shared by all those tribes whose aboriginal and treaty title claims fall within the modern boundaries of Texas. In an ultimate historical irony, they found themselves denied compensation by the Indian Claims Commission which Congress established in 1946 to hear and adjudicate all Indian claims against the United States for a just and final settlement. For claims outside Texas, many tribes have won substantial indemnities for unconscionably low initial compensations for ceded lands, for federal failures to protect their lands and other resources against encroachment, and for shortcomings in federal trusteeship of tribal funds. In many cases those awards have provided the badly needed capital base for social and economic programs of resurgent tribes.

For more than twenty years the Claims Commission denied federal responsibility for Indian claims in Texas: the Republic of Texas had never recognized aboriginal titles; the State of Texas had retained title to its public domain upon entering the Union, so the United States rejected responsibility for lands to which it never held title. Only in 1969, responding to an appeal filed by the Lipan Apache Tribe, did the Court of Claims rule that the United States was indeed liable for losses suffered by the Indians whose lives and property it had failed to protect against the Texans. The decision cited provisions in the Claims Commission Act for extralegal or moral claims which could make the United States responsible for damage to Indian tribes even on lands to which it never held title.

That decision signaled the reopening of all those Indian claims in Texas hitherto denied. Not only has the federal government firmly contested all claims in these adversary proceedings, but the costly tangle of litigation has also been worsened by tribes with conflicting claims, warring amongst themselves no less vigorously in twentieth-century courts than on eighteenth-century prairies. Consequently, tribes have yet to collect compensation for their mid-nineteenth-century losses at the hands of Texans abetted by United States troops.

---

live in Oklahoma, largely within the jurisdiction of the Anadarko Agency. A general council of the adult members conducts the tribal business.

Most of the tribes affected are now based in Oklahoma, where they were concentrated on reservations after their expulsion from Texas.[4] Within a generation they found their lands allotted in severalty and themselves subject to a determined federal program designed to obliterate tribal cultures as barriers to assimilation. Tribal identities stubbornly survived that battering, though at a grim cost of poverty and social dislocation for many of the people. Tribal governments do function: some now project programs of economic and cultural reconstruction for which claims indemnities could afford crucial capital.

Among the claimants are the Tiguas of Texas, perhaps the most remarkable of all survivals. Descendants of the Pueblo refugees who came south with the Spaniards in the 1680's, principally from Isleta, they virtually dropped out of sight after losing their lands to Texans in the 1870's. In the 1960's they were newly recognized, still functioning as a community around their old Mission Nuestra Señora del Carmen in the Ysleta section of southeastern El Paso, in grave poverty. They recovered their legal identity as a tribe, incorporating under the jurisdiction of the State of Texas rather than the federal government, but retaining their right to sue the United States for its failure to protect their lands as guaranteed in the Treaty of Guadalupe Hidalgo. The 126 Tigua families, altogether some 451 persons, have regained some lands and are developing some tribal enterprises under the aegis of the Texas Commission for Indian Affairs, with the financial as well as the administrative assistance of the State. A favorable settlement of their claims before the Indian Claims Commission would immeasurably strengthen their tribal reconstruction effort.

Surely no one foresaw, much less intended, that redress under the Indian Claims Act would falter upon technicalities of land title in Texas. Nor was it anticipated that the enlightened executive calls for just new Indian policies would founder upon a time of disarray in this powerful republic, not unlike the recurring crises that often balked the pious intents of the Spanish Crown. By March 1968, the political strain and the economic drain of undeclared war in Southeast Asia were so deeply undermining President Johnson's ambitious domestic programs that his Indian policies stood small chance of comprehensive implementation in that waning year of his administration.

Greater disappointments awaited those who pinned their hopes

---

[4] Populations of those groups who figure in this history are estimated at 6,500 Comanches, 600 Wichitas (including, but not limited to, the Wacos, Wichitas, Kichais, and Tawakonis), 2,000 Caddos, and 57 Tonkawas.

on President Nixon's promises of "a new era in which the Indian future is determined by Indian acts and Indian decisions." More than a year later the Council of Tribal Chairmen, despairing of true reforms as long as the Bureau of Indian Affairs lies subject to the conflicts of interest inherent in the Department of the Interior, demanded that the Bureau be transferred directly into the Executive Office of the President. Not only did their demand win no response from the Nixon administration; the overwhelming scandals of succeeding months taught the sobering lesson that the White House is no certain bulwark against either ineptness or corruption. Nor was there leadership forthcoming from the National Council on Indian Opportunity, a super executive policy mechanism chaired by a Vice-President otherwise preoccupied, who hardly convened it in the nearly five years before he resigned his office in disgrace.

What of Congressional responsibility? Countless hearings on Indian problems have been held and countless more proposed. Pending are several bills to facilitate Indian self-determination and to redress long-standing grievances. But Congressional promises of urgent priorities for Indian affairs inevitably fade in a climate of chronic emergency: the agonizing question of presidential impeachment, then the extraordinary remedy of presidential resignation; the unwonted shortages of food, fiber, and energy; the baffling coincidence of economic recession and inflation.

Storms brewed in other men's worlds pose no unprecedented test for Indian peoples who survived the best intentions and the worst performances of Hapsburgs and Bourbons. Some have learned as well as suffered much in the interval. To this mid-twentieth-century ordeal of Democrats and Republicans they bring not only their practiced endurance, but an important new collective sense of outrage and of determination to shape their own destinies at last.

BIBLIOGRAPHY

The principal archival sources of this study are the Bexar Archives, now in the University of Texas Archives at Austin (cited as BA), and the Spanish Archives of New Mexico, now in the State of New Mexico Records Center at Santa Fe (SANM). For materials from the Archivo General de Indias (AGI) and the Archivo General y Pública de la Nación (AGN), I have relied upon microfilm holdings of the Bancroft Library and the University of Texas Library, as well as the Dunn and Cunningham transcripts in the University of Texas Archives.

Published Works Cited

Adams, Eleanor B. "Bishop Tamarón's Visitation of New Mexico, 1760." *New Mexico Historical Review* 28 (1953):81–114, 192–221, 291–315; 29 (1954): 41–47.

———. "Fray Silvestre and the Obstinate Hopi." *New Mexico Historical Review* 38 (1963): 97–138.

Allain, Mathé. "LeBlanc de Villenuefve in Natchitoches." *Louisiana Studies* 4 (1965): 41–46.

Allen, Henry Easton. "The Parrilla Expedition to the Red River." *Southwestern Historical Quarterly* 43 (1939): 53–71.

Armijo, Isidro, ed. "Information Communicated by Juan Candelaria, Resident of This Villa de San Francisco Xavier de Alburquerque, Born 1692—Age 84." *New Mexico Historical Review* 4 (1929): 274–297.

Bancroft, Hubert Howe. *History of Arizona and New Mexico.* San Francisco: The History Company, Publishers, 1889.

———. *History of Texas and the North Mexican States.* 2 vols. San Francisco: The History Company, Publishers, 1890.

Bell, Robert E.; Jelks, Edward B; and Newcomb, W. W., Jr. *A Pilot Study of Wichita Indian Archaeology and Ethnohistory.* (Final Report for Grant GS-964, National Science Foundation, 1967.)

Benavides, Alonso de. *Fray Alonso de Benavides' Revised Memorial of 1634.* Translated and edited by Frederick Webb Hodge, George P. Hammond, and Agapito Rey. Coronado Historical Series, vol. 4. Albuquerque: University of New Mexico Press, 1945.

Benes, R. J. "Anza and Concha in New Mexico." *Journal of the West* 4 (1965): 63–76.

Bloom, Lansing B., ed. "A Campaign against the Moqui Pueblos under the Leadership of Governor and Captain-General Don Phelix Martínez, Beginning August 16th, 1716." *New Mexico Historical Review* 6 (1931): 158–226.

———. "A Glimpse of New Mexico in 1620." *New Mexico Historical Review* 3 (1928): 357–380.

———. "The Royal Order of 1620 to Custodian Fray Esteban de Perea." *New Mexico Historical Review* 5 (1930): 288–298.

Bobb, Bernard E. *The Viceregency of Antonio María Bucareli in New Spain, 1771–1779.* Austin: University of Texas Press, 1962.

Bolton, Herbert Eugene, ed. *Anza's California Expeditions.* 5 vols. Berkeley: University of California Press, 1930.

———, ed. *Athanase de Mézières and the Louisiana-Texas Frontier, 1768–1780.* 2 vols. Cleveland: Arthur H. Clark Company, 1914.

———. *Coronado, Knight of Pueblos and Plains.* Albuquerque: University of New Mexico Press, 1949.

———. *Pageant in the Wilderness: The Story of the Escalante Expedition to the Interior Basin.* Salt Lake City: Utah State Historical Society, 1950.

———, ed. *Spanish Exploration in the Southwest, 1542–1706.* New York: Charles Scribner's Sons, 1916.

———. *Texas in the Middle Eighteenth Century.* Berkeley: University of California Press, 1915.

Brinckerhoff, Sidney B., and Faulk, Odie B. *Lancers for the King: A Study of the Frontier Military System of Northern New Spain, with a translation of the Royal Regulations of 1772.* Phoenix: Arizona Historical Foundation, 1965.

Caruso, John Anthony. *The Mississippi Valley Frontier: The Age of French Exploration and Settlement.* New York: Bobbs-Merrill Company, Inc., 1966.

Caughey, John W. *Bernardo de Gálvez in Louisiana, 1776–1783.* Berkeley: University of California Press, 1934.

Chabot, Frederick C. *With the Makers of San Antonio.* San Antonio: Artes Gráficas, 1937.

Chamberlain, Robert S. "Castilian Backgrounds of the Repartimiento-Encomienda." *Contributions to American Anthropology and History,* V, 19–66. Washington D.C.: Carnegie Institution, 1939.

Chapman, Charles Edward. *The Founding of Spanish California: The Northwestward Expansion of New Spain, 1687–1783.* New York: Macmillan, 1916.

Chávez, Fray Angelico. "Pohé-Yemo's Representative and the Pueblo Revolt of 1680." *New Mexico Historical Review* 42 (1967):85–126.

Christiansen, Paige W. "Hugh O'Conor's Inspection of Nueva Vizcaya and Coahuila, 1773." *Louisiana Studies* 2 (1963): 157–175.

Clark, LaVerne Harrell. *They Sang for Horses: The Impact of the Horse on Navajo and Apache Folklore.* Tucson: University of Arizona Press, 1966.

Connor, Seymour V. "The Mendoza-López Expedition and the Location of San Clemente." *West Texas Historical Association Yearbook* 45 (1969): 3–29.

Dabbs, J. Autrey. "The Texas Missions in 1785." *Mid-America* 22 (1940): 38–58.

Delanglez, Jean. *The French Jesuits in Lower Louisiana (1700–1763)*. Catholic University of America Studies in American Church History, vol. 21. Washington, D.C.: Catholic University of America, 1953.

Documentos para la historia de Méjico. Series 3, edited by F. García Figueroa. Mexico City: Impr. de J. R. Navarro, 1857.

Domínguez, Francisco Atanasio. *The Missions of New Mexico, 1776*. Translated and edited by Eleanor B. Adams and Angelico Chávez. Albuquerque: University of New Mexico Press, 1956.

Dorsey, George A. *Mythology of the Wichita*. Washington: Carnegie Institution, 1904.

Driver, Harold E. *Indians of North America*. Chicago: University of Chicago Press, 1961.

Duffield, Lathel F. "The Taovayas Village of 1759: In Texas or Oklahoma?" *Great Plains Journal* 4 (1965): 39–48.

Dunn, William Edward. "Apache Relations in Texas, 1718–1750." *Texas State Historical Association Quarterly* 14 (1911): 198–274.

Espinosa, J. Manuel. *Crusaders of the Rio Grande*. Chicago: Institute of Jesuit History, 1942.

————, ed. *The First Expedition of Vargas into New Mexico, 1692*. Albuquerque: University of New Mexico Press, 1940.

————. "Journal of the Vargas Expedition into Colorado, 1694." *The Colorado Magazine* 16 (1939): 81–90.

Ewing, Russell Charles. "The Pima Uprising of 1751: A Study of Spanish-Indian Relations on the Frontier of New Spain." In *Greater America: Essays in Honor of Herbert Eugene Bolton*, pp. 259–280. Berkeley: University of California Press, 1945.

Faulk, Odie B. *The Last Years of Spanish Texas, 1778–1821*. The Hague: Mouton and Company, 1964.

Forbes, Jack D. *Apache, Navajo, and Spaniard*. Norman: University of Oklahoma Press, 1960.

Gálvez, Bernardo de. *Instructions for Governing the Interior Provinces of New Spain*. Translated and edited by Donald E. Worcester. Berkeley: The Quivira Society, 1951.

Gilpin, Laura. *The Enduring Navaho*. Austin: University of Texas Press, 1968.

Goodwin, Grenville. *Social Organization of the Western Apache*. Chicago: University of Chicago Press, 1942.

Habig, Marion A. *The Alamo Chain of Missions: A History of San Antonio's Five Old Missions*. Chicago: Franciscan Herald Press, 1968.

Hackett, Charles Wilson, ed. *Historical Documents Relating to New Mexico, Nueva Vizcaya, and Approaches Thereto, to 1773*. 3 vols. Washington, D.C.: Carnegie Institution, 1923–1927.

————, ed. *Pichardo's Treatise on the Limits of Louisiana and Texas*. 4 vols. Austin: University of Texas Press, 1931–1946.

————, ed. *Revolt of the Pueblo Indians of New Mexico and Otermín's Attempted Reconquest, 1680–1682*. 2 vols. Coronado Historical Series, vols. 8 and 9. Albuquerque: University of New Mexico Press, 1942.

Hammond, George P., ed. "The Zuñiga Journal, Tucson to Santa Fe: The

Opening of a Spanish Trade Route, 1788–1795." *New Mexico Historical Review* 6 (1931): 40–65.

————, and Rey, Agapito, eds. *Don Juan de Oñate, Colonizer of New Mexico, 1595–1628.* 2 vols. Coronado Historical Series, vols. 5 and 6. Albuquerque: University of New Mexico Press, 1953.

————, and Rey, Agapito, eds. *The Rediscovery of New Mexico, 1580–1594: The Explorations of Chamuscado, Espejo, Castaño de Sosa, Morlete, and Leyva de Bonilla and Humaña.* Coronado Historical Series, vol. 3. Albuquerque: University of New Mexico Press, 1966.

Hanke, Lewis. *The Spanish Struggle for Justice in the Conquest of America.* Philadelphia: University of Pennsylvania Press, 1949.

Harper (John), Elizabeth Ann. "The Taovayas Indians in Frontier Trade and Diplomacy, 1719 to 1768." *The Chronicles of Oklahoma* 31 (1953): 268–289.

————. "The Taovayas Indians in Frontier Trade and Diplomacy, 1769–1779." *Southwestern Historical Quarterly* 57 (1953): 181–201.

————. "The Taovayas Indians in Frontier Trade and Diplomacy, 1779–1835." *Panhandle-Plains Historical Review* 23 (1953): 1–32.

Hill, Willard W. "Some Navaho Culture Changes during Two Centuries (with a translation of the early eighteenth century Rabal Manuscript)." In *Essays in Historical Anthropology of North America.* Smithsonian Miscellaneous Collections, vol. 100, pp. 395–415. Washington D.C.: United States Government Printing Office, 1940.

Hodge, Frederick Webb, ed. "French Intrusion toward New Mexico in 1695." *New Mexico Historical Review* 4 (1929): 72–76.

Holder, Preston. "The Fur Trade as Seen from the Indian Point of View." In *The Frontier Re-examined,* edited by John Francis McDermott. Urbana: University of Illinois Press, 1967.

Hughes, Annie E. "The Beginning of Spanish Settlement in the El Paso District." *University of California Publications in History* 1 (1914): 293–333.

Instrucciones que los virreyes de Nueva España dejaron a sus sucesores; Añadense algunas que los mismos trajeron de la corte y otros documentos semejantes a las instrucciones. 2 vols. Mexico City: Impr. de I. Escalante, 1873.

John, Elizabeth Ann Harper. "Spanish Relations with the *Indios Bárbaros* on the Northernmost Frontier of New Spain in the Eighteenth Century." Ph.D. dissertation, University of Oklahoma, 1957.

Johnson, Leroy, Jr., and Jelks, Edward B. "The Tawakoni-Yscani Village, 1760: A Study in Archaeological Site Identification." *The Texas Journal of Science* 10 (1958): 405–422.

Jones, Oakah L., Jr. *Pueblo Warriors and Spanish Conquest.* Norman: University of Oklahoma Press, 1966.

Kelley, J. Charles. "Juan Sabeata and Diffusion in Aboriginal Tribes." *American Anthropologist* 57 (1955): 981–995.

Kerlérec, Louis Billouart de. "Projet de Paix et d'Alliance avec les Cannecis . . ." *Journal de la Société des Américanistes de Paris,* new series, 3 (1906): 67–76.

Kinnaird, Lawrence, ed. *Spain in the Mississippi Valley, 1765–1794, Trans-*

lations of Materials from the Spanish Archives in the Bancroft Library. 3 vols. Annual Report of the American Historical Association for the Year 1945, vols. 2, 3, and 4. Washington, D.C.: United States Government Printing Office, 1946.

Lafora, Nicolás de. *The Frontiers of New Spain: Nicolás de La Fora's Description, 1766–68.* Edited by Lawrence Kinnaird. Berkeley: The Quivira Society, 1958.

————. *Relación del viaje que hizo a los presidios internos, situados en la frontera de la América septentrional, perteneciente al rey de España.* Edited by Vito Alessio Robles. Mexico City: P. Robredo, 1939.

Linton, Ralph, ed. *Acculturation in Seven American Indian Tribes.* Gloucester, Mass.: P. Smith, 1963.

Loomis, Noel M., and Nasatir, Abraham P. *Pedro Vial and the Roads to Santa Fe.* Norman: University of Oklahoma Press, 1967.

Margry, Pierre, ed. *Découvertes et Établissements des Français dans l'Ouest et dans le Sud de l'Amérique Septentrionale, 1614–1754.* 6 vols. Paris: Imprimerie D. Jouaust, 1876.

Moorhead, Max L. *The Apache Frontier: Jacobo Ugarte and Spanish-Indian Relations in Northern New Spain, 1769–1791.* Norman: University of Oklahoma Press, 1968.

Nasatir, Abraham P., ed. *Before Lewis and Clark: Documents Illustrating the History of the Missouri, 1785–1804.* 2 vols. St. Louis: St. Louis Historical Documents Foundation, 1952.

Nathan, Paul D., trans., and Simpson, Lesley Byrd, ed. *The San Sabá Papers: A Documentary Account of the Founding and Destruction of San Sabá Mission.* San Francisco: John Howell Books, 1959.

Navarro García, Luis. *José de Gálvez y la Comandancia General de las Provincias Internas del Norte de Nueva España.* Seville: Consejo Superior de Investigaciones Científicas, 1964.

Nelson, Al B. "Juan de Ugalde and the Rio Grande Frontier, 1779–1790." Ph.D. dissertation, University of California, 1937.

Newcomb, W. W., Jr. *The Indians of Texas.* Austin: University of Texas Press, 1961.

O'Conor, Hugo de. *Informe de Hugo de O'Conor sobre el estado de las Provincias Internas del Norte, 1771–76.* Edited by Francisco R. Almada. Mexico City: Editorial Cultura, 1952.

Parsons, Elsie Clews. *Pueblo Indian Religion.* Chicago: University of Chicago Press, 1939.

Patten, Roderick B. "Miranda's Inspection of Los Almagres: His Journal, Report, and Petition." *Southwestern Historical Quarterly* 74 (1970): 223–254.

Pénigault, André. *Fleur de Lys and Calumet: Being the Pénicaut Narrative of French Adventure in Louisiana.* Edited by Richebourg Gaillard McWilliams. Baton Rouge: Louisiana State University Press, 1953.

Pfefferkorn, Ignaz. *Sonora: A Description of the Province.* Edited by Theodore E. Treutlein. Albuquerque: University of New Mexico Press, 1949.

Reeve, Frank D. "Early Navaho Geography." *New Mexico Historical Review* 31 (1956): 290–310.

————. "Navaho-Spanish Wars, 1680–1720." *New Mexico Historical Review* 33 (1958): 205–231.

————. "Seventeenth Century Navaho-Spanish Relations." *New Mexico Historical Review* 32 (1957): 36–52.

Rivera, Pedro de. *Diario y Derrotero de lo Caminado, Visto y Observado en la Visita que Hizo a los Presidios.* Edited by Vito Alessio Robles. *Archivo Histórico Militar Mexicano,* no. 2. Mexico City: Taller Autográfico, 1946.

Rowland, Donald. "The Sonora Frontier of New Spain, 1735–1745. In *New Spain and the Anglo-American West: Historical Contributions Presented to Herbert Eugene Bolton,* vol. 1, pp. 147–169. Lancaster, Pa.: Lancaster Press, Inc., 1932.

Scholes, France V. "Church and State in New Mexico, 1610–1650." *New Mexico Historical Review* 11 (1963): 9–58, 145–179, 282–293, 297–349; 12 (1937): 78–106.

————. "Documents for the History of the New Mexican Missions in the Seventeenth Century." *New Mexico Historical Review* 4 (1929): 46–51, 195–201.

————. "Juan Martínez de Montoya, Settler and Conquistador of New Mexico." *New Mexico Historical Review* 19 (1944): 337–342.

————. "The Supply Service of the New Mexican Missions in the Seventeenth Century." *New Mexico Historical Review* 5 (1930): 93–115, 186–210, 386–404.

Secoy, Frank Raymond. *Changing Military Patterns on the Great Plains (Seventeenth Century through Early Nineteenth Century).* Monographs of the American Ethnological Society, no. 21. Locust Valley, N.Y.: J. J. Augustin, 1953.

Simmons, Marc, ed. *Border Comanches: Seven Spanish Colonial Documents, 1785–1819.* Santa Fe: Stagecoach Press, 1967.

Spicer, Edward H. *Cycles of Conquest: The Impact of Spain, Mexico, and the United States on the Indians of the Southwest, 1533–1960.* Tucson: The University of Arizona Press, 1962.

————, ed. *Perspectives in American Indian Culture Change.* Chicago: University of Chicago Press, 1961.

Surrey, N. M. Miller. *The Commerce of Louisiana during the French Régime, 1699–1763.* New York: Columbia University Press, 1916.

Swanton, John R., ed. *Source Material on the History and Ethnology of the Caddo Indians.* Bureau of American Ethnology, Bulletin no. 132. Washington, D.C.: Smithsonian Institution, 1942.

Thomas, Alfred Barnaby, ed. *After Coronado: Spanish Exploration Northeast of New Mexico, 1696–1727.* Norman, University of Oklahoma Press, 1935.

————, ed. "Antonio de Bonilla and Spanish Plans for the Defense of New Mexico." In *New Spain and the Anglo-American West: Historical Contributions Presented to Herbert Eugene Bolton,* vol. 1, pp. 183–209. Lancaster, Pa.: Lancaster Press, Inc., 1932.

————, ed. *Forgotten Frontiers: A Study of the Spanish Indian Policy of Don Juan Bautista de Anza, Governor of New Mexico, 1777–1787.* Norman: University of Oklahoma Press, 1932.

———, ed. "Governor Mendinueta's Proposals for the Defense of New Mexico, 1772–1778." *New Mexico Historical Review* 6 (1931): 21–39.

———, ed. *The Plains Indians and New Mexico, 1751–1778: A Collection of Documents Illustrative of the History of the Eastern Frontier of New Mexico*. Coronado Historical Series, vol. 11. Albuquerque: University of New Mexico Press, 1940.

———. "San Carlos, A Comanche Pueblo on the Arkansas River, 1787." *The Colorado Magazine* 6 (1929): 79–91.

———, ed. *Teodoro de Croix and the Northern Frontier of New Spain, 1776–1783*. Norman: University of Oklahoma Press, 1941.

Tous, Gabriel. "Ramón's Expedition: Espinosa's Diary of 1716." *Mid-America* 12 (1929): 339–361.

Troike, Rudolph C. "A Pawnee Visit to San Antonio in 1795." *Ethnohistory* 11 (1964): 380–393.

Tunnell, Curtis D., and Newcomb, W. W., Jr. *A Lipan Apache Mission: San Lorenzo de la Santa Cruz, 1762–1771*. Texas Memorial Museum Bulletin, no. 14. Austin: Texas Memorial Museum, 1969.

Twitchell, Ralph Emerson, comp. *The Spanish Archives of New Mexico*. 2 vols. Cedar Rapids, Iowa: Torch Press, 1914.

Vigness, David M. "Don Hugo O'Conor and New Spain's Northeastern Frontier, 1764–1776." *Journal of the West* 6 (1967): 27–40.

Wallace, Ernest, and Hoebel, E. Adamson. *The Comanches: Lords of the South Plains*. Norman: University of Oklahoma Press, 1952.

Weddle, Robert S. *San Juan Bautista: Gateway to Spanish Texas*. Austin: University of Texas Press, 1968.

———. *The San Sabá Mission: Spanish Pivot in Texas*. Austin: University of Texas Press, 1964.

Weltfish, Gene. "The Question of Ethnic Identity: An Ethnohistorical Approach." *Ethnohistory* 6 (1959): 321–346.

Wisconsin State Historical Collections. Vol. 18. Madison: State Historical Society of Wisconsin, 1908.

Worcester, Donald E. "The Navaho during the Spanish Régime in New Mexico." *New Mexico Historical Review* 26 (1951): 101–118.

Wroth, Lawrence C. "The Frontier Presidios of New Spain: Books, Maps, and a Selection of Manuscripts Relating to the Rivera Expedition of 1724–1729." *The Papers of the Bibliographical Society of America* 43 (1951): 191–218.

Wyllys, Rufus Kay, ed. "Padre Luis Velarde's Relación of Pimería Alta, 1716." *New Mexico Historical Review* 6 (1931): 111–157.

INDEX

Note: Indian peoples have been distinguished in main entries by the use of caps and small caps. To facilitate chronological construction of subgroup histories, analysis is limited to generic entries.